PRINCIPLES OF INTERNATIONAL TRADE LAW

including

The World Trade Organization, NAFTA and the European Union

by

Ralph H. Folsom
Professor of Law
University of San Diego School of Law

CONCISE HORNBOOK SERIES™

Mat #41582150

Concise Hornbook Series and Westlaw are trademarks registered in the U.S. Patent and Trademark Office.

© 2014 LEG, Inc. d/b/a West Academic

> 444 Cedar Street, Suite 700
> St. Paul, MN 55101
> 1-877-888-1330

Printed in the United States of America

ISBN: 978-0-314-29140-0

Preface

———————

Principles of International Trade Law is part of West Academic Publishing's Concise Hornbook series. Its coverage commences in Part One with the World Trade Organization, followed by Part Two on Customs and Import Law, Part Three on Export Law, Part Four on Preferential Trading Arrangements (including NAFTA and the European Union), and ends in Part Five with coverage of Technology Transfers and Int'l Commercial Arbitration. Principles is intended to provide considerably more depth, analysis, citations and related documents than found in the West Nutshell on International Trade and Economic Relations.

Principles of International Trade Law can be used in connection with **any** international trade or international business transactions course book.

West Academic Publishing has a number of course books in these areas, including:

Jackson, Davey and Sykes, Int'l Economic Relations

Mavroidis and Wu, The Law of the World Trade Organization

Folsom, Gordon, Spanogle and Van Alstine, IBT: Int'l Trade and Economic Relations

Folsom, Gordon and Gantz, NAFTA and Free Trade in the Americas

Folsom, Gordon, Spanogle and Van Alstine, Int'l Business Transactions

Vagts, Dodge and Koh, Transnational Business Problems (Foundation Press)

Fellmeth, The Law of Int'l Business Transactions

Bermann, Goebel, Davey and Fox, European Union Law

Other law course books for which Principles of International Trade Law is suitable include:

Bhala, Int'l Trade Law

Guzman and Pauwelyn, Int'l Trade Law

Chow and Schoenbaum, Int'l Trade Law

Stephan, Int'l Trade and Investment

Westbrook, *Int'l Business Transactions*

Stephan and Roin, *Int'l Business and Economics*

Principles of International Trade Law can also be used as an inexpensive course book, notably in conjunction with the legal documents included in selected chapters and appended at the end.

Your feedback would be much appreciated.

Ralph H. Folsom

Professor of Law,
University of San Diego
School of Law

rfolsom@sandiego.edu

June 2014

Summary of Contents

PART 5. ADDITIONAL INTERNATIONAL
TRADE LAW TOPICS

Table of Contents

PART 4. PREFERENTIAL TRADE AGREEMENTS

PART 5. ADDITIONAL INTERNATIONAL
TRADE LAW TOPICS

PRINCIPLES OF INTERNATIONAL TRADE LAW

including

The World Trade Organization, NAFTA and the European Union

Part 1

WORLD TRADE LAW

Chapter 1

THE ESSENTIALS OF INTERNATIONAL TRADE LAW

Table of Sections

NOTE: A Directory of coverage in this book of the World Trade Organization (WTO) agreements is presented in Section 1.3 below.

Selected provisions of the GATT 1947 and 1994, various WTO agreements, and the WTO Dispute Settlement Understanding (DSU) are appended at the end of this book or at the end of certain chapters. See the Table of Contents for their location.

---

§ 1.0   International Trade and Bilateral Treaties

International trade law has a long and controversial history. Many nations, especially in their early stages of development, are

3

fearful of trade across borders. International trade is a competitive force, one that typically shakes up domestic economic interests. It is a powerful engine of change, creating winners and losers in its path. The law of international trade, for better or worse, shapes the scope and direction of this force.

The United States in its early years sheltered "infant" agricultural and industrial sectors behind protective tariffs and regulatory restraints. When the Great Depression of the 1930s arrived, the United States enacted highly protective tariffs under the Smoot-Hawley Tariff Act of 1930 intended to wall off its economy from foreign competition, in theory "saving American jobs for American citizens". Other nations around the world retreated from international trade through similarly protective laws. Fear of foreign trade (and foreigners) reached a zenith that most economists agree deepened and prolonged the Great Depression. World War II rescued the United States from the Depression, but did nothing to remove the Smoot-Hawley tariffs and encourage other nations to do likewise. International trade law was at a crossroads.

Despite its economic power and leadership in the development of modern trade law, the United States retains some of its early fear and concerns about international commerce. This is particularly apparent when U.S. free trade agreements are debated and undertaken, but also when the U.S. controls exports of goods and technology. *See* Chapter 10 and Section 2.4. Little wonder then that developing nations, many not much more than 50 years old and created out of colonial empires, hesitate to embrace the panoply of modern international trade law. Some developed nations are unusually dependent on international trade in goods and services. The Netherlands, for example, depend on exports for over 75% of their Gross Domestic product (GDP). Roughly 50% of the GDPs of Sweden, Germany and Switzerland derive from exports. Canada, New Zealand, France and Britain come in at about 25%, with the United States at approximately 12%.

The need to balance the protection of local industries from harm by foreign competitors and the encouragement of trade across national borders is a recurrent theme in the law of international business transactions. There has been a shift in recent years toward freer international trade reflected notably in diminished restrictions on imported goods and services. However, problems associated with imports and exports across borders still arise because of restrictive laws and practices which impede or distort trade.

Common devices include tariff barriers (e.g., import duties and export duties), as well as nontariff trade barriers (NTBs) such as quotas, import and export licensing procedures, safety, environmental, health and other regulatory standards, complex customs procedures, and government procurement policies. For example, France once required that all video recorders entering France had to do so through a small customs post at Poitiers and carry documentation written in French. Product distribution practices have been an effective NTB in Japan. The United States has a host of NTB restraints, reviewed in Chapter 7. Lastly, not all trade inhibiting barriers are government-made. Private sector cartel restraints can also keep international trade from reaching its full potential. *See* Chapter 19.

Bilateral Trade Treaties

Early efforts by countries to limit disruptive trade practices were traditionally found in bilateral treaties of Friendship, Commerce and Navigation (FCN), some of which remain in force. Such treaties opened the territory of each signatory to greater imports, at times controversially under "unequal treaty" terms favoring European nations and the United States in Asia, for example. Bilateral FCN treaty clauses were usually linked to other preferential trade agreements. Such linkage was most often accomplished through a reciprocal "most favored nation" (MFN) clause. In a MFN clause, both parties agree not to extend to any other nation trade arrangements which are more favorable than available under the bilateral treaty, unless the more favorable trade arrangements are immediately *also* available to the other FCN signatory. FCN treaties also focused on promoting foreign investment across borders, shipping and basic trade and investment principles of "national treatment" . . . the right to be taxed, regulated and generally treated in the same legal manner as domestic businesses.

At this point, the United States has moved beyond many of its FCN treaties to bilateral Trade and Investment Framework Agreements (TIFAs), Free Trade Agreements (FTAs) and Bilateral Investment Treaties (BITs). All three can be found at www.ustr.gov. FCN trade and investment law principles, notably MFN and national treatment, carry over into these agreements. TIFAs are centered on dialogue about trade and investment issues. They often precede the more advanced legal regimes of FTAs and BITs.

The United States has numerous TIFAs with individual countries and regional economic groups. The U.S. has TIFAs with Angola, Ghana, Liberia, Mauritius, Mozambique, Nigeria, Rwanda, South Africa and the Common Market for Eastern and Southern Africa (COMESA), the East African Community, the West African Economic and monetary Union (WAEMU) and the South African

Customs Union (titled as a Trade, Investment and Development Agreement). The U.S. also has TIFAs with Algeria, Bahrain, the Caribbean Common Market (CARICOM), Egypt, the Gulf Cooperation Council, Georgia, Iceland, Iraq, Kuwait, Lebanon, Libya, Oman, Qatar, Saudi Arabia, Switzerland, Tunisia, Turkey, Ukraine, the United Arab Emirates, Uruguay and Yemen. Additional TIFAs have been concluded with Afghanistan, collectively with five Central Asian nations, the Maldives, Nepal, Pakistan, Sri Lanka, the ASEAN group (Association of South East Asian Nations), Brunei, Cambodia, Indonesia, Malaysia, New Zealand, the Philippines, Thailand and Vietnam.

In various parts of the world, two or more countries have joined in customs unions or free trade areas in order to facilitate trade between those countries, and to acquire increased bargaining power in trade negotiations. The European Union and NAFTA are prime examples. Hundreds of bilateral and multilateral free trade agreements now lattice the globe, many replacing older FCN treaties. The free trade agreements of the United States are reviewed in Chapters 2 and 16. But the most dramatic and far reaching trade agreements in modern times originate from the General Agreement on Tariffs and Trade (GATT, 1947) and its successor, the World Trade Organization (WTO). Commencing in 1995, the WTO package of international trade agreements establishes a legal baseline for some 160 member states. *See* Section 1.3 for a list of the WTO agreements and directions as to their coverage in this book.

In the materials that follow, we move first to a review of the GATT (1947). The GATT was an international arrangement with over one hundred countries as Contracting States which regularly held multilateral trade negotiations (MTN) seeking ways of making international trade more open. These periodic negotiations cumulatively reduced tariff barriers by an average of up to eighty percent below those existing in the Great Depression. For example, after the most recent multilateral negotiations completed in 1994, average tariff rates of developed countries on dutiable manufactured imports were cut from 6.3 percent to 3.9 percent. In addition, considerable international trade now crosses borders duty free. Tariff reductions and eliminations are one of the success stories of GATT (1947). *See* Section 1.2.

But not all nations participated in the GATT 1947 or are members of its replacement, the WTO. By the 1970s, nontariff trade barriers (NTBs) began to be addressed by the GATT, including agreements designed to lessen NTBs such as complex customs valuation procedures, import licensing systems, product standards, subsidies and countervailing duties, and dumping practices. But the GATT NTB agreements were optional, and most of the developing world membership opted out. By the 1990s international trade law was once again at a crossroad.

§ 1.1   The General Agreement on Tariffs and Trade, Core MFN and National Treatment Principles

United States, British and other participants in the 1994 Bretton Woods, New Hampshire meetings recognized a post-War need to reduce trade obstacles in order to foster freer trade. They envisioned the creation of an International Trade Organization (ITO) to achieve the desired result. Fifty-three countries met in Havana in 1948 to complete drafting the Charter of an ITO that would be the international organizational umbrella underneath which negotiations could occur periodically to deal with tariff reductions and other trade law matters. A framework for such negotiations had already been staked out in Geneva in 1947, in what was expected to be only a transitional document, the General Agreement on Tariffs and Trade (GATT 1947) in goods.

Twenty-three nations participated in that first GATT session, India, Chile, Cuba and Brazil representing the developing world. China participated; Japan and West Germany did not. Stringent trading rules for goods (and only goods) were adopted only where there were no special interests of major participants to alter them. The developing nations objected to many of the strict rules, arguing for special treatment justified on development needs, but they achieved few successes in drafting GATT 1947. Some commenters believe GATT 1947 was in essence a deal struck between the United States and Europe, especially Britain.

The ITO Charter was never ratified. The United States Congress in the late 1940s was unwilling to join more new international organizations. Thus U.S. ratification of the ITO Charter could not be secured. Nonetheless, moving by way of the President Truman's power to make executive agreements, the United States did join twenty-one other countries, as Contracting Parties, in signing a Protocol of Provisional Application of the General Agreement on Tariffs and Trade (61 Stat.Pts. 5, 6) (popularly called the "GATT 1947 Agreement").

One notable feature of this protocol was the exemption of existing trade restraints of the Contracting States. Because of the failure to create the ITO, the GATT 1947 Agreement evolved from its "provisional" status into the premier international trade body, GATT the **organization** based in Geneva. It was through this organization that tariffs were steadily reduced over decades by means of increased membership and GATT negotiating Rounds. Today, the GATT 1947 Agreement has been replaced by the substantially similar GATT 1994 Agreement, part of the World Trade Organization "package" of trade agreements that took effect in 1995. *See* Section 9.3. The United States, having denied the creation of the ITO in the late 1940s, had to wait more that forty years for a second bite at the apple. When that opportunity finally came, the U.S. was among the strongest proponents of the WTO.

Trade in Goods: MFN Treatment

One of the central features of GATT 1947 and 1994 is Article I, which makes a general commitment to the long standing practice of "most favored nation treatment" (MFN) by requiring each Contracting Party to accord unconditional MFN status to goods from all other Contracting Parties. Thus, any privilege or tariff granted by a Contracting Party to products imported from any other country (not necessarily a WTO member) must also be "immediately and unconditionally" granted to any "like product" imported from any Contracting Parties. Article 1 of the GATT (1947) and (1994) spells out the golden rules of MFN trading:

> With respect to customs duties and charges of any kind imposed on or in connection with importation or exportation or imposed on the international transfer of payments for imports or exports, and with respect to the method of levying such duties and charges, and with respect to all rules and formalities in connection with importation and exportation, and with respect to all matters referred to in paragraphs 2 and 4 of Article III, any advantage, favour, privilege or immunity granted by any contracting party to any product originating in or destined for any other country shall be accorded immediately and unconditionally to the like product originating in or destined for the territories of all other contracting parties. (emphasis added).

MFN principles essentially ban de jure and de facto tariff and trade discrimination. Goods in transit between WTO member states are exempt from transit duties or charges. For leading WTO Appellate Body decisions on the application of MFN rules, see EC-Bananas, WT/DS27/AB/R (1997), Canada-Autos, WT/DS139/AB/R (2000). There are two major exceptions to the MFN obligation of Article I: Free trade areas and customs unions (see Chapter 15) and differential and more favorable treatment of goods from developing countries (see Chapter 2). General exceptions contained in GATT Article XX and XXI (see below) may also apply.

Trade in Goods: National Treatment

GATT Article III incorporates the practice of according "national treatment" to imported goods by providing, with enumerated exceptions, that they shall receive the same tax and regulatory treatment as domestic goods. In this context, national treatment requires that "like products" of the exporting GATT Contracting State be treated no less favorably than domestic products of the importing State under its laws and regulations concerning sale, internal resale, purchase, transportation and use. Physical properties, consumer perspectives and tariff classifications all contribute to evaluating the "likeness" of products. See EC-Asbestos, WT/DS 135/AB/R (2001). In addition to film distribution quotas (Article IV), two major exceptions apply to Article III: Government procurement policies (see Section 1.10), and authorized subsidization of domestic industries (see Chapter 5).

The core text of Article III provides:

The contracting parties recognize that internal taxes and other internal charges, and laws, regulations and requirements affecting the internal sale, offering for sale, purchase, transportation, distribution or use of products, and internal quantitative regulations requiring the mixture, processing or use of products in specified amounts or proportions, should not be applied to imported or domestic products so as to afford protection to domestic production.

The products of the territory of any contracting party imported into the territory of any other contracting party shall not be subject, directly or indirectly, to internal taxes or other internal charges of any kind in excess of those applied, directly or indirectly, to like domestic products. Moreover, no contracting party shall otherwise apply internal taxes or other internal charges to imported or domestic products in a manner contrary to the principles set forth in paragraph 1. * * * *

The products of the territory of any contracting party imported into the territory of any other contracting party shall be accorded treatment no less favorable than that accorded to like products of national origin in respect of all laws, regulations and requirements affecting their internal sale, offering for sale, purchase, transportation, distribution or use. The provisions of this paragraph shall not prevent the application of differential internal transportation charges which are based exclusively on the economic operation of the means of transport and not on the nationality of the product.

Where GATT does permit non-discriminatory "duties, taxes and other charges," the powers of a Contracting Party are limited even as to these devices. First, GATT Article X requires that notice be given of any new or changed national regulations which affect international trade, by requiring the prompt publication of those "laws, regulations, judicial decisions and administrative rulings of general application." Second, the Contracting Parties commit themselves "from time to time" to a continuing series of multilateral tariff negotiations (MTN) to seek further reductions in tariff levels and other barriers to international trade. Such negotiations are to be "on a reciprocal and mutually advantageous basis." GATT negotiated tariff rates (called "concessions" or "bindings"), which are listed in the "Tariff Schedules", are deposited with GATT by each participating country. These concessions must be granted to imports from any Contracting Party, both because of the GATT requires MFN treatment, and also because Article II specifically requires use of the negotiated rates.

The 1947 GATT Agreement and its subsequent multinational negotiating rounds were quite successful in reducing tariff duty levels on trade in goods. *See* Section 1.2 below. This was its original purpose, and the mechanism was well-adapted to accomplishing that purpose. However, its effectiveness was also limited to trade in goods, and primarily to reduction of tariffs in such trade. It was not designed to affect trade in services, trade-related intellectual property rights or trade-related investment measures. As tariff duty rates declined, the trade-distorting effects of these other issues became more important.

Trade in Goods: General Exceptions

Even within "trade in goods," the 1947 GATT had limitations. It included a Protocol of Provisional Application which allowed numerous grandfathered exceptions to Members' obligations under the GATT Agreement. The Protocol exempted from GATT disciplines the national laws of Member States which were already enacted and in force at the time of adoption of the Protocol. This "grandfather clause" no longer applies under GATT 1994.

Framers of GATT 1947 were well aware that a commitment to freer trade could cause serious, adverse economic consequences from time to time within part or all of a country's domestic economy, particularly its labor sector. The GATT 1947 and 1994 contains at least seven safety valves (in nine clauses of the Agreement) to permit a country, in appropriate circumstances, to respond to domestic pressures while remaining a participant in GATT. Two safety valves deal with antidumping duties and countervailing government subsidies. *See* Chapters 4 and 5. Another important safety valve concerns "safeguard procedures." *See* Chapter 6.

General omnibus exceptions to the GATT are established in Chapter XX, notably for measures "necessary" to protect public morals, and human, animal and plant life or health. *See* U.S.-Shrimp, WT/DS 58/AB/R (1998) (protection of endangered sea turtles). Evaluating whether measures are "necessary" requires consideration of reasonably available alternative approaches to achieve public policy goals. *See* Brazil-Tyres, WT/DS332/AB/R (2007) (ban on imports of retreaded tires upheld) and EC-Asbestos, WT/DS/AB/R (2001) (ban on asbestos imports upheld). Another general exception concerns measures "relating to" the conservation of exhaustible natural resources. *See* China-Raw Materials, WT/DS 394, 395, 398 (Panel, 2011) (export quota on bauxite and export duty on fluorspar did not relate to conservation). Other general exceptions concern trade in gold and silver, prison labor, protection of national treasures, commodity agreements, government stabilization plans and products in general or local short supply.

All of these general exceptions are subject to the qualifying language of the Article XX "chapeau": They may not be applied in an arbitrary or unjustifiably discriminatory manner, or constitute a disguised restriction on international trade. *See* U.S.-Shrimp, 21.5, WT/DS58/AB/RW (2001) (unjustifiable and arbitrary discrimination found in U.S. shrimp import restraints intended to conserve endangered sea turtles). For additional examples of the application of these exceptions and its chapeau, see Sections 1.7, 7.4 and 7.5.

Chapter XXI of the GATT preserves the right of member states to act in ways it considers necessary for the protection of its essential security interests. WTO members, in accordance with GATT Articles XII, XV and XVIII, may also generally undertake trade and monetary exchange restraints necessary to deal with their balance of payments needs.

§ 1.2   The GATT/WTO Multinational Trade Negotiations (Rounds)

Under the auspices of GATT 1947 Article XXVIII, the Contracting Parties committed themselves to hold periodic multinational trade negotiations (MTN or "Rounds"). They completed eight such Rounds with the GATT membership steadily increasing:

Geneva (1947) with 19 countries

Annecy (1948) with 27 countries

Torquay (1950) with 33 countries

"Dillon Round" Geneva (1960–62) with 36 countries

"Kennedy Round" Geneva (1964–67) with 74 countries

"Tokyo Round" Geneva (1973–79) with 85 countries

"Uruguay Round" Geneva (1986–94) with 128 countries

The WTO Doha Round (2001–   ) is marginally ongoing.

The largest exporters by volume of particular goods generally take the lead on tariff reduction negotiations. While the first five Rounds concentrated on item by item tariff reductions, the "Kennedy Round" (1964–1967) was noted for its achievement of across-the-board tariff reductions. In 1961, GATT began to consider how to approach the increasing trade disparity with the developing world. In 1964, GATT adopted Part IV, which introduced a principle of "diminished expectations of reciprocity". Reciprocity remained a goal, but developed nations would not expect concessions from developing nations which were inconsistent with developmental needs. For the developing nations, non-reciprocity meant freedom to protect domestic markets from import competition. Import substitution was a major focus of developmental theory in the 1960s, and developing nations saw keeping their markets closed as a way to save these domestic industries. Part IV of GATT 1947 resulted in a substantial growth in developing nation Contracting Parties.

Although they also sought preferential treatment of their exports, that was a demand which would remain unsatisfied for another decade and longer. *See* Sections 2.10–2.16 covering GATT approved "generalized tariff preference" (GSP) schemes.

The "Tokyo Round" (1973–1979) engendered agreements about several areas of nontariff barrier (NTB) trade restraints. Nearly a dozen major agreements on nontariff barrier issues were produced in the Tokyo Round. In the early 1970s, national and regional generalized preference schemes (GSP) developed to favor the exports of developing nations. The foreign debt payment problems of the developing nations suggest that they need to generate revenue to pay these debts, and that developmental theory must shift from import substitution to export promotion.

In 1986, the "Uruguay Round" of multilateral trade negotiations began at a Special Session of the GATT Contracting States. This Uruguay Round included separate negotiations on trade in goods and on trade in services, with separate groups of negotiators dealing with each topic. Subtopics for negotiation by subgroups included nontariff barriers, agriculture, subsidies and countervailing duties, intellectual property rights and counterfeit goods, safeguards, tropical products, textiles, investment policies, and dispute resolution. The negotiating sessions were extraordinarily complex, but were able to achieve a successful conclusion at the end of 1993, giving birth to the World Trade organization in 1995.

WTO Negotiating Rounds

In 1999 an attempt at launching a "Seattle Round" led by President Clinton failed with violence in the streets. Two years later, the "Doha Round" was successfully launched in Qatar covering all existing WTO fields as well as E-commerce, trade and the environment, debt and finance, and special and differential treatment and assistance for developing countries. Developed WTO countries have been pushing foreign investment, competition policy, transparency in procurement, and trade facilitation topics. At Cancun in 2003, the WTO developing nations rejected these topics, focusing on agricultural trade barriers to their exports.

Scheduled for completion in 2005, the Doha Round of WTO negotiations collapsed in July 2008 after marathon sessions. India and China, in particular, insisted upon Special Safeguard Mechanisms against surges in agricultural imports, provisions the U.S. and EU did not accept. The members were in agreement on nearly all other areas of the Doha Round negotiations. In 2013, WTO members agreed on a "Bali Package" concerning trade facilitation focused on customs law. At this writing, the Doha Round remains on life support, which has caused many nations to accelerate their participation in bilateral and regional free trade agreements. *See* Chapter 15.

§ 1.3   The World Trade Organization (WTO): Directory of Agreements, Admission

The WTO is the product of the Uruguay Round of GATT negotiations, which was successfully completed in 1994. The Uruguay Round produced a package of agreements, the Agreement Establishing the World Trade Organization and its Annexes, which include the General Agreement on Tariffs and Trade 1994 (GATT 1994) and a series of Multilateral Trade Agreements (the Covered Agreements).[1] These agreements extend way beyond trade in goods to trade in services, trade-related intellectual property rights, trade-

---

[1]   *See* 33 Int. Legal Mat. 1130 (1994).

related investment measures, and a binding system of dispute settlement. All of the Covered Agreements are non-negotiable; they are mandatory. Four Plurilateral Trade Agreements are optional, though two of these Agreements (Dairy and Bovine Meat) have been rescinded.

GATT 1947 and GATT 1994 are two distinct agreements. GATT 1994 incorporates the provisions of GATT 1947, except for the Protocol of Provisional Application, which is expressly excluded. Thus, the problems created by exempting the existing national laws at the time of the adoption of the Protocol have been avoided by this exclusion. Otherwise, in cases involving a conflict between GATT 1947 and GATT 1994, GATT 1947 controls. The WTO will be guided by the decisions, procedures and customary practices under GATT. The WTO package of agreements are routinely construed in light of the Vienna Convention on the Interpretation of Treaties. *See, e.g.,* EC-Chicken, WT/DS269/AB/R (2005).

Annexed to the WTO Agreement are several Multilateral Trade Agreements. As to trade in goods, they include Agreements on Agriculture, Textiles, Antidumping, Subsidies and Countervailing Measures, Safeguards, Technical Barriers to Trade, Sanitary and Phytosanitary Measures, Pre-shipment Inspection, Rules of Origin, and Import License Procedures. In addition to trade in goods, they include a General Agreement on Trade in Services and Agreements on Trade-Related Aspects of Intellectual Property Rights and Trade-Related Investment Measures.

Affecting all of these agreements is the Understanding on Rules and Procedures Governing the Settlement of Disputes (DSU). All of the Multilateral Trade Agreements are generally binding on all members of the World Trade Organization. Moreover, should a conflict arise between GATT 1994 and one of these Agreements, the latter prevails. Hence in WTO dispute proceedings where a conflict may exist, panels are required to first examine the specific Multilateral Agreement before taking up the GATT 1994 issue. *See* EC-Sardines, WTO/DS231/AB/R (2002) and U.S.-Internet Gambling, WT/DS 285/AB/R (2005).

Existing WTO members may declare "non-application" of all these Agreements vis-à-vis new members, thus opting out of their application to them. The United States, for example, declared non-application of the WTO Agreements to Armenia, Moldova, Georgia, Mongolia and the Kyrgyz Republic when those nations joined the WTO, although these declarations were subsequently revoked for all but Moldova.

In addition to the Multilateral Trade Agreements, there are also Plurilateral Trade Agreements, which are annexed to the WTO Agreement. These agreements, however, are not binding on all WTO members, and states can choose to adhere to them or not. They include Agreements on Government Procurement, Trade in Civil Aircraft, International Dairy (rescinded), and an Arrangement Regarding Bovine Meat (rescinded). Member states which do not join the plurilateral trade agreements do not receive reciprocal benefits under them. Participating members agree to utilize the DSU to settle Plurilateral Trade Agreement disputes.

WORLD TRADE ORGANIZATION AGREEMENTS

AGREEMENT ESTABLISHING THE WORLD TRADE ORGANIZATION

ANNEX 1A: AGREEMENTS ON TRADE IN GOODS

1   General Agreement on Tariffs and Trade 1994

   (a) Understanding on the Interpretation of Article II:1(b) (tariff concessions)

   (b) Understanding on the Interpretation of Article XVII (state trading enterprises)

   (c) Understanding on Balance-of-Payments Provisions

   (d) Understanding on the Interpretation of Article XXIV (free trade areas and customs unions) *See Chapter 15.*

   (e) Understanding on the Interpretation of Article XXV (waivers)

   (f) Understanding on the Interpretation of Article XXVIII (modification of tariff schedules)

   (g) Understanding on the Interpretation of Article XXXV (non-application of GATT)

2   GATT 1994 *(See Section 1.3)*

3   Agreement on Agriculture *(See Section 1.8)*

4   Agreement on Sanitary and Phytosanitary Measures *(See Section 1.7)*

5   Agreement on Textiles and Clothing *(See Section 1.6)*

6   Agreement on Technical Barriers to Trade *(See Section 1.7)*

7   Agreement on Trade-Related Investment Measures *(See Section 1.12)*

8   Agreement on Implementation of Article VI (antidumping and countervailing duties) *See Chapters 4 and 5.*

9   Agreement on Implementation of Article VII (customs valuation) *See Chapter 3.*

10   Agreement on Preshipment Inspection

11   Agreement on Rules of Origin *(See Section 1.10)*

12   Agreement on Import Licensing Procedures *(See Section 1.6)*

13   Agreement on Subsidies and Countervailing Measures *(See Chapter 5)*

14   Agreement on Safeguards *(See Chapter 6)*

ANNEX 1B: General Agreement on Trade in Services and Annexes *(See Section 1.9)*

ANNEX 1C: Agreement on Trade-Related Aspects of Intellectual Property Rights, Including Trade in Counterfeit Goods *(See Section 1.11)*

ANNEX 2:   Understanding on Rules and Procedures Governing the Settlement of Disputes *(See Sections 1.14 and 1.15)*

ANNEX 3:   Trade Policy Review Mechanism *(See Section 1.4)*

ANNEX 4:   Plurilateral Trade Agreements

ANNEX 4(a) Agreement on Trade in Civil Aircraft

ANNEX 4(b) Agreement on Government Procurement (See Section 1.13)

ANNEX 4(c) International Dairy Arrangement (rescinded)

ANNEX 4(d) Arrangement Regarding Bovine Meat (rescinded)

In addition, Accession Agreements undertaken by new members may add to or subtract from the WTO package of mandatory multilateral agreements. China, for example, agreed to the application of special "safeguard" rules against its exports for a limited period of time after its WTO admission in 2001. *See* Section 6.12.

The duties of the World Trade Organization are to facilitate the implementation, administer the operations and further the objectives of all these agreements. Its duties also include the resolution of disputes under the agreements, reviews of trade policy and cooperation with the International Monetary Fund (IMF) and the World Bank. To achieve these goals, the WTO Agreement provides a charter for the new organization, but for only minimalist institutional and procedural capabilities, and no substantive competence. Thus, there is a unified administration of pre-existing and new obligations under all agreements concerning trade in goods, including the Uruguay Round Agreements. In addition, the administration of the new obligations on trade in services, intellectual property and foreign investment were brought under the same roof.

The WTO as an institution has no power to bring actions on its own initiative. Under the provisions of the WTO Agreement, only the members of WTO can initiate actions under the Dispute Settlement Understanding. Enforcement of WTO obligations is primarily through permitting members to retaliate or cross retaliate against other members, rather than by execution of WTO institutional orders. *See* Section 1.6 below. As Article 3.2 of the DSU suggests, many panel and Appellate Body decisions utilize the Vienna Convention on Interpretation of Treaties to clarify the meaning of the WTO package of agreements.

Admission to the WTO

The existing 130 or so members of GATT 1947 became the WTO's founding member states. Admission to the World Trade Organization is in common practice by "consensus." In theory, this gives each member a veto over applicant countries, though a formal two-thirds affirmative vote could be employed. In reality, no nation wishing to join has ever formally been vetoed, though many have been long delayed. Iran's desire to join has basically been frustrated by U.S. refusal to negotiate on WTO entry. It took, for example, well over a decade to negotiate acceptable terms of entry for the People's Republic of China in 2001, Vietnam in 2007 and Russia in 2012. Such negotiations are handled individually by member states, not by the WTO as an organization. United States negotiations with China were particularly lengthy and difficult, one principal issue being whether China should be admitted as a developing or developed nation, which is normally a self-selected choice. The issue was fudged, with China treated differently within the WTO mandatory package of agreements. China's admission also brought in Chinese Taipei (Taiwan).

Essentially, applicant counties make an offer of trade liberalization commitments and compliance with the mandatory Covered Agreements to join the WTO. This offer is renegotiated with interested member states, some 40 nations regarding China, including the European Union which negotiates as a unit (NAFTA does not). Regarding China, the last member to reach agreement on WTO admission was Mexico, which extracted stiff promises against the dumping of Chinese goods. The various trade commitments made by the applicant in these bilateral negotiations are consolidated into a final accession protocol, which is then approved by "consensus." At this writing there are approximately 160 WTO member states. Any member may withdraw with six months' notice.

§ 1.4   WTO Decision-Making

The World Trade Organization is structured in three tiers. One tier is the Ministerial Conference, which meets biennially and is composed of representatives of all WTO members. Each member state has an equal voting weight. This is unlike the representation in the IMF and World Bank where there is weighted voting, and financially powerful states have more power over the decision-making process. The Ministerial Conference is responsible for all WTO functions, and is able to make any decisions necessary. It has the power to authorize new multilateral negotiations and to adopt the results of such negotiations. The Ministerial Conference, by a three-fourths vote, is authorized to grant waivers of obligations to members in exceptional circumstances. It also has the power to adopt interpretations of Covered Agreements. When the Ministerial Conference is in recess, its functions are performed by the General Council.

The second tier is the General Council which has executive authority over the day to day operations and functions of the WTO. It is composed of representatives of all WTO Members, and each member has an equal voting weight. It meets whenever it is appropriate. The General Council also has the power to adopt interpretations of Covered Agreements.

The third tier comprises the councils, bodies and committees which are accountable to the Ministerial Conference or General Council. Ministerial Conference committees include Committees on Trade and Development, Balance of Payment Restrictions, Budget, Finance and Administration. General Council bodies include the Dispute Settlement Body, the Trade Policy Review Body, and Councils for Trade in Goods, Trade in Services and Trade-Related Intellectual Property Rights. The Councils are all created by the WTO Agreement and are open to representatives of all member states. The Councils also have the authority to create subordinate organizations. Other committees, such as the Committee on Subsidies and Countervailing Measures are created by specific individual agreements.

Trade Policy Review Mechanism

Of the General Council bodies, the two which are most important are the Dispute Settlement Body (DSB) and the Trade Policy Review Body (TPRB). The DSB is a special meeting of the General Council, and therefore includes all WTO members. It has responsibility for resolution of disputes under all the Covered Agreements, discussed in more detail in Section 1.14 under Dispute Resolution.

The purpose of the Trade Policy Review Mechanism (TPRM) is to improve adherence to the WTO agreements and obligations, and to obtain greater transparency. In that regard, the TPRM supplements the general trade law transparency requirements of Chapter X of the GATT. Individual Members of WTO each prepare a "Country Report" on their trade policies and perceived adherence to the WTO Covered Agreements. The WTO Secretariat also prepares a report on each Member, but from the perspective of the Secretariat.

The Trade Policy Review Body (TPRB) then reviews the trade policies of each member based on these two reports. At the end of the review, the TPRB issues its own report concerning the adherence of the member's trade policy to the WTO Covered Agreements. The TPRB has no enforcement capability, but the report is sent to the next meeting of the WTO Ministerial Conference. It is then up to the Ministerial Conference to evaluate the trade practices and policies of the member.

Consensus Rules

The process of decision-making in the WTO Ministerial Conference and General Council relies upon "consensus" as the norm, just as it did for decision-making under GATT 1947. "Consensus", in this context means that no member formally objects to a proposed decision. Thus, consensus is not obtained if any one member formally objects, and has often been very difficult to obtain, which proved to be a weakness in the operation of GATT. However, there are many exceptions to the consensus formula under WTO, and some new concepts (such as "inverted consensus") which are designed to ease the process of decision-making under WTO.

Article IX(1) of the WTO Agreement first provides that "the practice of decision-making by consensus" followed under GATT shall be continued. The next sentence of that provision, however, states that "where a decision cannot be arrived at by consensus, the matter at issue shall be decided by voting", except where otherwise provided. The ultimate resolution of the conflict between these two sentences is not completely clear.

There are a number of exceptions to the requirement for consensus that are expressly created under the WTO Agreement. One such exception is decisions by the Dispute Settlement Body, which has its own rules (see Section 1.14). Another set of exceptions concerns decisions on waivers, interpretations and amendments of the Covered Agreements. Waivers of obligations may be granted and amendments adopted to Covered Agreements only by the Ministerial Conference. Amendments of Multilateral Trade Agreements usually require a consensus, but where a decision on a proposed amendment cannot obtain consensus, the decision on that amendment is to be made in certain circumstances by a two-thirds majority vote. In "exceptional circumstances", the Ministerial Conference is authorized to grant waivers of obligations under a Covered Agreement by a three-fourths vote. Another exception to the consensus requirement allows procedural rules in both the Ministerial Conference and the General Council to be decided by a majority vote of the members, unless otherwise provided.

Operationally speaking, the WTO membership rarely meets in its entirety. Alliances and groups within the membership meet to undertake WTO decisions. For example, the "Cairns Group" of 18 member-states has focused on agricultural trade issues and endured as a group for some time. Groups and alliances often shift depending upon the subject matter.

§ 1.5   WTO Agreements and U.S. Law

The WTO Covered Agreements concern not only trade in goods, but also trade in services (GATS), trade-related aspects of intellectual property (TRIPS) and trade-related investment measures (TRIMs). The basic MFN and national treatment concepts that GATT 1947 applied to trade in goods (see Section 1.1) are now applied to these areas through GATS and TRIPS. The basic concepts of GATT 1947 and its associated agreements are elaborated and clarified through interpretive "understandings". In addition, there is an attempt to transform all protectionist measures relating to agriculture (such as import bans and quotas, etc.) into only tariff barriers, which can then be lowered in subsequent MTN Rounds (a process known as "tariffication"). Some of the WTO provisions, particularly those concerning trade in goods, are discussed in more detail below in relation to United States trade law.

The United States enacted legislation to implement WTO and the Covered Agreements on December 3, 1994. The implementing legislation was submitted to Congress under the "fast track" procedures of 19 U.S.C.A. § 2112. The statutory authority for "fast track" procedures also required that the President give 90 days' notice of his intention to enter into such an agreement. Fast track required that the WTO Agreements be considered by Congress as negotiated by the President, with no Congressional amendments via the implementing legislation. Nevertheless, the Uruguay Round Agreements Act of 1994 was adopted with relatively little controversy. Similar fast track procedures were in place for the Doha Round of WTO negotiations under the Trade Promotion Authority Act of 2002, but expired in July of 2007.

GATT 1947, GATT 1994, the WTO Agreement and the other Covered Agreements have not been ratified as treaties. They therefore comprise international obligations of the United States only to the extent that they are incorporated in United States' implementing legislation. GATT 1947 was not considered controlling by the courts of the United States, which have always held themselves bound only to the U.S. legislation actually enacted.[2] The WTO Covered Agreements will be considered to have a non-self-executed status, and therefore are likely to be regarded in the same manner as GATT 1947.

§ 1.6   Import/Export Quotas and Licensing, Textiles and Clothing

In addition to requiring MFN and national treatment, GATT 1947 and 1994 prohibits use of certain kinds of quantitative restrictions. Subject to exceptions such as balance of payment crises, Article XI prohibits "prohibitions or restrictions" on imports and it specifically prohibits the use of "quotas, import or export licenses or other measures" to restrict imports from a Contracting Party. Quotas include voluntary export restrain agreements. See Japan-Semiconductors, GATT Panel Report (1988). If utilized, Article XIII requires non-discrimination in quantitative trade restrictions, by barring an importing Contracting State from applying any prohibition or restriction to the products of another Contracting State, "unless the importation of the like product of *all* third countries . . . is similarly prohibited or restricted." (emphasis added).

---

[2]   *See, e.g.*, Suramerica de Aleaciones Laminadas, C.A. v. United States, 966 F.2d 660 (Fed.Cir.1992).

The WTO has significantly reduced the number of trade quotas. By 2005, the Agreement on Textiles eliminated quotas long maintained under the Multi-Fiber Arrangement. *See* Section 1.7. Voluntary export restraints (quotas) are severely limited by the Safeguards Agreement. *See* Section 6.3. In addition, the WTO removes trade quotas by advancing "tariffication," replacing quotas with tariffs—sometimes even at extraordinarily high tariff rates. Tariffication is the approach adopted in the WTO Agricultural Agreement. *See* Section 9.9.

Quantity restrictions, such as numerical quotas on the importation or exportation of goods continue to exist, despite GATT Article XI which calls for their elimination, subject to a number of broadly worded exceptions to relieve critical shortages, to ensure domestic price controls, and to remediate short supply conditions. "Tariff-rate quotas" admit a specified quantity of goods at a preferential rate of duty. Once imports reach that quantity, tariffs are normally increased. WTO disputes concerning quotas have resulted in a number of panel and Appellate Body decisions that largely treat import rules that can create de facto quantitative restraint effects as prohibited by Article XI. For example, in *India-Autos* (WTO/DS16/AB/R (2002) "trade balancing" rules requiring producers to export in order to import were held to breach Article XI.

The Agreement on Textiles eliminated in 2005 the quotas long maintained under the Multi-Fibre Arrangement. The demise of MFA textile quotas in 2005, as widely expected, accelerated Chinese and other Asian textile exports to the United States. Responding to domestic pressures, the United States repeatedly invoked special safeguard protections against textile and clothing imports during the ten-year phase-out period that ended in 2005. Since then the average U.S. bound and applied tariff on textile products has been around 8 percent.

Import (but not export) licensing schemes are allowed when quotas are permitted. On export licensing, see Section 1.6. International concern about delays which result from cumbersome import licensing procedures was manifested in the 1979 Tokyo Round MTN Import Licensing Code (which most developing countries refused to sign). The United States adhered to this Code, as did a reasonable number of other developed nations. The Uruguay Round made the Agreement on Import Licensing Procedures (1994) binding on all World Trade Organization members. The Agreement's objectives include facilitating the simplification and harmonization of import licensing and licensing renewal procedures, ensuring adequate publication of rules governing licensing procedures, and reducing the practice of refusing importation because of minor variations in quantity, value or weight of the import item under license.

§ 1.7   GATT/WTO Nontariff Trade Barrier Codes, TBT and SPS Codes

There are numerous nontariff trade barriers applicable to imports. Many of these barriers arise out of safety and health regulations. Others concern the environment, consumer protection, product standards and government procurement. Many of the relevant rules were created for legitimate consumer and public protection reasons. They were often created without extensive consideration of their international impact as potential nontariff trade barriers. Nevertheless, the practical impact of legislation of this type is to ban the importation of nonconforming products. Thus, unlike tariffs which can always be paid, and unlike quotas which permit a certain amount of goods to enter the market, nontariff trade barriers have the potential to totally exclude foreign exports.

Multilateral GATT negotiations since the end of World War II have led to a significant decline in world tariff levels, particularly on trade with developed nations. As steadily as tariff barriers have disappeared, nontariff trade barriers (NTBs) have emerged. Health and safety regulations, environmental laws, rules regulating products standards, procurement legislation and customs procedures are often said to present NTB problems.

Negotiations over nontariff trade barriers dominated the Tokyo Round of the GATT negotiations during the late 1970s. A number of optional NTB "codes" (sometimes called "side agreements") emerged from the Tokyo Round. These concerned subsidies, dumping, government procurement, technical barriers (products standards), customs valuation and import licensing. In addition, specific agreements regarding trade in bovine meats, dairy products and civil aircraft, as well as government procurement, were also reached. The United States accepted all of these NTB codes and agreements except the one on dairy products. Most of the necessary implementation of these agreements was accomplished in the Trade Agreements Act of 1979. Nearly all of the developing members of GATT opted out of these NTB codes.

Additional NTB codes were agreed upon under the Uruguay Round ending in late 1994 and became part of the WTO legal regime. All of the NTB areas covered by the Tokyo Round Codes were revisited, and new codes created for sanitary and phyto-sanitary measures (SPS), trade-related investment measures (TRIMs), preshipment inspection, rules of origin, escape clause safeguards and trade-related intellectual property rights (TRIPs). Unlike the Tokyo Round Codes, the WTO nontariff barrier codes (save a few plurilateral codes) are **mandatory** for all members. The United States Congress approved and implemented these Codes, along with the optional WTO Procurement Code, in December of 1994 under the Uruguay Round Agreements Act.

One problem with nontariff trade barriers is that they are so numerous. Intergovernmental negotiation intended to reduce their trade restricting impact is both tedious and difficult. There are continuing attempts through the World Trade Organization to come to grips with additional specific NTB problems. Furthermore, various trade agreements of the United States have been undertaken in this field. For example, the Canada–United States Free Trade Area Agreement and the NAFTA built upon the existing GATT agreements in attempting to further reduce NTB problems between the United States, Canada and Mexico.

SPS Code

The SPS Code strongly encourages the use of international SPS standards, such as the Codex Alimentarius Commission. But member states may proceed to enact their own nondiscriminatory SPS rules, subject to the Code's mandates, notably that they be based upon risk assessments and scientific evidence. There is some suggestion in the decisions of the WTO Appellate Body that SPS measures must be "proportional" to the risks involved. See *Japan-Apples*, WT/DS245/AB/R (2003).

Some of the difficulties of these NTBs are illustrated in the *EU Beef Hormones* case (WT/DS 26/AB/R (1998). The Sanitary and Phytosanitary Code (SPS Code) basically requires adherence to international food standards, or a scientific basis for regulatory rules governing food products. The EU, adhering to "precautionary principles," banned imports of growth-enhancing hormone-treated beef from the U.S. and Canada as a health hazard. The Appellate Body ruled in 1997 under the SPS Code that, since the ban was stricter than international standards, the EU needed scientific evidence to back it up. The Appellate Body noted the EU had failed to undertake a scientific risk assessment, and the EU's scientific reports did not provide any rational basis to uphold the ban. In fact, the primary EU study had found no evidence of harm to humans from the growth-enhancing-hormones. If the "relevant scientific evidence is insufficient", there is limited recognition of precautionary principles in Article 5.7 of the SPS Code.

The Appellate Body concluded that the ban violated the EU's SPS obligations, and required the EU to produce scientific evidence to justify the ban within a reasonable time, or to revoke the ban. Arbitrators later determined that 15 months was a reasonable time. But the EU failed to produce such evidence and the U.S. retaliated (as authorized) by imposing substantial tariffs on EU imports. Late in 2004, the EU commenced WTO proceedings asserting that new scientific studies and precaution justified its ban and required removal of U.S. retaliation. This WTO proceeding also went against the EU, again in the absence of adequate proof of scientific basis. *See* U.S.-Continued Suspension in EC-Hormones, WT/320/AB/R (2008). Finally, in 2009, a phased four year settlement of the *Beef Hormones* dispute was reached. The U.S. got a higher quota to export hormone-free beef to the EU in return for phasing out its retaliatory tariffs on EU goods.

TBT Code

Widespread use of "standards" requirements as NTB import restraints resulted in 1979 in the GATT Agreement on Technical Barriers to Trade (called the "Standards Code"). This Code was made operative in the United States by the Trade Agreements Act of 1979, and was followed by a reasonable number of other developed nations.

Its successor is the WTO Agreement on Technical Barriers to Trade (1994) (TBT Code). By explicit provision in Article 1.5 of the TBT Code, the SPS Code takes precedence over the TBT Code. The Appellate Body has held that both Codes take precedence over GATT 1994 issues. The TBT Code is binding on all WTO members. It strongly favors conforming use of international product standards, such as those of the International Standards Organization. See EC-Sardines, WT/DS231/AB/R (2002) (EC marketing rule not based on Codex Alimentarius standard). In general, the TBT Code deals with the problem of manipulation of product standards and labels, product testing procedures, and product certifications in order to slow or stop imported goods. To this end, the TBT Code requires NTBs to be not more trade restrictive than necessary to effectuate legitimate governmental objectives.

The TBT Code provides, in part and subject to some exceptions, that imported products shall be accorded treatment (including testing treatment and certification) no less favorable than that accorded to like products of national origin or those originating in any other country. It also requires that WTO members establish a central office for standards inquiries, publish advance and reasonable notice of requirements that are applicable to imported goods, and provide an opportunity for commentary by those who may be affected adversely. The TBT Code establishes an international committee to deal with alleged instances of noncompliance. For U.S. implementation of the TBT Code, see Section 7.4.

Various United States TBT, notably dolphin-safe and imported meat origin labels as well as flavored cigarette standards, have been challenged in WTO dispute settlement proceedings. *See* Section 7.5.

§ 1.8   The WTO Agreement on Agriculture

Agricultural issues played a central role in the Uruguay Round negotiations and are critical to the Doha Round as well. More than any other issue, they delayed completion of the Uruguay Round from 1990 to 1993. The agreement reached in December of 1993 is a trade liberalizing, market-oriented effort. Each country has made a number of commitments on market access, reduced domestic agricultural support levels and export subsidies. The United States Congress approved these commitments in December of 1994 by adopting the Uruguay Round Agreements Act.

Broadly speaking nontariff barriers (NTBs) to international agricultural trade are replaced by tariffs that provide substantially the same level of protection. This is known as "tariffication." It applies to virtually all NTBs, including variable levies, import bans, voluntary export restraints and import quotas. *See* Chile-Price Band System, WT/DS207/AB/R (2002). Tariffication applies specifically to U.S. agricultural quotas adopted under Section 22 of the Agricultural Adjustment Act. All agricultural tariffs, including those converted from NTBs, are to be reduced by 36 and 24 percent by developed and developing countries, respectively, over 6 and 10 year periods. Certain minimum access tariff quotas apply when imports amount to less than 3 to 5 percent of domestic consumption. An escape clause exists for tariffed imports at low prices or upon a surge of importation depending upon the existing degree of import penetration.

Regarding domestic support for agriculture, some programs with minimal impact on trade are exempt from change. These programs are known as "green box policies." They include governmental support for agricultural research, disease control, infrastructure and food security. Green box policies were also exempt from GATT/WTO challenge or countervailing duties for 9 years. Direct payments to producers that are not linked to production are also generally exempt. This will include income support, adjustment assistance, and environmental and regional assistance payments. Furthermore, direct payments to support crop reductions and *de minimis* payments are exempted in most cases.

After removing all of the exempted domestic agricultural support programs, the agreement on agriculture arrives at a calculation known as the Total Aggregate Measurement of Support (Total AMS). This measure is the basis for agricultural support reductions under the agreement. Developed nations reduced their Total AMS by 20 percent over 6 years, developing nations by 13.3 percent over 10 years. United States reductions undertaken in 1985 and 1990 meant that little or no U.S. action was required to meet this obligation. Agricultural export subsidies of developed nations were reduced by 36 percent below 1986–1990 levels over 6 years and the quantity of subsidized agricultural exports by 21 percent. Developing nations had corresponding 24 and 14 percent reductions over 10 years.

All conforming tariffications, reductions in domestic support for agriculture and export subsidy alterations were essentially exempt from challenge for 9 years within the GATT/WTO on grounds such as serious prejudice in export markets or nullification and impairment of agreement benefits. However, countervailing duties could be levied against all unlawfully subsidized exports of agricultural goods except for subsidies derived from so-called national "green box policies" (discussed in Chapter 5). In *U.S.- Upland Cotton* (WTO/DS267/AB/R (2005), the Appellate Body affirmed that member states must not only conform to the Agreement on Agriculture, but also the SCM Agreement. In that decision, U.S. compliance with the Agriculture Agreement was acknowledged, but its "Step-2" payments to cotton users favoring domestic over imported cotton (local content subsidies) were held to violate the SCM Agreement.

§ 1.9   The General Agreement on Trade in Services (GATS)

Because protectionist barriers to international trade in services were stifling, the United States and other developed countries insisted that there should be a General Agreement on Trade in Services (GATS). In the United States, services account for over two-thirds of the Nation's GDP and provide jobs for nearly two-thirds of the work force. Services account for almost one-third of U.S. exports in sectors such as tourism, education, construction, telecommunications, transport and health. In contrast, most developing nations are minimal exporters of services, save by means of exporting their people . . . but migration was not included as a subject under the GATS.

Market access for services is a major focus of the General Agreement on Trade in Services (GATS), a product of the Uruguay

Round of Negotiations. The GATS defines the supply of services broadly to include providing services across borders or inside member states with or without a commercial presence therein. Apart from ensuring transparency of national regulatory controls over services, the core GATS Article XVII commitment is to afford most-favored-nation treatment to service providers, subject to country-specific, preferential trade agreement or labor market integration agreement exemptions, such as audio-visual services in the EU.

In addition, each WTO member state made under GATS XVI specific schedule of commitments (concessions) on opening up their markets in services' sectors negotiated using the WTO Services Sectoral Classification List: Business services; communication; construction; distribution; educational; environmental; financial; health-related and social services; tourism; recreational and sporting; transport; and other services. They further agreed under Article XVI to provide national treatment to their services' commitment schedule. For example, to what degree may foreign banks or foreign economic consultants provide services, and are they entitled to national treatment?

The answers to those questions will be found in the GATS specific commitments of each member. Much to its consternation, the United States was found to have failed to exclude Internet gambling services under its GATS commitments' schedule. This caused Antigua-Barbuda to prevail in a dispute that alleged U.S. gambling laws discriminatorily prohibited its right to export such services to the U.S. market. *See* U.S.-Gambling, WT/DS285/AB/R (2007). The United States also lost the argument that its Internet gambling services' restraints were justifiable on public morals' grounds. This argument failed as discriminatory under the "chapeau" of the GATS Article XIV general exceptions (similar to GATT Article XX general exceptions discussed in Section 1.1).

Special "GATS Rules" govern use of safeguards against surges of services' imports, subsidies applicable to services' exports, and government procurement of services. General GATS exceptions apply (for example, government supplied services), as do national security GATS exceptions.

National laws that restrict the number of firms in a market, that are dependent upon local "needs tests", or that mandate local incorporation are regulated by the GATS. Various "transparency" rules require disclosure of all relevant laws and regulations, and these must be administered reasonably, objectively and impartially. Specific service market access and national treatment commitments are made by various governments in schedules attached to the agreement. These commitments may be modified or withdrawn after 3 years, subject to a right of compensation that can be arbitrated. Certain mutual recognition of education and training for service-sector licensing occurs. State monopolies or exclusive service providers may continue, but must not abuse their positions. Detailed rules are created in annexes to the GATS on financial, telecommunications and air transport services. Under the Telecommunications Reference Paper (TRP), for example, the United States successfully argued that Telmex had abused its monopoly position in Mexico by charging discriminatory, non-cost-oriented connection fees for foreign calls. *See* Mexico—Telecoms, WT/DS204/AB/R (2004).

The U.S. Congress approved and implemented the GATS agreement in December of 1994 under the Uruguay Round Agreements Act. Subsequently, early in 1995, the United States refused to extend most-favored-nation treatment to financial services. The European Union, Japan and other GATS nations then entered into an interim 2-year agreement which operated on MFN principles. Financial services were revisited in 1996–97 with further negotiations aimed at bringing the United States into the fold. These negotiations bore fruit late in 1997 with 70 nations (including the United States) joining in an agreement that covers 95 percent of trade in banking, insurance, securities and financial information. This agreement took effect March 1, 1999.

The GATS has reduced unilateral U.S. action under Section 301 to gain access to foreign markets for U.S. service providers. This reduction flows from U.S. adherence to the Dispute Settlement Understanding (DSU) that accompanies the WTO accords. The DSU obligates its signatories to follow streamlined dispute settlement procedures under which unilateral retaliation is restrained until the offending nation has failed to conform to a World Trade Organization ruling.

GATS Disputes

GATS, and the 1996 Protocol on Telecommunications and 1997 Protocol on Financial Services, have generated only a handful of WTO disputes. Here is a sampling of them:

1.   EC—Regime for the Importation, Sale and Distribution of Bananas, WT/DS27/AB/R (1997) (traders of goods may also be traders of services, such as wholesaling or retailing, GATS Articles II and XVII apply to de jure and de facto discrimination).

2. Canada—Certain Measures Concerning Periodicals, WT/DS31/AB/R (1997) (GATT and GATS co-exist, no override).

3. Canada—Certain Measures Affecting The Automotive Industry, WT/DS139,142/R (2000) (coverage under GATS must be determined before assessment of consistency with GATS obligations).

4. Mexico—Measures Affecting Telecommunication Services WT/DS204/R(2004)(Mexican cross-border interconnection rates not cost-oriented and unreasonable in breach of Telecoms Annex, failure to allow access to private leased-circuits also violated commitments) (settled with rate reductions and increased access).

5. United States—Measures Affecting The Cross-Border Supply of Gambling and Betting Services, WT/DS 285/AB/R (2005) (gambling included in U.S. recreational services' commitments, U.S. import ban amounted to "zero quota" in breach of GATS Article XVI, necessary to protect public morals under Article XIV defense but discriminatory enforcement regarding Interstate Horseracing Act fails to meet "chapeau" requirements) (U.S. pays compensation to all GATS signatories except Antigua and Barbuda, the complaining party. . . . $21 million retaliation authorized in 2008).

6. China—Certain Measures Affecting Electronic payment Systems, WT/DS413/R (2012) (discriminatory restraints on foreign electronics payment services' suppliers violate GATS commitments).

§ 1.10   The WTO and Rules of Origin

The Uruguay Round accord on rules of origin is, in reality, an agreement to agree. A negotiations schedule was established along with a WTO Committee to work with the Customs Cooperation Council on harmonized rules of origin. Certain broad guiding principles for the negotiations are given and considered binding until agreement is reached. These principles are:

- Rules of origin applied to foreign trade must not be more stringent than applied to domestic goods.

- Rules of origin must be administered consistently, uniformly, impartially and reasonably.

- Origin assessments must be issued within 150 days of a request and remain valid for three years.

- New or modified rules or origin may not be applied retroactively.

- Strict confidentiality rules apply to information submitted confidentially for rule of origin determinations.

To date, no WTO agreement on rules of origin has been reached.

§ 1.11   The WTO TRIPs Agreement, U.S. Special 301 Procedures

The Uruguay Round accords of late 1993 include an agreement on trade-related intellectual property rights (TRIPs). This agreement is binding upon the roughly 160 nations that are members of the World Trade Organization. In the United States, the TRIPs agreement has been ratified and implemented by Congress under the Uruguay Round Agreements Act. There is a general requirement of national and most-favored-nation treatment among the parties.

Many developed nations had been trying unsuccessfully to promote expanded intellectual property rights through the U.N.-created World Intellectual Property Rights Organization (WIPO). WIPO agreements are not mandatory, and much of the developing world had declined to opt into their terms. Much to the benefit of private parties in the developed world, the TRIPs Code covers the gamut of intellectual property. It has de facto become a near-global IP Code.

On copyrights, there is protection for computer programs and databases, rental authorization controls for owners of computer software and sound recordings, a 50-year motion picture and sound recording copyright term, and a general obligation to comply with the Berne Convention (1971 version)(except for its provisions on moral rights).

On patents, the Paris Convention (1967 version) prevails, 20-year product and process patents are available "in all fields of technology", including pharmaceuticals and agricultural chemicals. However, patents can be denied when necessary to protect public morals or order, to protect human, animal or plant life or health, and to avoid serious environmental prejudice. The TRIPs provisions did not stop the Indian Supreme Court in 2013 from denying Novartis a patent on its cancer drug, Gleevac. The court took the view that Novartis was engaged in "evergreening", i.e., making small, inconsequential changes to existing patents and that Indian law could require proof of "improved therapeutic efficacy" before a patent grant.

Article 31 of the TRIPs permits compulsory licensing of patents in national emergencies or other circumstances of extreme urgency, subject to a duty to reasonably compensate the patent owner. Thailand has issued compulsory licenses on a range of cancer, heart disease and AIDS drugs. There is considerable controversy over pharmaceutical patents based on traditional medicines of indigenous peoples, which some see as bio-piracy. Proposals have been made to amend TRIPs to require disclosure of the origins of bio-patents, obtain informed consent from the indigenous communities involved, and share the benefits of such patents.

Note that by incorporating the Berne and Paris conventions, TRIPs and the WTO DSU become an enforcement mechanism for those longstanding treaties. For trademarks, the Paris Convention also rules, service marks become registrable, internationally prominent marks receive enhanced protection, the linking of local marks with foreign trademarks is prohibited, and compulsory licensing is banned. But gray market trading and related IP issues are explicitly not covered by TRIPs, allowing each WTO member state to differ on such law. *See* Chapter 9.

In addition, trade secret protection is assisted by TRIPs rules enabling owners to prevent unauthorized use or disclosure. These rules closely parallel those of NAFTA. *See* Section 16.8. Integrated circuits are covered by rules intended to improve upon the Washington Treaty. Lastly, protection of industrial designs and geographic indicators of product origin (e.g., Canadian Whiskey) are also part of the TRIPs regime.

Mandatory IP infringement and anti-counterfeiting remedies are included in the TRIPs, for both domestic and international trade protection. There are specific provisions governing injunctions, damages, judicial and customs seizures, and discovery of evidence. Willful trademark counterfeiting and copyright piracy on a commercial scale must be criminalized. Counterfeit goods may not be re-exported by customs authorities in an unaltered state.

The Medicines Agreement

Late in 2001, the Doha Round of WTO negotiations were launched. These negotiations have reconsidered the TRIPs agreement, particularly as it applies to developing nations. Their compliance deadline for the TRIPs' rules on patents for pharmaceuticals was extended to 2016, thereby allowing a continuation of cheaper, local generics. In addition, a Declaration on the TRIPs Agreement and Public Health was issued at the Qatar Ministerial Conference. This 20001 Declaration includes the following statement:

We agree that the TRIPs Agreement does not prevent Members from taking measures to protect public health. Accordingly, while reiterating our commitment to the TRIPs Agreement, we affirm that the Agreement can and should be interpreted and implemented in a manner supportive of WTO Members' right to protect public health and, in particular, to promote access to medicines for all.

A "Medicines Agreement" waiver (2003) and amendment to TRIPs (2005) implement this Declaration. Compulsory licensing and/or importation of generic copies of patented medicines needed to address developing nation public health problems are authorized. Such activities may not pursue industrial or commercial policy objectives, and different packaging and labeling must be used in an effort at minimizing the risk of diversion of the generics to developed country markets. Under pressure from the United States, a number of more advanced developing nations (such as Mexico, Singapore and Qatar) agreed not to employ compulsory licensing except in situations of national emergency or extreme urgency. Canada, China, the EU, India, South Korea and other members, on the other hand, have licensed production of drugs for nations incapable of pharmaceutical production.

Special 301—Prioritization of U.S. Intellectual Property Rights Disputes

The Special 301 procedures established by the 1988 Omnibus Trade and Competitiveness Act are permanent features of United States trade legislation. These procedures are located in Section 182 of the Trade Act of 1974.[3] Under these procedures the United States Trade Representative is required to identify foreign countries that deny adequate and effective protection of intellectual property rights, or deny fair and equitable access to United States persons that rely upon intellectual property protection. The USTR is given discretion to determine whether to designate certain of these countries to be "priority countries."

If so designated, a mandatory Section 301 investigation (see Section 14.4) must follow in the absence of a determination that this would be detrimental to U.S. economic interests or a negotiated settlement of the intellectual property dispute. Once designated, Special 301 investigations and retaliations against priority countries must ordinarily be decided within 6 months by the USTR. Whether to retaliate or not is discretionary with the USTR, but retaliation is not authorized if the country in question enters into good faith negotiations or makes "significant progress" in bilateral

---

[3]   19 U.S.C.A. § 2242.

or multilateral negotiations towards increased protection for intellectual property rights. Many commentators have observed that unilateral use of Section 301 prior to creation of the WTO helped push the U.S. agenda in the TRIPs negotiations. Since 1994, if the dispute is covered by the WTO TRIPs agreement, the United States must avoid using unilateral Section 301 trade sanctions and pursue WTO dispute settlement. *See* Section 1.14.

In identifying priority foreign countries in the intellectual property field, Section 182 indicates that the USTR is to prioritize only those countries that have the most "onerous or egregious" practices, whose practices have the greatest adverse impact on United States products, and are not entering into good faith negotiations bilaterally or multilaterally to provide adequate and effective protection of intellectual property rights.[4] For these purposes, the term "persons that rely on intellectual protection" covers those involved in copyrighted works of authorship or those involved in the manufacture of products that are patented or subject to process patents.[5] Interestingly, this definition does not include those who rely on United States trademarks.

However, the relevant definitions include trademarks in connection with the denial by foreign countries of adequate and effective protection of intellectual property rights. The definition of practices that deny fair and equitable market access in connection with intellectual property rights appear to be limited to copyrights and patents. This denial must constitute a violation of provisions of international law or international agreements to which both the United States and that country are parties or otherwise constitute a discriminatory nontariff trade barrier.[6]

Regular reports to Congress are required of the USTR by Section 182. The USTR has chiefly placed foreign country intellectual property practices on watch lists rather than formally designating priority countries. These watch lists are divided as between "priority watch lists" and "secondary watch lists." Many nations have been listed by the USTR since 1989 in this fashion. This has the practical effect of placing pressure on those nations to enter negotiations with the United States that will improve their protection of intellectual property rights.

The use of these lists gives the USTR more room to negotiate settlements with the countries concerned. For example, the USTR formally named China, India and Thailand as the first "priority

---

[4]   19 U.S.C.A. § 2422(b).

[5]   19 U.S.C.A. § 2242(d).

[6]   Id.

countries" for Special 301 purposes. The formal process of negotiation backed up by a mandatory Section 301 investigation and potential sanctions was begun. Thailand was cited for its failure to enforce copyrights and for the absence of patent protection for pharmaceuticals. India was named because its patent laws are deficient from the U.S. perspective, particularly on compulsory licensing and the absence of pharmaceutical protection. Extensive book, video, sound recording and computer software piracy in India was also cited.

United States Special 301 investigations and watch lists, now including "Out-of-Cycle Reviews of Notorious Markets", have continued relentlessly in spite of the WTO TRIPs agreement. The USTR has filed numerous TRIPs complaints with the WTO. *See* Section 1.15. Filings have been made, for example, against Denmark, Sweden, Ireland, Ecuador, Greece, Portugal, India, Russia, Pakistan, Turkey and, not surprisingly, China.

TRIPs Disputes

Dozens of TRIPs complaints have been initiated under WTO dispute settlement procedures. Most have been settled, but a few have resulted in WTO Panel and Appellate Body Reports. Here is a sampling of those disputes:

1. India—Patent Protection for Pharmaceutical and Agricultural Chemical Products, WT/DS50/AB/R (1998)("mailbox rule" patent applications for subjects not patentable in India until 2005 inadequate, denial of exclusive marketing rights in breach of TRIPs Article 70.9).

2. Canada—Term of Patent Protection, WT/DS170/AB/R (2000) (pre-TRIPs Canadian patents must receive 20 year term).

3. U.S.—Section 110 (5) Copyright Act, WT/DS160/R (2000) (copyright exemption for "homestyle" dramatic musical works consistent with Berne Convention, "business use" exemption inconsistent with Berne and therefore in breach of TRIPs) (settled by payment).

4. Canada—Pharmaceutical Patents, WT/DS114/R (2000) (Canadian generic pharmaceutical regulatory review and stockpiling patent rights' exceptions not sufficiently "limited").

5. U.S.—Section 211 Appropriations Act, WT/DS176/AB/R (2002) (prohibition against registering marks confiscated by Cuban government, e.g. HAVANA

CLUB rum, without original owner's consent violates Paris Convention and TRIPs, trade names covered by TRIPs).

6. EC—Trademarks and Geographical Indications WT/DS 174,290/R (2005) (EC regulation violates national treatment and most-favored treatment obligations to non-EC nationals, procedural violations also found).

7. China—Measures Affecting The Protection and Enforcement of Intellectual Property Rights, WT/DS362/R (2009) (China's implementation of TRIPs upheld as to criminal law thresholds and disposal of confiscated, infringing goods by customs authorities, rejected as to denial of copyright protection for works not authorized for release in China).

8. China—Measures Affecting Trading Rights and Distribution Services for Certain Publications and Audiovisuals Entertainment Products, WT/DS363/AB/R (2009) (China's ADV restrictions limited to state-owned or approved channels violate WTO Accession Protocol, GATT 1994 and GATS; Restraints not necessary to protect public morals).

9. European Communities—Information Technology Tariffs, WT/DS375–377 (2010) (EU tariffs on cable converter boxes with Net capacity, flat panel computer screens and printers that also scan, fax or copy violated 1996 Information Technology Agreement zero tariff rules).

§ 1.12 Trade-Related Investment Measures (TRIMs)

The WTO package of mandatory agreements includes TRIMs, Trade-Related Investment Measures. This is the only WTO agreement concerning foreign investment law, an area which is almost devoid of common international rules. The WTO is a trade law organization, hence its coverage of foreign investment is only "trade-related". In practice, this means that TRIMs is almost exclusively concerned with "performance requirements", i.e. national rules requiring designated performances by foreign investors. There are 14 performance requirements enumerated in and broadly prohibited by TRIMs. They fall into three general categories: (1) Local content rules; (2) Trade balancing rules; and (3) Export requirements.

Regarding performance requirements, TRIMs tracks the GATT Article III rule of "national treatment" and Article XI proscription against quotas. But member states may "deviate temporarily" from these principles, thus undermining their impact. Trade-related investment practices which are deemed inconsistent with TRIMs are listed illustratively in an Annex. These include minimum domestic content rules (say 50% of the value of the foreign investor's products must be sourced locally), limitations on imports used in production, the linkage of allowable imports to export requirements, export quotas or percentage of production requirements, and restrictions on foreign exchange designed to limit imports.

Perhaps because of their limited scope and soft prohibition, there have been very few TRIMs disputes. The United States and others did succeed in challenging Indonesia's local content requirements for autos. See Indonesia—Certain Measures Affecting the Automobile Industry, WT/DS/AB/R 54, 55, 59 & 64 (1998).

§ 1.13   The Optional WTO Public Procurement Code

Where public procurement is involved, and the taxpayer's money is at issue, virtually every nation has some form of legislation or tradition that favors buying from domestic suppliers. The Tokyo Round GATT Procurement Code was not particularly successful at opening up government purchasing. Relatively few GATT members and the United States adhered to that Procurement Code. This was also partly the result of the 1979 Code's many exceptions. For example, the Code did not apply to contracts below its threshold amount of $150,000 SDR (about $171,000 since 1988), service contracts, and procurement by entities on each country's reserve list (including most national defense items). Because procurement in the European Union and Japan is often decentralized, many contracts fell below the SDR threshold and were therefore GATT exempt. By dividing up procurement into smaller contracts national preferences were retained. United States government procurement tends to be more centralized and thus more likely to be covered by the GATT Code. This pattern may help explain why Congress restrictively amended the Buy American Act in 1988.

The Uruguay Round WTO Procurement Code took effect in 1995 and replaced the 1979 Tokyo Round GATT Procurement Code. The WTO Code (revised in 2014) expanded the coverage of the prior GATT Code to include procurement of services, construction, government-owned utilities, and some state and local (sub-central) contracts. The U.S. and the European Union applied the new Code's provisions on government-owned utilities and sub-central contracts as early as April 15, 1994. Other participants include Armenia,

Aruba, Chinese Taipei (Taiwan), Iceland, Japan, Korea, Israel, Lichtenstein, Norway, Singapore and Switzerland. Each participating country lists covered procuring entities and covered goods and services in Annexes, subject to contract thresholds and general exceptions. Nearly all developing nations have opted out of the WTO Procurement Code, though China has expressed interest in it.

Various improvements to the procedural rules surrounding procurement practices and dispute settlement under the WTO Code attempt to reduce tensions in this difficult area. For example, an elaborate system for bid protests is established. Bidders who believe the Code's procedural rules have been abused will be able to lodge, litigate and appeal their protests. The WTO Procurement Code became part of U.S. law in December of 1994 under the Uruguay Round Agreements Act. The United States has made, with few exceptions, all procurement by executive agencies subject to the Federal Acquisition Regulations under the Code's coverage (i.e., to suspend application of the normal Buy American preferences to such procurement). Thirteen U.S. states have not ratified the WTO Procurement Code. The economic stimulus and auto bail-out legislation of the Obama administration raised questions of U.S. compliance with the Code.

Chapter 10 of the North American Free Trade Area Agreement opened government procurement to U.S., Canadian and Mexican suppliers on contracts as small as $25,000. However, the goods supplied must have at least 50 percent North American content. These special procurement rules effectively created an exception to the GATT Procurement Code which otherwise applied. The thresholds are $50,000 for goods and services provided to federal agencies and $250,000 for government-owned enterprises (notably PEMEX and CFE). These regulations are particularly important because Mexico, unlike Canada, has not traditionally joined in GATT/WTO procurement codes. However, Chapter 10 does not cover state and provincial procurement. In December 2011 Canada-U.S. procurement provisions were incorporated in a long awaited agreement to expand the WTO Procurement Code. This expansion selectively brings more types of procurement contracts, notable service contracts, and more sub-central government entities within the Code's coverage. Contract value thresholds are also selectively lowered.

§ 1.14 WTO Dispute Settlement

GATT 1947 did not have an institutional charter, and was not intended to become an international organization on trade. It did later develop institutional structures and acquired quasi-organizational status, but there was always a lack of structure. This lack was most often perceived in the somewhat over-stated inability of GATT to resolve disputes which were brought to it. Indeed, GATT 1947 members could block the formation of a panel to hear a dispute. Moreover, GATT panel decisions could be blocked by the losing state! Hence most GATT 1947 dispute settlement panel reports were un-adopted, and as such "the GATT acquis" is said to merely provide guidance in the context of WTO dispute settlement. *See* Japan-Alcoholic Beverages II, WTO/DS/R 8, 10, 11 (1996).

The WTO provides a unified, mandatory, and exclusive intergovernmental system for settling trade disputes governed by WTO law through the Dispute Settlement Understanding (DSU) using the Dispute Settlement Body (DSB). There are no private remedies, though private sector interests are often motivating elements. In the United States, private parties and their attorneys can attempt to trigger WTO dispute settlement proceedings by filing complaints with the U.S. Trade Representative (USTR), a presidential appointee. Whether to pursue WTO trade law complaints is entirely discretionary for the USTR. Under the terms of the DSU, the USTR can pursue complaints of breach of WTO agreement obligations, or nullification or impairment of benefits accruing under WTO agreements.

The DSB is a special assembly of the WTO General Council, and includes all WTO members. There are six stages in the resolution of disputes under WTO: 1) Consultation; 2) Panel establishment, investigation and report; 3) Appellate review of the panel report; 4) Adoption of the panel and appellate decision; 5) Implementation of the decision adopted, and 6) Authorized retaliation. There is also a parallel process for binding arbitration, if both parties agree to submit this dispute to arbitration, rather than to a DSB panel. In addition, the party subject to an adverse decision may seek arbitration as a matter of right on issues of compliance and authorized retaliation.

Although the DSU offers a unified dispute resolution system that is applicable across all sectors and all WTO Covered Agreements, there are many specialized rules for disputes which arise under them. Such specialized rules appear in the Agreements on Textiles, Antidumping, Subsidies and Countervailing Measures, Technical Barriers to Trade, Sanitary and Phyto-sanitary Measures, Customs Valuation, General Agreement on Trade in Services, Financial Services and Air Transport Services. The special provisions in these individual Covered Agreements govern, where applicable, and prevail in any conflict with the general provisions of the DSU.

Under WTO, unlike under GATT 1947, the DSU practically assures that panels will be established upon request by a member state. Further, under WTO, unlike GATT 1947, the DSU virtually ensures the adoption of unmodified panel and appellate body decisions. It accomplishes this by requiring the DSB to adopt panel reports and appellate body decisions automatically and without amendment unless they are rejected by a consensus of all members. This "inverted consensus" requires that all members of the DSB, including the state that prevailed in the dispute, decide to reject the dispute resolution decision. Not surprisingly, this has never happened because if any member formally favors that decision (the winner in the dispute for example), it becomes binding. This inverted consensus requirement is imposed on both the adoption of panel reports or appellate body decisions and also on the decision to establish a panel.

The potential resolutions of a dispute under DSU range from a "mutually satisfactory solution" agreed to by the parties under the first, or consultation phase, to authorized retaliation under the last, or implementation phase. The preferred solution is always any resolution that is mutually satisfactory to the parties. After a panel decision, there are three types of remedies available to the prevailing party, if a mutually satisfactory solution cannot be obtained. One is for the respondent to bring the measure found to violate a Covered Agreement into conformity with the Agreement. A second is for the prevailing Member to receive compensation from the respondent which both parties agree is sufficient to compensate for any injury caused by the measure found to violate a Covered Agreement.

Finally, if no such agreement can be reached, a prevailing party can be authorized to suspend some of its concessions under the Covered Agreements to the respondent. These suspended concessions, called "retaliation," can be authorized within the same trade sector and agreement; or, if that will not create sufficient compensation, can be authorized across trade sectors and agreements.

The entire WTO dispute resolution process, from filing a complaint to authorized retaliation, can take roughly three years. One perspective on WTO dispute settlement seeks a rule-oriented use of the "rule of law". The other seeks a power-oriented use of diplomacy. The United States and less developed countries have traditionally sought to develop a rule-oriented approach to international trade disputes. The European Union and Japan have traditionally sought to use the GATT/WTO primarily as a forum for diplomatic negotiations, although the EU now ranks second in number of WTO dispute proceedings. These different views created part of the conflict at the December 1999 Seattle WTO meeting (which failed to launch the Millennium Round). If the DSB is a court, its proceedings should be open and "transparent." However, if it is just another form of government-to-government diplomacy, that has always been held in secret.

Phase 1, Consultation

Any WTO Member who believes that the Measures of another Member are not in conformity with the Covered Agreements may call for consultations on those measures. The respondent has ten days to reply and must agree to enter into consultation within 30 days. If the respondent does not enter into consultations within the 30 day period, the party seeking consultations can immediately request the establishment of a panel under DSU, which puts the dispute into Phase 2.

Once consultations begin, the parties have 60 days to achieve a settlement. The goal is to seek a positive solution to the dispute, and the preferred resolution is to reach whatever solution is mutually satisfactory to the parties. If such a settlement cannot be obtained after 60 days, the party seeking consultations may request the establishment of a panel under DSU, which moves the dispute into Phase 2.

WTO member third parties with an interest in the subject-matter of the consultations may seek to be included in them. If such inclusion is rejected, they may seek their own consultations with the other member state. Alternatives to consultations may be provided through the use of conciliation, mediation or good offices, where all parties agree to use the alternative process. Any party can terminate the use of conciliation, mediation or good offices and then seek the establishment of a panel under DSU, which also will move the dispute into Phase 2.

Phase 2, Panel Establishment, Investigation and Report

If consultations between the parties fail, the party seeking the consultations (the complainant) may request the DSB to establish a panel to investigate, report and resolve the dispute. The DSB must establish such a panel upon request, unless the DSB expressly decides by consensus not to establish the panel. Since an "inverted consensus" is required to reject the establishment of the panel and the complainant member must be part of that consensus, it is almost guaranteed that a panel will be established. Roughly 100 panels were established in the first five years of operation of the DSU, and many more since then.

Almost any WTO member state may intervene in the dispute. No specific legal or trade interest in the dispute is required since every WTO member has a legal interest in seeing that WTO rules are observed. Hence, for example, the United States intervened in the *Bananas* dispute between Latin American exporters and the European Union. One measure of the significance of the dispute is how many and which WTO members join either side of the dispute . . . resulting in say seven states against ten.

The WTO Secretariat maintains a list of well-qualified persons who are available to serve as panelists, mainly international trade law specialists drawn from the world of law practice, the academe and government service. The panels are usually composed of three individuals from that list who are not citizens of either party. If the parties agree, a panel can be composed of five such individuals. The parties can also agree to appoint citizens of a party to a panel. Panelists may be either nongovernmental individuals or governmental officials, but they are to be selected so as to ensure their independence. Thus, there is a bias towards independent individuals who are not citizens of any party. If a citizen of a party is appointed, his government may not instruct that citizen how to vote, for the panelist must be independent. By the same reasoning, a governmental official of a non-party member state who is subject to instructions from his or her government would not seem to fit the profile of an independent panelist.

The WTO Secretariat proposes nominations of the panelists. Parties may not normally oppose the nominations, except for "compelling reasons." The parties are given twenty days to agree on the panelists and the composition of the panel. If such agreement is not forthcoming, the WTO Director-General is authorized to appoint the panelists, in consultation with other persons in the Secretariat.

Complaints brought to DSB panels can involve either violations of Covered Agreements, or non-violation nullification and impairment of benefits under the Covered Agreements. A prima facie case of nullification impairment arises when one member infringes upon the "obligations assumed under a Covered Agreement." Such infringement creates a presumption against the infringing member, but the presumption can be rebutted by a showing that the complaining member state has suffered no adverse effect from the infringement. A classic nullification and impairment complaint concerns use of government subsidies after tariff reductions cause increased imports. See the *Australian Subsidy* case, 2 GATT Panel B.I.S.D. 188 (1950).

The panels receive pleadings and rebuttals and hear oral arguments. Panels can also engage in fact development from sources outside those presented by the parties. Thus, the procedure has aspects familiar to civil law courts. A panel can, on its own initiative, request information, including from experts selected by the panel. It can also obtain confidential information in some circumstances from an administrative body which is part of the government of a member state, without any prior consent from that state. A panel can establish its own group of experts to provide reports on factual or scientific issues. In a series of rulings commencing with the *Shrimp-Turtles* decision in 1998, the WTO Appellate Body has affirmed the right of panels and itself to elect to receive unsolicited informational and argumentative briefs or letters from non-governmental organizations (NGOs), business groups and law firms representing persons interested in the dispute.

A panel is obligated to produce two objectively assessed written reports—an interim and a final report. These reports are normally drafted by the WTO Secretariat, subject to review by the panelists. A panel is supposed to submit a final written report to the DSB within six months of its establishment. The report will contain its findings of fact, findings of law, a decision and the rationale for its decision. Before the final report is issued, the panel is supposed to provide an interim report to the parties. The purpose of this interim report is to apprize the parties of the panel's current analysis of the issues and to permit the parties to comment on that analysis. The final report of the panel need not change any of the findings or conclusions in its interim report, unless the panel is persuaded to do so by a party's comments. However, if it is not so persuaded, it is obligated to explain in its final report why not. At this writing, well over 200 WTO panel reports have been issued.

The decisions in panel reports are final as to issues of fact. The decisions in panel reports are not necessarily final as to issues of law. Panel decisions on issues of law are subject to review by the Appellate Body, which is Phase 3, and explained below. Any party can appeal a panel report, and appeals are usually taken.

Phase 3, Appellate Review of the Panel Report

Appellate review of panel reports is available at the request of any party, unless the DSB rejects that request by an "inverted consensus." There is no threshold requirement for an appellant to present a substantial substantive legal issue. Thus, most panel decisions are appealed as a matter of course. However, the Appellate Body can only review the panel reports on questions of law or legal interpretation.

The Appellate Body is a new institution in the international trade organization and its process. GATT 1947 had nothing comparable to it. The Appellate Body is composed of seven members (or judges) who are appointed by the DSB to four-year terms. Each judge may be reappointed, but only once, to a second four-year term. Each judge is to be a recognized authority on international trade law and the Covered Agreements. To date, Appellate Body members have been drawn mostly from the academe and retired justices. They have come from Germany, Japan, Egypt, India, New Zealand, the Philippines, Argentina, China, the United States and other WTO member nations.

The review of any panel decision is performed by three judges out of the seven. The parties do not, however, have any influence over which judges are selected to review a particular panel report. There is a schedule, created by the Appellate Body, for the rotation for sitting of each of the judges. Thus, a party might try to appear before a favored judge by timing the start of the dispute settlement process to arrive at the Appellate Body at the right moment on the rotation schedule, but this limited approach has major difficulties.

The Appellate Body receives written submissions from the parties and has 60, or in some cases 90, days in which to render its decision. The Appellate Body review is limited to issues of law and legal interpretation. The panel decision may be upheld, modified, or reversed by the Appellate Body decision. Appellate Body decisions are anonymous, and ex parte communications are not permitted. Appellate Body decisions do not represent binding precedent. That said, many have observed a desire on the part of the Appellate Body to achieve consistency and a willingness to discuss its prior rulings when rendering decisions.

Phase 4, Adoption of the Panel or Appellate Body Decision

Appellate Body determinations are submitted to the DSB. Panel decisions which are not appealed are also submitted to the DSB. Once either type of decision is submitted, the DSB must automatically adopt them without modification or amendment at its next meeting unless the decision is rejected by all members of the DSB acting by "inverted consensus", which has never happened.

An alternative to Phases 2 through 4 is arbitration, if both parties agree. The arbitration must be binding on the parties, and there is no appeal from the arbitral tribunal's decision to the DSB or Appellate Body.

Phase 5, Implementation of the Decision Adopted

Once a panel or Appellate Body decision is adopted by the DSB, implementation is a three-step process. In the first step, the member found to have a measure which violates its WTO obligations has "a reasonable time" (usually 15 months) to bring those measures into conformity with its WTO obligations. That remedy is the preferred one, and this form of implementation is the principal goal of the WTO dispute settlement system. To date, most disputes have resulted in compliance in this manner. If the adequacy of compliance is disputed, such disputes typically return to the WTO panel that rendered decision on the merits. The panel then determines, acting as an arbitrator, the amount (if any) of authorized retaliation. The retaliation process is discussed below.

Compensation

If the violating measures are not brought into conformity within a reasonable time, the parties proceed to the second step. In that second step, the parties negotiate to reach an agreement upon a form of compensation which will be granted by the party in violation to the injured party. Such compensation will usually comprise trade concessions by the violating party to the injured party, which are over and above those already available under the WTO and Covered Agreements. The nature, scope, amount and duration of these additional concessions is at the negotiating parties' discretion, but each side must agree that the final compensation package is fair and is properly related to the injury caused by the violating measures. Presumably, any such concessions need not be extended under MFN principles to all WTO members.

Few such compensation agreements have ever been achieved, though the United States compensated most of the membership after losing a dispute to Antigua about whether it had "reserved" (excepted) Internet gambling from coverage under the GATS. *See* Section 1.9. The United States also compensated the EU in a copyright dispute involving small business use of music, and Brazil after losing a subsidies dispute concerning cotton. *See* Section 1.16.

Phase 6, Authorized Retaliation

Both "compensation" and "retaliation" provide only for indirect enforcement of DSB decisions. There is no mechanism for direct enforcement by the WTO of its decisions through WTO orders to suspend trade obligations. Commentators differ on whether retaliation will be an effective implementation device. The division represented by these conflicting views represents two different approaches to the nature of both international law and international trade law.

If the parties cannot agree on an appropriate amount of compensation within twenty days, the complainant may proceed to the third step. In the third step, the party injured by the violating measures seeks authority from the DSB to retaliate against the party whose measures violated its WTO obligations. Thus complainant seeks authority to suspend some of its WTO obligations in regard to the respondent. The retaliation must ordinarily be within the same sector and agreement as the violating measure. "Sector" is sometimes broadly defined, as all trade in goods, and sometimes narrowly defined, as in individual services in the Services Sectoral Classification List. "Agreement" is also broadly defined. All the agreements listed in Annex IA to the WTO Agreement are considered a single agreement. If retaliation within the sector and agreement of the violating measure is considered insufficient compensation, the complainant may seek suspension of its obligations across sectors and agreements. This is known as "cross-sector retaliation."

The DSB must grant the complainant's request to retaliate within 30 days unless all WTO members reject it through an "inverted consensus." (Article 22.6, D.S.U.) However, the respondent may object to the level or scope of the retaliation. The issues raised by the objection will be examined by either the Appellate Body or by an arbitrator. The respondent has a right, even if arbitration was not used in Phases 2 through 4, to have an arbitrator review in Phase 5 the appropriateness of the complainant's proposed level and scope of retaliation. The arbitrator will also examine whether the proper procedures and criteria to establish retaliation have been followed. The Phase 5 arbitration is final and binding, and the arbitrator's decision is not subject to DSB review.

In addition to objecting to the level of authorized retaliation, the responding WTO member may simultaneously challenge the assertion of noncompliance (Article 21.5, D.S.U.). This challenge will ordinarily be heard by the original panel and must be resolved within 90 days. Thus the request for authorized retaliation and objections thereto could conceivably be accomplished before noncompliance is formally determined. In practice, WTO dispute settlement has melded these conflicting procedures such that compliance and retaliation issues are decided together, typically by the original panel.

Retaliation in Action

Retaliation has rarely been authorized and even less rarely imposed. The amount of a U.S. retaliation permitted against the EU after the WTO *Bananas* and *Beef Hormones* decisions were not implemented by the EU was contested. The arbitration tribunals for this issue were the original WTO panels, which did not allow the entire amount of the almost $700 million in retaliatory tariffs proposed by the United States. The U.S. was authorized and levied retaliatory tariffs amounting to about $300 million against European goods because of the EU failure to implement those WTO decisions.

Since 2000, Congress has authorized rotating WTO retaliatory tariffs in "carousel" fashion upon different goods. The threat of carousel retaliation contributed to an April 2001 settlement of the *Bananas* dispute. In 2009, a four year settlement of the *Beef Hormones* dispute was reached. The U.S. gets a higher quota to export hormone-free beef to the EU in return for phasing out its retaliatory tariffs on EU goods. The U.S. threat of carousel sanctions was again instrumental to this settlement.

Perhaps the most dramatic use of retaliation occurred in a tax subsidy dispute. The amount of EU retaliation permissible after the U.S. lost (for the second time) under WTO subsidy rules concerning Internal Revenue Code extraterritorial export tax preferences (FISCs) was disputed. A WTO panel, serving as an arbitrator, authorized approximately $4 *billion* in EU retaliation against U.S. exports. This retaliation commenced in March of 2004 and escalated monthly until the U.S. capitulated by amending the I.R.C. late in 2004.

Cross-Sector Retaliation

In a landmark ruling, a WTO panel acting as an arbitrator authorized Ecuador to remove protection of intellectual property rights regarding geographical indicators, copyrights and industrial designs on European Union goods for sale in Ecuador. This authorization was part of Ecuador's $200 million compensation in the *Bananas* dispute. The WTO panel acknowledged that Ecuador imports mostly capital goods and raw materials from the European Union and that imposing retaliatory tariffs on them would adversely harm its manufacturing industries. This risk supported "cross-retaliation" under Article 22.3 of the DSU outside the sector of the EU trade violation.

Allowance of cross-sector IP retaliation was probably the most critical driver behind the 2001 settlement of the *Bananas* dispute. Cross-sector retaliation was also authorized against the U.S. after losing a GATS dispute to Antigua on Internet gambling restraints. The United States settled this dispute with nearly all WTO members save Antigua via compensation. At this writing, Antigua is still debating whether and how to retaliate.

§ 1.15 ____U.S. Involvement in WTO Dispute Resolution

The WTO dispute resolution process has been invoked more frequently than many expected. The United States has been a complainant or a respondent in dozens of disputes since 1995, as has China since its membership in 2001. The sampling of disputes summarized below illustrates the WTO dispute settlement process in action.

United States WTO Disputes

The United States lost a dispute initiated by Venezuela and Brazil concerning U.S. standards for reformulated and conventional gasoline. The offending U.S. law was amended to conform to the WTO ruling. It won on a complaint initiated jointly with Canada and the European Union regarding Japanese taxes on alcoholic beverages. Japan subsequently changed its law. When Costa Rica complained about U.S. restraints on imports of underwear, the U.S. let the restraints expire prior to any formal DSB ruling at the WTO. Similar results were reached when India complained of U.S. restraints on wool shirts and blouses. The United States won a major dispute with Canada concerning trade and subsidies for periodicals This celebrated *Sports Illustrated* dispute proved that WTO remedies can be used to avoid Canada's cultural industries exclusion under NAFTA. *See* Section 16.1.

In the longstanding *Bananas* dispute noted above, the United States joined Ecuador, Guatemala, Honduras and Mexico in successfully challenging EU import restraints against so-called "dollar bananas." The EU failed to comply with the Appellate Body's ruling, and retaliatory measures were authorized and imposed . . . tariffs on EU goods by the United States and cross-sector IP retaliation by Ecuador and others. In April 2001, the *Bananas* dispute was settled on terms that generally converted EU quotas to tariffs by 2006, though limited preferential quotas for ACP exporters were retained. A patent law complaint by the U.S. against India prevailed in the DSB and ultimately brought changes in Indian law regarding pharmaceuticals and agricultural chemicals.

In *Beef Hormones,* also noted above, the European Union lost twice before the Appellate Body for want of proof of a "scientific basis" for its ban on hormone beef. It refused to alter its import restraints and absorbed $200 million in retaliatory tariffs on selected exports to Canada and the United States. In 2009, an arguably pro-European settlement was reached. The U.S. effectively got a higher quota to export hormone-free beef to the EU, in return for phasing out over four years its retaliatory tariffs on EU goods. The U.S. threat of carousel sanctions, i.e. rotating goods subject to retaliation, was instrumental to this settlement. Meanwhile, because the U.S. beef industry failed to timely ask for a continuation of the retaliatory tariffs, the Federal Circuit ruled in 2010 that they expired in 2007. Refunds were given to importers of EU products who paid those tariffs.

The United States prevailed against Argentina regarding tariffs and taxes on footwear, textiles and apparel. It lost a challenge (strongly supported by Kodak) to Japan's distribution rules regarding photo film and paper. In this dispute the U.S. elected *not* to appeal the adverse WTO panel ruling to the Appellate Body. In contrast, the European Union took an appeal which reversed an adverse panel ruling on its customs classification of computer equipment. The U.S. had commenced this proceeding. Opponents in many disputes, Japan, the United States and the European Union united to complain that Indonesia's National Car Programme was discriminatory and in breach of several WTO agreements. They prevailed and Indonesia altered its program.

India, Malaysia, Pakistan and Thailand teamed up to challenge U.S. shrimp import restraints enacted to protect endangered sea turtles. The WTO Appellate Body generally upheld their complaint and the U.S. has moved to comply. The adequacy of U.S. compliance is being challenged by Malaysia. The European Union and the United States jointly opposed Korea's discriminatory taxes on alcoholic beverages. This challenge was successful and Korea now imposes flat non-discriminatory taxes. The United States also complained of Japan's quarantine, testing and other agricultural import rules. The U.S. won at the WTO and Japan has changed its procedures.

In a semiconductor dumping dispute, Korea successfully argued that the U.S. was not in compliance with the WTO Antidumping Agreement. The United States amended its law, but Korea has instituted further proceedings alleging that these amendments are inadequate. The United States did likewise after Australia lost a subsidies dispute relating to auto leather. The reconvened WTO panel ruled that Australia had indeed failed to conform to the original adverse DSB decision. A U.S. challenge concerning India's quotas on imports of agricultural, textile and industrial products was upheld. India and the United States subsequently reached agreement on a timeline for removal of these restraints.

Closer to home, New Zealand and the United States complained of Canada's import/export rules regarding milk. Losing at the WTO, Canada agreed to a phased removal of the offending measures. The United States also won against Mexico in an antidumping dispute involving corn syrup, but lost a "big one" when the Appellate Body determined that export tax preferences granted to "Foreign Sales Corporations" of U.S. companies were illegal. Another "big one" went in favor of the United States. The European Union challenged the validity under the DSU of unilateral retaliation under Section 301 of the Trade Act of 1974. Section 301 has been something of a bete noire in U.S. trade law (see Chapter 14), but the WTO panel affirmed its legality in light of Presidential undertakings to administer it in accordance with U.S. obligations to adhere to multilateral WTO dispute settlement.

U.S. involvement in WTO dispute settlement continues to be extensive. The Appellate Body ruled that U.S. countervailing duties against British steel based upon pre-privatization subsidies were unlawful. The European Union prevailed before a WTO panel in its challenge of the U.S. Antidumping Act of 1916, since repealed. U.S. complaints against Korean beef import restraints and procurement practices were upheld. Canada's patent protection term was also invalidated by the WTO under a U.S. complaint. European Union complaints concerning U.S. wheat gluten quotas and the royalty free small business provisions of the Fairness in Music Licensing Act of 1998 have been sustained. The *Wheat Gluten* dispute questions the legality of U.S. "causation" rules in escape clause proceedings under Section 201 of the Trade Act of 1974.

A WTO Panel ruled in 2002 that the Byrd Amendment violates the WTO antidumping and subsidy codes. The Byrd Amendment (Continued Dumping and Subsidy Act of 2000) authorizes the Customs Service to forward AD and CVD duties to affected domestic producers for qualified expenses. Eleven WTO members including the EU, Canada and Mexico challenged the Amendment. This ruling was affirmed by the WTO Appellate Body and retaliation was authorized. Late in 2005, the U.S. repealed the Byrd Amendment, subject to a contested two-year phase out. The Appellate Body also ruled against Section 211 of the Omnibus Appropriations Act of 1998 denying trademark protection in connection with confiscated assets (the "HAVANA CLUB" dispute). U.S. compliance with these rulings has been slow in forthcoming. The United States and other complainants prevailed in a 2002 WTO proceeding against Indian local content and trade balancing requirements for foreign auto manufacturers. These requirements violated the TRIMs agreement.

In March of 2004, the European Union commenced raising tariffs against U.S. goods under the WTO retaliation authorized out of the FSC/export tax subsidy dispute. Monthly increments were planned until either the U.S. complied or the EU reached the maximum of roughly $4 billion annually it was authorized to retaliate. In the Fall of 2004, the United States repealed the extraterritorial income exclusion and the EU subsequently removed its retaliatory tariffs. In 2004, also, Antigua-Barbuda won a WTO panel ruling under the GATS against certain U.S. Internet gambling restraints. Retaliation was authorized, and the U.S. settled with nearly all members by offering compensation. The U.S. won a panel decision against Mexico's exorbitant telecom interconnection rates, but lost a 2004 cotton subsidy challenge by Brazil. Retaliation by Brazil was authorized.

The United States also lost a second dispute with the EU about pre-privatization countervailable subsidies, in particular the legality of the U.S. "same person" methodology. The U.S. won a SPS dispute against Japanese quarantine of U.S. apples, while losing an important softwood lumber "zeroing" methodology complaint brought by Canada. In 2006, the Mexico–United States "sugar war" came to a head before the Appellate Body. Mexico's 20% soft drink tax on beverages not using cane sugar, its 20% distribution tax on those beverages, and related bookkeeping requirements were found to violate GATT Article III and not exempt under Article XX(d). Subsequently, the two countries settled their dispute by agreeing, effective in 2008, to free trade in sugar and high fructose corn syrup. Further in 2006, the U.S. failed to persuade the Appellate Body to require the European Union under GATT Article X (3) to undertake a major overhaul of its customs law system targeting inconsistencies therein among the 28 member states.

In 2010, the United States agreed to pay $147 million annually to provide technical assistance to Brazilian cotton farmers. In return, Brazil has suspended retaliatory tariffs and cross-sector IP sanctions authorized by the WTO because of U.S. cotton subsidy violations. In 2009, a WTO panel ruled that Airbus had received $20 billion in illegal EU "launch" subsidies. By 2010, that same panel found Boeing the recipient of $5 billion in federal research contract subsidies that violated the WTO Subsidies Code.

The United States has also settled a number of disputes prior to WTO panel decisions, and remains in consultation on other disputes that may be decided by a WTO panel. For the latest summary of all WTO disputes, including many not involving the United States, see www.wto.org.

§ 1.16 ____China Involvement in WTO Disputes

China, a member since 2001, is involved in a growing number of WTO disputes. Here is a sampling of those disputes.

Canada, the European Union and the United States complained against Chinese duties on imported auto parts (10 percent) that rose to those on complete autos (25 percent) if the imported parts exceeded a fixed percentage of the final vehicle content or price, or if specific combinations of imported auto parts were used in the final vehicle. In addition, extensive record keeping, reporting and verification requirements were imposed when Chinese auto companies used imported parts. In July of 2008, a WTO panel ruled that these "internal charges" violated Articles III (2) and III (4) of the GATT and China's accession commitments. The core Panel ruling, affirmed by the Appellate Body, found China's auto parts measures discriminatory in favor of domestic producers, a violation of the national treatment standard for taxes and regulations. This ruling marked the first time since China's admission in 2001 that it was held in breach of its WTO commitments and obligations.

Less than one month after losing this dispute, China enacted a clever "green tax" on gas-guzzling autos, most of which just happen to be imported. The sales tax on cars with engine capacities over 4.1 litres has been doubled to 40%. Autos with engines between 3 and 4.1 litres are taxed at 25%, up from 15%. Most Chinese-made cars have engines with 2.5 litres or less. Autos with engines between 1 and 3 litres remain taxed at 8% and 10%. The smallest cars with engines below 1 litre have their sales tax reduced from 3 to 1 percent. This green tax could achieve protective results similar to China's Auto Parts tariff structure and could be challenged under GATT Article III.

Other disputes challenging China's compliance with WTO law are pending. They concern China's auto export subsidies and CVDs on auto imports, protection and enforcement of intellectual property rights (2009 WTO panel ruled against China), trade and distribution of publications and audiovisual entertainment products and services (2009 Appellate Body ruled against China), commodity export tariffs and restrictions (2012 WTO Appellate Body ruled against China), application of Chinese AD to U.S. grain-oriented flat rolled steel (GOES) (2012 WTO Appellate Body ruled against China), discriminatory treatment of foreign electronic payment services (2012 WTO panel ruled against China), and eport restrictions on rare earths (WTO Panel ruled against China in 2014). The United States is a complaining party to all of these disputes.

China, in turn, has challenged U.S. safeguard measures applied to Chinese steel exports (2010 WTO Panel rejected challenge) and tires (2011 WTO Panel rejected challenge). It has challenged U.S. antidumping and countervailing duties on paper products from China (2011 WTO Panel ruled against U.S. dual assessment of AD and CVD duties, such double remedies were ruled WTO illegal in 2014), as well as U.S. AD on Chinese solar panels. China has also applied AD duties to U.S. exports, e.g. chicken.

Part 2

CUSTOMS AND IMPORT LAW

Chapter 2

UNITED STATES TRADE AND TARIFF LAW

Table of Sections

Sec.

§ 2.0   U.S. International Trade Legislation and Administrative Authorities

U.S. international trade law is primarily found in the frequently amended Tariff Act of 1930 and the Trade Act of 1974. Much of the content of these statutes is derived from World Trade Organization principles. Additional statutes of note include the NAFTA Implementation Act of 1993, the Uruguay Round Agreements Act of 1994, the Export Administration Act of 1979, the Foreign Corrupt Practices Act of 1977, and the Caribbean Basin Economic Recovery Act of 1983.

The international trade of the United States is regulated by a number of different governmental bodies. The International Trade Administration is part of the Commerce Department, which in turn is part of the Executive Branch of the federal government. The Commerce Department also contains the Office of Export Licensing and the Office of Anti-boycott Compliance. *See* Chapters 10 and 12. U.S. economic sanctions are administered by the Treasury Department, and international arms controls by the Department of State. *See* Chapter 11. The International Trade Commission is an independent federal government agency, and the Court of International Trade is part of the Judicial Branch of the United States government. Lastly, the Office of the United States Trade Representative works directly under the President.

The international trade of the United States is regulated by a number of different governmental bodies. The International Trade Administration is part of the Commerce Department, which in turn is part of the Executive Branch of the federal government. The Commerce Department also contains the Office of Export Licensing and the Office of Anti-boycott Compliance. The International Trade Commission is an independent federal government agency, and the Court of International Trade is part of the Judicial Branch of the United States government. Lastly, the Office of the United States Trade Representative works directly under the President.

§ 2.1   ___U.S. International Trade Administration (ITA)

The Commerce Department's International Trade Administration (ITA) is an administrative agency. In broadest terms, the ITA is to foster, promote and develop world trade, and to bring U.S. companies into the business of selling overseas. At a practical level, the ITA is designed to be helpful to the individual business by providing it with information concerning the "what, where, how and when" of imports and exports, such as information sources, requirements for a particular trade license, forms for an international license agreement or procedures to start a business in a foreign country. The ITA provides business data and educational programs to United States businesses.

In addition to these duties, the ITA also decides whether there are subsidies in countervailing duty (CVD)[1] cases, or sales at less than fair value in antidumping duty (AD) cases.[2] Prior to 1980, such decisions were made by the Treasury Department. The ITA is not, however, involved in decision-making in escape clause (Section 201), market disruption (Section 406) and unfair import practices (Section 337) proceedings.

§ 2.2   ____U.S. International Trade Commission (ITC)

The United States International Trade Commission (ITC) is an independent bipartisan agency created in 1916 by an act of Congress. The ITC is the successor to the United States Tariff Commission. In 1974, the name was changed and the ITC was given additional authority, powers and responsibilities. The Commission's present powers and duties include preparing reports pertaining to international economics and foreign trade for the Executive Branch, the Congress, other government agencies and the public. To carry out this responsibility, the ITC conducts investigations which entail extensive research, specialized studies and a high degree of expertise in all matters relating to the commercial and international trade policies of the United States.

Statutory investigations conducted by the ITC include unfair import trade practice determinations (Section 337 proceedings),[3] domestic industry injury determinations in antidumping and countervailing duty cases,[4] and safeguard and market disruption import relief recommendations.[5] The ITC also advises the President about probable economic effects on domestic industries and consumers of modifications on duties and other trade barriers incident to proposed trade agreements with foreign countries.

The ITC is intended to be a quasi-judicial, bipartisan, independent agency providing trade expertise to both Congress and the Executive. Congress went to great lengths to create a bipartisan body to conduct international trade studies and provide reliable

---

[1]   See Chapter 5.
[2]   See Chapter 4.
[3]   See Chapter 8.
[4]   See Chapters 4 and 5.
[5]   See Chapter 6.

expert information. The six Commissioners of the ITC are appointed by the President and confirmed by the United States Senate for nine year terms, unless appointed to fill an unexpired term. The presence of entrenched points of view is inhibited because a Commissioner who has served for more than five years is not eligible for reappointment. Not more than three Commissioners may be members of the same political party.

The Chairman and Vice-Chairman are designated by the President for two year terms. No Chairman may be of the same political party as the preceding Chairman, nor may the President designate two Commissioners of the same political party as Chairman and Vice-Chairman. Congress further guaranteed the independence of the ITC from the Executive Branch by having its budget submitted directly to the Congress. This means that its budget is not subject to review by the Office of Management and Budget.

§ 2.3 ____U.S. Court of International Trade (CIT)

The United States Court of International Trade (CIT) is an Article III court under the United States Constitution for judicial review of civil actions arising out of import transactions and certain federal statutes affecting international trade. It grew out of the Board of General Appraisers (a quasi-judicial administrative unit within the Treasury Department which reviewed decisions by United States Customs officials concerning the amount of duties to be paid on imports in actions arising under the tariff acts) and the United States Customs Court which had essentially the same jurisdiction and powers. The President, with the advice and consent of the Senate, appoints the nine judges who constitute the Court of International Trade. Not more than five of the nine judges may belong to any one political party.

The geographical jurisdiction of the Court of International Trade extends throughout the United States, and it is also authorized to hold hearings in foreign countries. The court has exclusive subject-matter jurisdiction to decide any civil action commenced against the United States, its agencies or its officers arising from any law pertaining to revenue from imports, tariffs, duties or embargoes or enforcement of these and other customs regulations. This includes disputes regarding trade embargoes, quotas, customs classification and valuation, country of origin determinations and denials of protests by the U.S. Customs Service.

The court's exclusive jurisdiction also includes any civil action commenced by the United States that arises out of an import transaction, and authority to review final agency decisions concerning antidumping and countervailing duty matters, the eligibility of workers, firms and communities who are economically harmed by foreign imports for trade adjustment assistance, disputes concerning the release of confidential business information, and decisions to deny, revoke or suspend the licenses of customs brokers. However, the CIT does *not* have jurisdiction over disputes involving restrictions on imported merchandise where public safety or health issues are raised. This limitation on CIT jurisdiction arises because such issues involving domestic goods would be determined by other regulatory bodies, and only referral to United States District Courts can ensure uniform treatment of both imports and domestically produced goods.

The standard for the judicial review exercised by the CIT varies from case to case. In some instances, such as confidentiality orders, a *de novo* trial is undertaken. In others, notably antidumping and countervailing duty cases, the standard is one of substantial evidence, or arbitrary, capricious or unlawful action, or an abuse of discretion. In trade adjustment assistance litigation, the administrative determinations are considered conclusive absent substantial evidentiary support in the record with the CIT empowered to order the taking of further evidence. Unless otherwise specified by statute, the Administrative Procedure Act governs the judicial review by the CIT of U.S. international trade law.

The CIT possesses all the remedial powers, legal and equitable, of a United States District Court, including authority to enter money judgments for or against the United States, but with three limitations. First, in an action challenging a trade adjustment ruling, the court may not issue an injunction or writ of mandamus. Second, the CIT may order disclosure of confidential information only as specified in Section 777(c)(2) of the Tariff Act of 1930. Third, the CIT may order only declaratory relief for suits brought under the provision allowing the court accelerated review because of a showing of irreparable harm.

The CIT must ordinarily give due deference to Customs Service regulations under *Chevron* rules[6] even when undertaking *de novo* review.[7] However, the Supreme Court has ruled that *Chevron* does not apply to product classification decisions by the Customs Service.[8] CIT decisions are first appealed to the Court of Appeals for

---

[6]   Chevron, U.S.A., Inc. v. Natural Resources Defense Council, Inc., 467 U.S. 837, 104 S.Ct. 2778, 81 L.Ed.2d 694 (1984).

[7]   United States v. Haggar Apparel Co., 526 U.S. 380, 119 S.Ct. 1392, 143 L.Ed.2d 480 (1999).

[8]   United States v. Mead Corp., 533 U.S. 218 (2001). See Section 3.1.

the Federal Circuit (formerly to the Court of Customs and Patent Appeals), and ultimately to the United States Supreme Court.

§ 2.4   The USTR, Free Trade Agreements and U.S. Fast Track Negotiations

Removing trade barriers is usually done on a reciprocal basis, and requires lengthy bargaining and negotiations between the sovereigns. Congress is not adapted to carry on such negotiations, so it routinely delegates limited authority to the President to negotiate agreements reducing trade restrictions. Recent efforts to reduce trade restrictions have been multilateral, bilateral and trilateral. Congress has intermittently given quite broad authority to the President, or his representative, to reduce or eliminate United States tariffs on a reciprocal "fast track" basis, discussed below.

The USTR

In response to Section 1104 of the Trade Agreements Act of 1979,[9] the President reviewed the structure of the international trade functions of the Executive Branch. Although this did not lead to the establishment of a new Department of International Trade and Investment, it did lead to enhancement of the Office of the Special Representative for Trade Negotiations,[10] which has since been renamed the United States Trade Representative (USTR). The powers of the USTR were expanded and its authority given a legislative foundation. The USTR is appointed by the President, with the advice and consent of the Senate.[11] The Office of the USTR has been the principal vehicle through which tariff and trade negotiations have been conducted on behalf of the United States. Among other things, the USTR has had continuing responsibility in connection with implementation of the WTO Agreements and U.S. free trade agreements. The USTR is the contact point for persons who desire an investigation of instances of noncompliance with any trade agreement.

In 1988, the duties of the USTR were significantly expanded in conjunction with an overhaul of Section 301 of the Trade Act of 1974.[12] Section 301 creates a controversial unilateral trade remedy which principally has been used to obtain foreign market access for U.S. exports. Prior to 1988, the President directly administered Section 301. Thereafter, as amended by the Omnibus Trade and

---

[9]   P.L. 96–39.

[10]   The office had been established by an Executive Order in 1963.

[11]   19 U.S.C.A. § 2171.

[12]   See Chapter 14.

Competitiveness Act, the USTR assumed this role along with new duties governing the Super 301 and Special 301 procedures created in 1988. Moreover, since the 1988 Act expanded the coverage of Section 301 and introduced mandatory (not discretionary) remedies, the USTR became involved in many domestic industry complaints about foreign governments. Such complaints can reach breaches of international agreements as well as unjustifiable, unreasonable or discriminatory foreign country practices. *See* Chapter 14.

Free Trade Agreements

The USTR has negotiated about 20 free trade agreements for the United States (see below). Hundreds of free trade agreements (FTAs) lattice the world, including for example between the European Union and South Africa, Canada and Costa Rica, China and Chile, Japan and Singapore. Mexico has dozens of bilateral free trade agreements. At this point the only nation without a bilateral free trade deal is Mongolia. A variety of factors help explain why free trade has become the leading edge of international trade law and policy. Difficulties encountered in the Uruguay, "Seattle" and Doha Rounds of multilateral trade negotiations are certainly crucial. *See* Section 1.2. GATT/WTO regulatory failures regarding free trade and customs union agreements have also fueled this reality. *See* Chapter 15. Yet these "negatives" do not fully explain the global feeding frenzy of free trade agreements.

A range of attractions are also at work. For example, free trade agreements often extend to subject matters beyond WTO competence. Foreign investment law is a prime example, and many FTAs serve as investment magnets. Government procurement, optional at the WTO level, is often included in free trade agreements. Competition policy, labor and environmental matters absent from the WTO are sometimes covered as well. In addition, free trade agreements can reach beyond the scope of existing WTO agreements. Services are one "WTO-plus" area where this is clearly true. Intellectual property rights are also being "WTO-plussed" in bilateral free trade agreements. Whether this amounts to competitive trade liberalization or competitive trade imperialism is a provocative question.

"Fast Track" U.S. Trade Negotiations

Fast track originated as a compromise after Congress refused to ratify two major components of the Kennedy Round of GATT negotiations. When in place, fast track requires Congress to vote within 90 legislative days up or down, without amendments, on U.S. trade agreements. In return, Congress receives substantial notice and opportunity to influence U.S. trade negotiations conducted by the USTR. Congress also sets nonbinding trade negotiation objectives under fast track enabling legislation.

NAFTA and the Uruguay Round WTO agreements were negotiated and implemented under fast track procedures in place from 1991–1996. The bipartisan Trade Act of 2002 (P.L. 107–210) authorized President George W. Bush to negotiate international trade agreements on a fast track basis for five years. *See* 19 U.S.C. § 3801 et seq. President Bush and the USTR quickly completed, and Congress quickly approved, free trade agreements (FTAs) with Chile and Singapore. Thereafter U.S. FTAs with Morocco, Australia, Central America/Dominican Republic (CAFTA), Peru, Jordan, Oman, and Bahrain followed. Just prior to the expiration of fast track authority in July of 2007, President Bush signed FTA agreements with Colombia, Panama and Korea. Several years later these agreements were implemented by Congress under the Obama administration.

For U.S. free trade partners, fast track suggests that once they reach a deal with the USTR Congress cannot alter it. That said, in recent years Congress has effectively tacked on additional requirements via letters of intent, notably regarding labor and the environment. To date, Congress has been unwilling to grant fast track authority to President Obama, though several bills are pending at this writing. Nevertheless, recognizing that China is a rapidly developing economic superstar, the United States under the Obama administration is pursuing what resembles a "containment" strategy by promoting a "Trans-Pacific Partnership." This strategy seeks to bring the U. S., Australia, New Zealand, Chile, Peru, Malaysia, Brunei, Singapore and notably Vietnam into a broad trade, technology and investment alliance. Mexico, Canada and Japan have more recently joined these negotiations. In addition, in 2013, the USTR commenced negotiations with the European Union on a "Transatlantic Trade and Investment Partnership" agreement. Both of these negotiations are notably being undertaken without fast track authority.

§ 2.5   Overview of U.S. Tariffs and Duty Free Entry

The sections that follow focus on United States tariffs under the Harmonized Tariff Schedule (HTS). Column 1 tariffs, known as most-favored-nation (MFN) tariffs, are the lower and most likely to be applicable. Column 2 tariffs, originating in the Smoot-Hawley Tariff Act of 1930, are the higher and least likely to be applicable. United States tariffs generally take one of three forms. The most common is an ad valorem rate. Such tariffs are assessed in proportion to the value of the article. Tariffs may also be assessed at specific rates or compound rates. Specific rates may be measured by the pound or other weight. A compound rate is a mixture of an ad valorem and specific rate tariff. Tariff rate quotas involve limitations on imports at a specific tariff up to a certain amount. Imports in excess of that amount are not prohibited, but are subject to a higher rate of tariff. Thus tariff rate quotas tend to restrict imports that are in excess of the specified quota for the lower tariff level.

Duty Free Entry

Some goods may enter the United States at less than most-favored-nation tariff levels or duty free. This occurs because of special tariff preferences incorporated into United States law (outlined below). It is important to realize that these preferences create valuable trading opportunities for U.S. importers and exporters located in qualified nations. These people are the clients for whom lawyers work to secure duty free entry into the United States market. Duty free entry is, of course, the ultimate goal of all exporters and importers involved in United States trade. Various free trade and customs union agreements (including NAFTA and other FTAs of the United States) achieving duty free outcomes are discussed in Section 2.4 and Chapter 16.

Perhaps the widest of the U.S. duty free programs is known as the Generalized System of Preferences (GSP) adopted through the GATT. The GSP is a complex system of duty free tariff preferences benefiting selected goods originating in developing nations and intended to foster their economic improvement. A second program is the Caribbean Basin Economic Recovery Act of 1983 (also known as the Caribbean Basin Initiative), which permits certain goods to enter the United States market duty free. To a significant degree, the CBI duty free program was duplicated in the Andean Trade Preference Act of 1991 initially benefiting Colombian, Ecuadorian, Bolivian and Peruvian goods. Another important "duty free" category allows fabricated U.S.-made components shipped abroad for assembly to return to the U.S. without tariffs on the value of the components. Authorization for this importation is found in Section 9802.00.80 of the Harmonized Tariff Schedule. Goods of this type are subject to a United States Customs duty limited in amount to the value added by foreign assembly operations. This provision is perhaps best known in connection with Latin American maquiladoras.

The least restrictive rules of origin for duty free entry of goods into the United States apply to its insular possessions. These include American Samoa, Guam, Johnson Island, Kingman Reef,

Midway Islands, Puerto Rico, the U.S. Virgin Islands and Wake Island. Generally speaking, goods from such possessions may contain up to 70 percent foreign value and still be admitted duty free.

Some of these duty free programs overlap and effectively compete with each other. It might be helpful to think of them in terms of concentric geographic circles. The widest circle is Section 9802.00.80 which applies to the entire globe. The next circle represents the GSP system and most developing nations. Inside that circle is the Caribbean Basin Initiative, the Andean Initiative, and U.S. insular possessions followed by NAFTA and other U.S. free trade agreements. A manufacturer based in the Caribbean may seek duty free entry into the United States market under Section 9802.00.80, the GSP program or the CBI, but not U.S. free trade agreements, save the Dominican Republic. To most developing nations, these are selectively discriminatory duty free programs that undermine their GSP benefits.

Unusual trade opportunities can arise by linking U.S. duty free entry programs with those of the European Union (EU). For example, the Union has its own complicated and different GSP program, its equivalent of Section 9802.00.80, and two selective duty free programs for developing nations. The latter are known as its Mediterranean Policy and Cotonou Convention. A producer in Israel can quite possibly gain duty free access to the EU (under its Mediterranean Policy) and to the United States (under the Israeli-U.S. FTA). A producer in Jamaica might achieve similar results under the Cotonou Convention, the CBI and/or the GSP programs of the EU and the United States.

§ 2.6   The Origins of United States Tariffs

Article I, Section 8, of the United States Constitution authorizes Congress to levy uniform tariffs on imports. Tariff legislation must originate in the House of Representatives. Although tariffs were primarily viewed as revenue-raising measures at the founding of the nation, it was not long before tariffs became used for openly protectionist purposes. The Tariff Act of 1816 initiated this change in outlook. During much of the Nineteenth Century, the United States legislated heavy protective tariffs. These were justified as necessary to protect the country's infant industries and to force the South to engage in more trade with the North (not with Europe). Exceptions were made to the high level of tariffs for selected United States imports under conditional most-favored-nation reciprocity treaties. The first of these treaties involved Canada (1854) and Hawaii (1875).

As the United States moved into the 20th Century, additional tariffs in excess of the already high level of protection were authorized. "Countervailing duty" tariffs were created in 1890 to combat export subsidies of European nations, particularly Germany. After 1916, additional duties could also be assessed if "dumping practices" were involved. Early American dumping legislation was largely a reaction to marketplace competition from foreign cartels. Throughout all of these years the constitutionality of protective tariffs was never clearly resolved.

In 1928, however, the United States Supreme Court firmly ruled that the enactment of protective tariffs was constitutional.[13] This decision, followed by the crash of the stock market in 1929, led to the enactment of the Smoot-Hawley Tariff Act of 1930. The Act set some of the highest rates of tariff duties in the history of the United States. It represents the last piece of tariff legislation that Congress passed without international negotiations. These tariffs remain part of United States law and are generally referred to as "Column 2 tariffs" under the Harmonized Tariff Schedule (HTS).

Since 1930, changes in the levels of tariffs applicable to goods entering the United States have chiefly been achieved through international trade agreements negotiated by the President and affirmed by Congress. During the 1930s and 40s, the Smoot-Hawley tariffs generally applied unless altered through bilateral trade agreements. The Reciprocal Trade Agreements Act of 1934[14] gives the President the authority to enter into such agreements, and under various extensions this authority remains in effect today. An early agreement of this type was the Canadian Reciprocal Trade Agreement of 1935.

§ 2.7   Column 1 U.S. Tariffs and the GATT/WTO

The Trade Agreements Extension Act of 1945 authorized the President to conduct multilateral negotiations in the trade field. It was out of this authority that the General Agreement on Tariffs and Trade (GATT) was negotiated. The GATT became effective on January 1, 1948 and was implemented in the United States by executive order. Indeed, despite its wide-ranging impact on United States tariff levels since 1948, the GATT was never ratified by the United States Congress. Nevertheless, it is the source of the principal tariffs assessed today on imports into the United States. These duties, known as most-favored-nation (MFN) tariffs or "Column 1 tariffs," have been dramatically reduced over the years

---

[13]   J.W. Hampton, Jr. & Co. v. United States, 276 U.S. 394, 48 S.Ct. 348, 72 L.Ed. 624 (1928).

[14]   48 Stat. 943 (1934).

through successive rounds of trade negotiations. See the sample U.S. tariff schedule excerpted in Section 3.4. They are unconditional MFN tariffs, meaning that reciprocity is not required in order for them to apply. Multilateral tariff agreements have predominated over bilateral negotiations since 1948.

The term "most-favored-nation" is misleading in its suggestion of special tariff arrangements. It is more appropriate and since 1998 officially correct to think of MFN tariffs as the "normal" level of U.S. tariffs, to which there are exceptions resulting in the application of higher or lower tariffs. After the Tokyo Round of GATT negotiations in 1978, the average MFN tariff applied to manufactured imports into the United States was approximately 5.6 percent. Reductions in this level to approximately 3.5 percent have been accomplished under the Uruguay Round of 1994. That said, unusually high Column 1 tariffs apply selectively: 10% to certain shoes and 25% to certain trucks, for example.

Tariff cuts on a wide range of information technology products were agreed to late in 1996. By the year 2000, the United States, the European Union and most of East Asia had abolished tariffs on computers, electrical capacitors, calculators, ATM's, fax and answering machines, digital copiers and video cameras, computer diskettes, CD-ROM drives, computer software, fiber optical cables and hundreds of other items. This agreement covers more than 90 percent of all information technology trade.

In early 1997, agreement on liberalizing trade and reducing tariffs on basic telecommunications equipment was reached by 69 nations. This agreement took effect Feb. 5, 1998. Later that year, a WTO declaration imposed standstill obligations on all members to continue to refrain from applying customs duties to electronic commerce while negotiations are underway for more permanent rules in this area.

§ 2.8   Column 2 U.S. Tariffs

Between 1948 and 1951 the United States granted Column 1 most-favored-nation tariff treatment to goods originating from virtually every part of the world. Commencing in 1951, goods originating in nations controlled by communists were withdrawn from such tariff treatment. This had, and to some degree continues to have, the effect of treating the importation of goods from communist nations under Column 2 United States tariff headings. See the sample U.S. tariff schedule excerpted in Section 3.4. As a practical matter, very few such imports can overcome the high Smoot-Hawley tariffs embodied in Column 2.

The designation of which nations are "communist" for these purposes has varied over time. Yugoslavia was generally not treated as a communist country and its goods therefore entered under Column 1 MFN tariffs. Goods from the Balkans presently do so as well. Central and Eastern European nations were sometimes treated as communist countries, particularly during the 1950s and 1960s. This is no longer the case, and at this point nearly every European and Baltic nation has been granted MFN status under United States tariff law. Belarus, Kazakhstan, Turkmenistan, Georgia, Azerbaijan, Tajikistan, Moldova, Kyrgyzstan, Armenia, Uzbekistan, the Russian Federation and Ukraine are also MFN beneficiaries.

It is perhaps more useful, therefore, to indicate those nations that do not presently benefit from most-favored-nation tariff treatment. These include Cuba and North Korea. Goods from some of these nations are totally embargoed as a matter of national security; the law in this area is covered in Chapter 11. The most current listing of those nations whose products are subject to Column 2 tariffs can be found in General Headnote 3(b) to the HTS.

§ 2.9   The Jackson-Vanik Amendment

Section 402 of the 1974 Trade Act governs American grants of most-favored-nation tariff status.[15] This is commonly known as the "Jackson-Vanik Amendment." Under its terms, no products from a nonmarket economy nation may receive MFN treatment, nor may that country participate in U.S. financial credit or guaranty programs, whenever the President determines that it denies its citizens the right or opportunity to emigrate, imposes more than nominal taxes on visas or other emigration documents, or imposes more than nominal charges on its citizens as a result of their desire to leave.

These statutory conditions are widely thought to have been the product of United States desires to have the Soviet Union permit greater exodus of its Jewish population during the early 1970s. However, the passage of the Jackson-Vanik Amendment was an important factor in the Soviet decision to withdraw from a broad trade agreement with the United States at that time, and led to sharply curtailed Jewish emigration from the Soviet Union.

The application of Jackson-Vanik by the President is subject to a waiver by executive order whenever the President determines that such a waiver will substantially promote the objectives of freedom of emigration and the President has received assurances

---

[15]   19 U.S.C.A. § 2432.

that the emigration practices of a particular nonmarket economy nation will lead substantially to the achievement of those objectives. If the President decides to exercise this waiver authority, the waiver must be renewed annually and reported to Congress. These reports and the exercise of presidential waivers have over the years been contentious.

Congressional Veto

At one point Congress had the power to veto presidential waivers under the Jackson-Vanik Amendment. However, a 1983 decision of the United States Supreme Court strongly suggested that these veto powers were unconstitutional.[16] The Customs and Trade Act of 1990 amended the Trade Act of 1974 so as to permit Congress to jointly resolve against presidential Jackson-Vanik waivers. These resolutions can be vetoed by the President, and the President's veto can in turn by overridden by Congress. It is thought that these amendments resolved the constitutional problems associated with Congressional vetoes of presidential action.

Congress and the President disagreed significantly over the renewal of most-favored-nation treatment for Chinese goods. Questions surrounding China's emigration policies, and its general human rights record, were downplayed by U.S. authorities for many years prior to Tiananmen Square. As internal discord within China increased, especially in Tibet and more generally in connection with the Democracy Movement, the Jackson-Vanik amendment came to the forefront of Sino-American trade relations. President Bush's renewal of China's most favored nation status in 1990, 1991 and 1992 was heavily criticized.

China and Jackson-Vanik

Jackson-Vanik became the political fulcrum of Sino-American trade relations. Congress threatened but did not achieve a veto of the President's renewal of MFN tariffs for Chinese goods. Early in 1992, Congress adopted the United States–China Act of 1991. This law would have prohibited the President from recommending further extensions of MFN status to China unless he reported that the PRC had accounted for citizens detained or accused in connection with Tiananmen Square and had made significant progress in achieving specified objectives on human rights, trade and weapons proliferation. President Bush Sr. vetoed the Act and the Congress was unable to override that veto.

---

[16]   See Immigration and Naturalization Service v. Chadha, 462 U.S. 919, 103 S.Ct. 2764, 77 L.Ed.2d 317 (1983).

In 1993, President Clinton renewed China's MFN status subject to some general human-rights conditions, including "significant progress" in releasing political prisoners, allowing international groups access to prisons and respect for human rights in Tibet. This seemed to pacify Congress for the moment. But it engendered hostility and resistance in China. Less publicly, the United States business community opposed the linkage of human rights to MFN tariffs as its PRC trade and investment commitments and opportunities were endangered. China, meanwhile, had developed the world's fastest growing economy and it decided to force the issue. If anything, abuse of human rights in the PRC actually increased early in 1994, notably prior to a well-publicized visit of the U.S. Secretary of State.

With Congress increasingly split on the issue, President Clinton made an historic reversal in policy. In June of 1994, he renewed China's MFN tariff status without human rights conditions, limiting its coverage only as regards Chinese-made ammunition and guns. President Clinton renewed China's MFN tariff status each year after 1994. Congress did not seek to override these decisions. In 1998, for the first time, President Clinton waived the Jackson-Vanik requirements for Vietnam. President George W. Bush did likewise. This waiver survived Congressional scrutiny. It opened the door to EXIMBANK and OPIC programs, as well as Column 1 MFN tariffs on Vietnamese goods entering the United States.

WTO members like China since 2001, Vietnam since 2007 and Russia since 2012 receive MFN tariff status automatically and unconditionally. Hence the Jackson-Vanik amendment no longer has significant application.

§ 2.10 U.S. Generalized System of Tariff Preferences (GSP)—Statutory Authorization

The Generalized System of Preferences (GSP) originated in United Nations dialogues between the developed and the developing world. The third world successfully argued that it needed special access to industrial markets in order to improve and advance their economies. One problem with this approach is that it is contrary to the unconditional most-favored-nation principle contained in the GATT. Nevertheless, in 1971 the GATT authorized its parties to establish generalized systems of tariff preferences for developing nations. The European Union, Japan and nearly all other developed nations adopted GSP systems before the United States. Although similar in purpose, each of these systems is governed by a unique body of law of the "donor" country.

It was not until the Trade Act of 1974 that a GSP system was incorporated into United States tariff law. The Trade Act authorized GSP tariff preferences for ten years. The program was renewed in the Trade Act of 1984 for an additional nine years ending in July 1993. Incremental extensions have since been made pending a program review. The Trade Promotion Authority-Trade Adjustment Assistance Act of 2002 (TPA-TAA) renewed the GSP program through 2006 retroactive to its expiration on Sept. 30, 2001. Various GSP renewals have followed. At this point, tens of billions worth of goods enter the U.S. market duty free under the GSP program, but it is estimated that more imports could achieve this status if traders better understood the GSP.

Title V of the Trade Act of 1974 contains the provisions authorizing the United States GSP program.[17] The United States GSP system, as presently operated, designates certain nations as "beneficiary developing countries." Unless a country is so designated, none of its imports can enter duty free under the GSP program. In addition, only selected goods are designated "eligible articles" for purposes of the GSP program. Thus, for duty free entry under the GSP program to occur, the goods must originate from a beneficiary nation and qualify as eligible articles.

§ 2.11   U.S. Generalized System of Tariff Preferences—USTR Petition Procedures

Any United States producer of an article that competes with GSP imports can file a petition with the United States Trade Representative (USTR) to have a country or particular products withdrawn from the program. This petitioning procedure can also be used in the reverse by importers and exporters to obtain product or beneficiary country status under the United States GSP program. The President is given broad authority to withdraw, suspend or limit the application of duty free entry under the GSP system.[18] Specific products from specific countries may be excluded from GSP benefits. In one case, for example, the President's decision to withdraw GSP benefits for "buffalo leather and goat and kid leather (not fancy)" from India was affirmed.[19] In another decision, the President's discretionary authority to deny GSP benefits to cut flowers from Colombia was similarly upheld.[20]

The President is required to take into consideration the impact of duty free entry on U.S. producers of like or directly competitive

---

[17]   19 U.S.C.A. §§ 501–506.
[18]   See 19 U.S.C.A. § 2464(a).
[19]   Florsheim Shoe Co. v. United States, 744 F.2d 787 (Fed.Cir.1984).
[20]   Sunburst Farms, Inc. v. United States, 797 F.2d 973 (Fed.Cir.1986).

products. There is a set of regulations, codified at 15 C.F.R. Part 2007, which details the petitioning procedures used in connection with the certification of GSP eligible products or countries. These regulations require the domestic competitor to cite injury caused by duty free GSP imports. Within 6 months after the petition is filed, and a review by the United States Trade Representative (USTR) acting with the advice of the International Trade Commission (ITC) has been undertaken, a decision on the petition will be rendered by the USTR.

§ 2.12   U.S. Generalized System of Tariff Preferences—Competitive Need Limitations

There are two statutory limitations on the applicability of duty free GSP entry. These are known as the "competitive need" limitations. They are found in Section 504 of the Trade Act of 1974, codified at 19 U.S.C.A. § 2464(c). The first statutory limitation focuses upon dollar volumes. Duty free entry is not permitted to any eligible product from a beneficiary country if during the preceding year that country exported to the United States more than a designated dollar volume of the article in question. There is a statutory formula for establishing this dollar volume limitation. In recent years, the maximum dollar volume limitation has ranged between 75 and 80 million dollars. The second statutory limitation on duty free GSP entry is framed in terms of percentages. Duty free entry is denied to products if during the preceding year the beneficiary country exported to the United States 50 percent or more of the total U.S. imports of that particular product.[21]

A complex system of waivers applies to the competitive need formulae. These are administered by the USTR and the President acting on advice of the International Trade Commission.[22] Basically, there are five possibilities for waivers of the competitive need limitations. The first can occur if the President decides that there is no like or directly competitive article produced in the United States and the imported product is exempt from the percentage but not the dollar value competitive need limitation. The second can occur under circumstances where the President determines that the imports in question are *de minimis*.

The third possibility involves imports from the least developed developing nations, after notice to Congress. A list of these countries can be found in HTS General Note 3(c)(ii)(B). A fourth opportunity for a competitive need waiver exists when there has

---

[21]   See West Bend Co. v. United States, 10 C.I.T. 146 (1986) (competitive impact still must be proven).

[22]   See 19 U.S.C.A. § 2464(c).

been an historical preferential trade relationship between the United States and the source country, and there is a trade agreement between that country and the United States, and the source country does not discriminate against or otherwise impose unjustifiable or unreasonable barriers to United States commerce.

Lastly, the President is authorized to waive the competitive need requirements of the GSP program if the International Trade Commission decides that the imports in question are not likely to have an adverse effect on the United States industry with which they compete, and the President determines that such a waiver is in the national economic interest.[23] In making waiver determinations, the President must consider generally the extent to which the beneficiary country has assured the United States that it will provide equitable and reasonable access to its markets and basic commodity resources. The President must also consider the extent to which the country provides adequate and effective means for foreigners to secure and exercise intellectual property rights.

Once a waiver of the competitive need limitations is granted, it remains in effect until circumstances change and the President decides that it is no longer justified. Attorneys can play a useful role in monitoring Department of Commerce trade statistics to determine how close imports are coming under the competitive need formulae to restriction. By shifting to purchases of similar goods from another country, importers can preserve duty free entry and avoid the effects of these statutory restraints.

§ 2.13 U.S. Generalized System of Tariff Preferences—Country Eligibility

Thousands of products from over one hundred countries benefit from duty free GSP entry into the United States.[24] A list of GSP qualified nations and territories is presented in HTS General Note 3(c)(ii). Goods from insular possessions of the United States (e.g., American Samoa and the U.S. Virgin Islands) ordinarily receive duty free GSP entry "no less favorable" than allowed GSP beneficiary nations.[25]

The President's power over the list of eligible countries and eligible products is wide and politically sensitive. For example, the President is required to evaluate, in determining whether a country is eligible under the U.S. GSP program, if it is upholding

---

[23]   See 19 U.S.C.A. § 2464(c)(3)(A).

[24]   See Executive Order 11888 (Nov. 24, 1975, 40 F.R. 55276, extensively amended, for a detailed listing of eligible products and countries).

[25]   19 U.S.C.A. § 2462(d).

"internationally recognized workers' rights." Such rights include the right of association, the right to organize and bargain collectively, a prohibition against forced or compulsory labor, a minimum age for employment of children, and acceptable working conditions (minimum wages, hours of work, and occupational safety and health.)[26] In 2002, the definition of "core worker rights" for GSP country eligibility purposes was updated to include the ILO prohibition on the worst forms of child labor. The President must report annually to the Congress on the status of internationally recognized workers' rights in every GSP beneficiary country, but the issue is not open to private challenge.[27]

The President must also consider whether the foreign country is adequately protecting United States owners of intellectual property, (compliance with TRIPs is not necessarily sufficient), and whether its investment laws adversely affect U.S. exports. In addition, when designating GSP beneficiary nations, the Trade Act requires the President to take into account various factors which amount to a U.S. agenda on international economic relations:

(1) The desires of the country;

(2) Its level of economic development;

(3) Whether the EU, Japan or others extend GSP treatment to it;

(4) The extent to which the country provides equitable and reasonable access to its markets and its basic commodity resources, and the extent to which it will refrain from unreasonable export practices;

(5) The extent to which it provides adequate and effective intellectual property rights; and

(6) The extent to which it has taken action to reduce trade distorting investment practices (including export performance requirements) and reduced barriers to trade in services.[28]

No communist nations and no oil restraining OPEC nations (Indonesia, Ecuador and Venezuela are excepted) may benefit from the GSP program. Furthermore, the President must not designate countries that grant trade preferences to other *developed* nations. The President must also consider, in making GSP decisions, whether beneficiary countries are cooperative on drug enforcement, whether they are expropriators of U.S. property interests, whether

---

[26]   19 U.S.C.A. 2462(a).

[27]   See International Labor Rights Education & Research Fund v. Bush, 752 F.Supp. 495 (D.D.C.1990), *affirmed* 954 F.2d 745 (D.C.Cir.1992).

[28]   19 U.S.C.A. § 2462(c).

they offer assistance to terrorists, and whether they are willing to recognize international arbitration awards. The President may waive the expropriation requirement if it is determined that the country in question has paid prompt, adequate and effective compensation or entered into good faith negotiations or arbitration with the intent to do so.

The statutory bar against communist, oil restricting OPEC and preferentially trading countries as GSP beneficiaries is absolute. The bar against expropriating, drug dealing, denials of arbitration award enforcement, terrorist aiding and workers' rights non-recognition beneficiaries is discretionary with the President. The goods of such nations may still qualify if the President determines that GSP duty free entry would be in the national economic interest of the United States.[29]

In applying these country eligibility criteria, past Presidents have disqualified a variety of nations from the U.S. GSP program. For example, Romania, Nicaragua, Paraguay, Chile, Burma, the Central African Republic and Liberia have all been disqualified in the past for failure to meet the workers' rights standards. Argentina and Honduras have lost GSP benefits for perceived failures to adequately protect U.S. pharmaceutical patents. Panama under General Noriega was rendered ineligible because of the failure to cooperate on narcotics. Intellectual property piracy led to the suspension of Ukraine's country eligibility in the GSP program.

The President's review of a country's eligibility under the GSP program is ongoing. This led to the reinstatement of GSP beneficiary nations. Russia was made a GSP beneficiary by President Clinton. Any country designated as a beneficiary nation under the GSP program that is subsequently disqualified by exercise of Presidential discretion, or graduated, must receive 60 days' notice from the President with an explanation of this decision.[30] This, in effect, presents the opportunity to reply and negotiate.

Since the GSP program originated within the GATT/WTO nearly all the beneficiary countries are members of that organization. It is not, however, mandatory for a developing nation to be a member of the WTO in order to receive GSP trade benefits from the United States. China is a WTO member, but for other reasons its goods do not qualify for GSP duty free entry. Other nations whose goods are not eligible are specifically listed in the Trade Act: Australia, Austria, Canada, European Union States,

---

[29]   19 U.S.C.A. § 2462(b).
[30]   19 U.S.C.A. § 2462(a).

Finland, Iceland, Japan, Monaco, New Zealand, Norway, Republic of South Africa, Sweden, and Switzerland.[31]

§ 2.14 U.S. Generalized System of Tariff Preferences—Product Eligibility

For each designated GSP beneficiary country, the President also issues a list of products from that country eligible for duty free entry into the United States. The statutory authorization for the United States GSP program generally excludes leather products, textiles and apparel,[32] watches,[33] selected electronics and, certain steel, footwear and categories of glass from being designated as eligible articles.[34] All these goods are thought to involve particular "import sensitivity."

The UNCTAD Certificate of Origin Form A is ordinarily required of the foreign exporter when GSP eligible merchandise is involved. Complex "rules of origin" determine where goods are from for purposes of the United States GSP program. Basically, for goods to originate in a beneficiary country, at least 35 percent of the appraised value of those goods must be added in that nation.[35] The statutory rules of origin for GSP eligible goods are found in 19 U.S.C.A. § 2463(b).[36]

---

[31]   19 U.S.C.A. § 2462(b).

[32]   See Luggage and Leather Goods Mfrs. of America, Inc. v. United States, 588 F.Supp. 1413 (C.I.T.1984) (man-made fiber flat goods are textile and apparel articles).

[33]   See North American Foreign Trading Corp. v. United States, 600 F.Supp. 226 (C.I.T.1984), *affirmed* 783 F.2d 1031 (Fed.Cir.1986) (exemption for watches includes solid-state digital watches).

[34]   19 U.S.C.A. § 2463(c).

[35]   See Madison Galleries, Ltd. v. United States, 870 F.2d 627 (Fed.Cir.1989).

[36]   19 U.S.C.A. § 2463(b). Eligible articles qualifying for duty-free treatment:

(b)(1) The duty-free treatment provided under section 501 shall apply to any eligible article which is the growth, product, or manufacture of a beneficiary developing country if—

(A) that article is imported directly from a beneficiary developing country into the customs territory of the United States; and

(B) the sum of (i) the cost or value of the materials produced in the beneficiary developing country or any 2 or more countries which are members of the same association of countries which is treated as one country under section 502(a)(3), plus (ii) the direct costs of processing operations performed in such beneficiary developing country or such member countries is not less than 35 percent of the appraised value of such article at the time of its entry into the customs territory of the United States.

(2) The Secretary of the Treasury, after consulting with the United States Trade Representative, shall prescribe such regulations as may be necessary to carry out this subsection, including, but not limited to, regulations providing that, in order to be eligible for duty-free treatment under this title, an article must be wholly the growth, product, or manufacture of a beneficiary developing country, or must be a new or different article of commerce which

A federal Circuit Court of Appeals has ruled that a "two-stage" substantial transformation process must also occur in order to qualify goods for GSP purposes.[37] Thus, the value of U.S.-grown corn did not count towards meeting the 35 percent requirement because the intermediate products into which it was turned did not qualify as Mexican in origin for lack of substantial transformation into a new and different article of commerce.[38] But the assembly of integrated circuits in Taiwan from slices containing many integrated circuit chips, gold wire, lead frame strips, molding compound and epoxy (all of which were U.S. in origin) did constitute a substantial transformation of such items into a new article of commerce. Thus the circuits could be deemed from Taiwan for purposes of the 35 percent value added GSP rule.[39]

One unusual feature of the rules of origin for the United States GSP program is that which favors selected regional economic groups. Goods made in the ANDEAN pact, ASEAN or CARICOM may be designated as "one country" for purposes of origin. So too may goods produced in the East African Community, the West African Economic and Monetary Union and the Southern African Development Community. This means that the value added requirement as applied in these regions is met if 35 percent of the value added has been created inside each group as opposed to inside any one nation of the group. It is notable that many other third world regional economic groups are not similarly treated, e.g. MERCOSUR, and the Gulf Council of the Middle East.

§ 2.15   U.S. Generalized System of Tariff Preferences—Graduation

As nations develop, U.S. law either bars their participation in the GSP program absolutely or vests discretion in the President to remove nations or products from its scope. Developing nations with

---

has been grown, produced, or manufactured in the beneficiary developing country; but no article or material of a beneficiary developing country shall be eligible for such treatment by virtue of having merely undergone—

(A) simple combining or packaging operations, or

(B) mere dilution with water or mere dilution with another substance that does not materially alter the characteristics of the article.

[37]   See Torrington Company v. United States, 764 F.2d 1563 (Fed.Cir.1985). See generally Cutler, United States Generalized System of Preferences: the Problem of Substantial Transformation, 5 North Carolina Journal of International Law & Commercial Regulation, 393 (1980).

[38]   Azteca Mill. Co. v. United States, 890 F.2d 1150 (Fed.Cir.1989).

[39]   Texas Instruments Inc. v. United States, 681 F.2d 778 (C.C.P.A.1982). See Madison Galleries, Ltd. v. United States, 688 F.Supp. 1544 (C.I.T.1988) (blank porcelain from Taiwan substantially transformed when painted and fired in Hong Kong).

a per capita gross national product in excess of $8,500 are totally ineligible for GSP duty free entry. The Bahamas, Bahrain, Brunei, Israel, Nauru and Bermuda have been disqualified under this rule. In addition, the President has a broad authority to "graduate" countries from the United States GSP program. The basic concept here is that certain nations are sufficiently developed so as to not need the benefits of duty free entry into the United States market. Discretionary graduation is based on an assessment of the economic development level of the beneficiary country, the competitive position of the imports and the overall national economic interests of the United States.[40]

In recent years, Presidents have been graduating more and more products from countries like India and Brazil. In January of 1989, President Reagan graduated all products from Hong Kong, Singapore, South Korea and Taiwan. At that time, these countries were the source of about 60 percent of all goods benefiting from the United States GSP program. Mexico then emerged as the chief beneficiary country under the program until late in 1993 when all of its products were removed from the GSP treatment in anticipation of the North American Free Trade Agreement. In 1997, President Clinton graduated Malaysia entirely from the GSP program. Other U.S. free trade partners, such as Jordan, Morocco and Peru, have also been eliminated as beneficiary countries. *See* Section 2.4.

§ 2.16 U.S. Generalized System of Tariff Preferences—Judicial and Administrative Remedies

Legal challenges to presidential revocations of duty free GSP treatment were originally filed with the U.S. Customs Court. This was the case despite contentions of inadequate legal remedies in that court and the fact that plaintiff could not pursue class action relief except in federal district court.[41] Litigation involving the GSP program is now commenced in the U.S. Court of International Trade.

The goods entering the United States duty free through the GSP program remain subject to the possibility of escape clause relief under Section 201 of the Trade Act of 1974.[42] Moreover, such goods may also be restrained pursuant to Section 232 of the Trade

---

[40]   See 47 Fed.Reg. 31,099, 31,000 (July 16, 1982).
[41]   Barclay Industries, Inc. v. Carter, 494 F.Supp. 912 (D.D.C.1980).
[42]   See 19 U.S.C.A. § 2251 and Chapter 15.

Expansion Act of 1962 in the name of the national security of the United States.[43]

§ 2.17   U.S. Caribbean Basin Initiative (CBI)

The European Union has had for many years a policy which grants substantial duty free entry into its market for goods originating in Mediterranean Basin countries. The United States has duplicated this approach for the Caribbean Basin. This is accomplished through the Caribbean Basin Economic Recovery Act of 1983 (19 U.S.C. 2701–2707). For these purposes, the Caribbean Basin is broadly defined to include nearly all of the islands in that Sea, and a significant number of Central and South American nations bordering the Caribbean. So defined, there are 28 nations which could qualify for purposes of the United States Caribbean Basin Initiative.

As with the GSP program, the Caribbean Basin Initiative (CBI) involves presidential determinations to confer beneficiary status upon any of these eligible countries. However, unlike the GSP, there are no presidential determinations as to which specific products of these countries shall be allowed into the United States on a duty free basis. All Caribbean products except those excluded by statute are eligible. Moreover, there is no "competitive need" or annual per capita income limits under the CBI. Lastly, unlike the GSP program which must be renewed periodically, the Caribbean Basin Initiative is a permanent part of the U.S. tariff system.

The United States has maintained a steady trade surplus with Caribbean Basin countries. Leading export items under the CBI are typically beef, raw cane sugar, medical instruments, cigars, fruits and rum. The leading source countries have often been the Dominican Republic, Costa Rica and Guatemala, now all U.S. free trade partners. The value of all CBI duty free imports now exceeds $1 billion annually, but CBI countries fear a diversion of trade and investment to Mexico and Central America as the North American Free Trade Agreement (NAFTA) and the Central American Free Trade Agreement (CAFTA) mature.

§ 2.18   ____CBI Country Eligibility

The President is forbidden from designating Caribbean Basin Initiative beneficiaries if they are communist, have engaged in expropriation activities, nullified contracts or intellectual property rights of the U.S. citizens, failed to recognize and enforce arbitral awards, given preferential treatment to products of another

---

[43]   See 19 U.S.C.A. § 2463(c)(2).

developed nation, broadcast through a government-owned entity United States copyrighted material without consent, failed to sign a treaty or other agreement regarding extradition of United States citizens, failed to cooperate on narcotics enforcement, or failed to afford internationally recognized workers' rights. For these purposes, the definition of workers' rights enacted in connection with the GSP program applies.[44] Since 2000, CBI countries must also show a commitment to implementing WTO pledges.

These prohibitions notwithstanding, the President can still designate a Caribbean Basin country as a beneficiary if he or she determines that this will be in the national economic or security interest of the United States. However, this can be done only in connection with countries that are disqualified as being communist, expropriators, contract or intellectual property nullifiers, non-enforcers of arbitral awards, unauthorized broadcasters, or those who fail to provide for internationally recognized workers' rights. Thus, if a Caribbean nation is disqualified because it grants preferential trade treatment to products of another developed nation or refuses to sign an extradition treaty with the United States, there is no possibility of its designation as a beneficiary nation under the Caribbean Basin Initiative. As with the GSP statutory requirements, if the basis for the disqualification is expropriation or nullification of benefits, the President may override this disqualification if that nation is engaged in payment of prompt, adequate and effective compensation or good faith negotiations intended to lead to such compensation.

In addition, the President is required to take various factors into account in designating beneficiary countries under the Caribbean Basin Initiative. These include:

(1) The desire of that country to participate;

(2) The economic conditions and living standards of that nation;

(3) The extent to which the country has promised to provide equitable and reasonable access to its markets and basic commodity resources;

(4) The degree to which it follows accepted GATT rules on international trade;

(5) The degree to which it uses export subsidies or imposes export performance requirements or local content requirements which distort international trade;

---

[44]   See § 10.9, supra.

(6) The degree to which its trade policies help revitalize the region;

(7) The degree to which it is undertaking self-help measures to promote its own economic development;

(8) Whether it has taken steps to provide internationally recognized workers' rights;

(9) The extent to which it provides adequate and effective means for foreigners to secure and enforce exclusive intellectual property rights;

(10) The extent to which the country prohibits unauthorized broadcasts of copyrighted material belonging to U.S. owners; and

(11) The extent to which the country is prepared to cooperate with the United States in connection with the Caribbean Basin Initiative, particularly by signing a tax information exchange agreement.

Under these criteria, the President has designated a large number of the 28 eligible nations as beneficiary countries under the Caribbean Basin Initiative. These include Antigua and Barbuda, Aruba, the Bahamas, Barbados, Belize, the British Virgin Islands, Costa Rica, Dominica, the Dominican Republic, El Salvador, Grenada, Guatemala, Guinea, Haiti, Honduras, Jamaica, Monserrat, the Netherlands Antilles, Nicaragua, Panama, St. Christopher-Nevis, St. Lucia, St. Vincent and the Grenadines, and Trinidad and Tobago. Cuba is not even listed among the nations eligible for consideration in connection with the Caribbean Basin Initiative. Some of these countries are now U.S. free trade partners and therefore no longer CBI eligible. *See* Section 2.4.

U.S. Presidents have typically required of each potential beneficiary a concise written presentation of its policies and practices directly related to the issues raised by the country designation criteria listed in the Caribbean Basin Economic Recovery Act. Wherever measures were in effect which were inconsistent with the objectives of these criteria, U.S. presidents have sought assurances that such measures would be progressively eliminated or modified. For example, the Dominican Republic promised to take steps to reduce the degree of book piracy and the Jamaican and Bahamian governments promised to stop the unauthorized broadcast of U.S. films and television programs.[45]

---

[45]   19 U.S.C.A. § 2702.

§ 2.19 _____CBI Product Eligibility

Unless specifically excluded, all products of Caribbean Basin nations are eligible for duty free entry into the United States market. Certain goods are absolutely excluded from such treatment.[46] These include footwear, canned tuna, petroleum and petroleum derivatives, watches, and certain leather products. It should be noted that this listing of "import sensitive" products is different from but overlaps with that used in connection with the United States GSP program. Since 2000, products ineligible for CBI benefits enter at reduced tariff levels corresponding to Mexican goods under NAFTA . . . so-called "NAFTA parity".

One of the most critical of the products that may enter the United States on a duty free basis is sugar. But the President is given the authority to suspend duty free treatment for both sugar and beef products originating in the Caribbean Basin or to impose quotas in order to protect United States domestic price support programs for these products.[47] Sugar exports have traditionally been critical to many Caribbean Basin economies. Nevertheless, sugar import quotas into the United States from the Caribbean have been steadily reduced in recent years. For example, by 1988 the sugar quota allocations for some CBI countries reached a low of 25 percent of their 1983 pre-Caribbean Basin Initiative allocations.[48] Many consider the few duty free import benefits obtained under the Initiative to be more than counterbalanced by the loss in sugar exports to the United States market.

The rules of origin for determining product eligibility in connection with the Caribbean Basin Initiative are virtually the same as discussed previously under the GSP.[49] As a general rule, a substantial transformation must occur and a 35 percent value added requirement is imposed (but 15 percent may come from the United States). This percentage is calculated by adding the sum of the cost or value of the materials produced in the beneficiary country or two or more beneficiary countries plus the direct cost of processing operations performed in those countries.[50] It should be noted that this approach effectively treats all of the CBI-eligible nations as a regional beneficiary since the 35 percent required value can be cumulated among them.

---

[46]   See 19 U.S.C.A. § 2703(b).

[47]   19 U.S.C.A. § 2073(c) and (d).

[48]   See Fox, Interaction of the Caribbean Basin Initiative and U.S. Domestic Sugar Price Support: A Political Contradiction, 8 Mississippi College Law Review 197 (1988).

[49]   See HTS General Note 3(c)(v).

[50]   19 U.S.C.A. § 2703(a).

As under the GSP program, the President is given broad powers to suspend duty free treatment with reference to any eligible product or any designated beneficiary country.[51] Import injury relief under Section 201 of the Trade Act of 1974 can be invoked in connection with Caribbean Basin imports. And the equivalent of that relief is authorized specifically for agricultural imports upon similar determinations by the Secretary of Agriculture.[52] The effects of these protective proceedings may be diminished in the context of Caribbean Basin imports.

Whenever the International Trade Commission is studying whether increased imports are a substantial cause of serious injury to a domestic industry under Section 201 or its agricultural equivalent, the ITC is required to break out the Caribbean Basin beneficiary countries. The President is given the discretion if he or she decides to impose escape clause relief to suspend that relief relative to Caribbean Basin imports. A similar discretion is granted to the President in connection with national security import restraints under Section 232 of the Trade Expansion Act of 1962. However, these discretionary provisions relate only to those goods that are eligible for duty free entry under the Caribbean Basin Initiative.[53]

In 1986, President Reagan initiated a special program for textiles produced in the Caribbean. Essentially, this program increases the opportunity to sell Caribbean textile products when the fabric involved has been previously formed and cut in the United States. If this is the case, there are minimum guaranteed access levels. This program is run in conjunction with Section 9802.00.80 of the Harmonized Tariff Schedule of the United States.[54] *See* Section 2.21.

The U.S.-Caribbean Basin Trade Partnership Act of 2000 grants duty-free and quota-free access to the U.S. market for apparel made from U.S. fabric and yarn. Apparel made from CBI fabric is capped for duty free into the United States. CBI textiles and apparel are subject to market surge safeguards comparable to those under NAFTA. Late in 2006, duty free treatment of Haitian apparel products was expanded under the HOPE Act. In certain cases, Haiti may utilize third country fabrics and still ship apparel duty free into the United States.

---

[51]   19 U.S.C.A. § 2702(e).

[52]   19 U.S.C.A. § 2703(f).

[53]   See 29 U.S.C.A. § 2703(e).

[54]   See 51 Fed.Reg. 21,208 (June 11, 1986).

§ 2.20   U.S. Andean Trade Preferences

The Andean Trade Preference Act (ATPA) of 1991[55] authorizes the President to grant duty free treatment to imports of eligible articles from Colombia, Peru, Bolivia and Ecuador. Venezuela is not included as a beneficiary country under this Act. The Andean Trade Preference Act is patterned after the Caribbean Basin Economic Recovery Act of 1983. Goods that ordinarily enter duty free into the United States from Caribbean Basin nations will also enter duty free from these four Andean countries. The same exceptions and exclusions discussed above in connection with the Caribbean Basin Initiative generally apply. However, while the CBI is a permanent part of United States Customs law, the ATPA was only authorized initially for a period of ten years. Furthermore, the guaranteed access levels for Caribbean Basin textile products, separate cumulation rules for antidumping and countervailing duty investigations, and the waiver of the Buy American Act for procurement purposes are not authorized by the ATPA.

The Andean Trade Preference Act was renewed by the TPA-TAA through February 2006 retroactive to its expiry Dec. 4, 2001. Periodic renewals have followed. Textile and apparel products, and most other products previously excluded, are now included under the ATPA. Country eligibility for enhanced benefits includes consideration of steps taken to comply with WTO obligations, the protection of worker rights and combating corruption. Broadly speaking, the passage of the ATPA represents fulfillment of the elder President Bush's commitment to assist these nations economically in return for their help in containing narcotics. Peru and Colombia are now U.S. free partners, a status that removes ATPA benefits. Free trade negotiations with Ecuador and Bolivia have not succeeded, leaving their Andean benefits uncertain. Ecuador has renounced ATPA benefits, and the Act expired July 31, 2013.

§ 2.21   U.S. African Trade Preferences

The Africa Growth and Opportunity Act of 2000[56] granted duty-free and quota-free access to the U.S. market for apparel made from U.S. fabric and yarn. Apparel made from African fabric is capped for duty free entry. The least developed sub-Saharan countries enjoy duty-free and quota-free apparel access regardless of the origin of the fabric. In 2008, the so-called "abundant supply" provision of AGOA was repealed, thus assuring least-developed

---

[55]   Public Law 102–82, 19 U.S.C.A. § 3201 et seq.
[56]   Public Law No. 106–200, 114 Stat. 252.

country textile exports to the United States. U.S. imports of AGOA textiles using third country fabrics have also been liberalized.

The Act also altered U.S. GSP rules to admit certain previously excluded African products on a duty-free basis, including petroleum, watches and flat goods. Sub-Saharan countries can export almost all products duty-free to the United States. These countries are encouraged to create a free trade area with U.S. support. African exports are subject to import surge (escape clause) protection and stringent rules against transshipments between countries for purposes of taking advantage of U.S. trade benefits.

§ 2.22   Section 9802.00.80 of the USHTS

Section 9802.00.80 of the Harmonized Tariff Schedule of the United States (formerly Section 807.00 of the Tariff Schedule of the United States) is an unusual "duty free" provision.[57] This section allows for the duty free importation of United States fabricated components that were exported ready for assembly abroad. If qualified, goods assembled abroad containing U.S. components are subject only to a duty upon the value added through foreign assembly operations regardless of where assembled.

In order for this to be the case, Section 9802.00.80 requires that the components be fabricated and a product of the United States, that they be exported in a condition ready for assembly without further fabrication, that they not lose their physical identity by change in form, shape or otherwise, and that they not be advanced in value or improved in condition abroad except by being assembled and except by operations incidental to the assembly process such as cleaning, lubricating and painting.

---

[57]   Harmonized Tariff Schedule of the United States (2013) (edited):

9802.00.80 Articles, except goods of heading 9802.00.90 and goods imported under provisions of subchapter XIX of this chapter and goods imported under provisions of

subchapter XX, assembled abroad in whole or in part of fabricated components, the product of the United States, which (a) were exported in condition ready for assembly

without further fabrication, (b) have not lost their physical identity in such articles by change in form, shape or otherwise, and (c) have not been advanced in value or

improved in condition abroad except by being assembled and except by operations incidental to the assembly process such as cleaning, lubricating and painting. . . .

A duty upon he full value of A duty upon value of the imported the full value of the imported article, the imported article, less the article, less the less the cost or cost or value of cost or value of such products value of such of the United such products of States.

The regulations issued in connection with Section 9802.00.80 indicate that there are other incidental operations which will not disqualify components from duty free re-entry into the United States. These include removing rust, grease, paint or other preservative coatings, the application of similar preservative coatings, the trimming or other removal of small amounts of excess material, adjustments in the shape or form of a component required by the assembly that is being undertaken, the cutting to length of wire, thread, tape, foil or similar products, the separation by cutting of finished components (such as integrated circuits exported in strips), and the calibration, testing, marking, sorting, pressing and folding and assembly of the final product.[58]

In contrast, the regulations also provide examples of operations that are not considered incidental to assembly for these purposes. These examples include the melting of ingots to produce cast metal parts, the cutting of garments according to patterns, painting which is intended to enhance the appearance or impart distinctive features to the product, chemical treatment so as to realize new characteristics (such as moisture-proofing), and the machining, polishing or other treatment of metals which create significant new characteristics or qualities.[59]

If all of the Section 9802.00.80 criteria are met, the tariff that will be assessed upon the imported assembled product will be limited to a duty upon the full value of that product less the cost or value of U.S. made components that have been incorporated into it.[60] Those who seek to take advantage of Section 9802.00.80 must provide the United States Customs Service with a Foreign Assembler's Declaration and Certification. This is known as Form 3317. The assembly plant operator certifies that the requirements of Section 9802.00.80 are met, and the importer declares that this certification is correct.

Billions of dollars of ordinarily tariffed value have been excluded as a result of this Customs law provision. Motor vehicles, semiconductors, office machines, textiles and apparel, and furniture are good examples of the kinds of products assembled abroad with fabricated U.S. components so as to meet the requirements of Section 9802.00.80. Historically, many of these products have been assembled in Japan, Germany or Canada. In more recent times, the assembly operations to which Section 9802.00.80 frequently applies have more commonly been found in the developing world.

---

[58]   19 C.F.R. § 10.16(b).

[59]   19 C.F.R. § 10.16(c).

[60]   See generally 19 C.F.R. § 10.14 et seq.

§ 2.23 ___Maquiladoras

Section 9802.00.80 is applicable to goods imported into the United States from anywhere in the world. However, it is most frequently associated with maquiladoras. Maquiladoras are "in-bond" assembly plants that often take advantage of the duty free potential of Section 9802.00.80. Maquiladoras enjoyed a phenomenal popularity after 1982 when the Mexican peso was dramatically devalued. This had the practical effect of rendering Mexican labor costs lower than those of Taiwan, Hong Kong, Singapore and South Korea. These Asian nations were traditionally low-cost assembly plant centers. In 1995, Mexican labor costs were dramatically lowered when the peso crashed once again.

Since 1982, thousands of maquiladoras have been established in Tijuana, Ciudad Juarez, Neuvo Laredo and other border cities. They provide Mexico with hundreds of thousands of jobs and are a major source of foreign currency earnings. Electronics, apparel, toys, medical supplies, transport equipment, furniture and sporting goods are examples of the types of industries that have been attracted south of the border. United States components, when assembled in maquiladoras and qualifying under Section 9802.00.80, are exported and then reimported on a duty free basis. Maquiladoras have been developed throughout the Caribbean Basin and Central America. Much to the frustration of organized labor, such offshore assembly operations exemplify the internalization of the United States manufacturing sector.

The maquiladora industry enjoyed explosive growth before and in the early years of NAFTA. Mexican law, like Section 9802.00.80, supported this growth. Various decrees permit goods to enter Mexico on a duty free basis *under bond* for purposes of assembly in maquiladoras. Mexican law permits duty free importation of equipment, technology and components for six months. At the end of that period the goods must be exported from Mexico, typically back to the United States. Except with special permission, which has been increasingly granted by the authorities, maquiladora-assembled goods may not enter the Mexican market. Investors may own maquiladoras, typically using 30-year land trusts (fideicomiso) and Mexican subsidiaries. Alternatively, they may lease assembly plant space from a Mexican company and operate a maquiladora from that space. The simplest way to enter into maquiladora operations is to contract with a company to assemble the goods in question ("shelter operations").

Until late in 1993, there was also a link between the United States System of Generalized Preferences (GSP) and Mexican maquiladoras. Under the rules of origin that govern the GSP program, if at least 35 percent of the value of a maquiladora product was of Mexican origin, it could qualify entirely for duty free entry into the United States. The possibility of this result caused many users of maquiladoras to seek out Mexican suppliers in order to try to meet the 35 percent rule of origin. This incentive was enhanced by the fact that South Korea, Singapore, Taiwan and Hong Kong were all graduated from the United States GSP program in 1989. Mexico was the largest source of GSP qualified goods entering the United States market prior to December, 1993 when all of its products were removed from the GSP program as a result of NAFTA.

The net result of the United States and foreign laws like that of Mexico in this area is to create an interdependent legal framework mutually supportive of maquiladora operations. Many have characterized this legal framework as a "co-production" or "production sharing" arrangement between the two countries. However, utilization of maquiladoras is not limited to U.S. firms or United States' components. Japanese and Korean companies have become major investors in maquiladora industries. To the extent that they utilize U.S. components, they may benefit from the duty free entry provisions of Section 9802.00.80.

In 1998, Mexico's Ministry of Commerce and Industry Development (SECOFI) published an amended Maquiladora Decree. The revised Decree streamlines regulation of maquiladoras in Mexico, notably reducing SECOFI's discretion to deny, suspend or cancel maquiladora programs. A translation of the Decree can be found at www.natlaw.com. Mexico was responding, in part, to increased assembly plant competition from Asia, especially China after its 2001 admission to the WTO. At this stage, some firms have moved their plants to Asia where lower labor costs often prevail. Nevertheless, rising Chinese labor and shipping costs have actually caused some assembly plants to migrate back to Mexico.

The North American Free Trade Area incorporating Mexico, Canada and the United States creates an incentive to invest in Mexico. Nearly all Mexican-made goods are able to enter the United States market on a duty free basis. NAFTA phased out over seven years the duty free entry Section 9802.00.80 benefits applied to Mexican maquiladoras, but not as regards goods assembled with United States components elsewhere in the Americas.

There seems to be an evolutionary cycle in assembly plants-from cheap raw labor to more skill-oriented operations to capital-intensive manufacturing. One of the most interesting comparative questions is whether there is also an evolutionary process in the

applicable laws of these countries. In other words, what legal
regimes do developing nations have to adopt in order to first attract
assembly operations and do they evolve from extremely
accommodating to more demanding as the cycle reaches completion?
Or, does the manufacturer's ability to go elsewhere to even cheaper
labor markets (e.g., from Mexico to Guatemala to Haiti, or from
Hong Kong to the People's Republic of China to Vietnam) constantly
temper the legal regimes regulating assembly plants?

§ 2.24 ____Section 9802.00.80 Case Law

There is a surprisingly large body of case law interpreting
Section 9802.00.80. Much of it was developed when this provision
was formally known as Section 807 of the Tariff Schedule of the
United States.

One issue is whether the United States components have been
advanced in value or improved in condition abroad. If this is the
case, duty free re-entry into the United States is prohibited. An
early decision of the Court of Customs and Patent Appeals held that
the export of U.S. fish hooks, which were assembled abroad into
individually packaged assortments so as to meet the requirements
of retail purchasers in the United States, were not advanced in
value or improved in condition so as to be disqualified.[61] In another
decision, U.S. revolvers were re-chambered in Canada such that
they no longer fired with accuracy .38 caliber bullets as originally
designed. This change in condition caused the revolvers to be
disqualified under Section 9802.00.80.[62] United States tomatoes
shipped to Canada in bulk and sorted, graded as to color and size,
and repackaged in smaller cartons were not changed, advanced in
value or improved in condition so as to be disqualified from duty
free re-entry.[63]

The buttonholing in Mexico of U.S. shirt components (cuffs and
collar-bands) did not advance them in value nor improve their
condition as a result of this incidental operation.[64] But polyester
fabric exported from the United States to Canada where it was dyed
and processed, and then exported back to the United States as
finished fabric did advance in value and changing of the condition of

---

[61]   United States v. John V. Carr & Son, Inc., 496 F.2d 1225 (C.C.P.A.1974).

[62]   A.D. Deringer, Inc. v. United States, 386 F.Supp. 518, 73 Cust.Ct. 144 (1974).

[63]   Border Brokerage Co., Inc. v. United States, 314 F.Supp. 788, 65 Cust.Ct. 50
(1970).

[64]   United States v. Oxford Industries, Inc., 668 F.2d 507 (C.C.P.A.1981). See
United States v. Mast Industries, Inc., 668 F.2d 501 (C.C.P.A.1981) (buttonholing
and pocket slitting operations incidental to assembly process do not lead to duty free
entry disqualification.)

the U.S. component so as to disqualify it from duty free entry.[65] Similarly, glass pieces produced in annealed form in the United States which were sent to Canada for heat treatment and returned for use as pieces of tempered glass were not capable of benefiting from duty free entry.[66] Terminal pins of U.S. origin were shipped to Mexico and incorporated into header assemblies and relays. This operation constituted an assembly which did not advance the value of the terminals nor improve their condition.[67]

Another requirement of Section 9802.00.80 is that the United States component be fabricated and ready for assembly without further fabrication. Circuit boards for computers made in the United States from foreign and U.S. parts qualify as fabricated components for these purposes.[68] In this case, the programmable read only memory (PROM) was programmed in the United States causing it to undergo a substantial transformation and become a United States product. Aluminum foil, tabs, tape, paper and Mylar made in the United States and shipped to Taiwan in role form where they were used together with other articles of U.S. origin to produce aluminum electrolytic capacitors were not eligible for duty free entry because they were not "fabricated components" upon departure from the United States to Taiwan.[69] The fact that gold wire made in the United States was not cut until used for transistors assembled in Taiwan did not make it a U.S. component that was not ready for assembly abroad without further fabrication. The cutting of the gold wire was an incident of the assembly process.[70] But the assembly in Ecuador of flattened cylinders and ends into tuna fish cans which were then packed with tuna and shipped back to the United States did not qualify under Section 9802.00.80.[71]

The failure to lock knitting loops to keep the knitting from unraveling in the United States meant that knitted glove shelves were not exported in a condition ready for assembly without further fabrication. The importer of those gloves was not entitled to duty free entry for the value of the shelves.[72] On the other hand, pantyhose tubes made in the United States were fully constructed

---

[65]   Dolliff & Co., Inc. v. United States, 455 F.Supp. 618 (Cust.Ct.1978), *affirmed* 599 F.2d 1015 (C.C.P.A.1979).

[66]   Guardian Industries Corp. v. United States, 3 C.I.T. 9 (1982).

[67]   Sigma Instruments, Inc. v. United States, 565 F.Supp. 1036 (C.I.T.), *affirmed* 724 F.2d 930 (Fed.Cir.1983).

[68]   Data General Corp. v. United States, 4 C.I.T. 182 (1982).

[69]   General Instrument Corp. v. United States, 67 Cust.Ct. 127 (1971).

[70]   General Instrument Corp. v. United States, 462 F.2d 1156 (C.C.P.A.1972).

[71]   Van Camp Sea Food Co. v. United States, 73 Cust.Ct. 35 (1974).

[72]   Zwicker Knitting Mills v. United States, 613 F.2d 295 (C.C.P.A.1980).

and secured from un-raveling by stitches. A closing operation did not create a new toe portion and the goods were permitted the benefits of Section 9802.00.80.[73] Likewise the joinder of molten plastic to the upper portion of a shoe abroad did not prevent the shoe vamp from duty free entry upon return to the United States. This operation did not constitute further fabrication of the vamp.[74]

The scoring and breaking of silicon slices along designated "streets" was an incidental operation to the assembly of transistors and therefore the slices were entitled to duty free entry into the United States.[75] Magnet and lead wire made in the U.S. and exported to Taiwan where it was wound into coils and cable harness put into television deflection yolks were entitled to duty free entry.[76] The two-step assembly process in this case did not defeat the application of Section 9802.00.80. The burning of slots and holes in steel Z-beams in order to incorporate them into railroad cars was an operation incidental to the assembly process and therefore the beams were not dutiable.[77]

For Section 9802.00.80 to apply the components must be assembled abroad. It has been held that a needling operation causing fibers to be entwined with exported fabric in order to create papermaker's felts constituted an assembly abroad for these purposes.[78] Likewise the adhesion of Canadian chemicals to sheets of the United States polyester involved an assembly.[79]

Another requirement of Section 9802.00.80 is that the components not lose their physical identity by change in form, shape or otherwise. Fabric components used to make papermaker's felts which were needled abroad and thus perforated with holes and changed in width did not lose their physical identity and therefore continued to qualify for duty free re-entry.[80] The absence of a loss of physical identity was apparently included as a requirement of Section 9802.00.80 in order to exclude U.S. components that are chemical products, food ingredients, liquids, gases, powders and the like. These products would presumably lose their physical identity when "assembled" abroad.[81]

---

[73]   L'Eggs Products, Inc. v. United States, 704 F.Supp. 1127 (C.I.T.1989).

[74]   Carter Footwear, Inc. v. United States, 669 F.Supp. 439 (C.I.T.1987).

[75]   United States v. Texas Instruments, Inc., 545 F.2d 739 (C.C.P.A.1976).

[76]   General Instrument Corp. v. United States, 499 F.2d 1318 (C.C.P.A.1974).

[77]   Miles v. United States, 567 F.2d 979 (C.C.P.A.1978).

[78]   E. Dillingham, Inc. v. United States, 470 F.2d 629 (C.C.P.A.1972).

[79]   C.J. Tower & Sons of Buffalo, Inc. v. United States, 304 F.Supp. 1187 (Cust.Ct.1969).

[80]   E. Dillingham, Inc. v. United States, 470 F.2d 629 (C.C.P.A.1972).

[81]   See United States v. Baylis Bros., Co., 451 F.2d 643 (C.C.P.A.1971).

§ 2.25 U.S. Antidumping, Countervailing and Other Special Tariffs

In addition to its GATT/WTO negotiated MFN tariffs, the United States and other WTO member states are authorized in appropriate circumstances to assess special tariffs. Antidumping duties are authorized to counteract dumping practices (sales of goods abroad at prices below those in the country of export). *See* Chapter 4. Countervailing tariffs are authorized in response to selected foreign government subsidies that benefit their exports. *See* Chapter 5. Occasionally, as well, additional tariffs may be assessed under escape clause (safeguard) proceedings when imports surge. *See* Chapter 6.

Chapter 3

CUSTOMS CLASSIFICATION, VALUATION AND ORIGIN

Table of Sections

For coverage of European Union customs law, see Chapter 18.

§ 3.0   Customs Classification, Valuation and Origin of Imports

There are trillions of dollars of annual imports into the United States each year. To calculate import duties, you must first determine the classification, country of origin and the customs valuation of goods. In other words, what is it, where is it from, and what is its customs value? U.S. customs officials make these decisions routinely and in large volume. In some cases, the importer (and the exporter) may disagree with those decisions. This chapter concentrates on the customs process, those who play a role in the process, and some of the difficulties that may arise.

All foreign goods entering the United States must be identified in a process called classification. Classification takes two forms, determining the nature of the product, and the product's country of origin. The first classification looks to the nature of a product, such as whether an imported doll wig made from human hair should be classified as a wig of human hair, part of a doll, or as a toy.[1] Fortunately, there is a set of widely used Harmonized Tariff System (HTS) rules governing the classification of goods. The second looks at the country or countries where a product was made. For example, if the doll wig was made in Argentina from human hair from Cuba, is the doll wig a product of Argentina or Cuba? This form of classification by country will likely involve national rules of origin.

Knowing the nature of the product allows Customs to determine the proper tariff within the HTS system. But because tariffs differ from nation to nation, knowing the country of origin informs Customs which tariff "column" to use. For example, different U.S. tariffs apply to countries granted most favored nation (MFN) status, countries denied such status, or countries with preferential or duty free tariff levels such as Canada and Mexico under the North American Free Trade Agreement (NAFTA), Caribbean Basin beneficiaries under the Caribbean Basin Economic Recovery Act, or other such agreements noted in Chapter 2. Additionally, identification of the country of origin informs Customs of products that cannot be imported at all, such as by reason of the United States embargo of Cuba.

But even when the product and its source of origin have been identified, Customs must know the value of the product before the

---

[1]   A hypothetical problem involving imported doll wigs and the process of classification and valuation was included in R. Folsom, M. Gordon & J. Spanogle, International Business Transactions: A Problem Oriented Coursebook 276 (2d ed. 1991). The hypothetical in the latest edition of this book involves classifying peanut butter-jelly swirl.

tariff can be determined. Assigning a value to an import is called valuation. Customs officials must be able to determine a value in order to calculate the appropriate import tariff, usually calculated as a percentage of the value. The task is easier if the product is entitled to duty free entry. In such case the valuation is not needed for purposes of collecting a tariff. But valuation remains useful for gathering information regarding the value of various classes of imports for statistical purposes.

§ 3.1 The U.S. Customs Service

The United States Customs Service, as part of the Department of the Treasury, administers the entry of goods into the Customs Territory of the United States, which includes the fifty states, the District of Columbia, and Puerto Rico.[2] This process allows Customs officials to detain and examine goods to determine compliance with all laws and regulations. Title 19 of the Code of Federal Regulations contains extensive regulations governing such entry.[3]

An importable item must "pass customs". Usually, the passage through customs and physical entry into a country occur simultaneously. When goods arrive at the United States border, the consignee (or an agent, such as a customs broker) files both "entry" and "entry summary" forms which are used to determine the classification, valuation, origin and conformity to product standards of the imported goods. At the same time, a deposit of the amount of estimated customs duties is made with customs officials. A procedure for immediate release of imported goods is available, as is the use of consolidated periodic statements for all entries made during a billing period.

Because the entry process requires the importer to classify and value goods, a Customs Service official must determine the correctness of the documentation presented by the importer. If the Customs official rejects the importer's documentation, the decision may be appealed to the District Director (Regional Commissioner if for the port of New York), and to the Commissioner of Customs.[4]

---

[2]   19 U.S.C.A. § 1500, granting Customs authority to appraise, classify and liquidate merchandise entering the United States.

[3]   Title 19 of the C.F.R. is divided into three chapters. Chapter I includes parts 1–199 entitles United States Customs Service, Department of the Treasury. Chapter II and Chapter III include parts 200 to the end and are entitled United States International Trade Commission, and International Trade Administration, Department of Commerce, respectively.

[4]   19 C.F.R. §§ 173–174. There is a process for omitting the review by the district director in certain instances, by application for "further review." See 19 C.F.R. § 174.23–174.27.

Customs' decisions may be reviewed by the judiciary.[5] Specifically, the United States Court of International Trade (CIT),[6] which has exclusive jurisdiction.[7] Appeals from the CIT may be made to the Court of Appeals for the Federal Circuit (CAFC).[8] From these specialized courts, appeals are ultimately made to the United States Supreme Court. In *United States v. Mead Corp.,* the U.S. Supreme Court held Customs Service classification rulings are not entitled to full administrative deference. Rather, such rulings are entitled to limited deference depending on their "thoroughness, logic and expertness, fit with prior interpretations, and any other sources of weight."[9]

As an additional precaution, on February 28, 2012, President Barack Obama, by way of an executive order, created the Interagency Trade Enforcement Center within the Office of the United States Trade Representative.[10] The primary purpose of the Center focuses on strengthening and coordinating the enforcement of U.S. trade rights under international law. The Order ensures compliance with domestic trade laws and international trade agreements through coordination between government agencies that have "trade related responsibilities."

§ 3.2   The Customs Cooperation Council (CCC)

Other international actors are also involved in classification and valuation, and play an important role.

The Customs Cooperation Council (CCC) is a Brussels-based organization formed under the Convention on the Commodity Description and Coding System (the Convention) as an administrative entity. Since 1970, the CCC has sought to develop an internationally accepted "Harmonized Commodity Coding and Description System." This system, called the Customs Cooperation Council Nomenclature (CCCN), gives nations a domestic law for classifying goods for all purposes, including the application of tariffs and gathering statistics. It was formerly known as the Brussels Tariff Nomenclature (BTN). The CCCN evolved into the Harmonized Tariff Schedule (HTS), which is the system in currently used by the United States.

---

[5]   See Dell Products v. U.S., 642 F.3d 1055 (Fed. Cir. 2011) (affirming an appeal from importer regarding Customs and Border Protection decision under Harmonized Tariff Schedule of the United States).

[6]   19 C.F.R. § 176.

[7]   The CIT is the successor to the Customs Court.

[8]   The CAFC is the successor to the Court of Customs and Patent Appeals.

[9]   533 U.S. 218, 121 S.Ct. 2164, 150 L.Ed.2d 292 (2001).

[10]   Exec. Order No. 13601, 77 Fed, Reg. 12981 (March 5, 2012).

The Customs Cooperation Council (CCC) is composed of four committees. These committees have worked closely with the HTS, however, only one remains active today, the Harmonized System Committee.

§ 3.3   International Sources of Law on Classification of Goods and Valuation

The process of classification (of the item and the country of origin) and valuation requires us to turn to separate rules. Classification of products or materials requires use of the Harmonized Tariff Schedule, adopted by the enactment of the Omnibus Trade and Competitiveness Act of 1988. Classification of the country of origin tends to focus on theory developed in cases, whereas the process of valuation utilizes provisions in the Tariff Act of 1930, which generally follow the GATT/WTO Customs Valuation Code. The statutory development of classification of products and valuation follows.

Classification of Goods

Although most nations used the internationally accepted Brussels Tariff Nomenclature (BTN), the United States refused to participate in the system. Instead, the United States used its own system of classification, found within the Tariff Schedule of the United States (TSUS). These two systems created very different classifications for United States exports destined to a nation using the BTN, and those classifications of products entering the United States from other nations. What might be very narrowly defined in one system, might be very broadly defined in another. It made achieving fairness in lower tariffs for certain products quite difficult. What was called a widget in the foreign nation, might be a gadget in the United States.

As a result of using a separate system, the United States became increasingly isolated, and it became apparent that the United States TSUS would have to give way to the BTN. In 1982, after much urging from other major trading partners, the United States began converting to the HTS, the effective successor to the BTN. The HTS is administered by the World Customs Organization (WCO) in Brussels. This conversion was completed by adoption of the HTS for all imports in the Omnibus Trade and Competitiveness Act of 1988, effective January 1, 1989.[11] Most United States exports enter other nations under the HTS, and now the same is true for products of those other nations entering the United States.

---

[11]   P.L. 100–418, title I, §§ 1202–1217, Aug. 23, 1988, 102 Stat. 1107. The HTS is not published in the U.S. Code. The United States International Trade Commission maintains the current version.

The HTS "nomenclature" has twenty sections, the majority of which group articles from similar branches of industry or commerce. For example, Section I covers live animals and animal products, Section II vegetable products, Section III animal or vegetable fats, Section IV prepared foodstuffs, and Section V mineral products. The twenty sections are subdivided into 99 chapters, which in total list approximately 5,000 article descriptions in the heading and sub-heading format. These provisions apply to all goods entering the customs territory of the United States. Most problems arise when it is possible to classify imported goods under more than one heading.

Valuation

For many years the United States used the American Selling Price (ASP) system to determine the value of an imported good. This system valued an imported good at the level of the usual wholesale price that the same product was offered for sale if manufactured and sold in the United States. Thus, the valuation had no relation to the cost of production in the foreign nation, which caused the system to be much criticized abroad.[12] Many other nations, especially in Europe, used a system based on the 1950 convention that established the Brussels Definition of Value. To many, the Brussels Definition was too general, and was not adopted by either the United States or Canada.

Harmonization of customs valuation became one of the most important topics at the 1979 GATT Tokyo Round, which produced the GATT Customs Valuation Code.[13] The United States abandoned the ASP when it adopted the GATT Customs Valuation Code in the Trade Agreements Act of 1979.[14] The GATT's approach to valuation differs significantly from the ASP because it values goods based on "positive" rather than "normative" economic principles. In other words, the Code values goods based on the transaction price (price paid or payable) and not what the value of the good should be. If the transaction price cannot be determined, several fallback methods in a descending order of applicability may be used.

Because the United States replaced the TSUS with the HTS for the classification of imports, and the ASP with the GATT Customs Valuation Code for valuation of imports, its classification and

---

[12]   Such criticism was quite expected since United States domestic producers could indirectly control the valuation applied to foreign competitors' imports.

[13]   Its importance is reflected by its adoption by the European Union, Canada and the United States, plus such major trading nations as Australia, Japan, Spain (prior to joining the EU) and Sweden, and even important developing nations such as Argentina, Brazil, and India.

[14]   19 U.S.C.A. § 1401a.

valuation systems obtained greater harmony with its major trading partners.

The Uruguay Round of negotiations ushered in the next stage of development of customs valuation. The World Trade Organization replaced the GATT, and incorporated customs valuation provisions rather than having them exist as a separate external code. The three principal amendments to the Customs Valuation Code are discussed below. The provisions, which allow pre-shipment inspection, are of considerable importance to customs procedures.[15] These provisions attempt to balance the interests of some nations in contracting with outside companies to determine whether imports were fairly valued in the invoice, with the interest of exporting nations to reduce or remove impediments to trade, not to increase them.

§ 3.4   Classification of Goods—Sample Provisions of the U.S. Harmonized Tariff System

In any classification dispute, two issues must be resolved: (1) under what category or categories is it proper to classify the goods; and, (2) if there are several permissible classifications, which one takes priority over the others? Although the HTS updates every five years to account for new products, obsolete products, and provide more thorough classifications, multiple classifications can still result.[16]

As to the first question, no provisions in the United States HTS (HTSUS) "General Rules of Interpretation" (GRI) purport to limit the categorization of a product to a single categorization. In other words, the General Rule of Interpretation 2 (GRI 2) is inclusive, not exclusory, and the GRI 3 assumes that multiple categorizations will occur.

To solve the issue of multiple classifications, the GRIs provide priorities among competing categories, and the GRI 3(c) provides a "last resort" provision for cases where all else fails. However, even within the GRI, interesting ambiguities exist. For example, even though an international treaty produced the HTS and attempts to avoid the now-repealed TSUS system, a U.S. court may consult

---

[15]   See Creskoff, Pre-Shipment Inspection Programs: The Myth of Inconsistency with GATT Customs Valuation Provisions, 35 Fed.Bar News & J. 83 (1988).

[16]   For example, since 2012, Chapter 3, covering "Fish and crustaceans, mollusks, and other aquatic invertebrates," has a new heading for aquatic invertebrates (i.e. sea urchin and jellyfish), which had previously been classified only under "Other" or "Not Elsewhere Included." See Harmonized Tariff Schedule of the U.S., Annotated for Statistical Reporting Purposes (USITC Publ. 4299).

prior U.S. cases under the TSUS to interpret GRI 3(a)'s preference for "the most specific description."[17]

In addition to the GRI, the U.S. has included "Additional U.S. Rules of Interpretation," and "General Notes" in the HTS. These allow any determined attorney to create additional interpretations, and have particular importance because it is unclear whether the General Notes prevail over the GRIs and the Additional U.S. Rules, or vice versa. The best example of these possible conflicts arises when one tries to determine the priority between competing classifications. Should one first attempt to use the provisions of GRI 3, including the "last resort" provision in GRI 3(c)? Or, should one first attempt to apply the General Notes, especially Note 3(f)? And, what is the role of the Additional U.S. Notes to the Chapter Headnotes?

Below is a small portion of the extensive classification schedule of the United States.[18] The provision illustrates two features of the HTS. First, the notes preceding the chart provide comments on what the chapter does or does not cover. And second, the illustration shows the schedule of tariffs in the various columns.

CHAPTER 67

PREPARED FEATHERS AND DOWN AND ARTICLES MADE OF FEATHERS OR OF DOWN; ARTIFICIAL FLOWERS; ARTICLES OF HUMAN HAIR

Notes

1.   This chapter does not cover:

(a) Straining cloth of human hair (heading 5911);

(b) Floral motifs of lace, of embroidery or other textile fabric (section XI);

(c) Footwear (chapter 65);

(d) Headgear or hair-nets (chapter 65);

(e) Toys, sports equipment, or carnival articles (chapter 95); or

(f) Feather dusters, powder-puffs or hair sieves (chapter 96).

---

[17]   See Mitsui Petrochemicals v. U.S., 21 C.I.T. 882, 887 (1997) (citing United States v. Siemens America, Inc., 653 F.2d 471 (C.C.P.A. 1981) (applying the "relative specificity" test under the Tariff Schedules of the United States)).

[18]   See Harmonized Tariff Schedule of the U.S., Annotated for Statistical Reporting Purposes (USITC Publ. 4299).

Heading Subheading	Stat. Suf. & cd	Article Description	Units of Quantity	Rates of Duty	
				General	Special
6703.00		Human hair, dressed, thinned, bleached or otherwise worked; wool or other animal hair or other textile materials, prepared for use in making wigs or the like:			
6703.00.30	00 1	Human hair	kg	Free	20%
6703.00.60	00 4	Other	kg	Free	35%
6704		Wigs, false beards, eyebrows and eyelashes, switches and the like, of human or animal hair or of textile materials; articles of human hair not elsewhere specified or included:			
		Of synthetic textile materials:			
6704.11.00	00 3	Complete wigs	No.	Free	35%
6704.19.00	00 5	Other	X	Free	35%
6704.20.00	00 2	Of human hair	X	Free	35%
6704.90.00	00 7	Of other materials	X	Free	35%

§ 3.5   Classification of Goods—Headings in the USHTS

The heading in the excerpt above is used under the General Rules of Interpretation to determine classification of products. Customs must apply the rule of relative specificity in the classification process, which requires that goods be classified under the provision that most specifically describes it. Here, false eyelashes made of human hair, for human adult use, appear to fall under Chapter 67 because it is an article of human hair. However, it seems that this commodity may fit under more than one heading. This potential problem will be discussed in the next section.

§ 3.6   Classification of Goods—Notes in the USHTS

The notes at the beginning of chapters in the HTS provide a useful tool in classification. They are to be used in addition to the terms of the headings, under the General Rules of Interpretation. For example, Note 1 in Chapter 67 states footwear cannot be classified under Chapter 67, but is the subject of Chapter 64. These "chapter notes" should not be confused with the Explanatory Notes to the Harmonized System, or the General Notes to the HTS.

§ 3.7   Classification of Goods—Columns in the USHTS

After looking through the applicable chapter notes, the next step is to look at the columns. The United States HTS utilizes a combined number system, including the six digits used internationally, and adding further digits for more subdivisions and statistical use. As seen in the above excerpt the first column, titled "Heading/Subheading", has eight digits. The first six are the heart of the HTS, and must be adopted by all contracting nations. The first two (67 in the excerpt) repeat the chapter. The second two designate the heading (03 for Human hair, etc., 04 for Wigs, etc., in the excerpt). The next two are subheadings. The additional two numbers provide further sub-subheadings (.30 for Human hair and .60 for Other in the excerpt),[19] and the columns titled "Stat. Suf. & cd" help maintain records for statistical purposes.

The three-column section entitled "Rates of Duty" discloses the rate of duty for the particular article. The Column 1 rates apply to nations that receive most favored nation (MFN) status. MFN tariffs are set by GATT/WTO negotiations and are now referred to officially as "normal" tariffs. The "General" column applies to most MFN nations. The "Special" column applies to nations that have tariff preferences, making these nations even more favored than the most favored. The tariffs may be commodities, which enter duty free or with less than the general MFN rate. The capital letters denote different special preferential tariff programs. For example, A means nations qualifying under the Generalized System of Preferences (GSP),[20] B means commodities under the Automotive Products Trade Act, C means products under the Agreement on Trade in Civil Aircraft, CA means commodities under the Canada–United

---

[19]   The use of an additional four digits is permitted by the Convention and other nations have adopted their own form of using these additional digits. Such use will lead to some lessening of the uniformity of the system.

[20]   An A* appears if a country is specifically ineligible.

States Free Trade Agreement, E means commodities under the Caribbean Basin Economic Recovery Act,[21] IL means commodities under the United States–Israel Free Trade Area, and NA means commodities under the North American Free Trade Agreement.

Column 2 applies to all nations, which are not entitled to Column 1 rates of duty. These countries are listed in General Note 3(b). They include principally nations under communist or socialist rule. Essentially these counties are "least" favored nations, although that term perhaps ought to be saved for those nations, which are excluded from trading with the United States altogether.

While it might seem the HTS offers a fairly easy resolution to classification, it does so only when a commodity clearly fits into one chapter, one heading, and if present one sub-heading. Fortunately, that is often the case, but many commodities are not clearly allocated within the system, and multiple possibilities for their classification may exist. This is the subject of much of the remainder of this chapter.

§ 3.8   Classification of Goods—Text and Application of the HTS General Rules of Interpretation

While the Customs Service classifies goods, the importer (also the foreign exporter) has an obvious interest in the classification, because when the goods are classified at a high rate of duty applicable, the transaction may not go forward. Thus, the United States importer may consider the classification themselves. If the importer's conclusion is not the same as the Customs Service (meaning undoubtedly that the latter will be a classification at a higher rate of duty), the importer may (1) decide not to import the goods, (2) pay the higher duty, or (3) challenge the Customs' determination.

The process of determination, whether conducted by Customs or the importer, must use the rules of interpretation of the United States (e.g. the General Rules of Interpretation and the Additional U.S. Rules of Interpretation).[22] A walk through those rules illustrates how difficult the classification process can be.

---

[21]   The symbol E* appears if a country is ineligible.

[22]   Harmonized Tariff Schedule of the United States (2010)

GENERAL RULES OF INTERPRETATION:

Classification of goods in the tariff schedule shall be governed by the following principles:

1. The table of contents, alphabetical index, and titles of sections, chapters and sub-chapters are provided for ease of reference only; for legal purposes, classification shall be determined according to the terms of the headings and

any relative section or chapter notes and, provided such headings or notes do not otherwise require, according to the following provisions:

2. (a) Any reference in a heading to an article shall be taken to include a reference to that article incomplete or unfinished, provided that, as entered, the incomplete or unfinished article has the essential character of the complete or finished article. It shall also include a reference to that article complete or finished (or falling to be classified as complete or finished by virtue of this rule), entered unassembled or disassembled.

(b) Any reference in a heading to a material or substance shall be taken to include a reference to mixtures or combinations of that material or substance with other materials or substances. Any reference to goods of a given material or substance shall be taken to include a reference to goods consisting wholly or partly of such material or substance. The classification of goods consisting of more than one material or substance shall be according to the principles of rule 3.

3. When, by application of rule 2(b) or for any other reason, goods are, *prima facie*, classifiable under two or more headings, classification shall be effected as follows:

(a) The heading which provides the most specific description shall be preferred to headings providing a more general description. However, when two or more headings each refer to part only of the materials or substances contained in mixed or composite goods or to part only of the items in a set put up for retail sale, those headings are to be regarded as equally specific in relation to those goods, even if one of them gives a more complete or precise description of the goods.

(b) Mixtures, composite goods consisting of different materials or made up of different components, and goods put up in sets for retail sale, which cannot be classified by reference to 3(a), shall be classified as if they consisted of the material or component which gives them their essential character, insofar as this criterion is applicable.

(c) When goods cannot be classified by reference to 3(a) or 3(b), they shall be classified under the heading which occurs last in numerical order among those which equally merit consideration.

4. Goods which cannot be classified in accordance with the above rules shall be classified under the heading appropriate to the goods to which they are most akin.

5. In addition to the foregoing provisions, the following rules shall apply in respect of the goods referred to therein:

(a) Camera cases, musical instrument cases, gun cases, drawing instrument cases, necklace cases and similar containers, specially shaped or fitted to contain a specific article or set of articles, suitable for long-term use and entered with the articles for which they are intended, shall be classified with such articles when of a kind normally sold therewith. This rule does not, however, apply to containers which give the whole its essential character;

(b) Subject to the provisions of rule 5(a) above, packing materials and packing containers entered with the goods therein shall be classified with the goods if they are of a kind normally used for packing such goods. However, this provision is not binding when such packing materials or packing containers are clearly suitable for repetitive use.

6. For legal purposes, the classification of goods in the subheadings of a heading shall be determined according to the terms of those subheadings and any related subheading notes and, *mutatis mutandis*, to the above rules, on the understanding that only subheadings at the same level are comparable. For the purposes of this rule, the relative section, chapter and subchapter notes also apply, unless the context otherwise requires.

Headings and Relevant Section or Chapter Notes (Rule 1)

The legal classification of a good is determined according to (1) the terms of the *headings*; (2) any relative *section*; and (3) *chapter notes*.[23] This means the section, chapter and sub-headings are subordinated to the headings in importance. If the headings and notes do not otherwise require, one turns to the additional provisions of the General Rules,[24] and also to the Additional U.S. Rules of Interpretation.[25] The General Rules specifically note that the "table of contents, alphabetical index, and titles of sections, chapters and sub-chapters" are only for reference, not legal classification.[26]

Heading References to Articles (Rule 2(a))

When any reference in a heading is to an *article,* as opposed to a material or substance, the reference is to be understood to include that article in an incomplete or unfinished state as long as it "has the essential character" of the complete or finished article.[27] The reference also includes that article unassembled or disassembled.[28] This emphasis on the *material* as well as on the *function* of the good replaces emphasis on how the goods were used under the TSUS.

Heading References to a Material or Substance (Rule 2(b))

If the reference heading describes a *material* or *substance,* as opposed to an article, it should be understood to refer to mixtures or combinations of that material or substance with other materials or substances.[29] Also, any reference to goods of a given material or substance should include a reference to goods consisting wholly or partly of such material or substance. The obvious problem with this is that when the goods are only partly of a material or substance, the other party may have its own classification. This can also occur when there are mixtures or combinations. The Rules acknowledge this and require one to move on to Rule 3.

---

[23]   General Rules of Interpretation 1.

[24]   Id.

[25]   The Additional U.S. Rules of Interpretation are found immediately following the General Rules in the HTS, as adopted in the United States. These additional rules often include methods of interpretation used under the prior classification system in the United States. *See* Section 3.9.

[26]   General Rules of Interpretation 1.

[27]   General Rules 2(a).

[28]   Id. Rule 2 generally follows the previous position under the TSUS.

[29]   General Rules 2(b).

Classification under Two or More Headings—Most Specific Description (Rule 3(a)).

When goods may be classified under two or more headings,[30] the most specific description is preferred over the *more general description.*[31] This rule parallels the long used "rule of relative specificity," and decisions under that rule may continue to be of some use.[32] However, if each possible heading refers only to a *part* of the material or substances in mixed or composite goods, or of the items in a set for retail sale,[33] the headings must be considered equally specific. This is so even if one heading provides a more complete or precise description of the goods.[34] If this occurs, one must move to Rule 3(b).

Classification under Two or More Headings—Essential Character (Rule 3(b)).

If an item cannot be classified under the most specific description test in Rule 3(a), then it must be classified with regard the material or component that gives the items their *essential character.*[35] While no similar provision existed in the TSUS[36] and the HTS does not strictly define "essential character," it has some parallel under the TSUS definition of the term "almost wholly of." Even some United States cases hold "almost wholly of" may be used while defining "essential character." However, the determination is fact-intensive[37] and should still be made on a case-by-case basis.

Classification under Two or More Headings—Last in Numerical Order (Rule 3(c)).

If classification is not possible using either the most specific description or essential character tests, the rules move from a substantive classification method to one based simply on location. More specifically, the proper classification is the one heading, which

---

[30] This applies to Rule 2(b) discussed above and to any other situation where two or more headings seem possibly applicable.

[31] General Rules 3(a).

[32] That includes the doctrine that an *eo nomine* description prevails over headings having only general or functional descriptions.

[33] In April 2011, the Federal Circuit held that "goods put up in sets for retail sale" include goods that are packaged together in a certain manner at the time they enter the United States, and does not include secondary materials that the customer must purchase separately. Dell Prod. LP v. U.S., 642 F.3d 1055, 1060 (Fed. Cir. 2011).

[34] General Rules 3(a).

[35] General Rules 3(b).

[36] A "chief value" determination applied, no less capable of exact determination.

[37] CamelBak Prod. LLC v. United States, 649 F.3d 1361, 1369 (Fed. Cir. 2011).

occurs last in numerical order among those which might be applicable.[38]

Goods Unclassifiable under Rules 1–3—"Most Akin" (Rule 4)

When no headings appear directly applicable, the goods should be classified under the heading the goods are *most akin*. While this test has been used very infrequently, it is essentially a "do the best the headings allow" test, and may result in two or more headings being equally "most akin." In such case one should try to find which is "more" akin. However, if uncertainty still results, move on to Rule 5.

Specially Shaped or Fitted Cases for Goods—Classed with Their Contents (Rule 5(a))

Containers, such as camera cases, musical instrument cases, gun cases, drawing instrument cases, and necklace cases, which are "specially shaped or fitted" are classified with the goods they serve, if they enter with those goods and are suitable for long term.[39]

However, the rule does not apply if the containers give the whole its essential character. For example, expensive carved tea caddies containing tea would not be classified as tea, because the container is not shaped to fit the tea (as is a musical instrument case) and the container gives the whole (tea plus caddy) the essential character.

Packing Materials and Containers—Classed with Their Contents (Rule 5(b))

Subject to the provisions of Rule 5(a), packing materials and containers that enter with goods are classified as the goods if they are the normal kind used in packaging or containers.[40] However, this is not true when the materials or containers are suitable for repetitive use.

Rules 5(a) and (b) are specific and apply only in limited situations. In fact, in most cases when a clear classification cannot be determined after using Rule 4, it will be necessary to go on to the final General Rule 6 for additional guidance.

Subheadings and Subheading Notes (Rule 6)

The subheadings, found in the first "Heading/Subheading" column of each chapter in the tariff schedules define goods more specifically than the heading. When subheadings or subheading notes are used, and two or more subheadings on the same level

---

[38]   General Rules 3(c).
[39]   General Rules 5(a).
[40]   General Rules 5(b).

seem applicable, the process follows the outline in the rules discussed above.[41]

§ 3.9 Classification of Goods—The Additional U.S. Rules of Interpretation

The six General Rules of Interpretation make up the classification system provided by the HTS. However, when the United States adopted this system, it added its own rules, called the "Additional U.S. Rules of Interpretation."[42] In addition to applying the General Rules, these rules must also be examined to determine whether a use is (1) consistent with the General Rules; (2) helpful where the General Rules do not lead to a satisfactory conclusion; or (3) in conflict with the conclusion reached under the General Rules.

Classification Controlled by Use Other Than Actual Use (U.S. Rule 1(a))

If a classification is controlled by use other than actual use, and there is no special language or context mandating otherwise, it must be the use in the United States . . . more specifically, the use in the United States at, or immediately prior to, the time of importation. Furthermore, the controlling use must be the *principal* use (which exceeds any other single use).[43] This requirement steps away from the Rule's past reference to chief use (which exceeds all other uses).

Classification Controlled by Actual Use (U.S. Rule 1(b))

This rule is similar to that above. However, to satisfy this provision, the imported goods must, (1) be the use intended at the time of importation, (2) the goods are so used, and (3) proof thereof

---

[41]   General Rules 6.

[42]   **ADDITIONAL U.S. RULES OF INTERPRETATION**

1. In the absence of special language or context which otherwise requires—

(a) a tariff classification controlled by use (other than actual use) is to be determined in accordance with the use in the United States at, or immediately prior to, the date of importation, of goods of that class or kind to which the imported goods belong, and the controlling use is the principal use;

(b) a tariff classification controlled by the actual use to which the imported goods are put in the United States is satisfied only if such use is intended at the time of importation, the goods are so used and proof thereof is furnished within 3 years after the date the goods are entered;

(c) a provision for parts of an article covers products solely or principally used as a part of such articles but a provision for "parts" or "parts and accessories" shall not prevail over a specific provision for such part or accessory; and

(d) the principles of section XI regarding mixtures of two or more textile materials shall apply to the classification of goods in any provision in which a textile material is named.

[43]   U.S. Rules 1(a).

is furnished within three years after the date the goods are entered.[44]

Parts and Accessories—General v. Specific (U.S. Rule 1(c))

Where a provision specifically describes a part or accessory, it must be used over a general "parts and accessories" provision.[45] Thus, the import of bicycle chains would be classified as bicycle chains if described specifically, and not under a "catch-all" "other parts and accessories" category. This rule provides consistency with the General Rules' preference for specificity, even though the General Rules do not specifically contain a rule for parts.[46]

Textile Materials (U.S. Rule 1(d))

The principles of section XI, which govern mixtures of two or more *textile* materials, apply to any goods in any provision where textile materials are named.[47] Textiles have their own mystique, and are subject to special trading rules throughout the world. These provisions assure the special rules of classification for textile materials are applied throughout the tariff schedules wherever textile material is mentioned.

Conflicts between General Rules and Additional U.S. Rules

When a conflict arises between the application of the General Rules and the Additional U.S. Rules, no guidance exists within the rules to handle that situation. However, it seems likely that the Additional U.S. Rules would supplant as well as supplement the General Rules. But, the likelihood for such conflict is slim because the Additional U.S. Rules were not intended to set forth views where the United States differs with the HTS. Instead, the Rules provide a necessary supplement.

Fair and accurate application of the above rules is not an easy task, and certainly does not mean that all reasonable minds (including those found in the Customs Service) will reach the same conclusion. However, another important source should be considered while classifying products, the "United States Customs Service, Guidance for Interpretation of Harmonized System."

---

[44]   U.S. Rules 1(b).

[45]   U.S. Rules 1(c).

[46]   However, individual chapter and section notes sometimes include parts rules.

[47]   U.S. Rules 1(d).

§ 3.10 Classification of Goods—United States Customs Service, Guidance for Interpretation of Harmonized System

When the HTS was adopted in 1989, some questions existed as to how Customs would classify some of the materials developed over the years. Of specific concern was the use of the Explanatory Notes to the Harmonized System, and reports of the Nomenclature Committee, which administered the Customs Cooperation Council (CCC) Nomenclature. Additionally, how letters from the Secretariat of the CCC would be used was unclear, and rulings and regulations from the customs administrations of other nations. The United States Customs Service soon issued the *Guidance for Interpretation of Harmonized System.*[48] The guide makes several points quite clear.

The United States Customs Service does not seek uniformity of interpretation with other nations. While the Harmonized System Committee (HSC) under Article 7 of the Convention functions to provide uniformity, the United States Customs Service does not. To illustrate, the United States does not to alter "sections, chapters, headings or subheadings" of the HTS, and will consider background documents to avoid such alterations. However, the Customs Service will not purposely make its interpretations of the HTS consistent with the interpretations of other HTS member nations. If serious inconsistencies in interpretation result, the HTS will likely be modified to minimize the inconsistency, such as by further refining the classification.

Use of Explanatory Notes to the Harmonized System. These notes are the official interpretation of the Harmonized System created by the Customs Cooperation Council. According to the Custom Service, Customs should use the notes as a useful tool, providing guidance, but should not treat them as dispositive.[49] Further, because the Explanatory Notes are amended from time to time and reflect changes in interpretation, they should be consulted periodically as changes are adopted. The only other documents given this status by Congress are the "similar publications of the Council," which essentially refers to the Compendium of Classification Opinions (below) because it is the only similar publication.

Use of the Compendium of Classification Opinions. The Harmonized System Committee (HSC) writes these opinions on the classification of different products. They are the result of requests presented to

---

[48]   54 Fed.Reg. 35127 (1989).
[49]   See Conf.Rep. No. 100–576, 100th Cong., 2d Sess. 549 (1988).

the HSC, and have the same weight as Explanatory Notes. Additionally, the Opinions are the official interpretation of the HSC on the particular issue decided.

Harmonized System Committee Reports. In addition to opinions, the HSC periodically issues reports on various subjects. While they do not have the same weight as the Explanatory Notes or Compendium of Classification Opinions, they may be helpful in determining the intention of the HSC. However, the reports of committees within the HSC, such as the Nomenclature Committee, carry virtually no weight, but may nevertheless be of some assistance in interpretation. Of even less use are the "working documents" of the Nomenclature and Classification Directorate of the CCC. They are the basis of discussions in HSC sessions, but they may not necessarily reflect the intent of the HSC.

Rulings of Other Countries. Because other nations that have adopted the HTS use the same General Rules of Interpretation, Section and Chapter Notes, and first six digits in the classification tables, their customs administration decisions are sometimes presented to the United States Customs Service. In general, U.S. Customs does not follow other nations' rulings because their decisions "may have been subject to political realities or domestic regulations which are different from our own." The meaning of this has not been further defined, but illustrates that there may be political pressure to classify goods so as to more readily admit them to, or more readily exclude them from, the United States. In any event, these foreign rulings are considered "merely instructive of how others" classify imports.

Position Papers. Before a session of the HSC, U.S. Customs, the International Trade Commission, and the Bureau of Census prepare position papers for the session. These papers do not reflect Customs' position in the interpretation of the HTS and are considered to have no value, although they are occasionally circulated and obtained by importers or their counsel.

These notes, opinions, reports, rulings and papers all add to the process of interpretation, a layer which did not exist before the adoption of the HTS by the United States. Awareness of their use by the Customs Service may be helpful to United States counsel, but should not expect to be given weight beyond that announced by the Customs Service as described above.

§ 3.11 Classification of Goods—Decisions of United States Courts

While it may seem strange to suggest that decisions of United States courts may not be applicable in interpreting the HTS, that may be correct for decisions interpreting the prior TSUS.[50] Interpretations of the United States HTS must follow the procedure outlined above. Certainly decisions rendered subsequent to the adoption of the HTS in 1988, which interpret the HTS, will be useful. But in many cases decisions have little usefulness because they apply to a narrow set of issues affecting specific goods where two or more classification possibilities exist. Although the HTS has a different process, the approach used in the past may find use in the future. Thus, some earlier decisions may be useful to understand the analytical process used by the courts.[51]

For example, prior United States decisions applying the rule of relative specificity may be used in interpreting General Rule of Interpretation Rule 3(a), which uses a kind of "rule of relative specificity" under the wording "most specific description."[52]

§ 3.12 Rules of Origin

The second form of classification determines the country of origin of the items to be imported. Unlike, the determination of the proper classification discussed above, the country of origin determination discloses whether Column 1 or Column 2 rates of duty apply. If Column 1 rates of duty apply, the goods may qualify for preferential or duty free treatment, if from a country of origin that qualifies under "Special" in Column 1. The Court of International Trade requires importers seeking preferential tariff treatment to verify the country of origin of their goods. "Reasonable care" must be exercised, not just simple reliance on the exporter's assertions of origin. Failures in this regard can result in collection of lost duties and penalties.[53]

Additionally, knowing the country of origin uncovers more general prohibitions of trade with that country, because the United

---

[50] See JVC Company of America v. United States, 234 F.3d 1348 (Fed.Cir.2000).

[51] For example, the Mattel, Inc. v. United States decision, 287 F.Supp. 999 (Cust.Ct.1968), might be used when the issue involves priority of one classification over another.

[52] See, e.g., Great Western Sugar Co. v. United States, 452 F.2d 1394 (C.C.P.A.1972).

[53] United States v. Golden Ship Trading Co., 2001 WL 65751 (C.I.T.2001) (T-shirts imported from Dominican Republic under Caribbean Basin Act were from China).

States nearly always has several nations with which it does not trade by legislative or presidential declaration.[54] The United States may also put limits on products entering from a specific foreign nation. This limitation may be the result of a formal quota,[55] or an informal voluntary restraint agreement (VRA). VRAs have in the past covered a wide range of products (e.g., steel, vehicles, electronics), and have been a device adopted by the United States (and other areas such as the European Union) as executive policy in order to discourage legislative action to establish mandatory and involuntary quotas to reduce trade imbalances.[56] VRAs are now generally prohibited under the WTO Safeguards Agreement (1995).

Counsel representing an importer must know the framework for determining the country of origin of articles.[57] Eligibility of entry often depends on country of origin determination.[58] Country of origin law does not have as consolidated a framework as for classification of the goods discussed above. Although the classification is dealt with exclusively in the HTS, working within that system is not a simple matter. Determination of the country of origin requires using rules that may apply in a spectrum of different areas. While there are several references to various aspects of the rule of origin in different sources of law, the *substantial transformation* test (treated below) in its various costumes, has traditionally been *the* test.

In 2008, the Bureau of Customs and Border Protection proposed shifting to a single uniform approach to determine the origin of imported goods.[59] Although Customs and Border Protection withdrew the proposal, if adopted, it would have abandoned the historic test for the "substantial transformation" of foreign goods. The proposal elicited so many responses that the time for public comment on the proposal was extended twice. Most of the responses opposed the proposal because the rule could have substantially impacted the cost of entry into the United States, place undue burdens on those in the trading community, and cause the

---

[54] These prohibitions may extend to both exports and imports, but may have certain exceptions, such as medical supplies.

[55] Quotas are regulated by the Customs Service. See 19 C.F.R. Part 132.

[56] See, e.g., Note, Voluntary Restraint Agreements: Effects and Implications of the Steel and Auto Cases, 11 N.C.J. Int'l L. & Com.Reg. 101 (1986).

[57] Counsel may wish to obtain a ruling from Customs in advance of importation. See 19 C.F.R. §§ 177.1–177.11.

[58] The United States must know whether the country of origin is one entitled to most favored nation treatment.

[59] Uniform Rules of Origin for Imported merchandise, Notice of Proposed Rulemaking, 73 FR 43,385 (2008).

importation process to become more complex.[60] Eventually, in 2010 the Bureau of Customs and Border Protection abandoned the proposal.

Under the proposed WTO Agreement on Rules of Origin, there will be an effort to harmonize the rules of origin on a world-wide basis. A committee of experts is charged with creating rules which are "objective, understandable, and predictable." They are likely to differ from the core U.S. rule. Special rules of origin apply to the various U.S. duty free entry programs, most notably NAFTA which relies principally on changes in tariff classifications and regional value content to determine which goods may freely be traded. *See* Section 16.3. It is expected that any WTO agreement on rules of origin may adopt similar approaches.

§ 3.13 ____U.S. Rules of Origin—Sources of Law

Trade Agreements Act of 1979. Section 308 of the Trade Agreements Act provides various definitions, including the rule of origin for eligible products.[61] The definition focuses on the concept of substantial transformation,[62] leaving the courts to interpret the meaning of substantial transformation. This is the fallback or general U.S. rule of origin for goods for purposes of tariff collection, absent more specific legislative rules. For example, all U.S. free trade agreements, the GSP, and the CBI have their own rules of origin. *See* Chapters 2 and 16.

Code of Federal Regulations, Country of Origin Marking. Part 134 of 19 C.F.R. provides rules governing the country of origin *marking,* which on occasion may be different from a product's origin for purposes of assessing tariffs. The regulations define articles subject to the marking, with special rules for articles repacked or manipulated, and ones usually combined with another article.[63] Rules also specify how containers or holders must be marked,[64] exceptions to the marking requirements,[65] method and location of marking,[66] and the consequences of finding articles not legally

---

[60]   Vivian C. Jones and Michael F. Martin, INTERNATIONAL TRADE: RULES OF ORIGIN, Cong. Res. Serv., RL 34524 at 2 (January 5, 2012).

[61]   19 U.S.C.A. § 2518.

[62]   "An article is a product of a country or instrumentality only if (i) it is wholly the growth, product, or manufacture of that country or instrumentality, or (ii) in the case of an article which consists in whole or in part of materials from another country or instrumentality, it has been substantially transformed into a new and different article of commerce with a name, character, or use distinct from that of the article or articles from which it was so transformed." 19 U.S.C.A. § 2518(4)(B).

[63]   19 C.F.R. §§ 134.13–134.14.

[64]   19 C.F.R. §§ 134.21–134.26.

[65]   19 C.F.R. §§ 134.31–134.36.

[66]   19 C.F.R. §§ 134.41–134.47.

marked.[67] Essentially, the consequences for not properly marking a good are (1) properly mark the goods; (2) return the goods to the foreign nation; or (3) destroy the goods.[68]

Generally, a single country of origin must be determined for labeling purposes, even though the product may have been made in several countries. The country of origin, as determined by Customs, may not disclose other nations that may have participated in the process. While this may be important to the United States consumer, who may not wish to purchase products from a country substantially benefiting from the sale, it is not important to the determination of the official country of origin for marking purposes.

Special Rules—The North American Free Trade Agreement (NAFTA). In drafting the NAFTA, as with drafting the earlier Canada–United States Free Trade Agreement, there was considerable concern that products entering the United States, as products of Canada or Mexico, actually had little fabrication or processing in those countries. To prevent this, special NAFTA rules of origin (discussed in Chapter 16) were adopted, which include articles governing customs procedures for the certification of origin.

The procedures create a North American "Certificate of Origin" and require extensive verification provisions. The exporter provides the Certificate of Origin when the importer tries to claim the duty free tariff treatment offered by the NAFTA.[69] However, a Certificate of Origin is not required for goods valuing $1,000 or less, or where a member state has waived their use.[70] A member state may conduct verification through written questionnaires, visits to the premises exporter/producer, or other procedures the member states agree.[71] Verification is of considerable concern to the United States because it does not want Mexico to be used as a base for transshipping products from outside the NAFTA area, especially from Asia. The Court of International Trade requires importers seeking preferential tariff treatment to verify the country of origin of their goods. "Reasonable care" must be exercised, which requires more than simple reliance on the exporter's assertions of origin. Failure to do so can result in collection of lost duties and penalties.[72]

---

[67]   19 C.F.R. §§ 134.51–134.55.

[68]   19 C.F.C. § 134.51(a).

[69]   NAFTA Art. 501.

[70]   NAFTA Art. 503.

[71]   NAFTA Art. 506.

[72]   United States v. Golden Ship Trading Co., 2001 WL 65751 (Ct. Intl' Trade 2001) (T-shirts imported from Dominican Republic under Caribbean Basin Act were from China).

Decisions of United States Courts. There are several areas where Customs is required to determine the country of origin. However, the determinations sometimes lead to problems. For example, products from countries that the United States does not trade may be transshipped through a country that the United States does trade. Products from countries subject to high rates of duty in Column 2 may be transshipped through countries subject to lower rates of duty in Column 1. Products with most favored nation status, Column 1 rates of duty, may be transshipped through a country with special access, such as a Caribbean nation. Exporters from a nation that has agreed to a voluntary restraint agreement may try to exceed the agreed upon numbers by having the products transshipped through a nation without such a quota. As the United States enters into free trade agreements such as NAFTA, other nations may attempt to take advantage of that relationship by having goods transshipped through Canada or Mexico into the United States.

Fortunately, some case law has evolved, addressing the country of origin issue. Those cases, which involve one specific area, may be helpful in addressing another. For example, a case that has identified the country of origin may be useful in determining whether the agreed amount under a voluntary restraint agreement has been exceeded.[73] Or it may be helpful where products are allegedly violating the rules of the generalized system of preferences. Thus, when dealing with a country of origin issue, cases outside the scope of the form of entry (i.e., GSP, NAFTA, etc.) must be consulted.[74]

§ 3.14 ____U.S. Rules of Origin—Substantial Transformation Test

While some consistency in the identification of the country of origin exists, the process requires more than simply reading the label, which states the country of origin. Because a nation may do little more to an item than sew on the country of origin label, the product itself must be measured.

Substantial Transformation Test

The principal focus in a U.S. country of origin determination examines whether the product was substantially transformed in the

---

[73]   See, e.g., Superior Wire, A Div. of Superior Products Co. v. United States, 669 F.Supp. 472 (C.I.T.1987), *affirmed* 867 F.2d 1409 (Fed.Cir.1989).

[74]   See Ferrostaal Metals Corp. v. United States, 664 F.Supp. 535, 538 (C.I.T.1987) (case law does not suggest that the court should depart from "policy-neutral rules governing substantial transformation in order to achieve wider import restrictions in particular cases.").

country claiming the country of origin status.[75] One of the bedrock cases defining substantial transformation in the United States, an early United States Supreme Court decision, involves drawbacks.[76] The Court held substantial transformation occurs when a product is transformed into a new and different article "having a distinctive *name, character or use.*"[77] However, while this case provides a standard, it has been applied in many different ways.[78] For example, while a name change alone would not always be sufficient, such as from "wire" to "wire rod,"[79] a court held that changing heat-treated steel to galvanized steel was sufficient. More specifically, because the annealing process involved substantial manufacturing, which ultimate strengthened the steel and made it resistant to corrosion, it caused a substantial transformation to occur.[80]

Courts tend to concentrate on changes in *character* or *use* rather than in the name of the product. Also, they often develop subtests appropriate for a particular kind of article. For example, whether a *significant value* was added, or *additional costs* were incurred. But each test leads to some subjective evaluation, which provides a sort of sense of whether the product is really from the state country. While the substantial transformation test has been criticized,[81] it remains the generally applicable U.S. law.

However a U.S. court reaches a decision on a substantial transformation question, it is likely to have considered most of the following changes:

1. Change in name (and change in tariff classification);

2. Change in physical appearance;

3. Change in material substance (at each stage of manufacture);

4. Change in apparent use;

---

[75]   This test is in the Trade Agreements Act of 1979. See 19 U.S.C.A. § 2518(4)(B).

[76]   Anheuser-Busch Brewing Ass'n v. United States, 207 U.S. 556, 28 S.Ct. 204, 52 L.Ed. 336 (1908).

[77]   Id. at 562, 28 S.Ct. at 206.

[78]   But it is applied by the courts. See, e.g., Texas Instruments Inc. v. United States, 681 F.2d 778, 782 (C.C.P.A.1982).

[79]   See Superior Wire, A Div. of Superior Products Co. v. United States, 669 F.Supp. 472 (C.I.T.1987) (the court noted that in recent years the focus was on a change in use or character).

[80]   Ferrostaal Metals Corp. v. United States, 664 F.Supp. 535 (C.I.T.1987) (there was a "significant altering" of the "mechanical properties and chemical composition of the steel").

[81]   Maxwell, Formulating Rules of Origin for Imported Merchandise: Transforming the Substantial Transformation Test, 23 J. Int'l L. & Econ. 669 (1990).

5.   Change in value of item in the mind of the consumer;

6.   Additional capital vested in article;

7.   Additional labor vested in article;

8.   Type of processing;

9.   Effect of processing; and

10. Change in method of distribution.

There is no secret formula for determining which factor, if any, plays the most significant role. Little wonder Canada, Mexico and other U.S. partners insisted on creating different rules of origin when agreeing to free trade. *See* Section 16.3.

§ 3.15   Valuation—The Law of the GATT/WTO

Of the several codes adopted by the GATT in the Tokyo Round and renewed in the Uruguay WTO Round, the Agreement on the Implementation of Article VII of the General Agreement on Tariffs and Trade (GATT Customs Valuation Code) is of considerable importance to the United States.[82] While Article VII of the GATT 1947, titled "Valuation for Customs Purposes," established a form of transaction value, it was not until the Customs Valuation Code was adopted that the form of valuation by a descending order of tests was introduced. This form of valuation was incorporated into the United States law in 1979, and is the source of law one must consider for valuation of U.S. imports.

§ 3.16   Valuation—United States Law

The law applicable to valuation can be found in the United States Tariff Act of 1930, as amended. However, the United States' commitment to the GATT Customs Valuation Code, and the successor World Trade Organization must be considered.

For the most part, the United States Tariff Act of 1930 incorporates the GATT Customs Valuation Code of 1979.[83] However, because the United States adopted that GATT Code in 1979 amendments to the Tariff Act of 1930, some of the prior methods of interpretation of valuation may continue to be considered by courts.[84]

---

[82]   Geneve, 1979, GATT, 26th Supp. BISD 116 (1980). See Davey, Customs Valuation: Commentary on the GATT Customs Valuation Code (1989).

[83]   19 U.S.C.A. § 1401a. See Sherman, Reflections on the New Customs Valuation Code, 12 Law & Pol'y Int'l Bus. 119 (1980).

[84]   The same is true of other areas with pre-Code established procedures. See Snyder, Customs Valuation in the European Economic Community, 11 Georgia J. Int'l & Comp.L. 79 (1981).

§ 3.17 Valuation—Appraisal of Imported Merchandise

Imports of merchandise are valued according to a series of alternative methods,[85] but not alternative methods in the sense that Customs may use any method it chooses. Nor may Customs reject information provided if based on the use of generally accepted accounting procedures.[86] The methods of valuation are set forth in the order of use. Most valuations never go beyond the first, the transaction value.

§ 3.18 Valuation—Transaction Value

All merchandise imported into the United States must be appraised. First, Customs considers the transaction value of the merchandise.[87] The transaction value is often referred to as the *invoice value* because in the absence of over or under invoicing, it would be the value of the transaction. The statute describes the transaction value as the *price actually paid or payable*.[88] In other words, it is the price when sold for exportation to the United States, also known as the wholesale price.[89] This may be confusing where there are several contracts, in addition to the actual contract between the buyer-seller. This situation can occur as between a party to the sale and the party's parent entity,[90] or between a foreign seller and United States company acquiring items purchased by the foreign seller from a foreign manufacturer.[91]

Also, the transaction value may include some elements that create doubt as to application of duties. For example, quota charges clearly separated on the invoice are nevertheless includable.[92]

---

[85]   Merchandise is defined as of the same class or kind as other merchandise if within a group or range which is produced by a particular industry or industrial sector. 19 U.S.C.A. § 1401a(e)(2).

[86]   19 U.S.C.A. § 1401a(g)(3).

[87]   19 U.S.C.A. § 1401a(a)(1)(A).

[88]   19 U.S.C.A. § 1401a(b)(1). Price actually paid or payable is defined in 19 U.S.C.A. § 1401a(b)(4). Disbursements by the buyer for the benefit of the seller are included, as when the buyer disburses some funds to the agent's seller who assists in bringing about the sale. Moss Mfg. Co., Inc. v. United States, 714 F.Supp. 1223 (C.I.T.1989), *affirmed* 896 F.2d 535 (Fed.Cir.1990). The price payable may be determined by a clear, definite and agreed pre-importation formula. Del Monte Corp. v. United States, ___ F.3d ___ (Fed. Cir. 2013).

[89]   As of January 1, 2011, Customs and Border Protection.

[90]   Nissho Iwai American Corp. v. United States, 786 F.Supp. 1002 (C.I.T.1992), *aff'd in part, rev'd in part* 982 F.2d 505 (Fed.Cir.1992) (holding the master contract between the buyer and seller controls, rather than the contract price paid by the seller's Japanese company's parent to primary manufacturer).

[91]   See Brosterhous, Coleman & Co. v. United States, 737 F.Supp. 1197 (C.I.T.1990).

[92]   Generra Sportswear Co. v. United States, 905 F.2d 377 (Fed.Cir.1990).

Rebates to the price actually paid or payable made after the merchandise has entered the United States are disregarded in determining the transaction value.[93] However, dividing the assembly (service) price from the consumer (sale of goods) price for made-to measure clothing does not relieve the importer from duty on the former portion, the full cost is subject to duty.[94]

Transaction Value: Associated Costs

Five other categories of associated costs must be also added to the transaction value. Some are costs, which may be part of the price paid or payable, but some are costs, which, if not subject to tariffs, could be split off from the price of the goods and paid separately, thus avoiding or evading proper duty.[95] These additional costs subject to duty are:

1.   Packing costs incurred by the buyer.[96] If incurred by the seller they would be part of the price paid for the merchandise, probably buried in the price of the goods.

2.   All selling commission incurred by the buyer with respect to the imported merchandise.[97]

3.   The value of any assist, apportioned as appropriate.[98] An assist includes a very broad range of benefits, and is the subject of an extensive definitional provision.[99]

4.   Any royalty or license fee related to the goods, which the buyer pays directly or indirectly as a condition of the sale.[100] This can be a difficult provision to interpret. However, if a buyer pays a flat fee per year directly to the designer of the goods, no matter how many are sold, the buyer may escape duty. But, any payment related to the number sold seems subject to duty.

---

[93]   19 U.S.C.A. § 1401a(b)(4)(B). See Allied Int'l v. United States, 795 F.Supp. 449 (C.I.T.1992) (importer has the burden of showing that the rebate occurred on or before date of entry).

[94]   E.C. McAfee Co. v. United States, 842 F.2d 314 (Fed.Cir.1988).

[95]   See All Channel Products v. United States, 787 F.Supp. 1457 (C.I.T.1992), *judgment affirmed* 982 F.2d 513 (Fed.Cir.1992) (inland freight charges separately invoiced properly included in transaction value); United States v. Arnold Pickle & Olive Co., 659 F.2d 1049, 68 C.C.P.A. 85 (1981) (inspection costs).

[96]   19 U.S.C.A. § 1401a(b)(1)(A).

[97]   19 U.S.C.A. § 1401a(b)(1)(B). See Jay-Arr Slimwear Inc. v. United States, 681 F.Supp. 875 (C.I.T.1988).

[98]   19 U.S.C.A. § 1401a(b)(1)(C).

[99]   19 U.S.C.A. § 1401a(h)(1). See, e.g., Texas Apparel Co. v. United States, 883 F.2d 66 (Fed.Cir.1989), *cert. denied* 493 U.S. 1024, 110 S.Ct. 728, 107 L.Ed.2d 747 (1990) (sewing machine costs constitute an assist in manufacturing jeans). See Collins, The Concept of Assist as Applied to Customs Valuation of Imported Merchandise, 1991 Detroit Col.L.R. 239.

[100]   19 U.S.C.A. § 1401a(b)(1)(D).

5.   Any direct or indirect accrual to the seller from the subsequent resale, disposal, or use of the goods.[101] This prevents the sale at a low base price, with the buyer required to pass on a percentage to the seller after the goods are resold.

The price paid or payable shall be increased by any of the above five additions, if it can be shown that they have not already been included in the price paid or payable by "sufficient" information.[102] The statute defines sufficient information as that which "establishes the accuracy of such amount, difference, or adjustment."[103] Where sufficient information is not available, and it seems like one or more of the five additional amounts exist, the transaction value is not determinable, and one must move to the next section in the chronology of applicable provisions.[104]

Appraised Value

Where the transaction value is determinable, as discussed above, it will be considered the *appraised* value only if certain further conditions exist. The first of these conditions requires the buyer to dispose of or use the goods without restriction, except restrictions that (1) are required by law, (2) limit resale to a geographical area, or (3) do not substantially affect the value.[105]

The second condition requires that there may not be any condition or consideration affecting the sale of or the price paid or payable where the value of the condition or consideration cannot be determined.[106]

The third states that no part of the proceeds from the use or resale may accrue directly or indirectly to the seller, unless that amount is calculable under the provisions noted above.[107]

The fourth requires the buyer and seller to be either unrelated, or if related that the transaction is acceptable.[108] Because buyers and sellers are often related through a parent and subsidiary relationship, the statute sets forth special rules. Often the prices reflected in transfers within an organization do not truly reflect arm's length prices because they want to avoid taxes, avoid tariff

---

[101]   19 U.S.C.A. § 1401a(b)(1)(E).

[102]   19 U.S.C.A. § 1401a(b)(1).

[103]   19 U.S.C.A. § 1401a(b)(5).

[104]   Id.

[105]   19 U.S.C.A. § 1401a(b)(2)(A)(i).

[106]   19 U.S.C.A. § 1401a(b)(2)(A)(ii).

[107]   19 U.S.C.A. § 1401a(b)(2)(A)(iii). The above provision is 19 U.S.C.A. § 1401a(b)(1)(E).

[108]   19 U.S.C.A. § 1401a(b)(2)(A)(iv).

duties, or for other purposes.[109] The transaction value in such a transaction will be the appraised value, as long as (1) the circumstances of the sale do not suggest the relationship influenced the price, and (2) the transaction value approximates the transaction value in an unrelated parties' transaction, the deductive value, or computed value for identical or similar merchandise.[110]

This exception introduces the concepts of *deductive* value and *computed* value, both alternative valuations methods discussed below. The exception also requires defining both *identical* merchandise and *similar* merchandise.[111] The comparison values referred to above must be values for merchandise entering the United States on or around the same time as the merchandise in question.

The values used for comparison purposes usually consists of identical or similar goods,[112] however, varying method of sales may distort the comparison between the goods. Consequently, the values used must consider these differences, if based on sufficient information, in commercial levels, quantity levels and any costs, commissions, values, fees and proceeds in § 1401a(b)(1), discussed above.[113]

Items Not Included in Transaction Value

While the above identifies provisions designating the composition of the transaction value, specific items should not be included in the transaction value, including:

First, transaction value should not include any reasonable cost or charge for either: (1) construction, erection, assembly, or maintenance of, or technical assistance to the merchandise after importation or (2) transportation after importation.[114]

Second, transaction value should not include the customs duties or other federal taxes imposed upon importation, nor federal excise tax.[115]

---

[109]   Transfer pricing is discussed in chapter 24.

[110]   19 U.S.C.A. § 1401a(b)(2)(B).

[111]   19 U.S.C.A. § 1401a(h)(2) & (4).

[112]   See Walter Holm & Co. v. United States, 3 C.I.T. 119 (1982) (use of value of exports of cantaloupes through Laredo, Texas, to determine value of same items through Nogales, Arizona).

[113]   19 U.S.C.A. § 1401a(b)(2)(C).

[114]   19 U.S.C.A. § 1401a(b)(3)(A). International transportation is separately excluded in 19 U.S.C.A. § 1401a(b)(4)(A).

[115]   19 U.S.C.A. § 1401a(b)(3)(B).

Transaction Value of Identical and Similar Merchandise

This material largely draws from the material above applicable to transaction value. The identical merchandise value method is used when the transaction value cannot be determined or used. When the identical merchandise value cannot be used, the similar merchandise value should be used.[116] Where the transaction value has been determined above for identical merchandise or for similar merchandise, as defined in the statute,[117] it must be adjusted. This adjustment requires consideration of all different commercial level or quantity level of sales for identical or similar merchandise.[118] It must also be based on sufficient information. Where two or more comparison transactions exist, the appraisal of the imported merchandise will be based on the lower or lowest of the comparison values.[119]

§ 3.19 Valuation—Deductive Value

The most important question is when will the deductive method of valuation be used? Deductive value should be used when the above transaction value does not lead to an acceptable determination to Customs.[120] However, the importer may request that the computed value discussed below be used in place of the deductive value.[121] If computed value does not prove possible, the deductive value must be used next.[122]

Deductive value may be applied to the merchandise being appraised, or to either identical or similar merchandise.[123] The deductive value focuses on unit value,[124] and constitutes the most appropriate value as determined in one of three ways.

The first method applies when the merchandise imported is sold (1) in the condition as imported, and (2) at or about the date of

---

[116]   19 U.S.C.A. §§ 1401a(a)(1)(B) & (C).

[117]   19 U.S.C.A. § 1401a(h)(2) & (4).

[118]   19 U.S.C.A. § 1401a(c)(2).

[119]   Id.

[120]   19 U.S.C.A. § 1401a(a)(1)(D).

[121]   19 U.S.C.A. § 1401a(a)(2).

[122]   Id.

[123]   19 U.S.C.A. § 1401a(d)(1).

[124]   Unit value is the price the merchandise is sold (1) in the greatest aggregate quantity, (2) to unrelated persons, (3) at the first commercial level after importation (at level i and ii discussed below), or after further processing (at level iii discussed below), (4) in a total volume which is both greater than the total volume sold at any other unit price, and sufficient to establish the unit price. 19 U.S.C.A. § 1401a(d)(2)(B).

importation. The deductive value is the unit price at which the merchandise is sold in the greatest quantity.[125]

The second method applies when the merchandise imported is sold in the condition as imported, but not at or about the date of importation. The deductive value in this case is the unit price at which the merchandise is sold in the greatest quantity, but within 90 days after importation.[126]

The third method is where the merchandise is neither sold in the condition imported nor within 90 days after importation. The deductive value is the unit price at which the merchandise, after further processing, is sold in the greatest quantity within 180 days of importation.[127] This third method only applies at the election of the importer and upon notification to the customs officer.[128]

If the deductive method applies, some reductions from the unit price may result, including commissions, additions for profit and expenses, costs of domestic and international transportation, customs duties and other federal taxes on the merchandise. If the third method of deductive value is used, the costs of additional processing may reduce the unit price.[129] However, deductions for profits and expenses must be consistent with profits and expenses in the United States for similar merchandise, and any state or local taxes on the importer relating to the sale of the merchandise is considered an expense.[130]

There may also be an increase to the unit price, if such costs have not already been included, amounting to the packing costs incurred by the importer or buyer.[131]

A final provision requires one to disregard any sale to a person who supplies an assist for use in connection with the merchandise.[132]

Where deductive value is inapplicable, or where the importer has chosen to pass over deductive value, the next method is computed value.

---

[125]   19 U.S.C.A. § 1401a(d)(2)(A)(i).
[126]   19 U.S.C.A. § 1401a(d)(2)(A)(ii).
[127]   19 U.S.C.A. § 1401a(d)(2)(A)(iii).
[128]   Id.
[129]   19 U.S.C.A. § 1401a(d)(3)(A).
[130]   19 U.S.C.A. § 1401a(d)(3)(B).
[131]   19 U.S.C.A. § 1401a(d)(3)(C).
[132]   19 U.S.C.A. § 1401a(d)(3)(D).

§ 3.20   Valuation—Computed Value

Computed value should be used when transaction and deductive value methods do not provide an appropriate result. However, the importer may skip over the deductive value tests and go straight to the computed value test.[133] The computed value determination consists of the sum of four parts.[134]

First, computed value considers the cost or value of materials and fabrication or processing,[135] but it does not include any internal tax by the exporting country if the tax is remitted upon exportation.[136]

Second, compute value considers the profit and expenses of the amount usually associated with the same kind of merchandise.[137] They are based on producer's profits and expenses, unless inconsistent with those for sales of the same class or kind of merchandise by producers in the country exporting to the United States, in which case there is a calculation of such profits and expenses using the "sufficient information" procedure.[138] For example, freight costs incurred through the shipment of tomato paste from Mexico to the United States should be included in the computed value.[139] Also, the costs of a warranty for aircraft should be included as profit, less expenditures the manufacturer-seller establishes as incurred by the warranty obligations in curing defects.[140]

Third, computed value includes any assist if not already included in the amount above.[141] Computing the value of jeans would allow the addition of the cost or value of the sewing machines

---

[133]   19 U.S.C.A. § 1401a(a).

[134]   19 U.S.C.A. § 1401a(e)(1). For cases which have used the constructed value approach, see Campbell Soup Co., Inc. v. United States, 107 F.3d 1556 (Fed. Cir. 1997) (calculating the computed value of transported tomato paste from Mexico to United States); New York Credit Men's Adjustment Bureau, Inc. v. United States, 314 F.Supp. 1246 (Cust.Ct.1970), *affirmed* 342 F.Supp. 745 (Cust.Ct.1972).

[135]   19 U.S.C.A. § 1401a(e)(1)(A). See Texas Apparel Co. v. United States, 698 F.Supp. 932 (C.I.T.1988), *affirmed* 883 F.2d 66 (Fed.Cir.1989), *cert. denied* 493 U.S. 1024, 110 S.Ct. 728, 107 L.Ed.2d 747 (1990).

[136]   19 U.S.C.A. § 1401a(e)(2)(A).

[137]   19 U.S.C.A. § 1401a(e)(1)(B). See Braniff Airways, Inc. v. United States, 2 C.I.T. 26 (1981).

[138]   19 U.S.C.A. § 1401a(e)(2)(B).

[139]   Campbell Soup Co., Inc. v. United States, 107 F.3d 1556 (Fed. Cir. 1997).

[140]   Braniff Airways, Inc. v. United States, 2 C.I.T. 26 (1981).

[141]   19 U.S.C.A. § 1401a(e)(1)(C).

used to produce the jeans.[142] Finally, packing costs are included in the computed value.[143]

§ 3.21 Valuation—Value When Other Methods Are Not Effective

If the value cannot be determined under the above-discussed methods, there is a final method for calculating value. It is to derive a value using the methods set forth above, and then adjusting them to the extent necessary to achieve a reasonable result.[144] But in making such an appraisal, the statute prohibits using any of seven items:[145]

(1) United States selling price of United States produced merchandise,

(2) Any system using the higher of two alternatives,

(3) Domestic market price in country of exportation,

(4) Cost of production for identical or similar merchandise which differs from such cost of production determined under the computed value method,

(5) Price for export to a country other than the United States,

(6) Minimum values, or

(7) Arbitrary or fictitious values.

As first noted, transaction value expressed in the invoice is used in the vast majority of cases. However, when challenges to transaction value appear, the procedure may become more complex. While any of the determinations of Customs may be challenged, the cost of such challenge for all but the largest importers will often result in paying the Customs determined value, or not importing the goods. Counsel should calculate the possible rates of duty under all the possible alternatives and should only import the products if the rate of duty is acceptable and does not cause the price for resale to be either excessive, or more than would result from using United States products which may cost more to produce, but do not have added duty.

---

[142] Texas Apparel Co. v. United States, 698 F.Supp. 932 (C.I.T.1988), *affirmed* 883 F.2d 66 (Fed.Cir.1989), *cert. denied* 493 U.S. 1024, 110 S.Ct. 728, 107 L.Ed.2d 747 (1990).

[143] 19 U.S.C.A. § 1401a(e)(1)(D).

[144] 19 U.S.C.A. § 1401a(f)(1).

[145] 19 U.S.C.A. § 1401a(f)(2).

Chapter 4

ANTIDUMPING DUTIES

Table of Sections

Sec.

For coverage of external European Union law on antidumping duties, see Section 18.5. No antidumping duties apply to internal EU trade. For NAFTA coverage, see Section 16.10.

§ 4.0   Antidumping and Countervailing Duties

The core of the GATT (1947) and (1994) agreements is the principle of binding tariffs applied equally to all WTO member states, the most-favored-nation (MFN) principle. These tariffs, negotiated in the various GATT/WTO Rounds, are commonly referred to as MFN tariffs. The national tariff levels of the WTO member states reflect these negotiated MFN tariffs. In the United States tariff code, MFN tariffs are referenced as Column 1 tariffs. *See* Chapter 2.

The GATT/WTO system allows, however, certain exceptions to MFN tariff levels. The two most important are "antidumping duties" (ADs) and "countervailing duties" (CVDs). Such duties are intended to "remedy" what the GATT/WTO has agreed are unfair international trade practices. Think of them as special tariffs which, in authorized circumstances, are additional to MFN tariffs. This Chapter will analyze antidumping duties; Chapter 5 will examine the subject of governmental subsidies and the response of countervailing duties.[1]

Antidumping duties are a permissible trade response where an enterprise prices its goods for sale in the country of importation at a level that is less than that charged for comparable sales in the home country (*i.e.*, at "less than fair value" (LTFV)). Hence AD generally counteract private sector discriminatory pricing. Countervailing duties are a permissible response to certain "subsidies" given in another country that favor its exports in the international marketplace. Hence CVD counteract governmental subsidies. AD and CVD cannot simultaneously be applied. *See* U.S.-AD and CVD Duties (China), WT/DS 379/AB/R (2011).

§ 4.1   WTO Authorized Trade Remedies

The WTO system recognizes and permits both antidumping duties and countervailing duties, providing of course the respective requirements are satisfied. Each "trade remedy" also is governed by a separate Agreement ("Code") that provides more detail on the circumstances under which member states may impose these exceptional duties. Because the AD and CVD Codes are mandatory in the WTO system, they provide the foundation for a reasonably

---

[1]   Chapter 6 examines a third allowed response to import competition: temporary "safeguard" (or "escape clause") measures. This form of governmental protection against import competition is substantially less common and not based upon the premise that unfair international trade practices have occurred.

uniform body of legal rules for trade remedies among the roughly 160 WTO member states.

Under the WTO Antidumping Agreement (AD Code) and the WTO Subsidies and Countervailing Measures Agreement (CVD Code), a country may impose a special duty on products of another WTO member state only if two requirements are met. First, the country must find sufficient evidence of an unfair trade practice, either dumping (sales at less than fair value) or prohibited or actionable subsidies. Second, the practice must cause a sufficiently significant injury to a domestic industry. In the case of dumping or subsidies, this requires proof that the practice has caused or threatens to cause "material injury" to a domestic industry, or that it has "materially retarded" the establishment of such an industry. Thus, the substantive grounds for the determination of the existence of "dumping" and of a "countervailable (actionable) subsidy" are different, but the domestic injury standard is essentially the same.

Neither of these trade remedies in favor of domestic producers is based on any notion of reciprocity. That is, neither arises because another country has restricted the importation of U.S. goods into its markets. Antidumping and countervailing duties instead address unfair selling prices of dutiable imported goods.

§ 4.2   Dumping—What Is It and Why Is It Done?

Dumping involves an exporter selling goods abroad at a price that is less than the price charged for the same goods in the home market (the "normal" or *"fair"* value). This alone is not sufficient however. Antidumping duties are allowed as a trade response only if the practice causes or threatens to cause a material injury to an industry in the export market. Dumping is recognized by most of the trading world as an unfair practice (akin to price discrimination as an antitrust offense). As noted, dumping is the subject of a special WTO Code that defines when dumping occurs, what constitutes a material injury, and the rules for the calculation of an allowed antidumping duty response.

The economics of dumping arise from a producer's opportunity to compartmentalize the overall market for its product, thus permitting it to offer the product for sale at different prices in different geographic areas. Only if trade barriers or other factors insulate each market sector from others is there opportunity to vary substantially the product's price in different sectors of the global market. For example, a producer can securely "dump" products in an overseas market at cheap prices and at high volume only if it can be sure that the product market in its home country is immune from (return) penetration by these products. The objectives of dumping range include increasing marginal revenues, ruining a competitor's market position, and developing a new market on an expeditious basis.

On the other hand, a sale at less than the home price may not necessarily represent an unfair trade practice. It may instead merely result from a short-term need to introduce new products, sell off excess inventory, or conduct a distress sale in difficult financial circumstances. Indeed, "dumping" products in order to establish a foothold in a new foreign market or to raise brand awareness in an existing market may make sense as a marketing technique. Consumers, at least in the short term, are typically enthusiastic about obtaining goods at "dumped" prices. Hence there is considerable debate about the economic rationality of categorizing dumping an unfair trade practice. Nevertheless, a substantial body of international trade law seeks to identify dumping and counteract it through AD tariffs.

§ 4.3   The WTO Antidumping Agreement (1994)

The law regarding dumping has repeatedly been the subject of discussion in the various rounds of negotiations under GATT and (later) the WTO. A technical area, antidumping remedies were for many years principally used by developed nations to protect against competition from developing country imports. Then, in a remarkable transfer of legal technology, the principles endorsed by various GATT antidumping agreements took hold in newly developing countries. Today, antidumping duties are as likely to be imposed on U.S. exports by Mexico, India or China, as vice-versa. Antidumping proceedings remain the preferred trade remedy of domestic producers. India, the European Union, the United States and Argentina are the most frequent users of antidumping remedies, with products from China and EU states by far the top target of antidumping duties.

Late in 1993, the Uruguay Round of GATT negotiations came to a successful conclusion and President Clinton notified Congress of his intent to sign the many "covered agreements" that resulted from those negotiations. One of those agreements is yet another attempt at a codification of antidumping law. As a basic matter Article VI of the longstanding GATT grants WTO member states the right to impose antidumping duties. But the more detailed standards for such duties are set forth in a separate WTO Agreement, "The Agreement on Implementation of Article VI of GATT 1994."

The WTO Antidumping Agreement, adapted from the earlier Tokyo Round GATT "Antidumping Code," focuses upon dumping determinations (particularly criteria for allocating costs) and material injury determinations (particularly causation). The WTO Antidumping Agreement provides that dumping occurs with respect to a product if its export price is less than the "normal value." It defines the "normal value" of a good as the comparable price, in the ordinary course of trade, for the same or a similar product "when destined for consumption in the exporting country." Thus, in evaluating whether an export price constitutes dumping, the best baseline for comparison is the domestic sales price of comparable goods in the exporting country (*i.e.*, the home country).

However, such comparable sales may not be available, either because comparable products are not sold domestically or because the usual retail transaction there is not comparable (*e.g.*, leasing rather than a sale). In that situation, the WTO Antidumping Agreement provides a hierarchy of alternative computation methods to achieve an approximate evaluation. Among these alternatives, the preferred one uses the *price* for the same or a similar product in the ordinary course of trade for export to a third country. The next preferred alternative is to calculate the *cost* of production of the exported goods in the country of origin, plus a reasonable amount for profits and for administrative, selling and any other general costs. In either case, the value thus determined is then compared against the price charged on the export price to the import country.

The WTO Agreement has detailed rules that permit a member state to impose an antidumping duty only if a sale at less than fair value has caused a sufficient injury to a domestic industry.

Because the United States has agreed to abide by the WTO Antidumping Agreement, each of these requirements is reflected in conforming provisions of the U.S. Tariff Act of 1930. The remaining Sections of this Chapter will examine in detail these rules of antidumping law.

The WTO Antidumping Agreement also has a few special rules that are worthy of emphasis. First, it forbids duties for *de minimis* dumping, defined as less than two percent of the product's export price; in such cases member states must terminate any antidumping investigations immediately. Second, the Agreement permits "cumulation" of imports—*i.e.*, imports of the same goods from more than one country—if the dumping from each is more than *de minimis* and this is otherwise appropriate under the circumstances. Third, it recognizes, but does not expressly allow or disallow, antidumping petitions by employees and their union representatives. Fourth, the Agreement obligates member states to notify the WTO of any changes to their domestic antidumping laws as well as any related administrative actions. More generally, a special WTO "Committee on Anti-Dumping Practices" oversees implementation of the Agreement by member states.

Finally, when another member state challenges the imposition of antidumping duties before the WTO, the Dispute Settlement Body (DSB) panel may rely on the facts developed in the domestic administrative proceedings and must accept those facts if the domestic evaluation "was unbiased and objective, even if the panel might have reached a different conclusion." The WTO Agreement also expressly allows for "competing, reasonable interpretations" of its obligations under the domestic law of its member states.

§ 4.4   The Evolution of U.S. Antidumping Law

The United States was an early advocate of the perspective that dumping constitutes an unfair trade practice. Indeed, complaints about dumping were recorded as the subject of a protest by Secretary of the Treasury Alexander Hamilton in 1791. In general, U.S. antidumping statutes compare the price at which articles are imported or sold within the United States with their price in the country of production at the time of their export to the United States. This approach was first established by the Antidumping Act of 1916, a rarely-invoked criminal statute prohibiting "predatorily low price levels."[2] This statute, which also created a private remedy for treble damages, required proof of an intent to seriously injure or destroy a U.S. industry. The European Union, Japan, and other states successfully challenged this 1916 Act in WTO dispute settlement proceedings as inconsistent with the Antidumping Agreement. The pressure of the adverse rulings by the WTO's DSB ultimately led the United States to repeal the Act in 2004.

The modern U.S. rules and procedures governing antidumping duties are set forth in a statute that is still known as the Tariff Act of 1930.[3] Congress has enacted amendments to this statute numerous times. The most important of these for present purposes came through the Uruguay Round Agreements Act of 1994 (URAA),[4] by which Congress amended the Tariff Act to implement the numerous Uruguay Round WTO agreements, including the Antidumping Agreement. Finally, the Code of Federal Regulations

---

[2]   15 U.S.C. §§ 71–77.

[3]   Codified at 19 U.S.C. §§ 1671–1677g.

[4]   Public Law No. 103–465, 108 Stat. 4809.

contains more detailed rules on the requirements for, calculation of, and process for assessing antidumping duties.[5]

U.S. law places authority for administering antidumping law in two different governmental agencies.[6] Generally, the Secretary of Commerce (which in turn has delegated specific authority to its International Trade Administration (ITA)) is the "Administering Authority."[7] The ITA is responsible for all administration determinations except those relating to injury to a domestic industry. Injury determinations are the responsibility of the International Trade Commission (ITC).[8] To provide guidance on the application of the applicable statutory and regulatory rules, the International Trade Administration publishes an "Antidumping Manual," the most recent version of which is from 2009.[9]

Sections 12.5 through 12.19 below will examine in detail the substantive rules of U.S. law on antidumping determinations. In brief, and in conformity with the WTO Antidumping Agreement, the fundamental determination under U.S. law is whether a sale is at "less than fair value" (LTFV).[10] This requires a comparison of the U.S. price of imported goods with their "normal value." "Normal value" is usually determined by the price charged for the goods in the exporter's *domestic* market (the home market) in the ordinary course of business.[11] The ITA then compares this value with the price of the goods for export to the United States.[12] As noted, the ITC separately makes determinations on injury and causation in antidumping proceedings. In order to impose antidumping duties, the Tariff Act requires an affirmative determination by the ITC that a challenged practice presents an actual or threatened "material injury" to a domestic industry, or that it has "materially retarded" the establishment of such an industry.[13]

If sales are both at LTFV and cause or threaten "material injury" to a domestic industry, then the Tariff Act declares that an

---

[5]   The principal U.S. antidumping regulations are found in 19 C.F.R. Part 351.

[6]   For more on the administrative processes governing antidumping duties see Sections 4.22 through 4.25.

[7]   19 U.S.C. § 1677(1). Prior to 1980, the Treasury Department was the "administering authority", but the Secretary of Commerce was so designated in 1980. *See President's Reorganization Plan No. 3 of 1979*, 44 Fed. Reg. 69,273 (1979), and Executive Order 12188, 45 Fed. Reg. 989 (1980).

[8]   19 U.S.C. §§ 1673(2) and 1677(2).

[9]   Import Administration Antidumping Manual (2009), available at http://ia.ita.doc.gov/admanual/index.html.

[10]   19 U.S.C. § 1673(1).

[11]   19 U.S.C. §§ 1673(1), 1677b. *See also* Sections 4.6–4.9.

[12]   19 U.S.C. §§ 1673(1), 1677a. *See also* Section 4.10.

[13]   19 U.S.C. § 1673(2). *See also* Sections 4.12–4.18.

antidumping duty "shall be imposed."[14] Thus, antidumping duties are a statutory remedy, one which the President cannot veto or affect (except by the extraordinary act of the negotiating an international trade agreement).

§ 4.5　The Basic U.S. Dumping Determination

The ITA determines whether foreign merchandise[15] is, or is likely to be, sold in the United States at less than fair value (LTFV) by comparing the foreign market value (the "normal value") of the goods to the price charged for export to the United States. If the former exceeds the latter, dumping has occurred. Much turns, therefore, on the definitions of these two central concepts. Sections 12.6 through 12.9 below will examine the calculation of the foreign market value. Section 12.10 below will then analyze the appropriate comparison price regarding the export of the goods to the United States.

If a sale is at LTFV and meets the statutory material injury requirement, then the Tariff Act provides that an antidumping duty "shall be imposed."[16] The amount of the duty will correspond to the "dumping margin." The ITA normally compares the "weighted-average" foreign market value with the "weighted-average" U.S. price for the dumped product.[17] The term "weighted average dumping margin" is a percentage that is determined with reference to the "aggregate dumping margins" of the exporter or producer for the type of products at issue.[18] For large capital goods, however, the ITA will typically use the actual normal value and the U.S. price on a transaction-to-transaction basis.[19] Whichever calculation method is used, the "dumping margin"—and thus the amount of the antidumping duty—corresponds to the amount by which the foreign market "normal value" of the goods exceeds the price charged in the export to the United States.[20] The dumping margin may be different for similar merchandise from different foreign states, and may also be different for different manufacturers from the same foreign state.

§ 4.6　＿＿Foreign Market Value ("Normal Value")

The first step in the analysis is to determine the appropriate value of the allegedly dumped goods in a relevant foreign market.

---

[14]　19 U.S.C. § 1673.

[15]　Antidumping law generally does not apply to services, but also is not limited to "cash-only sales." *See* U.S. v. Eurodif S. A., 555 U.S. 305 (2009).

[16]　19 U.S.C. § 1673.

[17]　19 U.S.C. § 1677(35)(B).

[18]　*Id.*

[19]　19 U.S.C. § 1677(35)(A).

[20]　*Id.*

The Tariff Act refers to this value as the "normal value."[21] It recognizes three different measures for this normal value:

Home Market Price. The standard measure of the "normal value" is the price at which the foreign merchandise is first sold for consumption—in usual quantities, in the ordinary course of trade, and preferably at the same level of trade—in the exporting country ("home market price").[22]

Third Country Price. If, however, sales in the home market are nonexistent or too small to form an adequate basis for comparison (usually, less than five percent of the U.S. total), then export sales to other countries may be used ("third country price").[23] Sales intended to establish fictitious markets in the source country, however, cannot be considered.[24]

Constructed Value. If comparable merchandise is not offered for sale either in the home market or for export to other countries, the ITA is authorized to calculate a "constructed" value.[25] In such a case, the ITA will build a figure using one of three methodologies: (1) the producer's actual costs and profit for the specific product under investigation; (2) the producer's actual costs and profit for similar products; *or* (3) a weighted average of other producers' actual costs and profit for the category of products under investigation.[26] If the foreign producer is in a non-market economy, then the ITA will construct an appropriate value based either on various "factors of production" or on "surrogate country prices."[27]

The time and place for determining the normal value is often crucial. The Tariff Act requires that the relevant time for measuring the sales in the foreign country must "reasonably correspond]" to the time used to calculate the comparison export price to the United States.[28] That is the time when the product is "first sold (or agreed to be sold) before the date of importation by the producer or exporter of the subject merchandise outside of the United States to an unaffiliated purchaser in the United States."[29] That is also the

---

[21] 19 U.S.C. § 1677b.

[22] 19 U.S.C. § 1677b(a)(1)(B)(i).

[23] 19 U.S.C. § 1677b(a)(1)(B)(ii).

[24] 19 U.S.C. § 1677b(a)(2).

[25] 19 U.S.C. § 1677b(a)(4), (e).

[26] 19 U.S.C. § 1677b(e).

[27] 19 U.S.C. § 1677b(c). For more detail on this issue see Section 4.9.

[28] 19 U.S.C. § 1677b(a)(1)(A).

[29] 19 U.S.C. § 1677a(a).

date for determining the appropriate exchange rate for converting prices in foreign currency into U.S. dollars.[30]

In determining foreign market value, the ITA may use averaging and generally recognized sampling techniques whenever there is a significant volume of sales or number of adjustments.[31] The authority to select averages and statistical sampling "rests exclusively" with the Secretary of Commerce (and thus the ITA).[32]

When the goods are manufactured in one country and then shipped to another, from which they are exported to the United States, a question arises as to which foreign country is the relevant one. The Act provides a partial answer. Generally, the price in country of transshipment (the "intermediate country") is the correct one *unless*:

(A) The producer knew at the time of the sale that the subject merchandise was destined for exportation;

(B) The goods are merely transshipped through the intermediate country;

(C) Sales of the goods in the intermediate country are too small to form an adequate basis for comparison; or

(D) The goods are not produced in the intermediate country.[33]

Other issues relating to the determination of foreign market value are discussed below. These problems include issues arising out of sales at less than the costs of production; constructed values; imports from nonmarket economy countries; special rules for multinational corporations; and adjustments necessary to ensure a proper comparison of value with price.

§ 4.7   ____Sales Below Cost Disregarded

The central question in most antidumping proceedings is whether and to what degree the foreign producer or exporter is selling its goods in the home market below the cost of production. Sales are below cost if they do not recover total costs, both fixed and variable, over a commercially reasonable period. Thus, a significant volume of sales by a foreign producer at prices that cover only its variable costs can be disregarded by the ITA in its calculation of the foreign market value of the goods. The Tariff Act explicitly

---

[30]   *See* 19 U.S.C. § 1677b–1.
[31]   19 U.S.C. § 1677f–1.
[32]   19 U.S.C. § 1677f–1(a).
[33]   19 U.S.C. § 1677(a)(3).

authorizes the ITA to disregard sales at less than the cost of production when it makes its "normal value" determinations.[34]

The ITA will investigate this issue whenever it "has reasonable grounds to believe or suspect" that sales of the goods under investigation "have been made at prices which represent less than the cost of production." If the ITA determines that such sales (a) have occurred "within an extended period of time in substantial quantities," and (b) "were not at prices which permit recovery of all costs within a reasonable period of time," then it "may" disregard the sales in determining the "normal value."[35] Thus, recovery of start-up costs may be prorated over commercially reasonable periods. A decision to disregard sales below cost from the normal value calculation naturally raises the average cost and thus increases the potential to find dumping. A decision to include such sales has the opposite effect.

If the ITA disregards sales as below the cost of production, it will make its "normal value" determination based on the remaining sales of the goods "in the ordinary course of trade."[36] And if no sales are made in the ordinary course of trade, the ITA must instead use the "constructed value" of the goods.[37]

§ 4.8 _____Nonmarket Economy Constructed Values

The ITA will always use the "constructed value" to determine the foreign market value of imports from nonmarket economy countries.[38] The actual prices used in the exporter's (home) foreign market are deemed irrelevant because they are assumed to be determined bureaucratically and not by market forces. That is, they are not sufficiently subject to the forces of competition to form an accurate standard for comparison.

The Tariff Act delegates to the ITA the authority to determine when imports are from a "nonmarket economy country,"[39] and then insulates that administrative determination from judicial review.[40] The Act nonetheless gives the ITA a basic definition—whether the country's economy operates on "market principles" so that home market sales reflect "fair value." It then provides five factors to

---

[34]   19 U.S.C. § 1677b(b).
[35]   *Id.*
[36]   *Id.*
[37]   *See* Section 4.9.
[38]   19 U.S.C. § 1677b(c).
[39]   19 U.S.C. § 1677(18)(A), (C).
[40]   19 U.S.C. § 1677(18)(D).

consider.[41] The factors include the convertability of the foreign country's currency, the extent to which wages and prices are determined by government action or free bargaining, the extent of government ownership of the means of production, and the receptivity to private foreign investment.[42] Although the Act speaks in terms of a country by country decision, the ITA has more often analyzed the particular industrial segment involved, for example with allegedly dumped exports from China. Many WTO members have recognized China as a market economy, and the accession provision allowing treatment of China as a nonmarket economy expires in 2016.

If the imports are from a nonmarket economy (NME) country, the Act directs the ITA to "construct" a foreign market value by determining the factors of production (labor, materials, energy, capital, etc.) actually used by the NME to produce the imported goods.[43] The ITA then determines a value for each of those factors of production according to the prices or costs in a market economy that is appropriate under the circumstances. Surrogate countries are appropriate if they are "at a level of economic development comparable to that of the nonmarket economy country" and also are "significant producers of comparable merchandise."[44]

The Act then directs the ITA to add to the cost of production— again, as constructed based on the factors of production— appropriate amounts for general expenses, profits, and the packaging of the goods for shipment to the United States. The amounts for general expenses and profits are to be derived from sales of the same class or kind of merchandise in the "country of exportation,"[45] but this term simply means an "appropriate" market economy country.

In recognition of some of the difficulties with a "cost of production" approach, the Act provides an exception to the constructed value method outlined above, by allowing the use of a different method of constructing a foreign market value for imports from a NME. The ITA may use this alternative method if it finds that the best available information on the factors of production is not adequate. In such cases, the ITA will find a "surrogate" market economy country that produces the goods that are the same as or similar to the merchandise imported from the NME, and base the foreign market value on the price of the goods imported from the

---

[41]   19 U.S.C. § 1677(18)(B).
[42]   *Id.*
[43]   19 U.S.C. § 1677b(c)(1).
[44]   19 U.S.C. § 1677b(c)(4).
[45]   19 U.S.C. § 1677b(e)(1)(B).

surrogate country.[46] Such a construction methodology does not require the ITA to break the pricing of the goods into factors of production.

Several problems arise in the application of this scheme. First, "appropriate" market economy countries may be limited or unavailable. Second, the surrogate market economy countries selected may be obviously inappropriate, when compared to the level of economic development of the NME. Third, producers in such countries may not furnish the necessary information, even though the ITA is authorized to use the "best available information."[47] Fourth, there is no necessary relationship between the price so constructed by the ITA and any price that the NME producer may decide to charge. This leaves the NME producer or exporter always open to antidumping duties, and there is no pre-transaction analytical path for avoiding such duties.

§ 4.9   ____Market Economy Constructed Values

The ITA may use constructed values not only for imports from NME countries, but in other circumstances as well. It is directed to construct a foreign market value whenever merchandise comparable to the imported merchandise is not offered for sale either in the home market of the foreign producer or exporter or for export from that home market to other countries.[48] A constructed foreign market value is also to be used when so many sales in the home market are below cost of production, and therefore are disregarded, such that the remaining sales provide an inadequate basis for determining foreign market value.[49]

In such a case, the ITA will calculate the foreign market value based on one of three methodologies: (1) the producer's actual costs, plus sales, general, and administrative expenses, and plus a profit for the specific product under investigation; or (2) the producer's actual costs and profit for the products in the same category as those under investigation; or (3) a weighted average of other producers' actual costs and profit for the category of products under investigation.[50]

The Act also has a special rule for determining the foreign market value of merchandise produced by a corporation with production facilities in two or more countries. This "special rule for certain multinational corporations" applies when there are

---

[46]   19 U.S.C. § 1677b(c)(2).

[47]   19 U.S.C. § 1677b(c)(1).

[48]   19 U.S.C. § 1677b(a)(2).

[49]   19 U.S.C. § 1677b(b).

[50]   19 U.S.C. § 1677b(e)

insufficient sales by that producer in its home market on which to base a comparison of its export sales to the United States.[51] If the foreign market value of the goods produced in the country of exportation is less than the price of the goods produced in the corporation's facilities in another country, the ITA "shall" construct a foreign market value which reflects the price of the goods produced in the non-exporting country.

§ 4.10 United States Price

To determine whether dumping exists, the ITA will compare the foreign market value ("normal value") of the goods with the price charged for export to the United States. The Tariff Act recognizes two different methods for calculating this price:

Export Price. The ITA generally uses the "export price" for the price of the goods for exportation to the United States. This is the price at which the goods are first sold *outside* of the United States to an unaffiliated person before the goods are imported into the United States.[52] The standard example of this is when a foreign producer or exporter contacts an unaffiliated U.S. business in order to distribute a foreign product in the United States and the parties agree on the sale terms (price, quantity, delivery, etc.).

Constructed Export Price. If, however, the foreign exporter first sells the goods to an *affiliated* person outside the United States— such that this "export" price is not a reliable one—, then the ITA may use the "constructed export price."[53] This is the price at which the goods are first sold to an unaffiliated person *in* the United States irrespective of whether it occurs before or after importation. This typically occurs when a foreign exporter or producer first sells to a U.S. subsidiary, and in that case the relevant price is that charged by the subsidiary to the first unaffiliated U.S. buyer.

§ 4.11 ____"Like Product" Determinations and Required Adjustments

All of the analysis above depends upon a comparison of the prices of a "foreign like product,"[54] a concept also relevant in injury determinations by the ITC.[55] Because merchandise sold in foreign markets is often different, due to cultural, technical or legal constraints, the determination of comparability of merchandise sold in the foreign market to the imported merchandise is often a crucial

---

[51]   19 U.S.C. § 1677b(d).

[52]   19 U.S.C. § 1677a(a).

[53]   19 U.S.C. § 1677a(b).

[54]   19 U.S.C. § 1677b(a)(1)(A), (B).

[55]   *See* Section 4.13.

one. The Act provides a definition, with a hierarchy of criteria.[56] Thus, merchandise that is identical in physical characteristics, and produced in the same country by the same person as the imported merchandise, is to be categorized as a "foreign like product."[57]

If such identical merchandise is not available, the ITA next looks for merchandise that is (a) produced in the same country by the same person, (b) has similar component materials, and (c) is approximately equal in value to the imported merchandise.[58]

If none of these reference points is available, the ITA is to look at merchandise that (a) is produced in the same country by the same person, (b) is of "the same general class or kind as the subject merchandise," and (c) in the judgment of the ITA "may reasonably be compared with" the imported merchandise.[59] In practice, the ITA considers similarities in the physical characteristics, use and expectations of ultimate purchasers, including advertising of the product, and distribution channels.

A considerable number of adjustments are necessary to obtain comparable prices for goods sold in home markets and for export to the United States. To determine the United States price, packing costs and container costs are added to the purchase price or exporter's sales price, if they are not already included in that price.[60] If generally applicable taxes are either not collected or are rebated by the exporting government, these also may be included in the determining United States price.

Adjustments deducted from the purchase price or exporter's sales price include any expenses, such as freight or insurance, included in that price and attributable to the costs of bringing the goods from the country of export to the United States and most export taxes of the exporting country.[61] Deductions also are appropriate for any commissions and other expenses for selling in the United States and for the costs of additional processing or assembly in the United States after importation and before sale.[62] However, the additional cost of U.S. product liability insurance is not a permitted adjustment.[63]

---

[56]   19 U.S.C. § 1677(16).

[57]   19 U.S.C. § 1677(16)(A).

[58]   19 U.S.C. § 1677(16)(B).

[59]   19 U.S.C. § 1677(16)(C).

[60]   19 U.S.C. § 1677a(d)(1).

[61]   19 U.S.C. § 1677a(d)(2).

[62]   19 U.S.C. § 1677a(e).

[63]   *See* Carlisle Tire & Rubber Co. v. United States, 622 F. Supp. 1071 (C.I.T. 1985).

Adjustments and exchange rate conversions are also made to determine the foreign market value of the goods. Exchange rate conversions are required whenever the foreign market price or the United States price is not in U.S. dollars. The rates for the relevant sales period as determined quarterly by the Federal Reserve Bank of New York are ordinarily used except when those rates are fluctuating rapidly. In such cases, the ITA will test whether the dumping margin remains if the rates from the prior quarter are used. If the margin disappears, the dumping is attributed to exchange rate fluctuations and the ITA may determine that no dumping occurred.

To obtain an equivalent of the United States price, the ITA will add to the foreign market value an amount equal to the packing costs and container costs for shipment to the United States.[64] Allowances may be made for sales at different trade levels (wholesale versus retail), quantity or production cost discounts, differences in the circumstances of sale, and physical differences in the merchandise.[65] Differences in the circumstances of the sale include credit terms, warranties, servicing, technical assistance, and advertising allowances. Adjustments for cost differences in the circumstances of sale are allowed even if they do not give rise to comparable price increases in the foreign market. This is true even if they involve rebates or discounts not made available to all purchasers.[66] These decisions reflect the substantial deference the courts give to the ITA on the important issue of adjustments to its price and value calculations.

§ 4.12 The U.S. Injury Determination

Antidumping proceedings in the United States are conducted in two stages. In the second stage, the International Trade Commission (ITC) must determine whether the dumping has caused material injury to concerned domestic industries.[67] The following sections review the material injury determination under U.S. law, including market definition, injury factors, and causation.

The injury determination by the ITC involves three separate inquiries:

(1) First, the ITC must define the relevant "domestic like product" and relevant domestic industry;

---

[64] 19 U.S.C. § 1677b(a)(1), last paragraph.

[65] 19 U.S.C. § 1677b(a)(b).

[66] *See* Zenith Radio Corp. v. United States, 783 F.2d 184 (Fed.Cir.1986).

[67] 19 U.S.C. § 1673(2).

(2) Second, the ITC must determine whether that industry is suffering or threatened with a sufficiently serious injury; and

(3) Third, the ITC must determine whether a causal link exists between the injury and the sale at LTFV (*i.e.*, the dumping).

The most import of these steps is the determination of whether a domestic industry is suffering a sufficient injury due to a dumping practice. The Tariff Act provides that an affirmative injury determination is required when an industry in the United States is materially injured or is threatened with material injury by reason of dumped imports, or the establishment of an industry in the United States is materially retarded.[68] Both the "material injury"[69] and the "threat of material injury"[70] standards apply to established industries, and substantial overlap exists between the two. Nonetheless, the Act makes clear that they are independent grounds for a sufficient injury to justify antidumping duties.[71]

§ 4.13 ____The "Like Product" and Relevant Domestic Industry Determinations

In order to assess "material injury," the ITC and the ITA must first identify the relevant products and relevant domestic industry affected by an alleged dumping practice. The ITA necessarily focuses on which foreign products are like those alleged to be dumped in the United States. For its part, the ITC must define the relevant domestic industry that produces like products in order to make its injury determinations.

The term "domestic like product" is defined by the Tariff Act as one that is "like, or in the absence of like, most similar in characteristics and uses with" to the foreign product under investigation. WTO Appellate Body rulings suggest that products are "like" when they are "directly competitive or substitutable". *See* Korea-Alcoholic Beverages, WT/DS75/AB/R (1999). The "like product" determination is a factual issue for which the ITC weighs six relevant factors: "(1) physical characteristics and uses; (2) common manufacturing facilities and production employees; (3) interchangeability; (4) customer perceptions; (5) channels of distribution; and, where appropriate, (6) price."[72]

Separately, the ITA and the ITC must define the relevant domestic industry potentially affected by dumped products. The

---

68 Id.

69 19 U.S.C. § 1677(7).

70 19 U.S.C. § 1677(7)(F).

71 19 U.S.C. § 1673(2).

72 Cleo Inc. v. U.S., 501 F.3d 1291, 1295 (Fed. Cir. 2007).

Tariff Act defines the relevant "domestic industry" as those domestic producers, "as a whole," of a "domestic like product" or as those producers "whose collective output of a domestic like product constitutes a major proportion" of the total domestic production.[73] Although these definitions apply to both the ITA and the ITC, they do not always agree on the outcome. The ITA and ITC may assess injury on a geographically regional basis if local producers sell most of their production in the regional market, and the demand in the regional market is not supplied by other U.S. producers outside that region.[74]

The determination of domestic "like products" and the relevant domestic industry can be decisive for ITA dumping determinations, but especially for ITC injury determinations. Some early cases on the subject, which have paved the way for later determinations, illustrate the point. In one early case, for example, the ITC excluded large screen TVs from the U.S. domestic industry definition. This had the effect of giving Japanese TV exports a much larger market share in the United States, thus supporting an affirmative injury determination.[75] In another early decision, the ITC narrowly defined the relevant U.S. industry as the canned mushrooms industry, noting that fresh and canned mushrooms were not always interchangeable. This narrow market definition again supported a preliminary injury determination.[76]

Variations on the theme of defining "domestic like products" can occur if the ITC decides it is appropriate to exclude domestic companies that also import the allegedly dumped goods or are related to the importer or foreign producer.[77] The ITC may also define the domestic industry regionally in situations where this reflects market realities.[78] Thus, which U.S. firms the ITC chooses to include or exclude in its "domestic like product" definition is an important threshold issue in material injury analysis.

§ 4.14   ____Material Injury

There are two potential perspectives on the appropriate meaning of "material." The first is that the term means any economic harm that is more than trivial, inconsequential, or *de minimis*. The second is that it contemplates a higher threshold,

---

[73]   19 U.S.C. § 1677(4)(A).

[74]   19 U.S.C. § 1677(4)(C).

[75]   *See Television Sets from Japan*, U.S.I.T.C. Publ. No. 367 (March 1971).

[76]   Canned Mushrooms from the People's Republic of China, U.S.I.T.C. Publ. No. 1324 (Dec. 1982).

[77]   19 U.S.C. § 1677(4)(B).

[78]   19 U.S.C. § 1677(4)(C).

something not quite as hurtful as the "serious injury" required for safeguard relief,[79] but yet still serious in the ordinary sense of that word. The consensus view is that the spirit of Article VI of the GATT embraces the higher standard.

The Tariff Act defines material injury as "harm which is not inconsequential, immaterial, or unimportant."[80] (The same standard applies in CVD proceedings[81] and much of the law in the area is therefore interchangeable.) In assessing this essential "material injury" standard, the Act *requires* the ITC to consider three factors:

(1) The volume of imports of the merchandise subject to investigation;

(2) The effect of these imports on prices in the United States for like products; and

(3) The impact of these imports on domestic producers of like products, but only in the context of domestic U.S. production operations.[82]

The Act also *permits* the ITC to consider "such other economic factors as are relevant to the determination regarding whether there is material injury by reason of imports."[83]

The ITC is required to explain its analysis of each factor considered and the relevance of each to its determination.[84] The Tariff Act nonetheless provides that the "presence or absence" of any of the three mandatory factors should "not necessarily give decisive guidance" to the ITC in its material injury determination, and the ITC is not required to give any particular weight to any one factor.[85] The factors are examined through extensive statistical analyses. This analysis occurs on industry-wide basis and not on a company-by-company basis. The ITC may select whatever time period best represents the business cycle, best captures the competitive conditions in the industry, and most reasonably allows it to determine whether an injury exists.[86]

---

[79]   *See* Chapter 6.

[80]   19 U.S.C. § 1677(7)(A).

[81]   *See* Chapter 5.

[82]   19 U.S.C. § 1677(7)(B)(i). *See also* Angus Chemical Co. v. United States, 140 F.3d 1478 (Fed. Cir. 1998)(holding that consideration of these three factors is mandatory).

[83]   19 U.S.C. § 1677(7)(B)(ii).

[84]   19 U.S.C. § 1677(7)(B).

[85]   19 U.S.C. § 1677(7)(E)(ii).

[86]   19 U.S.C. § 1677(7)(C).

The Tariff Act also gives detailed guidance for the ITC's assessment of each of the three mandatory considerations for a material injury determination:

Volume of Imports

The Tariff Act requires the ITC to consider the absolute volume of imports or any increase in volume of imports in evaluating the volume of imports subject to investigation. This assessment may be made in relation to production or consumption in the United States. The standard in this evaluation is whether the volume of imports, viewed in any of the above ways, is significant.[87]

Data relating to the volume of imports are an important factor in the ITC's injury determinations. In particular, the ITC is more concerned with the dynamics of the market share, such as a significant increase in market penetration, than it is with the size of market share. It is also primarily concerned with the effects that market share changes might have on profits and lost sales. Injury can be found when an a specific producer has a small market share, but imports from its home country as a whole are increasing rapidly, such that the U.S. domestic industry must reduce its prices in response. On the other hand, a large market share for the importer, coupled with increases in production, domestic shipments, exports, employment and profits of the domestic industry, may indicate that no material injury is occurring.

Price Effects

While price issues are obviously crucial to any determination of dumping margins, they have no strict correlation to injury determinations. However, under the Tariff Act, the ITC may consider the effect of the dumped imports upon prices for like products in the domestic market. This is done to the extent that such a consideration assists in evaluating whether (1) there is significant "price underselling" in the imported merchandise as compared with the price of like products of the United States;[88] and (2) the effect of the imported merchandise is otherwise to depress domestic prices to a significant degree or to prevent price increases that otherwise would occur.[89]

If there is no price underselling, but instead the exporters cut their U.S. prices to effectively meet price competition from U.S. producers, this is traditionally considered only "technical dumping" and precludes a finding of material injury. The rationale for this

---

[87]   19 U.S.C. § 1677(7)(C)(i).

[88]   19 U.S.C. § 1677(7)(C)(ii)(I).

[89]   19 U.S.C. § 1677(7)(C)(ii)(II).

approach focuses upon the purposes behind antidumping law, *i.e.*, to prevent unfair dumping not to protect against pro-competitive trade practices. Thus, technical dumping constitutes a defense to U.S. material injury determinations.

Price underselling is not a *per se* basis for a finding of injury. For example, if the demand for the product is not price sensitive, price underselling will not be a central consideration. Price underselling in fact may be irrelevant, even if domestic producers are losing sales in the United States, if their inability to sell goods is not attributable to dumped imports. For example, the industry's decline may have been caused by its failure to develop, produce, and market a competitive product. (The next Section will analyze causation issues in more detail.)

Substantial underselling, on the other hand, will lead to an affirmative injury finding where the market is price sensitive. The ITC looks for a pervasive pattern of underselling. If the ITC finds that demand for a specific product is price sensitive and importers are engaging in price underselling, it will then examine whether domestic producers are being forced into price suppression[90] or actual price cutting.[91] Because price suppression can be as severe a burden to domestic producers as can an actual price cutting, the ITC will find an injury if it determines that, in order to respond to dumping practices, domestic producers have lowered or have been unable to raise their prices to accommodate rising costs.

Domestic Industry Impact

The impact on a domestic industry of an allegedly dumped product commonly is the most important consideration in the ITC's injury analysis. Because of this, the Tariff Act provides supplemental factors for the ITC to consider. These include (1) actual and potential decline in "output, sales, market share, profits, productivity, return on investments, and utilization of capacity," (2) impact on domestic prices, (3) actual and potential "negative effects on cash flow, inventories, employment, wages, growth, ability to raise capital, and investment," (4) actual and potential negative effects "on the existing development and production efforts of the domestic industry," and (5) in specific cases, the magnitude of the margin of dumping.[92]

---

[90] Price suppression arises when the domestic industry can affect smaller price increases on those articles directly competitive with dumped imports than it can on those articles that directly compete with non-dumped imports.

[91] Price cutting arises when the domestic industry is compelled to lower its prices to meet the prices of dumped imports in an attempt to protect its market share.

[92] 19 U.S.C. § 1677(7)(C)(iii).

The ITC must evaluate all these relevant economic factors within the context of the business cycle and conditions of competition in the affected industry.[93] But the ITC traditionally relies primarily on two of the factors in making this determination. First, the industry must be in a distressed or a stagnant condition. Second, the low domestic price levels must be a factor in the industry's difficulties (*e.g.*, high unemployment or low capacity utilization rate), and these low prices must be having a serious negative effect on profits.

The ITC will often base an affirmative determination of material injury on severe downward trends in profitability among domestic producers. In one early case, the ITC found that a drop in the ratio of net profit to sales from 5.55 percent to 1.05 percent over a three year period, coupled with a 75 percent decline in the aggregate profit in the relevant industry in the same period, justified an affirmative determination of material injury.[94] Thus, it is not necessary that an industry suffer an actual loss as a prerequisite to a finding of material injury. On the other hand, simply because an industry is experiencing a decline in profitability does not require a finding of material injury due to dumping. Other factors unrelated to dumping, such as general economic conditions and industry over expansion, may be the cause.

The effect of dumped imports on employment in the relevant domestic industry often is a significant factor. Employment data are not dispositive, because decreases in the level or rate of employment may be due to a broad spectrum of economic factors unrelated to dumping. The economic downturn that commenced in 2008 provides ample proof of this point. Nonetheless, sudden changes in domestic employment during the period of dumping can be an important signal for the ITC that dumping is causing a material injury. For example, in one early case the ITC found that a thirty-five percent drop in employment during the period of dumping was a reasonable indication of material injury.[95] On the other hand, an increase in employment levels and hours worked can be a strong indication that dumping did not cause a material injury to the relevant industry.

Finally, the utilization of plant capacity can be a significant factor in material injury determinations. Again, however, such capacity utilization data commonly is affected by a variety of factors. For example, the ITC found a reasonable indication of

---

[93]   19 U.S.C. § 1677(7)(C), last paragraph.

[94]   Sugars and Syrups from Canada, 46 Fed. Reg. 51,086 (1981).

[95]   Montan Wax from the German Democratic Republic, 45 Fed. Reg. 73,821 (1980).

material injury from the fact that capacity utilization in the affected industry fell from 88 percent to 77 percent in two years.[96] In contrast, the ITC found no material injury in a case where capacity utilization similarly dropped from 85 to 77 percent, because in that instance frequent equipment breakdowns and quality control disruptions were the actual cause of the decline.[97]

§ 4.15   Threat of Material Injury

The ITC may also make an affirmative determination of injury if it finds that dumped imports represent a "threat of material injury" to a domestic industry. The Tariff Act lists a variety of "economic factors" that the ITC "shall consider" in making such a determination in an antidumping proceeding:

(1) Any "unused production capacity or imminent, substantial increase in production capacity in the exporting country . . . indicating the likelihood of substantially increased imports" into the United States;

(2) "A significant rate of increase of the volume or market penetration of imports. . . . indicating the likelihood of substantially increased imports":

(3) Whether imports are coming to the U.S. "at prices that are likely to have a significant depressing or suppressing effect on domestic prices, and are likely to increase demand for further imports";

(4) The existing inventories of the imported products;

(5) The potential that the low prices for the imports will cause other production facilities in the foreign country to switch to the products at issue;

(6) "The actual and potential negative effects on the existing development and production efforts" of the industry in the United States.[98]

Beyond these, the Tariff Act requires the ITC to consider "any other demonstrable adverse trends that indicate the probability" of a material injury to a domestic industry.[99]

The Tariff Act obligates the ITC to consider these factors "as a whole" in making a determination of a threat of material injury. Therefore, the presence or absence of any one factor is not

---

[96]   Carbon Steel Wire Rod from Brazil, Belgium, France, and Venezuela, 47 Fed. Reg. 13,927 (1982).

[97]   Crystal from Austria and Italy, 45 Fed. Reg. 31,830 (1980).

[98]   19 U.S.C. § 1677(7)(F)(i).

[99]   *Id.*

determinative. In any event, the determination "may not be made on the basis of mere conjecture or supposition."[100]

The case of *Rhone Poulenc, S.A. v. United States* represents a good example of the analysis of the *threat* of material injury standard.[101] That case involved the shipment of package anhydrous sodium metasilicate from France to the United States. The U.S. industry comprised four companies, only one of which was demonstrably injured. *Rhone Poulenc* was an appeal to the U.S. Court of International Trade (CIT) from an ITC decision concerning the "threat of material injury" standard. The court first rejected the importers' argument that the market penetration by imports is the crucial fact in determining whether such a threat exists. Instead, the court found that it is proper for the ITC to consider, in determining the likelihood of future injury, the developing trends in all the indicators used to determine whether an actual injury has occurred. These indicators of actual injury include the volume of imports, the effect of imports on prices, and the impact of the imports on the domestic industry. The court also held that the ITC also may look at likely future conduct of the producers or exporters of the dumped products.

§ 4.16 ___Material Retardation

The Tariff Act recognizes as an independent ground for an affirmative injury determination by the ITC that a dumped import product has "materially retarded" the establishment of an industry in the United States. The standard for "material retardation" is applied to new industries, *i.e.*, those that have made a substantial commitment to begin production, or have recently begun production.[102] As the ITA notes in its Antidumping Manual, however, this ground "has rarely been asserted by a petitioner in an antidumping duty investigation. Nearly all antidumping investigations have been initiated on the basis of petitions by established manufacturers of the domestic like product."[103]

§ 4.17 Causation

Causation of material injury by dumping is a required element in addition to, and independent of, the finding of material injury, threat of material injury or the material retardation of the establishment of a domestic industry. As a practical matter,

---

[100]   19 U.S.C. § 1677(7)(F)(ii).

[101]   592 F. Supp. 1318 (C.I.T. 1984).

[102]   For a rare analysis of this standard see BMT Commodity Corp. v. United States, 667 F. Supp. 880 (C.I.T. 1987), *affirmed* 852 F.2d 1285 (Fed. Cir.1988), *cert. denied*, 489 U.S. 1012 (1989).

[103]   Antidumping Manual, *supra* footnote 9, Ch. 18, I, § III.D.

however, the two separate inquiries (injury and causation) are closely linked. As a result, when it has found a material injury from a dumping practice the ITC has tended to make an affirmative injury determination without a lengthy analysis of the causal link between them. In a negative injury determination, on the other hand, the ITC may engage in a rather detailed analysis of causation.

The Tariff Act requires a simple causation element: that the material injury to a domestic industry is "by reason of" the dumped imports.[104] Again, the same standard applies in CVD proceedings and the law in this area is largely interchangeable.[105] The causation requirement is not a high one. Imports need only be *a* cause material injury, and need not be the most substantial or primary cause of injury suffered by domestic industry.[106] The "by reason of" standard nonetheless "mandates a showing of causal—not merely temporal—connection between the LTFV goods and the material injury."[107] The Tariff Act does not require that the ITC use any particular methodology in making such a determination, and it "need not isolate the injury caused by other factors from injury caused by unfair imports."[108] Nonetheless, the Federal Circuit has made clear that "causation is not shown if the subject imports contributed only 'minimally or tangentially to the material harm.'"[109]

In short, the causation element of an affirmative injury determination can be satisfied if the dumped products contribute in any noteworthy way to the conditions of the domestic injury.[110] Under this "contributing cause" standard, causation of injuries may be found despite the absence of correlation between dumped imports and the alleged injuries if there is substantial evidence that the volume of dumped imports was a contributing factor to the price depression experienced by the domestic injury.

---

[104]   19 U.S.C. § 1673(2).

[105]   *See* Section 5.18.

[106]   *See* Nippon Steel Corp. v. Int'l Trade Comm'n, 345 F.3d 1379, 1381 (Fed. Cir. 2003) (observing that "'dumping' need not be the sole or principal cause of injury").

[107]   Gerald Metals, Inc. v. United States, 132 F.3d 716, 720 (Fed. Cir. 1997).

[108]   Bratsk Aluminium Smelter v. U.S., 444 F.3d 1369, 1373 (Fed. Cir. 2006)(*quoting* Taiwan Semiconductors Industry Ass'n v. Int'l Trade Comm'n, 266 F.3d 1339, 1345 (Fed. Cir. 2001)).

[109]   *Id.*, 444 F.3d at 1373 (*quoting* Gerald Metals, Inc. v. U.S., 132 F.3d 716, 722 (Fed. Cir. 1997)).

[110]   Antidumping Manual, *supra* footnote 9, Ch. 18, I, § III.F (observing that:[t]he courts have held that this causation standard is satisfied if the dumped imports contribute, more than minimally or tangentially, to the injured condition of the domestic industry").

In examining the causal link between the dumped imports and the material injury, the ITC must consider other causal factors that might be responsible for the alleged injury. The Federal Circuit has observed that, for example, "the increase in volume of subject imports priced below domestic products and the decline in the domestic market share are not in and of themselves sufficient to establish causation."[111] On this reasoning, the Federal Circuit has held that the ITC must consider "fairly traded imports" of non-dumped products as a relevant "other economic factor" for causation inquiries.[112] Thus, the ITC may uncover other major causes for the problems of the domestic industry. These may include huge unnecessary expenses, chronic excess capacity, inefficiency, poor quality, price sensitivity or increased domestic competition. Nonetheless, the presence of such major alternative causes of injury does not foreclose the possibility that imports have been *a* contributing cause of the industry's problems.[113]

The ITC may, but is not required to, consider the margin of dumping when evaluating causation. In practice the margin of dumping is an important factor in the ITC's causation analysis. If the dumping margin is slight or substantially lower than the margin of underselling, this may indicate that the injury was not caused by the dumped imports. The imports will still be able to undersell domestic producers, even if the prices of the imports are raised to their fair values. If, on the other hand, the dumping margin is higher than the margin of underselling, thereby enabling the foreign exporters to undersell domestic producers, the dumping can be the cause of the material injury because the foreign exporters may be able to undersell only because of the higher dumping margin.

§ 4.18 ____Cumulative Causation

Can "material injury" be caused by imports from exporters from more than one country through the cumulative effect of many small injuries? There are arguments against cumulating each source of dumping to determine whether it is a cause of injury. For example, cumulation could penalize small suppliers who would not have caused injury if their dumping had been examined in isolation.

---

[111]   *See* Bratsk Aluminium Smelter v. U.S., 444 F.3d 1369, 1374 (Fed. Cir. 2006).

[112]   *See, e.g.,* Gerald Metals, Inc. v. United States, 132 F.3d 716, 723 (Fed.Cir.1997).

[113]   *See, e.g.,* Iwatsu Electric Co., Ltd. v. United States, 758 F. Supp. 1506 (C.I.T.1991) (regarding small telephone systems); United Engineering & Forging v. United States, 779 F. Supp. 1375 (C.I.T.1991), *opinion after remand* 14 ITRD 1748 (C.I.T.1992)(regarding crankshafts).

Nevertheless, the WTO Antidumping Agreement expressly permits cumulation.[114]

In turn, the Tariff Act requires that the ITC cumulatively assess the impact of reasonably coincident dumped imports from two or more countries if the imports compete with like U.S. products. In specific, the Act requires the ITC to "cumulatively assess the volume and price effects of imports of the subject merchandise from all countries" with respect to which antidumping petitions were initiated on the same day, "if such imports compete with each other and with domestic like products in the United States market."[115] An exception exists, however, for imports from beneficiary countries of the Caribbean Basin Initiative.[116] The injury to a domestic industry is measured by the cumulated results of dumping on the ground that an injury caused by "many nibbles" is just as harmful as one caused by "one large bite." Cumulation also provides administrative ease, since the ITC is not required to allocate the amount of injury caused by each individual exporter.

The CIT has observed that to support a cumulation decision, the ITC "must find a reasonable overlap of competition between imports from the subject countries and the domestic like product."[117] In applying this "reasonable overlap" test, the ITC traditionally has applied a "four factor" test: "(1) fungibility; (2) sales or offers in the same geographic markets; (3) common or similar channels of distribution; and (4) simultaneous presence."[118]

§ 4.19 Negligible Dumping

The Tariff Act requires that an investigation be terminated with a negative injury determination if imports of the subject merchandise are negligible. The Act defines imports as "negligible" if they "account for less than 3 percent of the volume of all such merchandise imported into the United States" during a defined twelve-month period."[119] In the case of cumulated imports from a number of countries,[120] however, the "negligible threshold rises to seven percent.[121] In computing import volumes for these purposes,

---

[114] *See* Antidumping Agreement, art. 3.3.

[115] 19 U.S.C. § 1677(7)(G)(i). *See also* Hosiden Corp. v. Advanced Display Mfrs. of America, 85 F.3d 1561 (Fed. Cir. 1996).

[116] 19 U.S.C. § 1677(7)(G)(ii)(III).

[117] Nucor Corp. v. U.S., 594 F. Supp. 2d 1320, 1347 (C.I.T. 2008) (*quoting* Noviant OY v. United States, 451 F. Supp. 2d 1367, 1379 (C.I.T. 2006), *aff'd*, Nucor Corp. v. U.S. 601 F.3d 1291 (Fed. Cir. 2010).

[118] Nucor Corp. v. U.S., 594 F. Supp. 2d 1320, 1347 (C.I.T. 2008).

[119] 19 U.S.C. § 1677(24)(A)(i).

[120] *See* Section 4.18.

[121] 19 U.S.C. § 1677(24)(A)(ii).

the ITC "may make reasonable estimates on the basis of available statistics."[122]

§ 4.20   Other U.S. Antidumping Law Issues

Congress ratified and implemented the Uruguay Round accords of 1994 under the Uruguay Round Agreements Act (URAA).[123] For present purposes, the most significant aspect of the URAA was the amendment of the Tariff Act to conform to the WTO Antidumping Agreement. In nearly all respects, therefore, the important rules on dumping determinations as described in the Sections above conform to the requirements of the Antidumping Agreement. Nonetheless, the URAA brought about a few more specific changes that are worthy of emphasis here.

De Minimis Dumping

First, the URAA amended the Tariff Act to address "*de minimis*" dumping.[124] In specific, the Tariff Act now requires that, in making its preliminary determination, the administrating authority (the Secretary of Commerce/ITA) disregard any weighted average dumping margin less than two percent ad valorem or the equivalent specific rate for the subject merchandise. Any weighted average dumping margin that is *de minimis* must also be disregarded by the administrating authority when making its final determinations.[125]

Statutory Time Limits

A significant new effect from the adoption of the URAA is the imposition of strict new statutory timelines for dumping determinations by the ITA. In the case of an antidumping petition, the ITA must make an initial determination within twenty days after the date on which a petition is filed. This time limit may be extended to forty days in any case where the ITA is required to poll or otherwise determine support for the petition by the industry and exceptional circumstances exist.[126] Time limits are also imposed on the ITC in its determination of whether there is a reasonable indication of injury.[127] Separately, the ITC must conduct a review no later than five years after an antidumping duty order is issued to determine whether revoking the order would likely lead to continuation or recurrence of dumping and material injury. Known

---

[122]   19 U.S.C. § 1677(24)(C).
[123]   Public Law No. 103–465, 108 Stat. 4809.
[124]   19 U.S.C. 1673b(b)(3).
[125]   19 U.S.C. 1673d(a).
[126]   19 U.S.C. 1673a(c).
[127]   19 U.S.C. 1673b(a).

as the "sunset provision," this new requirement will result in periodic reviews of antidumping (and countervailing duty) orders.

Notice and Comment

The URAA requires that the ITC provide all parties to a proceeding with an opportunity to comment, prior to a formal decision, on *all* information collected in the investigation.

Other Issues

The URAA requires the ITC to consider the magnitude of the dumping margin (although not the magnitude of the margin of subsidization) in making material injury determinations. It also authorizes an adjustment to sales-below-cost calculations to accommodate start-up costs,[128] a new rule thought to be particularly beneficial to high-tech products. It also adds a new "captive production" section intended to remove such internal sales from ITC injury determinations.[129]

§ 4.21 U.S. Antidumping Procedures—Petition and Response

In an antidumping proceeding, the ITA determines whether the imports are being sold at less than fair value (LTFV), and the ITC makes a separate determination concerning injury to the domestic industry making like or similar products.

United States antidumping proceedings may be initiated by a petition of the Commerce Department itself or by a union or aggrieved business (or by a group association of aggrieved workers or businesses).[130] The petition requirements are set forth by regulation.[131] In general, antidumping proceedings involve the ITA first making a determination that a petition adequately alleges the relevant statutory requirements. But before initiating an investigation, the ITA must find that a sufficient percentage of the affected domestic industry supports the petition—for Tariff Act requires that a petition be filed "by or on behalf of" the entire domestic industry.[132] Generally, this requires that the industry or workers who support the petition account for (a) at least twenty-five percent of the total industry, and (b) at least fifty percent of those

---

[128]   19 U.S.C. § 1677b(f)(1)(c).

[129]   19 U.S.C. § 1677b(f)(1)(c)(iii).

[130]   19 U.S.C. § 1673a.

[131]   *See* 19 C.F.R. § 351.202.

[132]   19 U.S.C. § 1673a(b).

that have actually expressed an opinion for or against the petition.[133]

After an initial investigation, the ITA then makes a "preliminary determination"—based on the "best information available at the time"—on whether there is "a reasonable basis to believe" that the relevant standard is met.[134] Such information cannot include any information furnished by respondents or a respondent's government. In other words, the ITA accepts or rejects the petition almost entirely on the basis of the information supplied by the petitioner.

Once the petition is accepted, the proceeding becomes genuinely adversarial if (as is commonly the case) the parties alleged to be dumping respond to the questionnaires on sales volumes and prices that the ITA creates and later verifies through on-site investigations. It is rare for the "defense" to have more than one month to respond. Any failure to respond or permit verification risks an ITA dumping decision on the "best information available," *i.e.* most likely the petitioner's or other respondent's submissions.[135] Because this obviously is an undesirable result, the best information available rule functions much like a subpoena. Most respondents answer the ITA's questionnaires. Protective orders preserve the confidentiality of the often strategically valuable information submitted to the ITA and ITC in dumping proceedings.[136] Such orders ordinarily preclude release to corporate counsel engaged in competitive decision-making, but permit release to outside counsel and outside experts.

§ 4.22 ___Administrative Determinations

Antidumping proceedings under U.S. law involve four stages. The ITC first makes a "preliminary determination" that, again "based on the best information available to it" at that time, there is "a reasonable indication" that the challenged practice presents a real or threatened material injury to the affected domestic industry.[137] Use of the best information available test encourages responses to DOJ dumping questionnaires by opponents. If the ITC makes such a finding, the ITA then makes a preliminary determination whether there is "a reasonable basis to believe" that goods are being sold at LTFV.[138] If the ITA makes such a

---

[133]   19 U.S.C. § 1673a(c)(4).
[134]   19 U.S.C. § 1673a(c).
[135]   *See* 19 U.S.C. § 1677e(b).
[136]   19 U.S.C. § 1677f.
[137]   19 U.S.C. § 1673b(a).
[138]   19 U.S.C. § 1673b(b).

preliminary determination, it proceeds to make a "final determination" concerning sales at LTFV.[139] If the ITA finds sales at LTFV as a final determination, the ITC then must make a final determination concerning injury.[140] Thus the chain of decision-making in antidumping proceedings runs as follows:

ITC Preliminary Injury Determination

ITA Preliminary Dumping Determination

ITA Final Dumping Determination

ITC Final Injury Determination

Congress has repeatedly amended U.S. antidumping law so as to accelerate the rate at which these determinations are made. At this point, it is common for the proceeding to be completed within one year. U.S. antidumping duties are then and in the future assessed retrospectively for each importation such that the amount payable varies for each importer and transaction.

Any goods imported after an ITA preliminary determination of sales at LTFV (Stage Two) will be subject to any antidumping duties imposed later, after final determinations are made.[141] In customs law parlance, liquidation of the goods is suspended. In "critical circumstances," the antidumping duties will also be imposed on goods entered 90 days *before* suspension of liquidation.[142] Critical circumstances exist when there is a prior history of dumping or the importer knew or should have known that the sales were below fair value, and there have been massive imports over a relatively short period of time.[143] Because the ITA has demonstrated a willingness to order retroactive antidumping duties and need not find injury as a result of the massive imports, the importer's risks in such a case may be substantial.

§ 4.23 _____The Importance of the ITA Preliminary Dumping Determination

As a practical matter, the ITA's *preliminary* determination that dumping has occurred will place significant, often overwhelming, pressure on the importers of the covered goods. This is so because at that point any covered goods become subject to antidumping duties that are ultimately determined once the ITA and ITC complete their investigations and make any affirmative final determinations. The

---

[139] 19 U.S.C. § 1673d(a).

[140] 19 U.S.C. § 1673d(b).

[141] 19 U.S.C. § 1673b(d).

[142] 19 U.S.C. 1673b(e).

[143] 19 U.S.C. 1673b(e)(1).

preliminary determination, therefore, tends to discourage or even cut off the imports, because at that point importers generally must post cash or bonds to cover any duties as determined by the ITA in its preliminary determination. At a minimum, they likely will have to raise their import prices—unless and until either the ITA or the ITC makes a contrary final determination once the agencies have completed their respective administrative proceedings.

Thus, once a petition is filed, importers will not know what their liabilities for duties will be and must post an expensive bond in the meantime to gain entry. Foreign exporters frequently raise their "United States prices" to the level of home market prices soon after such a preliminary determination. If they do, antidumping law will have accomplished its essential purpose. However, the U.S. Tariff Act disfavors termination of the proceeding on the basis of voluntary undertakings of compliance.[144]

United States antidumping proceedings may be settled by the ITA if the respondents formally agree to cease exporting to the United States within six months or agree to revise their prices so as to eliminate the margin of the dumping.[145] Because price revision agreements are hard to monitor, they are disfavored by the ITA. But an agreement to cease exports also cancels any outstanding suspension of liquidation. The total time secured in this manner may allow foreigners a window of opportunity to establish market presence prior to shifting production to the United States. If requested, the ITA and ITC may proceed to their final determinations after a settlement is agreed. If the respondents prevail, normal trading will resume; but if the petitioners prevail, the settlement agreement will remain in effect. The ITA monitors all settlement agreements and may assess civil penalties (in addition to antidumping duties) in the event of a breach.[146]

§ 4.24   U.S. Antidumping Duty Reviews

The ITA final determination of sales at LTFV establishes the amount of any antidumping duties. Because duties are not imposed to support any specific domestic price, they are set at the "margin of dumping" (the amount the "normal value" exceeds the United States price).[147] In the ordinary case, antidumping duties are retroactive to the date of the suspension of liquidation that occurred when the ITA preliminarily found dumping. However, if the ITC final determination is one of threatened (not actual) domestic

---

[144]   19 U.S.C. § 1673c.

[145]   19 U.S.C. § 1673c(b).

[146]   19 U.S.C. § 1673c(i).

[147]   19 U.S.C. § 1677(35).

injury, the duties usually apply as from the ITC's final decision and not retroactively to the suspension date.

The antidumping duty remains in force only as long as the dumping occurs. Upon request, annual ITA reviews are conducted.[148] The ITA also may review and revoke or modify any antidumping order if changed circumstances warrant such an action, but the burden of proof is on the proponent.[149] In accordance with the WTO Antidumping Agreement, the ITA must also conduct a review of finial antidumping determinations every five years.[150]

Problems in assessing and collecting antidumping duties may arise because the antidumping duty order applies to goods that do not exactly correspond to normal U.S. Harmonized Tariff Schedule (HTS) classifications. While the ITA is given some leeway to modify an antidumping order to accommodate such problems, it may not use them as an excuse to exclude merchandise falling within the scope of the order. Where, on the other hand, merchandise was deliberately excluded from the original antidumping order, the ITA may not subsequently include that merchandise in an anti-circumvention order (see immediately Section 4.26 below).[151]

§ 4.25 ____Anti-circumvention

In 1988, Congress enacted important amendments to Tariff Act to address the "circumvention" of antidumping duties. These "anti-circumvention" rules entered into force while the subject was under discussion in the GATT Uruguay Round negotiations. Ultimately, the WTO Antidumping Agreement included no substantive rules on anti-circumvention, but also did not forbid the practice.

The Tariff Act addresses circumvention in a variety of ways. First, it allows the ITA to ignore fictitious markets in the source country when calculating the foreign market "normal value."[152] Moreover, the ITA may include within the scope of an antidumping order merchandise "completed or assembled" in the United States if such merchandise includes "parts or components produced in the foreign country" that is the original subject of the order.[153] The principal requirements are that the process of completion or assembly in the United States is "minor or insignificant" and the

---

[148] 19 U.S.C. § 1675(a).

[149] 19 U.S.C. § 1675(b).

[150] 19 U.S.C. § 1675(c).

[151] See, e.g., Wheatland Tube Co. v. United States, 161 F.3d 1365 (Fed.Cir.1998).

[152] 19 U.S.C. § 1677b(a)(5).

[153] 19 U.S.C. § 1677j(a).

value of the components themselves is a "significant portion of the total value of the merchandise.[154]

Similarly, when the exporter ships the components to a third country for assembly and subsequent exportation to the United States, such circumvention efforts can be defeated by extending an antidumping order to those goods as well.[155] Again, such an action is appropriate if the assembly in the third country is "minor or insignificant" and the components themselves represent the principal value of the merchandise.[156]

§ 4.26 Appeals—United States Courts

A party to an administrative antidumping proceeding may appeal an adverse final determination of the ITA or ITC to the U.S. Court of International Trade (CIT). The CIT was established in 1980 as the successor to the U.S. Court of Customs. The CIT is an Article III court, and its nine judges are appointed by the President with the Advice and Consent of the Senate. The CIT possesses all the powers in law and equity of a U.S. District Court, including the authority to enter money judgments against the United States, but with three general limitations. These limitations (a) prohibit its issuance of injunctions or writs of mandamus in challenges to trade adjustment rulings, (b) allow it to issue only declaratory relief in suits for accelerated review of pre-importation administrative actions, and (c) limit its power to order disclosure of confidential information to a narrowly defined class of cases.

The CIT has "exclusive" subject matter jurisdiction over suits against the United States, its agencies, or its officers arising from any law pertaining to revenue from imports, tariffs, duties or embargoes, or the enforcement of such laws and certain related regulations. The court's exclusive jurisdiction also includes any civil action commenced by the United States that arises out of an import transaction, as well as the authority to review final agency decisions concerning antidumping duties and countervailing duties as well as eligibility for trade adjustment assistance.

CIT decisions may be appealed first to the Court of Appeals for the Federal Circuit (formerly the Court of Customs and Patent Appeals), and ultimately to the U.S. Supreme Court.

---

[154] 19 U.S.C. § 1677j(a)(2).

[155] 19 U.S.C. § 1677j(b).

[156] *Id.*

§ 4.27   Appeals—International Tribunals

International institutions also play an increasingly significant role in the resolution of trade disputes. The most important of these is the WTO's Dispute Settlement Body ("DSB"). Dissatisfied parties in domestic administrative proceedings may convince their government to challenge an adverse antidumping before the DSB based on alleged violations of the WTO Antidumping Agreement. As Chapter 1 examines in detail, proceedings before the DSB are governed by a separate WTO Agreement, the Dispute Settlement Understanding (DSU). The DSU generally provides that the involved member states first must pursue consultations. If those consultations are not successful, either party may request that the DSB establish a panel to investigate the dispute and issue a written report. Panel decisions are appealable on issues of law to the WTO's Appellate Body.

Three points are worthy of emphasis concerning proceedings before the DSB. First, since the WTO came into being in 1994, dispute settlement before the DSB, once initiated, is compulsory and binding.[157] Second, this dispute settlement option is not open to private litigants, only member state governments may file an action before the DSB. Finally, although formally binding, the WTO has no direct power to compel compliance with its decisions. Nonetheless, it may order compensation for the aggrieved state(s) or authorize retaliatory trade sanctions, and these may provide a significant incentive for an offending state to bring its domestic law into compliance.

Separately, a special international institution exists for trade disputes involving the three member states of the North American Free Trade Agreement (NAFTA)—the U.S., Canada, and Mexico. NAFTA uniquely provides for resolution of antidumping disputes through "bi-national panels." Such panels apply the domestic law of the importing country, and provide a substitute for judicial review of the decisions of administrative agencies of the importing country. Indeed, the initiation of a review under NAFTA divests the CIT of jurisdiction over the same dispute. Although the decisions of such bi-national panels are not formally binding in U.S. law, the ITA or ITC may decide to review any administrative action to conform to an adverse panel decision, including through a revocation or reduction of antidumping duties.

---

[157]   For more detail, see Section 1.14.

§ 4.28 ____WTO Rulings on U.S. Antidumping Law, Zeroing, The Byrd Amendment

The WTO Appellate Body (AB) has taken a restrictive view of what constitutes permissible antidumping duties and in fact has repeatedly ruled against the United States in disputes with other countries. In the *Thai-steel from Poland* dispute, for example, the WTO rejected a cursory material injury determination by the ITC, stressing that all relevant economic factors must be considered. Similarly, in the *United States–Hot-Rolled Steel from Japan* dispute, the AB found bias in the determination of normal value when low-priced sales from a respondent to an exporter were automatically excluded. The AB also indicated that injury determinations must include an analysis of captive production markets in addition to merchant markets. It thus observed that causation in such determinations must be rigorously scrutinized.

Separately, a WTO panel ruled that the Commerce Department's refusal to revoke an antidumping order against South Korean DRAMS was inconsistent with Article 11.2 of the Antidumping Agreement. Hence, U.S. regulations regarding the likelihood of continued dumping after a three-year hiatus are suspect under the Antidumping Agreement. The Court of International Trade, on the other hand, has found that the U.S. regulations in question are consistent with the WTO Antidumping Agreement. The Court took the position that the WTO panel ruling was not binding precedent, merely persuasive.

The Zeroing Controversy

In a series of decisions that ran through 2006, the WTO's Appellate Body also repeatedly ruled against "zeroing," a methodology used in dumping margin calculations by the United States, the EU and other WTO members. To understand this practice, first note that a foreign producer likely will have numerous sales in its home country. As a result, in order to calculate the "home market price," the ITA must use the *average* price from all such sales.[158] This average price is then compared to the "export price" to yield the dumping margin. Under zeroing, however, the ITA in effect considered only those home market sales that were *above* the export price; for sales *below* the export price, it simply assigned a "zero" (*i.e.*, not a negative number). Because on average this meant a higher home country comparison price, it also resulted in a higher average dumping margin.

---

[158] *See* 19 U.S.C. § 1677(35).

In a series of decisions, WTO panels declared that this practice violates United States' obligations under the Article 2.4 of the Antidumping Agreement.[159] Notwithstanding these decisions, the Federal Circuit has repeatedly upheld the methodology as a reasonable interpretation of the actual language in the Tariff Act.[160] In response to the repeated adverse rulings by the WTO, and the 2013 Federal Circuit judgment in *Union Steel,* the ITA has discontinued the practice of zeroing in antidumping investigations but maintained it in antidumping duty reviews.[161]

The "Byrd Amendment" Controversy

The WTO Appellate Body also ruled against the United States with respect to the Continued Dumping and Subsidy Offset Act of 2000 (CDSOA, also known as the "Byrd Amendment"). The controversial aspect of that Act was a mechanism under which the U.S. government funneled the antidumping duties that it collected back to the members of the affected domestic industry. As a result, CDSOA in effect subsidized domestic industries through antidumping procedures, because it made those industries the financial beneficiaries of any duties ultimately assessed.

Nine other member states of the WTO promptly challenged CDSOA pursuant to the procedures set forth in the WTO's Dispute Settlement Understanding (DSU). *See* Chapter 1. Following unsuccessful negotiations, a WTO panel concluded that CDSOA was inconsistent with Articles 5.4, 18.1, and 18.4 of the antidumping Agreement (as well as various provisions of other WTO Agreements). The United States then appealed to the WTO's Appellate Body (AB).

In its ruling, the AB first observed that CDSOA was subject to the obligations in the Antidumping Agreement because it was a "specific action against" dumping. It also found that the only permitted responses to dumping under the Antidumping Agreement are "definitive antidumping duties, provisional measures and price undertakings." The AB ultimately concluded that, because CDSOA did not fall into any of these allowed responses to dumping, it was

---

[159] *See, e.g.*, Appellate Body Report, *United States—Laws, Regulations and Methodology for Calculating Dumping Margins ("Zeroing")*, ¶ 222, WT/DS294/AB/R, adopted May 9, 2006.

[160] *See, e.g., Corus Staal BV v. U.S. Dep't of Commerce*, 395 F.3d 1343 (Fed. Cir. 2005); *Union Steel v. United States*, ___ F.3d ___ (Fed. Cir. 2013) (use of zeroing permissible in administrative reviews but not antidumping investigations).

[161] *See Antidumping Proceedings: Calculation of the Weighted Average Dumping Margin and Assessment Rate in Certain Antidumping Proceedings*, 75 Fed. Reg. 81533 (Dep't Commerce Dec. 28, 2010); *Union Steel, supra* note 160.

inconsistent with U.S. obligations under the Antidumping Agreement.[162]

When the United State failed to comply with this decision, the WTO authorized the claimant countries to retaliate in their domestic trade laws as permitted under Article 22 of the DSU.[163] Congress then bowed to the pressure created by the WTO decisions and repealed CDSOA effective October 1, 2007.

§ 4.29 Text of the WTO Antidumping Agreement

(Agreement on Implementation of Article VI of the General Agreement on Tariffs and Trade 1994)

(Selected Provisions)

PART I

Article 1

Principles

An anti-dumping measure shall be applied only under the circumstances provided for in Article VI of GATT 1994 and pursuant to investigations initiated[1] and conducted in accordance with the provisions of this Agreement. The following provisions govern the application of Article VI of GATT 1994 in so far as action is taken under anti-dumping legislation or regulations.

Article 2

Determination of Dumping

2.1   For the purpose of this Agreement, a product is to be considered as being dumped, i.e. introduced into the commerce of another country at less than its normal value, if the export price of the product exported from one country to another is less than the comparable price, in the ordinary course of trade, for the like product when destined for consumption in the exporting country.

2.2   When there are no sales of the like product in the ordinary course of trade in the domestic market of the exporting country or when, because of the particular market situation or the low volume of the sales in the domestic market of the exporting country,[2] such sales do not permit a

---

[162]   *See Appellate Body Report, United States—Continued Dumping and Subsidy Offset Act of 2000*, WT/DS217/R, WT/DS234/R, Jan. 16, 2003.

[163]   *See, e.g., United States—Continued Dumping and Subsidy Offset Act of 2000, Original Complaint by Canada—Recourse to Arbitration by the United States under Article 22.6 of the DSU*, WT/DS234/ARB/CAN, 31 August 2004.

[1]   The term "initiated" as used in this Agreement means the procedural action by which a Member formally commences an investigation as provided in Article 5.

[2]   Sales of the like product destined for consumption in the domestic market of the exporting country shall normally be considered a sufficient quantity for the determination of the normal value if such sales constitute 5 per cent or more of the sales of the product under consideration to the importing Member, provided that a

proper comparison, the margin of dumping shall be determined by comparison with a comparable price of the like product when exported to an appropriate third country, provided that this price is representative, or with the cost of production in the country of origin plus a reasonable amount for administrative, selling and general costs and for profits.

2.2.1 Sales of the like product in the domestic market of the exporting country or sales to a third country at prices below per unit (fixed and variable) costs of production plus administrative, selling and general costs may be treated as not being in the ordinary course of trade by reason of price and may be disregarded in determining normal value only if the authorities[3] determine that such sales are made within an extended period of time[4] in substantial quantities[5] and are at prices which do not provide for the recovery of all costs within a reasonable period of time. If prices which are below per unit costs at the time of sale are above weighted average per unit costs for the period of investigation, such prices shall be considered to provide for recovery of costs within a reasonable period of time.

2.2.1.1   For the purpose of paragraph 2, costs shall normally be calculated on the basis of records kept by the exporter or producer under investigation, provided that such records are in accordance with the generally accepted accounting principles of the exporting country and reasonably reflect the costs associated with the production and sale of the product under consideration. Authorities shall consider all available evidence on the proper allocation of costs, including that which is made available by the exporter or producer in the course of the investigation provided that such allocations have been historically utilized by the exporter or producer, in particular in relation to establishing appropriate amortization and depreciation periods and allowances for capital expenditures and other development costs. Unless already reflected in the cost allocations under this sub-paragraph, costs shall be adjusted appropriately for those non-recurring items of cost which benefit future and/or current production,

---

lower ratio should be acceptable where the evidence demonstrates that domestic sales at such lower ratio are nonetheless of sufficient magnitude to provide for a proper comparison.

[3]   When in this Agreement the term "authorities" is used, it shall be interpreted as meaning authorities at an appropriate senior level.

[4]   The extended period of time should normally be one year but shall in no case be less than six months.

[5]   Sales below per unit costs are made in substantial quantities when the authorities establish that the weighted average selling price of the transactions under consideration for the determination of the normal value is below the weighted average per unit costs, or that the volume of sales below per unit costs represents not less than 20 per cent of the volume sold in transactions under consideration for the determination of the normal value.

or for circumstances in which costs during the period of investigation are affected by start-up operations.[6]

2.2.2 For the purpose of paragraph 2, the amounts for administrative, selling and general costs and for profits shall be based on actual data pertaining to production and sales in the ordinary course of trade of the like product by the exporter or producer under investigation. When such amounts cannot be determined on this basis, the amounts may be determined on the basis of:

> (i) the actual amounts incurred and realized by the exporter or producer in question in respect of production and sales in the domestic market of the country of origin of the same general category of products;

> (ii) the weighted average of the actual amounts incurred and realized by other exporters or producers subject to investigation in respect of production and sales of the like product in the domestic market of the country of origin;

> (iii) any other reasonable method, provided that the amount for profit so established shall not exceed the profit normally realized by other exporters or producers on sales of products of the same general category in the domestic market of the country of origin.

2.3   In cases where there is no export price or where it appears to the authorities concerned that the export price is unreliable because of association or a compensatory arrangement between the exporter and the importer or a third party, the export price may be constructed on the basis of the price at which the imported products are first resold to an independent buyer, or if the products are not resold to an independent buyer, or not resold in the condition as imported, on such reasonable basis as the authorities may determine.

2.4   A fair comparison shall be made between the export price and the normal value. This comparison shall be made at the same level of trade, normally at the ex-factory level, and in respect of sales made at as nearly as possible the same time. Due allowance shall be made in each case, on its merits, for differences which affect price comparability, including differences in conditions and terms of sale, taxation, levels of trade, quantities, physical characteristics, and any other differences which are also demonstrated to affect price comparability.[7] In the cases referred to in paragraph 3, allowances for costs, including duties and taxes, incurred

---

[6]   The adjustment made for start-up operations shall reflect the costs at the end of the start-up period or, if that period extends beyond the period of investigation, the most recent costs which can reasonably be taken into account by the authorities during the investigation.

[7]   It is understood that some of the above factors may overlap, and authorities shall ensure that they do not duplicate adjustments that have been already made under this provision.

between importation and resale, and for profits accruing, should also be made. If in these cases price comparability has been affected, the authorities shall establish the normal value at a level of trade equivalent to the level of trade of the constructed export price, or shall make due allowance as warranted under this paragraph. The authorities shall indicate to the parties in question what information is necessary to ensure a fair comparison and shall not impose an unreasonable burden of proof on those parties.

2.4.1   When the comparison under paragraph 4 requires a conversion of currencies, such conversion should be made using the rate of exchange on the date of sale,[8] provided that when a sale of foreign currency on forward markets is directly linked to the export sale involved, the rate of exchange in the forward sale shall be used. Fluctuations in exchange rates shall be ignored and in an investigation the authorities shall allow exporters at least 60 days to have adjusted their export prices to reflect sustained movements in exchange rates during the period of investigation.

2.4.2   Subject to the provisions governing fair comparison in paragraph 4, the existence of margins of dumping during the investigation phase shall normally be established on the basis of a comparison of a weighted average normal value with a weighted average of prices of all comparable export transactions or by a comparison of normal value and export prices on a transaction-to-transaction basis. A normal value established on a weighted average basis may be compared to prices of individual export transactions if the authorities find a pattern of export prices which differ significantly among different purchasers, regions or time periods, and if an explanation is provided as to why such differences cannot be taken into account appropriately by the use of a weighted average-to-weighted average or transaction-to-transaction comparison.

2.5   In the case where products are not imported directly from the country of origin but are exported to the importing Member from an intermediate country, the price at which the products are sold from the country of export to the importing Member shall normally be compared with the comparable price in the country of export. However, comparison may be made with the price in the country of origin, if, for example, the products are merely transshipped through the country of export, or such products are not produced in the country of export, or there is no comparable price for them in the country of export.

2.6   Throughout this Agreement the term "like product" ("produit similaire") shall be interpreted to mean a product which is identical, i.e. alike in all respects to the product under consideration, or in the absence of such a product, another product which, although not alike in all respects,

---

8   Normally, the date of sale would be the date of contract, purchase order, order confirmation, or invoice, whichever establishes the material terms of sale.

has characteristics closely resembling those of the product under consideration.

2.7   This Article is without prejudice to the second Supplementary Provision to paragraph 1 of Article VI in Annex I to GATT 1994.

Article 3

Determination of Injury[9]

3.1   A determination of injury for purposes of Article VI of GATT 1994 shall be based on positive evidence and involve an objective examination of both *(a)* the volume of the dumped imports and the effect of the dumped imports on prices in the domestic market for like products, and *(b)* the consequent impact of these imports on domestic producers of such products.

3.2   With regard to the volume of the dumped imports, the investigating authorities shall consider whether there has been a significant increase in dumped imports, either in absolute terms or relative to production or consumption in the importing Member. With regard to the effect of the dumped imports on prices, the investigating authorities shall consider whether there has been a significant price undercutting by the dumped imports as compared with the price of a like product of the importing Member, or whether the effect of such imports is otherwise to depress prices to a significant degree or prevent price increases, which otherwise would have occurred, to a significant degree. No one or several of these factors can necessarily give decisive guidance.

3.3   Where imports of a product from more than one country are simultaneously subject to anti-dumping investigations, the investigating authorities may cumulatively assess the effects of such imports only if they determine that *(a)* the margin of dumping established in relation to the imports from each country is more than *de minimis* as defined in paragraph 8 of Article 5 and the volume of imports from each country is not negligible and *(b)* a cumulative assessment of the effects of the imports is appropriate in light of the conditions of competition between the imported products and the conditions of competition between the imported products and the like domestic product.

3.4   The examination of the impact of the dumped imports on the domestic industry concerned shall include an evaluation of all relevant economic factors and indices having a bearing on the state of the industry, including actual and potential decline in sales, profits, output, market share, productivity, return on investments, or utilization of capacity; factors affecting domestic prices; the magnitude of the margin of dumping; actual and potential negative effects on cash flow, inventories, employment, wages, growth, ability to raise capital or investments. This list is not

---

[9]   Under this Agreement the term "injury" shall, unless otherwise specified, be taken to mean material injury to a domestic industry, threat of material injury to a domestic industry or material retardation of the establishment of such an industry and shall be interpreted in accordance with the provisions of this Article.

exhaustive, nor can one or several of these factors necessarily give decisive guidance.

3.5   It must be demonstrated that the dumped imports are, through the effects of dumping, as set forth in paragraphs 2 and 4, causing injury within the meaning of this Agreement. The demonstration of a causal relationship between the dumped imports and the injury to the domestic industry shall be based on an examination of all relevant evidence before the authorities. The authorities shall also examine any known factors other than the dumped imports which at the same time are injuring the domestic industry, and the injuries caused by these other factors must not be attributed to the dumped imports. Factors which may be relevant in this respect include, *inter alia,* the volume and prices of imports not sold at dumping prices, contraction in demand or changes in the patterns of consumption, trade restrictive practices of and competition between the foreign and domestic producers, developments in technology and the export performance and productivity of the domestic industry.

3.6   The effect of the dumped imports shall be assessed in relation to the domestic production of the like product when available data permit the separate identification of that production on the basis of such criteria as the production process, producers' sales and profits. If such separate identification of that production is not possible, the effects of the dumped imports shall be assessed by the examination of the production of the narrowest group or range of products, which includes the like product, for which the necessary information can be provided.

3.7   A determination of a threat of material injury shall be based on facts and not merely on allegation, conjecture or remote possibility. The change in circumstances which would create a situation in which the dumping would cause injury must be clearly foreseen and imminent.[10] In making a determination regarding the existence of a threat of material injury, the authorities should consider, *inter alia,* such factors as:

   (i) a significant rate of increase of dumped imports into the domestic market indicating the likelihood of substantially increased importation;

   (ii) sufficient freely disposable, or an imminent, substantial increase in, capacity of the exporter indicating the likelihood of substantially increased dumped exports to the importing Member's market, taking into account the availability of other export markets to absorb any additional exports;

   (iii) whether imports are entering at prices that will have a significant depressing or suppressing effect on domestic prices, and would likely increase demand for further imports; and

   (iv) inventories of the product being investigated.

---

[10]   One example, though not an exclusive one, is that there is convincing reason to believe that there will be, in the near future, substantially increased importation of the product at dumped prices.

No one of these factors by itself can necessarily give decisive guidance but the totality of the factors considered must lead to the conclusion that further dumped exports are imminent and that, unless protective action is taken, material injury would occur.

3.8   With respect to cases where injury is threatened by dumped imports, the application of anti-dumping measures shall be considered and decided with special care.

Article 4

Definition of Domestic Industry

4.1   For the purposes of this Agreement, the term "domestic industry" shall be interpreted as referring to the domestic producers as a whole of the like products or to those of them whose collective output of the products constitutes a major proportion of the total domestic production of those products, except that:

> (i) when producers are related[11] to the exporters or importers or are themselves importers of the allegedly dumped product, the term "domestic industry" may be interpreted as referring to the rest of the producers;

> (ii) in exceptional circumstances the territory of a Member may, for the production in question, be divided into two or more competitive markets and the producers within each market may be regarded as a separate industry if *(a)* the producers within such market sell all or almost all of their production of the product in question in that market, and *(b)* the demand in that market is not to any substantial degree supplied by producers of the product in question located elsewhere in the territory. * * *

4.2   When the domestic industry has been interpreted as referring to the producers in a certain area, i.e. a market as defined in paragraph 1(ii), anti-dumping duties shall be levied only on the products in question consigned for final consumption to that area. When the constitutional law of the importing Member does not permit the levying of anti-dumping duties on such a basis, the importing Member may levy the anti-dumping duties without limitation only if *(a)* the exporters shall have been given an opportunity to cease exporting at dumped prices to the area concerned or otherwise give assurances pursuant to Article 8 and adequate assurances in this regard have not been promptly given, and *(b)* such duties cannot be levied only on products of specific producers which supply the area in question.

---

[11]   For the purpose of this paragraph, producers shall be deemed to be related to exporters or importers only if *(a)* one of them directly or indirectly controls the other; or *(b)* both of them are directly or indirectly controlled by a third person; or *(c)* together they directly or indirectly control a third person, provided that there are grounds for believing or suspecting that the effect of the relationship is such as to cause the producer concerned to behave differently from non-related producers. For the purpose of this paragraph, one shall be deemed to control another when the former is legally or operationally in a position to exercise restraint or direction over the latter.

4.3   Where two or more countries have reached under the provisions of paragraph 8(a) of Article XXIV of GATT 1994 such a level of integration that they have the characteristics of a single, unified market, the industry in the entire area of integration shall be taken to be the domestic industry referred to in paragraph 1.

4.4   The provisions of paragraph 6 of Article 3 shall be applicable to this Article.

Article 5

Initiation and Subsequent Investigation

5.1   Except as provided for in paragraph 6, an investigation to determine the existence, degree and effect of any alleged dumping shall be initiated upon a written application by or on behalf of the domestic industry.

5.2   An application under paragraph 1 shall include evidence of *(a)* dumping, *(b)* injury within the meaning of Article VI of GATT 1994 as interpreted by this Agreement and *(c)* a causal link between the dumped imports and the alleged injury. Simple assertion, unsubstantiated by relevant evidence, cannot be considered sufficient to meet the requirements of this paragraph. The application shall contain such information as is reasonably available to the applicant on the following:

(i) the identity of the applicant and a description of the volume and value of the domestic production of the like product by the applicant. Where a written application is made on behalf of the domestic industry, the application shall identify the industry on behalf of which the application is made by a list of all known domestic producers of the like product (or associations of domestic producers of the like product) and, to the extent possible, a description of the volume and value of domestic production of the like product accounted for by such producers;

(ii) a complete description of the allegedly dumped product, the names of the country or countries of origin or export in question, the identity of each known exporter or foreign producer and a list of known persons importing the product in question;

(iii) information on prices at which the product in question is sold when destined for consumption in the domestic markets of the country or countries of origin or export (or, where appropriate, information on the prices at which the product is sold from the country or countries of origin or export to a third country or countries, or on the constructed value of the product) and information on export prices or, where appropriate, on the prices at which the product is first resold to an independent buyer in the territory of the importing Member;

(iv) information on the evolution of the volume of the allegedly dumped imports, the effect of these imports on prices of the like product in the domestic market and the consequent impact of the imports on the domestic industry, as demonstrated by relevant factors and indices having a bearing on the state of the domestic industry, such as those listed in paragraphs 2 and 4 of Article 3.

5.3   The authorities shall examine the accuracy and adequacy of the evidence provided in the application to determine whether there is sufficient evidence to justify the initiation of an investigation.

5.4   An investigation shall not be initiated pursuant to paragraph 1 unless the authorities have determined, on the basis of an examination of the degree of support for, or opposition to, the application expressed by domestic producers of the like product, that the application has been made by or on behalf of the domestic industry.[12] The application shall be considered to have been made "by or on behalf of the domestic industry" if it is supported by those domestic producers whose collective output constitutes more than 50 per cent of the total production of the like product produced by that portion of the domestic industry expressing either support for or opposition to the application. However, no investigation shall be initiated when domestic producers expressly supporting the application account for less than 25 per cent of total production of the like product produced by the domestic industry.

* * *

5.6   If, in special circumstances, the authorities concerned decide to initiate an investigation without having received a written application by or on behalf of a domestic industry for the initiation of such investigation, they shall proceed only if they have sufficient evidence of dumping, injury and a causal link, as described in paragraph 2, to justify the initiation of an investigation.

* * *

Article 6

Evidence

6.1   All interested parties in an anti-dumping investigation shall be given notice of the information which the authorities require and ample opportunity to present in writing all evidence which they consider relevant in respect of the investigation in question.

6.1.1   Exporters   or   foreign   producers   receiving questionnaires used in an anti-dumping investigation shall be given at least 30 days for reply. Due consideration should be given to any request for an extension of the 30-day period and, upon cause shown, such an extension should be granted whenever practicable.

6.1.2   Subject to the requirement to protect confidential information, evidence presented in writing by one interested

---

[12]   Members are aware that in the territory of certain Members employees of domestic producers of the like product or representatives of those employees may make or support an application for an investigation under paragraph 1.

party shall be made available promptly to other interested parties participating in the investigation.

6.1.3 As soon as an investigation has been initiated, the authorities shall provide the full text of the written application received under paragraph 1 of Article 5 to the known exporters and to the authorities of the exporting Member and shall make it available, upon request, to other interested parties involved. Due regard shall be paid to the requirement for the protection of confidential information, as provided for in paragraph 5.

6.2 Throughout the anti-dumping investigation all interested parties shall have a full opportunity for the defence of their interests. To this end, the authorities shall, on request, provide opportunities for all interested parties to meet those parties with adverse interests, so that opposing views may be presented and rebuttal arguments offered. Provision of such opportunities must take account of the need to preserve confidentiality and of the convenience to the parties. There shall be no obligation on any party to attend a meeting, and failure to do so shall not be prejudicial to that party's case. Interested parties shall also have the right, on justification, to present other information orally.

* * *

6.5 Any information which is by nature confidential (for example, because its disclosure would be of significant competitive advantage to a competitor or because its disclosure would have a significantly adverse effect upon a person supplying the information or upon a person from whom that person acquired the information), or which is provided on a confidential basis by parties to an investigation shall, upon good cause shown, be treated as such by the authorities. Such information shall not be disclosed without specific permission of the party submitting it.

6.5.1 The authorities shall require interested parties providing confidential information to furnish non-confidential summaries thereof. These summaries shall be in sufficient detail to permit a reasonable understanding of the substance of the information submitted in confidence. In exceptional circumstances, such parties may indicate that such information is not susceptible of summary. In such exceptional circumstances, a statement of the reasons why summarization is not possible must be provided.

6.5.2 If the authorities find that a request for confidentiality is not warranted and if the supplier of the information is either unwilling to make the information public or to authorize its disclosure in generalized or summary form, the authorities may disregard such information unless it can be demonstrated to their satisfaction from appropriate sources that the information is correct.

6.6 Except in circumstances provided for in paragraph 8, the authorities shall during the course of an investigation satisfy themselves as to the accuracy of the information supplied by interested parties upon which their findings are based.

6.7 In order to verify information provided or to obtain further details, the authorities may carry out investigations in the territory of other Members as required, provided they obtain the agreement of the firms concerned and notify the representatives of the government of the Member in question, and unless that Member objects to the investigation.
* * *

6.8 In cases in which any interested party refuses access to, or otherwise does not provide, necessary information within a reasonable period or significantly impedes the investigation, preliminary and final determinations, affirmative or negative, may be made on the basis of the facts available. The provisions of Annex II shall be observed in the application of this paragraph.

* * *

6.10 The authorities shall, as a rule, determine an individual margin of dumping for each known exporter or producer concerned of the product under investigation. In cases where the number of exporters, producers, importers or types of products involved is so large as to make such a determination impracticable, the authorities may limit their examination either to a reasonable number of interested parties or products by using samples which are statistically valid on the basis of information available to the authorities at the time of the selection, or to the largest percentage of the volume of the exports from the country in question which can reasonably be investigated.

6.10.1 Any selection of exporters, producers, importers or types of products made under this paragraph shall preferably be chosen in consultation with and with the consent of the exporters, producers or importers concerned.

6.10.2 In cases where the authorities have limited their examination, as provided for in this paragraph, they shall nevertheless determine an individual margin of dumping for any exporter or producer not initially selected who submits the necessary information in time for that information to be considered during the course of the investigation, except where the number of exporters or producers is so large that individual examinations would be unduly burdensome to the authorities and prevent the timely completion of the investigation. Voluntary responses shall not be discouraged.

* * *

6.12 The authorities shall provide opportunities for industrial users of the product under investigation, and for representative consumer organizations in cases where the product is commonly sold at the retail level, to provide information which is relevant to the investigation regarding dumping, injury and causality.

6.13 The authorities shall take due account of any difficulties experienced by interested parties, in particular small companies, in supplying information requested, and shall provide any assistance practicable.

* * *

Article 7

Provisional Measures

7.1 Provisional measures may be applied only if:

(i) an investigation has been initiated in accordance with the provisions of Article 5, a public notice has been given to that effect and interested parties have been given adequate opportunities to submit information and make comments;

(ii) a preliminary affirmative determination has been made of dumping and consequent injury to a domestic industry; and

(iii) the authorities concerned judge such measures necessary to prevent injury being caused during the investigation.

7.2 Provisional measures may take the form of a provisional duty or, preferably, a security—by cash deposit or bond—equal to the amount of the anti-dumping duty provisionally estimated, being not greater than the provisionally estimated margin of dumping. Withholding of appraisement is an appropriate provisional measure, provided that the normal duty and the estimated amount of the anti-dumping duty be indicated and as long as the withholding of appraisement is subject to the same conditions as other provisional measures.

7.3 Provisional measures shall not be applied sooner than 60 days from the date of initiation of the investigation.

7.4 The application of provisional measures shall be limited to as short a period as possible, not exceeding four months or, on decision of the authorities concerned, upon request by exporters representing a significant percentage of the trade involved, to a period not exceeding six months. When authorities, in the course of an investigation, examine whether a duty lower than the margin of dumping would be sufficient to remove injury, these periods may be six and nine months, respectively.

7.5 The relevant provisions of Article 9 shall be followed in the application of provisional measures.

Article 8

Price Undertakings

8.1 Proceedings may[19] be suspended or terminated without the imposition of provisional measures or anti-dumping duties upon receipt of

---

[19] The word "may" shall not be interpreted to allow the simultaneous continuation of proceedings with the implementation of price undertakings except as provided in paragraph 4.

satisfactory voluntary undertakings from any exporter to revise its prices or to cease exports to the area in question at dumped prices so that the authorities are satisfied that the injurious effect of the dumping is eliminated. Price increases under such undertakings shall not be higher than necessary to eliminate the margin of dumping. It is desirable that the price increases be less than the margin of dumping if such increases would be adequate to remove the injury to the domestic industry.

8.2 Price undertakings shall not be sought or accepted from exporters unless the authorities of the importing Member have made a preliminary affirmative determination of dumping and injury caused by such dumping.

8.3 Undertakings offered need not be accepted if the authorities consider their acceptance impractical, for example, if the number of actual or potential exporters is too great, or for other reasons, including reasons of general policy. Should the case arise and where practicable, the authorities shall provide to the exporter the reasons which have led them to consider acceptance of an undertaking as inappropriate, and shall, to the extent possible, give the exporter an opportunity to make comments thereon.

8.4 If an undertaking is accepted, the investigation of dumping and injury shall nevertheless be completed if the exporter so desires or the authorities so decide. In such a case, if a negative determination of dumping or injury is made, the undertaking shall automatically lapse, except in cases where such a determination is due in large part to the existence of a price undertaking. In such cases, the authorities may require that an undertaking be maintained for a reasonable period consistent with the provisions of this Agreement. In the event that an affirmative determination of dumping and injury is made, the undertaking shall continue consistent with its terms and the provisions of this Agreement.

8.5 Price undertakings may be suggested by the authorities of the importing Member, but no exporter shall be forced to enter into such undertakings. The fact that exporters do not offer such undertakings, or do not accept an invitation to do so, shall in no way prejudice the consideration of the case. However, the authorities are free to determine that a threat of injury is more likely to be realized if the dumped imports continue.

8.6 Authorities of an importing Member may require any exporter from whom an undertaking has been accepted to provide periodically information relevant to the fulfilment of such an undertaking and to permit verification of pertinent data. In case of violation of an undertaking, the authorities of the importing Member may take, under this Agreement in conformity with its provisions, expeditious actions which may constitute immediate application of provisional measures using the best information available. In such cases, definitive duties may be levied in accordance with this Agreement on products entered for consumption not more than 90 days before the application of such provisional measures, except that any such retroactive assessment shall not apply to imports entered before the violation of the undertaking.

Article 9

Imposition and Collection of Anti-Dumping Duties

9.1   The decision whether or not to impose an anti-dumping duty in cases where all requirements for the imposition have been fulfilled, and the decision whether the amount of the anti-dumping duty to be imposed shall be the full margin of dumping or less, are decisions to be made by the authorities of the importing Member. It is desirable that the imposition be permissive in the territory of all Members, and that the duty be less than the margin if such lesser duty would be adequate to remove the injury to the domestic industry.

9.2   When an anti-dumping duty is imposed in respect of any product, such anti-dumping duty shall be collected in the appropriate amounts in each case, on a non-discriminatory basis on imports of such product from all sources found to be dumped and causing injury, except as to imports from those sources from which price undertakings under the terms of this Agreement have been accepted. The authorities shall name the supplier or suppliers of the product concerned. If, however, several suppliers from the same country are involved, and it is impracticable to name all these suppliers, the authorities may name the supplying country concerned. If several suppliers from more than one country are involved, the authorities may name either all the suppliers involved, or, if this is impracticable, all the supplying countries involved.

9.3   The amount of the anti-dumping duty shall not exceed the margin of dumping as established under Article 2.

* * *

Article 10

Retroactivity

10.1 Provisional measures and anti-dumping duties shall only be applied to products which enter for consumption after the time when the decision taken under paragraph 1 of Article 7 and paragraph 1 of Article 9, respectively, enters into force, subject to the exceptions set out in this Article.

* * *

Article 11

Duration and Review of Anti-Dumping Duties and Price Undertakings

11.1 An anti-dumping duty shall remain in force only as long as and to the extent necessary to counteract dumping which is causing injury.

11.2 The authorities shall review the need for the continued imposition of the duty, where warranted, on their own initiative or, provided that a reasonable period of time has elapsed since the imposition of the definitive anti-dumping duty, upon request by any interested party which submits positive information substantiating the need for a review. Interested parties shall have the right to request the authorities to examine whether the continued imposition of the duty is necessary to offset dumping, whether the injury would be likely to continue or recur if the duty were removed or varied, or both. If, as a result of the review under this paragraph, the authorities determine that the anti-dumping duty is no longer warranted, it shall be terminated immediately.

11.3 Notwithstanding the provisions of paragraphs 1 and 2, any definitive anti-dumping duty shall be terminated on a date not later than five years from its imposition (or from the date of the most recent review under paragraph 2 if that review has covered both dumping and injury, or under this paragraph), unless the authorities determine, in a review initiated before that date on their own initiative or upon a duly substantiated request made by or on behalf of the domestic industry within a reasonable period of time prior to that date, that the expiry of the duty would be likely to lead to continuation or recurrence of dumping and injury. The duty may remain in force pending the outcome of such a review.

11.4 The provisions of Article 6 regarding evidence and procedure shall apply to any review carried out under this Article. Any such review shall be carried out expeditiously and shall normally be concluded within 12 months of the date of initiation of the review.

11.5 The provisions of this Article shall apply *mutatis mutandis* to price undertakings accepted under Article 8.

Article 12

Public Notice and Explanation of Determinations

12.1 When the authorities are satisfied that there is sufficient evidence to justify the initiation of an anti-dumping investigation pursuant to Article 5, the Member or Members the products of which are subject to such investigation and other interested parties known to the investigating authorities to have an interest therein shall be notified and a public notice shall be given.

12.1.1 A public notice of the initiation of an investigation shall contain, or otherwise make available through a separate report, adequate information on the following:

(i) the name of the exporting country or countries and the product involved;

(ii) the date of initiation of the investigation;

(iii) the basis on which dumping is alleged in the application;

(iv) a summary of the factors on which the allegation of injury is based;

(v) the address to which representations by interested parties should be directed;

(vi) the time-limits allowed to interested parties for making their views known.

12.2 Public notice shall be given of any preliminary or final determination, whether affirmative or negative, of any decision to accept an undertaking pursuant to Article 8, of the termination of such an undertaking, and of the termination of a definitive anti-dumping duty. * * *

12.2.1   A public notice of the imposition of provisional measures shall set forth, or otherwise make available through a separate report, sufficiently detailed explanations for the preliminary determinations on dumping and injury and shall refer to the matters of fact and law which have led to arguments being accepted or rejected. Such a notice or report shall, due regard being paid to the requirement for the protection of confidential information, contain in particular:

(i) the names of the suppliers, or when this is impracticable, the supplying countries involved;

(ii) a description of the product which is sufficient for customs purposes;

(iii) the margins of dumping established and a full explanation of the reasons for the methodology used in the establishment and comparison of the export price and the normal value under Article 2;

(iv) considerations relevant to the injury determination as set out in Article 3;

(v) the main reasons leading to the determination.

12.2.2   A public notice of conclusion or suspension of an investigation in the case of an affirmative determination providing for the imposition of a definitive duty or the acceptance of a price undertaking shall contain, or otherwise make available through a separate report, all relevant information on the matters of fact and law and reasons which have led to the imposition of final measures or the acceptance of a price undertaking, due regard being paid to the requirement for the protection of confidential information. In particular, the notice or report shall contain the information described in subparagraph 2.1, as well as the reasons for the acceptance or rejection of relevant arguments or claims made by the exporters and importers, and the basis for any decision made under subparagraph 10.2 of Article 6.

12.2.3   A public notice of the termination or suspension of an investigation following the acceptance of an undertaking pursuant to Article 8 shall include, or otherwise make available through a separate report, the non-confidential part of this undertaking.

12.3 The provisions of this Article shall apply *mutatis mutandis* to the initiation and completion of reviews pursuant to Article 11 and to decisions under Article 10 to apply duties retroactively.

Article 13

Judicial Review

Each Member whose national legislation contains provisions on anti-dumping measures shall maintain judicial, arbitral or administrative tribunals or procedures for the purpose, *inter alia,* of the prompt review of administrative actions relating to final determinations and reviews of determinations within the meaning of Article 11. Such tribunals or procedures shall be independent of the authorities responsible for the determination or review in question.

Article 14

Anti-Dumping Action on Behalf of a Third Country

14.1 An application for anti-dumping action on behalf of a third country shall be made by the authorities of the third country requesting action.

14.2 Such an application shall be supported by price information to show that the imports are being dumped and by detailed information to show that the alleged dumping is causing injury to the domestic industry concerned in the third country. The government of the third country shall afford all assistance to the authorities of the importing country to obtain any further information which the latter may require.

14.3 In considering such an application, the authorities of the importing country shall consider the effects of the alleged dumping on the industry concerned as a whole in the third country; that is to say, the injury shall not be assessed in relation only to the effect of the alleged dumping on the industry's exports to the importing country or even on the industry's total exports.

14.4 The decision whether or not to proceed with a case shall rest with the importing country. If the importing country decides that it is prepared to take action, the initiation of the approach to the Council for Trade in Goods seeking its approval for such action shall rest with the importing country.

Article 15

Developing Country Members

It is recognized that special regard must be given by developed country Members to the special situation of developing country Members when considering the application of anti-dumping measures under this Agreement. Possibilities of constructive remedies provided for by this Agreement shall be explored before applying anti-dumping duties where they would affect the essential interests of developing country Members.

PART II

* * *

Article 17

Consultation and Dispute Settlement

17.1 Except as otherwise provided herein, the Dispute Settlement Understanding is applicable to consultations and the settlement of disputes under this Agreement.

17.2 Each Member shall afford sympathetic consideration to, and shall afford adequate opportunity for consultation regarding, representations made by another Member with respect to any matter affecting the operation of this Agreement.

17.3 If any Member considers that any benefit accruing to it, directly or indirectly, under this Agreement is being nullified or impaired, or that the achievement of any objective is being impeded, by another Member or Members, it may, with a view to reaching a mutually satisfactory resolution of the matter, request in writing consultations with the Member or Members in question. Each Member shall afford sympathetic consideration to any request from another Member for consultation.

17.4 If the Member that requested consultations considers that the consultations pursuant to paragraph 3 have failed to achieve a mutually agreed solution, and if final action has been taken by the administering authorities of the importing Member to levy definitive anti-dumping duties or to accept price undertakings, it may refer the matter to the Dispute Settlement Body ("DSB"). When a provisional measure has a significant impact and the Member that requested consultations considers that the measure was taken contrary to the provisions of paragraph 1 of Article 7, that Member may also refer such matter to the DSB.

17.5 The DSB shall, at the request of the complaining party, establish a panel to examine the matter based upon:

(i) a written statement of the Member making the request indicating how a benefit accruing to it, directly or indirectly, under this Agreement has been nullified or impaired, or that the achieving of the objectives of the Agreement is being impeded, and

(ii) the facts made available in conformity with appropriate domestic procedures to the authorities of the importing Member.

17.6 In examining the matter referred to in paragraph 5:

(i) in its assessment of the facts of the matter, the panel shall determine whether the authorities' establishment of the facts was proper and whether their evaluation of those facts was unbiased and objective. If the establishment of the facts was proper and the evaluation was unbiased and objective, even though the panel might have reached a different conclusion, the evaluation shall not be overturned;

(ii) the panel shall interpret the relevant provisions of the Agreement in accordance with customary rules of interpretation of public international law. Where the panel finds that a relevant provision of the Agreement admits of more than one permissible interpretation, the panel shall find the authorities' measure to be in conformity with the Agreement if it rests upon one of those permissible interpretations.

* * *

ANNEX II

BEST INFORMATION AVAILABLE IN TERMS OF PARAGRAPH 8 OF ARTICLE 6

1.   As soon as possible after the initiation of the investigation, the investigating authorities should specify in detail the information required from any interested party, and the manner in which that information should be structured by the interested party in its response. The authorities should also ensure that the party is aware that if information is not supplied within a reasonable time, the authorities will be free to make determinations on the basis of the facts available, including those contained in the application for the initiation of the investigation by the domestic industry.

2.   The authorities may also request that an interested party provide its response in a particular medium (e.g. computer tape) or computer language. * * *

3.   All information which is verifiable, which is appropriately submitted so that it can be used in the investigation without undue difficulties, which is supplied in a timely fashion, and, where applicable, which is supplied in a medium or computer language requested by the authorities, should be taken into account when determinations are made. If a party does not respond in the preferred medium or computer language but the authorities find that the circumstances set out in paragraph 2 have been satisfied, the failure to respond in the preferred medium or computer language should not be considered to significantly impede the investigation.

4.   Where the authorities do not have the ability to process information if provided in a particular medium (e.g. computer tape), the information should be supplied in the form of written material or any other form acceptable to the authorities.

5.   Even though the information provided may not be ideal in all respects, this should not justify the authorities from disregarding it, provided the interested party has acted to the best of its ability.

6.   If evidence or information is not accepted, the supplying party should be informed forthwith of the reasons therefor, and should have an opportunity to provide further explanations within a reasonable period, due account being taken of the time-limits of the investigation. If the explanations are considered by the authorities as not being satisfactory, the

reasons for the rejection of such evidence or information should be given in any published determinations.

7.   If the authorities have to base their findings, including those with respect to normal value, on information from a secondary source, including the information supplied in the application for the initiation of the investigation, they should do so with special circumspection. In such cases, the authorities should, where practicable, check the information from other independent sources at their disposal, such as published price lists, official import statistics and customs returns, and from the information obtained from other interested parties during the investigation. It is clear, however, that if an interested party does not cooperate and thus relevant information is being withheld from the authorities, this situation could lead to a result which is less favourable to the party than if the party did cooperate.

Chapter 5

SUBSIDIES AND COUNTERVAILING DUTIES

Table of Sections

For coverage of external European Union subsidies and countervailing duties law, see Section 18.6. No CVD apply to internal EU trade. For NAFTA coverage, see Section 16.10.

§ 5.1   Subsidies and International Trade

Countervailing duties (CVDs) complement antidumping duties (ADs). Unfair international trade practices can arise either through practices of producers or exporters, or through unfair practices of foreign governments. The former are subject to AD law; the latter are subject to CVD law. Either can be equally harmful to domestic industries, which often simultaneously pursue both "trade remedies."

In theory, a countervailing duty offsets exactly the unfair subsidy. Proponents of countervailing duties argue that they are necessary to keep imports from being unfairly competitive based on foreign government support. Opponents argue that there is no coherent standard of "fairness" to justify a rational assessment of such duties. Such opponents also point out that it is often difficult to identify precisely when a subsidy exists as compared with general governmental actions to support beneficial commercial activity.

A member state of the World Trade Organization (WTO) may impose an increased tariff on an imported item beyond the regular tariff schedule as a "countervailing duty." Such duties are an authorized response to a foreign government providing a "prohibited" or "actionable" subsidy that permits their exporters to sell at lower prices in other countries. Government subsidies come in many forms, including tax reductions or rebates, tax credits, loan guarantees, below market financing, equity infusions and outright monetary grants. Rapidly developing countries routinely offer subsidies to foreign investors designed to generate exports.

But subsidies are not just a phenomenon in developing countries. The Internal Revenue Code is littered with subsidies that lower the cost of U.S. made goods. The Export-Import Bank (EXIMBANK)—the financing for which Congress extended and expanded in 2012—offers low cost loans to overseas buyers of U.S. products. Other developed countries have similar subsidy programs. In all cases, the critical legal issue is which subsidies may be countervailed by CVD duties under the rules of the WTO Agreement on Subsidies and Countervailing Measures (SCM).

§ 5.2   The WTO Agreement on Subsidies and Countervailing Measures (SCM)

International concern with unfair subsidies and countervailing duties is reflected in Articles VI, XVI, and XXIII of the General Agreement on Tariffs and Trade (GATT) 1947 and 1994. An optional Subsidies Code was created under the Tokyo Round of

GATT multilateral negotiations. In 1995, the mandatory WTO "Agreement on Subsidies and Countervailing Measures" (SCM Agreement) took effect. Like the WTO Antidumping Agreement, Congress approved and implemented the SCM Agreement through the Uruguay Round Agreements Act of 1994 (URAA).[1]

Under the SCM Agreement, government authorities in an importing member state may impose a CVD in the amount of the subsidy for as long as the subsidy continues. The SCM Agreement also provides substantive rules governing when, and under what circumstances, a member state may impose CVDs to offset a claimed governmental or "public body" subsidy. State-owned enterprises (SOEs) are not generally treated as public bodies unless performing governmental functions. *See* U.S.-AD and CVD Duties (tires), WT/DS 379/AB/R (2011) (Commercial finance by SOE banks in China). The CVD may only be imposed after an investigation, begun on the request of an affected industry, has demonstrated the existence of a prohibited or actionable "specific" subsidy that has adverse trade effects, such as injury to a domestic industry or "serious prejudice" to the interests of the importing state. *See* U.S.-Cotton, WT/DS 267/AB/RW (2008) (adverse price suppression trade effects constitute serious prejudice). Finally, there must be a causal link between the subsidy and the alleged injury.

Disputes over subsidies may occur either before national administrative authorities (according to prescribed procedures), or before the WTO's Dispute Settlement Body, or both.[2] In addition, a special WTO "Committee on Subsidies and Countervailing Measures" supervises the implementation of the SCM Agreement by the WTO member states.

The SCM Agreement generally defines a subsidy as a financial contribution provided by a government that confers a benefit on an exporter. The Agreement establishes three classes of subsidies:

(1) Prohibited subsidies (e.g., export subsidies, also known as "red light" subsidies, and always deemed specific);

(2) Actionable subsidies, *i.e.*, those that are permissible unless they cause adverse trade effects ("yellow light" subsidies); and

(3) Non-actionable and non-countervailable subsidies ("green light" subsidies). Under the terms of the SCM Agreement, however, the "green light" category expired in 2000.

The SCM Agreement also granted special exemptions for developing countries that permitted them to phase out their export

---

[1]   Public Law No. 103–465, 108 Stat. 4809.
[2]   *See* Sections 5.20 and 5.25.

subsidies and local content rules on a gradual basis. These exemptions were to have expired by 2003, but as of 2014, eighteen countries—principally in the Caribbean and Central America—continue to operate under an extension of this deadline granted by the WTO's Committee on Subsidies and Countervailing Measures.

The SCM Agreement also prescribes procedural rules for the investigation and imposition of CVDs by domestic authorities. These rules address, among other things, the initiation of CVD proceedings, the conduct of investigations, the calculation of the amount of the subsidy, and the right of all interested parties to present information. The Agreement also has special rules relating to subsidies that cause a "serious prejudice" to the interests of another member state, though some of these rules have lapsed. Finally, the SCM has rules on the gathering of evidence in CVD proceedings, on the imposition and collection of CVDs, on provisional measures, and on the permitted length of any allowed CVDs, typically five years. Agricultural subsidies that are not exempted by the WTO Agreement on Agriculture (see Section 1.8) can be challenged under the SCM Agreement.

§ 5.3   Historical Introduction to U.S. CVD Law

United States law has long considered the grant of a subsidy by a foreign government to aid its exporters to be an unfair trade practice. Laws granting a right to impose countervailing duties to counter unfair subsidies have existed since 1897, long before the creation of the GATT. The origin of U.S. laws against export "bounties" or "grants" can be traced to Section 5 of the Tariff Act of 1897.[3] For many years, this law vested almost complete discretion in the Treasury Department to levy CVDs as it saw fit. Several early CVD tariffs targeted tax subsidies on sugar exports.[4] And the U.S. Supreme Court essentially gave the Treasury Department *carte blanche* to impose CVDs whenever foreign government regulations favored exports reaching the United States.[5] Prior to the Trade Act of 1974, U.S. law on CVDs was largely administered as a branch of U.S. foreign policy, not as a private international trade remedy.[6] Indeed, it was not until 1974 that negative bounty or grant determinations by the Treasury Department became subject to judicial review. The Trade Act of 1974 also gave private parties a

---

[3]   30 Stat. 205.

[4]   *See* Downs v. United States, 187 U.S. 496 (1903)(relating to Russia); United States v. Hills Bros., 107 Fed. 107 (2nd Cir. 1901)(relating to the Netherlands).

[5]   *See* G.S. Nicholas & Co. v. United States, 249 U.S. 34 (1919).

[6]   *See* Energetic Worsted Corp. v. United States, 53 C.C.P.A. 36 (1966)(relating to wool from Uruguay); United States v. Hammond Lead Products, 440 F.2d 1024 (C.C.P.A. 1971), *cert. denied* 404 U.S. 1005 (1971) (relating to Mexican lead).

number of procedural rights, notably time limits for Treasury decisions on their petitions for CVD relief and mandatory publication of Treasury rulings. It is from this point, therefore, that a systematic body of case law interpreting and applying U.S. bounty, grant, and CVD provisions began to develop.

The next major development in the U.S. statutes governing this field arrived in the Trade Agreements Act of 1979. This Act, *inter alia,* codified the rules on the use of CVDs to counteract unfair "export subsidies" as agreed in the Tokyo Round GATT Subsidies Code. In addition, the 1979 Act authorized limited use of CVDs against foreign *domestic* subsidies, a subject the GATT Subsidies Code did not address. Furthermore, the 1979 Act adopted the GATT requirement of proof of an actual injury to a domestic industry.

The Uruguay Round Agreements Act of 1994 implemented the numerous changes of the WTO SCM Agreement into U.S. law. Most important, the URAA amended the Tariff Act of 1930 to reflect a rough arrangement similar to the "red light," "yellow light," and "green light" (now lapsed) categories of the SCM Agreement. The requirements of the Tokyo Round Subsidies Code relating to material injury continued in substantially the same form.

§ 5.4   Two Statutory U.S. Tests

The United States currently has two statutory structures on countervailing duties: Section 1671 of the Tariff Act of 1930 provides a test for products imported from countries that participate in the WTO SCM Agreement (or its equivalent)[7], as compared to products imported from other countries.[8]

The most important difference between the two is that for imports from a "Subsidies Agreement Country,"[9] CVDs may be imposed only upon an affirmative determination that a U.S. industry is "materially" injured, or threatened with such injury, or its development is materially retarded. For the relatively few other countries, CVDs may be imposed *without* any finding of injury to a domestic industry. In most other significant respects, the two tests are the same.[10] Nonetheless, with the continuing growth in the membership of the WTO (roughly now 160 member states), the

---

[7]   19 U.S.C. § 1671(a)(2).

[8]   19 U.S.C. § 1671(a)(1).

[9]   19 U.S.C. § 1671(b)(defining a "Subsidies Agreement Country" as a WTO member state or a country the President has determined has laws that are "substantially equivalent" to the SCM Agreement).

[10]   *But see* § 1671(c)(stating the other general requirements for the imposition of CVDs that do not apply for countries that are not "Subsidies Agreement Countries").

possibility of imposing CVDs without a showing of material injury is rapidly decreasing in significance.

§ 5.5   U.S. Implementation of the WTO SCM Agreement

The U.S. statutory provisions on countervailing duties are set forth principally in Section 1671 of the Tariff Act of 1930.[11] As derived from the SCM Agreement, Section 1671 imposes two general conditions on the imposition of countervailing duties. First, the International Trade Administration (ITA) in the Department of Commerce must determine that a foreign state is providing a prohibited or actionable subsidy to its exporters. Second, the International Trade Commission (ITC) must determine that imports benefiting from the subsidy injure, threaten to injure, or retard the establishment of a domestic industry.[12] This second condition embraces proof of causation, a difficult CVD and AD issue. If these conditions are met, a duty equal to the net subsidy "shall be imposed" upon the imports.

Like antidumping duties, countervailing duties are a statutory remedy, one which the President cannot veto or in general otherwise affect. If an injured U.S. industry believes that a countervailable subsidy exists, it may pursue CVD proceedings to their conclusion over the President's objection simply by refusing to withdraw a petition once filed.[13] The President nonetheless may have substantial influence in bringing a CVD proceeding to a positive end. Section 1671 allows the suspension of a proceeding if the subsidizing foreign government or exporters accounting for substantially all of the exports agree to cease exporting to the United States, or to eliminate the subsidy within six months.[14]

The subsidy may be eliminated by imposition of either an export tax or a price increase amounting to the net subsidy. In "extraordinary circumstances" benefiting the domestic industry, the ITA may also suspend a proceeding in the case of a settlement agreement reducing the subsidy by at least eighty-five percent and preventing price cutting in the United States.[15] These approaches, which are increasingly common, may effectively give exporters a brief window of opportunity to enter the U.S. market at subsidized price levels prior to shifting production to the United States.

---

[11]   19 U.S.C. § 1671 et seq.
[12]   19 U.S.C. § 1671(a).
[13]   19 U.S.C. § 1671c(a).
[14]   19 U.S.C. § 1671c(b).
[15]   19 U.S.C. § 1671c(c)(4).

Although the subsidy may arise from public or private sources, all U.S. determinations to date have involved foreign governmental subsidies. Thus, these cases are usually determined on a country-wide basis (for instance, solar panels from China). CVD orders usually apply to all imported goods of a particular tariff classification from a particular country—including indirect imports shipped via other countries. This is one of the few instances in which the GATT/WTO allows an importing country to engage in discriminatory conduct against one or a few member states.

The United States amended its rules on countervailing duties in 1994 to conform to the SCM Agreement. The amendments changed many concepts under U.S. law and, although with a slightly different structure, the U.S. rules on CVDs in large measure are consistent with the substance of the SCM Agreement. In nearly all respects, the important rules on the imposition of CVDs under U.S. law as described in the Sections below conform to the substance of the WTO SCM Agreement.

In general, the U.S. rules state that "there shall be imposed . . . a countervailing duty" if the ITA determines that an exporting country is providing, "directly or indirectly," a disallowed subsidy, and the ITC makes an affirmative injury determination.[16] Thus, U.S. law defines essentially three elements for the imposition of a CVD: (1) a "countervailable subsidy," (2) that is "specific," and (3) that causes or threatens to cause a material injury to a domestic industry.[17] If all three elements are satisfied, the ITA must impose a CVD "equal to the amount of the net countervailable subsidy."[18]

The following sections analyze in detail each of the three required elements for the imposition of a CVD.

§ 5.6   ___The Subsidy Requirement

The first step in the analysis for the imposition of a CVD is a finding of a "subsidy." This term is defined as a "financial contribution" by a governmental entity that confers a "benefit" on the producer or exporter of the subsidized product.[19] It includes governmental grants, loans, equity infusions, and loan guarantees, as well as tax credits and the failure to collect taxes. *See* U.S.-FSCs, WT/DS 108/AB/R (2000) (foregone taxes are subsidies). It can also include the governmental purchase or providing of goods or services on advantageous terms.[20] Further, direct governmental action is not

---

[16]   19 U.S.C. § 1671(a).
[17]   19 U.S.C. § 1671(2).
[18]   *Id.*
[19]   19 U.S.C. § 1677(5).
[20]   19 U.S.C. § 1677(5)(D).

required. A subsidy may also arise if a government provides any of the above through a private body.

A financial contribution provides a "benefit" if it grants an exporter a better deal than would be available through normal market mechanisms. The Tariff Act states that this "normally" occurs: (1) in the case of an equity infusion, "if the investment decision is inconsistent with the usual investment practice of private investors"; (2) in the case of a loan, if the recipient gains an advantage as against a "comparable commercial loan"; (3) in the case of a loan guarantee, if there is a difference between the fee the recipient paid as compared to the fee for "a comparable commercial loan"; (4) in the case of governmental goods or services, if they "are provided for less than adequate remuneration"; and (5) in the case of goods purchased from the exporter, if the goods are purchased "for more than adequate remuneration."[21]

§ 5.7 ____The Specificity Requirement

In addition to a financial contribution that confers a benefit, the Tariff Act requires that the resulting subsidy be "specific" to a particular industry or enterprise. This is where U.S. law uses a slightly different structure as compared to the SCM Agreement (although, again, the substance is largely the same). U.S. law thus refers to "export subsidies" (see § 5.8 below) to correspond to the "prohibited" (red light) subsidies under the SCM Agreement. These are deemed to be specific as a matter of law. Similarly, U.S. law refers to "domestic subsidies" (see § 5.9 below) to correspond to "actionable" (yellow light) subsidies under the SCM Agreement. These may be subject to CVDs if they cause "adverse trade effects" based on a variety of further factual considerations.

Two other categories originally recognized under the SCM Agreement, and incorporated into U.S. law, have lapsed.[22] A so-called "dark amber" subsidy was one that exceeded five percent of the cost basis of the product, or provided debt forgiveness, or covered the operating losses of a specific enterprise industry more than once. The dark amber provisions lapsed in 2000. The "green light" category of allowed subsidies—for industrial research and development, regional development, and adaptation of existing facilities to new environmental standards—also lapsed after five years and was not renewed.[23]

---

[21]   19 U.S.C. § 1677(5)(E).

[22]   *See* 19 U.S.C. § 1677(5B)(A)–(E).

[23]   *See* Section 5.2.

§ 5.8   Export Subsidies

The clearest example of a specific subsidy is a direct export incentive provided by a foreign government, such as an export credit on taxes or export loan guarantees at less than commercial rates. U.S. CVD law provides that a subsidy is an "export subsidy," and thus is specific as a matter of law, if "in law or in fact" it is "contingent upon export performance," even where that condition is only one of several.[24] The same applies for a subsidy that is "conditioned upon the use of domestic goods over imported goods" ("import substitution subsidy").[25]

These rules correspond to the "prohibited" (red light) subsidies under the SCM Agreement. Annex I to the SCM Agreement also provides an "Illustrative List of Export Subsidies." A footnote to the SCM Agreement explains that a subsidy also is contingent on exports if it is "in fact tied to actual or anticipated exportation or export earnings."[26] A 2011 WTO Appellate Body decision in the long-running dispute between the European Union and the United States over aircraft subsidies explained that this concept applies, "[w]here the evidence shows, all other things being equal, that the granting of the subsidy provides an incentive to skew anticipated sales towards exports."[27] Although U.S. law does not expressly incorporate the language of the SCM Agreement footnote, a fair interpretation of the definition of an "export subsidy" would seem to capture it.

Other examples of an export subsidy might include governmental loans at below market interest rates or with uncompensated deferrals of payments of the principal. If these benefits are used to induce the building of a plant with a capacity too large for the local market, an export subsidy may exist. Outright cash payments to exporters, export tax credits, and accelerated depreciation benefits for exporters provide additional examples of clearly countervailable export subsidies.

More difficulties arise in analyzing whether tax rebates confer the type of benefits that would equate with an export subsidy. Remission or deferral of, or exemption from, a direct tax on exports is a countervailable subsidy. But the remission of an indirect tax (sales tax, value added tax, etc.) is not a "specific" subsidy, as long as it is not excessive. However, a foreign government that makes

---

[24]   19 U.S.C. § 1677(5A)(B).

[25]   19 U.S.C. § 1677(5A)(C).

[26]   *See* SCM Agreement, art. 3.1(a), footnote 4.

[27]   *See Report, European Communities and Certain Member States—Measures Affecting Trade in Large Civil Aircraft,* ¶ 1047, WT/DS316/AB/ (May 18, 2011).

payments to exporters must show a clear link between the amount, eligibility, and purpose of the payments and the actual payment of indirect taxes, and then document the link.

At one time, the amount of a U.S. CVD would be reduced by the "non-excessive" amount of the remission of an indirect tax. The Tariff Act now provides, however, a definition of "net subsidy" that allows certain subtractions. These include (1) application fees to qualify for the subsidy, (2) any reduction in the value of the subsidy due to a governmentally mandated deferral in payment, and (3) export taxes intended to offset the subsidy.[28]

§ 5.9 ____Domestic Subsidies

The Tariff Act as amended by the URAA in 1994 generally covers the SCM Agreement category of "actionable" (yellow light) subsidies under the concept of a "domestic subsidy." Under the SCM Agreement such subsidies are permissible (and thus may not be subject to CVDs), but only if they do not cause "adverse trade effects."[29]

Under the Tariff Act, a domestic subsidy exists if as a matter of law or fact it is provided to a specific enterprise or industry, even if not linked to export performance.[30] The law lists four "guidelines" for determining whether a subsidy so qualifies as a domestic subsidy:

(1) If the subsidizing country "expressly limits access" to the subsidy to an enterprise or industry, then it is "specific as a matter of law."

(2) If the subsidy is in fact automatically granted to all enterprises or industries that meet written and objective criteria or conditions, it is "not specific as a matter of law."

(3) But a subsidy may be "specific as a matter of fact" where the actual recipients are limited in number; one enterprise or industry is the predominant user or receives a "disproportionately large amount" of the subsidy; or the manner in which the granting authority exercises its discretion indicates that one enterprise or industry is favored over others.

(4) Finally, a subsidy is specific if it is limited to an enterprise or industry in a "designated geographic region"

---

[28]   19 U.S.C. § 1677(6).

[29]   SCM Agreement, art. 5.

[30]   19 U.S.C. § 1677(5A)(D).

and is granted by the governmental authority of that region.[31]

For purposes of each of these guidelines, the Tariff Act makes clear that a reference to an enterprise or industry includes "a group of such enterprises or industries."[32]

§ 5.10 ____Upstream Subsidies

A foreign government may subsidize component parts or raw materials that are incorporated into a final exported product. The latter are called "upstream subsidies" and are subject to CVDs if they both bestow a competitive benefit on the product exported to the United States and have a significant effect on its cost of production.[33] A competitive benefit arises if the price of the subsidized "input product" (the component or raw material) to the producer of the final product is less than it would have been "in an arms-length transaction."[34] Upstream subsidies then become "countervailable subsidies" if this competitive benefit functions to create or support an import substitution subsidy or a domestic subsidy.[35]

The amount of the benefit from an upstream subsidy is determined by calculating the subsidy rate on the input and then determining what percentage of the cost of the final product is represented by the subsidized input. By regulation the ITA has stated that, if the subsidy so calculated represents more than five percent of the total cost, it will presume that there is a "significant effect;" and if it is less than one percent, it will presume no significant effect.[36] However, both presumptions are rebuttable, and the ITA also will consider the importance of price in the competitiveness of the final product.[37]

The Tariff Act has specialized rules for processed agricultural products. A subsidy provided to producers of a "raw agricultural product" is deemed to be provided to the producer of the processed agricultural product if (1) the demand for the "raw" product is substantially dependent upon the demand for the processed

---

[31]   19 U.S.C. § 1677(5A)(D)(i)–(iv).

[32]   19 U.S.C. § 1677(5A)(D), last paragraph.

[33]   19 U.S.C. § 1677–1(a). *See also* 19 U.S.C. § 1671(e)(providing for the inclusion of upstream subsidies in CVDs).

[34]   19 U.S.C. § 1677–1(b).

[35]   19 U.S.C. § 1677–1(a)(stating that an upstream subsidy is one "other than an export subsidy"); 19 U.S.C. §§ 1677(5)(C)(referring to import substitution subsidies), and 1677(5)(D)(referring to domestic subsidies).

[36]   19 CFR § 351.523(d)(1) (2013).

[37]   19 CFR § 351.523(d)(2) (2013).

product, and (2) the processing adds only limited value to the raw product.[38]

§ 5.11 ___*De Minimis* Subsidies

De minimis subsidies, defined in U.S. law as subsidies of "less than 0.5 percent *ad valorem,*" are disregarded and no CVD is imposed.[39] However, when the ITA calculates country-wide CVD rates, it uses a fair average of aggregate subsidy benefits to exports of all firms from that country. In making such calculations, the ITA must include not only sales by exporters who receive substantial subsidy benefits, but also sales by exporters who receive zero or *de minimis* subsidies, when calculating the weighted average benefit conferred.[40] Thus, in such circumstances, the CVD imposed may not exceed the weighted average benefit received by all exporters of the goods subject to the CVD proceeding. The *de minimis* 0.5 percent rule need not be utilized in sunset reviews of CVDs every five years.[41]

§ 5.12 ___CVDs and Nonmarket Economies

The subject of subsidies is particularly difficult with respect to non-market economies (NMEs). The longstanding view was that CVDs for products from NMEs were not appropriate because the NME government in effect is responsible for the entire economy. In accordance with this view, the Federal Circuit Court of Appeals ruled in 1986 that economic incentives given to encourage exportation by the government of an NME cannot create a "countervailable subsidy."[42] The court's rationale was that, even though an NME government provides export-oriented benefits, the NME can direct sales to be at any price, so the benefits themselves do not distort competition. The court also suggested that imports from NMEs with unreasonably low prices should be analyzed under the rules for antidumping duties.

For some time one strong view was that Congress implicitly approved of this reasoning when it enacted important amendments to the Tariff Act in 1988, and again in 1994. Those amendments addressed *dumping* from NMEs, but did not address *subsidies* for

---

[38]   19 U.S.C. § 1677–2.

[39]   Although the Tariff Act generally refers to one percent, see 19 U.S.C. § 1671b(b)(4), the ITA has refined the standard to .05 percent. *See* 19 CFR § 351.106(c)(1) (2013).

[40]   *See* Ipsco, Inc. v. United States, 899 F.2d 1192 (Fed.Cir.1990).

[41]   *See* Report of the Appellate Body, U.S. *CVD on Certain Corrosion—Resistant Steel Flat Products from Germany*, WT/DS213/AB/R (Dec. 19, 2002).

[42]   Georgetown Steel Corp. v. United States, 801 F.2d 1308 (Fed. Cir. 1986).

exports from NMEs.[43] Thus, for many years it was assumed that unfair trade practices by NMEs would only be subject to antidumping reviews and not CVD reviews. But in a major reversal, the Commerce Department in 2007 started pursuing CVD cases against China despite its NME status under U.S. trade law. In 2008, it then imposed CVD duties of up to 616% on steel pipe from China.[44] It did the same in 2010 for certain imports from Vietnam.[45]

In 2011 the Federal Circuit rejected this effort based on its reading of congressional intent in the substantial amendments of CVD law in 1994.[46] In March 2012, however, Congress annulled that decision by special legislation (Public Act 112–99). As a result, countervailing duties may be imposed retroactively to 2006 on goods from non-market economies such as China and Vietnam. China challenged this legislation before the WTO and lost in 2014. Many WTO members have recognized China as a market economy, and the accession provision allowing treatment of China as a nonmarket economy expires in 2016.

The criteria used to determine whether a country has a nonmarket economy in antidumping proceedings[47] will apply for U.S. countervailing duty law as well. These criteria focus principally upon government involvement in setting prices or production levels, private versus collective ownership, and market pricing of inputs.[48] Public Act 112–99 prohibits dual application of CVD and AD duties, a practice China successfully challenged before the WTO. *See* Section 4.0.

§ 5.13   The U.S. Injury Determination

CVD proceedings in the United States for Subsidies Agreement Countries (and only such countries[49]), are conducted in two stages. The ITA is responsible for assessing the substantive grounds for the imposition of a CVD.[50] In the second stage, the International Trade Commission (ITC) must determine whether the subsidization of the imported merchandise has caused or threatens material injury to a domestic industry.[51] The following sections review the material

---

[43]   *See, e.g.,* 19 U.S.C. §§ 1677b(c) and 1677(18).

[44]   *See* 73 Fed. Reg. 40,480 (July 15, 2008).

[45]   *See* 75 Fed. Reg. 23,670 (May 4, 2010).

[46]   *See* GPX Intern. Tire Corp. v. United States, 666 F.3d 732, 745 (Fed. Cir. 2011).

[47]   *See* Chapter 4.

[48]   *See id.*

[49]   *See* Section 5.2 (noting that an injury determination is required only for "Subsidies Agreement Countries").

[50]   *See generally* 19 U.S.C. § 1671(a)(1).

[51]   19 U.S.C. § 1671(a)(2).

injury determination under U.S. law, including market definition, injury factors, and causation. Injury determinations in CVD proceedings are almost identical to hose the ITC undertakes in AD proceedings. *See* Chapter 4.

The injury determination by the ITC involves three separate inquiries:

(1) First, the ITC must define the relevant "domestic like product" and relevant domestic industry;

(2) Second, the ITC must determine whether that industry is suffering or threatened with a sufficiently serious injury; and

(3) Third, the ITC must determine whether a causal link exists between the injury and the "countervailable subsidy."

The most important of these steps is the determination of whether a countervailable subsidy causes a sufficient injury to a domestic industry. The Tariff Act provides that an affirmative injury determination is required when an industry in the United States is materially injured or is threatened with material injury by reason of dumped imports, or the establishment of an industry in the United States is materially retarded.[52] Both the "material injury"[53] and the "threat of material injury"[54] standards apply to established industries, and substantial overlap exists between the two. Nonetheless, the Act makes clear that they are independent grounds for a sufficient injury to justify a CVD.[55]

The law governing the injury determination for the imposition of CVDs in nearly all significant respects is the same as that for imposing antidumping duties. Indeed, the definitions of the relevant product market, the relevant industry, and the three alternatives for an affirmative injury determination are essentially identical for CVDs and ADs. Thus, the analysis of the injury determination for CVDs below will often be the same as, or will liberally refer to, the injury analysis for ADs in Chapter 4.

§ 5.14 ____The "Like Product" and Relevant Domestic Industry Determinations

In order to assess "material injury," the ITC must first identify the relevant products and relevant domestic industry affected by a countervailable subsidy.

---

[52]   *Id.*

[53]   19 U.S.C. § 1677(7).

[54]   19 U.S.C. § 1677(7)(F).

[55]   19 U.S.C. § 1671(a)(2).

With regard to the product market, the Tariff Act uses the term "domestic like product." This term is defined, for both CVDs and ADs, as one that is "like, or in the absence of like, most similar in characteristics and uses with" to the foreign product under investigation. The "like product" determination is a factual issue for which the ITC weighs six relevant factors: "(1) physical characteristics and uses; (2) common manufacturing facilities and production employees; (3) interchangeability; (4) customer perceptions; (5) channels of distribution; and, where appropriate, (6) price."[56]

In a CVD proceeding, the ITC must define the relevant product and industry for an assessment of the harm caused by a subsidized product upon importation. The ITA will undertake a similar analysis in AD proceedings in order to determine the foreign market value ("normal value") for the imported merchandise.[57] Since the concept of "like product" is used for a different purpose, its definition need not necessarily be the same as that used by the ITA in determining whether dumping has occurred.[58]

Separately, the ITC in a CVD proceeding must define the relevant domestic industry potentially affected by a proscribed subsidy practice. The Tariff Act defines the relevant "domestic industry" as those domestic producers, "as a whole," of a "domestic like product" or as those producers "whose collective output of a domestic like product constitutes a major proportion" of the total domestic production.[59] Again, although these definitions apply to both the ITA and the ITC, they do not always agree on the outcome.

In addition, the ITC may create regional geographic product markets if the local producers sell most of their production in the regional market, and the demand in the regional market is not supplied by other U.S. producers outside that region.[60] If the relevant domestic injury in such a region is harmed, then there is material injury to a domestic industry.

§ 5.15 ____Material Injury

The Tariff Act defines material injury as "harm which is not inconsequential, immaterial, or unimportant."[61] (The same

---

[56] Cleo Inc. v. U.S., 501 F.3d 1291, 11294–1295 (Fed. Cir. 2007).

[57] *See* Section 4.6.

[58] Cleo Inc. v. U.S., 501 F.3d 1291, 1295 (Fed. Cir. 2007); Mitsubishi Elec. Corp. v. U.S., 898 F.2d 1577 (Fed.Cir.1990).

[59] 19 U.S.C. § 1677(4)(A).

[60] 19 U.S.C. § 1677(4)(C).

[61] 19 U.S.C. § 1677(7)(A).

standard applies in AD proceedings,[62] and again much of the law in the area is therefore interchangeable.) In assessing this essential "material injury" standard, the Act *requires* the ITC to consider three factors:

> (1) The volume of imports of the merchandise subject to investigation;

> (2) The effect of these imports on prices in the United States for like products; and

> (3) The impact of these imports on domestic producers of like products, but only in the context of domestic United States production operations.[63]

The Act also *permits* the ITC to consider "such other economic factors as are relevant to the determination regarding whether there is material injury by reason of imports."[64]

The ITC is required to explain its analysis of each factor considered and the relevance of each to its determination.[65] The Tariff Act nonetheless provides that the "presence or absence" of any of the three mandatory factors should "not necessarily give decisive guidance" to the ITC in its material injury determination, and the ITC is not required to assign any particular weight to any one factor.[66] The factors are examined through extensive statistical analyses. This analysis occurs on industry-wide basis and not on a company-by-company basis. The ITC may select whatever time period best represents the business cycle and competitive conditions in the industry and most reasonably allows it to determine whether an injury exists.[67]

The Tariff Act also gives detailed guidance for the ITC's assessment of each of the three mandatory considerations for a material injury determination. This guidance applies to both CVD and AD proceedings.

Volume of Imports. The Tariff Act requires the ITC to consider the absolute volume of imports or any increases in volume in evaluating the volume of imports subject to investigation. This assessment may be made in relation to production or consumption

---

[62]   *See* Section 4.14.

[63]   19 U.S.C. § 1677(7)(B)(i). *See also* Angus Chemical Co. v. United States, 140 F.3d 1478 (Fed.Cir.1998)(holding that consideration of these three factors is mandatory).

[64]   19 U.S.C. § 1677(7)(B)(ii).

[65]   19 U.S.C. § 1677(7)(B).

[66]   19 U.S.C. § 1677(7)(E)(ii).

[67]   19 U.S.C. § 1677(7)(C).

in the United States. The standard in this evaluation is whether the volume of imports, viewed in any of the above ways, is significant.[68]

Price Effects. Under the Tariff Act, the ITC must consider the effect of the subsidized imports on prices for like products in the domestic market. This is done to the extent that such a consideration assists in evaluating whether (1) there is significant price underselling by the imported merchandise as compared with the price of like products of the United States,[69] and (2) whether the effect of the imported merchandise is otherwise to depress domestic prices to a significant degree or to prevent price increases that otherwise would have occurred to a significant degree.[70]

Domestic Industry Impact. Similar to AD proceedings, the impact on a domestic industry of an allegedly subsidized product commonly is the most important consideration in the ITC's injury analysis. Because of this, the Tariff Act provides supplemental factors for the ITC to consider. These include: (1) actual and potential decline in "output, sales, market share, profits, productivity, return on investments, and utilization of capacity"; (2) impact on domestic prices; (3) actual and potential "negative effects on cash flow, inventories, employment, wages, growth, ability to raise capital, and investment"; and (4) actual and potential negative effects "on the existing development and production efforts of the domestic industry."[71]

The ITC must evaluate all these relevant economic factors within the context of the business cycle and conditions of competition in the affected industry.[72] But traditionally the ITC has relied primarily on two of the factors in making this determination. First, the industry must be in a distressed or a stagnant condition. Second, the low domestic price levels must be a factor in the industry's difficulties (*e.g.*, high unemployment or low capacity utilization rate), and these low prices must have a serious negative effect on profits.

The ITC will often base an affirmative determination of material injury on severe downward trends in profitability among domestic producers. But even in a case of declining profitability, increasing production, shipments, capacity, and market share may demonstrate to the ITC that the affected industry is in a healthy

---

[68]   19 U.S.C. § 1677(7)(C)(i).

[69]   19 U.S.C. § 1677(7)(C)(ii)(I).

[70]   19 U.S.C. § 1677(7)(C)(ii)(II). For more detail on the role of "price underselling" in the ITC's determination of injury see Section 4.14.

[71]   19 U.S.C. § 1677(7)(C)(iii).

[72]   19 U.S.C. § 1677(7)(C), last paragraph.

state.[73] Thus, the ITC may make a negative determination concerning material injury even if the industry is experiencing decreases in profitability.

Like AD proceedings, the effect of subsidized imports on employment in the relevant domestic industry may also be significant. Again, employment data are not dispositive due to the broad spectrum of economic factors that may affect such data, many of which may not be attributable to foreign subsidization. However, changes in domestic employment during the period under investigation are one factor to be considered. A decrease in employment during the period of investigation may be an indication of injury, whereas increasing employment commonly is a fact that supports a negative injury determination.

Finally, and again as in AD proceedings, plant capacity utilization can be an important factor. Falling capacity utilization may indicate material injury if no other explanation exists, but the ITC can make negative injury determinations despite falling capacity utilization, if the decline is caused by other factors, such as frequent equipment breakdowns and quality control disruptions.

§ 5.16 ____Threat of Material Injury

The ITC may also make an affirmative determination of injury if it finds that a proscribed subsidy practice represents a "threat of material injury" to a domestic industry. The Tariff Act lists a variety of "economic factors" that the ITC "shall consider" in making such a determination in an antidumping proceeding. Again, these factors apply for AD proceedings as well, and Chapter 4 analyzes them in detail.[74]

The Tariff Act nonetheless adds one "economic factor" that is relevant only for CVD proceedings. For such proceedings the ITC must also consider "the nature of the subsidy . . . and whether imports of the subject merchandise are likely to increase."[75]

§ 5.17 ____Material Retardation

For a CVD proceeding as well, the Tariff Act recognizes as an independent ground for an affirmative injury determination by the ITC that a dumped import product has "materially retarded" the establishment of an industry in the United States. This standard of

---

[73]   *See, e.g.,* Nucor Corp. v. U.S., 675 F. Supp. 2d 1340 (C.I.T. 2010)(relating to a revocation of CVDs after a review); American Spring Wire Corp. v. U.S., 590 F. Supp. 1273 (C.I.T. 1984), *affirmed sub nom.* Armco, Inc. v. U.S., 760 F.2d 249 (Fed. Cir. 1985).

[74]   *See* Section 4.15.

[75]   19 U.S.C. § 1677(7)(F)(i)(I).

its nature is relevant to new or nascent domestic industries. Like AD proceedings,[76] this ground for an affirmative injury determination has not been a significant one in CVD cases.

§ 5.18 _____Causation

In addition to sufficient injury to a domestic industry, the ITC must also find causation. As with AD proceedings, however, when the subsidization and material injury already exist, there is a natural tendency to make an affirmative determination for a CVD without a lengthy analysis of the causal link between the two. In a negative injury determination, on the other hand, the ITC may engage in a rather detailed analysis of causation.

The Tariff Act sets out a simple causation standard: that material injury must occur "by reason of" the subsidization of the imports.[77] The same standard applies in AD proceedings and once again the law in this area is largely interchangeable.[78] The Tariff Act does not require that the ITC use any particular methodology in making such a determination, and it "need not isolate the injury caused by other factors from injury caused by unfair imports."[79] Thus the causation requirement is not a high one. Imports need only be a cause of material injury, and need not be the most substantial or even primary cause.

The causation standard may be satisfied if the subsidized imports simply contribute to the conditions of the domestic injury. Under this "contributing cause" standard, causation may exist despite the absence of a correlation between subsidized imports and the alleged injuries, if substantial evidence exists that the volume of subsidized imports was a contributing factor in the price depression experienced by the domestic injury. Nonetheless, the Federal Circuit has made clear that "causation is not shown if the subject imports contributed only 'minimally or tangentially to the material harm.'"[80]

As in AD proceedings, the ITC must consider causal factors other than subsidies in CVD cases.[81] An industry that is prospering

---

[76] *See* Section 4.16.

[77] 19 U.S.C. § 1671(a)(2).

[78] *See* Section 4.17.

[79] Bratsk Aluminium Smelter v. U.S., 444 F.3d 1369, 1373 (Fed. Cir. 2006)(*quoting* Taiwan Semiconductors Industry Ass'n v. Int'l Trade Comm'n, 266 F.3d 1339, 1345 (Fed. Cir. 2001)).

[80] *Id.*, 444 F.3d at 1373 (*quoting* Gerald Metals, Inc. v. U.S., 132 F.3d 716, 722 (Fed. Cir. 1997)).

[81] Taiwan Semiconductors Industry Ass'n v. International Taiwan Semiconductors Industry Ass'n v. International Trade Com'n, 266 F.3d 1339, 1345 (Fed. Cir. 2001)(so holding with respect to an AD proceeding).

during times of greater import penetration will find it difficult to persuade the ITC that subsidized imports are the cause of any material injury to it. The existence of extraneous injury factors will not, however, necessarily preclude an affirmative finding of material injury for purposes of the Tariff Act, as long as the subsidies are a contributing cause to the material injury of the domestic industry. The ITC is not required to weigh the effects from the subsidized imports against the effects associated with other factors, if the subsidization is a contributing cause of the injury. Nonetheless, the ITC may uncover other major causes for the problems of the domestic industry. These may include huge unnecessary expenses, chronic excess capacity, inefficiency, poor quality, price sensitivity or increased domestic competition.

§ 5.19 ____Cumulative Causation

Similar to an AD proceeding,[82] the Tariff Act requires that the ITC cumulatively assess the impact of reasonably coincident subsidized imports from two or more countries if the imports compete with "like products" in the United States. In specific, the Act requires the ITC to "cumulatively assess the volume and price effects of imports of the subject merchandise from all countries" with respect to which CVD proceedings were initiated on the same day, "if such imports compete with each other and with domestic like products in the United States market."[83] The reasoning for this approach, again, is that the injury caused by "many nibbles" is just as harmful as that caused by "one large bite."

The Court of International Trade has observed that to support a cumulation decision, the ITC "must find a reasonable overlap of competition between imports from the subject countries and the domestic like product."[84] In applying this "reasonable overlap" test, the ITC traditionally has applied a four factor test: (1) the degree of fungibility; (2) the presence of sales or offers in the same geographic markets; (3) the existence of common or similar channels of distribution; and (4) whether there is a simultaneous presence in the relevant market.[85] However, neither the "reasonable overlap" test nor the four factors test is "singularly dispositive or the sole factors the ITC may consider."[86]

---

[82]   *See* Section 4.18.

[83]   19 U.S.C. § 1677(7)(G)(i).

[84]   Nucor Corp. v. U.S., 594 F. Supp. 2d 1320, 1347 (C.I.T. 2008) (*quoting* Noviant OY v. United States, 451 F. Supp. 2d 1367, 1379 (C.I.T. 2006), *aff'd*, Nucor Corp. v. U.S. 601 F.3d 1291 (Fed. Cir. 2010).

[85]   *Id.*, at 1347.

[86]   *Id.*

When cumulating, it is not necessary to find, for each country, a separate causal link between imports and U.S. material injury. Such multiple country cumulation should be distinguished from the "cross cumulation," which is also allowed by the Tariff Act. Cross cumulation involves consideration by the ITC of both dumped and subsidized imports into the United States. The net effect of U.S. rules on cumulation of import injury is to encourage petitioners to name as many countries as possible as the source of their problems and combine these in a single proceeding.

§ 5.20   U.S. Countervailing Duty Procedures

As noted above, the Tariff Act applies different rules for the imposition of CVDs depending on whether the source country is or is not a "Subsidies Agreement Country."[87] The major difference between the two is that for a "Subsidies Agreement Country" a determination of both a countervailable subsidy and an injury is required; for other countries, only a finding of a countervailable subsidy is necessary.[88] Thus, the administrative procedure for deciding whether to impose CVDs for a Subsidies Agreement Country is the same as that for antidumping duties[89] and involves the ITA and ITC (see below) making both preliminary and final determinations. But for subsidized products from other countries, a decision by the ITA will alone be sufficient to impose CVDs.

§ 5.21   ____Administrative Determinations

Two different governmental agencies are involved in administering U.S. CVD law: The International Trade Administration (ITA), which is part of the Commerce Department and thus the Executive Branch, and the International Trade Commission (ITC), which is an independent agency created by Congress.

The chain of decision-making in CVD proceedings depends on whether a Subsidies Agreement Country is involved. If not, the proceeding is totally before the ITA. This will be a two-stage proceeding:

ITA Preliminary Countervailable Subsidy Determination.

ITA Final Countervailable Subsidy Determination.

If, in contrast, a Subsidies Agreement Country is the source of the challenged goods, then a four-stage proceeding will apply:

---

87   *See* Section 5.4.
88   19 U.S.C. § 1671(a)(1), (2).
89   *See* Sections 4.21–4.23.

ITC Preliminary Injury Determination.

ITA Preliminary Countervailable Subsidy Determination.

ITA Final Countervailable Subsidy Determination.

ITC Final Injury Determination.

The CVD process may be initiated by either the Department of Commerce or by a union or business (or group or association of aggrieved workers or businesses).[90] The petition requirements are set forth by regulation.[91] Pre-filing contact with the ITA and (if necessary) the ITC can often resolve any problems regarding the contents of the petition. Petitioners may also access the ITA's library of information on foreign subsidy practices.

The ITA then first determines whether the petition alleges the elements necessary for the imposition of a duty, based on the best information available at the time.[92] In other words, the ITA essentially accepts or rejects the petition.

Once the petition is accepted, the ITC makes a preliminary determination as to a real or threatened material injury within forty-five days of the filing of the petition based on the best information available to it at that time.[93] If the ITC makes such a finding, the ITA must then make a preliminary determination on whether there is "a reasonable basis to believe" based on the best information available that there is a countervailable subsidy with respect to the covered merchandise.[94] The time for making this decision may be extended if the petitioner so requests, or if the ITA determines both that the parties are cooperating and that the case is extraordinarily complicated.[95] The time period may also be extended for "upstream subsidy" investigations.[96]

If the ITA makes a preliminary determination that a countervailable subsidy exists, it must, within seventy-five days, both make a "final determination" on the existence of a countervailable subsidy and calculate the amount of the proposed CVD.[97] If the ITA makes a positive finding on a countervailable subsidy, the ITC then must make a final determination on material injury within 120 days after the ITA's preliminary determination or

---

[90]   19 U.S.C. § 1671a(a), (b).

[91]   *See* 19 C.F.R. § 351.102.

[92]   19 U.S.C. § 1671a(b).

[93]   19 U.S.C. § 1671b(a).

[94]   19 U.S.C. § 1671b(b).

[95]   19 U.S.C. § 1671b(c).

[96]   19 U.S.C. § 1671b(h).

[97]   19 U.S.C. § 1671d(a).

forty-five days after the ITA's final determination.[98] If the ITA makes a negative preliminary determination, but then an affirmative final determination, the ITC must thereafter make its final determination within seventy-five days.[99]

In reaching their determinations, both the ITA and the ITC frequently circulate questionnaires to interested parties, including foreign governments and exporters. Since any failure to respond risks a determination on the "best information available," this results in the flow of significant and often strategically valuable business information to the government.

§ 5.22 ____The Importance of the ITA Preliminary Subsidy Determination

An ITA preliminary determination that a countervailable subsidy exists places great pressure on the importers of the foreign goods. Liquidation (entry at a determined rate of tariff) of all such merchandise is suspended by order of customs. Goods imported after an ITA preliminary determination of a countervailable subsidy will be subject to any CVD imposed later, after final determinations are made.[100] Such a preliminary determination, although subject to final determinations by the ITA and the ITC and appealable to the CIT, will effectively cut off further importation of the disputed goods unless an expensive bond is posted pending completion of the process.

The respondent importer thus will want a speedy resolution, as its total costs for the imports will have become uncertain. It is for this reason that the Tariff Act is replete with time provisions designed to protect the importer by requiring decisions within specified time limits (see § 5.21 above). As with antidumping proceedings, most CVD proceedings are completed within one year.

At one level, then, a useful intermediate goal in representing a petitioner is to obtain an ITA preliminary determination concerning a "subsidy" that meets the statutory requirements. The respondent's "defense" to such efforts must be organized quickly, usually within thirty days of the filing of a CVD petition. The importer's ability to present a defense is handicapped by the nature of CVD proceedings—the actual target of the petition is the subsidy practices of foreign governments.

Unlike most foreign exporters whose pricing decisions are the focus in AD proceedings, many foreign governments are loath to

---

[98]   19 U.S.C. § 1671d(b)(2).
[99]   19 U.S.C. § 1671d(b)(3).
[100]   19 U.S.C. § 1671b(d).

provide information necessary for an adequate response to a CVD complaint. Because the ITA and ITC are authorized to make decisions on the basis of the "best information available," any failure to adequately respond to a CVD complaint can contribute to adverse rulings. Moreover, responses by foreign governments and exporters to ITA questionnaires that cannot be verified by on-the-spot investigations are ignored and thus removed from the best information available for decision-making. This may leave only the petitioner's or other respondents' submissions for review—one-sided proceeding almost sure to result in affirmative determinations.

The respondent-importer's uncertainties over the amount of duty owed after a preliminary ITA determination that a countervailable subsidy exists can increase for Subsidies Agreement Countries if the ITA decides that "critical circumstances" are present. In such cases, the suspension of liquidation of the goods applies not only prospectively from the date of such determination, but also retrospectively for ninety days.[101] For other countries, moreover, there is *no* time limit on retroactively and no need for a "critical circumstances" determination.

§ 5.23 ____CVDs and Anti-circumvention

The ITA final determination of the existence of a subsidy establishes the amount of any CVDs. Because duties are not imposed to support any specific domestic price, they are set only to equal the amount of the net subsidy.[102] The CVDs remain in force as long as the subsidization continues.

Like antidumping duties,[103] the Tariff Act also has rules that address the "circumvention" of CVDs. First, the ITA may include within the scope of a CVD order merchandise "completed or assembled" in the United States if such merchandise includes "parts or components produced in the foreign country" that are the original subject of the order.[104] The principal requirements are that the process of completion or assembly in the United States is "minor or insignificant" and the value of the components themselves is a "significant portion of the total value of the merchandise.[105] Second, when the exporter ships components to a third country for assembly and subsequent exportation to the United States, such circumvention efforts can be defeated by extending an antidumping

---

[101] 19 U.S.C. § 1671b(e).

[102] 19 U.S.C. § 1671e.

[103] *See* Section 4.25.

[104] 19 U.S.C. § 1677j(a).

[105] 19 U.S.C. § 1677j(a)(2).

order to those goods as well.[106] Again, such an action is appropriate if the assembly in the third country is "minor or insignificant" and the value of the components represents a "significant portion" of the total value.

Many petitioners in countervailing duty cases also seek antidumping duties[107] and other relief through safeguard or market disruption proceedings.[108] Thus, domestic producers seeking relief from import competition will often use a "shotgun" approach to obtain protective relief.

§ 5.24   U.S. Court Appeals, Binational NAFTA Panels

Judicial review "on the record" of final (not preliminary) decisions by the ITA and the ITC in both CVD and AD proceedings may be sought before the Court of International Trade (CIT). In turn, CIT decisions may be appealed first to the Court of Appeals for the Federal Circuit, and ultimately to the U.S. Supreme Court.

For proceedings arising out of exports from Canada and Mexico, however, NAFTA provides for resolution of antidumping and countervailing duty disputes through binational panels.[109] Such panels apply the domestic law of the importing country, and provide a substitute for judicial review of the decisions of administrative agencies of the importing country. Indeed, the initiation of a review under NAFTA divests the CIT of jurisdiction over the same dispute. Although the decisions of such bi-national panels are not formally binding in U.S. law, the ITA or ITC may decide to review any administrative action to conform to an adverse panel decision, including through a revocation or reduction of countervailing duties.

§ 5.25   WTO Proceedings

International institutions also play an increasingly significant role in the resolution of trade disputes. The most important of these is the WTO's Dispute Settlement Body (DSB). Dissatisfied parties in domestic administrative proceedings may convince their government to challenge an adverse CVD determination before the DSB based on alleged violations of the WTO SCM Agreement. As Chapter 1 examines in detail, proceedings before the DSB are governed by a separate WTO Agreement, the Dispute Settlement Understanding (DSU).

---

[106]   19 U.S.C. § 1677j(b).

[107]   *See* Chapter 4.

[108]   *See* Chapter 6.

[109]   Canada-United States Free Trade Agreement (1989), Chapter 19; NAFTA (1994), Chapter 19. *See* Section 16.10.

The SCM Agreement also has special rules regarding the resolution of subsidy disputes. The multilateral procedure under WTO first provides for consultations between the complaining state and the subsidizing state. If these do not resolve the dispute within thirty days for a "red light" subsidy, or sixty days for a "yellow light" subsidy, either party is entitled to request that the DSB establish a panel to investigate the dispute and issue a written decision and report. The DSB panel will have ninety days (red light), or 120 days (yellow light), to investigate and prepare its report. The panel report is appealable on issues of law to the Appellate Body. The Appellate Body has thirty days (red light), or sixty days (yellow light), to decide the appeal. Panel and Appellate Body decisions are adopted without modification by the DSB unless rejected by an "inverted consensus."

If a prohibited or actionable subsidy is found to exist, the subsidizing state is obligated under the WTO to withdraw the subsidy. If the subsidy is not withdrawn within a six month period, the AB may authorize the complaining state to take countermeasures. Such countermeasures need not be in the form of countervailing duties, but may instead comprise increased tariffs by the complaining state on exports from the subsidizing state.

A classic, longstanding pair of subsidy disputes concerning Boeing and Airbus aircraft have been decided by the Appellate Body. In 2011, the European Union and various member states were found to have illegally subsidized Airbus, mainly through "launch aid", by $22 billion (WT/DS316/AB/R (May 18, 2011). In 2012, the Appellate Body determined that the U.S. and various state governments had subsidized Boeing by about $4.3 billion under procurement contracts and tax loopholes (WT/DS353/AB/R (March 12, 2012). At this writing, neither side seems inclined to comply with these rulings, no settlement is in sight, and hence mutual trade retaliation could occur.

§ 5.26 Text of WTO Agreement on Subsidies and Countervailing Measures (SCM)

(Selected Provisions)

PART I: GENERAL PROVISIONS

Article 1

Definition of a Subsidy

1.1 For the purpose of this Agreement, a subsidy shall be deemed to exist if:

(a)(1) there is a financial contribution by a government or any public body within the territory of a Member (referred to in this Agreement as "government"), i.e. where:

(i) a government practice involves a direct transfer of funds (e.g. grants, loans, and equity infusion), potential direct transfers of funds or liabilities (e.g. loan guarantees);

(ii) government revenue that is otherwise due is foregone or not collected (e.g. fiscal incentives such as tax credits)[1];

(iii) a government provides goods or services other than general infrastructure, or purchases goods;

(iv) a government makes payments to a funding mechanism, or entrusts or directs a private body to carry out one or more of the type of functions illustrated in (i) to (iii) above which would normally be vested in the government and the practice, in no real sense, differs from practices normally followed by governments;

or

(a)(2) there is any form of income or price support in the sense of Article XVI of GATT 1994;

and

(b) a benefit is thereby conferred.

1.2   A subsidy as defined in paragraph 1 shall be subject to the provisions of Part II or shall be subject to the provisions of Part III or V only if such a subsidy is specific in accordance with the provisions of Article 2.

Article 2

Specificity

2.1   In order to determine whether a subsidy, as defined in paragraph 1 of Article 1, is specific to an enterprise or industry or group of enterprises or industries (referred to in this Agreement as "certain enterprises") within the jurisdiction of the granting authority, the following principles shall apply:

(a) Where the granting authority, or the legislation pursuant to which the granting authority operates, explicitly limits access to a subsidy to certain enterprises, such subsidy shall be specific.

---

[1]   In accordance with the provisions of Article XVI of GATT 1994 (Note to Article XVI) and the provisions of Annexes I through III of this Agreement, the exemption of an exported product from duties or taxes borne by the like product when destined for domestic consumption, or the remission of such duties or taxes in amounts not in excess of those which have accrued, shall not be deemed to be a subsidy.

(b) Where the granting authority, or the legislation pursuant to which the granting authority operates, establishes objective criteria or conditions[2] governing the eligibility for, and the amount of, a subsidy, specificity shall not exist, provided that the eligibility is automatic and that such criteria and conditions are strictly adhered to. The criteria or conditions must be clearly spelled out in law, regulation, or other official document, so as to be capable of verification.

(c) If, notwithstanding any appearance of non-specificity resulting from the application of the principles laid down in subparagraphs (a) and (b), there are reasons to believe that the subsidy may in fact be specific, other factors may be considered. Such factors are: use of a subsidy programme by a limited number of certain enterprises, predominant use by certain enterprises, the granting of disproportionately large amounts of subsidy to certain enterprises, and the manner in which discretion has been exercised by the granting authority in the decision to grant a subsidy.[3] In applying this subparagraph, account shall be taken of the extent of diversification of economic activities within the jurisdiction of the granting authority, as well as of the length of time during which the subsidy programme has been in operation.

2.2   A subsidy which is limited to certain enterprises located within a designated geographical region within the jurisdiction of the granting authority shall be specific. It is understood that the setting or change of generally applicable tax rates by all levels of government entitled to do so shall not be deemed to be a specific subsidy for the purposes of this Agreement.

2.3   Any subsidy falling under the provisions of Article 3 shall be deemed to be specific.

2.4   Any determination of specificity under the provisions of this Article shall be clearly substantiated on the basis of positive evidence.

PART II: PROHIBITED SUBSIDIES

Article 3

Prohibition

3.1   Except as provided in the Agreement on Agriculture, the following subsidies, within the meaning of Article 1, shall be prohibited:

---

[2]   Objective criteria or conditions, as used herein, mean criteria or conditions which are neutral, which do not favour certain enterprises over others, and which are economic in nature and horizontal in application, such as number of employees or size of enterprise.

[3]   In this regard, in particular, information on the frequency with which applications for a subsidy are refused or approved and the reasons for such decisions shall be considered.

(a) subsidies contingent, in law or in fact,[4] whether solely or as one of several other conditions, upon export performance, including those illustrated in Annex I[5];

(b) subsidies contingent, whether solely or as one of several other conditions, upon the use of domestic over imported goods.

3.2   A Member shall neither grant nor maintain subsidies referred to in paragraph 1.

Article 4

Remedies

4.1   Whenever a Member has reason to believe that a prohibited subsidy is being granted or maintained by another Member, such Member may request consultations with such other Member.

* * *

4.4   If no mutually agreed solution has been reached within 30 days[6] of the request for consultations, any Member party to such consultations may refer the matter to the Dispute Settlement Body ("DSB") for the immediate establishment of a panel, unless the DSB decides by consensus not to establish a panel.

4.5   Upon its establishment, the panel may request the assistance of the Permanent Group of Experts (referred to in this Agreement as the "PGE") with regard to whether the measure in question is a prohibited subsidy. If so requested, the PGE shall immediately review the evidence with regard to the existence and nature of the measure in question and shall provide an opportunity for the Member applying or maintaining the measure to demonstrate that the measure in question is not a prohibited subsidy. The PGE shall report its conclusions to the panel within a time-limit determined by the panel. The PGE's conclusions on the issue of whether or not the measure in question is a prohibited subsidy shall be accepted by the panel without modification.

4.6   The panel shall submit its final report to the parties to the dispute. The report shall be circulated to all Members within 90 days of the date of the composition and the establishment of the panel's terms of reference.

4.7   If the measure in question is found to be a prohibited subsidy, the panel shall recommend that the subsidizing Member withdraw the subsidy without delay. In this regard, the panel shall specify in its

---

[4]   This standard is met when the facts demonstrate that the granting of a subsidy, without having been made legally contingent upon export performance, is in fact tied to actual or anticipated exportation or export earnings. The mere fact that a subsidy is granted to enterprises which export shall not for that reason alone be considered to be an export subsidy within the meaning of this provision.

[5]   Measures referred to in Annex I as not constituting export subsidies shall not be prohibited under this or any other provision of this Agreement.

[6]   Any time-periods mentioned in this Article may be extended by mutual agreement.

recommendation the time-period within which the measure must be withdrawn.

4.8 Within 30 days of the issuance of the panel's report to all Members, the report shall be adopted by the DSB unless one of the parties to the dispute formally notifies the DSB of its decision to appeal or the DSB decides by consensus not to adopt the report.

4.9 Where a panel report is appealed, the Appellate Body shall issue its decision within 30 days from the date when the party to the dispute formally notifies its intention to appeal. When the Appellate Body considers that it cannot provide its report within 30 days, it shall inform the DSB in writing of the reasons for the delay together with an estimate of the period within which it will submit its report. In no case shall the proceedings exceed 60 days. The appellate report shall be adopted by the DSB and unconditionally accepted by the parties to the dispute unless the DSB decides by consensus not to adopt the appellate report within 20 days following its issuance to the Members.

4.10 In the event the recommendation of the DSB is not followed within the time-period specified by the panel, which shall commence from the date of adoption of the panel's report or the Appellate Body's report, the DSB shall grant authorization to the complaining Member to take appropriate countermeasures, unless the DSB decides by consensus to reject the request.

4.11 In the event a party to the dispute requests arbitration under paragraph 6 of Article 22 of the Dispute Settlement Understanding ("DSU"), the arbitrator shall determine whether the countermeasures are appropriate.

4.12 For purposes of disputes conducted pursuant to this Article, except for time-periods specifically prescribed in this Article, time-periods applicable under the DSU for the conduct of such disputes shall be half the time prescribed therein.

PART III: ACTIONABLE SUBSIDIES

Article 5

Adverse Effects

No Member should cause, through the use of any subsidy referred to in paragraphs 1 and 2 of Article 1, adverse effects to the interests of other Members, i.e.:

(a) injury to the domestic industry of another Member;

(b) nullification or impairment of benefits accruing directly or indirectly to other Members under GATT 1994 in particular the benefits of concessions bound under Article II of GATT 1994;

(c) serious prejudice to the interests of another Member.

This Article does not apply to subsidies maintained on agricultural products as provided in Article 13 of the Agreement on Agriculture.

Article 6

Serious Prejudice

[Note: The provisions of Art. 6(1) have "sunset" under Art. 31, and have not been renewed.]

6.2 Notwithstanding the provisions of paragraph 1, serious prejudice shall not be found if the subsidizing Member demonstrates that the subsidy in question has not resulted in any of the effects enumerated in paragraph 3.

6.3 Serious prejudice in the sense of paragraph (c) of Article 5 may arise in any case where one or several of the following apply:

(a) the effect of the subsidy is to displace or impede the imports of a like product of another Member into the market of the subsidizing Member;

(b) the effect of the subsidy is to displace or impede the exports of a like product of another Member from a third country market;

(c) the effect of the subsidy is a significant price undercutting by the subsidized product as compared with the price of a like product of another Member in the same market or significant price suppression, price depression or lost sales in the same market;

(d) the effect of the subsidy is an increase in the world market share of the subsidizing Member in a particular subsidized primary product or commodity[17] as compared to the average share it had during the previous period of three years and this increase follows a consistent trend over a period when subsidies have been granted.

6.4 For the purpose of paragraph 3(b), the displacement or impeding of exports shall include any case in which, subject to the provisions of paragraph 7, it has been demonstrated that there has been a change in relative shares of the market to the disadvantage of the non-subsidized like product (over an appropriately representative period sufficient to demonstrate clear trends in the development of the market for the product concerned, which, in normal circumstances, shall be at least one year). "Change in relative shares of the market" shall include any of the following situations: (*a*) there is an increase in the market share of the subsidized product; (*b*) the market share of the subsidized product remains constant in circumstances in which, in the absence of the subsidy, it would have declined; (*c*) the market share of the subsidized product declines, but at a slower rate than would have been the case in the absence of the subsidy.

6.5 For the purpose of paragraph 3(c), price undercutting shall include any case in which such price undercutting has been demonstrated

---

[17] Unless other multilaterally agreed specific rules apply to the trade in the product or commodity in question.

through a comparison of prices of the subsidized product with prices of a non-subsidized like product supplied to the same market. The comparison shall be made at the same level of trade and at comparable times, due account being taken of any other factor affecting price comparability. However, if such a direct comparison is not possible, the existence of price undercutting may be demonstrated on the basis of export unit values.

6.6   Each Member in the market of which serious prejudice is alleged to have arisen shall, subject to the provisions of paragraph 3 of Annex V, make available to the parties to a dispute arising under Article 7, and to the panel established pursuant to paragraph 4 of Article 7, all relevant information that can be obtained as to the changes in market shares of the parties to the dispute as well as concerning prices of the products involved.

6.7   Displacement or impediment resulting in serious prejudice shall not arise under paragraph 3 where any of the following circumstances exist[18] during the relevant period:

(a) prohibition or restriction on exports of the like product from the complaining Member or on imports from the complaining Member into the third country market concerned;

(b) decision by an importing government operating a monopoly of trade or state trading in the product concerned to shift, for non-commercial reasons, imports from the complaining Member to another country or countries;

(c) natural disasters, strikes, transport disruptions or other force majeure substantially affecting production, qualities, quantities or prices of the product available for export from the complaining Member;

(d) existence of arrangements limiting exports from the complaining Member;

(e) voluntary decrease in the availability for export of the product concerned from the complaining Member (including, inter alia, a situation where firms in the complaining Member have been autonomously reallocating exports of this product to new markets);

(f) failure to conform to standards and other regulatory requirements in the importing country.

6.8   In the absence of circumstances referred to in paragraph 7, the existence of serious prejudice should be determined on the basis of the information submitted to or obtained by the panel, including information submitted in accordance with the provisions of Annex V.

---

[18]   The fact that certain circumstances are referred to in this paragraph does not, in itself, confer upon them any legal status in terms of either GATT 1994 or this Agreement. These circumstances must not be isolated, sporadic or otherwise insignificant.

6.9   This Article does not apply to subsidies maintained on agricultural products as provided in Article 13 of the Agreement on Agriculture.

Article 7

Remedies

7.1   Except as provided in Article 13 of the Agreement on Agriculture, whenever a Member has reason to believe that any subsidy referred to in Article 1, granted or maintained by another Member, results in injury to its domestic industry, nullification or impairment or serious prejudice, such Member may request consultations with such other Member.

* * *

7.4   If consultations do not result in a mutually agreed solution within 60 days, any Member party to such consultations may refer the matter to the DSB for the establishment of a panel, unless the DSB decides by consensus not to establish a panel. The composition of the panel and its terms of reference shall be established within 15 days from the date when it is established.

7.5   The panel shall review the matter and shall submit its final report to the parties to the dispute. The report shall be circulated to all Members within 120 days of the date of the composition and establishment of the panel's terms of reference.

7.6   Within 30 days of the issuance of the panel's report to all Members, the report shall be adopted by the DSB unless one of the parties to the dispute formally notifies the DSB of its decision to appeal or the DSB decides by consensus not to adopt the report.

* * *

7.9   In the event the Member has not taken appropriate steps to remove the adverse effects of the subsidy or withdraw the subsidy within six months from the date when the DSB adopts the panel report or the Appellate Body report, and in the absence of agreement on compensation, the DSB shall grant authorization to the complaining Member to take countermeasures, commensurate with the degree and nature of the adverse effects determined to exist, unless the DSB decides by consensus to reject the request.

* * *

PART IV: NON-ACTIONABLE SUBSIDIES

Article 8

Identification of Non-actionable Subsidies

[Note: The provisions of Arts. 8 and 9 have "sunset" under Art. 31, and have not been renewed.]

* * *

Article 9

Consultations and Authorized Remedies

[Note: The provisions of Art. 8 and 9 have "sunset" under Art. 31, and have not been renewed.]

PART V: COUNTERVAILING MEASURES

Article 10

Application of Article VI of GATT 1994[35]

Members shall take all necessary steps to ensure that the imposition of a countervailing duty[36] on any product of the territory of any Member imported into the territory of another Member is in accordance with the provisions of Article VI of GATT 1994 and the terms of this Agreement. Countervailing duties may only be imposed pursuant to investigations initiated and conducted in accordance with the provisions of this Agreement and the Agreement on Agriculture.

Article 11

Initiation and Subsequent Investigation

11.1 Except as provided in paragraph 6, an investigation to determine the existence, degree and effect of any alleged subsidy shall be initiated upon a written application by or on behalf of the domestic industry.

11.2 An application under paragraph 1 shall include sufficient evidence of the existence of *(a)* a subsidy and, if possible, its amount, (b) injury within the meaning of Article VI of GATT 1994 as interpreted by this Agreement, and *(c)* a causal link between the subsidized imports and the alleged injury. Simple assertion, unsubstantiated by relevant evidence, cannot be considered sufficient to meet the requirements of this paragraph. The application shall contain such information as is reasonably available to the applicant on the following:

---

[35]   The provisions of Part II or III may be invoked in parallel with the provisions of Part V; however, with regard to the effects of a particular subsidy in the domestic market of the importing Member, only one form of relief (either a countervailing duty, if the requirements of Part V are met, or a countermeasure under Articles 4 or 7) shall be available. The provisions of Parts III and V shall not be invoked regarding measures considered non-actionable in accordance with the provisions of Part IV. However, measures referred to in paragraph 1(a) of Article 8 may be investigated in order to determine whether or not they are specific within the meaning of Article 2. In addition, in the case of a subsidy referred to in paragraph 2 of Article 8 conferred pursuant to a programme which has not been notified in accordance with paragraph 3 of Article 8, the provisions of Part III or V may be invoked, but such subsidy shall be treated as non-actionable if it is found to conform to the standards set forth in paragraph 2 of Article 8.

[36]   The term "countervailing duty" shall be understood to mean a special duty levied for the purpose of offsetting any subsidy bestowed directly or indirectly upon the manufacture, production or export of any merchandise, as provided for in paragraph 3 of Article VI of GATT 1994.

(i) the identity of the applicant and a description of the volume and value of the domestic production of the like product by the applicant. Where a written application is made on behalf of the domestic industry, the application shall identify the industry on behalf of which the application is made by a list of all known domestic producers of the like product (or associations of domestic producers of the like product) and, to the extent possible, a description of the volume and value of domestic production of the like product accounted for by such producers;

(ii) a complete description of the allegedly subsidized product, the names of the country or countries of origin or export in question, the identity of each known exporter or foreign producer and a list of known persons importing the product in question;

(iii) evidence with regard to the existence, amount and nature of the subsidy in question;

(iv) evidence that alleged injury to a domestic industry is caused by subsidized imports through the effects of the subsidies; this evidence includes information on the evolution of the volume of the allegedly subsidized imports, the effect of these imports on prices of the like product in the domestic market and the consequent impact of the imports on the domestic industry, as demonstrated by relevant factors and indices having a bearing on the state of the domestic industry, such as those listed in paragraphs 2 and 4 of Article 15.

11.3 The authorities shall review the accuracy and adequacy of the evidence provided in the application to determine whether the evidence is sufficient to justify the initiation of an investigation.

11.4 An investigation shall not be initiated pursuant to paragraph 1 unless the authorities have determined, on the basis of an examination of the degree of support for, or opposition to, the application expressed[38] by domestic producers of the like product, that the application has been made by or on behalf of the domestic industry.[39] The application shall be considered to have been made "by or on behalf of the domestic industry" if it is supported by those domestic producers whose collective output constitutes more than 50 per cent of the total production of the like product produced by that portion of the domestic industry expressing either support for or opposition to the application. However, no investigation shall be initiated when domestic producers expressly supporting the application account for less than 25 per cent of total production of the like product produced by the domestic industry.

---

[38] In the case of fragmented industries involving an exceptionally large number of producers, authorities may determine support and opposition by using statistically valid sampling techniques.

[39] Members are aware that in the territory of certain Members employees of domestic producers of the like product or representatives of those employees may make or support an application for an investigation under paragraph 1.

* * *

11.6 If, in special circumstances, the authorities concerned decide to initiate an investigation without having received a written application by or on behalf of a domestic industry for the initiation of such investigation, they shall proceed only if they have sufficient evidence of the existence of a subsidy, injury and causal link, as described in paragraph 2, to justify the initiation of an investigation.

* * *

11.9 An application under paragraph 1 shall be rejected and an investigation shall be terminated promptly as soon as the authorities concerned are satisfied that there is not sufficient evidence of either subsidization or of injury to justify proceeding with the case. There shall be immediate termination in cases where the amount of a subsidy is *de minimis*, or where the volume of subsidized imports, actual or potential, or the injury, is negligible. For the purpose of this paragraph, the amount of the subsidy shall be considered to be *de minimis* if the subsidy is less than 1 per cent ad valorem.

* * *

Article 12

Evidence

12.1 Interested Members and all interested parties in a countervailing duty investigation shall be given notice of the information which the authorities require and ample opportunity to present in writing all evidence which they consider relevant in respect of the investigation in question.

12.1.1   Exporters, foreign producers or interested Members receiving questionnaires used in a countervailing duty investigation shall be given at least 30 days for reply. Due consideration should be given to any request for an extension of the 30-day period and, upon cause shown, such an extension should be granted whenever practicable.

12.1.2   Subject to the requirement to protect confidential information, evidence presented in writing by one interested Member or interested party shall be made available promptly to other interested Members or interested parties participating in the investigation.

* * *

12.4 Any information which is by nature confidential (for example, because its disclosure would be of significant competitive advantage to a competitor or because its disclosure would have a significantly adverse effect upon a person supplying the information or upon a person from whom the supplier acquired the information), or which is provided on a confidential basis by parties to an investigation shall, upon good cause shown, be treated as such by the authorities. Such information shall not be disclosed without specific permission of the party submitting it.

12.4.1   The authorities shall require interested Members or interested parties providing confidential information to furnish non-confidential summaries thereof. These summaries shall be in sufficient detail to permit a reasonable understanding of the substance of the information submitted in confidence. In exceptional circumstances, such Members or parties may indicate that such information is not susceptible of summary.

In such exceptional circumstances, a statement of the reasons why summarization is not possible must be provided.

12.4.2   If the authorities find that a request for confidentiality is not warranted and if the supplier of the information is either unwilling to make the information public or to authorize its disclosure in generalized or summary form, the authorities may disregard such information unless it can be demonstrated to their satisfaction from appropriate sources that the information is correct.

12.5 Except in circumstances provided for in paragraph 7, the authorities shall during the course of an investigation satisfy themselves as to the accuracy of the information supplied by interested Members or interested parties upon which their findings are based.

12.6 The investigating authorities may carry out investigations in the territory of other Members as required, provided that they have notified in good time the Member in question and unless that Member objects to the investigation. Further, the investigating authorities may carry out investigations on the premises of a firm and may examine the records of a firm if *(a)* the firm so agrees and *(b)* the Member in question is notified and does not object. * * *

12.7 In cases in which any interested Member or interested party refuses access to, or otherwise does not provide, necessary information within a reasonable period or significantly impedes the investigation, preliminary and final determinations, affirmative or negative, may be made on the basis of the facts available.

* * *

12.10   The authorities shall provide opportunities for industrial users of the product under investigation, and for representative consumer organizations in cases where the product is commonly sold at the retail level, to provide information which is relevant to the investigation regarding subsidization, injury and causality.

12.11   The authorities shall take due account of any difficulties experienced by interested parties, in particular small companies, in supplying information requested, and shall provide any assistance practicable.

* * *

Article 13

Consultations

13.1 As soon as possible after an application under Article 11 is accepted, and in any event before the initiation of any investigation, Members the products of which may be subject to such investigation shall be invited for consultations with the aim of clarifying the situation as to the matters referred to in paragraph 2 of Article 11 and arriving at a mutually agreed solution.

13.2 Furthermore, throughout the period of investigation, Members the products of which are the subject of the investigation shall be afforded a reasonable opportunity to continue consultations, with a view to clarify the factual situation and to arriving at a mutually agreed solution.[44]

* * *

Article 14

Calculation of the Amount of a Subsidy in Terms of the Benefit to the Recipient

For the purpose of Part V, any method used by the investigating authority to calculate the benefit to the recipient conferred pursuant to paragraph 1 of Article 1 shall be provided for in the national legislation or implementing regulations of the Member concerned and its application to each particular case shall be transparent and adequately explained. Furthermore, any such method shall be consistent with the following guidelines:

(a) government provision of equity capital shall not be considered as conferring a benefit, unless the investment decision can be regarded as inconsistent with the usual investment practice (including for the provision of risk capital) of private investors in the territory of that Member;

(b) a loan by a government shall not be considered as conferring a benefit, unless there is a difference between the amount that the firm receiving the loan pays on the government loan and the amount the firm would pay on a comparable commercial loan which the firm could actually obtain on the market. In this case the benefit shall be the difference between these two amounts;

(c) a loan guarantee by a government shall not be considered as conferring a benefit, unless there is a difference between the amount that the firm receiving the guarantee pays

---

[44]   It is particularly important, in accordance with the provisions of this paragraph, that no affirmative determination whether preliminary or final be made without reasonable opportunity for consultations having been given. Such consultation may establish the basis for proceeding under the provisions of Part II, III, or X.

on a loan guaranteed by the government and the amount that the firm would pay on a comparable commercial loan absent the government guarantee. In this case the benefit shall be the difference between these two amounts adjusted for any differences in fees;

(d) the provision of goods or services or purchase of goods by a government shall not be considered as conferring a benefit unless the provision is made for less than adequate remuneration, or the purchase is made for more than adequate remuneration. The adequacy of remuneration shall be determined in relation to prevailing market conditions for the good or service in question in the country of provision or purchase (including price, quality, availability, marketability, transportation and other conditions of purchase or sale).

Article 15

Determination of Injury[45]

15.1 A determination of injury for purposes of Article VI of GATT 1994 shall be based on positive evidence and involve an objective examination of both *(a)* the volume of the subsidized imports and the effect of the subsidized imports on prices in the domestic market for like products[46] and *(b)* the consequent impact of these imports on the domestic producers of such products.

15.2 With regard to the volume of the subsidized imports, the investigating authorities shall consider whether there has been a significant increase in subsidized imports, either in absolute terms or relative to production or consumption in the importing Member. With regard to the effect of the subsidized imports on prices, the investigating authorities shall consider whether there has been a significant price undercutting by the subsidized imports as compared with the price of a like product of the importing Member, or whether the effect of such imports is otherwise to depress prices to a significant degree or to prevent price increases, which otherwise would have occurred, to a significant degree. No one or several of these factors can necessarily give decisive guidance.

15.3 Where imports of a product from more than one country are simultaneously subject to countervailing duty investigations, the investigating authorities may cumulatively assess the effects of such imports only if they determine that *(a)* the amount of subsidization established in relation to the imports from each country is more than *de*

---

[45]   Under this Agreement the term "injury" shall, unless otherwise specified, be taken to mean material injury to a domestic industry, threat of material injury to a domestic industry or material retardation of the establishment of such an industry and shall be interpreted in accordance with the provisions of this Article.

[46]   Throughout this Agreement the term "like product" ("produit similaire") shall be interpreted to mean a product which is identical, i.e. alike in all respects to the product under consideration, or in the absence of such a product, another product which, although not alike in all respects, has characteristics closely resembling those of the product under consideration.

minimis as defined in paragraph 9 of Article 11 and the volume of imports from each country is not negligible and *(b)* a cumulative assessment of the effects of the imports is appropriate in light of the conditions of competition between the imported products and the conditions of competition between the imported products and the like domestic product.

15.4 The examination of the impact of the subsidized imports on the domestic industry shall include an evaluation of all relevant economic factors and indices having a bearing on the state of the industry, including actual and potential decline in output, sales, market share, profits, productivity, return on investments, or utilization of capacity; factors affecting domestic prices; actual and potential negative effects on cash flow, inventories, employment, wages, growth, ability to raise capital or investments and, in the case of agriculture, whether there has been an increased burden on government support programmes. This list is not exhaustive, nor can one or several of these factors necessarily give decisive guidance.

15.5 It must be demonstrated that the subsidized imports are, through the effects[47] of subsidies, causing injury within the meaning of this Agreement. The demonstration of a causal relationship between the subsidized imports and the injury to the domestic industry shall be based on an examination of all relevant evidence before the authorities. The authorities shall also examine any known factors other than the subsidized imports which at the same time are injuring the domestic industry, and the injuries caused by these other factors must not be attributed to the subsidized imports. Factors which may be relevant in this respect include, *inter alia,* the volumes and prices of non-subsidized imports of the product in question, contraction in demand or changes in the patterns of consumption, trade restrictive practices of and competition between the foreign and domestic producers, developments in technology and the export performance and productivity of the domestic industry.

15.6 The effect of the subsidized imports shall be assessed in relation to the domestic production of the like product when available data permit the separate identification of that production on the basis of such criteria as the production process, producers' sales and profits. If such separate identification of that production is not possible, the effects of the subsidized imports shall be assessed by the examination of the production of the narrowest group or range of products, which includes the like product, for which the necessary information can be provided.

15.7 A determination of a threat of material injury shall be based on facts and not merely on allegation, conjecture or remote possibility. The change in circumstances which would create a situation in which the subsidy would cause injury must be clearly foreseen and imminent. In making a determination regarding the existence of a threat of material injury, the investigating authorities should consider, *inter alia,* such factors as:

---

[47]   As set forth in paragraphs 2 and 4.

(i) nature of the subsidy or subsidies in question and the trade effects likely to arise therefrom;

(ii) a significant rate of increase of subsidized imports into the domestic market indicating the likelihood of substantially increased importation;

(iii) sufficient freely disposable, or an imminent, substantial increase in, capacity of the exporter indicating the likelihood of substantially increased subsidized exports to the importing Member's market, taking into account the availability of other export markets to absorb any additional exports;

(iv) whether imports are entering at prices that will have a significant depressing or suppressing effect on domestic prices, and would likely increase demand for further imports; and

(v) inventories of the product being investigated.

No one of these factors by itself can necessarily give decisive guidance but the totality of the factors considered must lead to the conclusion that further subsidized exports are imminent and that, unless protective action is taken, material injury would occur.

15.8 With respect to cases where injury is threatened by subsidized imports, the application of countervailing measures shall be considered and decided with special care.

Article 16

Definition of Domestic Industry

16.1 For the purposes of this Agreement, the term "domestic industry" shall, except as provided in paragraph 2, be interpreted as referring to the domestic producers as a whole of the like products or to those of them whose collective output of the products constitutes a major proportion of the total domestic production of those products, except that when producers are related[48] to the exporters or importers or are themselves importers of the allegedly subsidized product or a like product from other countries, the term "domestic industry" may be interpreted as referring to the rest of the producers.

16.2 In exceptional circumstances, the territory of a Member may, for the production in question, be divided into two or more competitive markets and the producers within each market may be regarded as a separate industry if (a) the producers within such market sell all or almost all of their production of the product in question in that market, and (b) the

---

[48] For the purpose of this paragraph, producers shall be deemed to be related to exporters or importers only if (a) one of them directly or indirectly controls the other; or (b) both of them are directly or indirectly controlled by a third person; or (c) together they directly or indirectly control a third person, provided that there are grounds for believing or suspecting that the effect of the relationship is such as to cause the producer concerned to behave differently from non-related producers. For the purpose of this paragraph, one shall be deemed to control another when the former is legally or operationally in a position to exercise restraint or direction over the latter.

demand in that market is not to any substantial degree supplied by producers of the product in question located elsewhere in the territory. In such circumstances, injury may be found to exist even where a major portion of the total domestic industry is not injured, provided there is a concentration of subsidized imports into such an isolated market and provided further that the subsidized imports are causing injury to the producers of all or almost all of the production within such market.

16.3 When the domestic industry has been interpreted as referring to the producers in a certain area, i.e. a market as defined in paragraph 2, countervailing duties shall be levied only on the products in question consigned for final consumption to that area. When the constitutional law of the importing Member does not permit the levying of countervailing duties without limitation only if *(a)* the exporters shall have been given an opportunity to cease exporting at subsidized prices to the area concerned or otherwise give assurances pursuant to Article 18, and adequate assurances in this regard have not been promptly given, and *(b)* such duties cannot be levied only on products of specific producers which supply the area in question.

16.4 Where two or more countries have reached under the provisions of paragraph 8(a) of Article XXIV of GATT 1994 such a level of integration that they have the characteristics of a single, unified market, the industry in the entire area of integration shall be taken to be the domestic industry referred to in paragraphs 1 and 2.

16.5 The provisions of paragraph 6 of Article 15 shall be applicable to this Article.

Article 17

Provisional Measures

17.1 Provisional measures may be applied only if:

(a) an investigation has been initiated in accordance with the provisions of Article 11, a public notice has been given to that effect and interested Members and interested parties have been given adequate opportunities to submit information and make comments;

(b) a preliminary affirmative determination has been made that a subsidy exists and that there is injury to a domestic industry caused by subsidized imports; and

(c) the authorities concerned judge such measures necessary to prevent injury being caused during the investigation.

17.2 Provisional measures may take the form of provisional countervailing duties guaranteed by cash deposits or bonds equal to the amount of the provisionally calculated amount of subsidization.

17.3 Provisional measures shall not be applied sooner than 60 days from the date of initiation of the investigation.

17.4 The application of provisional measures shall be limited to as short a period as possible, not exceeding four months.

17.5 The relevant provisions of Article 19 shall be followed in the application of provisional measures.

Article 18

Undertakings

18.1 Proceedings may[49] be suspended or terminated without the imposition of provisional measures or countervailing duties upon receipt of satisfactory voluntary undertakings under which:

(a) the government of the exporting Member agrees to eliminate or limit the subsidy or take other measures concerning its effects; or

(b) the exporter agrees to revise its prices so that the investigating authorities are satisfied that the injurious effect of the subsidy is eliminated. Price increases under such undertakings shall not be higher than necessary to eliminate the amount of the subsidy. It is desirable that the price increases be less than the amount of the subsidy if such increases would be adequate to remove the injury to the domestic industry.

18.2 Undertakings shall not be sought or accepted unless the authorities of the importing Member have made a preliminary affirmative determination of subsidization and injury caused by such subsidization and, in case of undertakings from exporters, have obtained the consent of the exporting Member.

18.3 Undertakings offered need not be accepted if the authorities of the importing Member consider their acceptance impractical, for example if the number of actual or potential exporters is too great, or for other reasons, including reasons of general policy. Should the case arise and where practicable, the authorities shall provide to the exporter the reasons which have led them to consider acceptance of an undertaking as inappropriate, and shall, to the extent possible, give the exporter an opportunity to make comments thereon.

18.4 If an undertaking is accepted, the investigation of subsidization and injury shall nevertheless be completed if the exporting Member so desires or the importing Member so decides. In such a case, if a negative determination of subsidization or injury is made, the undertaking shall automatically lapse, except in cases where such a determination is due in large part to the existence of an undertaking. In such cases, the authorities concerned may require that an undertaking be maintained for a reasonable period consistent with the provisions of this Agreement. In the event that an affirmative determination of subsidization and injury is made, the

---

[49] The word "may" shall not be interpreted to allow the simultaneous continuation of proceedings with the implementation of undertakings, except as provided in paragraph 4.

undertaking shall continue consistent with its terms and the provisions of this Agreement.

18.5 Price undertakings may be suggested by the authorities of the importing Member, but no exporter shall be forced to enter into such undertakings. The fact that governments or exporters do not offer such undertakings, or do not accept an invitation to do so, shall in no way prejudice the consideration of the case. However, the authorities are free to determine that a threat of injury is more likely to be realized if the subsidized imports continue.

18.6 Authorities of an importing Member may require any government or exporter from whom an undertaking has been accepted to provide periodically information relevant to the fulfilment of such an undertaking, and to permit verification of pertinent data. In case of violation of an undertaking, the authorities of the importing Member may take, under this Agreement in conformity with its provisions, expeditious actions which may constitute immediate application of provisional measures using the best information available. In such cases, definitive duties may be levied in accordance with this Agreement on products entered for consumption not more than 90 days before the application of such provisional measures, except that any such retroactive assessment shall not apply to imports entered before the violation of the undertaking.

Article 19

Imposition and Collection of Countervailing Duties

19.1 If, after reasonable efforts have been made to complete consultations, a Member makes a final determination of the existence and amount of the subsidy and that, through the effects of the subsidy, the subsidized imports are causing injury, it may impose a countervailing duty in accordance with the provisions of this Article unless the subsidy or subsidies are withdrawn.

19.2 The decision whether or not to impose a countervailing duty in cases where all requirements for the imposition have been fulfilled, and the decision whether the amount of the countervailing duty to be imposed shall be the full amount of the subsidy or less, are decisions to be made by the authorities of the importing Member. It is desirable that the imposition should be permissive in the territory of all Members, that the duty should be less than the total amount of the subsidy if such lesser duty would be adequate to remove the injury to the domestic industry, and that procedures should be established which would allow the authorities concerned to take due account of representations made by domestic interested parties[50] whose interests might be adversely affected by the imposition of a countervailing duty.

19.3 When a countervailing duty is imposed in respect of any product, such countervailing duty shall be levied, in the appropriate amounts in

---

[50]   For the purpose of this paragraph, the term "domestic interested parties" shall include consumers and industrial users of the imported product subject to investigation.

each case, on a non-discriminatory basis on imports of such product from all sources found to be subsidized and causing injury, except as to imports from those sources which have renounced any subsidies in question or from which undertakings under the terms of this Agreement have been accepted. Any exporter whose exports are subject to a definitive countervailing duty but who was not actually investigated for reasons other than a refusal to cooperate, shall be entitled to an expedited review in order that the investigating authorities promptly establish an individual countervailing duty rate for that exporter.

19.4 No countervailing duty shall be levied on any imported product in excess of the amount of the subsidy found to exist, calculated in terms of subsidization per unit of the subsidized and exported product.

Article 20

Retroactivity

20.1 Provisional measures and countervailing duties shall only be applied to products which enter for consumption after the time when the decision under paragraph 1 of Article 17 and paragraph 1 of Article 19, respectively, enters into force, subject to the exceptions set out in this Article.

* * *

Article 21

Duration and Review of Countervailing Duties and Undertakings

21.1 A countervailing duty shall remain in force only as long as and to the extent necessary to counteract subsidization which is causing injury.

21.2 The authorities shall review the need for the continued imposition of the duty, where warranted, on their own initiative or, provided that a reasonable period of time has elapsed since the imposition of the definitive countervailing duty, upon request by any interested party which submits positive information substantiating the need for a review. Interested parties shall have the right to request the authorities to examine whether the continued imposition of the duty is necessary to offset subsidization, whether the injury would be likely to continue or recur if the duty were removed or varied, or both. If, as a result of the review under this paragraph, the authorities determine that the countervailing duty is no longer warranted, it shall be terminated immediately.

21.3 Notwithstanding the provisions of paragraphs 1 and 2, any definitive countervailing duty shall be terminated on a date not later than five years from its imposition (or from the date of the most recent review under paragraph 2 if that review has covered both subsidization and injury, or under this paragraph), unless the authorities determine, in a review initiated before that date on their own initiative or upon a duly substantiated request made by or on behalf of the domestic industry within a reasonable period of time prior to that date, that the expiry of the duty would be likely to lead to continuation or recurrence of subsidization and injury. The duty may remain in force pending the outcome of such a review.

21.4 The provisions of Article 12 regarding evidence and procedure shall apply to any review carried out under this Article. Any such review shall be carried out expeditiously and shall normally be concluded within 12 months of the date of initiation of the review.

21.5 The provisions of this Article shall apply *mutatis mutandis* to undertakings accepted under Article 18.

Article 22

Public Notice and Explanation of Determinations

22.1 When the authorities are satisfied that there is sufficient evidence to justify the initiation of an investigation pursuant to Article 11, the Member or Members the products of which are subject to such investigation and other interested parties known to the investigating authorities to have an interest therein shall be notified and a public notice shall be given.

22.2 A public notice of the initiation of an investigation shall contain, or otherwise make available through a separate report, adequate information on the following:

(i) the name of the exporting country or countries and the product involved;

(ii) the date of initiation of the investigation;

(iii) a description of the subsidy practice or practices to be investigated;

(iv) a summary of the factors on which the allegation of injury is based;

(v) the address to which representations by interested Members and interested parties should be directed; and

(vi) the time-limits allowed to interested Members and interested parties for making their views known.

22.3 Public notice shall be given of any preliminary or final determination, whether affirmative or negative, of any decision to accept an undertaking pursuant to Article 18, of the termination of such an undertaking, and of the termination of a definitive countervailing duty.
* * *

22.4 A public notice of the imposition of provisional measures shall set forth, or otherwise make available through a separate report, sufficiently detailed explanations for the preliminary determinations on the existence of a subsidy and injury and shall refer to the matters of fact and law which have led to arguments being accepted or rejected. Such a notice or report shall, due regard being paid to the requirement for the protection of confidential information, contain in particular:

(i) the names of the suppliers or, when this is impracticable, the supplying countries involved;

(ii) a description of the product which is sufficient for customs purposes;

(iii) the amount of subsidy established and the basis on which the existence of a subsidy has been determined;

(iv) considerations relevant to the injury determination as set out in Article 15;

(v) the main reasons leading to the determination.

22.5 A public notice of conclusion or suspension of an investigation in the case of an affirmative determination providing for the imposition of a definitive duty or the acceptance of an undertaking shall contain, or otherwise make available through a separate report, all relevant information on the matters of fact and law and reasons which have led to the imposition of final measures or the acceptance of an undertaking, due regard being paid to the requirement for the protection of confidential information. In particular, the notice or report shall contain the information described in paragraph 4, as well as the reasons for the acceptance or rejection of relevant arguments or claims made by interested Members and by the exporters and importers.

22.6 A public notice of the termination or suspension of an investigation following the acceptance of an undertaking pursuant to Article 18 shall include, or otherwise make available through a separate report, the non-confidential part of this undertaking.

22.7 The provisions of this Article shall apply *mutatis mutandis* to the initiation and completion of reviews pursuant to Article 21 and to decisions under Article 20 to apply duties retroactively.

Article 23

Judicial Review

Each Member whose national legislation contains provisions on countervailing duty measures shall maintain judicial, arbitral or administrative tribunals or procedures for the purpose, *inter alia,* of the prompt review of administrative actions relating to final determinations and reviews of determinations within the meaning of Article 21. Such tribunals or procedures shall be independent of the authorities responsible for the determination or review in question, and shall provide all interested parties who participated in the administrative proceeding and are directly and individually affected by the administrative actions with access to review.

* * *

PART VII: NOTIFICATION AND SURVEILLANCE

Article 25

Notifications

25.1 Members agree that, without prejudice to the provisions of paragraph 1 of Article XVI of GATT 1994, their notifications of subsidies shall be submitted not later than 30 June of each year and shall conform to the provisions of paragraphs 2 through 6.

25.2 Members shall notify any subsidy as defined in paragraph 1 of Article 1, which is specific within the meaning of Article 2, granted or maintained within their territories.

25.3 The content of notifications should be sufficiently specific to enable other Members to evaluate the trade effects and to understand the operation of notified subsidy programmes. * * *

25.6 Members which consider that there are no measures in their territories requiring notification under paragraph 1 of Article XVI of GATT 1994 and this Agreement shall so inform the Secretariat in writing.

* * *

25.10 Any Member which considers that any measure of another Member having the effects of a subsidy has not been notified in accordance with the provisions of paragraph 1 of Article XVI of GATT 1994 and this Article may bring the matter to the attention of such other Member. If the alleged subsidy is not thereafter notified promptly, such Member may itself bring the alleged subsidy in question to the notice of the Committee.

25.11 Members shall report without delay to the Committee all preliminary or final actions taken with respect to countervailing duties. Such reports shall be available in the Secretariat for inspection by other Members. Members shall also submit, on a semi-annual basis, reports on any counter-vailing duty actions taken within the preceding six months. The semi-annual reports shall be submitted on an agreed standard form.

* * *

PART VIII: DEVELOPING COUNTRY MEMBERS

Article 27

Special and Differential Treatment of Developing Country Members

27.1 Members recognize that subsidies may play an important role in economic development programmes of developing country Members.

27.2 The prohibition of paragraph 1(a) of Article 3 shall not apply to:

(a) developing country Members referred to in Annex VII.

(b) other developing country Members for a period of eight years from the date of entry into force of the WTO Agreement, subject to compliance with the provisions in paragraph 4.

27.3 The prohibition of paragraph 1(b) of Article 3 shall not apply to developing country Members for a period of five years, and shall not apply to least developed country Members for a period of eight years, from the date of entry into force of the WTO Agreement.

27.4 Any developing country Member referred to in paragraph 2(b) shall phase out its export subsidies within the eight-year period, preferably in a progressive manner. * * *

* * *

PART X: DISPUTE SETTLEMENT

Article 30

The provisions of Articles XXII and XXIII of GATT 1994 as elaborated and applied by the Dispute Settlement Understanding shall apply to consultations and the settlement of disputes under this Agreement, except as otherwise specifically provided herein.

PART XI: FINAL PROVISIONS

Article 31

Provisional Application

The provisions of paragraph 1 of Article 6 and the provisions of Article 8 and Article 9 shall apply for a period of five years, beginning with the date of entry into force of the WTO Agreement. Not later than 180 days before the end of this period, the Committee shall review the operation of those provisions, with a view to determining whether to extend their application, either as presently drafted or in a modified form, for a further period.

* * *

ANNEX I

ILLUSTRATIVE LIST OF EXPORT SUBSIDIES

(a) The provision by governments of direct subsidies to a firm or an industry contingent upon export performance.

(b) Currency retention schemes or any similar practices which involve a bonus on exports.

(c) Internal transport and freight charges on export shipments, provided or mandated by governments, on terms more favourable than for domestic shipments.

(d) The provision by governments or their agencies either directly or indirectly through government-mandated schemes, of imported or domestic products or services for use in the production of exported goods, on terms or conditions more favourable than for provision of like or directly competitive products or services for use in the production of goods for domestic consumption, if (in the case of products) such terms or conditions are more favourable than those commercially available[57] on world markets to their exporters.

(e) The full or partial exemption remission, or deferral specifically related to exports, of direct taxes[58] or social welfare charges paid or payable by industrial or commercial enterprises.[59]

---

[57]   The term "commercially available" means that the choice between domestic and imported products is unrestricted and depends only on commercial considerations.

[58]   For the purpose of this Agreement:

(f) The allowance of special deductions directly related to exports or export performance, over and above those granted in respect to production for domestic consumption, in the calculation of the base on which direct taxes are charged.

(g) The exemption or remission, in respect of the production and distribution of exported products, of indirect taxes in excess of those levied in respect of the production and distribution of like products when sold for domestic consumption.

(h) The exemption, remission or deferral of prior-stage cumulative indirect taxes on goods or services used in the production of exported products in excess of the exemption, remission or deferral of like prior-stage cumulative indirect taxes on goods or services used in the production of like products when sold for domestic consumption; provided, however, that prior-stage cumulative indirect taxes may be exempted, remitted or deferred on exported products even when not exempted, remitted or deferred on like products when sold for domestic consumption, if the prior-stage cumulative indirect taxes are levied on inputs that are consumed in the production of the exported product (making normal allowance for

---

The term "direct taxes" shall mean taxes on wages, profits, interests, rents, royalties, and all other forms of income, and taxes on the ownership of real property;

The term "import charges" shall mean tariffs, duties, and other fiscal charges not elsewhere enumerated in this note that are levied on imports;

The term "indirect taxes" shall mean sales, excise, turnover, value added, franchise, stamp, transfer, inventory and equipment taxes, border taxes and all taxes other than direct taxes and import charges;

"Prior-stage" indirect taxes are those levied on goods or services used directly or indirectly in making the product;

"Cumulative" indirect taxes are multi-staged taxes levied where there is no mechanism for subsequent crediting of the tax if the goods or services subject to tax at one stage of production are used in a succeeding stage of production;

"Remission" of taxes includes the refund or rebate of taxes;

"Remission or drawback" includes the full or partial exemption or deferral of import charges.

[59]   The Members recognize that deferral need not amount to an export subsidy where, for example, appropriate interest charges are collected. The Members reaffirm the principle that prices for goods in transactions between exporting enterprises and foreign buyers under their or under the same control should for tax purposes be the prices which would be charged between independent enterprises acting at arm's length. Any Member may draw the attention of another Member to administrative or other practices which may contravene this principle and which result in a significant saving of direct taxes in export transactions. In such circumstances the Members shall normally attempt to resolve their differences using the facilities of existing bilateral tax treaties or other specific international mechanisms, without prejudice to the rights and obligations of Members under GATT 1994, including the right of consultation created in the preceding sentence.

Paragraph (e) is not intended to limit a Member from taking measures to avoid the double taxation of foreign-source income earned by its enterprises or the enterprises of another Member.

waste).[60] This item shall be interpreted in accordance with the guidelines on consumption of inputs in the production process contained in Annex II.

(i) The remission or drawback of import charges in excess of those levied on imported inputs that are consumed in the production of the exported product (making normal allowance for waste); provided, however, that in particular cases a firm may use a quantity of home market inputs equal to, and having the same quality and characteristics as, the imported inputs as a substitute for them in order to benefit from this provision if the import and the corresponding export operations both occur within a reasonable time period, not to exceed two years. This item shall be interpreted in accordance with the guidelines on consumption of inputs in the production process contained in Annex II and the guidelines in the determination of substitution drawback systems as export subsidies contained in Annex III.

(j) The provision by governments (or special institutions controlled by governments) of export credit guarantee or insurance programmes, of insurance or guarantee programmes against increases in the cost of exported products or of exchange risk programmes, at premium rates which are inadequate to cover the long-term operating costs and losses of the programmes.

(k) The grant by governments (or special institutions controlled by and/or acting under the authority of governments) of export credits at rates below those which they actually have to pay for the funds so employed (or would have to pay if they borrowed on international capital markets in order to obtain funds of the same maturity and other credit terms and denominated in the same currency as the export credit), or the payment by them of all or part of the costs incurred by exporters or financial institutions in obtaining credits, in so far as they are used to secure a material advantage in the field of export credit terms.

Provided, however, that if a Member is a party to an international undertaking on official export credits to which at least twelve original Members to this Agreement are parties as of 1 January 1979 (or a successor undertaking which has been adopted by those original Members), or if in practice a Member applies the interest rates provisions of the relevant undertaking, an export credit practice which is in conformity with those provisions shall not be considered an export subsidy prohibited by this Agreement.

(l) Any other charge on the public account constituting an export subsidy in the sense of Article XVI of GATT 1994.

---

[60]   Paragraph (h) does not apply to value-added tax systems and border-tax adjustment in lieu thereof; the problem of the excessive remission of value-added taxes is exclusively covered by paragraph (g).

* * *

ANNEX IV

CALCULATION OF THE TOTAL AD VALOREM SUBSIDIZATION (PARAGRAPH 1(A) OF ARTICLE 6)

1.   Any calculation of the amount of a subsidy for the purpose of paragraph 1(a) of Article 6 shall be done in terms of the cost to the granting government.

2.   Except as provided in paragraphs 3 through 5, in determining whether the overall rate of subsidization exceeds 5 per cent of the value of the product, the value of the product shall be calculated as the total value of the recipient firm's sales in the most recent 12-month period, for which sales data is available, preceding the period in which the subsidy is granted.

3.   Where the subsidy is tied to the production or sale of a given product, the value of the product shall be calculated as the total value of the recipient firm's sales of that product in the most recent 12-month period, for which sales data is available, preceding the period in which the subsidy is granted.

4.   Where the recipient firm is in a start-up situation, serious prejudice shall be deemed to exist if the overall rate of subsidization exceeds 15 per cent of the total funds invested. For purposes of this paragraph, a start-up period will not extend beyond the first year of production.

5.   Where the recipient firm is located in an inflationary economy country, the value of the product shall be calculated as the recipient firm's total sales (or sales of the relevant product, if the subsidy is tied) in the preceding calendar year indexed by the rate of inflation experienced in the 12 months preceding the month in which the subsidy is to be given.

6.   In determining the overall rate of subsidization in a given year, subsidies given under different programmes and by different authorities in the territory of a Member shall be aggregated.

7.   Subsidies granted prior to the date of entry into force of the WTO Agreement, the benefits of which are allocated to future production, shall be included in the overall rate of subsidization.

8.   Subsidies which are non-actionable under relevant provisions of this Agreement shall not be included in the calculation of the amount of a subsidy for the purpose of paragraph 1(a) of Article 6.

ANNEX V

PROCEDURES FOR DEVELOPING INFORMATION CONCERNING SERIOUS PREJUDICE

1.   Every Member shall cooperate in the development of evidence to be examined by a panel in procedures under paragraphs 4 through 6 of Article 7. The parties to the dispute and any third-country Member concerned shall notify to the DSB, as soon as the provisions of paragraph 4

of Article 7 have been invoked, the organization responsible for administration of this provision within its territory and the procedures to be used to comply with requests for information.

2.   In cases where matters are referred to the DSB under paragraph 4 of Article 7, the DSB shall, upon request, initiate the procedure to obtain such information from the government of the subsidizing Member as necessary to establish the existence and amount of subsidization, the value of total sales of the subsidized firms, as well as information necessary to analyze the adverse effects caused by the subsidized product.[66] This process may include, where appropriate, presentation of questions to the government of the subsidizing Member and of the complaining Member to collect information, as well as to clarify and obtain elaboration of information available to the parties to a dispute through the notification procedures set forth in Part VII.[67]

3.   In the case of effects in third-country markets, a party to a dispute may collect information, including through the use of questions to the government of the third-country Member, necessary to analyse adverse effects, which is not otherwise reasonably available from the complaining Member or the subsidizing Member. This requirement should be administered in such a way as not to impose an unreasonable burden on the third-country Member. In particular, such a Member is not expected to make a market or price analysis specially for that purpose. The information to be supplied is that which is already available or can be readily obtained by this Member (e.g. most recent statistics which have already been gathered by relevant statistical services but which have not yet been published, customs data concerning imports and declared values of the products concerned, etc.). However, if a party to a dispute undertakes a detailed market analysis at its own expense, the task of the person or firm conducting such an analysis shall be facilitated by the authorities of the third-country Member and such a person or firm shall be given access to all information which is not normally maintained confidential by the government.

4.   The DSB shall designate a representative to serve the function of facilitating the information-gathering process. The sole purpose of the representative shall be to ensure the timely development of the information necessary to facilitate expeditious subsequent multilateral review of the dispute. In particular, the representative may suggest ways to most efficiently solicit necessary information as well as encourage the cooperation of the parties.

5.   The information-gathering process outlined in paragraphs 2 through 4 shall be completed within 60 days of the date on which the matter has been referred to the DSB under paragraph 4 of Article 7. The information obtained during this process shall be submitted to the panel

---

[66]   In cases where the existence of serious prejudice has to be demonstrated.

[67]   The information-gathering process by the DSB shall take into account the need to protect information which is by nature confidential or which is provided on a confidential basis by any Member involved in this process.

established by the DSB in accordance with the provisions of Part X. This information should include, *inter alia,* data concerning the amount of the subsidy in question (and, where appropriate, the value of total sales of the subsidized firms), prices of the subsidized product, prices of the non-subsidized product, prices of other suppliers to the market, changes in the supply of the subsidized product to the market in question and changes in market shares. It should also include rebuttal evidence, as well as such supplemental information as the panel deems relevant in the course of reaching its conclusions.

6.   If the subsidizing and/or third-country Member fails to cooperate in the information-gathering process, the complaining Member will present its case of serious prejudice, based on evidence available to it, together with facts and circumstances of the non-cooperation of the subsidizing and/or third-country Member. Where information is unavailable due to non-cooperation by the subsidizing and/or third-country Member, the panel may complete the record as necessary relying on best information otherwise available.

7.   In making its determination, the panel should draw adverse inferences from instances of non-cooperation by any party involved in the information-gathering process.

8.   In making a determination to use either best information available or adverse inferences, the panel shall consider the advice of the DSB representative nominated under paragraph 4 as to the reasonableness of any requests for information and the efforts made by parties to comply with these requests in a cooperative and timely manner.

9.   Nothing in the information-gathering process shall limit the ability of the panel to seek such additional information it deems essential to a proper resolution to the dispute, and which was not adequately sought or developed during that process. However, ordinarily the panel should not request additional information to complete the record where the information would support a particular party's position and the absence of that information in the record is the result of unreasonable non-cooperation by that party in the information-gathering process.

* * *

Chapter 6

SAFEGUARD PROCEEDINGS, TRADE ADJUSTMENT ASSISTANCE

Table of Sections

For coverage of European Union safeguards law, see Section 18.3. For NAFTA coverage, see Section 16.3.

-----

§ 6.1   Temporary Relief from Import Competition

Safeguard ("escape clause") and market disruption proceedings are anticipated by Article XIX of the General Agreement on Tariffs and Trade (GATT). A WTO "Safeguards Agreement" emerged from the Uruguay Round of negotiations.[1] In contrast to the statutory remedies against dumping and countervailable subsidies reviewed in Chapters 4 and 5, safeguard proceedings are not targeted at unfair international trade practices. Rather, the goods are assumed

-----

[1]   *See* Section 6.3.

to be fairly traded but imports are in such an unexpected volume that temporary protection is appropriate to allow the domestic industry to adjust to the new competitive environment.

In the United States, businesses may seek protection from import competition by initiating what are known as "escape clause" (safeguard) proceedings under the Trade Act of 1974. Escape clause proceedings can involve imports from anywhere in the world, and are authorized by Section 201 of the Trade Act.[2] Escape clause proceedings are also typically found in the free trade agreements of the United States.

In addition, "market disruption proceedings" can also provide temporary relief from import competition. Market disruption proceedings concern imports from communist nations and are authorized by Section 406 of the 1974 Trade Act.[3] They are similar but not identical to escape clause proceedings. Either may result in the imposition of U.S. import restraints, or presidential negotiation of export restraints from the source country.

Import injury relief available under the Trade Act of 1974 is basically of two kinds: (1) Presidential relief designed to temporarily protect domestic producers of like or directly competitive products; and (2) governmental assistance to workers and firms economically displaced by import competition. This assistance is intended to enhance job opportunities and competitiveness. Protective relief tends to be awarded when the President believes that U.S. industry needs time to adjust. Governmental assistance is seen as a means to accommodate the injury caused by import competition. In either case, adjustment to import competition is the longer term goal, hopefully resulting in more competitive U.S. industries and markets.

§ 6.2 ____ The Impact of Limited U.S. Judicial Review

Because of the President's power over escape clause and market disruption remedies, judicial review of these proceedings and remedies is very limited. As the Federal Circuit observed in *Corus Group PLC. v. International Trade Commission*, "under the escape clause provision of the Trade Act of 1974, '[f]or a court to interpose, there has to be a clear misconstruction of the governing statute, a significant procedural violation, or action outside delegated authority."[4] This flows from the President's broad

---

[2]   19 U.S.C. § 2251.

[3]   19 U.S.C. § 2436.

[4]   352 F.3d 1351, 1361 (Fed. Cir. 2003)(*quoting* Maple Leaf Fish Co. v. United States, 762 F.2d 86, 89 (Fed. Cir. 1985).

constitutional powers over foreign affairs. Derivatively, the actions of the International Trade Commission (ITC, or Commission) in these proceedings are likewise sheltered from extensive judicial review.[5] This means that the decisions of the ITC are critical to obtaining escape clause relief.

GATT/WTO compensation duties, U.S. free trade agreements, presidential prerogatives, and important amendments to Section 201 in 1988 and 1994 have significantly reduced the potential for protective trade relief. During the 1990s, there were very few Section 201 or Section 406 proceedings. Since 2003, the ITC has not instituted any Section 201 proceedings (although it has instituted six under a special rule related to Chinese imports arising from China's accession to the WTO)[6]. The main focus of U.S. escape clause relief has instead become trade adjustment assistance, as Sections 6.14 and 6.15 discuss in detail.

§ 6.3   The WTO Safeguards Agreement

One of the important "Codes" of the Uruguay Round negotiations is the "WTO Agreement on Safeguards." It concerns escape clause and related "gray area" protective measures. Under the Safeguards Agreement, the imposition of temporary protective relief from increased imports (absolutely or relatively) does not require a showing of any unfair trade practice, such as dumping or subsidies. But the injury standard is seemingly higher: Such duties are only permitted only where increased imports cause a "*serious injury or threat thereof*" (emphasis added) to a domestic industry. For antidumping duties and countervailing duties, the standard is merely "material" injury.[7] In addition, reaching back to language found in Article XIX of the GATT, the WTO Appellate Body has ruled that safeguards may be imposed only when the surge of imports is result from "unforeseen developments".[8]

The Safeguards Agreement permits escape clause measures "only to the extent necessary" to prevent or remedy such an injury and to "facilitate adjustment." Such measures are allowed for a maximum of four years, and on a progressively decreasing basis. Upon a further investigation, a member state may extend the measures, but not beyond a total period of eight years.

---

[5]   *Id. See also* Maple Leaf Fish Co. v. United States, 762 F.2d 86 (Fed. Cir. 1985).

[6]   *See* Section 6.12.

[7]   *See* Sections 4.12, 5.13.

[8]   *See* Argentina-Footwear (EC), WT/DS56 (1998); U.S. Steel Safeguards, WT/DS248 (2003).

Perhaps the most important provision of the Safeguards Agreement is that it expressly prohibits a member state from seeking, undertaking, or maintaining voluntary export or import restraint agreements (VERs or OMAs).[9] These were quite common, especially by developed countries to protect against unwanted imports, prior to the adoption of the Safeguards Agreement in 1994.

Protective safeguard remedies are often in the form of tariff increases and tariff rate quotas (TRQs). In general, such remedies must be applied on an MFN-basis to imports regardless of their source. Exporting countries with substantial interests at stake are entitled, absent satisfactory compensation, to suspend trade concessions benefiting the safeguarding country. The duty to compensate can generally be avoided if the safeguard action is for less than three years, responds to absolute import increases, and conforms to the provisions of the Safeguards Code.

Typically, the affected exporters suspend concessions, then de-activate those suspensions while challenging conformity in WTO proceedings. The suspended concessions come back into force after three years, or a WTO ruling of nonconformity with the Safeguards Code, whichever is sooner. Special rules limit the use of safeguard measures against imports from developing countries, and allow such countries to impose safeguard measures to protect domestic industries for up to ten years. The utilization of protective safeguard measures cannot generally be followed by a second usage in the same product market within two years or half the duration of the first use.

Congress implemented the Safeguards Agreement accords in December of 1994 through the Uruguay Round Agreements Act.[10] This Act changed a number of rules of U.S. law relating to escape clause relief. The most notable of these changes were: (1) clarifications of the meaning of significant terms, such as "domestic industry," "serious injury," and "threat of serious injury"; (2) changes to the duration of relief to provide an initial period of up to four years and an overall limit of eight years; (3) a requirement that any relief actions exceeding one year be "phased down at regular intervals" during the relief period; (4)permissible ITC investigations at the request of the President or on petition by industry with respect to continuing a relief measure; (5) certain new rules to protect confidential business information collected as part of a

---

9   *See* Safeguards Agreement, art. 11.
10   Public Law No. 103–465, 108 Stat. 4809.

proceeding; and (6) an allowance of expedited proceedings in "critical circumstances."[11]

The more general effect of URAA was to bring U.S. escape clause law into compliance with the Safeguards Agreement. Except as to certain doubts noted below, the standards and procedures for the granting of escape clause relief as described in the Sections below conform to the substance of the WTO's Safeguards Agreement. At this stage, the United States and the European Union almost never invoke safeguards, but developing nations (for example India, Indonesia and Turkey) have frequently done so.

§ 6.4   U.S. Safeguard Proceedings—Petitions

Decisions about the granting of escape clause relief are made by the President upon the recommendation of the ITC. Any entity that is representative of an industry, including a "trade association, firm, certified or recognized union, or group of workers," may file a petition requesting such import relief.[12] The petition must state the "specific purposes" for any requested action "which may include facilitating the orderly transfer of resources to more productive pursuits, enhancing competitiveness, or other means of adjustment to new conditions of competition."[13] The ITC also must initiate an escape clause proceeding at the request of the President, the United States Trade Representative, and certain congressional committees, and may do so "on its own motion."[14]

The Trade Act indicates that the purposes of the safeguards relief is to facilitate the orderly transfer of resources to more productive pursuits, enhance competitiveness, or otherwise assist an industry to adjust to new conditions of competition.[15] The petition may request provisional relief pending the outcome of an escape clause proceeding. Petitions under Section 201 also must show that a substantial number of the companies or workers in the industry support the petition, as the Trade Act requires that the petitioning "entity" be "representative of an industry."[16] In this sense, the petitioner is like a class action representative. While it is not necessary for all companies or workers in the industry to support the petition, a substantial proportion must do so because Section 201 is focused upon industry-wide relief.

---

[11]   A summary of these changes is available in the International Trade Commission's "Annual Report" of 1995.

[12]   19 U.S.C. § 2252(a)(1).

[13]   19 U.S.C. § 2252(a)(2).

[14]   19 U.S.C. § 2252(b)(1)(A).

[15]   19 U.S.C. § 2252(a)(2).

[16]   19 U.S.C. § 2252(a)(1).

The petitioner industry or worker group may—and is well advised to—submit its own specific plan "to facilitate positive adjustment to import competition" during the term of any protective relief.[17] This is often done because the Commission is required in conducting its escape clause investigation to seek information on actions being taken or planned by the firms and workers in the industry to make a positive adjustment to import competition. Moreover, the Commission is authorized to accept "commitments" regarding such action if it affirmatively determines that the statutory criteria of Section 201 are met.[18]

§ 6.5 _____ITC Investigations

Upon the filing of a petition that meets the statutory requirements, the ITC must then "promptly" begin an investigation to determine whether the import competition meets the statutory standard for temporary escape clause relief.[19] Separately, if the industry is unable to adequately document its case for escape clause relief, it may be possible to convince the Commission to do this on its own under what is known as a general Section 332 investigation.[20] If successful, a Section 332 investigation will shift the burden and the cost of preparing a Section 201 proceeding from the industry or its representatives to the Commission.

As the Commission's investigation proceeds, it will develop an extensive questionnaire to send to domestic producers. This questionnaire focuses on the kinds of information the Commission needs to obtain in order to assess the statutory criteria for escape clause relief. Although industry members typically support escape clause relief, they may not wish to reveal all the information requested in the questionnaire. In this case, the ITC can obtain subpoena enforcement from the U.S. District Court for the District of Columbia.[21]

The hearings held by the ITC in connection with escape clause proceedings involve testimony under oath with the right of cross examination by opposing parties. Thus, for example, importers that do not wish to see restrictive measures imposed may oppose the domestic industry and its witnesses. The various procedures governing escape clause investigations by the ITC defined in 19 C.F.R. Parts 201 and 206. The entire ITC investigation normally takes about six months.

---

[17]   19 U.S.C. § 2252(a)(4).
[18]   19 U.S.C. § 2252(a)(4)–(7).
[19]   19 U.S.C. § 2252(b)(1)(A).
[20]   19 U.S.C. § 1332.
[21]   19 U.S.C. § 1333(b).

§ 6.6   U.S. Statutory Criteria for Safeguard Relief

Section 201 of the Trade Act of 1974 requires proof of an increase in imports which substantially causes or threaten to causes serious injury to domestic industries producing like or directly competitive articles.[22] The ITC traditionally has divided this statutory standard for escape clause relief into three separate criteria. In order to make an affirmative determination on an escape clause petition, the ITC must find, as it stated in the famous (or infamous) *Steel Safeguards* determination, that:

> "(1) Imports of the subject article are in *increased quantities* . . . ;
>
> (2) The domestic industry producing an article that is like or directly competitive with the imported article is *seriously injured or threatened with serious injury*; and
>
> (3) The article is being imported in such increased quantities as to be a *substantial cause* of serious injury or threat of serious injury to the domestic industry."[23]

Of these three, the causation and injury criteria are the most consequential. They are the subject of separate analysis in Sections 6.8 and 6.9 below.

The increased quantity of imports test is comparatively uncontroversial. But for clarity the Trade Act emphasizes that the required "increase" in imports may be "either actual or relative to domestic production," and in consideration of imports from all sources. Relative increases occur when domestic production declines when measured against imports. Imports could thus decline but be relatively increasing if domestic production is declining at an even faster rate.[24]

§ 6.7   ____Relevant Domestic Industry

The focus of an escape clause proceeding is the harm to a domestic industry. Thus, the ITC must first identify what the relevant domestic industry is. But this in turn requires an identification of the relevant domestic products affected by the imports. The Trade Act focuses on the domestic industry that "produc[es] an article like or directly competitive with the imported article."[25] In determining what constitutes a "like product," the ITC

---

[22]   19 U.S.C. § 2251(a).

[23]   *See* U.S. International Trade Commission—*Steel*, Investigation No. TA–201–73, at 27 (Pub. No. 3479, Dec., 2001).

[24]   *See* 19 U.S.C. § 2252(c)(1)(C).

[25]   19 U.S.C. § 2252(b)(1)(A).

has traditionally consider a wide variety of factors, including "the physical properties of the product, its customs treatment, its manufacturing process (*i.e.*, where and how it is made), its uses, and the marketing channels through which the product is sold."[26]

Escape clause proceedings nonetheless commonly involve disputes as to the definition of the "competitive" imported article. Typically, domestic producers will want to define the imported article broadly so as to enhance the possibility of proving domestic injury as well as of obtaining broader relief. Importers of the product in question will want to define the imported article narrowly or in terms of separate categories so as to minimize the potential for escape clause remedies.

One issue concerning the definition of the domestic industry is whether it can involve various stages of processing. In other words, the issue is whether the imports must be at the same level of processing as the domestic industry. Once a uncertain area, the Trade Act now specifically states that various stages of processing can be considered in defining the relevant imported product. This has the practical effect of allowing the imported article to be at a different level of process from that which causes injury to the domestic industry.[27]

The next step is to identify the relevant domestic industry with respect to the relevant competitive products. The Trade Act defines the relevant "domestic industry" as either all of the producers of the articles at issue or "those producers whose collective production of the like or directly competitive article constitutes a major proportion of the total domestic production" of those articles.[28]

Having defined the industry, the Commission then must decide which particular companies belong to it. This is not always easy. In the ITC's automobile investigation during the serious economic downturn of the 1970s, for example, the Commission had to decide whether dealers and independent parts suppliers were part of the same domestic industry. It found that neither were part of the domestic industry because the dealers did not produce any article, and the independent suppliers of parts did not produce products that were like or directly competitive with the final product.[29]

---

[26]   *See* U.S. International Trade Commission—*Steel*, Investigation No. TA–201–73, at 30 (Pub. No. 3479, Dec., 2001).

[27]   *See* 19 U.S.C. § 2481(5).

[28]   19 U.S.C. § 2252(c)(6)(A).

[29]   *See* U.S. International Trade Commission—*Certain Motor Vehicles and Certain Chassis and Bodies Thereof*, Investigation No. TA–201–44, Publication No. 1110 (Dec. 1980).

To guide this difficult issue, the Trade Act provides specific instructions to the ITC: First, if a domestic company is also an importer, the ITC may only consider that part of the business that relates to domestic production to be in the domestic industry.[30] Second, if a domestic company produces more than one article, the ITC may treat as part of such domestic industry "only that portion or subdivision of the producer which produces the like or directly competitive article."[31] Finally, if the domestic producers are concentrated in one geographic area of the country and the imports also are concentrated in that area, the ITC may treat as the relevant domestic industry "only that segment of the production located in such area."[32]

§ 6.8   Substantial Causation

The issue of causation commonly is among the most controversial in escape clause proceedings. As a general matter, the Trade Act requires that the ITC "investigate any factor which in its judgment may be contributing to increased imports of the article under investigation."[33] But it also provides that the ITC "shall" consider the condition of the domestic industry not only at the specific time of the petition but over "the course of its relevant business cycle."[34]

The Trade Act defines "substantial cause" as "a cause which is important and not less than any other cause."[35] Thus, as the ITC has observed, "increased imports must be both an important cause of the serious injury or threat and a cause that is equal to or greater than any other cause."[36] The Act directs the ITC to consider all relevant economic factors, including "an increase in imports (either actual or relative to domestic production) and a decline in the proportion of the domestic market supplied by domestic producers."[37] As a more general matter, the Trade Act obligates the ITC to "examine factors other than imports" that may be the cause of an injury to a domestic industry.[38] However, the ITC may not aggregate the cause of declining demand associated with a recession

---

[30]   19 U.S.C. § 2252(c)(4)(A).

[31]   19 U.S.C. § 2252(c)(4)(B).

[32]   19 U.S.C. § 2252(c) (4)(C).

[33]   19 U.S.C. § 2252(c)(5).

[34]   19 U.S.C. § 2252(c)(2).

[35]   19 U.S.C. § 2252(b)(1)(B).

[36]   *See* U.S. International Trade Commission—*Steel*, Investigation No. TA–201–73, at 34 (Pub. No. 3479, Dec., 2001).

[37]   19 U.S.C. § 2252(c)(1)(C).

[38]   19 U.S.C. § 2252(c)(2)(B).

or economic downturn into "a single cause" of serious injury or threat of injury.[39]

Of its nature, the adjective "substantial" leaves considerable latitude to the ITC in making its determinations of import injury under Section 201. The difficulty with the "substantial cause" element comes in determining whether increased imports are "equal to or greater than" the myriad of other competing factors that may cause harm to an industry. Management may be inept; labor may be underproductive or overly costly; general economic trends may be predominantly negative; and technological innovations may be causing obsolescence. Myriad causes may be at play. Whether one cause is more substantial than another is often very difficult to pinpoint with precision.

The issue of causation also may be affected by political currents at the ITC. For example, the controversial *Steel* decision of 2001 was initiated by the U.S. Trade Representative and clearly unfolded in an atmosphere of political support for the steel industry at the highest levels of government.[40] In another controversial case, ITC refused to consider a general recession as a more substantial cause for a decline in the U.S. motorcycle industry.[41] On this point, Congress was forced to step in to clarify by express language that, also noted above, the ITC may not aggregate the causes of declining production associated with a general economic downturn into a single cause.[42] The point of this rule is that increasing imports may also be a "substantial cause" of a serious injury to a domestic industry even during a serious recession.

Economic Factors

The Trade Act requires that the ITC not only "investigate" other contributing factors, but also that it then "take into account all economic factors which it considers relevant" in making its ultimate determination.[43] In carrying out this obligation, the ITC in fact has considered a wide array of causes in past decisions, including the following alternative causes of injury to domestic industries:

(1) Consumer cycles that affect product purchases;

(2) Fundamental changes in consumption;

---

[39]   19 U.S.C. § 2252(c)(2)(A).

[40]   *See* U.S. International Trade Commission—*Steel*, Investigation No. TA–201–73 (Pub. No. 3479, Dec., 2001).

[41]   U.S. International Trade Commission—*Heavy Weight Motorcycles, & Engines & Power Train Subassemblies Therefor*, Investigation No.TA–201–47 (1983).

[42]   *See* 19 U.S.C. § 2252(c).

[43]   19 U.S.C. § 2252(c)(1).

(3) Governmental regulation;

(4) Industry competition;

(5) Management decision making;

(6) Trends in imports, domestic consumption and production;

(7) Price changes in the product market;

(8) Business cycle changes;

(9) Labor contract negotiations; and

(10) World price and competitive conditions.[44]

Finally, the legislative history of the Trade Act expressly identified other types of causes that may be more important than increased imports, including "changes in technology or in consumer tastes, domestic competition from substitute products, plant obsolescence, or poor management."[45]

§ 6.9   Serious Injury

A less developed, but nonetheless also potentially controversial, area of ITC determinations under Section 201 involves the question of what constitutes "serious injury" to the domestic industry. The statutory criteria indicate that loss of production should be the relevant inquiry, whereas loss of market share is relevant primarily to causation.

The Trade Act defines a "serious injury" as "a significant overall impairment in the position of the domestic industry."[46] In making its determinations with reference to a serious injury to a domestic industry, the Trade Act requires the ITC to take into account the following specific "economic factors":

(1) The significant idling of productive facilities;[47]

(2) The inability of a significant number of firms to carry out domestic production at a reasonable level of profit; and

(3) Significant unemployment or underemployment within the domestic industry.[48]

---

[44]   For a review of these alternative causation factors, see especially U.S. International Trade Commission—*Carbon & Certain Alloy Steel Products*, Publication 1553 (July 1984).

[45]   *See* Sen. Rep. No. 93–1298, at 121 (1974).

[46]   19 U.S.C. § 2252(c)(6)(C).

[47]   The term "significant idling of productive facility" includes the closing of plants or underutilization of production capacity. *See* 19 U.S.C. § 2252(c)(6)(B).

[48]   19 U.S.C. § 2252(c)(1)(A).

Due to the decline in safeguards proceedings in recent years, most of the ITC authority on the serious injury test comes from some time ago. An exception is the *Steel* safeguards case from 2001, which is examined in Section 6.13 below. From its earlier cases, the ITC has interpreted the term "serious injury" to mean damage of a grave or important proportion.[49] In a decision denying relief to U.S. cigar producers, the Commission determined that a marked decline in U.S. consumption of large cigars was a more important cause of injury than import competition.[50] Similarly, it found that a decline in housing construction was more important to the injury suffered by door manufacturers than was import competition.[51] In most of its decisions concerning causation and serious injury, the Commission ordinarily reviews the economic trends over the past five years so as to screen out temporary problems.

The Trade Act also states that a mere "threat" of serious injury is sufficient. This means a "serious injury that is clearly imminent."[52] The Act provides further guidelines on this alternative injury standard as well. It directs the ITC to consider:

(1) Declines in sales or market share and higher and growing inventories as well as downward trends in production, profits, wages or employment in the domestic industry;

(2) The extent to which the industry is unable to generate adequate capital to finance modernization or maintain existing levels of research and development; and

(3) The extent to which the United States market is the focal point for the diversion of exports of the article in question by reason of trade restraints in other countries.[53]

In actual practice, however, there may be little difference between evaluating actual and threatened injury in escape clause proceedings.

Whether there is serious injury or threat of serious injury will of course depend upon the definition of the domestic industry. This is a bit like deciding the relevant market in United States antitrust litigation. Sub-markets, including sub-product markets and sub-

---

[49]   U.S. International Trade Commission—*Bolts, Nuts & Screws of Iron or Steel*, Publication 747, (Nov. 1975).

[50]   U.S. International Trade Commission—Wrapper Tobacco, Publication 746 (Nov. 1975).

[51]   U.S. International Trade Commission—*Birch Plywood Door Skins*, Publication 743 (Oct. 1975).

[52]   *See* 19 U.S.C. § 2252(c)(6)(D).

[53]   *See* 19 U.S.C. § 2252(c)(1)(A).

geographic markets, can clearly be domestic industries for purposes of Section 201. The ITC has in fact used tariff classifications of the United States in order to determine the domestic industry. Using such classifications has the practical feature of allowing identifiable tariff relief if that is ultimately granted.

Because the injury determination is closely tied to the definition of the affected domestic industry, the parties typically attempt to promote either a broader or narrower definition depending on whether they are the petitioner or respondent industry. Importers may contest the definition initially offered by the domestic industry so as to decrease the perception that like or directly competitive products are at risk or to reduce the measurement of increase in imports. The definition of the industry will also impact on the question of causation. This was a principal issue in the *Heavy Weight Motorcycles* case. In that highly controversial decision, the Commission ruled that imported sub-assemblies were not directly competitive with domestic sub-assemblies because the imports were captively consumed.[54]

Similar issues were raised in the automobile investigation. The domestic industry argued that passenger cars should be defined as a single industry producing automobiles and light trucks. Importers opposed to the escape clause proceeding sought to subdivide the industry into large automobiles and small automobiles. The Commission ultimate determined that three different industries were involved, passenger automobiles, light trucks, and medium-heavy weight trucks.[55]

§ 6.10   USITC Safeguard Relief Recommendations

The statute requires the ITC to report its findings to the President within 120 days after the petition is filed.[56] If the ITC determines that the case is "extraordinarily complicated," the deadline is extended to 150 days.[57] If the ITC decides that the statutory criteria of Section 201 are met, it "shall" make recommendations to address the serious injury or threat thereof to the domestic industry as well as consider the most effective means

---

[54]   *See* U.S. International Trade Commission—*Heavy Weight Motorcycles*, Investigation No. TA–201–47, Publication No. 1342 (Feb. 1983).

[55]   *See* U.S. International Trade Commission—*Certain Motor Vehicles and Certain Chassis and Bodies Thereof*, Investigation No. TA–201–44, Publication No. 1110 (Dec. 1980).

[56]   19 U.S.C. § 2252(b)(2)(A).

[57]   19 U.S.C. § 2252(b)(2)(B).

to allow that industry to make a positive adjustment to import competition.[58]

The Trade Act authorizes the Commission to choose from a menu of relief options. It may recommend an increase in or the imposition of a tariff or a tariff rate quota, modification or imposition of an import quota, various trade adjustment measures including trade adjustment assistance, or any combination of these options.[59] No initial recommended relief may exceed four years and, if renewed, the total may not exceed eight years.[60] In addition, the Commission may recommend that the President initiate international negotiations to address the underlying cause of the increase in imports.[61] Interestingly, only those members of the ITC who voted in affirmatively on the satisfaction of the Section 201 criteria in the first place are eligible to vote on the recommendations to the President. Dissenting members appear to have no input on relief recommendations.[62]

The ITC's report to the President will also include any adjustment plans submitted by the domestic industry in its petition and any commitments made by firms and workers in that industry in order to facilitate positive adjustment to import competition.[63] The Commission's report must also analyze the long and short term economic effects of the relief it recommends. The report to the President is advisory, but if the President decides not to follow any recommended import relief, Congress may pass a joint resolution by majority vote of both houses disapproving of the President's action. The President may veto this joint resolution, but of course Congress may override that veto. If this were to occur, then the Commission's original relief recommendations would be implemented.[64]

§ 6.11 ____Presidential Relief Decisions

The Trade Act authorizes the President to grant escape clause relief *only if* the ITC has made an affirmative finding that the increased imports have caused or threaten to cause serious injury to a domestic industry.[65] But if the ITC makes an affirmative finding, the Act requires the President to take "all appropriate and feasible

---

58   19 U.S.C. § 2252(e).

59   19 U.S.C. § 2252(e)(2).

60   *See* 19 U.S.C. § 2252(e)(2), § 2253(e).

61   19 U.S.C. § 2252(e)(4)(A).

62   19 U.S.C. § 2252(e)(6).

63   19 U.S.C. § 2252(e)(5)(B).

64   *See* 19 U.S.C. § 2253(b), (c).

65   *See* 19 U.S.C. § 2253(a)(1)(A).

action within his power" to facilitate efforts by the industry to make "a positive adjustment to import competition."[66]

Presidential Discretion

Notwithstanding the mandatory nature of this language, the President, as the Federal Circuit has observed, "has broad latitude to determine the type of action to take."[67] The President need not follow the ITC's relief recommendations. Thus, even though the word "shall" is used, the Act leaves substantial discretion to the President in defining the appropriate protective action. In other words, unlike antidumping and countervailing duty proceedings, the President has effective control over whether any relief will be given in a Section 201 proceeding, and what form that relief will take. Indeed, the President need not take any action at all.

If the President decides to provide escape clause relief, the Trade Act gives the President "an expansive, non-exclusive list"[68] of available relief measures. These include tariffs, a tariff rate quota, an import quota, adjustment assistance, orderly marketing agreements with foreign countries,[69] an allocation among importers by auction of import licenses, international negotiations, legislative proposals, or any combination thereof.[70] Duty free treatment under the Generalized System of Tariff Preferences of the United States is automatically suspended if the President decides to impose an escape clause proceeding tariff.

In deciding whether to undertake escape clause relief, the President is directed to take into account the ITC's report, the extent to which the workers and firms in the industry are benefiting from trade adjustment assistance,[71] the efforts being made by the industry to make a positive adjustment to import competition, the likelihood of effectiveness of relief in facilitating such adjustment, and the short and long term economic and social costs of the relief relative to their short and long term economic and social benefits.[72]

The President must also consider other factors related to the national economic interest of the United States, including but not limited to, the economic and social costs if relief is not granted, the

---

[66] *Id.*

[67] Corus Group PLC. v. International Trade Com'n. 352 F.3d 1351, 1354 (Fed. Cir. 2003).

[68] *Id.*

[69] As noted in Section 6.3 above, however, the WTO Safeguards Agreement expressly prohibits such agreements to limit import competition. *See also* Safeguards Agreement, art. 11.

[70] 19 U.S.C. § 2253(a)(3).

[71] *See* Sections 6.14 and 6.15.

[72] 19 U.S.C. § 2253(a)(2)(A)–(E).

impact on consumers and on competition in domestic markets, and the impact on United States industries if other nations were to take retaliatory action.[73] Consumer interests have sometimes been critical of the President's decision to grant escape clause relief. Various presidents have noted that such relief can as a practical matter increase prices to consumers and that this would be adverse to the national economic interests of the United States. The argument that escape clause relief may cause inflation in the United States is a variation on this theme.

The Trade Act further directs the President to consider the extent to which there is a diversion of foreign exports to the U.S. markets by reason of foreign restraints, the potential for circumvention of any relief taken, the national security interests of the United States, and those factors that the Commission is required to consider in reaching its recommendations.[74]

These considerations have frequently caused Presidents to deny escape clause relief. This is consistent with the President's primary role in the foreign affairs. Thus, for example, the President once decided not to grant escape clause relief regarding imports of copper when doing so might have influenced then-pending negotiations under the auspices of GATT and with UNCTAD about the commodities trade.[75] A similar refusal to grant relief in connection with imports of copper was based on the need for the U.S. exporters of copper to obtain adequate export earnings.[76] In the latter case, the President expressly declared that "granting import relief is not consistent with our national economic interest."[77]

Limits on Escape Clause Relief

Although the President has almost unlimited discretion on the form of escape clause relief, the Trade Act places some outer limits: First, because escape clause relief is intended to be temporary, no relief ordered by the President may exceed four years initially, and eight years in total; second no increase in tariff resulting from escape clause proceedings can exceed fifty percent *ad valorem* of the rate existing at the time of the escape clause proceeding; finally, if the ordered relief exceeds one year, it "shall be phased down at regular intervals during the period in which [it] is in effect."[78]

---

[73]   19 U.S.C. § 2253(a)(2)(F).

[74]   19 U.S.C. § 2253(a)(2)(G)–(J).

[75]   Domestic Copper Industry, 43 Fed. Reg. 49523 (Oct. 24, 1978).

[76]   *See* Copper Import Relief Determination, 49 Fed. Reg. 35609 (1984).

[77]   *Id.*

[78]   19 U.S.C. § 2253(e).

Petitioners in escape clause proceedings should consider in advance which form of relief they hope to receive. Tariffs may not provide effective relief because of floating currency values. For example, if the dollar declines in value, imports will become cheaper and the negative impact of tariffs might be offset. On the other hand, if dollar values are rising, this will cause tariffs to be an effective form of protection because imports become notably more expensive. Thus, tariff relief may or may not provide the type of protection the petitioners anticipate. For one thing, the importers may simply pay the increased tariffs if allowed by the economics of the market.

One reason why protective escape clause relief is difficult to obtain is that the WTO Safeguards Agreement entitles most trading partners to seek compensation for the adverse effects of any relief granted by another member state. Formal retaliation through a return suspension of concessions on exports generally is prohibited for three years. But because escape clause proceedings do not concern any unfair trade practice, protective relief measures typically are a source of substantial friction in world trade. This perspective helps explain why the President frequently decides that it is not in the economic interest of the United States to impose escape clause relief or, if granted, decides to terminate the relief earlier than originally ordered.

The President has provided escape clause relief in relatively few instances. Again, Congress can (but never has chosen to) override any presidential denial of escape clause or market disruption relief recommended by the ITC. Congress can do so by adopting a joint resolution of disapproval. Once this is enacted, the President is required to adopt the import relief previously recommended by the Commission. However, the President may veto this joint resolution, in which case an override of the President's veto is required to obtain relief.[79]

Review of Relief

If the President decides to impose protective escape clause relief, the ITC must monitor the granted relief during the period it is in effect.[80] The President also may later decide to reduce, modify, terminate, or extend the relief.[81] The level of the relief granted, however, cannot be increased. In the subsequent proceedings, the Commission's role is advisory, but if the period of relief exceeds three years, it must provide reports to the President and Congress

---

[79]   *See* 19 U.S.C. § 2253(b), (c).
[80]   19 U.S.C. § 2254(a).
[81]   19 U.S.C. § 2254(b).

on any continuing injury and on the progress of the domestic industry in adjusting to import competition.[82] The President may alter existing escape clause relief if he or she finds that the domestic industry has failed to make adequate efforts to adjust to import competition, the circumstances have sufficiently changed to warrant a reduction or termination in relief, or upon the request of the domestic industry.[83]

Amendments to the Trade Act of 1974 adopted in 1988, and reaffirmed in the URAA in 1994, promote the goal of adjustment to import competition instead of trade protection relief. This is accomplished by strongly encouraging the submission of adjustment plans and commitments by petitioners for Section 201 relief, and by expanding the range of remedies the Commission may recommend to the President in escape clause proceedings to *any* action that will facilitate adjustment.

Further, the standards for presidential relief mandate a determination that the relief will facilitate efforts by the domestic industry to make a positive adjustment to import competition. Finally, the Trade Act requires increased monitoring of Section 201 relief plans and imposes time limits on any relief granted by the President. Thus, as compared to the past Section 201 of the Trade Act is now considerably less protectionist and more adjustment-oriented.

§ 6.12   Special U.S. Safeguard Rules for Chinese Imports

In addition to the general rule in Section 201, U.S. law has a special provision—which arose in connection with China's accession to the WTO in 2001—for safeguard measures relating to imports from China. Because of worries over a flood of inexpensive Chinese imports, these "Section 421" safeguard measures require only that increased imports be a "significant cause" of a "material" injury to a domestic industry.[84] These standards are significantly lower than for regular safeguard measures, which (as noted above) require a cause that is "equal to or greater than any other cause" and a real or threatened "serious" injury to a domestic industry.

In recent years, the special Section 421 safeguards rule has played a much more significant role than traditional Section 201 proceedings. Between 2003 and 2013, the ITC initiated six investigations under Section 421, but none under Section 201. A

---

[82]   19 U.S.C. § 2254(a)(2).

[83]   19 U.S.C. § 2254(b)(1).

[84]   19 U.S.C. § 2451(a), (c).

prominent example is President Obama's imposition in June 2009 of protective tariffs of 35% on vehicle tires from China.[85] Pursuant to the special authorization for such actions in China's WTO Accession Protocol, however, the United States may not initiate such China-specific actions after the end of 2013.

§ 6.13   WTO Rulings on U.S. Safeguard Actions

The rulings of the WTO's Appellate Body concerning the Safeguards Agreement have strictly limited the use of escape clause remedies. Indeed, the United States has lost a number of related disputes before the WTO, including in complaints brought by Australia and New Zealand on lamb; by the European Union on wheat gluten; by India and Pakistan on wool shirts and blouses; by South Korea on line pipe; and by Japan and numerous others on steel.

In 2001 alone, the Appellate Body (AB) ruled against the United States in three separate safeguard cases. In *U.S.-Wheat Gluten from the EC*, the AB emphasized the critical issue of causation. The AB found that the ITC's causation analysis lacked clarity and inadequately addressed factors other than imports that may have caused domestic industry injury. It also criticized the U.S. for a failure to give timely notice and to allow for a "meaningful exchange" in the required consultations. In *U.S.-Lamb Meat from New Zealand*, the AB reiterated that all causation factors must be isolated and examined. Further, it rejected the "domestic industry" definition adopted by the ITC because growers were included. Both of these decisions also emphasized the need for the ITC to find "unforeseen developments" in its injury determinations. The third 2001 AB ruling against U.S. safeguard measures concerned cotton yarn from India and Pakistan. In this decision, the AB rejected an exclusion of vertically integrated yarn producers from the definition of "domestic industry."

In its 2002 decision on U.S. safeguards on line pipe from Korea, the WTO similarly criticized the ITC for a "mere assertion" that challenged imports were "an important cause of serious injury and . . . not less than any other cause." More generally, the AB has repeatedly emphasized that the U.S. may not exclude consideration of imports from NAFTA countries (Canada and Mexico) in making safeguard determinations.

The U.S. Steel Safeguards Case

Perhaps the most controversial recent escape clause action by the United States was the imposition of tariffs on steel by President

---

[85]   *See* Proclamation No. 8414, 74 Fed. Reg. 47,861 (Sept. 17, 2009).

Bush in 2002. The ITC found, following an extensive investigation and numerous hearings, that certain categories of steel imports caused, or threatened to cause, serious injury to the domestic steel industry. President Bush then imposed on the covered steel products annually decreasing tariffs of up to thirty percent, although only for a three year period.[86] This escape clause relief was tempered by exclusions for selected steel from selected countries. Most Australian and Japanese steel products, for example, were not subject to the extra U.S. tariffs. About half of all EU steel imports were exempt. Canada and Mexico, as members of NAFTA, were fully exempt.

Opponents promptly challenged the imposition of the safeguard measures in both U.S. courts and the WTO. The Federal Circuit upheld the action as a matter of domestic law.[87] But numerous WTO member states then challenged the imposition of this safeguard relief before the WTO's Dispute Settlement Body. In 2003, the Appellate Body ultimately ruled that the special U.S. tariffs on steel were illegal under the WTO Safeguards Agreement.[88]

The AB held that the U.S. erred in utilizing the protective tariffs some four years after the surge of steel imports during the Asian economic meltdown of the late 1990s, and in excluding NAFTA partners Canada and Mexico. It also found that the ITC failed properly to address the requirement of "unforeseen developments." Although the AB acknowledged that the term does not appear in the Safeguards Agreement, it reiterated its earlier holdings that the Agreement must be understood against the backdrop of GATT Article XIX, which conspicuously includes such a requirement.

The European Union then threatened over $2 billion annually in retaliatory tariffs on U.S. exports of clothing, citrus, and boats, products thought to be politically damaging to the Bush Administration. But before the WTO could authorize such sanctions, President Bush—pursuant to corresponding authority in the Trade Act[89]—terminated the tariffs in December 2003. He stated that the effectiveness of the tariffs "ha[d] been impaired by changed economic circumstances."[90]

---

[86]   *See* Proclamation No. 7529, 67 Fed. Reg. 10553 (Mar. 5, 2002).

[87]   *See* Corus Group PLC v. ITC, 352 F.3d 1351 (Fed. Cir. 2003).

[88]   *See* Appellate Body Report, *U.S.-Definitive Safeguard Measures on Imports of Certain Steel Products*, WT/DS248/AB/R, *et al.* (adopted Dec. 10, 2003).

[89]   19 U.S.C. § 2254(b)(1).

[90]   *See* Proclamation No. 7741, 68 Fed. Reg. 68,483, ¶ 6 (Dec. 4, 2003).

Interestingly, in the meantime domestic interests separately petitioned the ITA and ITC to impose CVDs or ADs on many of the same products. Reasoning that the temporary safeguard measures effectively mitigated the damaging effects of imports, the ITC concluded that there was no material injury to justify responsive duties on either basis.[91]

§ 6.14 U.S. Trade Adjustment Assistance— Individual and Company Assistance Criteria

The idea of trade adjustment assistance has its origins in programs intended to assist people who were dislocated when the European Community (now Union) was established. Its adoption in the United States has had a checkered history, particularly as regards Congressional willingness to fund trade adjustment assistance. The first authority for such assistance was provided in the Trade Expansion Act of 1962. However, no assistance was actually provided until 1969.

The Trade Act of 1974 made trade adjustment assistance a greater possibility. But dramatic increases in payments to workers under the program during the early 1980s caused the Reagan Administration to seek to repeal the Trade Adjustment Assistance Program. During the 1980s, tighter eligibility requirements and shrinking budgetary allocations reduced the scope of the program. It was not until the Omnibus Trade and Competitiveness Act of 1988 that significant funds were committed to trade adjustment assistance and the program was reauthorized through 1993.

Nonetheless, actual payment of adjustment assistance to workers occurred slowly, and assistance to companies was extremely difficult to obtain. Trade adjustment assistance programs of the United States were consolidated and expanded in 2002, including for the first time worker assistance with health insurance, coverage of "secondary workers," a new pilot program on wage insurance for older workers, benefits for family farmers and ranchers, and expanded training and income support.

Trade adjustment assistance is designed to provide financial relief to workers (and, to a lesser extent, firms) for the effects of the increased imports—not to prevent, reduce, or restrict the imports. Escape clause relief is always considered temporary, but adversely affected workers may obtain "adjustment assistance" payments and other displacement benefits for a longer period.

Trade adjustment assistance decisions are made by the U.S. Department of Labor. Such assistance does not require an

---

[91]   *See* Nucor Corp. v. U.S., 414 F.3d 1331 (Fed. Cir. 2005).

affirmative determination by the ITC on import injuries (as is required for protective relief, *see* above). Adjustment assistance also is available to workers whose plants relocate to U.S. free trade partners, or GSP, CBI, Andean or African trade preference countries.

Congress expanded the trade adjustment assistance (TAA) programs significantly 2009 and 2011. Such expansions and extensions of trade adjustment assistance often are closely connected with the granting of Trade Promotion Authority ("fast track") by Congress to the President for free trade agreements, as well as to actual congressional approval of such agreements once concluded by the President. An example is the extension of the enhanced TAA programs in 2011 in connection with the approval of the free trade agreements with South Korea, Colombia, and Panama.

Among the variety of benefits and services now available for eligible workers are the following: employment counseling and job referrals; job search allowances for travel and related costs; "relocation allowances" to cover moving expenses; retraining assistance; and, perhaps most important, simple income support after state unemployment benefits have run out. The expanded TAA programs also allow financial assistance for health insurance as well as special wage subsidies for workers over fifty.

Petitions and DOL Determinations

U.S. law permits petitions for trade adjustment assistance by a "group of workers," unions, or "employers of such workers."[92] Generally, three groups of workers may be eligible for adjustment assistance: (1) those who have lost their jobs because increased imports caused significant harm to production by their former employer; (2) those who lost their jobs because increased imports caused their former employer to shift production to a foreign country; and (3) "adversely affected secondary workers"—those who lost their jobs with a supplier of a primary firm harmed by increased imports.[93]

Distilled to its essence, the Trade Act requires for a grant of trade adjustment assistance that the Secretary of Labor determine the existence of two elements:

---

[92]   19 U.S.C. § 2271.

[93]   19 U.S.C. §§ 2271(a), 2272(b). For a case analyzing the special requirements for "adversely affected secondary workers" see Former Employees of Southeast Airlines v. U.S. Secretary of Labor, 774 F .Supp. 2d 1333 (C.I.T 2011).

First, there must be *negative employment effects* from trade in the form of the loss or threatened loss of jobs by "a significant number or proportion of the workers" in a firm.

Second, there must be evidence of *causation*. The Secretary may find such causation in one of two ways:

- Sales or production by the firm have decreased absolutely, (b) imports of directly competitive goods (or their component parts) or services have increased, *and* (c) the increase in imports "contributed importantly" to the loss or threatened loss of the workers' jobs;

or

- the workers' firm moved production or services to a foreign country or has begun importing its products or services from a foreign country, *and* (b) either of these things "contributed importantly" to the loss or threatened loss of the workers' jobs.[94]

These criteria are related to but not identical with those considered by the ITC in connection with escape clause proceedings. For example, the term "contributed importantly" means a cause which is important but not necessarily more important than any other cause.[95] This is a lesser standard than the required "substantial causation" for Section 201 proceedings.[96] Whether imports are "like or directly competitive" with domestic products is a question of interchangeability or substitutability. The fact that imports are actually decreasing does not *per se* eliminate the possibility of trade adjustment assistance. The critical issue is whether those imports have "contributed importantly" to unemployment.[97]

Adjustment Assistance for Companies

Congress also has authorized a separate, but more limited, program of Trade Adjustment Assistance for Firms (TAAF) which is administered by the Department of Commerce.[98] Assistance to companies is primarily limited to technical aid.[99] Companies may receive adjustment assistance only if the Secretary of Commerce finds that a significant number of their workers have been

---

[94]   19 U.S.C. § 2272(a).

[95]   19 U.S.C. § 2272(c)(1).

[96]   *See* Section 6.8.

[97]   For an analysis of the importance of the "contributed importantly" standard in a long-running disagreement between the Secretary of Labor and the Court of International Trade see Chen v. Solis, 2009 WL 2058659 (C.I.T 2009).

[98]   *See* 19 U.S.C. § 2341.

[99]   *See* 19 U.S.C. § 2342(b).

separated or threatened with separation, that sales or production have decreased absolutely, and that increased importation of like or directly competitive articles contributed importantly to these results.[100] Agricultural firms may apply for adjustment assistance. Although once authorized by statute, Congress has not been willing to fund trade adjustment assistance for communities impacted by import competition.

A grant of trade adjustment assistance does not require an affirmative determination by the ITC on import injuries (as is required for protective relief, *see* above). Such separate assistance flows from the separate determinations by the Secretaries of Labor and Commerce under the Trade Act of 1974. One important difference is the fact that in adjustment assistance proceedings the effect of imports on the industry as a whole is not at issue. The focus is instead on specific workers and specific companies. Whenever the ITC commences an investigation for purposes of Section 201 escape clause proceedings, the Secretary of Labor is required to begin a parallel investigation as to the likelihood and number of workers who may be certified as eligible for trade adjustment assistance. The Secretary of Labor then prepares a report which is forwarded to the President along with the report of the ITC concerning the escape clause petition.

§ 6.15   ____Secretary of Labor Determinations

The Trade Act gives considerable discretion to the Secretary of Labor in making trade adjustment assistance determinations. The Court of International Trade has thus held that it will uphold a grant of such assistance "if it is supported by substantial evidence on the record and is otherwise in accordance with law."[101] Substantial evidence merely means "such relevant evidence as a reasonable mind might accept as adequate to support a conclusion."[102]

In making determinations as to worker eligibility, the Secretary of Labor must obtain from the workers' firm whatever information he or she "determines to be necessary to make the certification."[103] This may be done "through questionnaires and in such other manner as the Secretary determines appropriate."[104] The

---

[100]   *See* 19 U.S.C. § 2341(c).

[101]   *See* Former Employees of Western Digital Technologies, Inc. v. U.S. Secretary of Labor, 2012 WL 7006347, at *3 (C.I.T 2012) and 19 U.S.C. § 2395(b).

[102]   Former Emps. of Barry Callebaut v. Chao, 357 F.3d 1377, 1380–81 (Fed. Cir. 2004)(quoting Universal Camera Corp. v. NLRB, 340 U.S. 474, 477 (1951)).

[103]   19 U.S.C § 2272(d).

[104]   *Id.*

Secretary may also seek additional information from officials or employees of the workers' firm, officials of customers of the workers' firm, and officials of "certified or recognized unions" for the workers.[105] The Trade Act also expressly gives the Secretary *subpoena* powers.[106] But he or she must ensure confidentiality for any secret business information gathered in the process.[107]

The Secretary of Labor may conduct investigations in any reasonable manner.[108] But he or she must publish notice of the fact that an eligible group of workers has filed a petition for certification for trade adjustment assistance benefits, and must publish a summary of the determinations on that petition in the Federal Register.[109]

Once an investigation is commenced "the Labor Department is vested with considerable discretion in the conduct of its investigation of trade adjustment assistance claims."[110] Nonetheless, "there exists a threshold requirement of reasonable inquiry" by the Secretary.[111] This means, for example, that petitioners do not have a right to a trial-type hearing with cross examination of the witnesses of the Department of Labor as part of the process of determining eligibility for trade adjustment assistance. If, however, the CIT finds that the Department did not conduct a "reasonable inquiry," it may remand the case to require further investigation.[112]

Until recently, services were not covered by worker adjustment assistance programs. Thus, in the 1970s and 1980s courts held that workers engaged in airline services, automobile services, and shipyard maintenance services were not impacted by the importation of "articles" within the meaning of the Trade Act.[113] As amended, the Trade Act now expressly covers workers that have lost their jobs because, among other reasons, their employer either (a) has lost sales or production due to "imports of articles *or services*

---

[105]   *Id.*

[106]   19 U.S.C. § 2272(d)(3)(B).

[107]   19 U.S.C. § 2272(d)(3)(C).

[108]   Abbott v. Donovan, 570 F. Supp. 41 (C.I.T. 1983), *appeal after remand* 588 F. Supp. 1438 (1984).

[109]   19 U.S.C. § 2271(a)(3).

[110]   Former Employees of Invista, S.A.R.L. v. U.S. Sec'y of Labor, 714 F. Supp. 2d 1320, 1329 (C.I.T 2010).

[111]   *Id.* (quoting Former Employees of Hawkins Oil & Gas, Inc. v. U.S. Sec'y of Labor, 814 F. Supp. 1111, 1115 (1993)).

[112]   *See* 19 U.S.C. § 2395(b) and Former Employees of Fairchild Semi-Conductor Corp. v. U.S. Sec'y of Labor, 2008 WL 1765519 (C.I.T 2008).

[113]   *See, e.g.,* Woodrum v. United States, 737 F.2d 1575 (Fed. Cir. 1984); Miller v. Donovan, 568 F. Supp. 760 (C.I.T. 1983); Pemberton v. Marshall, 639 F.2d 798 (D.C. Cir. 1981); Fortin v. Marshall, 608 F.2d 525 (1st Cir.1979).

like or directly competitive with articles produced *or services* supplied by" the employer,[114] or (b) shifted work to a foreign country "in the production of articles or the supply of *services* like or directly competitive with articles which are produced or *services* which are supplied by" the employer.[115]

§ 6.16   Text of WTO Agreement on Safeguards

(Selected Provisions)

Having in mind the overall objective of the Members to improve and strengthen the international trading system based on GATT 1994;

Recognizing the need to clarify and reinforce the disciplines of GATT 1994, and specifically those of its Article XIX (Emergency Action on Imports of Particular Products), to re-establish multilateral control over safeguards and eliminate measures that escape such control;

Recognizing the importance of structural adjustment and the need to enhance rather than limit competition in international markets; and

Recognizing further that, for these purposes, a comprehensive agreement, applicable to all Members and based on the basic principles of GATT 1994, is called for;

Hereby *agree* as follows:

Article 1

General Provision

This Agreement establishes rules for the application of safeguard measures which shall be understood to mean those measures provided for in Article XIX of GATT 1994.

Article 2

Conditions

1. A Member[1] may apply a safeguard measure to a product only if that Member has determined, pursuant to the provisions set out below, that such product is being imported into its territory in such increased quantities, absolute or relative to domestic production, and under such

---

[114]   19 U.S.C. § 2272(a)(2)(A).

[115]   19 U.S.C. § 2272(a)(2)(B).

[1]   A customs union may apply a safeguard measure as a single unit or on behalf of a member State. When a customs union applies a safeguard measure as a single unit, all the requirements for the determination of serious injury or threat thereof under this Agreement shall be based on the conditions existing in the customs union as a whole. When a safeguard measure is applied on behalf of a member State, all the requirements for the determination of serious injury or threat thereof shall be based on the conditions existing in that member State and the measure shall be limited to that member State. Nothing in this Agreement prejudges the interpretation of the relationship between Article XIX and paragraph 8 of Article XXIV of GATT 1994.

conditions as to cause or threaten to cause serious injury to the domestic industry that produces like or directly competitive products.

2.   Safeguard measures shall be applied to a product being imported irrespective of its source.

* * *

Article 4

Determination of Serious Injury or Threat Thereof

1.   For the purposes of this Agreement:

(a) "serious injury" shall be understood to mean a significant overall impairment in the position of a domestic industry;

(b) "threat of serious injury" shall be understood to mean serious injury that is clearly imminent, in accordance with the provisions of paragraph 2. A determination of the existence of a threat of serious injury shall be based on facts and not merely on allegation, conjecture or remote possibility; and

(c) in determining injury or threat thereof, a "domestic industry" shall be understood to mean the producers as a whole of the like or directly competitive products operating within the territory of a Member, or those whose collective output of the like or directly competitive products constitutes a major proportion of the total domestic production of those products.

2.   (a) In the investigation to determine whether increased imports have caused or are threatening to cause serious injury to a domestic industry under the terms of this Agreement, the competent authorities shall evaluate all relevant factors of an objective and quantifiable nature having a bearing on the situation of that industry, in particular, the rate and amount of the increase in imports of the product concerned in absolute and relative terms, the share of the domestic market taken by increased imports, changes in the level of sales, production, productivity, capacity utilization, profits and losses, and employment.

(b) The determination referred to in subparagraph (a) shall not be made unless this investigation demonstrates, on the basis of objective evidence, the existence of the causal link between increased imports of the product concerned and serious injury or threat thereof. When factors other than increased imports are causing injury to the domestic industry at the same time, such injury shall not be attributed to increased imports.

(c) The competent authorities shall publish promptly, in accordance with the provisions of Article 3, a detailed analysis of the case under investigation as well as a demonstration of the relevance of the factors examined.

Article 5

Application of Safeguard Measures

1.   A Member shall apply safeguard measures only to the extent necessary to prevent or remedy serious injury and to facilitate adjustment. If a quantitative restriction is used, such a measure shall not reduce the quantity of imports below the level of a recent period which shall be the average of imports in the last three representative years for which statistics are available, unless clear justification is given that a different level is necessary to prevent or remedy serious injury. Members should choose measures most suitable for the achievement of these objectives.

2.   (a) In cases in which a quota is allocated among supplying countries, the Member applying the restrictions may seek agreement with respect to the allocation of shares in the quota with all other Members having a substantial interest in supplying the product concerned. In cases in which this method is not reasonably practicable, the Member concerned shall allot to Members having a substantial interest in supplying the product shares based upon the proportions, supplied by such Members during a previous representative period, of the total quantity or value of imports of the product, due account being taken of any special factors which may have affected or may be affecting the trade in the product.

(b) A Member may depart from the provisions in subparagraph (a) provided that consultations under paragraph 3 of Article 12 are conducted under the auspices of the Committee on Safeguards provided for in paragraph 1 of Article 13 and that clear demonstration is provided to the Committee that (*i*) imports from certain Members have increased in disproportionate percentage in relation to the total increase of imports of the product concerned in the representative period, (*ii*) the reasons for the departure from the provisions in subparagraph (a) are justified, and (*iii*) the conditions of such departure are equitable to all suppliers of the product concerned. The duration of any such measure shall not be extended beyond the initial period under paragraph 1 of Article 7. The departure referred to above shall not be permitted in the case of threat of serious injury.

Article 6

Provisional Safeguard Measures

In critical circumstances where delay would cause damage which it would be difficult to repair, a Member may take a provisional safeguard measure pursuant to a preliminary determination that there is clear evidence that increased imports have caused or are threatening to cause serious injury. The duration of the provisional measure shall not exceed 200 days, during which period the pertinent requirements of Articles 2 through 7 and 12 shall be met. Such measures should take the form of tariff increases to be promptly refunded if the subsequent investigation referred to in paragraph 2 of Article 4 does not determine that increased imports have caused or threatened to cause serious injury to a domestic industry. The duration of any such provisional measure shall be counted as a part of the initial period and any extension referred to in paragraphs 1, 2 and 3 of Article 7.

Article 7

Duration and Review of Safeguard Measures

1.   A Member shall apply safeguard measures only for such period of time as may be necessary to prevent or remedy serious injury and to facilitate adjustment. The period shall not exceed four years, unless it is extended under paragraph 2.

2.   The period mentioned in paragraph 1 may be extended provided that the competent authorities of the importing Member have determined, in conformity with the procedures set out in Articles 2, 3, 4 and 5, that the safeguard measure continues to be necessary to prevent or remedy serious injury and that there is evidence that the industry is adjusting, and provided that the pertinent provisions of Articles 8 and 12 are observed.

3.   The total period of application of a safeguard measure including the period of application of any provisional measure, the period of initial application and any extension thereof, shall not exceed eight years.

4.   In order to facilitate adjustment in a situation where the expected duration of a safeguard measure as notified under the provisions of paragraph 1 of Article 12 is over one year, the Member applying the measure shall progressively liberalize it at regular intervals during the period of application. If the duration of the measure exceeds three years, the Member applying such a measure shall review the situation not later than the mid-term of the measure and, if appropriate, withdraw it or increase the pace of liberalization. A measure extended under paragraph 2 shall not be more restrictive than it was at the end of the initial period, and should continue to be liberalized.

5.   No safeguard measure shall be applied again to the import of a product which has been subject to such a measure, taken after the date of entry into force of the WTO Agreement, for a period of time equal to that during which such measure had been previously applied, provided that the period of non-application is at least two years.

6.   Notwithstanding the provisions of paragraph 5, a safeguard measure with a duration of 180 days or less may be applied again to the import of a product if:

(a) at least one year has elapsed since the date of introduction of a safeguard measure on the import of that product; and

(b) such a safeguard measure has not been applied on the same product more than twice in the five-year period immediately preceding the date of introduction of the measure.

Article 8

Level of Concessions and Other Obligations

1.   A Member proposing to apply a safeguard measure or seeking an extension of a safeguard measure shall endeavour to maintain a substantially equivalent level of concessions and other obligations to that existing under GATT 1994 between it and the exporting Members which would be affected by such a measure, in accordance with the provisions of paragraph 3 of Article 12. To achieve this objective, the Members concerned may agree on any adequate means of trade compensation for the adverse effects of the measure on their trade.

2.   If no agreement is reached within 30 days in the consultations under paragraph 3 of Article 12, then the affected exporting Members shall be free, not later than 90 days after the measure is applied, to suspend, upon the expiration of 30 days from the day on which written notice of such suspension is received by the Council for Trade in Goods, the application of substantially equivalent concessions or other obligations under GATT 1994, to the trade of the Member applying the safeguard measure, the suspension of which the Council for Trade in Goods does not disapprove.

3.   The right of suspension referred to in paragraph 2 shall not be exercised for the first three years that a safeguard measure is in effect, provided that the safeguard measure has been taken as a result of an absolute increase in imports and that such a measure conforms to the provisions of this Agreement.

Article 9

Developing Country Members

1.   Safeguard measures shall not be applied against a product originating in a developing country Member as long as its share of imports of the product concerned in the importing Member does not exceed 3 per cent, provided that developing country Members with less than 3 per cent import share collectively account for not more than 9 per cent of total imports of the product concerned.[2]

2.   A developing country Member shall have the right to extend the period of application of a safeguard measure for a period of up to two years beyond the maximum period provided for in paragraph 3 of Article 7. Notwithstanding the provisions of paragraph 5 of Article 7, a developing country Member shall have the right to apply a safeguard measure again to the import of a product which has been subject to such a measure, taken after the date of entry into force of the WTO Agreement, after a period of time equal to half that during which such a measure has been previously applied, provided that the period of non-application is at least two years.

---

[2]   A Member shall immediately notify an action taken under paragraph 1 of Article 9 to the Committee on Safeguards.

Article 10

Pre-existing Article XIX Measures

Members shall terminate all safeguard measures taken pursuant to Article XIX of GATT 1947 that were in existence on the date of entry into force of the WTO Agreement not later than eight years after the date on which they were first applied or five years after the date of entry into force of the WTO Agreement, whichever comes later.

Article 11

Prohibition and Elimination of Certain Measures

1.   (a) A Member shall not take or seek any emergency action on imports of particular products as set forth in Article XIX of GATT 1994 unless such action conforms with the provisions of that Article applied in accordance with this Agreement.

(b) Furthermore, a Member shall not seek, take or maintain any voluntary export restraints, orderly marketing arrangements or any other similar measures on the export or the import side.[3,4] These include actions taken by a single Member as well as actions under agreements, arrangements and understandings entered into by two or more Members. Any such measure in effect on the date of entry into force of the WTO Agreement shall be brought into conformity with this Agreement or phased out in accordance with paragraph 2.

(c) This Agreement does not apply to measures sought, taken or maintained by a Member pursuant to provisions of GATT 1994 other than Article XIX, and Multilateral Trade Agreements in Annex 1A other than this Agreement, or pursuant to protocols and agreements or arrangements concluded within the framework of GATT 1994.

2.   The phasing out of measures referred to in paragraph 1(b) shall be carried out according to timetables to be presented to the Committee on Safeguards by the Members concerned not later than 180 days after the date of entry into force of the WTO Agreement. These timetables shall provide for all measures referred to in paragraph 1 to be phased out or brought into conformity with this Agreement within a period not exceeding four years after the date of entry into force of the WTO Agreement, subject to not more than one specific measure per importing Member,[5] the duration of which shall not extend beyond 31 December 1999. Any such exception

---

[3]   An import quota applied as a safeguard measure in conformity with the relevant provisions of GATT 1994 and this Agreement may, by mutual agreement, be administered by the exporting Member.

[4]   Examples of similar measures include export moderation, export-price or import-price monitoring systems, export or import surveillance, compulsory import cartels and discretionary export or import licensing schemes, any of which afford protection.

[5]   The only such exception to which the European Communities is entitled is indicated in the Annex to this Agreement.

must be mutually agreed between the Members directly concerned and notified to the Committee on Safeguards for its review and acceptance within 90 days of the entry into force of the WTO Agreement. The Annex to this Agreement indicates a measure which has been agreed as falling under this exception.

3.   Members shall not encourage or support the adoption or maintenance by public and private enterprises of non-governmental measures equivalent to those referred to in paragraph 1.

* * *

Article 14

Dispute Settlement

The provisions of Articles XXII and XXIII of GATT 1994 as elaborated and applied by the Dispute Settlement Understanding shall apply to consultations and the settlement of disputes arising under this Agreement.

ANNEX

EXCEPTION REFERRED TO IN PARAGRAPH 2 OF ARTICLE 11

Members concerned	Product	Termination
EC/Japan	Passenger cars, off road vehicles, light commercial vehicles, light trucks (up to 5 tonnes), and the same vehicles in wholly knocked-down form (CKD sets).	31 December 1999

Chapter 7

U.S. IMPORT CONTROLS AND NONTARIFF TRADE BARRIERS

Table of Sections

For European Union coverage of NTBs, see Sections 17.4–17.6. For NAFTA coverage, see Section 16.3. For texts of the WTO TBT and SPS Codes, see the Appendix to this book.

§ 7.1   U.S. Import Quotas and Licenses

Goods imported into the United States may have to qualify within numerical quota limitations imposed on that item or upon that kind of item. "Tariff-rate quotas" admit a specified quantity of goods at a preferential rate of duty. Once imports reach that quantity, tariffs are normally increased.

If a quota system is created, a fundamental subsidiary issue is: How will the quotas be allocated? The U.S. Customs Service generally administers quotas on a first-come, first-served basis. This approach creates a race to enter goods into the United States. One potential allocation method is through the use of licenses, which would be the documentation for administration of such quantitative restrictions. Licensing of imports can have trade restrictive effects. International concern about delays which result from cumbersome licensing procedures was manifested in the 1979 Tokyo Round MTN Import Licensing Code (which most developing countries refused to sign). The United States adhered to this Code, as did a reasonable number of other developed nations.

The Uruguay Round made the Agreement on Import Licensing Procedures (1994) binding on all World Trade Organization members. The Agreement's objectives include facilitating the simplification and harmonization of import licensing and licensing renewal procedures, ensuring adequate publication of rules governing licensing procedures, and reducing the practice of refusing importation because of minor variations in quantity, value or weight of the import item under license. *See* Section 1.6.

The President is authorized to sell U. S. import licenses at public auctions.[1] One advantage of an auction system is its revenue raising potential. The U.S. Tariff Act of 1930 also provides that to the extent practicable and consistent with efficient and fair administration, the President is to insure against inequitable sharing of imports by a relatively small number of larger importers.[2] In fact, allocating quotas among U.S. importers rarely happens. Rather, in the past, quotas have been part of a "voluntary restraint" or orderly market agreement between the U.S. and one or more foreign governments, and represent adherence by those governments to U.S. initiatives.

These negotiations have typically concentrated on obtaining foreign government agreement to limitations on exportation of their products into the U.S. market, and have not pursued limitations on who might use the resulting allocations. Voluntary export restraints (VERs) and orderly marketing agreements (OMAs) limiting exports into the U.S. market have been applied to textiles, autos, steel, machine tools and semiconductors. Their use is now severely limited by the WTO Agreement on Safeguards. *See* Section 6.3.

Agricultural and Meat Import Quotas

The United States has employed import quotas for many years. Tariff-rate quotas have been applied to dairy products, olives, tuna fish, anchovies, brooms, and sugar, syrups and molasses. Quite a few absolute quotas originate under Section 22 of the Agricultural Adjustment Act.[3] These quotas are undertaken when necessary to United States farm price supports or similar agricultural programs. They have been used on animal feeds, dairy products, chocolate, peanuts, and selected syrups and sugars. U.S. quotas and tariff-rate quotas on sugar and sugar-containing products, designed to reinforce U.S. price support and loan programs, have notably increased domestic costs well above world prices. Between 2000 and 2012, for example, the average price of U.S. sugar was more than double world-wide average prices. These quotas are administered by the Department of Agriculture by allocating certificates to sugar

---

[1]   19 U.S.C.A. § 2581.
[2]   Id.
[3]   7 U.S.C.A. § 624.

exporting countries. Only Mexico, under NAFTA, is permitted unlimited sugar exports into the United States. Some U.S. agricultural quotas have been "tariffied" under the WTO Agreement on Agriculture. *See* Section 1.8.

The Agricultural Act of 1949 requires the President to impose global import quotas on Upland Cotton unless the Secretary of Agriculture determines that its average price exceeds certain statutory limits.[4] This provision tends to be countercyclical to market forces for cotton in the United States, meaning the greater the U.S production of cotton, the more restrictive the quota. Brazil successfully challenged parts of this program in a WTO dispute proceeding, but it has largely remained in place under a U.S. settlement that makes payments to Brazilian cotton growers. *See* Section 1.15. A similar countercyclical system applies under the Meat Import Act of 1979. To avoid meat import quotas, the president usually negotiates "voluntary restraint" agreements with major meat exporting countries such as Australia.

Other U.S. Import Quotas

The United States sometimes imposes import restraints for national security or foreign policy reasons. Many of these restraints originate from Section 232 of the Trade Expansion Act of 1962. This provision authorizes the President to "adjust imports" whenever necessary to the national security of the country. Trade embargoes are sometimes imposed on all the goods from politically incorrect nations (e.g., Cuba). *See* Chapter 11. The Burmese Freedom and Democracy Act of 2003 (Public Law 108–61) banned the importation of Burmese goods, in protest against repression of democracy in that country. Recognizing pro-democracy developments in Myanmar, this ban was lifted in 2012. Trade embargoes have been periodically imposed on all or some imports from other countries, such as Libya, Iraq, and Iran.

Product-specific import bans also exist for selected goods, e.g., narcotic drugs and books urging insurrection against the United States.[5] The importation of "immoral" goods is generally prohibited[6], even for private use, and the obscenity of such items is decided by reviewing the community standards at the port of entry.[7] Generally, as well, goods produced with forced, convict, indentured

---

[4]   7 U.S.C.A. § 1444.

[5]   21 U.S.C.A. § 171 and 19 U.S.C.A. § 1305.

[6]   19 U.S.C.A. § 1305.

[7]   United States v. Various Articles of Obscene Merchandise, 536 F.Supp. 50 (S.D.N.Y.1981).

or bonded child labor is excluded from the United States.[8] The 1997 Bonded Child Labor Elimination Act amended 19 U.S.C. § 1307 to prohibit the U.S. importation of goods produced by "bonded child labor." Such labor is defined as work or service exacted by confinement against his or her will from persons under age 15 in payment for debts of parents, relatives or guardians, or drawn under false pretexts.

Generally speaking, the United States maintains an open market for competitive trade in services. One major exception is maritime transport. In this area, the U.S. protects its domestic industry from import competition under the Merchant Marine Act of 1920 ("Jones Act") and other statutes. For example, the shipment of Alaskan oil is reserved for U.S.-flag vessels as is the supply of offshore drill rigs. The Jones Act most notably prohibits foreign vessels from transporting goods or passengers between U.S. ports and on U.S. rivers, lakes and canals. The reservation of goods for U.S.-flag ships (such trade is known as cabotage) is very significant economically, amounting to billions annually, with a heavy concentration in petroleum products.

§ 7.2   U.S. Nontariff Trade Barriers (NTBs)

There are numerous nontariff trade barriers applicable to United States imports. Many of these barriers arise out of federal or state safety and health regulations. Others concern the environment, consumer protection, product standards and government procurement. Some 40 U.S. government agencies are involved with enforcing NTBs. Many of the relevant rules were created for legitimate consumer and public protection reasons. They were often created without extensive consideration of their international impact as potential nontariff trade barriers. Nevertheless, the practical impact of legislation of this type is to ban the importation of non-conforming products from the United States market. Thus, unlike tariffs which can always be paid, and unlike quotas which permit a certain amount of goods to enter the United States market, nontariff trade barriers have the potential to totally exclude foreign exports.

---

[8]   19 U.S.C.A. § 1307. Section 1307 bans products of convict, forced and indentured labor. See China Diesel Imports, Inc. v. United States, 870 F.Supp. 347 (C.I.T. 1994) (Chinese government documents referring to factory as "Reform through Labor Facility" probative of convict labor origin of goods; exclusion order affirmed; U.S. consumption demand exception applies only to forced and indentured labor). On standing to sue to block importation of prohibited labor goods, see McKinney v. United States Department of Treasury, 799 F.2d 1544 (Fed.Cir.1986) (causal link between imports and clear economic injury must be shown).

The diversity of regulatory approaches to products and the environment makes it extremely difficult to generalize about nontariff trade barriers. The material in this Chapter concerns health restrictions relating to food, safety restrictions relating to consumer products, environmental auto emissions standards and selected other NTBs. These areas have been chosen merely as examples of the types of NTB barriers to the United States market, and are by no means exhaustive. Special NTB rules apply in the context of the Canada-U.S. Free Trade Agreement and the NAFTA. *See* Chapter 16. Sanitary and phytosanitary (SPS) measures dealing with food safety and animal and plant health regulations are the subject of a WTO SPS Code, as are products standards generally (TBT Code). *See* Section 1.7.

The European Union and the United States, and (separately) Canada and the U.S., have reached Mutual Recognition Agreements on certain product standards. The Agreements attempt to reduce the trade restraining potential of regulations applicable to telecommunications equipment, medical devices, pharmaceuticals, recreational craft, electrical safety and electromagnetic compatibility. Each side promises to test their exports according to the other's standards. A second test in the country of importation should no longer be necessary.

§ 7.3　U.S. Public Procurement Preferences as NTBs

Where public procurement is involved, and the taxpayer's money is at issue, virtually every nation has some form of legislation or tradition that favors buying from domestic suppliers. In federal nations like the United States, these rules can also be found in state and local purchasing requirements.

Buy American Act

The principal United States statute affecting imports in connection with government procurement is the Buy American Act of 1933.[9] This Act requires the government to buy American unless the acquisition is for use outside the U.S.,[10] there are insufficient quantities of satisfactory quality available in the U.S., or domestic purchases would be inconsistent with the public interest or result in unreasonable costs.

---

[9]　41 U.S.C.A. §§ 10a–10d.

[10]　See the U.S. Balance of Payments Program, 48 C.F.R. § 225.302 et seq., creating procurement preferences for materials used outside the U.S. but suspended if the Code on Procurement applies.

As currently applied, the United States Buy American Act requires federal agencies to treat a domestic bid as unreasonable or inconsistent with the public interest only if it exceeds a foreign bid by more than six percent (customs duties included) or ten percent (customs duties and specific costs excluded). Exceptions to this general approach exist for reasons of national interest, certain designated small business purchases, domestic suppliers operating in areas of substantial unemployment and demonstrated national security needs. Bids by small businesses and companies located in labor surplus areas are generally protected by a 12 percent margin of preference. Bids from U.S. companies are considered foreign rather than domestic when the materials used in the products concerned are below 50 percent American in origin. These rules apply to civil purchasing by the United States government,[11] but are suspended for purchasing subject to the GATT/WTO Procurement Codes as implemented by the Trade Agreements Act of 1979 and the Uruguay Round Agreements Act of 1994. *See* Section 1.13.

The Department of Defense has its own Buy American rules. Generally speaking, a 50 percent price preference (customs duties excluded) or a 6 or 12 percent preference (customs duties included) whichever is more protective to domestic suppliers is applied. However, intergovernmental "Memoranda of Understanding" (MOU) on defense procurement provide important exceptions to the standard Department of Defense procurement rules.[12] Additional procurement preferences are established by the Small Business Act of 1953.[13] Under this Act, federal agencies may set-aside certain procurement exclusively for small U.S. businesses. In practice, the federal government normally sets aside about 30 percent of its procurement needs in this fashion. Special set-aside rules apply to benefit socially and economically disadvantaged minority-owned businesses. These preferences are exempt from U.S. adherence to the GATT/WTO Procurement Codes under a U.S. reservation.

A number of federal statutes also contain specific Buy American requirements. These include various GSA, NASA and TVA appropriations' bills, the 1941 Berry Amendment (mandating mostly U.S. food, clothing tents and flags for troops), the AMTRAK Improvement Act of 1978,[14] the Public Works Employment Act of

---

[11]   See Executive Order No. 10582 (Dec. 17, 1954), 19 Fed.Reg. 8723 *as amended by* Exec. Order No. 11051 (Sept. 27, 1962), 27 Fed.Reg. 9683 and Exec. Order No. 12148, July 20, 1979, 44 Fed.Reg. 43239.

[12]   See Self-Powered Lighting, Ltd. v. United States, 492 F.Supp. 1267 (S.D.N.Y.1980).

[13]   15 U.S.C.A. §§ 631–648. See 48 C.F.R. §§ 19.000–.902.

[14]   Pub.L. 95–421.

1977,[15] various highway and transport acts,[16] the Clean Water Act of 1977,[17] and the Rural Electrification Acts of 1936 and 1938.[18] Many of these statutes involve federal funding of state and local procurement. Most are generally excluded from the GATT/WTO Procurement Codes as applied by the United States.

A practice known as "unbalanced bidding" has arisen in connection with the Buy American Act. Unbalanced bidding involves the use of United States labor and parts by foreigners in sufficient degree so as to overcome the bidding preferences established by law for U.S. suppliers. This occurs because the United States value added is *not* included in the calculations of the margin of preference for the U.S. firms. Thus foreign bids minus the value of work done in the U.S. are multiplied by the 6, 12 or 50 percent Buy American Act preference. If the U.S. bids are above the foreign bids but within the margin of preference, the U.S. bidder gets the contract. If the U.S. bids are higher than the foreign bids plus the margin of preference, the foreigners get the contract.[19]

GATT/WTO Procurement Codes

The optional Tokyo Round GATT Procurement Code was not particularly successful at opening up government purchasing. Only Austria, Canada, the twelve European Union states, Finland, Hong Kong, Israel, Japan, Norway, Singapore, Sweden, Switzerland and the United States adhered to the Procurement Code. This was also partly the result of the 1979 Code's many exceptions. For example, the Code did not apply to contracts below its threshold amount of $150,000 SDR (about $171,000 since 1988), service contracts, and procurement by entities on each country's reserve list (including most national defense items). Because procurement in the European Union and Japan is often decentralized, many contracts fall below the SDR threshold and were therefore exempt. By dividing up procurement into smaller contracts national preferences were retained. U.S. government procurement tends to be more centralized and thus more likely covered by the Code. This pattern helps explain why Congress restrictively amended the Buy American Act in 1988.

The Buy American Act generally conformed to the GATT Code on Government Procurement negotiated during the Tokyo Round. However, Congress expressed its displeasure with the degree to

---

[15]   42 U.S.C.A. § 6705.
[16]   See, e.g., Highway Improvement Act of 1982, Pub.L. 97–424.
[17]   33 U.S.C.A. § 1295.
[18]   7 U.S.C.A. § 903.
[19]   See Allis-Chalmers Corp. v. Friedkin, 635 F.2d 248 (3d Cir. 1980).

which that Code opened up sales opportunities for United States firms abroad. It therefore amended the Buy American Act in 1988 to deny the benefits of the Procurement Code when foreign governments are not in good standing under it. United States government procurement contracts are also denied to suppliers from countries whose governments "maintain . . . a significant and persistent pattern of practice or discrimination against U.S. products or services which results in identifiable harm to U.S. businesses."[20] Presidential waivers of these statutory denials may occur in the public interest, to avoid single supply situations or to assure sufficient bidders to provide supplies of requisite quality and competitive prices.

The European Union was one of the first to be identified as a persistent procurement discriminator by the USTR. This identification concerns longstanding heavy electrical and telecommunications disputes that were partly settled by negotiation. The remaining disputes led to U.S. trade sanctions and European retaliation. This did not occur with Greece, Spain and Portugal (where the EU procurement rules do not apply), and with Germany which broke ranks and negotiated a path breaking bilateral settlement with the U.S. Japan was also identified as a persistent procurement discriminator in the construction, architectural and engineering areas.

The Uruguay Round Procurement Code replaced the Tokyo Round agreement. It is one of very few WTO agreements that is optional. About 35 developed nations currently participate, limited by listings of applicable procurement entities and goods and services, with most contract thresholds approximating $180,000. China is actively seeking to join the Procurement Code, negotiating with the existing Code signatories. The WTO Code expands coverage to include procurement of services, construction, government-owned utilities, and some state and local (sub-central) contracts. Various improvements to the procedural rules surrounding procurement practices and dispute settlement attempt to reduce tensions in this difficult area. For example, an elaborate system for bid protests is established and since 2014 electronic bid submissions must be allowed. Bidders who believe the Code's procedural rules have been abused will be able to lodge, litigate and appeal their protests. The United States has agreed, with few exceptions, to bring all procurement by executive agencies subject to the Federal Acquisition Regulations under the Code's coverage (i.e., to suspend application of the normal Buy American preferences to such procurement).

---

[20]   41 U.S.C.A. § 10d.

Most U.S. states have voluntarily agreed to adhere to the WTO Procurement Agreement. The United States, amid considerable controversy, adopted "Buy American" steel rules in the Obama administration economic stimulus plan (the American Recovery and Reinvestment Act of 2009), exempting WTO Procurement Code participants and U.S. free trade agreements. Additional Buy American preferences were created by the Obama administration auto bail-out plans and other legislation.

State, Local and NAFTA Procurement Preferences

In addition to the Buy American Act, state and local purchasing requirements may inhibit import competition in the procurement field. For example, California once had a law which made it mandatory to purchase American products. This law was declared unconstitutional as an encroachment upon the federal power to conduct foreign affairs.[21] A Massachusetts ban on contracts with companies invested in Burma was preempted by federal sanctions adopted in 1997 against Burma.[22]

State statutes which have copied the federal Buy American Act, on the other hand, and incorporated public interest and unreasonable cost exceptions to procurement preferences, have generally withstood constitutional challenge.[23] A Pennsylvania statute requiring state and local agencies to ensure that contractors do not provide products containing foreign steel was upheld by the Third Circuit Court of Appeals.[24] This case illustrated the inapplicability of the Tokyo Round Procurement Code to state and local purchasing requirements.[25]

Chapter 13 of the 1989 Canada–United States Free Trade Area Agreement opens government procurement to U.S. and Canadian suppliers on contracts as small as $25,000. However, the goods supplied must have at least 50 percent U.S. and Canadian content. The NAFTA also establishes distinct procurement regulations. The thresholds are $50,000 for goods and services provided to federal agencies and $250,000 for government-owned enterprises (notably

---

[21]   Bethlehem Steel Corp. v. Board of Commissioners of the Department of Water and Power of the City of Los Angeles, 276 Cal.App.2d 221, 80 Cal.Rptr. 800 (1969).

[22]   Crosby v. National Foreign Trade Council, 530 U.S. 363, 120 S.Ct. 2288, 147 L.Ed.2d 352 (2000).

[23]   See K.S.B. Technical Sales Corp. v. North Jersey District Water Supply Commission of the State of New Jersey, 75 N.J. 272, 381 A.2d 774 (1977), *appeal dismissed* 435 U.S. 982, 98 S.Ct. 1635, 56 L.Ed.2d 76 (1978).

[24]   Trojan Technologies, Inc. v. Pennsylvania, 916 F.2d 903 (3d Cir.1990), *cert. denied* 501 U.S. 1212, 111 S.Ct. 2814, 115 L.Ed.2d 986 (1991).

[25]   See Southwick, Binding the States: A Survey of State Law Conformance with Standards of the GATT Procurement Code, 13 U.Pa.J.Int'l Bus.L. 57 (1992).

PEMEX and CFE). These regulations are particularly important because Mexico, unlike Canada, has not traditionally joined in GATT/WTO procurement codes. They do not apply to states, provinces or municipalities.

§ 7.4   U.S. Product Standards, TBT Code Implementation

Widespread use of "standards" requirements as NTB import restraints resulted in 1979 in the optional GATT Agreement on Technical Barriers to Trade (called the "Standards Code").[26] This Code was made operative in the United States by the Trade Agreements Act of 1979,[27] and was followed by a reasonable number of other nations. Its successor is the Uruguay Round Agreement on Technical Barriers to Trade (1994) (TBT). This agreement is binding on all WTO members. In general, this Code deals with the problem of countries' manipulation of product standards, product testing procedures, and product certifications in order to slow or stop imported goods.

The TBT Code provides, in part and subject to some exceptions, that imported products shall be accorded treatment (including testing treatment and certification) no less favorable than that accorded to like products of national origin or those originating in any other country. It also requires that participating nations establish a central office for standards inquiries, publish advance and reasonable notice of requirements that are applicable to imported goods, and provide an opportunity for commentary by those who may be affected adversely. The Code establishes an international committee to deal with alleged instances of noncompliance.

Under United States law,[28] state and federal agencies may create standards which specify the characteristics of a product, such as levels of quality, safety, performance or dimensions, or its packaging and labeling. However, these "standards-related activities" must not create "unnecessary obstacles to U.S. foreign trade," and must be demonstrably related to "a legitimate domestic objective" such as protection of health and safety, security, environmental or consumer interests. Sometimes there is a conflict between federal and state standards. For example, federal law

---

[26]   See 18 Int'l Legal Mat. 1079.
[27]   19 U.S.C.A. § 1531 et seq.
[28]   19 U.S.C.A. § 2531.

licensing endangered species' articles preempted California's absolute ban on trade in such goods.[29]

The Office of the USTR is charged with responsibility for implementation of the Standards Code within the United States.[30] The Secretary of Commerce maintains a "standards information center" (National Bureau of Standards, National Center for Standards and Certification Information), in part to "serve as the central national collection facility for information relating to standards, certification systems, and standards-related activities, whether such standards, systems or activities are public or private, domestic or foreign, or international, regional, national, or local [and to] make available to the public at . . . reasonable fee . . . copies of information required to be collected."[31]

The diversity of U.S. regulatory approaches to products and the environment makes it extremely difficult to generalize about nontariff trade barriers. In 2008, all imports wood products (even toothpicks) were subjected to new Lacey Act criminal rules that inhibit trade. Wood derived from illegal logging, for example, has been denied entry and seized by U.S. Customs. Gibson Guitar Corp. paid about $300,000 to settle alleged violations of the Lacey Act.

All foods imported into the United States are subject to inspection for their wholesomeness, freedom from contamination, and compliance with labeling requirements (including the nutritional labeling rules). This examination is conducted by the Food and Drug Administration using samples submitted to it by the United States Customs Service. If these tests result in a finding that the food products cannot be imported into the United States, they must be exported or destroyed. The Food Safety Modernization Act of 2007 anticipates regulations that will require importers to verify and oversee compliance with U.S. food safety rules.

The Bioterrorism Act of 2002 requires all U.S. and foreign food companies selling in the United States to register with the Food and Drug Administration. Importers must notify the FDA in advance and in detail of food shipments, and keep records of suppliers and customers. The FDA can detain any food deemed a risk, including late or missing notice items.

U.S. Consumer and Environmental Law NTBs

The Consumer Products Safety Act bars the importation of consumer products which do not comply with the standards of the

---

[29] Man Hing Ivory and Imports, Inc. v. Deukmejian, 702 F.2d 760 (9th Cir.1983).

[30] 19 U.S.C.A. §§ 2541, 2552.

[31] 19 U.S.C.A. § 2544.

Consumer Products Safety Commission. Exporters of consumer products must certify that their goods conform to applicable United States safety and labeling standards. Any product that has a defect which is determined to constitute a "substantial product hazard" or is imminently hazardous may be banned from the United States market. The Customs Service may seize any such nonconforming goods. These goods may be modified in order to conform them to U.S. Consumer Products Safety Commission requirements. Otherwise, such goods must be exported or destroyed, an end result notably applied in 2007 to children's toys from China.

United States environmental or conservation laws notably affecting international trade include:

- The Endangered Species Act of 1973 prohibiting import/export of endangered species.

- The "Pelley Amendment" authorizing import restraints against fish products of nations undermining international fisheries or wildlife conservation agreements.

- The High Seas Driftnet Fisheries Enforcement Act of 1992 banning imports of fish, fish products and sport fishing gear from countries violating the United Nations driftnet moratorium.

- The Sea Turtle Conservation Act prohibiting shrimp imports harvested with adverse effects on sea turtles first used in 1993 against shrimp from several Caribbean nations and now applicable globally to Thailand, India, China and Bangladesh among others.

- The Wild Bird Conservation Act banning imports of tropical wild birds.

- The Antarctic Marine Living Resources Convention Act prohibiting import/export of living resources.

- The African Elephant Conservation Act restricting ivory imports.

- The Lacey Act prohibiting imports of fish, wildlife, plant and wood that violate foreign laws.

U.S. GATT/WTO Product Standards Disputes

United States standards have been attacked in international tribunals as violating international obligations. Sometimes the standards have been upheld, sometimes not. For example, a binational arbitration panel established under Chapter 18 of the Canada-U.S. FTA issued a decision upholding a United States law setting a minimum size on lobsters sold in interstate commerce. The panel found that, since the law applied to both domestic and foreign lobsters, it was not a disguised trade restriction. On the other hand, in 1991, a GATT panel found that United States import restrictions designed to protect dolphin from tuna fishers did violate the GATT. The panel ruled that GATT did not permit any import restrictions based on environmental concerns, whether they were considered disguised trade restrictions or not. This decision suggested repeal of a number of United States laws which concern health, safety and environmental conditions in exporting nations. A 1994 decision by a second GATT panel recognized the legitimacy of extraterritorial environmental regulations, but ruled against the tuna boycott of the U.S. because of its focus on production methods.

In 1998, the WTO Appellate Body ruled against a U.S. ban on shrimp imports from nations that fail to use turtle exclusion devises comparable to those required under U.S. law. The Appellate Body found the U.S. ban "arbitrary" and "unjustifiable". The standards of other nations have also been challenged as violations of GATT obligations. For example, the United States has criticized European Union bans of imports of meat from the United States, first for containing certain hormones, later for unsanitary conditions in U.S. meatpacking facilities. In 1997, and again in 2004, the WTO Appellate Body ruled against the EU hormone-treated beef ban, citing lack of an adequate scientific basis as required under the WTO SPS Code. *See* Section 1.7.

In 2012, the WTO Appellate Body determined that the United States ban on flavored cigarettes, as applied to clove cigarettes from Indonesia, breached the TBT Code national treatment standard. The Appellate Body noted particularly the discriminatory allowance for sale in the U.S. of menthol flavored cigarettes. WT/DS 406/AB/R (April 23, 2012).

§ 7.5   U.S. Import Labeling Rules, TBT Disputes

The United States requires clear markings of countries of origin on imports. This can be perceived, especially by those abroad, as a nontariff trade barrier intended to promote domestic purchases. Section 304 of the Tariff act of 1930 establishes the basic rules for origin markings.[32] Every imported article of foreign origin (or its container) must be marked conspicuously, legibly, indelibly and as permanently as practical in English so as to indicate to ultimate purchasers its country of origin.[33] Violation of these rules

---

[32]   19 U.S.C.A. § 1304.

[33]   See Precision Specialty Metals, Inc. v. United States, 116 F.Supp.2d 1350 (C.I.T.2000).

can result in additional tariffs of up to 10 percent. Intentional removal or alteration of markings is a crime.[34]

In 2008, Mexico initiated WTO proceedings against U.S. "dolphin-safe" label rules embodied in the 1990 Dolphin Protection Consumer Information Act, and a Ninth Circuit decision (*Earth Island Institute v. Hogarth*, 494 F.3d 757 (2007)) requiring zero use of purse seine nets for such labels. In 2010, the U.S. commenced NAFTA proceedings seeking to force Mexico to withdraw its WTO complaint and re-file it under NAFTA. "Standards" disputes are supposed to be resolved exclusively under NAFTA Chapter 20 procedures and trade rules that strongly favor national laws. In 2011, a WTO panel held in favor of Mexico's complaint, which Mexico declined to re-file under NAFTA. The WTO Appellate Body affirmed (WT/DS381/AB/R (July13, 2012), ruling that the U.S. dolphin-safe label rules violated the national treatment standard of the WTO TBT Code. *See* Section 1.7.

In 2008, as part of the Farm Bill, new Lacey Act import disclosure and country of origin requirements were broadly created for plants and wood products. *See* Section 7.5. Additional import disclosure and origin "COOL" rules for meat and meat products were also legislated in the 2008 Farm Bill. The COOL rules were successfully challenged by Canada and Mexico before the WTO. The Appellate Body declared them discriminatory, and violations of TBT Code national treatment obligations. WT/DS384 and 386/AB/R (July 23, 2012).

The principle sanction for failure to properly mark imports is the imposition of statutory tariffs of 10 percent ad valorem, which are imposed in addition to regular duties and even if the goods would ordinarily enter the U.S. duty free. Importers ordinarily receive notice from the Customs Service and an opportunity to comply with marking requirements. Any untimely failure to comply can result in liquidated damages proceedings by Customs against the importer. The amount of damages assessed will vary with the frequency and circumstances of the offense, and will be assessed as a percentage of the appraised value of the merchandise.

In severe cases, Customs may seek civil penalties under Section 592 of the Tariff Act of 1930.[35] This provision generally sanctions imports under false documents. Furthermore, criminal sanctions are also possible, either for use of false documents[36] or

---

[34]   19 U.S.C. 1304(c).
[35]   19 U.S.C.A. § 1592.
[36]   18 U.S.C.A. § 1001.

altering a required marking with concealment intended.[37] The latter penalties can rise to $250,000 or one year imprisonment or both. The severity of these sanctions must be measured against the temptation of traders to alter country of origin markings so as to obtain duty free or quota free entry of goods into the United States.

Various exceptions apply to the U.S. country of origin marking requirements.[38] These include goods that are incapable of being marked, goods economically prohibitive to mark (unless the failure to do so was a deliberate attempt at avoiding the law), or goods that will be injured if marked. If the containers will reasonably indicate origin to the ultimate consumer, or the import circumstances or character of the goods necessarily convey knowledge of their source, no marking is required.

Nor is it mandatory to mark goods not intended for resale, goods which when processed will obliterate the mark, goods over twenty years old and goods intended for export without entering U.S. commerce. Certain United States fishery products, products of U.S. possessions and products that originally came from the U.S. and are being imported are likewise exempt. Lastly, there is a "J-list" of specific goods that have been individually ruled exempt by the Secretary of the Treasury.[39] These include items like cordage, buttons, nails, etc., all of which must be marked by container.

Special regulations govern the marking requirements for imported textiles. These are created by the Textile Fiber Products Identification Act.[40] This Act is enforced by the U.S. Federal Trade Commission. It mandates disclosure of country of origin, generic fiber contents and the name or identification number of the manufacturer or marketer. Violation of the Textile Fiber Products Identification Act amounts to a violation of Section 5 of the Federal Trade Commission Act.[41] This means that F.T.C. cease and desist order proceedings, injunction actions, civil penalties and consumer redress relief can follow. Similar but not identical labeling requirements are established by the Wool Products Labeling Act[42] (country of origin required) and the Fur Products Labeling Act[43] (country of origin not required). These laws are also enforced by the Federal Trade Commission.

---

[37]   19 U.S.C.A. § 1304.
[38]   See 19 C.F.R. § 134.32.
[39]   See 19 C.F.R. § 134.33.
[40]   15 U.S.C.A. § 70–70K.
[41]   15 U.S.C.A. § 45.
[42]   15 U.S.C.A. § 68–68j.
[43]   15 U.S.C.A. § 69–69j.

Significant litigation has ensued under the Tariff Act country of origin requirements regarding when a U.S. manufacturer is to be deemed the "ultimate purchaser" which may render the goods exempt from marking. In a major decision by the Court of Customs and Patent Appeals, wooden brush handles from Japan were processed in the U.S. by inserting bristles which obliterated the marking. The CCPA, adopting a common rationale in U.S. customs law, held that the handles had undergone a "substantial transformation" into a new product in the United States and were thus subject only to container marking obligations.[44]

In contrast, when leather uppers for shoes were imported from Indonesia, the Court of International Trade required individual markings despite the attachment of soles in the U.S. and argument that a "substantial transformation" had taken place.[45] Gifts of products to ordinary consumers (umbrellas to racetrack patrons) may still require origin markings even if the donor would be exempt.[46]

Other litigation has focused on the duty to mark origin "conspicuously." The Court of International Trade initially reversed a "plainly erroneous" Customs Service position that frozen food markings at the rear of the package (Made in Mexico) were conspicuous.[47] The Court took the position that such markings did not give U.S. consumers realistic choices when shopping and noted the health risks associated with such goods. Subsequently, the Court of International Trade vacated this opinion.

---

[44]   United States v. Gibson-Thomsen Co., 27 C.C.P.A. 267 (1940), *superseded by regulation as stated in* Cumins Engine Co. v. United States, 83 F.Supp.2d 1366 (C.I.T.1999).

[45]   Uniroyal, Inc. v. United States, 542 F.Supp. 1026 (C.I.T.1982), *affirmed* 702 F.2d 1022 (Fed.Cir.1983).

[46]   Pabrini, Inc. v. United States, 630 F.Supp. 360 (C.I.T.1986).

[47]   Norcal/Crosetti Foods, Inc. v. United States Customs Service, 758 F.Supp. 729 (C.I.T.1991), *opinion vac'd* 790 F.Supp. 302 (C.I.T.1992).

Chapter 8

COUNTERFEIT AND IP
INFRINGING IMPORTS

Table of Sections

§ 8.1   Trade in Counterfeit Goods

Theft of intellectual property and use of counterfeit goods are rapidly increasing in developing and developed countries. Such theft is not limited to consumer goods (Pierre Cardin clothing, Rolex watches). Industrial products and parts (e.g., automotive brake pads) are now being counterfeited. Some countries see illegal technology transfers as part of their strategy for economic development. They encourage piracy or choose not to oppose it. Since unlicensed producers pay no royalties, they often have lower production costs than the original source. This practice fuels the fires of intellectual property piracy. Unlicensed low-cost reproduction of entire copyrighted books (may it not happen to this book) is said to be rampant in such diverse areas as Nigeria, Saudi Arabia, and South Korea. Apple computers have been inexpensively counterfeited in Hong Kong. General Motors estimates that about

40 percent of its auto parts are counterfeited in the Middle East. Recordings are duplicated almost everywhere without license or fee. The Internet fuels film and TV piracy . . . try a Google search. And the list goes on.

Among the industrialized countries, efforts occur to acquire (even by way of stealing) "leading edge" technology. One example in the 1980s involved attempted theft of IBM computer technology by Japanese companies ultimately caught by the F.B.I. In the United States, the Office of Export Administration uses the export license procedure to control strategic technological "diversions." But falsification of licensing documents by prominent Norwegian and Japanese companies allowed the Soviets to obtain the technology for making vastly quieter submarine propellers. In the ensuing scandal, "anti-Toshiba" trade sanctions were adopted in the United States. Leading Japanese executives resigned, which is considered the highest form of apology in Japanese business circles.

In 2009, U.S. officials seized about $260 million in counterfeit goods. Chinese gangs accounted for the bulk of these goods, which were most often footwear, consumer electronics, luxury goods and pharmaceuticals. U.S. military and civilian procurement agencies have begun actively targeting counterfeit suppliers. U.S. seizures of counterfeit goods rose to $1.26 billion in 2012 and $1.74 billion in 2013, again with China as the primary source. In 2012, the European Union seized over $1.3 billion in counterfeit goods, roughly two-thirds of which came from China. Cigarettes comprised the biggest counterfeit seizures. An Anti-Counterfeiting Trade Agreement (ACTA) has been in the works, though its future is in doubt and China is not expected to participate.

§ 8.2   Counterfeit Goods, U.S. Remedies

Legal protection against intellectual property theft and counterfeit goods is not very effective. The four principal U.S. remedies are: (1) seizure of goods by Customs; (2) infringement actions in federal courts; (3) criminal prosecutions or treble damages actions under the Trademark Counterfeiting Act of 1984; and (4) Section 337 proceedings. Each of these is discussed below.

The Anticounterfeiting Consumer Protection Act of 1996, Public Law 104–153 (110 Stat. 1386), made a number of statutory changes intended to combat counterfeiting. Trafficking in counterfeit goods is now an offense under the RICO Act (Racketeer Influenced and Corrupt Organizations Act). Importers must disclose the identity of any trademark on imported merchandise, ex parte seizures by law enforcement officers of counterfeit goods and vehicles used to transport them are widely authorized, damages and civil penalties that can be recovered from counterfeiters and importers were increased, and the Customs Service's authority to return counterfeit merchandise to its source (and potential re-entry into commerce) has been repealed. Customs must now destroy all counterfeit merchandise that it seizes unless the trademark owner otherwise consents and the goods are not a health or safety threat.

In the United States, the Copyright Felony Act of 1992 criminalized all copyright infringements. The No Electronic Theft Act of 1997 (NET) removed the need to prove financial gain as element of copyright infringement law, thus ensuring coverage of copying done with intent to harm copyright owners or copying simply for personal use. The Digital Millennium Copyright Act of 1998 (DMCA) brought the United States into compliance with WIPO treaties and created two new copyright offenses; one for circumventing technological measures used by copyright owners to protect their works ("hacking") and a second for tampering with copyright management information (encryption). The DMCA also made it clear that "webmasters" digitally broadcasting music on the internet must pay performance royalties. Criminal and civil sanctions apply.[1]

§ 8.3   U.S. Customs Service Seizures

United States trademark and copyright holders may register with the Customs Service and seek the blockade of pirated items made abroad. Such exclusions are authorized in the Tariff Act of 1930 and the Copyright Act of 1976.[2] The thrust of these provisions is that unauthorized imports bearing U.S. registered trademarks or copyrights may be seized by the Customs Service. Trade names that have been used for at least six months can also be recorded with the Customs Service.

Such recordation permits those names to receive the same relief accorded registered trademark and copyright holders when imports that counterfeit or simulate those trade names are found.[3] Since the trademark, copyright and trade name remedies are only available to United States citizens, distributors of foreign goods must ordinarily be assigned United States trademark rights held by foreigners. Such assignments would permit the distributor to seek a new registration from the Patent and Trademark Office so as to be able to invoke these trade remedies.

---

[1]   See, e.g., Universal City Studios, Inc. v. Shawn C. Reimerdes, 111 F.Supp.2d 294 (2000) (injunction against anti-encryption software).

[2]   See 19 U.S.C.A. § 1526(a) (trademarks) and 17 U.S.C.A. § 602(b) (copyrights). See also 19 C.F.R. § 133, Parts A, D.

[3]   See 19 C.F.R. § 133, Parts B, C.

The importation of semiconductor chip products or equipment that contains a semiconductor chip design or "mask work" registered with the U.S. Copyright Office is prohibited.[4] As with trademarks, copyrights and trade names, the owner of such a mask work may register it with the U.S. Customs Service or the U.S. International Trade Commission so as to invoke trade remedies which will preclude infringing products and equipment from entering into the United States. The Customs Service also administers a high-tech copyright protection program specially targeted at pirated computer programs.[5] Generally, the Customs Service will seize infringing programs if there is proof of access by the infringer and a "substantial similarity" between the imports and the registered program.[6]

U.S. Customs Seizure Procedures

There are some differences in Customs Service seizure proceedings depending upon whether the product seized is alleged to be a trademark counterfeit or a copyright counterfeit. The Customs Service rules indicate that in administrative hearings the burden is on the importer to demonstrate why allegedly counterfeit trademarked goods should be released, whereas the burden is on the copyright owner to prove that copyrighted goods are being pirated. These burdens are different because of the greater difficulties in proving copyright infringements.

The Second Circuit has ruled that the Customs Service must employ the "average purchaser test" in determining whether imports are counterfeits subject to seizure and forfeiture.[7] In this case, the Service had used experts to determine differences in the trademark such that it was deemed not a counterfeit (merely infringing) and therefore admissible if the confusing mark was obliterated. The consumer test mandated by the Second Circuit should give greater protection from counterfeits.

Attorneys invoking the Customs Service process frequently sense the inadequacy of relief against counterfeit goods. The first problem is simply knowing when counterfeit goods are likely to enter the United States market. The Customs Service has enormous duties and can only pay limited attention to the possibility that certain goods are pirated. This is understandable. How is the Customs Service officer to know that the goods are pirated? Can the

---

[4]   See 17 U.S.C.A. § 601(a).

[5]   See 19 C.F.R. § 133.31 et seq.

[6]   See Webster and Pryor, Customs Administration of the High-tech Copyright Protection Program, 73 J. Pat. & Trademark Off. Society 538 (1991).

[7]   Montres Rolex, S.A. v. Snyder, 718 F.2d 524 (2d Cir.1983), *cert. denied* 465 U.S. 1100, 104 S.Ct. 1594, 80 L.Ed.2d 126 (1984).

Customs Service do anything more than look at the invoice in a cursory way? Pirates often take great pains to imitate the logo and trademarks they are copying. This makes such piracy non-obvious.

Copyright piracy of sound recordings is even more difficult to ascertain. It cannot reasonably be expected of the Customs Service that they will play records and tapes in order to determine that they are counterfeit goods. To make customs relief effective it is necessary for private interests to notify the Customs Service that a suspected shipment of counterfeit goods is about to or has arrived in the United States. Companies are increasingly hiring private detectives in order to assist with this task. Private detectives might also be used to try to locate pirated copies and counterfeiting operations inside the United States.

ROMless Computers Case

A second frustration with Customs Service relief concerns narrow Customs Service interpretations, such as in the *ROMless Computers* case.[8] In that decision, the Customs Service refused to seize ROMless computers alleged to be in violation of Apple Computer Company copyrights. The practical effect of this decision was to permit ROMless computers to enter the U.S. market, and thereafter be altered in rather simple fashion so as to become effective competitors and arguably infringers of copyrights held by the Apple Computer Company. By removing the ROM (Read Only Memory operating system computer program) unit from the computers, the importers eliminated the only copyrighted element in the computer and thereby nullified attempts at blocking importation of these goods:

"Assuming without deciding that the making of the "ROMless" computers constitutes a contributory infringement against the copyright holder's copyrights, the importation of such merchandise is not prohibited by 17 U.S.C. 602(b). While the phrase "an infringement of copyright" arguably includes contributory copyright infringement, preventing the importation of "ROMless" computers would be inconsistent with other language in the statute. The objects against which the provisions of 17 U.S.C. 602(b) are directed are copies or phonorecords of a work that have been acquired outside the United States.

With regard to the very computer programs in issue, the statutory copyright requirement of fixation has been held to be satisfied through the embodiment of these programs in ROM devices. . . . Furthermore, computer programs contained in ROMs can be perceived, reproduced, or otherwise communicated therefrom

---

[8]   See 9 BNA U.S. Import Wkly 1062 (May 30, 1984).

with the aid of other computer equipment. Accordingly, the provisions of 17 U.S.C. 602(b) are operative against ROMs (or diskettes, tapes, or other devices for fixed storage of software) that contain unlawful reproductions of copyrighted computer software, for these items are copies within the meaning of that section. . . . Therefore, inasmuch as "ROMless" computers do not include such copies upon arrival in the United States, they may enter the country without violation of 17 U.S.C. 602(b)."

§ 8.4   Infringement Actions in U.S. Courts

Another alternative available to counsel attempting to assist U.S. firms combating foreign counterfeiting of their products is infringement relief, including temporary restraining orders, injunctions, damages and an award of the defendant's profits. The major problem with infringement relief is the inability of United States trademark, patent and copyright owners to get effective jurisdiction over and relief from foreign counterfeiters.

Infringement and contributory infringement actions can be used more effectively against the importers, distributors or retailers of counterfeit goods. But relief against one such party may merely shift counterfeit sales to another who must then be brought to court, and then another, and another, etc. While such proceedings can result in *ex parte* seizure orders of counterfeit goods already in the United States, they do not represent a long term solution to production of counterfeit goods in foreign jurisdictions.

Most injunctive and damages relief remains illusory, but it can sometimes be useful. For example, it has been held that counterfeit goods seized *ex parte* under the Lanham Trademark Act can be destroyed upon court order.[9] Civil remedies are *not* limited to simply removing the offending trademark.[10] That said, injunction remedies in federal courts for IP infringement have been stiffened by the Supreme Court.[11] Infringement and treble damages actions may be commenced in United States courts against importers and distributors of counterfeit goods, but service of process and jurisdictional barriers often preclude effective relief against foreign pirates. Even if such relief is obtained, counterfeiters and the sellers of counterfeit goods have proven adept at the "shell game," moving across the road or to another country to resume operations. Moreover, the mobility and economic incentives of counterfeiters

---

[9]   Fendi S.a.s. Di Paola Fendi E Sorelle v. Cosmetic World, 642 F.Supp. 1143 (S.D.N.Y.1986).

[10]   Id.

[11]   *See* eBay Inc v. MercExchange LLC, 547 U.S. 388 (2006).

have rendered the criminal sanctions of the Trademark Counterfeiting Act of 1984 (below) largely a Pyrrhic victory.

§ 8.5   U.S. Criminal Prosecutions

Many states have enacted criminal statutes to combat increased counterfeiting of goods and services in the United States. After much debate, Congress enacted the Trademark Counterfeiting Act of 1984.[12] Criminal penalties are established for anyone who "intentionally traffics or attempts to traffic in goods or services and knowingly uses a counterfeit mark on or in connection with such goods or services." Treble damages or profits (whichever is greater) and attorney fees may be recovered in civil actions unless there are "extenuating circumstances."

Ex parte seizure orders for counterfeit goods may be issued by the federal courts. Parallel imports of genuine or "gray market goods" (goods legitimately produced overseas but imported into the United States via unauthorized distribution channels, infra) and "overruns" (goods produced without authorization by a licensee) are expressly *excluded* from the Act's coverage. *See* Chapter 9. The real problem with criminal sanctions as a remedy for counterfeiting is to persuade public prosecutors to take these crimes seriously and to allocate law enforcement resources to them. However, in recent years, the Justice Department has significantly increased prosecutions of cyber-attacks and industrial espionage thefts of U.S. owned technology.

§ 8.6   International Solutions to Counterfeiting

International solutions to the problem of intellectual property piracy have been no less elusive. A draft "Anti-Counterfeiting Code" received close scrutiny in the Uruguay Round of negotiations. Although the TRIPs accord incorporates some coverage of counterfeiting (see Section 1.11), it is not the encompassing anti-counterfeiting code that the developed world sought. The TRIPs agreement does mandate border measures to block the release of counterfeit goods into domestic circulation. It also requires criminal penalties for willful trademark counterfeiting or copyright piracy undertaken on a commercial scale. However, the TRIPs agreement does not reject the practice of re-exportation of counterfeit merchandise. Re-exportation has the practical effect of pushing the problem on some other jurisdiction and does not represent a final solution from the point of view of the infringed party.

---

[12]   18 U.S.C.A. § 2320 et seq.

France and Italy have made it illegal to knowingly purchase counterfeit goods. For example, if a student buys a "Louis Vuitton" bag for $15 in a Paris or Florence flea market, he or she may be arrested, fined and imprisoned. Until recently, France went a step further. A government agency monitored Internet piracy. French offenders were subject to a "three strikes" rule: Two warnings were issued before Net access could be terminated and fines imposed by court order. South Korea and Taiwan also employ warnings and penalties against illegal downloading.

Various United States statutes authorize the President to withhold trade benefits from or apply trade sanctions to nations inadequately protecting the intellectual property rights of U.S. citizens. This is true of the Caribbean Basin Economic Recovery Act of 1983, the Generalized System of Preferences Renewal Act of 1984, the Trade and Tariff Act of 1984 (amending Section 301 of the 1974 Trade Act), and Title IV of the 1974 Trade Act as it applies to most-favored-nation tariffs. *See* Chapter 2.

Slowly this carrot and stick approach has borne fruit. Under these pressures for example, Singapore drafted a new copyright law, Korea new patent and copyright laws, and Taiwan a new copyright, patent, fair trade and an amended trademark law. Brazil introduced legislation intended to allow copyrights on computer programs. Though changes have been made, there is some doubt as to the rigor with which these laws will be enforced when local jobs and national revenues are lost.

§ 8.7   U.S. Section 337 Proceedings

Section 337 of the Tariff Act of 1930[13] provides exclusionary Customs Service remedies against the importation of counterfeit and infringing goods into the United States. Section 337 proceedings are administered by the U.S. International Trade Commission, which makes remedy recommendations (often "general exclusion orders") that are subject to veto by the President.

Statutory Provisions

Section 337 proceedings traditionally have involved some relatively complicated statutory provisions. Prior to 1988, the basic prohibition was against: (1) unfair methods of competition and unfair acts in the importation of goods (2) the effect or tendency of which is to destroy or substantially injure (3) an industry efficiently and economically operated in the U.S. Such importation was also prohibited when it prevented the establishment of an industry, or restrained or monopolized trade and commerce in the U.S. Section

---

[13]   19 U.S.C.A. 1337.

337 proceedings are *in rem* which explains why they are preferable to a series of *in personam* actions for infringement in the federal courts.

The Omnibus Trade and Competitiveness Act of 1988 revised Section 337. The requirement that the U.S. industry be efficiently and economically operated was dropped. Proof of injury to a domestic industry is *not* required in intellectual property infringement cases. The importation of articles infringing U.S. patents, copyrights, trademarks or semiconductor chip mask works[14] is specifically prohibited provided a U.S. industry relating to such articles exists or is in the process of being established. Such an industry exists if there is significant plant and equipment investment, significant employment of labor or capital, or **substantial** investment in exploitation of the intellectual property rights (including research and development or licensing). Licensing by itself has been held a sufficient basis for finding the existence of a domestic industry.[15] The substantial IP investment requirement (along with the public interest remedy rule, see Section 8.13) is thought by some to exclude use of Section 337 by patent trolls. This test has origins in prior ITC case law.[16] There is also prior case law on the question of whether an American industry is "in the process of being established."[17]

Determination of violations and the recommendation of remedies to the President under Section 337 is the exclusive province of the International Trade Commission (ITC). Most of the case law under Section 337 concerns the infringement of patents. Trademark, copyright and mask work infringements may also be

---

[14]   The Semiconductor Chip Protection Act of 1984 (17 U.S.C.A. §§ 901–914) provides a national system for the registration of original mask works. Only a mask work that was first commercially exploited in the United States, or which was owned by a national or domiciliary of the United States or a national, domiciliary, or sovereign authority of a foreign nation that is a party to a treaty affording protection to mask works to which the United States is also a party or a stateless person at the time of its first commercial exploitation outside the United States, is entitled to registration. The owner of a registered mask work has exclusive rights to reproduce the work by optical, electronic, or any other means and to import or distribute a semiconductor chip product in which the mask work is embodied. The violation of any of these exclusive rights would amount to infringement. However, the owner of a particular semiconductor chip product made by the owner of the mask work, or by any person authorized by the owner of the mask work, may import, distribute, or otherwise dispose of or use, but not reproduce, that particular semiconductor chip product without the authority of the owner of the mask work. Reverse engineering of the mask work is permitted for the purpose of teaching, analysis or evaluation or for the purpose of making another original mask work.

[15]   Interdigital Communications v. I.T.C., ___ Fed.3d ___ (Fed.Cir.2012).

[16]   See Airtight Cast-Iron Stoves, 3 ITRD 1158, U.S.I.T.C. Pub. No. 1126 (1980).

[17]   See Caulking Guns, 6 ITRD 1432, U.S.I.T.C. Pub. No. 1507 (1984).

pursued under Section 337.[18] In copyright cases, the petitioner must prove ownership of the copyright and the fact of copying.[19]

A 1989 GATT Panel ruled that Section 337 violated the national treatment provision of Article III (4) of the GATT 1947 agreement. The Panel was persuaded that goods imported into the United States were treated less favorably (i.e., more severely) under Section 337 in terms of patent infringement remedies than domestic goods in federal courts. Under the Uruguay Round Agreements Act, the U.S. made procedural changes, such as the allowance of counterclaims in Section 337y proceedings, intended to address the imbalance in patent infringement remedies. Federal district courts must stay infringement proceedings at the request of the respondent to a Section 337 action.

§ 8.8   Section 337 Proceedings—Complaint and Response

Section 337 complaints may be filed by domestic producers with the International Trade Commission in Washington, D.C., provided the complainants have not agreed by contract to litigate all disputes elsewhere.[20] The complainant must be a representative of the industry. The complaint itself must contain a statement of the facts alleged to constitute unfair import methods or acts. The complaint must also specify instances when unlawful importations occurred, the names and addresses of respondents, and if they exist, a description of any related court proceeding. The complaint must describe the domestic industry that is affected by the import practices and the petitioner's interest in that industry.

If the case involves intellectual property rights, detailed information regarding the patent, copyright, trademark or mask work must be provided. Lastly, the complaint must indicate what relief is sought.[21] Section 337 complainants are subject to the "duty of candor" recognized in *Convertible Rowing Exercisers.*[22] This duty is violated by (1) a failure to disclose material information or a submission of false material information and (2) an intent to mislead.

---

[18]   19 U.S.C.A. § 1337(a).

[19]   See Coin-Operated Audio-Visual Games and Components, 1981 WL 50518, U.S.I.T.C. Pub. No. 1160 (June 1981).

[20]   See Texas Instruments Inc. v. Tessera, Inc., 231 F.3d 1325 (Fed.Cir.2000) (agreement that all litigation must take place in California precludes Section 337 complaint).

[21]   C.F.R. § 210.20 (1990).

[22]   Inv. No. 337–TA–212, U.S.I.T.C. Pub. No. 2111 (1988).

Once a complaint is filed, or the Commission decides to start a Section 337 proceeding on its own initiative, an investigation is normally commenced. The Commission takes the position that it is not obliged to commence an investigation after the filing of a private complaint. Its Office of Unfair Imports (OUI) takes 30 days to examine the sufficiency of the complaint. This Office is an independent party in Section 337 proceedings charged with representing the public interest. Pre-filing review of draft complaints by the OUI is possible, and counsel for the respondents may also seek to have the OUI recommend against proceeding with a Section 337 complaint.

Although it is a rare event, the Commission occasionally has declined to pursue a Section 337 investigation. If this happens, the complaint is dismissed.[23] The Commission has maintained its discretionary authority to review Section 337 complaints despite statutory language which would appear to be mandatory.[24] Thus, it has dismissed complaints where there is insufficient data to support the allegations, or the allegations themselves are insufficient to prove a Section 337 violation.[25] The complainant may of course amend and refile its complaint. Furthermore, a rejection of Section 337 complaints by the Commission can be appealed to the Federal Circuit Court of Appeals.[26] The Commission serves the complaint on foreign parties, thus avoiding the delay of international service of process. Parties who fail to appear default, and can have exclusion orders automatically entered against them.

The respondents in Section 337 proceedings are given an opportunity to submit written briefs regarding the complaint. Such briefs should respond to each allegation in the complaint and set forth any defenses. Failure to provide a response to the complaint can result in a determination that the facts alleged in the complaint are deemed admitted.[27] For example, if the complaint is based upon patent infringement, the respondent would typically allege non-infringement by suggesting that the product is not covered by the patent and/or the invalidity of the patent. An unusual aspect of Section 337 proceedings is the appointment of an investigative attorney by the ITC to represent the public interest. This attorney

---

[23] See 19 C.F.R. § 210.12.

[24] See 19 U.S.C.A. § 1337(b)(1).

[25] See Certain Fruit Preserves in Containers Having Lids With Gingham Cloth Design, Docket 1056 (May 21, 1984); Certain Architectural Panels, Docket 1122 (November 30, 1984).

[26] See Syntex Agribusiness, Inc. v. U.S. International Trade Commission, 617 F.2d 290 (C.C.P.A.1980) and 659 F.2d 1038 (C.C.P.A.1981).

[27] 19 C.F.R. § 210.21.

is a party to the investigation and may participate in discovery and hearings to the full extent of the complainant and respondent.[28]

§ 8.9   Section 337 Proceedings—Temporary Relief

If the Commission decides, in the process of its investigation, that there is reason to believe that a violation of Section 337 has occurred, it may order the goods to be excluded from entry into the United States or permit entry only under a bond as a temporary remedy.[29] Such remedies require proof not only of the reasons to believe in the violation, but also of an immediate and substantial injury to the domestic industry in the absence of a temporary remedy.[30]

The statute requires that the Commission consider the public interest in making temporary remedial decisions in connection with Section 337. Thus, the Commission ends up balancing the probability of the complainant's success on the merits, the prospect for immediate and substantial harm to the domestic industry if no relief is granted, the harm to the respondent if such relief is granted, and the effect that temporary remedies would have on the public interest.[31] If the Commission is concerned that the complainant may possibly have filed a frivolous claim or that the harm to the respondent is particularly large, it can require the complainant to post a bond in order to get temporary relief. Decisions about temporary relief are made by the administrative law judge in the case, although they may be modified or vacated by the Commission upon review.[32]

§ 8.10   Section 337 Proceedings—Administrative Process

Section 337 investigations normally last one year but may be extended to eighteen months in complicated cases. This relatively short period has been described as "due process with dispatch." Section 337 investigations are the only investigations conducted by the International Trade Commission that are governed by the Administrative Procedure Act. Thus, the investigation will follow the established procedures for discovery under the Federal Rules of Civil Procedure, pre-hearing conferences, an initial determination of

---

[28]   19 C.F.R. § 210.4.
[29]   19 U.S.C.A. § 1337(e).
[30]   See Certain Apparatus, 12 ITRD 1841, U.S.I.T.C. Pub. No. 1132 (April 1981).
[31]   19 U.S.C.A. § 1337(e).
[32]   19 C.F.R. § 210.24(17).

the issues by an administrative judge, and final review by the Commission.[33]

One problem is the frequent need for extraterritorial discovery in Section 337 cases. Another issue is sanctions for abuse of discovery,[34] although findings of default can be made. Section 337 discovery responses are typically due in 10 days, much more rapidly than in civil litigation. Although the Commission is authorized to promulgate rules allowing costs and attorneys' fees as sanctions, it has not yet done so. In contrast, the Commission has aggressively enforced its protective orders against disclosure of confidential and business information of a proprietary character.[35] At any point during its investigation, the Commission may decide to settle the proceedings by consent order or by agreement of the parties. This happens reasonably often, especially when the parties to an intellectual property case agree to a licensing arrangement. In either case, the Commission will review the motion to terminate or a proposed consent order from the standpoint of the public interest in the proceeding. An arbitration agreement between parties who are contesting a Section 337 proceeding is no grounds for terminating the ITC investigation.[36]

When the International Trade Commission reviews the advisory decision of the administrative law judge in Section 337 proceedings, it need not undertake a review of that entire determination. It is sufficient for purposes of appeal that the Commission decides the case on the basis of a single dispositive issue. For example, in patent infringement litigation, if the Commission decides that there was no infringement, it need not render decisions concerning any other issues in the Section 337 proceeding.[37] Thus it was only this issue that could be appealed to the Federal Circuit Court of Appeals. Put another way, the only issues that can be appealed are those upon which the Commission has decided, and this is true even in cases concerning temporary relief under Section 337.[38]

---

[33]   See 19 C.F.R. §§ 2210.1–2210.71.

[34]   See Certain Concealed Cabinet Hinges and Mounting Plates, 12 ITRD 1841 (Jan. 8, 1990).

[35]   See Certain Electrically Resistive Monocomponent Toner, 10 ITRD 1672 (1988).

[36]   Farrel Corp. v. U.S. ITC, 949 F.2d 1147 (Fed.Cir.1991), *cert. denied* 504 U.S. 913, 112 S.Ct. 1947, 118 L.Ed.2d 551 (1992).

[37]   Beloit Corp. v. Valmet Oy, 742 F.2d 1421 (Fed.Cir.1984), *cert. denied* 472 U.S. 1009, 105 S.Ct. 2706, 86 L.Ed.2d 721 (1985).

[38]   See Warner Bros., Inc. v. U.S. International Trade Commission, 787 F.2d 562 (Fed.Cir.1986).

§ 8.11   Section 337 Proceedings—Sanctions

If the Commission ultimately decides that an unfair import method or act has been committed, it is authorized to issue a cease and desist order or an exclusion order barring the goods from entering the United States. Any violation of those orders is punishable by civil penalties up to $100,000 per day or twice the value of the merchandise in question. Final ITC determinations under Section 337 are appealed directly to the Federal Circuit Court of Appeals.

The Federal Circuit Court of Appeals has ruled that the ITC may impose civil penalties for violation of consent orders (as well as cease and desist orders) that terminate patent infringement investigations under Section 337.[39]

§ 8.12   Section 337 Proceedings—Settlements

As the Section 337 investigation proceeds, the complainant may move for a summary determination by the ITC. This is analogous to summary judgment under the Federal Rules of Civil Procedure.[40] If the complaint concerns patent infringement, one solution is for the parties to enter into a licensing agreement. However, the parties must give the Commission a copy of their complete agreement. The Commission's investigative attorney then comments on the settlement and the administrative law judge makes an initial decision as to whether to terminate the investigation on the basis of the settlement. This determination is sent to the Commission for final approval.[41] The purpose of these procedures is to insure that the public interest is preserved as part of the patent infringement dispute settlement.

In non-patent cases, the typical route for settlement is by consent order. To do this, a joint motion is filed by all of the complainants, the Commission's investigative attorney, and one or more of the respondents.[42] This typically occurs before the commencement of the hearing before the administrative law judge. Consent settlements of this type must contain admissions of all jurisdictional facts, waivers of rights to seek judicial review or other means of challenging the consent order, and an agreement that the enforcement, modification and revocation of the order will be undertaken pursuant to ITC rules. The consent order typically is

---

[39]   San Huan New Materials High Tech, Inc. v. ITC, 161 F.3d 1347 (Fed.Cir.1998).

[40]   19 C.F.R. § 210.50.

[41]   19 C.F.R. § 210.51.

[42]   19 C.F.R. § 211.20.

not deemed to constitute an admission of a violation of Section 337 and usually states that it is undertaken solely for settlement purposes.[43] There is a ten-day notice period which allows any interested party to comment on the proposed termination of a Section 337 proceeding on the basis of a consent order.[44]

§ 8.13   Section 337 Proceedings—ITC Public Interest Review

The International Trade Commission is not required to impose a Section 337 remedy if it finds a violation. Its remedial powers are discretionary. In deciding whether to accept proposed consent orders or to impose any remedy, the Commission is required to consider all of the public comments that have been received, the effect upon the public health and welfare of the United States, the effect upon competitive conditions in the U.S. economy, the effect on production of like or directly competitive articles in the United States, and its effect upon U.S. consumers.[45]

The Commission has rarely invoked the public interest exception to Section 337 relief. When it has, the domestic industry typically was unable to supply critically needed items[46] or the public's strong interest in the research overrode patent rights.[47] President Obama cited the public interest exception in vetoing a prominent exclusion order won by Samsung against Apple involving essential industry standard patents. *See* Section 8.15.

§ 8.14   Section 337 Proceedings—ITC General Exclusion and Cease and Desist Orders

The International Trade Commission may issue three different kinds of remedies under Section 337. The first is an exclusion order of a limited or general nature, and this type of relief predominates in intellectual property cases. The second is a cease and desist order, and this type of relief is often issued if there are significant inventories of the offending product already imported into the United States. The effect of such a cease and desist order is to prevent further distribution within the country. The Commission is expressly authorized to issue exclusion orders and cease and desist

---

[43]   19 C.F.R. § 211.22.

[44]   19 C.F.R. § 211.20.

[45]   19 U.S.C.A. § 1337(d), (e), (f).

[46]   See Automatic Crankpin Grinders, 2 ITRD 5121, U.S.I.T.C. Pub. No. 1022 (1979) (engine parts needed to meet fuel efficiency standards); Certain Fluidized Supporting Apparatus reported at 7 I.T.R.D. 1089 (1984).

[47]   Certain Inclined-Field Acceleration Tubes, 2 ITRD 5572 (1980).

orders together.[48] Unlike general exclusion orders, ITC cease and desist orders can lead to significant civil penalties.

In either case, the Commission may authorize entry of the goods under bond pending the President's final determination in the proceeding. The amount of the bond varies from case to case, but is generally intended to offset the competitive advantages that are perceived to exist. Such bonds have ranged upwards to 600 percent of the value of the imports.[49] Many Section 337 bonds have been determined by measuring the difference between the complainant's prices in the U.S. and the customs value of the imports. Forfeiture orders are relatively uncommon and typically follow notice by the Secretary of the Treasury that forfeiture would result from further importation of goods that offend Section 337.

Plaintiffs usually wish to obtain general exclusion orders in intellectual property cases. Such orders will keep out all infringing products. The problem with this approach is that it may unfairly bar the importation of goods that resemble but do not infringe the patented product. This is a generally undesirable result that the Commission will try to avoid.[50]

Consequently, the Commission requires those seeking general exclusion orders to prove a widespread pattern of unauthorized use of the patented invention and reasonable inferences that foreign manufacturers other than the respondents may attempt to enter the United States market with infringing goods.[51] A widespread pattern of unauthorized use can be demonstrated by the importation of the infringing goods by numerous companies, by pending foreign infringement suits based upon foreign patents which correspond to the United States patent at issue, or by other evidence which demonstrates a history of unauthorized foreign use of the invention.[52]

In providing evidence that it is reasonable to infer that other foreign manufacturers may attempt to enter the U.S. market, plaintiffs may offer proof of the established demand for the product, the existence of a distribution system in the United States for its marketing, the cost to foreigners of manufacturing or creating a facility capable of manufacturing the goods, the ease and number of foreign manufacturers who could retool so as to produce the

---

[48]   19 U.S.C.A. § 1337(f).

[49]   See Certain Cube Puzzles, supra.

[50]   See Certain Cloisonne Jewelry, 8 ITRD 2028, U.S.I.T.C. Pub. No. 1822 (March 1986).

[51]   See Certain Airless Spray Pumps and Components Thereof, 3 ITRD 2041, U.S.I.T.C. Pub. No. 1199 (1981).

[52]   Id.

offending article, and the cost of such retooling.[53] As these criteria suggest, obtaining a general exclusion order is not always easy, and certainly not automatic.

§ 8.15   Section 337 Proceedings—Presidential Veto

Any order issued by the International Trade Commission under Section 337 goes into effect immediately. However, the President may veto that order for public policy reasons.[54] Vetoes by the President of Commission orders in Section 337 proceedings are rare and not generally reviewable by the courts.[55] In 2013, however, President Obama vetoed an ITC-recommended general exclusion order sought by Samsung against importation of patent-infringing Apple iPhone and iPad devices. The President determined that the patents owned by Samsung comprised essential industry standards, subject to reasonable licensing requirements, and that it would not be in the public interest to exclude Apple's devices.[56] Not long thereafter, the President declined to veto an exclusion order recommendation that barred imports of Samsung phones found to be infringing Apple patents . . . no essential industry standards were involved.

The President has sixty days within which to make a decision concerning ITC orders under Section 337. If the President does not take action within this period, then the order becomes final.[57] Final ITC orders under Section 337 remain in effect until the Commission decides that there is no longer reason to continue the order.[58] Any violation of an outstanding ITC order under Section 337 can incur a civil penalty of up to $10,000 per day or twice the domestic value of the goods sold, whichever is greater.[59]

§ 8.16   Section 337—ITC Opinion Letters

The ITC follows the practice of issuing informal or formal opinion letters in connection with Section 337 matters. Requests for informal opinions from the ITC staff should be addressed to the Assistant General Counsel of the Commission. Formal opinions actually issued by the Commission itself may be obtained if the staff opinion letter is adverse or a formal opinion is just simply

---

[53]   Id.

[54]   19 U.S.C.A. § 1337(j).

[55]   Duracell, Inc. v. U.S. International Trade Commission, 778 F.2d 1578 (Fed.Cir.1985).

[56]   Certain Electronic Digital Media Devices and Components, ITC, 337–TA–796 (Aug. 9, 2013).

[57]   Id.

[58]   19 U.S.C.A. § 1337(k).

[59]   19 U.S.C.A. § 1337(j).

necessary. Requests for such opinions are filed with the Secretary of the Commission.[60]

§ 8.17   Section 337 Proceedings—General Exclusion of IP Infringing Imports

This section focuses on the application of Section 337 of the Tariff Act of 1930 to imports that infringe U.S. intellectual property rights. A 1989 decision by a General Agreement on Tariffs and Trade (GATT) panel ruled that Section 337 violates the national treatment provisions of Article III:4 of the GATT. The panel was persuaded that imported goods are treated less favorably (i.e., more severely) under Section 337 in terms of patent infringement remedies than domestic goods which are remedied in the federal courts. The panel's decision was ultimately adopted by the GATT Council and the U.S. indicated that it would consider ways to reach compliance after the TRIPs accord was finalized.

The Uruguay Round Agreements Act of 1994 did not alter the substance of Section 337 law. It did make procedural changes (such as allowance of counterclaims in Section 337 proceedings) intended to address the issue of an imbalance in patent infringement remedies. The federal district courts must stay infringement proceedings at the request of the respondent to Section 337 actions.

Patent Infringing Imports

While not quite a per se rule, it is nearly axiomatic that any infringement of United States patent rights amounts to an unfair import practice for purposes of Section 337.[61] Both product and process patents are entitled to protection under Section 337. In a major decision affecting biotechnology firms, the Federal Circuit Court of Appeals refused Section 337 relief when the U.S. patent owner had no claim either to the final product or the process used to create it even though the foreign party had to use the patented product to create the product being imported into the United States.[62] Had the same activity been undertaken in the U.S., an infringement would most probably have been found. Section 337 can be used to obtain exclusionary orders based upon misappropriation abroad of trade secrets of U.S. companies. Such complaints are governed by federal common law (not state law).[63]

---

[60]   19 C.F.R. § 211.54.

[61]   See Synthetic Star Sapphires, § 316, No. 13 (Sept. 1954), *aff'd sub nom.* In re Von Clemm, 229 F.2d 441 (C.C.P.A.1955).

[62]   Amgen, Inc. v. U.S. Int'l Trade Comm., 902 F.2d 1532 (Fed.Cir.1990).

[63]   See Tian Rui Group v. Int'l Trade Commission, _Fed. Cir._(2011) (misappropriation in China from licensees of wheel production trade secrets of U.S. manufacturer).

All legal and equitable defenses (but not counterclaims) may be presented, including attacks upon the validity or enforceability of the patent.[64] A patent license that required all "litigation" to take place in California barred pursuit of Section 337 relief.[65] The ITC's refusal to entertain a Section 337 proceeding because the complainant's patent was unenforceable due to prior inequitable conduct was upheld by the Federal Circuit Court of Appeals.[66] This decision illustrates the power of the ITC, as a practical matter, to rule on patent validity.

International Trade Commission decisions on patent validity, and Federal Circuit Court of Appeals opinions on appeal from the ITC, can be treated as preclusive fact findings under collateral estoppel principles in ordinary federal court proceedings.[67] Res judicata effect is ordinarily denied given the fundamental differences between ITC administrative and federal judicial proceedings concerning patent validity.[68]

Patent-based Section 337 proceedings are multiplying. ITC decisions take about 12 to 15 months, versus three to five years for federal court lawsuits. General exclusion orders are typically sought. Hearings are held before one of four administrative law judges specializing in patent law, with final decisions taken by the ITC. Infringing products are excluded from importation during the appeals process. About one-fourth of all 337 proceedings find infringements.

In 2007, in a major decision, the ITC excluded the importation of cell phones containing Qualcomm microchips found to infringe Broadcom patents. In 2012, Samsung succeeded before the ITC in alleging patent infringement by imported Apple cellphones, but the President denied a general exclusion order because the patents in question were part of an industry standard and thus he determined it was against the public interest to exclude the imports on the basis of such patent infringement. This was the first denial of ITC-recommended Section 337 relief since President Reagan. Apple's subsequent attempt to bar Samsung cellphones on patent infringement grounds were upheld by the ITC. Absent involvement of industry standards, no Presidential veto was forthcoming.

Invocation of Section 337 in patent disputes will be influenced by the U.S. Supreme Court's ruling in *KSR International Co. v.*

---

[64]   19 U.S.C.A. § 1337(c).

[65]   Texas Instruments Inc. v. Tessera, Inc., 231 F.3d 1325 (Fed.Cir.2000).

[66]   LaBounty Manufacturing, Inc. v. U.S. ITC, 958 F.2d 1066 (Fed.Cir.1992).

[67]   In re Convertible Rowing Exerciser Patent Litigation, 814 F.Supp. 1197 (D.Del.1993).

[68]   Id.

Teleflex, Inc. (April 30, 2007) where it unanimously held that a patent combining pre-existing elements is invalid if the combination is no "more than the predictable use of prior art elements according to their established functions" (obvious). Likewise, the Supreme Court's cautious consideration of business method patents in *Bilski v. Kappos* (June 28, 2010) will influence Section 337 disputes.

An increasing number of foreign owners of U.S. patents are invoking 337 procedures. About half of all such complaints are settled, often using cross-licensing among the parties. Section 337 proceedings can result in general exclusion orders permitting seizure of patent counterfeits at any U.S. point of entry. Apple Computer, for example, was able to get such an order against computers sold under the label "Orange" that contained infringing programs and color display circuits.[69] However, as previously noted, the Customs Service finds it extremely difficult when inspecting invoices and occasionally opening boxes to ascertain which goods are counterfeit or infringing. Many counterfeits do look like "the real thing." For most seizure remedies to work, the holder must notify the Customs Service of an incoming shipment of patent offending goods. Such advance notice is hard to obtain.

§ 8.18   Text of Section 337 (19 U.S.C.A 1337)

Unlawful activities; covered industries; definitions

(1) Subject to paragraph (2), the following are unlawful, and when found by the Commission to exist shall be dealt with, in addition to any other provision of law, as provided in this section:

(A) Unfair methods of competition and unfair acts in the importation of articles (other than articles provided for in subparagraphs (B), (C), (D), and (E)) into the United States, or in the sale of such articles by the owner, importer, or consignee, the threat or effect of which is—

(i) to destroy or substantially injure an industry in the United States;

(ii) to prevent the establishment of such an industry; or

(iii) to restrain or monopolize trade and commerce in the United States.

(B) The importation into the United States, the sale for importation, or the sale within the United States after importation by the owner, importer, or consignee, of articles that—

---

[69]   In Re Certain Personal Computers and Components Thereof, 6 ITRD 1140, 1984 Copr.L.Dec. p 25651, U.S.I.T.C. Pub. No. 1504.

(i) infringe a valid and enforceable United States patent or a valid and enforceable United States copyright registered under title 17; or

(ii) are made, produced, processed, or mined under, or by means of, a process covered by the claims of a valid and enforceable United States patent.

(C) The importation into the United States, the sale for importation, or the sale within the United States after importation by the owner, importer, or consignee, of articles that infringe a valid and enforceable United States trademark registered under the Trademark Act of 1946 [15 U.S.C. 1051 et seq.].

(D) The importation into the United States, the sale for importation, or the sale within the United States after importation by the owner, importer, or consignee, of a semiconductor chip product in a manner that constitutes infringement of a mask work registered under chapter 9 of title 17.

(E) The importation into the United States, the sale for importation, or the sale within the United States after importation by the owner, importer, or consigner, of an article that constitutes infringement of the exclusive rights in a design protected under chapter 13 of title 17.

(2) Subparagraphs (B), (C), (D), and (E) of paragraph (1) apply only if an industry in the United States, relating to the articles protected by the patent, copyright, trademark, mask work, or design concerned, exists or is in the process of being established.

(3) For purposes of paragraph (2), an industry in the United States shall be considered to exist if there is in the United States, with respect to the articles protected by the patent, copyright, trademark, mask work, or design concerned—

(A) significant investment in plant and equipment;

(B) significant employment of labor or capital; or

(C) substantial investment in its exploitation, including engineering, research and development, or licensing.

(4) For the purposes of this section, the phrase "owner, importer, or consignee" includes any agent of the owner, importer, or consignee.

(b) Investigation of violations by Commission

(1) The Commission shall investigate any alleged violation of this section on complaint under oath or upon its initiative. Upon commencing any such investigation, the Commission shall publish notice thereof in the Federal Register. The Commission shall conclude any such investigation and make its determination under this section at the earliest practicable time after

the date of publication of notice of such investigation. To promote expeditious adjudication, the Commission shall, within 45 days after an investigation is initiated, establish a target date for its final determination.

(2) During the course of each investigation under this section, the Commission shall consult with, and seek advice and information from, the Department of Health and Human Services, the Department of Justice, the Federal Trade Commission, and such other departments and agencies as it considers appropriate.

(3) Whenever, in the course of an investigation under this section, the Commission has reason to believe, based on information before it, that a matter, in whole or in part, may come within the purview of part II of subtitle IV of this chapter, it shall promptly notify the Secretary of Commerce so that such action may be taken as is otherwise authorized by such part II. If the Commission has reason to believe that the matter before it

(A) is based solely on alleged acts and effects which are within the purview of section 1671 or 1673 of this title, or

(B) relates to an alleged copyright infringement with respect to which action is prohibited by section 1008 of title 17, the Commission shall terminate, or not institute, any investigation into the matter. If the Commission has reason to believe the matter before it is based in part on alleged acts and effects which are within the purview of section 1671 or 1673 of this title, and in part on alleged acts and effects which may, independently from or in conjunction with those within the purview of such section, establish a basis for relief under this section, then it may institute or continue an investigation into the matter. If the Commission notifies the Secretary or the administering authority (as defined in section 1677(1) of this title) with respect to a matter under this paragraph, the Commission may suspend its investigation during the time the matter is before the Secretary or administering authority for final decision. Any final decision by the administering authority under section 1671 or 1673 of this title with respect to the matter within such section 1671 or 1673 of this title of which the Commission has notified the Secretary or administering authority shall be conclusive upon the Commission with respect to the issue of less-than-fair-value sales or subsidization and the matters necessary for such decision.

(c) Determinations; review

The Commission shall determine, with respect to each investigation conducted by it under this section, whether or not there is a violation of this section, except that the Commission may, by issuing a consent order or on the basis of an agreement between the private parties to the investigation, including an agreement to present the matter for arbitration, terminate any such investigation, in whole or in part, without making such a determination. Each determination under subsection (d) or (e) of this section shall be made on the record after notice and opportunity for a hearing in conformity with the provisions of subchapter II of chapter 5 of title 5. All legal and equitable defenses may be presented in all cases. A respondent may raise any counterclaim in a manner prescribed by the Commission. Immediately after a counterclaim is received by the Commission, the respondent raising such counterclaim shall file a notice of removal with a United States district court in which venue for any of the counterclaims raised by the party would exist under section 1391 of title 28. Any counterclaim raised pursuant to this section shall relate back to the date of the original complaint in the proceeding before the Commission. Action on such counterclaim shall not delay or affect the proceeding under this section, including the legal and equitable defenses that may be raised under this subsection. Any person adversely affected by a final determination of the Commission under subsection (d), (e), (f), or (g) of this section may appeal such determination, within 60 days after the determination becomes final, to the United States Court of Appeals for the Federal Circuit for review in accordance with chapter 7 of title 5. Notwithstanding the foregoing provisions of this subsection, Commission determinations under subsections (d), (e), (f), and (g) of this section with respect to its findings on the public health and welfare, competitive conditions in the United States economy, the production of like or directly competitive articles in the United States, and United States consumers, the amount and nature of bond, or the appropriate remedy shall be reviewable in accordance with section 706 of title 5. Determinations by the Commission under subsections (e), (f), and (j) of this section with respect to forfeiture of bonds and under subsection (h) of this section with respect to the imposition of sanctions for abuse of discovery or abuse of process shall also be reviewable in accordance with section 706 of title 5.

(d) Exclusion of articles from entry

(1) If the Commission determines, as a result of an investigation under this section, that there is a violation of this section, it shall direct that the articles concerned, imported by any person violating the provision of this section, be excluded from entry into the United States, unless, after considering the effect of such exclusion upon the public health and welfare, competitive conditions in the United States economy, the production of like or directly competitive articles in the United States, and United States consumers, it finds that such articles should not be excluded from entry. The Commission shall notify the Secretary of the Treasury of its action under this subsection directing such exclusion from entry, and upon receipt of such notice, the Secretary shall, through the proper officers, refuse such entry.

(2) The authority of the Commission to order an exclusion from entry of articles shall be limited to persons determined by the Commission to be violating this section unless the Commission determines that—

(A) a general exclusion from entry of articles is necessary to prevent circumvention of an exclusion order limited to products of named persons; or

(B) there is a pattern of violation of this section and it is difficult to identify the source of infringing products.

(e) Exclusion of articles from entry during investigation except under bond; procedures applicable; preliminary relief

(1) If, during the course of an investigation under this section, the Commission determines that there is reason to believe that there is a violation of this section, it may direct that the articles concerned, imported by any person with respect to whom there is reason to believe that such person is violating this section, be excluded from entry into the United States, unless, after considering the effect of such exclusion upon the public health and welfare, competitive conditions in the United States economy, the production of like or directly competitive articles in the United States, and United States consumers, it finds that such articles should not be excluded from entry. The Commission shall notify the Secretary of the Treasury of its action under this subsection directing such exclusion from entry, and upon receipt of such notice, the Secretary shall, through the proper officers, refuse such entry, except that such articles shall be entitled to entry under bond prescribed by the Secretary in an amount determined by the Commission to be sufficient to protect the complainant from any injury. If the Commission later determines that the respondent has violated the provisions of this section, the bond may be forfeited to the complainant.

(2) A complainant may petition the Commission for the issuance of an order under this subsection. The Commission shall make a determination with regard to such petition by no later than the 90th day after the date on which the Commission's notice of investigation is published in the Federal Register. The Commission may extend the 90-day period for an additional 60 days in a case it designates as a more complicated case. The Commission shall publish in the Federal Register its reasons why it designated the case as being more complicated. The Commission may require the complainant to post a bond as a prerequisite to the issuance of an order under this subsection. If the Commission later determines that the respondent has not violated the provisions of this section, the bond may be forfeited to the respondent.

(3) The Commission may grant preliminary relief under this subsection or subsection (f) of this section to the same extent as preliminary injunctions and temporary restraining orders may be granted under the Federal Rules of Civil Procedure.

(4) The Commission shall prescribe the terms and conditions under which bonds may be forfeited under paragraphs (1) and (2).

(f) Cease and desist orders; civil penalty for violation of orders

(1) In addition to, or in lieu of, taking action under subsection (d) or (e) of this section, the Commission may issue and cause to be served on any person violating this section, or believed to be violating this section, as the case may be, an order directing such person to cease and desist from engaging in the unfair methods or acts involved, unless after considering the effect of such order upon the public health and welfare, competitive conditions in the United States economy, the production of like or directly competitive articles in the United States, and United States consumers, it finds that such order should not be issued. The Commission may at any time, upon such notice and in such manner as it deems proper, modify or revoke any such order, and, in the case of a revocation, may take action under subsection (d) or (e) of this section, as the case may be. If a temporary cease and desist order is issued in addition to, or in lieu of, an exclusion order under subsection (e) of this section, the Commission may require the complainant to post a bond, in an amount determined by the Commission to be sufficient to protect the respondent from any injury, as a prerequisite to the issuance of an order under this subsection. If the Commission later determines that the respondent has not violated the provisions of this section, the bond may be forfeited to the respondent. The Commission shall prescribe the terms and conditions under which the bonds may be forfeited under this paragraph.

(2) Any person who violates an order issued by the Commission under paragraph (1) after it has become final shall forfeit and pay to the United States a civil penalty for each day on which an importation of articles, or their sale, occurs in violation of the order of not more than the greater of $100,000 or twice the domestic value of the articles entered or sold on such day in violation of the order. Such penalty shall accrue to the United States and may be recovered for the United States in a civil action brought by the Commission in the Federal District Court for the District of Columbia or for the district in which the violation occurs. In such actions, the United States district courts may issue mandatory injunctions incorporating the relief sought by the Commission as they deem appropriate in the enforcement of such final orders of the Commission.

(g) Exclusion from entry or cease and desist order; conditions and procedures applicable

(1) If—

    (A) a complaint is filed against a person under this section;

    (B) the complaint and a notice of investigation are served on the person;

(C) the person fails to respond to the complaint and notice or otherwise fails to appear to answer the complaint and notice;

(D) the person fails to show good cause why the person should not be found in default; and

(E) the complainant seeks relief limited solely to that person;

the Commission shall presume the facts alleged in the complaint to be true and shall, upon request, issue an exclusion from entry or a cease and desist order, or both, limited to that person unless, after considering the effect of such exclusion or order upon the public health and welfare, competitive conditions in the United States economy, the production of like or directly competitive articles in the United States, and United States consumers, the Commission finds that such exclusion or order should not be issued.

(2) In addition to the authority of the Commission to issue a general exclusion from entry of articles when a respondent appears to contest an investigation concerning a violation of the provisions of this section, a general exclusion from entry of articles, regardless of the source or importer of the articles, may be issued if—

(A) no person appears to contest an investigation concerning a violation of the provisions of this section,

(B) such a violation is established by substantial, reliable, and probative evidence, and

(C) the requirements of subsection (d)(2) of this section are met.

(h) Sanctions for abuse of discovery and abuse of process

The Commission may by rule prescribe sanctions for abuse of discovery and abuse of process to the extent authorized by Rule 11 and Rule 37 of the Federal Rules of Civil Procedure.

(i) Forfeiture

(1) In addition to taking action under subsection (d) of this section, the Commission may issue an order providing that any article imported in violation of the provisions of this section be seized and forfeited to the United States if—

(A) the owner, importer, or consignee of the article previously attempted to import the article into the United States;

(B) the article was previously denied entry into the United States by reason of an order issued under subsection (d) of this section; and

(C) upon such previous denial of entry, the Secretary of the Treasury provided the owner, importer, or consignee of the article written notice of—

(i) such order, and

(ii) the seizure and forfeiture that would result from any further attempt to import the article into the United States.

(2) The Commission shall notify the Secretary of the Treasury of any order issued under this subsection and, upon receipt of such notice, the Secretary of the Treasury shall enforce such order in accordance with the provisions of this section.

(3) Upon the attempted entry of articles subject to an order issued under this subsection, the Secretary of the Treasury shall immediately notify all ports of entry of the attempted importation and shall identify the persons notified under paragraph (1)(C).

(4) The Secretary of the Treasury shall provide—

(A) the written notice described in paragraph (1)(C) to the owner, importer, or consignee of any article that is denied entry into the United States by reason of an order issued under subsection (d) of this section; and

(B) a copy of such written notice to the Commission.

(j) Referral to President

(1) If the Commission determines that there is a violation of this section, or that, for purposes of subsection (e) of this section, there is reason to believe that there is such a violation, it shall—

(A) publish such determination in the Federal Register, and

(B) transmit to the President a copy of such determination and the action taken under subsection (d), (e), (f), (g), or (i) of this section, with respect thereto, together with the record upon which such determination is based.

(2) If, before the close of the 60-day period beginning on the day after the day on which he receives a copy of such determination, the President, for policy reasons, disapproves such determination and notifies the Commission of his disapproval, then, effective on the date of such notice, such determination and the action taken under subsection (d), (e), (f), (g), or (i) of this section with respect thereto shall have no force or effect.

(3) Subject to the provisions of paragraph (2), such determination shall, except for purposes of subsection (c) of this section, be effective upon publication thereof in the Federal Register, and the action taken under subsection (d), (e), (f), (g), or (i) of this section, with respect thereto shall be effective as provided in such subsections, except that articles directed to be excluded from entry under subsection (d) of this section or subject to a cease and desist order under subsection (f) of this section shall, until such determination becomes final, be entitled to entry under bond prescribed by the Secretary in an amount determined by the Commission to be sufficient to protect the complainant from any injury. If the determination becomes final, the bond may be forfeited to the complainant. The Commission shall

prescribe the terms and conditions under which bonds may be forfeited under this paragraph.

(4) If the President does not disapprove such determination within such 60-day period, or if he notifies the Commission before the close of such period that he approves such determination, then, for purposes of paragraph (3) and subsection (c) of this section such determination shall become final on the day after the close of such period or the day on which the President notifies the Commission of his approval, as the case may be.

(k) Period of effectiveness; termination of violation or modification or rescission of exclusion or order

(1) Except as provided in subsections (f) and (j) of this section, any exclusion from entry or order under this section shall continue in effect until the Commission finds, and in the case of exclusion from entry notifies the Secretary of the Treasury, that the conditions which led to such exclusion from entry or order no longer exist.

(2) If any person who has previously been found by the Commission to be in violation of this section petitions the Commission for a determination that the petitioner is no longer in violation of this section or for a modification or rescission of an exclusion from entry or order under subsection (d), (e), (f), (g), or (i) of this section—

    (A) the burden of proof in any proceeding before the Commission regarding such petition shall be on the petitioner; and

    (B) relief may be granted by the Commission with respect to such petition—

        (i) on the basis of new evidence or evidence that could not have been presented at the prior proceeding, or

        (ii) on grounds which would permit relief from a judgment or order under the Federal Rules of Civil Procedure.

(l) Importation by or for United States

Any exclusion from entry or order under subsection (d), (e), (f), (g), or (i) of this section, in cases based on a proceeding involving a patent, copyright, mask work, or design under subsection (a)(1) of this section, shall not apply to any articles imported by and for the use of the United States, or imported for, and to be used for, the United States with the authorization or consent of the Government. Whenever any article would have been excluded from entry or would not have been entered pursuant to the provisions of such subsections but for the operation of this subsection, an owner of the patent, copyright, mask work, or design adversely affected shall be entitled to reasonable and entire compensation in an action before the United States Court of Federal Claims pursuant to the procedures of section 1498 of title 28.

(m) "United States" defined

For purposes of this section and sections 1338 and 1340 of this title, the term "United States" means the customs territory of the United States as defined in general note 2 of the Harmonized Tariff Schedule of the United States.

(n) Disclosure of confidential information

(1) Information submitted to the Commission or exchanged among the parties in connection with proceedings under this section which is properly designated as confidential pursuant to Commission rules may not be disclosed (except under a protective order issued under regulations of the Commission which authorizes limited disclosure of such information) to any person (other than a person described in paragraph (2)) without the consent of the person submitting it.

(2) Notwithstanding the prohibition contained in paragraph (1), information referred to in that paragraph may be disclosed to—

(A) an officer or employee of the Commission who is directly concerned with—

(i) carrying out the investigation or related proceeding in connection with which the information is submitted,

(ii) the administration of a bond posted pursuant to subsection (e), (f), or (j) of this section,

(iii) the administration or enforcement of an exclusion order issued pursuant to subsection (d), (e), or (g) of this section, a cease and desist order issued pursuant to subsection (f) of this section, or a consent order issued pursuant to subsection (c) of this section,

(iv) proceedings for the modification or rescission of a temporary or permanent order issued under subsection (d), (e), (f), (g), or (i) of this section, or a consent order issued under this section, or

(v) maintaining the administrative record of the investigation or related proceeding,

(B) an officer or employee of the United States Government who is directly involved in the review under subsection (j) of this section, or

(C) an officer or employee of the United States Customs Service who is directly involved in administering an exclusion from entry under subsection (d), (e), or (g) of this section resulting from the investigation or related proceeding in connection with which the information is submitted.

Chapter 9

GRAY MARKET IMPORTS

Table of Sections

---

§ 9.1   Trade in Gray Market Goods

One of the most controversial areas of customs law concerns "gray market goods," goods produced abroad with authorization and payment but which are imported into unauthorized markets. Trade in gray market goods has dramatically increased in recent years, in part because fluctuating currency exchange rates create opportunities to import and sell such goods at a discount from local price levels. Licensors and their distributors suddenly find themselves competing in their home or other "reserved" markets with products made abroad by their own licensees.

Or, in the reverse, startled licensees find their licensor's products intruding on their local market shares. In either case, third party importers and exporters are often the immediate source of the gray market goods, and they have little respect for who agreed to what in the licensing agreement. When pressed, such third parties will undoubtedly argue that any attempt through licensing at allocating markets or customers is an antitrust or competition law violation.

In times of floating exchange rates, importers have found that by shopping around the world for gray market goods they can undercut local prices with "parallel imports." This explains in large part the dramatic growth in trade in gray market goods in recent years. Gray market goods have become an important source of price competition in the United States marketplace, particularly in years when the U.S. dollar is strong. Some retail firms, like K-Mart, are major traders of gray market goods.

A decline of the dollar against the Japanese yen or EURO would reduce the flow of gray market *imports* from those sources, but perhaps increase the flow of gray market *exports* from the U.S. to those countries. For example, assume a Cadillac sells in the U.S. for $30,000 and a Mercedes in Germany for 30,000 EUROs. At exchange rate of .75 EUROs to the dollar, the dollar is very strong. Mercedes sells in Germany for $22,500, Cadillac sells in the U.S. for 40,000 EUROs. This encourages importing cars bought in Germany to the U.S. The cars are converted to U.S. specifications for $2,000 and sold for $24,500 by nonauthorized companies, often independent Mercedes repair shops. Then the dollar drops in value to 1.50 EUROs. Now you must pay $45,000 in Germany to buy a Mercedes, but need only 20,000 EUROs to buy a Cadillac. This encourages exporting cars bought in the U.S. to Germany.

There is no international agreement, WTO or otherwise, concerning trade in gray market goods. Hence each jurisdiction is free to adopt its own rules. United Sates, European Union, Japanese and treatment of gray market goods in other jurisdictions are examined in this Chapter.

§ 9.2   U.S. Genuine Goods Exclusion Act, Text

In the early part of the century, gray market litigation provoked a Supreme Court decision blocking French cosmetics from entering the United States.[1] A United States firm was assigned the U.S. trademark rights for French cosmetics as part of the sale of the United States business interests of the French producer. The assignee successfully obtained infringement relief in federal district court against Katzel, an importer of the French product benefiting from exchange rate fluctuations. On appeal, the Second Circuit vacated this relief in a holding which followed a line of cases allowing "genuine goods" to enter the U.S. market in competition with established sources. The Supreme Court ultimately reversed the Second Circuit emphasizing the trademark ownership (not license) and independent public good will of the assignee as reasons for its reversal.

Genuine Goods Exclusion Act

Congress, before the Supreme Court reversal, passed the Genuine Goods Exclusion Act, now appearing as Section 1526 of the Tariff Act of 1930.[2] This Act bars *unauthorized importation* of goods

---

[1]   A. Bourjois & Co. v. Katzel, 260 U.S. 689, 43 S.Ct. 244, 67 L.Ed. 464 (1923).

[2]   19 U.S.C.A. § 1526. **Genuine Goods Exclusion Act;**

(a) Importation prohibited

Except as provided in subsection (d) of this section, it shall be unlawful to import into the United States any merchandise of foreign manufacture if such merchandise, or the label, sign, print, package, wrapper, or receptacle, bears a trademark owned by a citizen of, or by a corporation or association created or organized within, the United States, and registered in the Patent and Trademark Office by a person domiciled in the United States, under the provisions of sections 81 to 109 of title 15, and if a copy of the certificate of registration of such trademark is filed with the Secretary of the Treasury, in the manner provided in section 106 of said title 15, unless written consent of the owner of such trademark is produced at the time of making entry.

(b) Seizure and forfeiture

Any such merchandise imported into the United States in violation of the provisions of this section shall be subject to seizure and forfeiture for violation of the customs laws.

(c) Injunction and damages

Any person dealing in any such merchandise may be enjoined from dealing therein within the United States or may be required to export or destroy such merchandise or to remove or obliterate such trademark and shall be liable for the same damages and profits provided for wrongful use of a trade-mark, under the provisions of sections 81 to 109 of title 15.

(d) Exemptions; publication in Federal Register; forfeitures; rules and regulations

(1) The trademark provisions of this section and section 1124 of title 15, do not apply to the importation of articles accompanying any person arriving in the United States when such articles are for his personal use and not for sale if

(A) such articles are within the limits of types and quantities determined by the Secretary pursuant to paragraph (2) of this subsection, and

(B) such person has not been granted an exemption under this subsection within thirty days immediately preceding his arrival.

(2) The Secretary shall determine and publish in the Federal Register lists of the types of articles and the quantities of each which shall be entitled to the exemption provided by this subsection. In determining such quantities of particular types of trade-marked articles, the Secretary shall give such consideration as he deems necessary to the numbers of such articles usually purchased at retail for personal use.

(3) If any article which has been exempted from the restrictions on importation of the trade-mark laws under this subsection is sold within one year after the date of importation, such article, or its value (to be recovered from the importer), is subject to forfeiture. A sale pursuant to a judicial order or in liquidation of the estate of a decedent is not subject to the provisions of this paragraph.

(4) The Secretary may prescribe such rules and regulations as may be necessary to carry out the provisions of this subsection.

(e) Merchandise bearing counterfeit mark; seizure and forfeiture; disposition of seized goods

Any such merchandise bearing a counterfeit mark (within the meaning of section 1127 of title 15) imported into the United States in violation of the provisions of section 1124 of title 15, shall be seized and, in the absence of the written consent of the trademark owner, forfeited for violations of the customs laws. Upon seizure of such merchandise, the Secretary shall notify the owner of the trademark, and shall, after forfeiture, destroy the merchandise. Alternatively, if the merchandise is not unsafe or a hazard to health, and the Secretary has the consent of the trademark owner, the Secretary may obliterate the trademark where feasible and dispose of the goods seized—

bearing trademarks of U.S. citizens. Registration of such marks with the Customs Service can result in the seizure of unauthorized imports. Persons dealing in such imports may be enjoined, required to export the goods, destroy them or obliterate the offending mark, as well as pay damages. The Act has had a checkered history in the courts and Customs Service.

The Customs Service view (influenced by antitrust policy) was that genuine (gray market) goods may be excluded only when the foreign and U.S. trademark rights are not under common ownership or control, or those rights have been used without authorization. The practical effect of this position was to admit most gray market goods into the U.S., thereby providing substantial price competition, but uncertain coverage under manufacturers' warranty, service and rebate programs. Some firms, like K-Mart, excel at gray market importing and may provide independent warranty and repair service contracts. Since 1986, New York and California require disclosure that manufacturers' programs may not apply to sellers of gray market goods.

K Mart Decision

A split in the federal Courts of Appeal as to the legitimacy in light of the Genuine Goods Exclusion Act of the Customs Service position on gray market imports resulted in a U.S. Supreme Court

---

(1) by delivery to such Federal, State, and local government agencies as in the opinion of the Secretary have a need for such merchandise,

(2) by gift to such eleemosynary institutions as in the opinion of the Secretary have a need for such merchandise, or

(3) more than 90 days after the date of forfeiture, by sale by the Customs Service at public auction under such regulations as the Secretary prescribes, except that before making any such sale the Secretary shall determine that no Federal, State, or local government agency or eleemosynary institution has established a need for such merchandise under paragraph (1) or (2).

(f) Civil penalties

(1) Any person who directs, assists financially or otherwise, or aids and abets the importation of merchandise for sale or public distribution that is seized under subsection (e) of this section shall be subject to a civil fine.

(2) For the first such seizure, the fine shall be not more than the value that the merchandise would have had if it were genuine, according to the manufacturer's suggested retail price, determined under regulations promulgated by the Secretary.

(3) For the second seizure and thereafter, the fine shall be not more than twice the value that the merchandise would have had if it were genuine, as determined under regulations promulgated by the Secretary.

(4) The imposition of a fine under this subsection shall be within the discretion of the Customs Service, and shall be in addition to any other civil or criminal penalty or other remedy authorized by law.

ruling.[3] In an extremely technical, not very policy-oriented decision, the Supreme Court arrived at a compromise. The Customs Service can continue to permit entry of genuine goods when there is common ownership or control of the trademarks. The Service must seize such goods only when they were authorized (licensed), but the marks are not subject to common ownership or control. For these purposes, "common ownership or control" is defined as a 50 percent shareholding or the effective control of policy and operations. Gray market goods originating from such "affiliated companies" will still be allowed to enter the United States.[4]

However, a Fifth Circuit decision indicates that close and profitable business ties between a foreign trademark owner and the foreign owner of U.S. trademark rights do not amount to "common control." Rolex was thus able to obtain a Customs Service forfeiture ruling against gray market imports of its watches by Wal-Mart. The court applied a strict common ownership test to Section 526.[5] The Tenth Circuit affirmed summary judgment in favor of an Oklahoma company owning U.S. trademark rights to "Vittoria" for bicycle tires. The rights were transferred by an Italian company, the maker of the tires. The "common control" exception to gray market trademark protection did not apply because there was at most "a close business relationship" between the two companies.[6]

Many believe that the bulk of U.S. imports of gray market goods have continued under the Supreme Court's *K Mart* ruling. However, this perspective is somewhat undermined by treatment of gray market imports under other statutory regimes.

§ 9.3   U.S. Section 337 Remedies

An attempt in 1985 by Duracell to exclude gray market batteries alternatively under Section 337 of the Tariff Act of 1930 as an unfair import practice was upheld by the U.S. International Trade Commission, but denied relief by President Reagan in deference to the Customs Service position.[7]

---

[3]   K Mart Corp. v. Cartier, Inc., 486 U.S. 281, 108 S.Ct. 1811, 100 L.Ed.2d 313 (1988).

[4]   See 19 C.F.R. §§ 133.21(c), 133.2(d).

[5]   United States v. Eighty-Three Rolex Watches, 992 F.2d 508 (5th Cir.1993)., *cert. denied* 510 U.S. 991, 114 S.Ct. 547, 126 L.Ed.2d 449 (1993).

[6]   Vittoria North America, LLC v. Euro-Asia Imports, Inc., 278 F.3d 1076 (10th Cir.2001).

[7]   See Duracell, Inc. v. U.S. International Trade Commission, 778 F.2d 1578 (Fed.Cir.1985). Compare Bourdeau Bros. Inc. v. Int'l Trade Comm., 444 F.3d 1317 (2006) (goods produced in U.S., exported to Europe, importation can be blocked if materially different from goods sold in USA).

Absent veto by the president, Section 337 exclusion orders can be used against gray market imports. In one decision, the Federal Circuit Court of Appeals upheld the ITC's order against used Kubota-brand tractors.[8] This decision relies heavily on the existence of material differences between the gray market tractors and those distributed by authorized Kubota dealers in the U.S. These differences included parts and the absence of English-language labels and instructions.

§ 9.4   U.S. Trademark and Copyright Act Remedies

Section 42 of the Lanham Trademark Act prohibits the importation of goods that copy or simulate a registered U.S. trademark.[9] In *K Mart,* the U.S. Supreme Court specifically declined to review the legality of barring gray market goods under this provision. Some courts have denied relief under Section 42 against gray market imports. These cases stress the absence of consumer confusion when genuine goods are involved.[10] Other courts have reached conclusions that in the absence of adequate disclosure Section 42 is actionable against gray market goods that materially differ in physical content from those sold in the U.S.A.[11] When there are material differences, labeling suffices to avoid Section 42.[12]

A Second Circuit decision relying upon Section 32 of the Lanham Act also supports blocking imports of materially different gray market goods.[13] In this case, Cabbage Patch dolls produced in Spain under license came with birth certificates, adoption papers and instructions in Spanish, but were otherwise the same product. The U.S. manufacturer refused to register these dolls, leading to numerous complaints by parents and children. These complaints supported the court's injunction against importation of the dolls from Spain under Section 32. Section 32 provides trademark owners with remedies against persons who, without consent by the owner,

---

[8]   Gamut Trading Co. v. U.S. I.T.C., 200 F.3d 775 (Fed.Cir.1999).

[9]   15 U.S.C.A. § 1124.

[10]   See, e.g., Monte Carlo Shirt v. Daewoo International (America) Corp., 707 F.2d 1054 (9th Cir.1983); Bell & Howell: Mamiya Co. v. Masel Supply Co., Corp., 719 F.2d 42 (2d Cir.1983).

[11]   See Lever Bros. Co. v. United States, 877 F.2d 101 (D.C.Cir.1989); Ferrero U.S.A., Inc. v. Ozak Trading, Inc., 753 F.Supp. 1240 (D.N.J.1991), *affirmed* 935 F.2d 1281 (3d Cir.1991); Société Des Produits Nestle, S.A. v. Casa Helvetia, Inc., 982 F.2d 633 (1st Cir.1992); Lever Bros. Co. v. United States, 981 F.2d 1330 (D.C.Cir.1993).

[12]   See the U.S. Customs Service Regulation at 19 C.F.R. § 133.23.

[13]   Original Appalachian Artworks v. Granada Electronics, Inc., 816 F.2d 68 (2d Cir.1987), *cert. denied* 484 U.S. 847, 108 S.Ct. 143, 98 L.Ed.2d 99 (1987). Accord, Société Des Produits Nestle, S.A. v. Casa Helvetia, Inc., 982 F.2d 633 (1st Cir.1992).

use a "reproduction, counterfeit, copy or colorable imitation" of a mark so as to cause confusion, mistake or deception.[14] However, a Ninth Circuit decision relying of Sections 32 and 43(a) (country of origin markings) of the Lanham Act leads to the opposite conclusion, finding no support for the argument that gray market imports can be remedied under those provisions.[15]

Sections 103 and 602 of the Copyright Act provide that importing goods into the U.S. without the consent of copyright owners is an infringement.[16] But Section 109 limits the distribution rights of copyright owners under what is known as the "first sale doctrine."[17] This doctrine limits the owner's control over copies to their first sale or transfer. Two Third Circuit decisions split on the use of copyright law against gray market imports in spite of the first sale doctrine.[18] In *Sebastian,* the Third Circuit held that a U.S. manufacturer who sells goods with copyrighted labels to foreign distributors is barred by the first sale doctrine from obtaining import infringement relief. In *Scorpio,* where the goods were manufactured abroad under license by the U.S. copyright holder, such relief was granted.

The Supreme Court subsequently held that the first sale doctrine bars injunctive relief under the Copyright Act[19] against goods previously exported from the USA, and even if the goods are foreign made.[20]

§ 9.5   Treatment of Gray Market Imports in Japan and Europe

An excellent review of the treatment of gray market goods in other jurisdictions is presented in an article by Takamatsu.[21] This review is of particular interest to U.S. *exporters* of gray market goods. For the most part, his review indicates that other jurisdictions permit gray market goods to enter. This is true of the

---

[14]   15 U.S.C.A. § 1114.

[15]   NEC Electronics v. CAL Circuit Abco, Inc., 810 F.2d 1506 (9th Cir.1987), *cert. denied* 484 U.S. 851, 108 S.Ct. 152, 98 L.Ed.2d 108 (1987).

[16]   17 U.S.C.A. § 106.

[17]   17 U.S.C.A. § 109.

[18]   Columbia Broadcasting System v. Scorpio Music Distributors, 569 F.Supp. 47 (E.D.Pa.1983), *affirmed* 738 F.2d 424 (3d Cir.1984) (relief granted); Sebastian Int'l, Inc. v. Consumer Contacts (PTY), Ltd., 847 F.2d 1093 (3d Cir.1988) (relief denied).

[19]   Quality King Distributors, Inc. v. L'ANZA Research International, Inc., 523 U.S. 135, 118 S.Ct. 1125, 140 L.Ed.2d 254 (1998).

[20]   See Kirtsaeng v. John Wiley & Sons, ___ U.S. ___ (March 19, 2013) *reversing* Parfums Givenchy, Inc v. Drug Emporium, 38 F.3d 477 (9th Cir.1994)., *cert. denied* 514 U.S. 1004, 115 S.Ct. 1315, 131 L.Ed.2d 197 (1995).

[21]   Takamatsu, Parallel Importation of Trademarked Goods: A Comparative Analysis, 57 Wash.L.Rev. 433 (1982).

Parker Pen cases under Japanese law,[22] the *Maja* case under German law[23] and the *Agfa-Gevaert* case in Austria,[24] all of which are reviewed by Takamatsu. Canadian Superior Court law strongly supports free trade in gray market goods.[25]

The legal analysis contained in these opinions has been very influential in European Union law.[26] EU law basically posits that once goods subject to intellectual property rights of common origin have been sold on the market with authorization, the holders can no longer block importation of those goods ("parallel imports") through the use of national property rights. Such use is not thought to have been intended as part of the original grant of rights and is said to have been "exhausted" upon sale. An extensive body of law permits parallel imports (even of qualitatively different goods) as part of the promotion of the Common Market and rejects attempts to divide the market territorially along the lines of national property rights. Product labeling as to source and contents is thought sufficient notice to consumers that qualitatively different goods are involved.

In a major decision, the European Court of Justice ruled that trademark rights can be used to block gray market imports into the Common Market. These rights are not exhausted once the goods are voluntarily put into the stream of international commerce. An Austrian maker of high-quality sunglasses was therefore entitled to bar imports from Bulgaria.[27] In *Zino Davidoff, SA,* and *Levi Strauss* the European Court of Justice affirmed the right of trademark owners to block gray market sales of their goods sold at prices below those they utilize in the EU. No "implied consent" to gray market imports was found via the sale of goods outside the EU.[28]

---

[22]   NMC Co. v. Schulyro Trading Co., Feb. 20, 1970 (Osaka Dist. Ct., 234 Hanrei Taimuzu 57) reprinted in English at 16 Japanese Annual of Int'l Law 113 (1972) affirmed by Osaka High Court. See Nestle Nihon K.K. v. Sanhi Shoten (unreported Tokyo Dist.Ct. May 29, 1965) summarized in T. Doi, Digest of Japanese Court Decisions in Trademarks and Unfair Competition Cases (1971).

[23]   Fed.Sup.Ct. (W.Ger.) Jan. 22, 1964, 41 Bundesgerichtshof 84 summarized in 54 Trademark Rep. 452 (1964).

[24]   Agfa-Gevaert GmbH v. Schark, Sup.Ct. (Aus.), Nov. 30, 1970.

[25]   Consumers Distributing Co., Ltd. v. Seiko Time Canada Ltd., 1 Sup.Ct. 583 (1984). But see Mattel Canada Inc. v. GTS Acquisitions, 27 C.P.R.(3d) 358 (1989) (preliminary injunction against identical gray market goods).

[26]   See Chapters 17 and 19.

[27]   Silhouette International v. Hartlauer, 1998 WL 1043033 (July 16, 1998).

[28]   Cases C–414–99, 415/99 and 416/99, 2001 WL 1347061 (Levi jeans sold by supermarket in Britain) (Nov. 20, 2001).

Part 3

EXPORT LAW

Chapter 10

UNITED STATES EXPORT CONTROLS

Table of Sections

Sec.

---

§ 10.0 International Trade Law on Exports

Chapters 1 and 2 of this book explore the law of international trade, especially that of the World Trade Organization (WTO), as applied almost entirely to **imports**.

Why does the World Trade Organization fail to have equally extensive legal disciplines regarding **exports**?

The answer is less than clear. National export controls have certainly been less numerous, and therefore less on the international trade radar screen. Restricting exports is often counterintuitive to trade policy. Exports represent local production, employment and earnings, whereas imports may disrupt domestic companies, jobs and economic growth. Governments are therefore inclined to promote exports, not inhibit them. In the developing world, there has been a major policy shift away from import substitution in favor of export enhancement. Yet, apart from the law of export subsidies and countervailing duties (see Chapter 5) and to a degree the law of export quotas (see Section 1.6), the WTO package of agreements marginally touches upon export issues.

In the absence of WTO rules on export controls, member states have pursued different policies. The United States, one of the world's top exporters, shipping trillions of dollars of exports each year, has nevertheless maintained an extensive system of export controls. This system is the focus of this Chapter.

§ 10.1 U.S. Governance of Exports

United States export controls involve three primary laws and government agencies. The U.S. Dept. of Commerce, Bureau of Industry and Security (BIS), administers the Export Administration Act Regulations (EAR, 22 C.F.R. Parts 730–774), discussed in this chapter, and the U.S. anti-boycott laws, discussed in Chapter 12. The U.S. Dept. of the Treasury, Office of Foreign Asset Controls (OFAC), administers U.S. boycott/economic sanction laws, discussed in Chapter 11. Lastly, the U.S. Dept. of State administers the International Traffic in Arms Regulations (ITAR, 22 C.F.R. Parts 120–130) covering U.S. Munitions List Items, including notably technical data and defense services. The ITAR follow a "see-through" rule, which governs products containing controlled components. The United States also supports various non-proliferation treaties, and U.N. Security Council Resolution 1540 calling on all nations to enforce effective laws against non-state actors' possession and use of weapons of mass destruction, particularly for terrorist purposes.

Unlike the control of imports, U.S. laws regulating exports are briefer and rely on the issuance of extensive administrative regulations. For example, the *statutes* prohibiting U.S. persons from assisting boycotts against friendly nations fill only a few pages. But the *regulations* and examples of prohibited and permissible conduct fill dozens of pages in the Code of Federal Regulations. The statement of policy in the Export Administration Act, the primary source of U.S. export controls, indicates that it is only after consideration of the impact of restrictions on the economy that restrictive export regulations restrictions are to be adopted, and only to the extent necessary.[1]

U.S. exports are controlled for three reasons stated in the governing rules—(1) to protect against the drain of scarce materials and reduce inflation from foreign demand, (2) to further U.S. foreign policy and (3) to assure national security.[2] These goals are expressed in the principal export enactment, the Export Administration Act (EAA), and are implemented by means of licensing requirements.[3] But the EAA does not contain many substantive provisions regulating exports. They are contained in the Export Administration Regulations (EAR).

These regulations constitute an extensive set of provisions detailing the governance of U.S. exports and non-U.S. exports with more than *de minimis* U.S. content or technology, and re-exports thereof from foreign countries. For these purposes, "exports" include intracorporate transfers, electronic transmissions and disclosure of controlled technology to a foreign national in the United Staes ("deemed exports"), as well as financing the same. Following the "nationality of the goods", the EAR are primarily focused on the "end-use" or "end-user" of U.S. exports, including technology. The EAR rely heavily on "know your customer" determinations by exporters. Sanctions for violating the EAR are potentially severe (see Section 10.19). This leads to preventative lawyering under ongoing compliance and due diligence programs, with special emphasis on "dual use" (civil and military) goods and technology.

Control of U.S. exports is principally done by The Department of Commerce's Bureau of Industry and Security (BIS). But other departments also have some regulatory authority, especially the Department of State where the goods are "dual-use" items, meaning

---

[1]   50 U.S.C.A.App. § 2402.

[2]   15 C.F.R. § 730.6

[3]   The EAA of 1979 has been amended several times. It expired in 1994 but has been kept in force ever since by the President declaring a state of emergency under the International Emergency Economic Powers Act (IEEPA). 50 U.S.C.A. §§ 1701–1706. The President is required to report to Congress every six months on the national emergency. The report is more an outline of changes in export rules and actions taken than a disclosure of any conditions which any "reasonable man" might conclude constitute a national emergency. The Congress and the President have allowed the EAA to expire because of the continuing conflict between the Congress and the President regarding control over export trade. Unhappy with what Congress presents as a new framework for regulating exports, usually granting little discretion to the President to curtail exports to countries for U.S. foreign policy reasons, the President threatens a veto, the act is not passed, and the provisions of the old act remain in force under the International Emergency Economic Powers Act. Waiting for a "better" new law from Congress which does not so severely limit discretionary power of the President, with legislators annually predicting that it will be passed "this year", decades have passed without any expectation that a new law will be forthcoming "this year or next."

that they have both commercial and military application. Application for a license may be done electronically under the Simplified Network Application Process Redesign (SNAP-R), but only if the exporter has a BIS Company Identification Number (CIN). The BIS processes tens of thousands of export licenses annually, affecting billions of dollars of U.S. exports. In recent years, for example, high-tech goods involving encryption software and advance semiconductor chips with military applications have been a focus of these licenses.

§ 10.2 ____The Meaning of a "License"

Prior to 1996, exporters sent items abroad under either a "general" license or a "validated" license. The general license was used for most exports and did not require prior approval by the Department of Commerce. When most goods were shipped and a "Shipper's Export Declaration (SED)" was filled out, the SED constituted a general license. Validated licenses were issued only upon application to and approval by the Department of Commerce.

The current regulations eliminate the terms "general license" and "validated license". "License" refers to an authorization to export granted by the Department of Commerce. The change is to some degree a matter of semantics. General licenses, which were in a sense "self-granted", are abolished in favor of referring to such exports as exports permitted without any license. The new export "license" replaces the old "validated license." In 2012, the BIS processed over 23,000 export licenses for transactions valued at approximately $204 billion. Encryption-enabling goods and advanced semiconductor chips were high on the list of BIS export license concerns.

But much more was accomplished in the rearrangement of the regulations. The myriad of "special" licenses has been redone. There are now ten general prohibitions making up Part 736 of the C.F.R., rather than the previous scattering of the prohibitions throughout the regulations. These prohibitions indicate the circumstances where a license must be obtained. Note particularly that disclosure of controlled technology to a foreign national located *in the United States* constitutes a "deemed export". Transfers to foreign affiliates or subsidiaries within a corporate family are also treated as exports, as are electronic transmissions, donations and hand-carried items.

§ 10.3 U.S. Export Administration Regulations (EAR), Enhanced Proliferation Control Initiative (EPIC)

U.S. Export Administration Regulations[4] govern most export activity, including the issuance of licenses. The regulations are implemented and enforced by the Bureau of Industry and Security (BIS). The regulations include helpful provisions for exporters, which attempt to explain the regulations in simple terms. The regulations introduce the exporter to considerable new terminology.[5] The export of some commodities and technical data is absolutely prohibited, while other commodities are permitted to be exported under a range of lenient to severe restrictions.

Special provisions of the EAA apply to further control the proliferation of missiles, and chemical and biological weapons.[6] The EAR has integrated the role of the former Coordinating Committee for Multilateral Export Controls (COCOM), a group of nations which sought to keep sensitive material from communist dominated nations. COCOM was abolished soon after the Soviet Union was dismantled.[7]

The United States enacted the Enhanced Proliferation Control Initiative (EPCI), motivated by the Iraq conflict. This enactment seeks to establish greater control where commodities or technical data are destined for a prohibited nuclear, chemical or biological weapons or missile development use or end user. Considerable emphasis is placed on making the exporter aware of the nature of the buyer and where the items are going. The EPIC consists of Sections 744.1–744.6 of the C.F.R. EPIC addresses how technology and goods are *used* rather than by their *description*. They include essentially the "design, development, production, stockpiling, or use" of nuclear explosive devices, missiles, or chemical or biological weapons. The end result is that a license is required where otherwise it might not be. Exporters are thus given the responsibility to know more about their dual-use goods. The use of the EPCI in the control of weapons of mass destruction, especially after September 11, 2001, is clear.

The Department of Commerce has considerable discretion to allow or block exports when they are subject to licensing. In addition, certain *items* may be subject to mandatory controls, just as

---

4   15 C.F.R. §§ 730–774.

5   Terms are defined in 50 U.S.C.A.App. § 2415, and in 15 C.F.R. § 772

6   50 U.S.C.A.App. §§ 2410b and c.

7   COCOM expired in 1994. It has been replaced by the Wassenaar Arrangement, discussed below in § 10.34.

certain *destinations* may be subject to mandatory controls (e.g., a boycott that disallows most or all exports, such as with Cuba or North Korea). Actually, these mandatory controls allow some deviation, usually by the President rather than an agency exercising discretion. Some examples of mandatory controls include the Nuclear Non-Proliferation Act regulations governing exports that have nuclear explosive capability, unprocessed timber under the Forest Resources Conservation and Shortage Relief Act (FRCSRA 1990), oil for purposes of conservation or to establish reserves, and oil from certain locations such as the North Slope of Alaska. Exports are thus subject to a mix of regulations *by* different persons or agencies, *of* different products, *for* different purposes, and *to* different places.

§ 10.4 ____Steps for Using the EAR

Part 730 provides a general introduction to the EAR. It outlines the scope of the regulations, statutory authority, defines "dual use" exports (generally civil versus military), other agencies which participate in the regulation of exports, extraterritorial application of regulations, purposes of control, and limited situations requiring licenses. Part 732 includes the 29 steps for using the EAR. They include an overview, steps regarding the scope of the EAR, the ten general prohibitions, License Exceptions, Shipper's Export Declaration and other documents and records, and other requirements.

The overview notes some important questions to which the exporter must give thought, such as:

What is the item?

Where is it going?

Who will actually receive and use it?

What will the item be used for?[8]

Answers to these questions will help the exporter determine whether the EAR are applicable. The BIS maintains a list of "Red Flags" to assist with compliance and signal the need for further inquiries by exporter.

The first six steps regarding the scope of the EAR cover: (1) items subject to the exclusive jurisdiction of another federal agency; (2) publicly available technology and software; (3) re-export of U.S. origin items; (4) foreign made items incorporating less than a *de minimis* level of U.S. parts, components and materials; (5) foreign made items incorporating more than a *de minimis* level of U.S.

---

8   15 C.F.R. § 732.1.

parts, components and materials, and (6) foreign made items produced with certain U.S. technology for export to specified destinations.

§ 10.5   EAR—General Prohibitions[9]

If an export is subject to the EAR, the general prohibitions, as well as the License Exceptions, must be reviewed to determine if a license is necessary. This part informs the exporter of both the facts that make the proposed transaction subject to the general prohibitions, and the nature of the general prohibitions.

§ 10.6   EAR—Determination of the Applicability of the General Prohibitions, Re-exports

Five factors help determine the obligations of the exporter under the ten general prohibitions.[10] They are:

1.   Classification of the item using the Country Control List (CCL).

2.   Destination of the item using the CCL and Country Chart.

3.   End-user referring to a list of persons the exporter may not deal with.

4.   End-use.

5.   Conduct such as contracting, financing and freight forwarding in support of a proliferation project.

General Export Prohibitions

The ten general prohibitions follow, with commentary under the following headings:

1.   General Prohibition One—Export and re-export of controlled items to listed countries (Exports and Re-exports).

2.   General Prohibition Two—Re-export and export from abroad of foreign-made items incorporating more than a *de minimis* amount of controlled U.S. content (Parts and Components Re-exports).

3.   General Prohibition Three—Re-export and export from abroad of the foreign-produced direct product of U.S. technology and software (Foreign-Produced Direct Product Re-exports).

4.   General Prohibition Four—Engaging in actions prohibited by a denial order (Denial Orders).

---

[9]   15 C.F.R. Part 736.
[10]   15 C.F.R. § 736.2.

5. General Prohibition Five—Export or re-export to prohibited end-uses or end-users (End-Use End-User).

6. General Prohibition Six—Export or re-export to embargoed destinations (Embargo).

7. General Prohibition Seven—Support of Proliferation Activities (U.S. Person Proliferation Activity).

8. General Prohibition Eight—In transit shipments and items to be removed from vessels or aircraft (In transit).

9. General Prohibition Nine—Violation of any order, terms, and conditions (Orders, Terms, and Conditions).

10. General Prohibition Ten—Proceeding with transactions with knowledge that a violation has occurred or is about to occur (Knowledge Violation to Occur).

In preparing these prohibitions, the Commerce Department rejected a number of suggestions to liberalize existing re-export controls, such as to create a separate part for re-exports. Re-exports create a problem with the nation from which the item may be re-exported. That nation may object to any extraterritorial application of the U.S. rules. Indeed, foreign made products that include more than *de minimis* controlled U.S. content are also subject to the EAR.

§ 10.7   Overview of BIS Export Controls

The Commerce Control List (CCL—Part 774 of the EAR) is maintained by the BIS. The CCL includes all items (i.e., commodities, software, and technology) subject to BIS controls. The CCL does not include items exclusively governed by other agencies. But where there is shared governance, the CCL will note other agency participation. Knowing the Harmonized Code (customs classification for tariff purposes) Schedule B number does not help to determine whether or not an export license is required. That number is used by the Census Bureau for trade statistics. It is only the five-character Export Control Classification Number (ECCN) that will indicate whether or not an export license is required.

§ 10.8   ____The Commerce Control List (CCL)

The CCL is contained in Supplement No. 1 to Part 774. Supplement No. 2 to Part 774 contains the General Technology and Software Notes relevant to entries in the CCL. Commercial items that are not on the CCL are classified as "EAR99" and generally do not require licensing.

The CCL basic structure includes the following ten general categories:

0. Nuclear Materials, Facilities and Equipment (and Miscellaneous Items)

1. Materials, Chemicals, "Microorganisms," and Toxins

2. Materials Processing

3. Electronics

4. Computers

5. Telecommunications and Information Security

6. Sensors and Lasers

7. Navigation and Avionics

8. Marine

9. Propulsion Systems, Space Vehicles, and Related Equipment

Within each of the above ten categories are five different groups of items, identified by the letters A through E, as follows:

A. Systems, Equipment and Components

B. Test, Inspection and Production Equipment

C. Material

D. Software

E. Technology

To classify an item the exporter determines the general characteristics that will usually be expressed by one of the categories. Having the appropriate category, the next step is to match the characteristics and functions with one of the groups. For example, electronics equipment would be in category 3 and group A. The first digit and letter of the five-character ECCN would thus be 3A.

This pairing is followed by a number that signals the types of controls involved. The Reasons for Control are as follows:

0. National Security reasons (including Dual Use and International Munitions List) and Items on the NSG Dual Use Annex and Trigger List

1. Missile Technology reasons

2. Nuclear Nonproliferation reasons

3. Chemical & Biological Weapons reasons. . . .

9. Anti-terrorism, Crime Control, Regional Stability, Firearms Convention, Short Supply, Encryption, Computers and Significant Items

If electronics equipment is controlled for Missile Technology reasons, the EECN will read 3A1.

The final two numbers in the five-character EECN indicate its specific order within the category (first number) listed above . . . for example 3A106.

§ 10.9 ____License Requirements and Exceptions

Next to each ECCN is a brief description, followed by "License Requirements", "License Exceptions", and "List of Items Controlled" sections.

"License Requirements" identifies all possible Reasons for Control in order of precedence. Items within a particular ECCN number may be controlled for more than one reason. All the possible Reasons for Control are as follows:[11]

AT Anti-Terrorism

CB Chemical & Biological Weapons

CC Crime Control

CW Chemical Weapons Convention

EI Encryption Items

FC Firearms Convention

MT Missile Technology

NS National Security

NP Nuclear Nonproliferation

RS Regional Stability

SS Short Supply

SI Significant Items

SL Surreptitious Listening

UN United Nations Embargo

The applicable reasons appear in one of two columns in the License Requirements, entitled "Control(s)". The second column, entitled "Country Chart", identifies a column name and number for each applicable Reason for Control (e.g., CB Column 1). Once the exporter has determined that the item is controlled by a specific

---

[11]   15 C.F.R. § 738.2(d)(2)(i).

ECCN, information contained in the "License Requirements" section of the ECCN in combination with the Country Chart will allow a decision regarding the need for a license.

"License Exceptions" is used after it is determined that a license is required. It provides a brief eligibility statement for each ECCN-driven License Exception that may be applicable to the transaction. This is intended to help the exporter decide which ECCN-driven License Exception should be considered before submitting an application.[12] License Exceptions, the subject of Part 740, includes numerous categories. In the regulations, several exceptions were "bundled" under the grouping symbol LST (limited value shipments (LVS), shipments to group B countries (GBS), civil end-users (CIV), technology and software under restriction (TSR) and computers (APP)).

But objections by exporters with automated processes, who complained that an additional step was created, resulted in 1996 changes which dropped the LST, "de-bundled" the process, putting each exception into its own section. This makes them similar to other separated exceptions (i.e., temporary imports and exports (TMP), servicing and parts replacement (RPL), governments and international organizations (GOV), gift parcels and humanitarian donations (GFT), some technology and software (TSU), baggage (BAG), aircraft and vessels (AVS) and additional permissive re-exports (APR)). Part 740 is an extensive and important part of the EAR. It is followed by three supplements to Part 740, including (1) Country Groups, (2) meeting basic human needs, and (3) favorable treatment countries (ENC).

§ 10.10   ____The Commerce Country Chart (CCC)

Consulting the Country Chart is an essential step in determining the need for a license. It is useful in all cases except where short-supply reasons apply, or where there are unique entries.[13] The Country Chart is Supplement No. 1 to Part 738 of the EAR, and over several pages lists countries alphabetically. Territories, possessions, and departments are not listed, but are subject to the same rules as the governing country. On the right of the listed countries are the numerous columns identifying the various Reasons for Control. There may be one, two or three columns under a particular Reason for Control. They correlate to references in the License Requirements section of the applicable ECCN. There may be an "x" in one or more of the cells. Where it appears in more than one cell, there will be multiple reviews.

---

[12]   15 C.F.R. § 738.2(d)(2)(ii).
[13]   15 C.F.R. § 738.3.

§ 10.11   ____Determining the Need for a License[14]

Having determined that the item to be exported is controlled by a specific ECCN number, the exporter uses information in the "License Requirements" section of the ECCN entry in combination with the Country Chart. The need for a license is thus determined. Using the CCL "Controls" the exporter learns the reasons for control. Turning to the Country Chart and finding the appropriate country and the heading(s) for the reason(s), and with the column identifiers from the ECCN, the exporter looks for an "x". If an "x" is found in the cell on the Country Chart, the exporter knows a license is required.

A license application must be submitted unless a License Exception applies. Turning to the License Exceptions in the ECCN entry list, if a "yes" appears a further search of Part 740 will disclose whether an exception is available. Where there is no "x" in the cell on the Country Chart, a license is not required for control and destination, but one or more of General Prohibitions Four through Ten (see Section 10.6) may prohibit the export. One can thus go to Parts 758 and 762 for information on export clearance procedures and record keeping.

§ 10.12   U.S. Export Licenses—Advisory Opinions

A party who wishes to know whether a license is required may obtain an Advisory Opinion from the BIS.[15] Receipt of an opinion does not mean the subsequent application will be granted, opinions are not binding. But the BIS is likely to help the applicant in the preparation of an application which will meet the Advisory Opinion's requirements. An applicant may wish to avoid asking for an Advisory Opinion for fear that the opinion will be unfavorable. But if an export is made without an opinion and is in violation of the law, the sanctions may be severe.[16] Certainly, obtaining an unfavorable opinion and then exporting without a license creates a rather clear case of intent to disregard the law. But the Advisory Opinion is a good route to follow. If an unfavorable opinion is received, the BIS may explain what is required to obtain permission, unless the case is a clear one where no exports are permitted.

---

[14]   15 C.F.R. § 738.4.

[15]   15 C.F.R. § 748.3.

[16]   Persons convicted of a violation of any statute specified in § 11(h) of the EAA may not apply for any export license for ten years. 15 C.F.R. § 748.4(c).

Support documents may be required along with an application.[17] Numerous countries are exempt from the need of support documents, mostly (1) any exports or re-exports in the Western Hemisphere, (2) sales to government purchasers, and licenses submitted under special procedures, such as by A.I.D., or under the Special Comprehensive License procedure. When support documentation is required, the required data is to gain information about the disposition of the items, and to answer questions about national security controls and certain destinations. The transaction may require an End-User Certificate, or a Statement of Ultimate Consignee and Purchaser.[18]

§ 10.13 _____Issuance and/or Denial of Applications[19]

Part 750 of the EAR describes the BIS's process for reviewing a license application, including processing times, denials, revocations, issuance, duplicates, transfers, and shipping tolerances on approved licenses. The part also includes information on processing Advisory Opinion requests.

The BIS undertakes a complete review of the application, including an analysis of the license and support documentation, plus a consideration of the reliability of each party to the transaction, including any intelligence information. The Departments of Defense, Energy, State and the Arms Control and Disarmament Agency may also have review authority. Furthermore, the BIS may request review by other departments or agencies, which may agree to review, or waive review.

There has been a continuing dispute between Commerce and State over control of technology that seems to fall within the jurisdiction of each department. While the Arms Export Control Act gives State exclusive authority to issue jurisdiction determinations, Commerce has attempted to obtain concurrent authority to issue commodity jurisdiction determinations. Hearings were held in 1995 by the Senate Armed Services Committee after complaints that Commerce had issued export licenses for stealth technology that was under the jurisdiction of State. State intervened to stop the shipments, determined that they had jurisdiction, and denied the license. This kind of dispute has made it difficult to reach agreement on a new Export Administration Act. With proposals to abolish Commerce and transfer much of its export jurisdiction to

[17]   15 C.F.R. § 748.9.
[18]   See also 15 C.F.R. § 748.10–13, and Supplements.
[19]   15 C.F.R. Part 750.

State, the issue could become moot. There is little likelihood that State will agree to the transfer of any authority to Commerce.

Delay has been used by the government, especially by the Department of Defense, as a means of discouraging exports which might be permissible, but to which the Department objects. The *Daedalus Enterprises, Inc. v. Baldrige* case is an example.[20] Twenty-nine months after the filing of an application, the Department of Commerce had not reached a decision. The company had to seek a court order that the Secretary comply with the statutory timetable. There is little a company can do. It may not export the goods when the time period has expired if no response has been made by the government. It must go to court at each stage when the government fails to comply with the statute. Fortunately, the *Daedalus* case is an exception, and this kind of delay has been much diminished. The filing process is considerably improved. Furthermore, the President in 1996 made a major transfer of authority over encryption devices from the Department of State to the Department of Commerce.

§ 10.14 ____Timetable for Application Review

The BIS is required to resolve all applications, or refer them to the President, within 90 calendar days from the date of registration by the BIS. That is the date the BIS enters the application into the electronic license processing system.[21] Where there are deficiencies, the BIS tries to contact the applicant to obtain needed information. If no contact is made, the license is returned with notations of the deficiencies. This may cause a suspension in the processing time. If another department or agency is involved, or if government-to-government assurances or consultations are involved, there are additional time requirements for making requests and analyzing their results. When certain countries are involved, such as Congressional designated terrorist supporting nations, Congress may have to be notified, delaying the application for another 60 days.

§ 10.15 ____Issuance of a License[22]

A license is issued for a transaction, or series of transactions. The application may be approved in whole or in part. A license number is issued and a validation date. The license number must be used when discussing the license with the Department of Commerce. Nonmaterial changes may be made without obtaining a "Replacement" license.

---

20 563 F.Supp. 1345 (D.D.C.1983).
21 15 C.F.R. § 750.4.
22 15 C.F.R. § 750.7.

§ 10.16   _____Revocation or Suspension of a License[23]

All licenses may be revised, suspended, or revoked. This may occur without notice when the BIS learns that the EAR have been violated or are about to be violated. The exporter may have to stop a shipment about to be made, or if possible one that is already en route. When revocation or suspension occurs, the exporter is required to return the license to the BIS. Appeals from actions taken under the EAA or the EAR by the BIS are allowed for most actions.[24] There is an internal appeal process prior to appealing to the federal courts.

§ 10.17   _____Review of Export Applications by International Agencies

In December, 1995, 28 nations,[25] including the United States, agreed to establish a new export control regime that would assume some of the functions of the expired COCOM. The Wassenaar Arrangement on Export Controls for Conventional Arms and Dual-Use Goods and Technologies (the organizational meeting was in Wassenaar, the Netherlands; the secretariat was established in Vienna) fell short of U.S. expectations, not containing a requirement of prior notification of sales by one country to other countries in the group. A second concern is the lack of agreement on prohibiting dual-use goods and conventional weapons to civilian as well as military end-users in such nations as Iran, Iraq, Libya and North Korea. An additional concern is the lack of transparency in exchanging information on exports of dual use goods and conventional arms.

There are other multilateral export regimes, including the Nuclear Suppliers group (NSG), the Australia Group (AG), the Missile Technology Control Regime (MTCR), and the Technical Advisory Committees (TACs). It is reasonably safe to assume that the goals of these groups govern products carefully controlled under U.S. law.

---

[23]   15 C.F.R. § 750.8.

[24]   15 C.F.R. § 756.1.

[25]   Australia, Austria, Belgium, Canada, the Czech Republic, Denmark, Finland, France, Germany, Greece, Hungary, Iceland, Italy, Japan, Luxembourg, the Netherlands, New Zealand, Norway, Poland, Portugal, the Russian Federation, the Slovak Republic, Spain, Sweden, Switzerland, Turkey, the United Kingdom, and the United States. Several other nations have since joined.

§ 10.18   Shipper's U.S. Export Declaration (SED)

The exporter is responsible for following the regulations that govern carrying out the export.[26] This is so whether a license is issued or the exporter relies on a License Exception. The most important responsibility is the proper preparation of the Shipper's Export Declaration (SED), or Automated Export System (AES) record. They are primarily statements to the U.S. government used for gathering information to prepare trade statistics. There are numerous exemptions, such as gift parcels, aircraft and vessels, governments and international organizations, technology and software, and tools of trade.

As many as one-half the filings contain errors of omission or commission, according to the Bureau of Census and U.S. Customs Service. The two organizations have compared SEDs with outboard vessel manifests and discovered numerous inaccuracies in the vessel manifests as well as the SEDs. Cargo is often manifested not on the vessel actually carrying the goods, but on the manifest of a later departing vessel. The reason is the failure of exporters (and forwarders) to supply SEDs with complete and accurate information when the goods are shipped. This causes difficulties for Customs in detecting export law violations, and creates inaccurate trade statistics. Unless voluntary compliance improves, Customs may delay or detain an increasing number of shipments unless filings are presented with complete and accurate information.

§ 10.19   U.S. Sanctions—Fines, Suspensions and Revocation of Export Authority

Violation of laws and regulations governing U.S. exports brings into play both the basic law and the regulations. The EAA contains provisions governing violations of both the EAA and EAR.[27] The Export Administrative Regulations contain supplementary provisions, applying strict liability standards.[28] The general sanction for violations of the export laws, where the conduct was entered into *knowingly,* is a fine of the higher of $250,000 or twice the value of the exports.[29] This can obviously be *very* substantial.[30]

---

[26]   15 C.F.R. § 758.3.

[27]   50 U.S.C.A.App. § 2410. See www.bis.doc.gov, for considerable information concerning enforcement.

[28]   15 C.F.R. Part 764.

[29]   50 U.S.C.A. App. § 2410(a).

[30]   See United States v. Ortiz de Zevallos, 748 F.Supp. 1569, 1573 (S.D.Fla.1990), *judgment reversed* in United States v. Macko, 994 F.2d 1526 (11th Cir.1993). See also United States v. Brodie, 403 F.3d 123 (3d Cir. 2005).

Willful violations, with knowledge that the commodities or technology will be used to benefit, or are destined for, a controlled country, may result in a fine for business entities of the higher of $1 million per violation.[31] For individuals who engage in such willful violations the fine is $1,000,000 and/or 20 years imprisonment. This provision covers misuse of licenses.

Cases involving violations of the licensing requirements tend to be quite complex.[32] If the party exported to a controlled country commodities or technology under a license with knowledge that the commodities or technology were being used for military or intelligence gathering purposes, and willfully fails to report this use, the business entity fine is the same as above, the higher of $1 million or five times the value of the exports, but for the individual the imprisonment drops to five years, with the fine remaining the same, $250,000.[33] Even possession of goods or technology either with the intent to export in violation of the law, or knowing that the goods might be so exported, can result in a fine.

Perhaps the most severe statutory penalty in the EAA is in the civil penalty section. The Department of Commerce may impose a fine of $10,000 for violations (in certain cases up to $100,000), and they may *suspend or revoke the authority to export.*[34] This is a most severe sanction, used only in extreme cases. It was used in the Toshiba dispute, where Toshiba (Japan) and Köngsberg (Norway) enterprises sold to the Soviet Union technology allegedly useful for developing submarine propellers which would be sufficiently silent to avoid detection.[35] Debarment Lists can effectively "blacklist" foreign violators, barring U.S. firms from dealing with named parties, such as Dresser France in the Reagan-era Russian pipeline dispute. Temporary Denial Orders can also be employed against "related parties", as they were against Delft Instruments concerning the illegal export of munitions and night-vision devices. At one point, the Denial Order was extended to all 47 Delft companies located in 13 countries![36]

---

[31]   50 U.S.C.A. App. § 2410(b)(1).

[32]   United States v. Pervez, 871 F.2d 310 (3d Cir.1989); *cert. denied* 492 U.S. 925, 109 S.Ct. 3258, 106 L.Ed.2d 603 (1989).

[33]   50 U.S.C.A. App. § 2410(b)(2).

[34]   50 U.S.C.A. § 2410(c).

[35]   See Robert van den Hoven van Genderen, Cooperation on Export Control Between the United States and Europe: A Cradle of Conflict in Technology Transfer? 14 N.C.J.Int'l L. & Com.Reg. 391 (1989).

[36]   See Fitzgerald, Pierre Goes Online: Blacklisting and Secondary Boycotts in U.S. Trade Policy, 31 Vand. J. Trans. L. 1 (1998).

The result was enactment of the Multilateral Export Control Enhancements Act in 1988,[37] amending the EAA and providing trade prohibition sanctions for two to five years.[38] These sanctions are applied whether or not the other nations take action against their companies. The EAR repeat and expand upon these statutory sanctions. They further add provisions dealing with actions including "causing, aiding, or abetting" a violation,[39] and "solicitation and attempt", and "conspiracy."[40] More details are provided addressing misrepresentation and concealment of facts, or evasion,[41] failing to comply with reporting and record keeping requirements',[42] alterations of documents,[43] and acting contrary to the terms of a denial order.[44]

The political nature of export controls is emphasized by judicial refusal to agree to a settlement negotiated between a company accused of violations of the export laws and the Justice Department. In one instance a bargained $1 million fine was rejected by the court, which imposed a $3 million fine.[45]

§ 10.20   ____Administrative Proceedings and Denial Orders

Administrative procedures which supplement the U.S. Administrative Procedures Act, are the subject of a separate Part of the EAA and EAR.[46] They provide the framework for proceedings dealing largely with denial of export privileges and civil penalties. Appeals are the subject of several parts of the regulations.[47] The denial of export rights occurs principally either as an administrative sanction for violation of the EAR; or as a temporary measure when there is evidence of an imminent violation of the EAR. A denial order prohibits the party from any exports, unless there are exceptions in the order. The denial order states the extent

---

[37]   It was part of the 1988 Omnibus Trade and Competitiveness Act. See 50 U.S.C.A.App. § 2410a.

[38]   50 U.S.C.A.App. § 2410a.

[39]   15 C.F.R. § 764(2)(b).

[40]   15 C.F.R. § 764(2)(c) & (d).

[41]   15 C.F.R. § 764.2(g) & (h).

[42]   15 C.F.R. § 764.2(i).

[43]   15 C.F.R. § 764.2(j).

[44]   15 C.F.R. § 764.2(k).

[45]   United States v. Datasaab Contracting A.B., (D.D.C.Criminal No. § 84–00130, 4–27–84).

[46]   50 U.S.C.A.App. § 2412; 15 C.F.R. Parts 756, 764, and 766. One court has held that attorneys' fees of a prevailing defendant are not allowable under § 2412, because Congress did not make the equal Access to Justice Act part of the EAA. See Dart v. United States, 961 F.2d 284 (D.C.Cir.1992).

[47]   15 C.F.R. Part 764. See Iran Air v. Kugelman, 996 F.2d 1253 (D.C.Cir.1993).

to which exports are restricted. Because all denial orders are not the same, it is important to read carefully any specific denial order to determine the extent of the denial.

The denial order also affects persons dealing with the denied party.[48] The denied party may not be part of a transaction nor receive any benefit from a transaction. What are subject to regulation are essentially items of U.S. origin, or foreign items which require re-export permission. A person who deals with a denied party is not innocent if there is no knowledge of the denial status; everyone is responsible for knowing that any person with whom they engage in transactions is *not* on the denial list.

Licensed items to be shipped to a denied party may place the exporter at risk. The denial order must be checked to determine the extent of the loss of export privileges *if* the sale to the denied party is a product to be re-exported, or it releases controlled technical data to a denied foreign national. A person may buy products from a denied party in the United States, however, unless the intention is to subsequently export the product, which would give a "benefit" to the denied party. A transaction within a foreign country may be prohibited, as the foreign recipient of U.S. origin items may not sell them to a denied party even if the sale occurs within the foreign nation.[49] This purportedly applies whether the foreign firm is a U.S. subsidiary or not.

§ 10.21 _____Sanctions Against Designated Foreign Nationals

Although it is part of sanctions, being designated a foreign national merits separate consideration because it is so potentially restrictive. The Office of Foreign Assets Control (OFAC) in the Department of the Treasury may designate individuals and companies owned or controlled by, or acting for or on behalf of, targeted companies. They become so-called "specially designated nationals" or "SDNs." Their assets are blocked and U.S. persons are for the most part prohibited in dealing with them. The list of such designated nationals exceeds 550 pages. It can be a devastating designation and effectively end trade with the United States.

---

[48]   It could even limit employment of a denied party, to the extent that the party could not engage in transactions subject to the EAR.

[49]   This is not likely to be acceptable to the foreign country, which is apt to consider the prohibition an unreasonable extension of U.S. laws into its territory. A foreign court might order the transaction to take place.

Chapter 11

UNITED STATES BOYCOTT LAWS*

Table of Sections

Sec.

§ 11.1   U.S. Boycotts

U.S. boycott (embargo) laws deny or restrict import and export transactions by United States and other parties. As such, they represent a kind of ultimate import and export control system.

In the past few decades the United States has boycotted or embargoed goods from or to such countries as Cuba, Iran, Sudan, Burma, Syria, Iraq, Libya, Nicaragua, North Korea, South Africa, Rhodesia and Vietnam. The effectiveness of these boycotts in achieving political goals has been widely debated.[1] The U.S. boycotts have not all been unilateral. It has engaged in collective sanctions when many others have joined, such as the U.N. trade boycott against Iraq after the invasion of Kuwait,[2] or against Serbia and Montenegro after the Serbian-promoted invasion of Bosnia.[3] Less "collective" were the trade sanctions imposed on Argentina by the United States and the European Union after the Argentine invasion of the Falklands/Malvinas Islands.[4]

The United States has sometimes stood nearly alone among major nations in implementing boycotts, such as that directed against Cuba. Additionally, the United States has engaged in long term boycotts, notably against Cuba, and very brief boycotts, such

---

*   I am indebted to Prof. Michael Gordon for his work on a prior version of this chapter.

[1]   See Gary C. Hufbauer, Jeffrey J. Schott & Kimberly Ann Elliot, Economic Sanctions Reconsidered (1990).

[2]   See United Nations Security Council Resolution 661 (1990).

[3]   See United Nations Security Council Resolution 757 (1992).

[4]   See Domingo E. Acevedo, The U.S. Measures Against Argentina Resulting from the Malvinas Conflict, 78 Am.J.Int'l L. 323 (1984).

as limits on exports to Europe which might be used in the construction of a gas pipeline from the USSR after the Soviet invasion of Poland. The 2000 Trade Sanctions Reform and Export Enhancement Act prevents, except in extraordinary circumstances, use of unilateral agricultural and medical sector trade sanctions, provided only cash sales are involved. Despite doubts about their utility, there is little doubt that in the future unilateral or collective boycotts will continue to be part of U.S. foreign policy.

§ 11.2   U.S. Boycott Laws, OFAC Regulations

With whom the United States does not trade tends to be the decision of the President, although the Congress may act in special situations to deny trade benefits. Trade embargoes or other sanctions are often imposed quickly following some act which the U.S. President finds politically unacceptable. The Department of Commerce participates in the process of enforcing trade sanctions by controls on exports to various nations. Although Congress governs foreign commerce and specifically *exports* by means of the Export Administration Act, Congress tends to leave to presidential discretion the imposition of sanctions against specific countries.

This is not always the case, however. Congress may enact specific laws targeting particular nations. An example is the Cuban Democracy Act of 1992, which placed severe limitations on trade with Cuba, including trade by U.S. controlled subsidiaries abroad.[5] When Congress does act, it usually provides that its law will be carried out with additional regulations. The Export Administration Act (EEA) has substantial regulations that are enforced largely by the Department of Commerce.

OFAC

When Congress prohibits trade, or delegates such authority to the President, there is a shift of much of the enforcement (and enactment of regulations) responsibility from the Department of Commerce to the Department of the Treasury. Part of the reason is that Treasury has an extensive framework of regulations governing the control of foreign assets.[6] The Office of Foreign Assets Control (OFAC) of Treasury has jurisdiction over a broad range of controls on transactions between U.S. persons and persons in foreign countries.[7] When those latter persons are in certain foreign

---

[5]   Pub.L. No. 102–484, §§ 1706–12, 106 Stat. 2315, 2578–81 (1992).

[6]   31 C.F.R. Parts 500–585.

[7]   For a clash of OFAC and the Constitution see Looper v. Morgan, 1995 WL 499816 (S.D.Tex.1995) (regarding the search of an attorney's briefcase upon entry to the United States in search of documents supporting violations of the Libyan sanctions).

countries, the controls may prohibit nearly any form of "transaction" or "transfer". A transaction or transfer may involve money or goods or services. Certain transactions or transfers may be absolutely prohibited, others may be subject to special licensing.[8] The OFAC regulations extend to U.S. persons and permanent resident aliens no matter where located, to all persons and entities (including foreign branches and subsidiaries), and foreign branches of U.S. companies, but generally not foreign subsidiaries of U.S. firms (except Cuba). It is illegal to "facilitate" activities of non-U.S. persons that would be prohibited for U.S. persons, and OFAC construes "facilitation" broadly, for example bank financings.

The general regulations governing foreign assets control are followed by a series of mostly country-specific regulations.[9] These regulations vary in intensity of restrictiveness, but follow a general format including: (1) the relation of the regulations to other laws and regulations; (2) what transactions are prohibited; (3) definitions; (4) interpretations; (5) licensing process; (6) reports; (7) penalties; and (8) procedures. Some of the provisions are brief, others extensive. OFAC sanction programs target designated foreign countries, designated foreign entities and designated foreign individuals (the "SDN" List). Tens of thousands of persons and their related businesses are on the SDN List, most recently including Russian, Ukranian and Crimean names. To give an idea of how these restrictions function, the experience of Cuba is outlined in the following section.

OFAC Sanctions

The Office of Foreign Assets Control has two forms of sanctions. One is financial sanctions and asset freezes. Criminal sanctions generally range up to $1,000,000 per violation and up to 10 years in prison. Civil sanctions generally range between $12,000 and $250,000 per violation. The second form of sanction is trade and commercial embargoes. They may be used selectively or quite comprehensively. Selective sanctions may include blocking assets held in the United States, limitations on engaging in contracts, in travel, in transportation or even in exporting any goods or services. Selective sanctions have been used against various countries, including former "communist bloc" nations, South Africa, Iran and Angola. Comprehensive sanctions usually involve all the available

---

8   Licensing is in 31 C.F.R. Part 500, subpart E.

9   The consolidation of regulations as of July 1, 2009, included specific regulations for Burma, Cuba, Iran, Iraq, Sudan, Syria, Taliban (Afghanistan), Zimbabwe, the former Liberian Regime of Charles Taylor, and parts of the former Yugoslavia (Bosnian Serb-controlled areas of that Republic, Milosevic, and Kosovo).

options, and have been used against Cuba, Iran, Iraq, Sudan, Syria, Libya, North Korea and parts of the former Yugoslavia.

The Cuban sanctions discussed immediately below represent the most severe sanctions yet adopted. They were partly used as a model for the 1996 Iran and Libya Sanctions Act, often referred to as the D'Amato Act.[10] This Act, following the Libertad Act, requires the President to impose sanctions against *foreign* companies that invest more than $20 million a year in the development of petroleum resource production in Iran, or more than $40 million in Libya. The proposed $2 billion investment in Iran by the French Total company in the late 1990s generated a conflict between France and the United States over possible sanctions, which the U.S. President did not impose although he was under pressure to do so. If sanctions had been imposed, this matter quickly would have been taken to the WTO by the European Union on behalf of France.

State and Local Boycotts

Although the focus of this chapter is on federal law, in the past few years a number of state and local governments have adopted international boycott provisions. The provisions for the most part limit government procurement for reasons of perceived violations of human rights (a principal target has been Burma (Myanmar)), religious freedom (many countries), and the failure to deal with the return of Holocaust assets (Switzerland). These laws have created additional opposition among some foreign nations.

For example, the EU initiated a challenge under the WTO government procurement rules against a 1996 Massachusetts law addressed to Burma. Federal sanctions were authorized against Burma in 1997,[11] but the law did not discuss preemption. In a case against the Massachusetts law brought by the National Foreign Trade Council (NFTC), the federal district court, the federal circuit court and the U.S. Supreme Court all held for the NFTC.[12] The federal ruling caused the EU to withdraw its action under the WTO dispute resolution procedures.

---

[10]   Pub.L. No. 104–172, 110 Stat. 1541 (1996).

[11]   Omnibus Consolidated Appropriations Act, Pub.L. No. 104–208, § 570, 110 Stat. 3009, 3009–166–167, on September 30, 1996.

[12]   National Foreign Trade Council v. Baker, 26 F.Supp.2d 287 (D.Mass.1998), *aff'd*, National Foreign Trade Council v. Natsios, 181 F.3d 38 (1st Cir.1999), *aff'd sub nom.*, Crosby v. National Foreign Trade Council, 530 U.S. 363, 120 S.Ct. 2288, 147 L.Ed.2d 352 (2000) (holding Massachusetts' Burma law invalid under the Supremacy Clause because it threatens to frustrate federal statutory objectives).

§ 11.3   U.S. Boycotts: The Case of Cuba

The trade boycott of Cuba illustrates how the United States carries out a unilateral boycott. The Cuban boycott has endured longer than current sanctions against other nations. Furthermore, Cuba has received attention by Congress and the U.S. President of varying levels of forcefulness over the past three decades, often in direct relation to political campaigns.

Nationalization and the Start of the U.S. Boycott

The boycott of Cuba began as a response to the Cuban nationalization of all U.S. citizens' properties in 1959 and 1960,[13] and to the trade agreement concluded by Cuba with the USSR in February, 1960. The U.S. Congress amended the Sugar Act of 1948 giving the President authority to alter the Cuban sugar quota. The President used this authority during the height of the July, 1960, bitterness to nearly totally remove the extensive quotas, leaving Cuba with no access to the U.S. sugar market. In October, 1960, the President imposed an extensive embargo on shipments of goods to Cuba, except for nonsubsidized food, medicines and medical supplies.

With the cessation of diplomatic relations, the United States has continued the boycott without a break, but the intensity of the boycott has varied. The boycott provisions were amended in 1975 to allow foreign subsidiaries of U.S. companies to trade with Cuba. These amendments followed U.S. threats to tighten controls on foreign subsidiaries that caused several foreign governments to angrily denounce the policy, and even threaten nationalization of the companies. After 1975, U.S. subsidiaries abroad developed significant trade with Cuba. This trade angered anti-Castro groups in the United States, and led to the enactment of the Cuban Democracy Act in 1992. The Cuban Assets Control Regulations were amended to reflect the Act's strict provisions

The Libertad Act

Proponents of the Cuban Democracy Act kept urging adoption of a much harsher act, which would allow litigation by current U.S. citizens who were Cuban nationals at the time of the Castro expropriations, seeking compensation from persons currently using expropriated properties. This became the Cuban Liberty and Democratic Solidarity (Libertad) Act (more commonly known as

---

[13]   The expropriations effectively commenced under the Agrarian Reform Law on June 1, 1959, but did not reach their zenith until the resolutions issued under the authority of the major nationalization law of July, 1960. See Michael Wallace Gordon, The Cuban Nationalizations: The Demise of Foreign Private Property (1976).

Helms-Burton), enacted in March, 1996,[14] primarily because of the emotions aroused due to the shooting down of two U.S. civilian aircraft by Cuba near Cuban territory.

The Libertad Act included two very controversial sections. The first, Title III, created a right of action in U.S. courts for a U.S. national with a claim that Cuba expropriated property after January 1, 1959, against any person who is "trafficking" in such property. Trafficking is quite broadly defined, including not only such actions as selling, buying, leasing or transferring, but also engaging in a "commercial activity using or otherwise benefitting from confiscated property."[15]

The Libertad Act authorizes the President to suspend the effectiveness of Title III actions for successive periods of six months. President Clinton issued such suspension every six months beginning in August, 1996, throughout his term, and each president elected since has continued that practice. These suspensions were the only reason the European Union deferred its request for a panel under the WTO to challenge the extraterritorial effects of the Libertad Act. The United States has stated that it would use the national security defense under the WTO, and also in response to any similar challenge brought by Canada or Mexico under the NAFTA.[16]

The second important part of the Libertad Act, Title IV, requires that the Secretary of State deny visas for entry into the United States to corporate officers, principals, shareholders and even the spouse, minor children or agents of such persons, if they are trafficking in or have confiscated property.[17] This authority has been used against officials of Canadian, Israeli, and Mexican companies.

Other nations and organizations have responded in very strong terms against the Libertad Act by adopting blocking laws and enacting resolutions.[18] Cuba enacted its own response to the

---

[14]   Pub.L. No. 104–114, 110 Stat. 785 (Mar. 12, 1996).

[15]   Libertad Act § 4(13).

[16]   The use of the national security defense was strongly criticized in such a case, where there was no foreseeable security threat.

[17]   Id. at § 401.

[18]   See, e.g., Peter Glossop, Canada's Foreign Extraterritorial Measures Act and U.S. Restrictions on Trade with Cuba, 32 Int'l Lawyer 93 (1998); Mexico: Act to Protect Trade and Investment from Foreign Statutes which Contravene International Law, with Introductory note by Jorge Vargas, 36 Int'l Legal Materials 133 (1997); Douglas H. Forsythe, Introductory Note, Canada: Foreign Extraterritorial Measures Act Incorporating the Amendments Countering the U.S. Helms-Burton Act, 36 Int'l Legal Materials 111 (1997); Protecting Against the Effects of the Extraterritorial Application of Legislation Adopted by the Third

Libertad Act, which, *inter alia*, denies any possible compensation in a future settlement with the government of Cuba to anyone attempting to take advantage of the Libertad Act by using the U.S. courts under Title III.[19]

Finally, the Florida legislature largely deferred to the Miami Cuban-American groups and passed a state version of Helms-Burton, essentially a "feel good" action since the federal government had pre-empted governance of trade with Cuba. Florida later passed a law attempting to ban any Florida university researchers from traveling to Cuba using private funds, even if licensed by the federal government, and another, the 2008 Sellers of Travel Act, setting huge fees on federally authorized travel agencies in Florida that booked flights to Cuba. Both were quickly overturned by a federal district court.

Cuban Asset Control Regulations (CACR)

The Cuban Assets Control Regulations (CACR), approximately four dozen pages and nearly 150 separate provisions, are the principal regulations which govern trade with Cuba.[20] The application of the Regulations is limited by the Cuban Democracy Act, which removed administrative discretion in allowing some trade with Cuba from foreign subsidiaries. Furthermore, the Regulations may not conflict with the Trading with the Enemy Act,[21] or the Foreign Assistance Act of 1961, both as amended.[22] The administration of the Regulations is delegated to the Office of Foreign Assets Control (OFAC) of the Department of the Treasury.

The Regulations prohibit certain transactions and transfers, where Cuba or a Cuban national is involved. The scope is very wide, including various transfers involving (1) currency, securities, and gold or silver coin or bullion; (2) property or indebtedness; and (3) any form where the transfer is one which attempts to evade or avoid the first two prohibitions.[23] But the Secretary of the Treasury is given authority to authorize such transfers. Imports are prohibited

---

Country, E.U. Council Regulation 2271/96, 1996 O.J. (L 309), reprinted in 36 Int'l Legal Materials 127 (1997).

[19]   Ley de Reafirmacion de la Dignidad y Soberania Cubana (Ley No. 80), Dec. 24, 1996.

[20]   OFAC publishes a useful overview of the regulations.

[21]   The original powers of the President were in the Trading With the Enemy Act (TWEA) of 1917. The President delegated authority to Treasury in accordance with the TWEA. The International Emergency Economic Powers Act (IEEPA) was enacted in 1988 and substantially replaced the TWEA. The authority of the President continues under the IEEPA.

[22]   31 C.F.R. § 515.101.

[23]   31 C.F.R. § 515.201.

if (1) Cuban in origin,[24] (2) the goods have been in Cuba (including transported through), or (3) made from any Cuban parts.[25]

CACR Exceptions

There are few exceptions to the Cuban trade restrictions. One is a limited exception allowing trade in informational materials, such as some books.[26] More recently cash sales of certain agricultural products have been allowed. The trade prohibitions conclude with a restriction that disallows (1) any vessel which has entered a Cuban port for trade purposes from entering a U.S. port for 180 days after the departure from Cuba, or (2) any vessel carrying goods or passengers to or from Cuba (or goods in which a Cuban has any interest) from entering any U.S. port with such goods or passengers on board.[27]

The Regulations were modified in September, 2009, to increase allowed family visits and remittances, and increase permitted telecommunications. Additionally legislation in 2009 created a new *general* license to allow travel related transactions linked to commercial marketing of agricultural commodities, medicine, or medical devices. While general tourist travel is permitted, almost any U.S. national can find a group to travel with, especially church groups. The addition of the general license covering considerable travel has opened travel to many U.S. persons without Cuban relatives. The U.S. administration under President Obama seemed less inclined to source U.S. foreign policy towards Cuba in Miami, but there has been no major step toward removing the trade embargo. What has become important is an apparent relaxation by OFAC of zealous control demanded by a decreasing number of Cuban exiles.

U.S. Foreign Subsidiaries

The CACR prohibitions are followed by quite extensive definitions.[28] While nearly all of the definitions create little problem, one is of considerable importance to U.S. businesses with subsidiaries. A "person subject to the jurisdiction of the United States," upon whom the Regulations impose trade restrictions, includes, "any corporation, partnership, or association, wherever

---

[24]   See, e.g., United States v. Plummer, 221 F.3d 1298 (11th Cir.2000).

[25]   31 C.F.R. § 515.204.

[26]   31 C.F.R. § 515.206. But no cigars or rum. The regulations even prohibit a U.S. citizen or legal resident alien from smoking a Cuban cigar or drinking Cuban rum while in a third country. One might think that OFAC has more important things to do than produce and publish Cuban Cigar Updates.

[27]   31 C.F.R. § 515.207. These vessel restrictions were added to comply with § 1706(b) of the Cuban Democracy Act.

[28]   31 C.F.R. Subpart C.

organized or doing business, that is owned or controlled by persons" citizen or resident of the United States or where an entity is organized under the laws of the United States.[29] The meaning of "owned" or "controlled" is not included in the Regulations. The focus of the Cuban Democracy Act is to limit trade with Cuba from foreign subsidiaries of U.S. corporations. It has brought negative responses from the European Union (and separately from member states of the EU), Canada, Argentina, Mexico and the U.N. General Assembly. It is one more example of the extraterritorial application of U.S. laws, and one more example of foreign rejection of such application.

Until this point, the Regulations are mostly prohibitory. But the next section contains important provisions covering "licenses, authorizations, and statements of licensing policy."[30] These provisions authorize the Secretary of the Treasury to issue licenses in a wide variety of circumstances, including (1) for certain judicial proceedings to take place, (2) to determine persons to be unblocked nationals, (3) and to allow transfers by operations of law. The provisions of most importance for U.S. business interests allow some limited trade with Cuba by U.S. owned or controlled firms.[31]

But it was this provision which was the principal focus of the Cuban Democracy Act, which reversed a decade old policy allowing Treasury to license foreign subsidiaries to trade with Cuba.[32] The current law prohibits the issuance of any such licenses to contracts entered into after the enactment of the Cuban Democracy Act. The governments of the foreign nations in which many U.S. subsidiaries are located, however, have enacted laws which mandate that the subsidiaries disregard the U.S. restrictions. It must be assumed that some trade continues, without any attempt to obtain a license.

The subsequent subpart governs reports, and requires reports by any person engaging in any transaction subject to the Regulations.[33] Thus, a U.S. company trading through a subsidiary may twice violate the law, first by trading and second by failing to report the trade. Penalties are contained in the next provisions,[34] and are severe. Fines may reach $1 million for willful violations, with a maximum of $500,000 as civil penalties.[35] A U.S. firm in

---

[29]　31 C.F.R. § 515.329(d).

[30]　31 C.F.R. Subpart E.

[31]　31 C.F.R. § 515.559.

[32]　Cuban Democracy Act § 1706(a).

[33]　31 C.F.R. § 515.601.

[34]　31 C.F.R. Subpart F.

[35]　See United States v. Brodie, 403 F.3d 123 (3d Cir. 2005); United States v. Plummer, 221 F.3d 1298 (11th Cir. 2000); United States v. Macko, 994 F.2d 1526

violation of some of the CACR provisions may have a mitigating argument not present in the anti-boycott situation—to comply with the U.S. law means violation of the law of the nation in which the U.S. subsidiary is incorporated and operating.

(11th Cir. 1993); and United States v. Ortiz de Zevallos, 748 F.Supp. 1569 (S.D.Fla. 1990), all dealing with violations of the Cuban boycott rules.

Chapter 12

UNITED STATES ANTI-BOYCOTT LAW*

Table of Sections

Sec.

§ 12.1   The Arab Boycott of Israel

United States import and export controls[1] are generated under legislation intended to counteract the longstanding, though not terribly effective, Arab boycott of Israel. U.S. "anti-boycott" law attempts to restrict trading by individuals and firms that are deemed to support that boycott. Federal U.S. law was adopted exclusively because of the Arab boycott of Israel. But nowhere does the law specifically mention either Arabs or Israel. Instead, the law is directed to prohibiting U.S. persons from participating in or supporting boycotts by foreign nations against other foreign nations friendly to the United States. U.S. anti-boycott law is likely to remain on the books well after the Arab boycott expires.

The Arab nations employ an international primary, secondary and tertiary boycott of Israel. A primary boycott is where one

---

*   I am indebted to Prof. Michael Gordon for his work on a prior version of this chapter.

[1]   See generally Chapters 7 and 10.

nation, for example, Oman, refuses to deal with another, for
example, Israel. The boycott is secondary when the boycotting
nation (Oman) refuses to deal with any third party nation, such as
the United States, if that nation deals with the boycotted nation,
Israel. The tertiary boycott arises when the boycotting nation
(Oman) refuses to deal with the third party nation (the United
States), if any of the elements of its products are from a fourth
party nation company (e.g., The Netherlands) which trades with the
boycotted nation (e.g., Israel).

The boycott has been inconsistently applied by the Arab
nations. Where the product or project is of high priority, the Arab
nations either ignore their own boycott or grant a waiver.[2]

§ 12.2   U.S. Federal Anti-boycott Law

The Arab boycott of Israel led to the adoption of U.S. laws and
regulations essentially prohibiting U.S. persons from complying
with or supporting any boycott by a foreign nation against a nation
friendly to the United States.[3] Nowhere in the law is there any
direct reference to either Israel or any specific Arab nation.
Nevertheless, of 376 boycott requests notified to the Office of Anti-
boycott Compliance in 2011, 369 involved an Arab League member.
These provisions owe their existence to a long and bitter struggle
within Congress, and between Congress and the administration,
over the creation of rules that would prohibit U.S. companies from
assisting the Arab nations in their attempts to harm Israel.[4]

Prior to the enactment of federal export laws dealing with the
Arab boycott of Israel, several states enacted similar laws, and the
federal tax and antitrust laws were used to deter U.S. companies
from compliance with boycott requests. Although the boycott of
Israel by the Arab nations is the reason the federal law exists, there
has been some question raised about the applicability of the law to
foreign boycotts against South Africa. The Department of
Commerce interpreted the law as not applicable to the (since
terminated) boycotts against South Africa. The law does affect
many commercial relationships between U.S. persons and Middle
Eastern governments, private individuals and banks.

---

[2]   See Abrams v. Baylor College of Medicine, 581 F.Supp. 1570, 1576 n. 3
(S.D.Tex.1984) for an example of a waiver of the boycott regarding medical
equipment from a blacklisted company.

[3]   Export Administration Act of 1979, 50 App.U.S.C.A. § 2407; Export
Administrative Regulations, 15 C.F.R. Part 769.

[4]   The history of the boycott provisions is contained in Trane Co. v. Baldrige,
552 F.Supp. 1378 (W.D.Wis.1983). There are numerous references to Arab nations in
the Supplements to 15 C.F.R. Part 769, which include interpretations of the
regulations.

§ 12.3   U.S. Export Administration Act (EAA)

Enforcement of the federal anti-boycott laws lies largely within the Department of Commerce Bureau of Industry and Security. The Export Administration Act (EAA) governs the export of goods from the United States, including the anti-boycott provisions. These anti-boycott provisions, and the regulations, prohibit U.S. persons from participating in boycotts by a foreign nation against third nations that are friendly towards the United States. The statutory language is very broad, not unlike the concept of the U.S. antitrust laws. The EAA structure requires the President to issue regulations that prohibit any U.S. person from engaging principally in two different areas of activity, *refusals to deal* and *furnishing information*, if such actions further or support a boycott by one foreign nation against another foreign nation that is friendly to the United States.[5]

There is a further provision that applies particularly to banks, that prohibits certain actions with regard to letters of credit which also may further or support a boycott. These prohibitions are included in six sections of the law.[6] The law subsequently states that the regulations should provide exceptions governing some six classes of activity.[7] Reporting to the Secretary of Commerce is required of any request to furnish information.[8] Violations of these provisions are subject to the same statutes that govern other violations of the U.S. export laws. *See* Chapter 10.

§ 12.4   ____Export Administration Regulations (EAR)

The Export Administration Regulations (EAR) supplement the EEA.[9] They include very extensive examples of conduct which provide guidance in determining whether specific conduct may constitute an anti-boycott violation of the EAA and EAR. Many of the examples are of common occurrences where companies are in jeopardy of refusing to deal, or furnishing prohibited information. Use of these examples is essential to determining both the sense of the administration in interpreting the law, and the likelihood that the conduct in question may be challenged.

The examples in the regulations follow the pattern of the principal statute. Thus, the regulations begin (after a section with

---

5   50 App.U.S.C.A. § 2407(a)(1).
6   50 App.U.S.C.A. § 2407(a)(1)(A)–(F).
7   50 App.U.S.C.A. § 2407(a)(2)(A)–(F).
8   50 App.U.S.C.A. § 2407(b)(2).
9   15 C.F.R. Part 769.

definitions[10]) with examples of six classes of prohibited conduct,[11] and are followed by examples of six classes of exceptions.[12] Following the regulations are a series of 16 Supplements that include Department of Commerce interpretations of various provisions, with some suggested contractual provisions that may avoid challenges by the Department.

§ 12.5 ____Prohibited Intentional Actions

The purpose of the anti-boycott provisions is to prohibit any U.S. person "from taking or knowingly agreeing to take [certain actions] with intent to comply with, further, or support any boycott" against a country friendly to the United States.[13] It specifically exempts boycotts pursuant to U.S. law. The requirement of intent is essential, but what constitutes intent may seem marginal.

In *United States v. Meyer*,[14] the defendant Meyer was held to have knowledge that a form required by Saudi Arabia to have a trademark registered in that country was not used to obtain information needed for the registration, but to further the boycott of Israel. Meyer claimed that his actions were inadvertent and not intentional. But Meyer's knowledge and intention were rather clearly illustrated by his receipt of information from the Department of State that it could not notarize the form because of the boycott, and his subsequent acquisition of a notarization through the U.S.-Arab Chamber of Commerce. The *Meyer* decision involves a clear attempt to find a way past the law. It is thus not very helpful for a case where the intent is based on less apparent criteria.

§ 12.6 ____Refusals to Deal

The first prohibition in the EAA is against directly refusing to do business with or in the boycotted country (i.e. Israel), or with a national or resident of that country. Also prohibited is any refusal to do business with the boycotted country by agreement with or response to requests from any other person.[15] This means a U.S. company may not refuse to do business with Israel at the request of the central boycott office of the Arab nations in Damascus. Intent to refuse to do business is not established by the absence of any business relationship with the boycotted country.

---

[10]   15 C.F.R. § 769.1.

[11]   15 C.F.R. § 769.2.

[12]   15 C.F.R. § 769.3.

[13]   50 App.U.S.C.A. § 2407(a)(1).

[14]   864 F.2d 214 (1st Cir.1988).

[15]   50 App.U.S.C.A. § 2407(a)(1)(A).

The Export Administration Regulations, which include ten subsections further defining the meaning of refusing to do business, expand upon this prohibition.[16] The regulations make it clear that a refusal to do business may be established by a course of conduct as well as a specific refusal, or by a use of any "blacklist" or "whitelist". They emphasize, nevertheless, that intent to comply with or support a boycott is required.

Prior to 1985–86, the focus of the Department of Commerce was on reporting violations. But in 1986 the Department, concerned with its limited resources, began to concentrate on blacklists, religious discrimination and refusals to deal. These are viewed by the Department as the most serious violations.

The regulations attempt to cover many variations, but obviously cannot offer an example for each possible situation. Refusals to deal arise for reasons both directly related and totally unrelated to the boycott. When normally justified business reasons for refusing to deal begin to show a pattern of not dealing for reasons consistent with a boycott, the party is in some danger of a challenge from Commerce. But the law does include language of intent, which is most difficult to show from a pattern of conduct that indicates good business reasons for refusing to deal.

The regulations also suggest what does *not* constitute a refusal to do business, such as an agreement to comply generally with the laws of the boycotting country. There does not have to be an agreement not to do business. Compliance with a request, or a unilateral decision, if for boycott reasons, will suffice. These regulations raise one especially difficult issue—the use of a list of suppliers. The regulations give a specific example, although specific examples are usually left for the "examples" section.[17] A U.S. person under contract to provide management services for a construction contract may provide a list of qualified bidders for the client if the service is customary, and if qualified persons are not excluded because they are blacklisted.

Examples of Refusals to Deal

The regulations and especially the examples disclose the nearly unlimited possible configurations of fact situations that may give rise to problems. Consider only a few possible variations, from which numerous additional variations may be easily constructed:

Example 1. A U.S. company is doing business in Israel, but wants to do business in Arab nations while retaining the Israel

---

[16]   15 C.F.R. § 769.2(a). See also Supplements No. 6(a), 7, and 15(a) to Part 769.
[17]   15 C.F.R. § 769.2(a)(6).

business. This creates a problem if the Arab nations have alternative sources for the goods, especially from companies in nations which do not have anti-boycott laws, meaning essentially all other nations in the world.

Example 2. Same as above but the company would like to terminate the business in Israel because:

> (a) It believes in or doesn't really care about the boycott. The company is in danger of challenge by the Department of Commerce. But is a business likely to state that it believes in or doesn't care about the boycott?

> (b) The Israel business is not as large as the potential Arab nation's business and the company does not have the capacity to do business in both. As long as the decision is not boycott based, it is proper to drop the Israel business. But it may have to prove that its motives were business and not boycott based.

> (c) The company had planned to close the Israel business because it has been losing money. It had best be able to prove that loss.

Example 3. The company trades with Arab nations and would also like to do business with Israel. It knows if it does do business with Israel it may lose the business with the Arab nations.

Example 4. The same but the company is willing to drop the business with the Arab nations. It may do so without violating the boycott rules because Israel is not boycotting the Arab nations.

Example 5. The company is doing business in both Israel and Arab nations. The Arabs do not know this. The company wants to drop the Israel business because it fears that the Arabs will learn of that business and terminate very profitable Arab business.

§ 12.7 ____Discriminatory Actions

The second statutorily prohibited conduct is refusing to employ or otherwise discriminating against any U.S. person on the basis of race, religion, sex or national origin, where such conduct is intentional and in furtherance of an unlawful boycott.[18] This section addresses the Arab nations' attempts to injure Jewish people wherever they may live, rather than to harm Israel as a nation. Thus, a company may not refuse to employ Jewish persons so that it may gain favor with Arab clients. In one of the few court decisions

---

[18]   50 App.U.S.C.A. § 2407(a)(B). Even if employment discrimination is not boycott based, and thus not a violation of the EAA, it may violate other laws, such as civil rights legislation.

involving the anti-boycott provisions, Baylor College of Medicine was found to have persistently appointed non-Jewish persons for a project with Saudi Arabia.[19]

The antidiscrimination section of the EAA includes both refusals to employ and *other discrimination*. For example, a requirement that a U.S. company not use a six-pointed star on its packaging of products to be sent to the Arab nation would be a violation because it is part of the enforcement effort of the boycott. But it is not a violation if the demand is that no symbol of Israel be included on the packaging. The former is a religious symbol generally, the latter an acceptable request which does not include reference to any person's religion.[20] This illustrates a general attempt to acknowledge that the boycotting nations are entitled to have *some* control over what comes into their nation. They are entitled to say no imports may be stamped "Products of Israel", but they may not attack the Jewish religion more broadly by requiring certification that no religious symbols appear on any packages. The United States is attempting to say that Arab nations may have a right to engage in a primary boycott against Israel, but they may not draw U.S. persons into supporting that boycott.

The regulations governing discriminatory actions make it clear that such actions must involve "intent to comply with, further or support an unsanctioned foreign boycott."[21] The regulations further state that the boycott provisions do not supersede or limit U.S. civil rights laws.[22]

§ 12.8 _____Furnishing Information Regarding Race, Religion, Sex or National Origin

The third specific prohibition relates to the refusal to hire for reasons of race, religion, sex or national origin, discussed immediately above. This provision prohibits furnishing information with respect to race, religion, sex or national origin.[23] This brief provision is supplemented by regulations that state that it shall apply whether the information is specifically requested or offered voluntarily and whether stated in the affirmative or negative.[24]

---

[19]   Abrams v. Baylor College of Medicine, 581 F.Supp. 1570 (S.D.Tex.1984), *aff'd*, 805 F.2d 528 (5th Cir.1986). The case also deals with the issue of the right to bring a private action. Using the *Cort v. Ash* factors test, the court held that there is an implied right under the EAA.

[20]   These are examples included in 15 C.F.R. § 769.2(b), examples (viii) and (ix). See Supplement No. 6(b) & (c) to Part 769.

[21]   15 C.F.R. § 769.2(b)(2).

[22]   15 C.F.R. § 769.2(b)(3).

[23]   50 App.U.S.C.A. § 2407(a)(C).

[24]   15 C.F.R. § 769.2(c)(2).

Furthermore, prohibited information includes place of birth or nationality of the parents, and information in code words or symbols that would identify a person's race, religion, sex or national origin.[25] The regulations also reaffirm the element of intent.[26]

The examples in the regulations illustrate the difficulty of clearly defining "prohibited information". If the boycotting nation requests a U.S. company to give all employees who will work in the boycotting nation visa forms, and these visa forms request otherwise prohibited information, the company is not in violation for giving the forms to its employees or for sending the forms back to the boycotting country party. This is considered a ministerial function and not support of the boycott. But the company may not itself provide the information on race, religion, sex or nationality of its employees, if it meets the intent requirement. The company might certify that none of its employees to be sent to the boycotting nation are women, where the laws of the boycotting country prohibit women from working. The reason for the submission has nothing to do with the boycott.

§ 12.9 ____Furnishing Information Regarding Business Relationships—"Blacklists"

The fourth prohibition is one that is often at issue. It involves the use of blacklists. The Arab nations maintain a blacklist of persons and companies with whom they will not do business. Arab nations often ask a prospective commercial agreement party to certify that none of the goods will include components obtained from any companies on the blacklist.

Persons are prohibited from furnishing information about an extensive list of business activities ("including a relationship by way of sale, purchase, legal or commercial representation, shipping or other transport, insurance, investment, or supply"[27]), with an equally extensive list of business relationships ("with or in the boycotted country, with any business concern organized under the laws of the boycotted country, with any national or resident of the boycotted country, or with any other person which is known or believed to be restricted from having any business relationship with or in the boycotting country"[28]). At the end is a statement that the section does not prohibit furnishing "normal business information in a commercial context as defined by the Secretary." Thus, clients

---

[25]   15 C.F.R. § 769.2(c)(3).

[26]   15 C.F.R. § 769.2(c)(4).

[27]   50 App.U.S.C.A. § 2407(a)(D).

[28]   Id.

are very extensively governed with regard to the flow of information between the company and the boycotting country.

The regulations develop this already expansive section.[29] The prohibited information may not be given whether directly or indirectly requested or furnished on the initiative of the U.S. person.[30] The Secretary's definition of normal business in a commercial context is that related "to factors such as financial fitness, technical competence, or professional experience" as might be normally found in documents available to the public, such as "annual reports, disclosure statements concerning securities, catalogues, promotional brochures, and trade and business handbooks."[31] Such public information may not be supplied if in response to a boycott request.[32]

But it may be supplied if it could be used by the boycotting country to further the boycott—knowledge and intent on the part of the U.S. person is the key to making the furnishing of the information unlawful. There are numerous examples of this prohibition, many referring to use of blacklists. For example, a person may not certify that its suppliers are not on a furnished blacklist.[33] If a company is on the blacklist, or if it wishes to know whether it is on the blacklist, it may request such information.[34] That is not furnishing information. But if it furnishes information in order to be removed, it may be in violation. If a company believes it is on the blacklist but no longer would be listed were the Arab nations to know the true facts, supplying those facts may constitute a violation.[35] The same may occur when a company believes it is mistakenly listed, and wishes to make this known to the Arab nations. Companies have removed their names, but it must be done with great care.

The most publicized blacklist case involved Baxter International Inc., a large U.S. medical supply company.[36] As a result of an informant's disclosure, Baxter was investigated and charged with violating the EAA because of the way in which it

---

[29]   15 C.F.R. § 769.2(d).

[30]   15 C.F.R. § 769.2(d)(2)(ii).

[31]   15 C.F.R. § 769.2(d)(3).

[32]   15 C.F.R. § 769.2(d)(4).

[33]   15 C.F.R. § 769.2(d) example (x).

[34]   15 C.F.R. § 769.2(d) example (xv).

[35]   A U.S. subsidiary of the French cosmetics company L'Oreal provided the parent information to assist in removal from the blacklist. Providing this information and failing to report to the Commerce department led to L'Oreal agreeing to pay $1.4 million in civil penalties. See, e.g., Los Angeles Times, August 30, 1995, at Part D.

[36]   See, e.g., The Case Against Baxter International, Business Week, Oct. 7, 1991, pg. 106.

attempted to have its name removed from the Arab blacklist.[37] Commerce was prepared to charge Baxter and a senior officer with providing over 300 items of prohibited information to Syrian authorities and a Saudi Arabian firm. The company and the officer admitted civil and criminal violations and were assessed total civil penalties of $6,060,600—the highest at the time. The case would not have succeeded without the informant providing substantial documentation of the violations.

§ 12.10 ____Prohibition of Intentional Evasion

The EAA and the EAR regulations each include a section that states that no U.S. person may take any action with intent to evade the law.[38] Permitted activities are not to be considered an evasion of the law. An example of an evasion is placing a person at a commercial disadvantage or imposing on that person special burdens because that person is blacklisted or otherwise restricted from business relations for boycott reasons.[39] Another evasion may be use of risk-of-loss provisions that expressly impose a financial risk on another because of the import laws of a boycotting country, unless customarily used.[40] Two final suggested evasions are the use of dummy corporations or other devices to mask prohibited activities, or diverting boycotting country orders to a foreign subsidiary.[41]

§ 12.11 ____Reporting Requirements for Requests

Under the title "Foreign policy controls," the EAA includes very important provisions that require the reporting of the receipt of any request for the "furnishing of information, the entering into or implementing of agreements, or the taking of any other action" outlined in the policy section[42] of the EAA.[43] The receipt of any such request must be reported to the Secretary of Commerce. Failure to report boycott-associated requests is perhaps the most frequent violation of the EAA. The report must include any information the Secretary deems appropriate and must state whether the person intends to comply or has complied with the request. These reports are public records, except to the extent that certain confidential

---

[37]   See 5 OEL Insider 7 (Dec. 1993).

[38]   50 App. U.S.C.A. § 2407(a)(5); 15 C.F.R. § 769.4; see also Supplement No. 12 to Part 769 for an interpretation dealing with use of an agent.

[39]   15 C.F.R. § 769.4(c).

[40]   15 C.F.R. § 769.4(d).

[41]   15 C.F.R. § 769.4(e).

[42]   50 App. U.S.C.A. § 2402(5).

[43]   50 App. U.S.C.A. § 2407(b).

information is included that would cause a competitive
disadvantage to the reporting person.

The regulations include quite extensive provisions, covering (a)
the scope of reporting requirements, (b) the manner of reporting,
and (c) the disclosure of information.

Reporting Requirements

Whenever a person receives a written or oral request to take
any action in furtherance or support of a boycott against a friendly
foreign country it must be reported. The request may be to enter
into or implement an agreement. It may involve a solicitation,
directive, legend or instruction asking for information or action (or
inaction). The request must be reported whether or not the action
requested is prohibited, except as the regulations provide.[44] That
essentially means reporting is required if the person knows or has
reason to know that the purpose of the request is to enforce,
implement or otherwise support, further or secure compliance with
the boycott.[45]

When a request is received by a U.S. person located outside the
United States (subsidiary, branch, partnership, affiliate, office or
other controlled permanent foreign establishment), it is reportable
if received in connection with a transaction in interstate or foreign
commerce.[46] A general boycott questionnaire, unrelated to any
specific transaction, must be reported when that person has or
anticipates a business relationship with or in the boycotting
country, also in interstate or foreign commerce.

The reporting requirements apply whether the U.S. person is
an exporter, bank or other financial institution, insurer, freight
forwarder, manufacturer, or other person.[47] If the information about
a country's boycotting requirements is learned by means of the
receipt or review of books, pamphlets, legal texts, exporter's
guidebooks and other similar publications, it is not considered a
reportable request. The same is true of receipt of an unsolicited bid
where there is no intention to respond.[48]

---

[44]   15 C.F.R. § 769.6(a)(1).

[45]   15 C.F.R. § 769.6(a)(2).

[46]   Id., citing 15 C.F.R. §§ 769.1(c) and (d). The definition of "interstate or foreign
commerce" is the subject of a Department of Commerce interpretation in Supplement
No. 8 to Part 769.

[47]   15 C.F.R. § 769.6(a)(3).

[48]   15 C.F.R. § 769.6(a)(4). A definition of "unsolicited invitation to bid" is
included in Supplement No. 11 to Part 769.

Reporting Exemptions

The EAR regulations include ten specific requests that are not reportable. They were added because of the customary use of certain terms for boycott and non-boycott purposes, Congressional mandates for clear guidelines in uncertain areas, and the Department of Commerce's desire to reduce paperwork and costs. The non-reportable requests are:[49]

(i) Request to refrain from shipping goods on a carrier flying the flag of a particular country, or that is owned, chartered, leased or operated by a particular country or its nationals or residents; or a request for certification to such effect;

(ii) Request to ship goods, or refrain from shipping goods, on a prescribed route, or a certification request of either;

(iii) Request for an affirmative statement or certification regarding the country of origin of goods;

(iv) Request for an affirmative statement or certification of supplier's or manufacturer's or service provider's name;

(v) Request to comply with laws of another country except where it requires compliance with that country's boycott laws;

(vi) Request to individual for personal information about himself or family for immigration, passport, visa or employment requirements;

(vii) Request for an affirmative statement or certification stating destination of exports or confirming or indicating the cargo will be unloaded at a particular destination;

(viii) Request for certification from owner, master, charterer, or any employee thereof, that a vessel, aircraft, truck or other transport is eligible, permitted, nor restricted from or allowed to enter, a particular port, country or group of countries under the laws, rules, or regulations of that port, country or countries;

(ix) Request for certification from insurance company stating the issuing company has an agent or representative (plus name and address) in a boycotting country; or

(x) Request to comply with term or condition that vendor bears the risk of loss and indemnify the purchaser if goods are denied entry for any reason if this clause was in use by the purchaser prior to January 18, 1978.

The Department of Commerce periodically surveys domestic concerns to determine the worldwide scope of boycott requests

---

[49]   15 C.F.R. § 769.6(a)(5); see also Supplement No. 10(b) to Part 769.

received by U.S. subsidiaries and controlled affiliates regarding activities outside U.S. commerce.[50] This is intended to cover requests that would be required to be reported, but for the fact that they involve commerce outside the United States. Information collected from U.S. persons will include the number and nature of non-reportable requests received, action requested, action taken, and countries making such requests.

Manner of Reporting Requests

Every request must be reported; however, only the first need be reported when the same request is received in several forms.[51] But each different request regarding the same transaction must be reported. Each U.S. person receiving a request must report the request, but one person may designate another to make the report, such as a parent reporting on behalf of a subsidiary.[52]

Disclosure of Information

The third part of the regulations applying to reporting states that the reports shall become public records, except for "certain proprietary information."[53] The reporting party may certify that the disclosure of information relating to the (1) quantity, (2) description, or (3) value of any articles, materials or supplies (including technical data and other information), may place the company at a competitive disadvantage. In such case the information will not be made public.

But the reporting party must edit the public inspection copy of the accompanying documents as noted below, and the Secretary may reject the request for confidentiality for reasons either of disagreement regarding the competitive disadvantage, or of national interest in not withholding the information.[54] If such decision is made, the party must be given an opportunity to comment.

Because the report is made public, one copy must be submitted intact and the other may be edited in accordance with the above limitations. Any additional material considered confidential may also be deleted, as may be any material not required to be reported.[55] The copy is to be marked "Public Inspection Copy."

---

[50]   15 C.F.R. § 769.6(a)(7).
[51]   15 C.F.R. § 769.6(b)(1).
[52]   15 C.F.R. § 769.6(b)(2).
[53]   15 C.F.R. § 769.6(c)(1).
[54]   Id.
[55]   15 C.F.R. § 769.6(c)(2).

§ 12.12   U.S. Anti-boycott Violations and Enforcement

Violations and enforcement of the anti-boycott laws are subject to the same provisions as violations and enforcement of the export laws.[56] The enforcement of the anti-boycott laws has generated few court decisions. Most have involved issues of constitutionality, creation of private rights of action, or the statute of limitations.[57]

Several persons have had licenses suspended and fines exceeding $5 million have been levied. Most of these cases involved the receipt of requests for information from Arab countries. In instances where the companies had complied with the request, the Department of Commerce and the company usually agreed on a fine as part of a consent decree. The procedures were dealt with administratively, and the decisions are found only in some private reporters.[58] One of the largest civil penalties was imposed in a settlement with Baxter International Inc., in 1993. Baxter, a Swiss subsidiary, and an officer paid a penalty totaling $6,060,600. For all of 2011, eight companies paid penalties totaling only $129,300.

U.S. subsidiaries that carry out boycott activities of foreign parents are within the reach of the provisions. The French L'Oreal, S.A. cosmetics company requested information from two U.S. subsidiaries, Parbel of Florida, Inc. (formerly Helena Rubenstein, Inc.) and Cosmair, Inc., about their business relationships in or with Israel. More than 100 items of information were provided, and no report of the request was made to Commerce. The two subsidiaries (and individual corporate counsel for Cosmair) agreed to fines exceeding $1.4 million in 1995.

§ 12.13   U.S. Private Rights of Action

There is no clear indication whether the EAA includes a private right of action. A Texas federal district court, in *Abrams v. Baylor College of Medicine,*[59] addressed a claim by two Jewish medical students that Baylor University denied them opportunities when it excluded Jews from medical teams it sent to Saudi Arabia.

---

[56]   50 App.U.S.C.A. §§ 2410, 2411 and 2412. See supra, chapter 17. Considerable information on the boycotts is at www.bis.doc.gov, including major cases.

[57]   See United States v. Core Laboratories, Inc., 759 F.2d 480 (5th Cir.1985) (EAA and the statute of limitations); Abrams v. Baylor College of Medicine, 581 F.Supp. 1570 (S.D.Tex.1984), *aff'd* 805 F.2d 528 (5th Cir.1986) (EAA and affirming private right of action); Bulk Oil (ZUG) A.G. v. Sun Co., Inc., 583 F.Supp. 1134 (S.D.N.Y.1983), *aff'd* 742 F.2d 1431 (2d Cir.1984), *cert. denied* 469 U.S. 835, 105 S.Ct. 129, 83 L.Ed.2d 70 (1984) (EAA and rejecting private right).

[58]   See Int'l Boycotts (Business Law Inc.); Boycott L. Bull.

[59]   581 F.Supp. 1570 (S.D.Tex.1984), aff'd 805 F.2d 528 (5th Cir.1986).

The court found an implied right of action by applying the factors in the *Cort v. Ash* decision of the U.S. Supreme Court.[60] The Fifth Circuit upheld the decision. But in *Bulk Oil (ZUG) A.G. v. Sun Co.,* the Second Circuit rejected the existence of a private right of action, affirming a New York federal district court decision involving an accusation of violation of the anti-boycott provisions by failing to deliver oil to Israel.[61] The Seventh Circuit has also rejected private causes of action under U.S. anti-boycott law.[62]

---

[60]   422 U.S. 66, 95 S.Ct. 2080, 45 L.Ed.2d 26 (1975).

[61]   583 F.Supp. 1134 (S.D.N.Y.1983), *aff'd* 742 F.2d 1431 (2d Cir.1984), *cert. denied* 469 U.S. 835, 105 S.Ct. 129, 83 L.Ed.2d 70 (1984).

[62]   Israel Aircraft Ind. v. Sanwa Business Credit Corp., 16 F.3d 198 (7th Cir. 1994).

Chapter 13

THE U.S. FOREIGN CORRUPT PRACTICES ACT*

Table of Sections

§ 13.0 The U.S. Foreign Corrupt Practices Act (FCPA)

The Foreign Corrupt Practices Act of 1977 (FCPA) was enacted to reduce U.S. business participation in making payments or giving of items of value to foreign officials in an attempt to favorably

---

* I am indebted to Prof. Michael Gordon for his work on a prior version of this chapter.

influence government decisions.[1] The FCPA has been strongly enforced. Some 150 U.S. investigations are pending at this writing, encouraged by Dodd-Frank whistleblower rewards. While it has mostly concerned foreign investment practices, it has also been applied where corrupt practices favor U.S. exports. Anyone dealing with the FCPA should read the Department of Justice Resource Guide to the U.S. Foreign Corrupt Practices Act.

One difficulty with the FCPA is defining what constitutes a wrongful payment. Because the payment is made to a foreign official, cultural standards of that official's nation may affect the payment. Conflicts of interest by government officials may be governed by very different notions. While apparently no foreign country has written laws permitting foreign officials to accept bribes to influence their conduct, the "operational code" or unwritten law of many countries makes such conduct commonplace.

The FCPA imposes a U.S. ethic on conduct in the United States and abroad by U.S. persons, and to conduct within the United States by foreign persons. For 20 years, the United States stood almost alone in the global community on foreign corrupt practices law. Finally, in 1997, the Organization for Economic Cooperation and Development (OECD), comprised about 40 of the world's most developed nations, adopted a Convention on Combatting Bribery of Foreign officials in International Business Transactions. In 2004, the United Nations promulgated a widely ratified Convention against Corruption. Neither of these Conventions is a clone of the FCPA (see Section 13.4), but the lonely U.S. position on corrupt practices now has many allies.

§ 13.1   History of the FCPA

The FCPA resulted from disclosures made to the Special Investigator of the Watergate investigations that many U.S. corporations had made payments to foreign officials to favorably influence official government decisions. SEC investigations disclosed a large number of payments by U.S. corporations to foreign officials. Names of alleged recipients were disclosed, causing considerable embarrassment (Prince Bernard of the Netherlands), and even withdrawal or removal from office (Prime Minister

---

[1]   Public Law 95–213, 91 Stat. 1494, Dec.19, 1977. The law firm Sherman & Sterling produces a 400 page FCPA Digest of Cases and Review Releases Relating to Bribes to Foreign Officials under the Foreign Corrupt Practices Act of 1977 that is an excellent assist in dealing with bribes to foreign officials. In 2012, the U.S Department of Justice issued FCPA Guidelines.

Tanaka of Japan[2]) of national leaders. Ultimately, many consent agreements were concluded between the federal government and U.S. companies charged with making questionable payments. The agreements usually provided that names of foreign officials who received payments would be held confidential if the companies would disclose the payments.

Considerable debate ensued in the press, generally attacking the U.S. companies and including little about the way business was conducted in many other nations, where bribes were not only commonplace but a precondition to doing business. There were legitimate concerns that several large U.S. corporations' payments had been extremely harmful to U.S. foreign relations. Some new legislation was inevitable. Morality was at stake. Many foreign observers, especially from other major exporting nations, did not object to the proposed legislation. Preventing U.S. persons from making such payments would give foreign businesses a competitive advantage. Some foreign observers wondered why Americans needed to make such public disclosure of their moments of transgression. The inevitable legislation occurred in 1977 with the enactment of the FCPA.[3] It has had two principal amendments: in 1988 and 1998.

§ 13.2   FCPA Amendments in 1988

1988 amendments removed some of the strictness of the initial Act.[4] The level of conduct required to violate the FCPA was altered in favor of U.S. business by substantial elimination of the "reason to know" standard when payments made to agents might be passed on to foreign officials. The amendment requires that payments to agents must have been knowingly made, and includes a definition of such knowledge. One leading proponent of the original provision in the Senate was so incensed at the change that he suggested that the new loophole established by the amendment was "big enough to fly a Lockheed through." This author does not agree. *See* Section 13.12.

§ 13.3   FCPA Amendments in 1998

The FCPA was amended in 1998 to comply with U.S. obligations under the 1997 OECD Convention on Combating Bribery of Foreign Officials in International Business

---

[2]   Lockheed was alleged to have paid $1.4 million to Prime Minister Tanaka, which led to his removal and imprisonment. See 134 Cong. Rec. S9617–18 (July 14, 1988) (quoting statement of Senator Proxmire).

[3]   Pub.L. 95–213, 91 Stat. 1494, Dec. 19, 1977 (amending the Securities Exchange Act of 1934, 15 U.S.C.A. §§ 78q(b), 78dd, 78ff(a)).

[4]   15 U.S.C.A. §§ 78q(b), 78dd, 78ff(a).

Transactions.[5] The Convention included language, added to the FCPA, making it unlawful to make payments to gain "any improper advantage" in order to obtain or renew business. The FCPA was further amended to expand its scope to cover prohibited acts by "any person." Domestic concerns other than issuers and "other" persons are now covered. This makes the FCPA cover all *foreign* natural and legal persons who commit acts while in the United States.[6]

The amendments also reach payments by U.S. businesses and persons taking place wholly outside the United States, and payments to officials of international agencies. Finally, penalties for non-U.S. citizen employees and agents of U.S. employers and principals, previously limited to civil sanctions, now include the same criminal sanctions as for U.S. citizen employees and agents.

§ 13.4 OECD and United Nations Conventions, British Bribery Act

Transparency International, a European-based NGO, maintains a highly regarded global corruption perception index. *See* www.transparency.org. Every country is rated from very clean (e.g., Denmark) to highly corrupt (e.g., Somalia). Perhaps the most difficult "corruption" to address is that which is culturally ingrained, for example "ttokkap" (rice cake expenses) in Korea and "guanxi" in China. Both the industrial nations of the OECD and the United Nations have attempted to address corruption.

The OECD adopted a Convention on Combatting Bribery of Foreign officials in International Business Transactions in 1997. Enactment of laws in its member countries followed slowly, indeed Britain's Bribery Act did not arrive until 2010. That said, most the OECD membership now has anti-bribery law in place, notably in China, Russia, Nigeria, Brazil, France, Germany, India and Japan. The OECD also recommended prohibiting tax deductions for bribes, a recommendation that Canada and others have followed.

The British Bribery Act of 2010 may have been late in arriving, but is now widely perceived to be one of the most rigorous. It extends not just to payments to foreign officials, but also to private parties. Its coverage is broad in scope (for example, "grease payments" are not exempted) and its criminal and civil liability is strict, extending to essentially all firms doing business in the U.K. Hypothetically, therefore, the BBA reaches U.S. firms with U.K.

---

[5]   Pub.L. 105–366, Nov. 10, 1998 (International Anti-bribery & Fair Competition Act).

[6]   15 U.S.C.A. §§ 78dd–2, 78dd–3.

stock listings or sales offices, and those processing illegal payments via British banks. The BBA governs the activities of such firms around the world, say bribes in India. The Act applies to solicitation as well as receipt of bribes, and has no statute of limitations! It is tempered by an "adequate procedures" compliance defense not found in the FCPA.

The United Nations adopted a Convention against Corruption in 2004. The United States ratified this Convention in 2006, which did not require amendments to the FCPA. Some 170 nations have subscribed to the U.N. Convention, which includes cooperative provisions facilitating the recovery of corrupt payments "hidden" abroad by the officials who received them.

§ 13.5   FCPA—Who Is Covered?

In addition to limiting prohibited practices to certain kinds of payments, the drafters of the Act also had to consider the scope of coverage regarding who would fall within its prohibitions. That meant both which persons would be subject to an action for making prohibited payments, and which persons abroad had to be the recipients of the payments for the transaction to be unlawful. The amendments in 1998 expanded the scope of coverage of payors, extending to "any person", natural or legal, United States or foreign, acting within United States territory. Foreign firms simply using U.S. bank accounts or the U.S. mail are subject to the FCPA. Omitted are foreign persons acting outside the United States. But payments made via U.S. controlled foreign subsidiaries and branches fall within the Act, and good faith efforts to keep non-controlled foreign entities from violating the FCPA must be undertaken. Payments to officials, political parties, party officials, or candidates (except in some one-party states) are covered under the FCPA.

§ 13.6   FCPA—Prohibited and Exempted Payments, Sanctions

The FCPA makes it unlawful for an issuer of registered securities under § 12 of the Securities Exchange Act (SEA), or an issuer required to file reports under § 15(d) of the SEA, to make certain payments to foreign officials or other persons. The FCPA also requires those issuers to maintain accurate financial records which would disclose such payments. The Act additionally extends the scope of prohibited payments to any issuer *or domestic concern* making use of the mails or any means or instrumentality of interstate commerce.[7] This effectively extends liability to all corporations, in a manner not unlike the insider trading provisions of § 10 of the SEA. These rules focus on a shareholder's right to know if its corporation books are inaccurate, if management used corporate money to violate U.S. or foreign laws, if bribes were paid with corporate funds, or if payments were made to consultants with no accountability as to their disbursements.

The current FCPA remains relatively concise. After establishing accounting standards,[8] it prohibits payments by any person to foreign government or international organization officials directly, or by way of third persons, when such payments are for the purpose of influencing any act or decision of the foreign official,[9] inducing the foreign official to act or refrain from acting in violation of the official's duty,[10] inducing the foreign official to use influence with a foreign government or instrumentality to influence that government's or instrumentality's act or decision,[11] or to secure any improper advantage.[12] The beneficiary of the business obtained or retained need not be the person making the corrupt payment.

There is an important exception for routine government action,[13] which is further defined in a separate section.[14] The Act then establishes as an affirmative defense, cases where the payment was lawful under the *written* laws of the foreign country, or was a "reasonable and bona fide expenditure."[15] The Act defines of "foreign official", "public international organization", "knowing" and "routine governmental action."[16]

Section 78dd–1 and § 78dd–2 violations for making illegal payments are governed in these two different provisions, for issuers and domestic concerns, respectively, and their officers, directors, agents and shareholders acting on behalf of the entity. Each section leads to the same levels of penalties.[17]

---

[7]   15 U.S.C.A. §§ 78dd–1(a), 78dd–2(a). The latter part also defines both "domestic concern" and "interstate commerce." See § 78dd–2(h)(1) and (5).

[8]   15 U.S.C.A. § 78m(b).

[9]   15 U.S.C.A. § 78dd–1(a)(1)(A)(i).

[10]   15 U.S.C.A. § 78dd–1(a)(1)(A)(ii).

[11]   15 U.S.C.A. § 78dd–1(a)(1)(B).

[12]   15 U.S.C.A.§§ 78dd–1(a)(1)(A)(iii), 78dd–1(a)(2)(A)(iii), 78dd–1(a)(3)(A)(iii). The content of these provisions is essentially repeated in sections 78dd–2 and 78dd–3.

[13]   15 U.S.C.A. § 78dd–1(b).

[14]   15 U.S.C.A. § 78dd–1(f)(2).

[15]   15 U.S.C.A. § 78dd–1(c).

[16]   15 U.S.C.A. §§ 78dd–1(f), 78dd–2(h). Section 78dd–2(h) also defines "domestic concern" and "interstate commerce."

[17]   15 U.S.C.A. §§ 78ff(c) and 78dd–2(g).

The entities are subject to fines of not more than $2 million or double the intended benefit. The officers, directors, employees, agents, and shareholders acting on behalf of the concerns are subject to fines up to $250,000, or five years' imprisonment, or both, if the violation was willful.[18] Any fine imposed on a person under these provisions may not be paid or indemnified by the company directly or indirectly. These penalties illustrate that the U.S. government is serious about violations of the FCPA.[19] Individual and corporate civil penalties may also be assessed, along with disgorgement of corruptly obtained proceeds and debarment as a federal contractor. *See* Section 13.16 for examples of major fines and penalties secured by the federal government under the FCPA.

§ 13.7   FCPA—Accounting Standards

One approach used in the FCPA to discourage illegal payments is to require issuers subject to the SEA to maintain accounting records that assist in disclosing payments that might violate the substantive sections of the FCPA. The original law generated considerable criticism about standards that threatened harsh penalties for even slight, incorrect accounting entries. The standards further required considerable documentation of foreign transactions. The 1988 amendments addressed what was a concern for "reasonable detail" and "reasonable assurances" in internal accounting controls, and indicate that the Act does not cover technical or insignificant errors in record keeping. But records must be "accurately and fairly" . . . in other words a bribe must recorded as a bribe. Liability is to be imposed on persons who "knowingly circumvent or knowingly fail to implement a system of internal controls or knowingly falsify any book, record or account."[20]

The proof of accounting violations is mostly available in the United States, where the corporate books are located. But the books often disclose little to auditors, since payments may be made to persons who appear to be legitimate foreign consultants, and thus are listed only as payments made to consultants, not to foreign officials.

Section 78m(b) violations, the record-keeping and internal accounting-control standards section, may lead where there is a willful violation, or a willful and knowing making of a false or

---

[18]   Only willful violations are subject to criminal penalties. *See* Trane Co. v. O'Connor Securities, 718 F.2d 26 (2d Cir. 1983).

[19]   Two units of Litton Industries pleaded guilty in 1999 to fraud and conspiracy in making payments to obtain defense business in Greece and Taiwan. Litton agreed to pay $18.5 million to settle the matter (including an amount to reimburse the Department of Justice for the costs of the investigation).

[20]   15 U.S.C.A. § 78m(b)5.

misleading statement in filed applications, statements or reports, to a criminal penalty for individuals of not more than $5,000,000 and not more than 20 years imprisonment, or both.[21] Corporate criminal violations can result in up to $25 million fines or double the intended benefit. Individual and corporate civil penalties may also be assessed, along with disgorgement of corruptly obtained proceeds. *See* Section 13.16 for examples of major fines and penalties secured by the federal government under the FCPA.

§ 13.8   FCPA—What Is Given?

Persons who are subject to the Act may not "make use of the mails or any means or instrumentality of interstate commerce *corruptly*" where the act is "in furtherance of" any one of several actions, including an:

1.   Offer,

2.   Payment,

3.   Promise to pay, or

4.   Authorization of the payment

"of any money".

Or an:

1.   Offer,

2.   Gift,

3.   Promise to give, or

4.   Authorization of the giving

"of anything of value."[22]

Thus, the Act divides numerous "giving" actions between giving either money or anything of value. The fact that something offered, promised or given has a very small value does not remove it from the Act. There is no *de minimis* exemption. The exemptions exist in *to whom* the item is offered, promised or given, or *for what purpose* the item is offered, promised or given.

§ 13.9   FCPA—Acting "Corruptly"

The act of offering, promising or giving must be done *corruptly*. "Corruptly" is not defined in the FCPA. If all of the provisions are met, i.e., a payment is made to a defined foreign official and there is no statutory affirmative defense, does the government nevertheless

---

[21]   15 U.S.C.A. § 78ff(a). An exchange may be fined up to $2,500,000. Proof of no knowledge of the rule or regulation will avoid imprisonment. Id.

[22]   15 U.S.C.A. §§ 78dd–1(a), 78dd–2(a).

have to prove that the act was done corruptly? Or does the giving to a foreign official where there is no statutory defense constitute a corrupt act?

The word "corruptly" seems unnecessary. The FCPA prohibits certain conduct, about which persons might debate endlessly regarding whether it is corrupt conduct. One decision suggests that the word "corruptly" means that the court or jury determines whether the conduct violates the provisions of the Act, rather than meeting some external definition of "corrupt".[23] The party charged must be the one who acts corruptly. Carrying out an employer's instructions might not be acting corruptly.[24] Thus, an employee of a U.S. aircraft-maintenance contractor who made a "gesture" to the chief of maintenance for Nigerian Air Force cargo planes, in the form of purchasing airline tickets for the official's honeymoon, after the contract was awarded, was entitled to a new trial to determine whether the employee met the "corrupt" standard.[25]

An unusual comment in the Senate Committee Report on the 1977 Act stated:

> That the payment may have been first proposed by the recipient rather than the U.S. company does not alter the corrupt purpose on the part of the person paying the bribe. On the other hand true extortion situations would not be covered by this provision since a payment to an official to keep an oil rig from being dynamited should not be held to be made with the requisite corrupt purpose.[26]

This would be a useful defense where there is clearly an attempt to extort money from the company or individual. But it may be very difficult to prove, and may require the kind of dramatic case noted in the Senate Report.

§ 13.10   FCPA—Foreign Officials

The definition of a foreign official has long been debated. Defendants have argued that employees of state-owned or state-controlled companies are not foreign officials under the FCPA. Justice and the SEC disagree.

The offer, promise or gift may not be made to any person in any one of three classes. One class is a payment to any *foreign official* if the offer, promise or gift is either (1) to influence an official act or decision, induce an act or omission in violation of lawful duty, or

---

[23]   *See* United States v. Liebo, 923 F.2d 1308 (8th Cir.1991).

[24]   Id.

[25]   Id.

[26]   Senate Report No. 114, 95th Cong. 10 (1977).

secure any advantage, or (2) to induce the use of the official's influence with a foreign government or instrumentality in order to "affect or influence" any act thereof, and where the ultimate purpose is assisting the issuer in either obtaining or retaining business, or directing business to any person.[27]

The "obtaining or retaining" business language was discussed in *United States v. Liebo*, where the court held the standard had been met.[28] It later came before the court in *United States v. Kay*, where the Fifth Circuit found the "obtaining or retaining" business to mean more than bribes beyond payments sufficient only to "obtain or retain government contracts."[29] But it also held that bribes did not have to rise to the level of influencing awarding contracts to violate the Act.

In addition to defining "knowing", the Act offers some help in defining the term "foreign official."[30] A foreign official is any "officer or employee" of any foreign government, or department, agency or **instrumentality** thereof. "Official" is thus very broadly defined to include the lowest-level employee.[31] Also included are persons acting in an *official capacity* for or on behalf of a government.

Corrupt payments to international organizations and officers or employees of international organizations, including NGOs, were added in 1988. The addition of international organizations substantially expands the scope of the FCPA. When payments to only foreign *government* officials were covered, it was necessary to define "government." That is not always easy. Some entities, such as the Vatican, the PLO, or a territory over which there is some government control, may or may not be considered governments.

Case law suggests that foreign officials cannot be prosecuted under the FCPA.[32] But foreign nationals, otherwise subject to U.S. jurisdiction, fall under its scope.[33]

§ 13.11   FCPA—Foreign Political Party, Official or Candidate

An offer, promise or gift may not be made to any *foreign political party* or *official of that party* or *candidate for political*

---

[27]   15 U.S.C.A. §§ 78dd–1(a)(1), 78dd–2(a)(1).

[28]   923 F.2d 1308 (8th Cir.1991).

[29]   359 F.3d 738 (5th Cir.2004).

[30]   15 U.S.C.A. §§ 78dd–1(f)(1), 78dd–2(h)(2).

[31]   But the exceptions for routine government actions are most likely to apply to payments to relatively low-level employees.

[32]   United States v. Castle, 925 F.2d 831 (5th Cir. 1991).

[33]   Dooley v. United Technologies Corp., 803 F.Supp. 428 (D.D.C. 1992).

office, if it is (1) to influence such party in an official act or decision, induce an act or omission in violation of lawful duty, or secure any improper advantage, or (2) to induce the use of that party's influence with a foreign government or instrumentality to "affect or influence" any act thereof. The ultimate purpose must be to assist in either obtaining or retaining business, or directing business to any person.[34] "Candidate" may be difficult to define, since it may not be clear that a person is a candidate at the time of making a payment. The act does not specifically cover a person intending to become a candidate.

§ 13.12   FCPA—Any Person "While Knowing"

An offer, promise or gift may not be made to *any person,* while *knowing* it will be offered, promised or given to (1) a foreign official, (2) a foreign political party, (3) an official of a foreign political party, or (4) a candidate for foreign political office, where the purpose is the same as in the first two sections above.[35] This third category of persons to whom payments are prohibited governs payments to persons hired as agents or consultants, but adds the very important requirement that a payment to such third party be made "while knowing" that the money or item of value will be passed on to a prohibited person.

In the original Act, the language was "knowing or having reason to know."[36] The "having reason to know" language was the subject of continual criticism by business persons, who believed it created an unfair and ambiguous standard that placed the burden on the business to prove that its conduct was proper. Although proponents of the original language lost the fight to retain it in the 1988 amendments, a broad definition of "knowing" was added to the Act.

The definition of "knowing" states that knowing conduct is where either (1) the person is *aware* of the conduct, that "such circumstance" exists, or the result is "substantially certain" to occur, or (2) the person has a "firm belief" that such circumstance exists or the result is substantially certain to occur.[37] The provision then adds that the knowing standard is met if the person is "aware of a high probability" of the existence of such circumstance, *unless* the person "actually believes" that such circumstance does not exist.[38] The "high probability" language seems to carry the knowing

---

[34]   15 U.S.C.A. §§ 78dd–1(a)(3), 78dd–2(a)(3).

[35]   15 U.S.C.A. §§ 78dd–1(a)(3), 78dd–2(a)(3).

[36]   15 U.S.C.A. §§ 78dd–1(a)(3), 78dd–2(a)(3) (1977).

[37]   15 U.S.C.A. §§ 78dd–1(f)(2)(A), 78dd–2(h)(3)(A).

[38]   15 U.S.C.A. §§ 78dd–1(f)(2)(B), 78dd–2(h)(3)(B).

standard into the territory of a reason to know standard . . . and in any event hardly creates a loophole "big enough to fly a Lockheed through." Willful blindness or conscious avoidance are not likely to escape the FCPA.

§ 13.13   FCPA—"Grease" Payments

Probably many business persons have paid a small amount to a customs official to expedite the processing of goods in danger of spoilage or needed for an impatient customer. Congress did not wish to label as corrupt the myriad of minor "grease" payments made to government officials to do what they are supposed to do, but in a shorter period of time. The result is that corruption has a *de minimis* element, but it is not defined by a dollar amount. But even *de minimis* payments may be subject to the accounting requirements of the Act.

The original Act exempted payments for acts that were ministerial, using language that exempted payments to foreign government employees "whose duties are essentially ministerial or clerical."[39] The 1988 amendments changed that language to create an exception for "facilitating or expediting" payments when the purpose is to "expedite or to secure the performance of a routine governmental action."[40] A "routine governmental action" is defined in the Act,[41] in four specific sections and one general subsection. Payments are specifically allowed made when:

1.   Obtaining permits, licenses or other official documents which are part of the process of qualifying to do business in the country,

2.   Processing papers such as visas and work orders,

3.   Providing police protection, mail pick-up and delivery, or scheduling inspections which are associated with the performance of a contract or related to transit of goods across country, and

4.   Providing telephone service, power and water supply, loading and unloading cargo, or protecting perishables from deterioration.

A final, fifth class encompasses "actions of a similar nature."

Any decision by a foreign official about the terms of a new contract, the awarding of such contract, continuing business, or any

---

[39]   15 U.S.C.A. § 77dd–1(b) (1977).
[40]   15 U.S.C.A. §§ 78dd–1(b), 78dd–2(b).
[41]   15 U.S.C.A. §§ 78dd–1(f)(3), 78dd–2(h)(4).

action by any official involved in the process of new or renewal business is specifically **not** exempted.[42]

There is a very large gap between what is specifically allowed and what is specifically disallowed. One of the least clear areas involves the extent to which foreign officials may be entertained. Entertaining is not always motivated solely by courtesy. Foreign officials are usually entertained as part of the process of receiving the award of a contract, or establishing or continuing a business. The line of legitimacy must fall somewhere between reasonable expenses associated with normal business, and unreasonable expenses associated with unreasonable influence. Finding that line is helped by the special provisions providing affirmative defenses.[43]

§ 13.14   FCPA—Payments Lawful Under "Written" Laws

The FCPA establishes two basic classes of affirmative defenses. The first is when the payment, gift, offer or promise is lawful under the *written* laws and regulations of the foreign country.[44] Since nations rarely enact laws giving legitimacy to what may be common but corrupt practices of its officials, this section is likely to be of little use. Were it to allow payments where the *unwritten* laws, i.e., the expected and common practice, mandate payments, the loophole would be considerably wider than merely enough to fly a Lockheed through.

To be safe, counsel should obtain an opinion in writing from foreign local counsel that identifies the written law or regulation that allows a payment. It is of course possible that payments may be allowed to political campaigns under local written law, but not personally to serving officials to influence their official decisions.

§ 13.15   FCPA—"Reasonable and Bona Fide Expenditures"

The second specific affirmative defense is when the payment, gift, offer or promise is a "reasonable and bona fide expenditure, such as travel and lodging expenses" that a foreign official incurs, and which is *directly* related to either (1) the promotion, demonstration or explanation of products or services, or (2) the execution or performance of a contract.[45] While the first part of this section broadens the permissible payments, the second part

---

[42]   15 U.S.C.A. §§ 78dd–1(f)(3)(B), 78dd–2(h)(4)(B).
[43]   15 U.S.C.A. §§ 78dd–1(c), 78dd–2(c).
[44]   15 U.S.C.A. § 77dd–1(c)(1).
[45]   15 U.S.C.A. § 77dd–1(c)(2).

narrows it. Noticeably excluded are payments when the contract is being considered, either initially or for renewal. But a carefully crafted corporate policy might provide that even in the advance of obtaining a contract or having it renewed, payments to foreign officials are exclusively based on promotions, demonstrations and/or explanations relating to the performance of the contract if granted or renewed.

The Department of Justice issued an Opinion approving some planned paid travel for Chinese journalists to a Trace International event in China[46]. This DOJ procedure may be the best process to follow for travel expenses about which a corporation has some doubt.

§ 13.16   FCPA—U.S. Enforcement Actions

The severity of penalties for violations of the FCPA (see Sections 13.6 and 7) mandates close consideration of its provisions by all persons doing business abroad. Subsidiaries owned or controlled by publicly-traded U.S. companies fall within its jurisdictional scope. Violations of the FCPA are dealt with principally by the SEC (which monitors the record keeping) and the Department of Justice (which enforces the antibribery provisions). In the past decade, there has been a substantial increase in FCPA prosecutions. In 2010, the DOJ and SEC collected over $1.8 billion in FCPA fines and penalties. Comparatively few actions brought by the Department of Justice have reached the appellate courts. One example, involving the International Harvester Company, alleged participation in a series of charges relating to dealings with officials of Petroleos Mexicanos (PEMEX), the national oil company.[47]

Potentially corrupt payments by U.S. pharmaceutical companies in China have received extensive scrutiny. But it is not only the largest U.S. corporations which have been the subject of actions. Another action involved an individual who owned a postage stamp concession for a Caribbean island and who paid for flights for citizens to return to the island to vote for the reelection of the president, allegedly to influence the government to renew the concession.[48]

---

[46]   See 43 Int'l Lawyer 783 (2009). U.S. Dep't of Justice, Foreign Corrupt Practices Act Review, Opinion Procedure Release No. 08–03 (July 11, 2008).

[47]   The company pleaded guilty to conspiracy to violate the FCPA. See McLean v. International Harvester Co., 902 F.2d 372 (5th Cir.1990); McLean v. International Harvester Co., 817 F.2d 1214 (5th Cir.1987); Executive Legal Summary No. 5, Business Laws, Inc. 100.03 (Hancock ed., Oct. 1988).

[48]   Executive Legal Summary No. 5, Business Laws, Inc., 100.03, 100.04 (Hancock ed., Oct. 1988).

Investigations are often reported in the news, suggesting that U.S. persons and companies have not ceased making payments to foreign officials.[49] Some of the most controversial allegations have involved IBM and Mexico in 1993, during the sensitive negotiations for the North American Free Trade Agreement.[50] An Iranian-born British businessman was retained by IBM to be its agent in a tender bid for a new air-control system in Mexico City. The agent alleged that soon after a meeting with several Mexican officials at which they tried to obtain a $1 million bribe, IBM's bid was rejected and the contract given to the French Thomson Company. The agents' subsequent public disclosure and numerous newspaper articles led nowhere, but caused a sensation in Mexico. The Minister of Communications was ousted in a cabinet reorganization. The agent alleged that the Mexican government later tried to buy him off. IBM did not support the agent in his claims, and settled with the agent out of court.

The whole episode illustrates many problems. The U.S. government showed no inclination to become involved or investigate the matter. There were foreign policy problems, NAFTA priorities, perhaps a sense that the whole story was not implausible, but a realization that this is how things work. Aliases or no names, secret meetings, finger pointing, and leaks to the press are all part of the game. No one seems to have asked how the French Thomson Company got the bid so quickly after IBM was rejected.

IBM was later again in the news regarding an investigation of bribes in Argentina to obtain a $250 million contract to modernize the computer system for the Banco de la Nación.[51] IBM allegedly paid bribes to CCR, a computer systems company, in connection with obtaining a contract with Nación, money which soon found its way into Swiss accounts.[52]

Some significant recent prosecutions and settlements include Lucent Technologies, Inc., involving payments to Chinese officials and resulting in Lucent agreeing to pay penalties of $137 million. KBR/Halliburton settled for $579 million in 2009, BAE for $400 million in 2010, Johnson & Johnson for $70 million in 2011, Total of France $398 million in 2013, Alcoa $384 million in 2014 for bribes in Bahrain, and Hewlett-Packard $108 million in 2014 for bribes in

---

[49]   See, e.g., Some Weapons Makers Are Said To Continue Illicit Foreign Outlays, Wall St.J., Nov. 5, 1993, at 1, discussing GE, Teledyne Inc., Litton Industries, Inc., Loral Corp., and United Technologies Corp. problems.

[50]   See The Independent, August 29, 1993, Sunday Review at 2; The Financial Post, Oct. 27, 1993, at 13.

[51]   National Law Journal, Mar. 3, 1997, at B16.

[52]   Financial Times, Oct. 19, 1995, at 5.

Russia, Mexico and Poland. Daimler settled in 2010 with the SEC, agreeing to pay $185 million in FCPA fines ($96.3 million criminal and $91.4 million civil). Smaller sums have also been collected from AGA Medical Corporation involving China a $2 million fine, and Aibel Group Limited involving Nigeria and an agreed to $4.2 million fine.

Siemens AG paid bribes primarily in Argentina, Bangladesh and Venezuela and an agreed to fine of $800 million. The 2008 Siemens' FCPA settlement remains the largest to date. German and 20 other anti-bribery law enforcement authorities also pursued Siemans, which is reported to have spent over $1 billion in legal and accounting fees. The Siemens cases involved the Oil-for-Food program, which resulted in four other settlements against Akzo Nobel of the Netherlands for $3 million in penalties, against Flowserve Corporation for $10.55 million of criminal and civil penalties, against AB Volvo resulting in $12.6 million in penalties, and against Fiat for $17.8 million civil and criminal penalties.

There have also been increased individual prosecutions, including some high profile persons. Albert Stanley, CEO of KBR, a subsidiary of Halliburton, agreed to serve seven years in prison and pay $10.8 million in restitution. In 2010, the FBI conducted its first FCPA sting operation ("Shot Show"), resulting in the arrest of 22 executives from military and law enforcement products companies. The government has also seized personal assets (pensions, cars and homes) of violators as forfeited proceeds of bribery. Corporate compliance personnel may need prior DOJ/SEC approval, and government monitors given unfettered access to records and compliance processes.

A New York Times article in December 2012 covered more than three full pages describing bribes allegedly made by Wal-Mart in Mexico. The payments lead to a Department of Justice investigation, an expensive global in-house review of payments' practices by Wal-Mart (still costing $1 million **a day** in 2013), and a dramatic drop in the value of its stock.

§ 13.17   FCPA—Consent Decrees

Few of the FCPA cases investigated ever come to court.[53] Most cases are resolved by consent decrees. Corporations prefer to accept a negotiated fine rather than litigate in the federal courts.[54]

---

[53]   See United States v. McLean, 738 F.2d 655 (5th Cir.1984), *cert. denied* 470 U.S. 1050, 105 S.Ct. 1748, 84 L.Ed.2d 813 (1985).

[54]   The FCPA Reporter includes information regarding consent decrees and guilty pleas. The names of corporations charged are well known, including such

Furthermore, corporations usually prefer to avoid the publicity accompanying charges of making foreign payments corruptly. There is also the problem that the payment usually occurs in a foreign country and proof of the payment is difficult to establish. The foreign country is not likely to assist in allowing discovery or taking depositions.

§ 13.18   FCPA—DOJ Review Process

The FCPA requires the Department of Justice to establish a procedure allowing persons to request an opinion about proposed activity that might create some FPCA concern.[55] The first step is for the person or company to present to the Department of Justice details of the proposed transaction. The person or company may only rely upon a review letter signed by the Assistant Attorney General (or delegate) in charge of the criminal division. The procedure has not been used very often, possibly because of concern about identifying foreign officials and the consequences if the review request information is not held confidential.[56]

The 1988 amendments provide more definitional information of what may be allowed, and may lead to even less use of the review procedure. The DOJ has however rejuvenated the opinion procedure, and issued several opinions addressing disclosures, takeovers, acquisitions by auction, and payment of some travel expenses.[57]

§ 13.19   U.S. Private Rights of Action

There have not been many suits charging violations of the FCPA initiated by private individuals or companies against other private parties. One federal circuit court has held that there is no private right of action under the FCPA.[58] The case involved

---

companies as Ashland Oil, General Electric, Goodyear International, International Harvester, and Lockheed Martin.

[55]   15 U.S.C.A. §§ 78dd–1(e), 78dd–2(f). The review procedure is contained in 28 C.F.R. § 50.18.

[56]   Furthermore, information provided in a review request might be used against the person in a criminal prosecution. See John W. Bagby, Enforcement of the Accounting Standards in the Foreign Corrupt Practices Act, 21 Am.Bus.L.J. 213 (1983).

[57]   See 43 Int'l Lawyer 782–784 (2009).

[58]   Lamb v. Phillip Morris, Inc., 915 F.2d 1024 (6th Cir.1990), *cert. denied* 498 U.S. 1086, 111 S.Ct. 961, 112 L.Ed.2d 1048 (1991). See also Citicorp Int'l Trading Co., Inc. v. Western Oil & Refining Co., 771 F.Supp. 600 (S.D.N.Y.1991) (applying the well established four-part Cort v. Ash test to determine that there is no private cause of action); Shields on Behalf of Sundstrand Corp. v. Erickson, 710 F.Supp. 686 (N.D.Ill.1989) (violations of financial and accounting controls do not give rise to private right); Lewis v. Sporck, 612 F.Supp. 1316 (N.D.Cal.1985) (same conclusion).

donations Philip Morris allegedly promised a Venezuelan Children's Foundation (the wife of the President of Venezuela was the president of the Foundation) for benefits to Philip Morris in obtaining Venezuelan tobacco. Two U.S. tobacco producers sued Philip Morris for harm caused by the alleged violation of the FCPA (and antitrust law).

The *Lamb* decision is influential and law in the Sixth Circuit, but may not be the last word on the issue. With the recent substantial increase in enforcement by several governments, there may be a significant increase in bribery related private civil litigation. Shareholder derivative suits have become common once a FCPA investigation becomes public. Breach of fiduciary duty lawsuits under ERISA have also been pursued by pensioners.

§ 13.20   U.S. Employee Suits

The original 1977 Act included what was known as the Eckhardt provision, which did not allow government actions to be brought against employees without first going against the employer. The amendments in 1988 reversed this and allow such actions. An employer may now urge the government to bring suit directly against the employee who made the payment, even if the payment was authorized by other higher-level officers. The possibility of a scapegoat is back. But the scapegoat employee may not be without a remedy. That employee is likely to be or soon become a *former* employee, and may have an action against the company. Employees who are dismissed for refusing to comply with orders to make foreign payments may bring unlawful discharge suits, usually in the form of a breach of contract action, or become whistle-blowers and tell all to the government.[59]

Ashland Oil Inc., learned that firing an employee for refusing to make an illegal payment abroad is costly.[60] Ashland's vice-president William McKay was instructed but refused to make an illegal payment to an official in Oman. McKay later cooperated with SEC and IRS investigations of the payment. Another executive, Harry Williams, was sympathetic to McKay's attempt to change the corporate policy at Ashland. Both were soon no longer employed. They sued Ashland for wrongful discharge and received a verdict of nearly $70 million, later settled for $25 million.

A key to the settlement was a provision in McKay's employment contract that he would not be compelled to make

---

[59]   A whistle-blower's experience at GE is described in Some Weapons Makers Are Said To Continue Illicit Foreign Outlays, Wall St.J., Nov. 5, 1993, at 1.

[60]   See Marshall Sella, More Big Bucks in Jury Verdicts, 75 A.B.A. Journal 69 (July 1989). See also Williams v. Hall, 683 F.Supp. 639 (E.D.Ky.1988).

unlawful payments. It is an appropriate employment contract provision for an officer, because many states do not allow suits for termination in the absence of a contractual provision. Any suit commenced under such a contract provision would be based on the contract and not the FCPA. It would therefore not face the uncertain issue noted above of bringing private suits under the Act. Because it is a suit based on breach of the employment contract, it requires inquiry only regarding the company's act of demanding a payment that, if made, would be a violation.[61]

The FCPA itself does not provide any basis for a corporate employee to bring a claim against the corporation where the corporation appears to have made the employee the scapegoat for allegedly unlawful payments.[62] Nevertheless, Teledyne Systems faced another possible use of the FCPA: Whistle-blower suits. A significant military contractor, Teledyne became involved in several whistle-blower suits in the early 1990s. One filed by a former program manager for Teledyne in the Middle East alleged a payment to an Egyptian general to help obtain Air Force contracts.[63] Whistleblower awards under the Dodd-Frank Act are possible.

§ 13.21   U.S. Suits Charging Competitor with Violation of FCPA

A person or company believing that a competitor violated the FCPA and obtained business at the company's expense has several choices. First, a direct suit charging a violation of the FCPA may fail as in the case of the Philip Morris experience discussed above, because it is an attempt to bring a private cause of action.[64] Second, a suit might be based on violations of antitrust laws. A third choice is a violation of the Racketeer Influenced and Corrupt Organizations Act (RICO).[65] In each of the latter two actions, the corrupt payment would be *evidence* of the wrong alleged, but not used as the basis of the suit, and thus the suit would not fail as a disallowed private right of action. A fourth possible cause of action

---

[61]   See also Pratt v. Caterpillar Tractor Co., 149 Ill.App.3d 588, 102 Ill.Dec. 900, 500 N.E.2d 1001 (1986), *appeal denied* 114 Ill.2d 556, 107 Ill.Dec. 68, 506 N.E.2d 959 (1987), holding that the FCPA did not create a basis for a state claim of retaliatory discharge.

[62]   McLean v. International Harvester Co., 817 F.2d 1214 (5th Cir.1987), *appeal after remand* 902 F.2d 372 (5th Cir.1990).

[63]   See At Teledyne, A Chorus of Whistle-Blowers, Business Week, Dec. 14, 1992, at 40.

[64]   Lamb v. Phillip Morris, Inc., 915 F.2d 1024 (6th Cir.1990), *cert. denied* 498 U.S. 1086, 111 S.Ct. 961, 112 L.Ed.2d 1048 (1991).

[65]   18 U.S.C.A. §§ 1961–1968.

would be for tortious interference with a current or prospective business relationship.[66]

A RICO action was brought in *W.S. Kirkpatrick & Co., Inc. v. Environmental Tectonics Corp., Int'l.*[67] Environmental Tectonics was an unsuccessful bidder for a contract with the Nigerian Air Force. The company complained that Kirkpatrick had paid unlawful bribes to Nigerian officials. The company sued under the federal RICO statute. The court ruled that the act of state doctrine did not apply because the lawfulness of acts of a foreign government in its own territory were not at issue, but only the motives of foreign officials in accepting payments. The case was remanded. RICO thus may be an effective method for private suits involving violations of the FCPA.

Facing litigation by dismissed employees who refused to make illegal payments, and by competitors injured by such payments, not to mention multiple government prosecutions, companies may find it better to stop such payments rather than attempt to hide them. Many firms have developed serious internal policies and training programs which are intended both to prevent company officials from making such payments abroad, and to assure that they are in fact not made.

§ 13.22   FCPA Compliance Programs

The severity of sanctions and rise in FCPA proceedings over the past decade, combined with minimal jurisdictional requirements and major reputational and corrective action costs, have generated widespread adoption of company compliance policies and programs. Online and in-person training of all employees who might have contact with foreign officials has become commonplace. Such training sessions are repeated regularly, and placed in personnel files.

Vendors, customs brokers, transport carriers, construction and other service providers of U.S. corporations engaged in international business transactions are often subject to FCPA training requirements. Such third parties must also frequently submit to FCPA audits, and sign affidavits as to compliance and awareness of any FCPA risks. Some firms refuse to write checks to

---

[66]   See discussion in Citicorp Int'l Trading Co., Inc. v. Western Oil & Refining Co., Inc., 771 F.Supp. 600 (S.D.N.Y.1991).

[67]   493 U.S. 400, 110 S.Ct. 701, 107 L.Ed.2d 816 (1990) (antitrust laws). See Town of Kearny v. Hudson Meadows Urban renewal, 829 F.2d 1263 (3d Cir. 1987) (civil RICO) and United States v. Rubicam, 741 F.Supp. 334 (D.Conn. 1990) (Travel Act).

individuals, only businesses or governments, and refuse to make any grease payments.

International mergers and acquisitions, as a matter of due diligence, now routinely review of FCPA compliance risks. The surviving entity assumes FCPA liabilities. And, of course, record keeping and internal control compliance programs are essential to adhering to the strict FCPA accounting rules.

§ 13.23   Text of the Foreign Corrupt Practices Act

Public Law 95–213, 91 Stat. 1494, Dec. 19, 1977 (amending The Securities Exchange Act of 1934, 15 U.S.C.A. §§ 78q(b), 78dd, 78ff(a) (1976)); as amended by Public Law 100–418, 102 Stat. 1107, Aug. 23, 1988; as amended by Public Law 105–366, Nov. 10, 1998 (International Anti-Bribery & Fair Competition Act)

15 U.S.C. § 78m(b)

Accounting Standards

* * *

(2) Every issuer which has a class of securities registered pursuant to section 78*l* of this title and every issuer which is required to file reports pursuant to section 78o(d) of this title shall—

(A) make and keep books, records, and accounts, which, in reasonable detail, accurately and fairly reflect the transactions and dispositions of the assets of the issuer; and

(B) devise and maintain a system of internal accounting controls sufficient to provide reasonable assurances that—

(i) transactions are executed in accordance with management's general or specific authorization;

(ii) transactions are recorded as necessary (I) to permit preparation of financial statements in conformity with generally accepted accounting principles or any other criteria applicable to such statements, and (II) to maintain accountability for assets;

(iii) access to assets is permitted only in accordance with management's general or specific authorization; and

(iv) the recorded accountability for assets is compared with the existing assets at reasonable intervals and appropriate action is taken with respect to any differences.

* * *

15 U.S.C. § 78dd–1

Prohibited foreign trade practices by issuers

(a) **Prohibition.** It shall be unlawful for any issuer which has a class of securities registered pursuant to section 78*l* of this title or which is required to file reports under section 78*o*(d) of this title, or for any officer, director, employee, or agent of such issuer or any stockholder thereof acting on behalf of such issuer, to make use of the mails or any means or instrumentality of interstate commerce corruptly in furtherance of an offer, payment, promise to pay, or authorization of the payment of any money, or offer, gift, promise to give, or authorization of the giving of anything of value to—

(1) any foreign official for purposes of—

(A)(i) influencing any act or decision of such foreign official in his official capacity, (ii) inducing such foreign official to do or omit to do any act in violation of the lawful duty of such official, or (iii) securing any improper advantage; or

(B) inducing such foreign official to use his influence with a foreign government or instrumentality thereof to affect or influence any act or decision of such government or instrumentality,

in order to assist such issuer in obtaining or retaining business for or with, or directing business to, any person;

* * *

(3) any person, while knowing that all or a portion of such money or thing of value will be offered, given, or promised, directly or indirectly, to any foreign official, to any foreign political party or official thereof, or to any candidate for foreign political office, for purposes of—

(A)(i) influencing any act or decision of such foreign official, * * * in his or its official capacity, (ii) inducing such foreign official, * * * to do or omit to do any act in violation of the lawful duty of such foreign official, * * *, or (iii) securing any improper advantage; or

(B) inducing such foreign official * * * to use his or its influence with a foreign government or instrumentality thereof to affect or influence any act or decision of such government or instrumentality,

in order to assist such issuer in obtaining or retaining business for or with, or directing business to, any person.

(b) Exception for routine governmental action. Subsections (a) and (g) shall not apply to any facilitating or expediting payment to a foreign official, political party, or party official the purpose of which is to expedite or to secure the performance of a routine governmental action by a foreign official, political party, or party official.

(c) Affirmative defenses. It shall be an affirmative defense to actions under subsection (a) or (g) that—

(1) the payment, gift, offer, or promise of anything of value that was made, was lawful under the written laws and regulations of the foreign official's * * * country; or

(2) the payment, gift, offer, or promise of anything of value that was made, was a reasonable and bona fide expenditure, such as travel and lodging expenses, incurred by or on behalf of a foreign official * * * and was directly related to—

(A) the promotion, demonstration, or explanation of products or services; or

(B) the execution or performance of a contract with a foreign government or agency thereof.

(d) Guidelines by the Attorney General. Not later than one year after August 23, 1988, the Attorney General, after consultation with the Commission, the Secretary of Commerce, the United States Trade Representative, the Secretary of State, and the Secretary of the Treasury, and after obtaining the views of all interested persons through public notice and comment procedures, shall determine to what extent compliance with this section would be enhanced and the business community would be assisted by further clarification of the preceding provisions of this section and may, based on such determination and to the extent necessary and appropriate, issue—

(1) guidelines describing specific types of conduct, associated with common types of export sales arrangements and business contracts, which for purposes of the Department of Justice's present enforcement policy, the Attorney General determines would be in conformance with the preceding provisions of this section; and

(2) general precautionary procedures which issuers may use on a voluntary basis to conform their conduct to the Department of Justice's present enforcement policy regarding the preceding provisions of this section.

* * *

(e) Opinions of the Attorney General. (1) The Attorney General, after consultation with appropriate departments and agencies of the United States and after obtaining the views of all interested persons through public notice and comment procedures, shall establish a procedure to provide responses to specific inquiries by issuers concerning conformance of their conduct with the Department of Justice's present enforcement policy regarding the preceding provisions of this section. * * *

(f) Definitions. For purposes of this section:

(1)(A) The term "foreign official" means any officer or employee of a foreign government or any department, agency, or instrumentality thereof, or of a public international organization, or any person acting in an official capacity for or on behalf of any such government or department, agency, or instrumentality, or for or on behalf of any such public international organization.

(B) For purposes of subparagraph (A), the term "public international organization" means—

(i) an organization that is designated by Executive Order pursuant to section 1 of the International Organizations Immunities Act (22 U.S.C. § 288); or

(ii) any other international organization that is designated by the President by Executive order for the purposes of this section, effective as of the date of publication of such order in the Federal Register.

(2)(A) A person's state of mind is "knowing" with respect to conduct, a circumstance, or a result if—

(i) such person is aware that such person is engaging in such conduct, that such circumstance exists, or that such result is substantially certain to occur; or

(ii) such person has a firm belief that such circumstance exists or that such result is substantially certain to occur.

(B) When knowledge of the existence of a particular circumstance is required for an offense, such knowledge is established if a person is aware of a high probability of the existence of such circumstance, unless the person actually believes that such circumstance does not exist.

(3)(A) The term "routine governmental action" means only an action which is ordinarily and commonly performed by a foreign official in—

(i) obtaining permits, licenses, or other official documents to qualify a person to do business in a foreign country;

(ii) processing governmental papers, such as visas and work orders;

(iii) providing police protection, mail pick-up and delivery, or scheduling inspections associated with contract performance or inspections related to transit of goods across country;

(iv) providing phone service, power and water supply, loading and unloading cargo, or protecting perishable products or commodities from deterioration; or

(v) actions of a similar nature.

(B) The term "routine governmental action" does not include any decision by a foreign official whether, or on what terms, to award new business to or to continue business with a particular party, or any action taken by a foreign official involved in the decisionmaking process to encourage a decision to award new business to or continue business with a particular party.

(g) Alternative Jurisdiction

(1)   It shall also be unlawful for any issuer organized under the laws of the United States, or a State, territory, possession, or commonwealth of the United States or a political subdivision thereof and which has a class of securities registered pursuant to section 12 of this title or which is required to file reports under section 15(d) of this title, or for any United States person that is an officer, director, employee, or agent of such issuer or a stockholder thereof acting on behalf of such issuer, to corruptly do any act outside the United States in furtherance of an offer, payment, promise to pay, or authorization of the payment of any money, or offer, gift, promise to give, or authorization of the giving of anything of value to any of the persons or entities set forth in paragraphs (1), (2), and (3) of this subsection (a) of this section for the purposes set forth therein, irrespective of whether such issuer or such officer, director, employee, agent, or stockholder makes use of the mails or any means or instrumentality of interstate commerce in furtherance of such offer, gift, payment, promise, or authorization.

(2) As used in this subsection, the term "United States person" means a national of the United States (as defined in section 101 of the Immigration and Nationality Act (8 U.S.C. § 1101)) or any corporation, partnership, association, joint-stock company, business trust, unincorporated organization, or sole proprietorship organized under the laws of the United States or any State, territory, possession, or commonwealth of the United States, or any political subdivision thereof.

15 U.S.C. § 78dd–2

Prohibited foreign trade practices by domestic concerns

(a) Prohibition. It shall be unlawful for any domestic concern, other than an issuer which is subject to section 78dd–1 of this title. [At this point, the language for the most part follows that of section 77dd–1, except injunctive relief is specifically allowed. Domestic concerns include individuals who are citizens, nationals or residents of the United States, or essentially any form of business with a principal place of business in the United States, or organized in one of the United States, or a territory, possession or commonwealth of the United States.]

* * *

(g) Penalties

(1)(A) Any domestic concern that is not a natural person and that violates subsection (a) or (i) [alternative jurisdiction] of this section shall be fined not more than $2,000,000.

(B) Any domestic concern that is not a natural person and that violates subsection (a) or (i) of this section shall be subject to a civil penalty of not more than $10,000 imposed in an action brought by the Attorney General.

(2)(A) Any natural person that is an officer, director, employee, or agent of a domestic concern, or stockholder acting on behalf of such domestic concern, who willfully violates subsection (a) or (i) of this section shall be fined not more than $100,000 or imprisoned not more than 5 years, or both.

(B) Any natural person that is an officer, director, employee, or agent of a domestic concern, or stockholder acting on behalf of such domestic concern, who violates subsection (a) or (i) of this section shall be subject to a civil penalty of not more than $10,000 imposed in an action brought by the Attorney General.

(3) Whenever a fine is imposed under paragraph (2) upon any officer, director, employee, agent, or stockholder of a domestic concern, such fine may not be paid, directly or indirectly, by such domestic concern.

* * *

15 U.S.C. § 78dd–3

Prohibited foreign trade practices by persons other than issuers or domestic concerns

(a) Prohibition. It shall be unlawful for any person other than an issuer that is subject to section 30A of the Securities Exchange Act of 1934 or a domestic concern, (as defined in section 104 of this Act), or for any officer, director, employee, or agent of such person or any stockholder thereof acting on behalf of such person, while in the territory of the United States, corruptly to make use of the mails or any means or instrumentality of interstate commerce or to do any other act in furtherance of an offer, payment, promise to pay, or authorization of the payment of any money, or offer, gift, promise to give, or authorization of the giving of anything of value to—[At this point, the language follows that of active 78dd–1, except injunctive relief similar to that in section 78dd–2.]

* * *

(e) Penalties

(1)(A) Any juridical person that violates subsection (a) of this section shall be fined not more than $2,000,000.

(B) Any juridical person that violates subsection (a) of this section shall be subject to a civil penalty of not more than $10,000 imposed in an action brought by the Attorney General.

(2)(A) Any natural person who willfully violates subsection (a) of this section shall be fined not more than $100,000 or imprisoned not more than 5 years, or both.

(B) Any natural person who violates subsection (a) of this section shall be subject to a civil penalty of not more than $10,000 imposed in an action brought by the Attorney General.

(3) Whenever a fine is imposed under paragraph (2) upon any officer, director, employee, agent, or stockholder of a person, such fine may not be paid, directly or indirectly, by such person.

(f) Definitions. For purposes of this section:

(1) The term "person," when referring to an offender, means any natural person other than a. national of the United States (as defined in 8 U.S.C. § 1101) or any corporation, partnership, association, joint-stock company, business trust, unincorporated organization, or sole proprietorship organized under the law of a foreign nation or a political subdivision thereof.

* * *

15 U.S.C. § 78ff

Penalties

(a) Willful violations; false and misleading statements. Any person who willfully violates any provision of this chapter (other than section 78dd–1 of this title), or any rule or regulation thereunder the violation of which is made unlawful or the observance of which is required under the terms of this chapter, or any person who willfully and knowingly makes, or causes to be made, any statement in any application, report, or document required to be filed under this chapter or any rule or regulation thereunder or any undertaking contained in a registration statement as provided in subsection (d) of section 78o of this title, or by any self-regulatory organization in connection with an application for membership or participation therein or to become associated with a member thereof, which statement was false or misleading with respect to any material fact, shall upon conviction be fined not more than $1,000,000, or imprisoned not more than 10 years, or both, except that when such person is a person other than a natural person, a fine not exceeding $2,500,000 may be imposed; but no person shall be subject to imprisonment under this section for the violation of any rule or regulation if he proves that he had no knowledge of such rule or regulation.

* * *

(c) Violations by issuers, officers, directors, stockholders, employees, or agents of issuers

(1)(A) Any issuer that violates subsection (a) or (g) of Section 30A of this title shall be fined not more than $2,000,000.

(B) Any issuer that violates subsection (a) or (g) of Section 30A of this title shall be subject to a civil penalty of not more than $10,000 imposed in an action brought by the Commission.

(2)(A) Any officer, director, employee, or agent of an issuer, or stockholder acting on behalf of such issuer, who willfully violates subsection (a) or (g) of Section 30A of this title shall be fined not more than $10,000, or imprisoned not more than 5 years, or both.

(B) Any officer, director, employee, or agent of an issuer, or stockholder action on behalf of such issuer, who violates subsection (a) or (g) of Section 30A of this title shall be subject to a civil penalty of not more than $10,000 imposed in an action brought by the Commission.

(3) Whenever a fine is imposed under paragraph (2) upon any officer, director, employee, agent or stockholder of an issuer, such fine may not be paid, directly or indirectly, by such issuer.

Chapter 14

UNILATERAL U.S. SECTION 301 TRADE SANCTIONS

Table of Sections

Sec.

§ 14.1   Foreign Country Practices and U.S. Export Access

Section 301 of the Trade Act of 1974 (19 U.S.C. 2411) is one of the most highly political remedies concerning United States trade relations. Basically, this section applies when United States rights or benefits under international trade agreements are at risk or when foreign nations engage in unjustifiable, unreasonable or discriminatory conduct. Thus Section 301 is primarily focused on the activities of foreign governments. Although it has been used to protect United States markets from foreign imports, Section 301 has been most notably applied to open up foreign markets to United States exports, investments and intellectual property rights. The focus has been on foreign market access for U.S. goods and services.

Most Section 301 proceedings have been resolved through negotiations leading to alteration of foreign country practices. Ultimately, if the President or United States Trade Representative (USTR) is not satisfied with any negotiated result in connection with a Section 301 complaint, the United States may undertake unilateral retaliatory trade measures. Unlike subsidy, dumping, and safeguard proceedings (see Chapters 4, 5 and 6), Section 301 of the Trade Act of 1974 has no origins in or other imprimatur of legitimacy from the GATT/WTO. Indeed, the **unilateral** nature of

Section 301 is thought by many to run counter to the multilateral approach to trade relations.

Although the U.S. has been a strong supporter of the GATT over the years, Section 301 reflects U.S. frustration with multilateral methods and procedures. It has received hostile responses from United States trade partners, especially after the amendments to Section 301 implemented in 1988 through the Omnibus Trade and Competitiveness Act.

The offenses under Section 301 are primarily subject to the authority of the United States Trade Representative as opposed to the President. The 1988 Act also introduced the concept of mandatory versus discretionary retaliation. Offenses for which retaliation is mandatory involve the breach of international agreements to which the United States is a party, and unjustifiable trade practices. The USTR has discretionary authority to retaliate under Section 301 regarding unreasonable or discriminatory practices of foreign countries.

Brazil lodged but did not actively pursue a complaint about Section 301 during the Uruguay Round negotiations. Late in 1999, a panel of the World Trade Commission concluded that Section 301 was not inconsistent with U.S. obligations under the WTO (WTO/DS 152/1). The panel relied heavily on President Clinton's Congressionally approved statement that the U.S. would refrain from Section 301 retaliation until the WTO has ruled on disputes falling within its domain. Should some future U.S. administration fail to adhere to this policy, the WTO panel indicated that Section 301 would violate the WTO Dispute Settlement Understanding.

§ 14.2   The Evolution of Section 301

The origins of Section 301 can be traced to a trade dispute between the United States and the European Community (now Union) during the 1960s. This dispute became known as "the Chicken War." Basically, United States chicken producers had mechanized and developed a large export market in the European Union. The Union sought to protect its smaller chicken producers and did so by establishing a minimum price for imported chicken. This had the effect of drastically curtailing United States exports into the European market.

At that time, there was no vehicle through which the United States growers could express their complaints over this practice. Nevertheless, the United States government sought to resolve the dispute through the nullification and impairment provisions of Article XXIII of the GATT. These attempts failed and ultimately the

United States imposed unilateral trade restraints upon European Union exports as a matter of compensation for the minimum import price program. In the Chicken War, the retaliatory tariffs concerned brandy, trucks and potato starch. These trade restraints, while arguably compensating the United States as a nation, did little to satisfy the chicken exporters. In other words, the remedy was not linked to the source of the complaint, a reality that remains in Section 301 law.

As the Chicken War was in progress, the Trade Expansion Act of 1962 was adopted. Section 252 of that Act specifically authorized the President to retaliate against foreign import restrictions imposed in breach of GATT obligations. Furthermore, the President was authorized to impose higher tariffs or other import restraints on the products of countries that established burdensome restraints upon U.S. exports of agricultural goods. The latter could be imposed regardless of whether the import restraints of the foreign country constituted a breach of the GATT. Section 252 of the Trade Expansion Act of 1962 thus preceded and anticipated Section 301 of the Trade Act of 1974.

The President exercised retaliatory authority under Section 252 only twice. Both cases involved the imposition of import restraints because of agricultural disputes. Between 1974 and 1979, the first of the private petitions for Section 301 action were considered. However the typical result was to refer the dispute to the GATT organization, which deliberated at length and effectively turned the disputes into issues for review during the Tokyo Round of GATT negotiations concluded in 1979. Congress was not happy with these results, and in the Trade Agreements Act of 1979 imposed a variety of time limitations in connection with Section 301 complaints. Congress also expanded the range of complaints that could be filed, and on balance sought to rejuvenate Section 301.

From 1979 through the 1980s, the number of Section 301 investigations initiated by private complaints increased considerably. Through the Trade and Tariff Act of 1984, Congress continued to seek to make Section 301 an effective trade remedy. Its availability for complaints in the field of intellectual property rights and trade involving services was made clear. Nevertheless, a significant number of these complaints were still being referred to the GATT and its remarkably slow dispute settlement procedures. Through the Omnibus Trade and Competitiveness Act of 1988, Congress expressed its displeasure with GATT as a dispute settlement forum. Congress amended the law to indicate that under appropriate circumstances Section 301 investigations and remedies could proceed notwithstanding the fact that GATT dispute settlement had not run its full course. At the same time, Congress switched the ultimate authority for determining Section 301 offenses and Section 301 remedies from the President to the United States Trade Representative.

The bottom line after all of these legislative efforts on the part of Congress to invigorate Section 301 is that it became a significant forum for opening up foreign markets to United States exports. For examples, see Chapter 14. This forum can be accessed by private initiative, as well as governmental action.

§ 14.3   The Impact of the WTO Dispute Settlement Understanding

United States membership in the World Trade Organization since 1995 has committed it to multilateral dispute settlement of disputes arising out of the numerous WTO agreements. If the dispute is covered by a WTO agreement, the United States is obliged to pursue remedies under the WTO Dispute Settlement Understanding (DSU). See Chapter 1.

Section 301 petitions falling within the scope of the WTO routinely trigger USTR complaints with the multilateral Dispute Settlement Body. The United States has been involved in more WTO disputes (as a complaining and responding party) than any other member country. The DSU creates procedures under which unilateral retaliation is restrained until the offending nation has failed to conform to a WTO panel or Appellate Body ruling. Retaliation is then authorized by the WTO in an amount equal to the damages incurred. See Chapter 1.

When a petition concerns subject matter not covered by a WTO agreement (media goods) or a country that is not a WTO member (Iran), Section 301 and its unilateral remedies remain in full force and effect.

§ 14.4   Section 301—Mandatory Versus Discretionary Offenses and Remedies

Section 301 of the Trade Act of 1974 vests in the United States Trade Representative the power to determine when the *rights* of the United States under any trade agreement are being denied, when foreign country practices are inconsistent with or otherwise denying the *benefits* to the United States of trade agreements, or foreign countries are engaged in unjustifiable practices that burden or restrict United States commerce. An affirmative finding by the USTR in connection with any of the above requires **mandatory** retaliation on the part of the United States "subject to Presidential direction."[1]

The USTR is not required to take action whenever the dispute has been adjudicated within the GATT/WTO and there has been a finding that United States rights under a trade agreement are not being denied, or that the foreign country practices under dispute are not in violation of nor impair the benefits of the United States under any trade agreement. In addition, the USTR does not have to take retaliatory action if he or she determines that the foreign country in question is taking satisfactory measures to grant the rights of the United States under a trade agreement, or has agreed to eliminate or phase out the practices that are in dispute. If this is not possible, but the foreign country agrees to provide the United States with compensatory trade benefits satisfactory to the USTR, no mandatory retaliation will take place. In extraordinary cases, the USTR need not undertake retaliatory action if that would have an adverse impact on the United States economy substantially out of proportion to the benefits of that, or would cause serious harm to the national security of the United States.[2]

Section 301 also authorizes the USTR to determine when foreign countries are engaged in unreasonable or discriminatory practices that burden or restrict United States commerce. If such findings are reached, the Trade Representative (subject to directives from the President) may decide to undertake retaliatory action.[3] Hence, these offenses do not require mandatory retaliation; they are **discretionary**.

With reference to both mandatory and discretionary actions under Section 301, the USTR is authorized to withdraw the benefits of trade agreements enjoyed by the foreign country engaging in the offending activities, impose tariffs or other import restrictions upon the goods of those nations, and enter into binding international agreements to eliminate or phase out the unfair practices or to provide the United States with compensatory trade benefits. If the dispute concerns services, and many Section 301 disputes have been focused upon services, the USTR may restrict any "service sector access authorization" under United States law. Presumably, for example, the USTR subject to presidential directives could deny access to foreign banks by withholding licenses from federal authorities. It is less clear, but appears possible, that the USTR

---

[1]   19 U.S.C.A. § 2411.
[2]   19 U.S.C.A. § 2411(a)(2).
[3]   19 U.S.C.A. § 2411(b).

could order state authorities to deny similar access to the services sector.[4]

One problem with Section 301 remedies is that they need not necessarily benefit those who have been injured by foreign country practices. Thus, for example, if the complaint concerns European Union export subsidies on wheat, the ultimate retaliatory action taken by the United States may involve the imposition of tariffs upon European wine. Similarly, if the dispute concerns the intellectual property rights afforded pharmaceuticals in Brazil, the ultimate Section 301 remedy may impose quotas or other trade restraints upon Brazilian hardwoods.

§ 14.5   Section 301—Statutory Definitions

The provisions of Section 301 are remarkably broad and open-ended in language. The statute therefore seeks to define with greater specificity some of the important terms involved. These definitions are found in Section 301(d) of the Trade Act of 1974.[5] One important definition provides an expansive interpretation of the appropriate international commerce to which Section 301 applies. For these purposes, commerce includes trade in goods and services, and foreign direct investment by United States persons with implications for trade in goods or services.

The statutory definitions of unreasonableness reviewed above were greatly expanded in 1988. This suggests that the most likely avenue of success under Section 301 is in pleading unreasonable practices. Foreign country practices are *"unreasonable"* if they are unfair and inequitable, regardless of whether they are in violation of or inconsistent with the international legal rights of the United States. Unreasonable practices include those which deny fair and equitable opportunities for the establishment of a business abroad, those which provide inadequate or ineffective protection of intellectual property rights, those which deny market opportunities as a result of systematic anticompetitive activities of private firms, and those which constitute export targeting (defined to mean any government scheme designed to assist its exporters in becoming more competitive). Unreasonable practices include those which constitute a persistent pattern of conduct that denies workers the right to associate, organize or bargain collectively. They also include practices which tolerate forced or compulsory labor, fail to provide a minimum working age for children, or fail to provide general standards on minimum wages, hours of work and occupational safety and health requirements.

---

[4]   19 U.S.C.A. § 2411(c)(2).

[5]   19 U.S.C.A. § 2411(d).

However, Section 301(d) indicates that foreign country practices are not to be treated as unreasonable if the USTR determines that nation is taking action which demonstrates a significant and tangible advancement towards providing the rights and standards discussed above or that the practices in question are not inconsistent with the level of economic development of the foreign country. Where appropriate, the absence or presence of reciprocal opportunities in the United States for foreign nationals shall be taken into account in determining whether any particular practice is unreasonable.

It is important to bear in mind that this lengthy definition of unreasonable foreign country practices coincides with discretionary USTR action if such practices are found. The other discretionary category under Section 301 includes foreign country practices which are *"discriminatory."* Section 301(d) defines discriminatory as any practice which denies national or most favored nation treatment to United States goods, services or investment. The prohibition against *"unjustifiable"* foreign country practices is expanded by a definition which indicates that such practices must violate or be inconsistent with the international legal rights of the United States. These include those which deny national or most favored nation treatment, the right of establishment or the protection of intellectual property rights. Unjustifiable practices, if determined to exist by the USTR, mandate retaliatory action by the United States.

Perhaps the most critical difference in the Section 301(d) definitions of Section 301 offenses concerns "international legal rights". This is part of the definition of unjustifiable practices, but not found in connection with unreasonable or discriminatory practices. There is no requirement that unreasonable, discriminatory or unjustifiable practices violate or contradict any international agreement to which the United States is a party. Thus the international legal rights which must be breached in order to find an unjustifiable practice may turn upon the customary international law of trade.

§ 14.6 Section 301—Petitioning and Procedures

Section 302 of the Trade Act of 1974 permits any interested person to file a petition with the United States Trade Representative requesting action under Section 301. Complaints from U.S. industries have in fact driven most Section 301 proceedings, and they can be screened by the USTR before filing. The USTR is given 45 days within which to determine whether to initiate an investigation. Interested parties may include but are not limited to domestic companies and workers, representatives of consumer interests, U.S. exporters, and any industrial users of goods or services potentially affected by Section 301 actions.[6]

The Trade Representative's powers to initiate investigations under Section 301 appear to be completely discretionary. That is to say, if the USTR is not persuaded by the petition and supporting documents, no Section 301 procedures will be commenced. This is true for both mandatory and discretionary action under Section 301. However, if the USTR decides not to initiate an investigation, he or she must inform the petitioner of the reasons why and publish notice of that determination together with its reasons in the Federal Register.[7]

If the USTR decides to initiate an investigation under Section 301, he or she then publishes a summary of the petition and is required to provide an opportunity for the presentation of views including a public hearing. The USTR may self-initiate Section 301 investigations.[8] The USTR is not required to initiate any investigation if he or she determines that to do so would be detrimental to United States economic interests.[9]

Once an investigation under Section 301 is launched, either by petition or self-initiation, the USTR must consult with the foreign country alleged to have engaged in unfair trade practices. If a mutually acceptable solution is not reached, and the complaint concerns a breach of an international agreement to which the United States is a party, the USTR is obliged to commence dispute settlement procedures as provided for in that agreement.[10] WTO dispute settlement procedures are frequently invoked as a consequence.

The regulations which detail the procedures and conduct of investigations in connection with Section 301 are found at 15 C.F.R. 2006 et seq. An interagency committee composed of staff from the Departments of State, Treasury, Commerce, Justice, Agriculture, Labor and the Council of Economic Advisors is involved in the decisionmaking under Section 301. This Committee is sometimes called the "Section 301 Committee" and its report and advice will be considered by the USTR in making Section 301 determinations. The input of this Committee does not diminish the discretion of the USTR in deciding whether to commence a Section 301 investigation.

---

[6]   19 U.S.C.A. § 2411(d)(9).

[7]   19 U.S.C.A. § 2412(a).

[8]   19 U.S.C.A. § 2412(b).

[9]   19 U.S.C.A. § 2412(b).

[10]   19 U.S.C.A. § 2413(a).

Private Sector Petitions

When a petition is received from the private sector alleging a Section 301 offense, the USTR typically notifies the country that is the object of the complaint. That country may supply any relevant information it chooses. In the absence of such a response, the USTR is entitled to proceed on the basis of the "best information available."[11] This will often as a practical matter be the information submitted by the petitioner or otherwise derived from the Section 301 Committee or other independent sources. Thus the procedures utilized in Section 301 make it imperative that private petitioners properly document the nature of their complaint.

The rules require that a private petition for Section 301 action describe the petitioner's interest that is allegedly impacted by the foreign country practice about which the petitioner is complaining. If the complaint is based upon international agreements to which the United States is a party and the denial of rights thereunder, this must be clearly cited and documented. The petition must specifically identify the foreign country alleged to be engaging in a Section 301 offense. It must identify the specific product or service which is the subject of the complaint. Most importantly, the petition must show exactly how the practice in question is inconsistent with a trade agreement or is otherwise unjustifiable, unreasonable or discriminatory and that it burdens or restricts United States commerce. Lastly, the petitioner must indicate whether any other requests for relief under the Trade Act of 1974 or other United States law have been filed.

Once the USTR determines to initiate an investigation under Section 301, the petitioner has 30 days to submit a written request for a public hearing.[12] Any other interested person can also submit an application for such a hearing. Section 305 of the Trade Act of 1974 allows U.S. companies and other interested persons to essentially request of the USTR information necessary to substantiate a Section 301 complaint. Such requests have the practical effect of obliging the USTR to provide any such available information, and perhaps even to require the USTR to contact foreign governments in order to satisfy this request for information. Such requests can amount to a kind of preliminary Section 301 investigation before formal investigations are initiated.[13]

---

[11]   15 C.F.R. § 2006.4.

[12]   19 U.S.C.A. § 2414(b).

[13]   See 19 U.S.C.A. § 2411(d)(2).

§ 14.7   Section 301—USTR Determinations

Since the amendments of 1988, the USTR is required to make a determination of whether foreign country practices are actionable under Section 301 regardless of whether any retaliatory action is taken. For many years disputes concerning export subsidies, particularly export subsidies of the European Union, dominated Section 301 proceedings.[14] Whenever Section 301 complaints involve an alleged breach of United States benefits under an existing international agreement, such as the package of WTO agreements, the USTR must initiate the dispute settlement procedures of that agreement. This commitment has significantly reduced the number of unilateral trade remedies imposed since 1995 by the United States under Section 301.

The USTR is required to determine whether unfair practices have occurred under Section 301 within certain time limits. These are 12 months in cases involving export subsidies and practices not covered by trade agreements, 18 months in trade agreement cases other than subsidies unless the dispute settlement procedures of the relevant agreement are concluded earlier. Generally speaking, the USTR must determine whether a Section 301 offense has occurred in all instances where an investigation has been commenced within a 12-month deadline. These time limits could pressure the USTR into making a determination before the international dispute settlement procedures of the WTO or other trade agreements are concluded.[15]

§ 14.8   Section 301 in Action

Prior to the arrival of the WTO in 1995, there were a large number of complaints, investigations and unilateral U.S. remedies undertaken via Section 301 of the Trade Act of 1974. In some instances, complaints under Section 301 were dismissed by the President or USTR as without merit. In other instances, the complaints led to a GATT dispute settlement panel which decided against the position of the United States. This had the effect of terminating the Section 301 proceeding. Since 1995, many private Section 301 complaints to the USTR alleging trade agreement violations have triggered WTO dispute settlement proceedings.

Section 301 complaints are sometimes resolved to the satisfaction of those concerned through international negotiations.

---

[14]   See Bishop, The Multilateral Trade Negotiations, Subsidies and the Great Plains Wheat Case, 16 International Lawyer 339 (1982).

[15]   See generally Bliss, The Amendments to Section 301: An Overview and Suggested Strategies for Foreign Response, 20 Law & Policy of International Business 501 (1989).

For example, in the early 1970s, a shipping company complained about the discriminatory practices of the government of Guatemala. The United States undertook negotiations with that government and reached an agreement satisfactory to the complainant.[16] In the same year, Canada had been imposing a quota on the importation of eggs from the United States. A trade association complaint to the USTR led to negotiations and an increase in this quota.[17] An exporter of thrown silk to Japan complained about the difficulties in obtaining import licenses for such silk. This complaint led to the threat of retaliatory action against Japanese-made silk products. However, subsequent negotiations resulted in an agreement which caused the Japanese to remove their import licensing restraints.[18]

A lengthy Section 301 complaint concerned European Union tariff restraints in connection with the export of Florida citrus products. In this case, the GATT (pre-WTO) did not provide an adequate dispute resolution forum, and the United States decided to retaliate by imposing substantial tariffs on European pasta products. Europe in turn retaliated with tariff increases on U.S. walnuts and lemons. Ultimately the United States and the European Union agreed to mutual elimination of the tariffs in question. This result did not really resolve the underlying dispute concerning the export of citrus products from the United States to Europe.[19]

One Section 301 complaint involved the Cigar Association of America. This complaint was against Japanese practices which had the effect of raising the price on U.S. cigars and making them difficult to market in Japan. International negotiations led to the formation of a GATT dispute settlement panel. However, this panel did not need to complete its task because the Japanese government agreed to substantial reductions in the relevant tariffs and retail requirements.[20]

While many Section 301 complaints have concerned export opportunities for United States firms, some have involved import competition. For example, a complaint was filed against Taiwanese subsidies of rice exports. International negotiations led to an agreement limiting these subsidized exports such that the Section 301 complaint was withdrawn.[21]

---

[16]   See 41 Fed.Reg. 26758 (1976).

[17]   41 Fed.Reg. 9430 (1976).

[18]   43 Fed.Reg. 8876 (1978).

[19]   See 50 Fed.Reg. 26143 (1985).

[20]   See 44 Fed.Reg. 19083 (1979), 44 Fed.Reg. 64938 (1979) and 46 Fed.Reg. 1388, 1389 (1981).

[21]   See 48 Fed.Reg. 56289 (1983), 49 Fed.Reg. 10761 (1984).

The United States Trade Representative has occasionally commenced Section 301 proceedings on its own initiative. For example, the Brazilian "informatics policy" was challenged in this manner. This policy discriminated against foreign computer and high technology imports principally through local content requirements and the grant of exclusive monopolies. International negotiations, backed up by a threat by the United States to suspend the benefits for Brazil under the U.S. Generalized System of Tariff Preferences, eventually resulted in an opening of the Brazilian informatics market.[22]

Another self-initiated Section 301 proceeding concerned Korea's restraints on foreign insurance companies. Korean law was discriminatory and failed to give foreign companies the same benefits that domestic firms obtained. An international settlement was reached between the United States and Korea which gave access to that market for life and non-life insurance.[23] Korea was also the object of another Section 301 investigation concerning its intellectual property rights. These were thought to be inadequate, particularly in the copyright area. International negotiations led to the creation of a comprehensive copyright system for Korea, including coverage of computer software. Amendments were also made to the Korean patent laws and the country joined the Universal Copyright Convention.[24]

Several Section 301 disputes were resolved with Thailand. Following Section 301 success at opening the Japanese, Taiwanese and South Korean markets to United States cigarettes, the first dispute concerned Thai tariffs on U.S. cigarettes. United States producers petitioned under Section 301, and a lengthy investigation resulted in the formation of a GATT dispute settlement panel. This panel ruled against the tariffs and Thailand removed them.[25] A second Section 301 complaint by the International Intellectual Property Alliance and others led to an investigation focused on Thai piracy of audio and video cassettes. A substantial Thai industry had developed around such activities. The USTR threatened removal of Thailand's GSP duty free tariff entry benefits and the imposition of a total U.S. barrier to Thai imports. Thailand capitulated and announced copyright reforms targeted at cassette piracy.[26]

A longstanding dispute between the United States and Japan concerning semiconductor products resulted in a Section 301

---

[22]   See 51 Fed.Reg. 35993.

[23]   See 51 Fed.Reg. 29443.

[24]   See 51 Fed.Reg. 29445.

[25]   55 Fed.Reg. 49724 (USTR 1990).

[26]   56 Fed.Reg. 67114 (USTR 1991).

complaint in the late 1980s. The essence of the complaint was that a prior agreement concerning trade in such products between the two nations had been breached and therefore the United States intended to impose tariffs on certain imports from Japan.[27] The United States argued that Japan had not opened up its market sufficiently to foreign semiconductor manufacturers and had not avoided dumping of Japanese-made semiconductors in various markets around the world. Thus the heart of this complaint was that the benefits of an international agreement previously made were being denied to the United States and that this constituted a burden or restraint on U.S. commerce. The United States did impose additional duties on Japanese data processing machines, rotary drills and color television sets. However, these duties were suspended when the USTR found improved compliance by the Japanese with the semiconductor agreement.[28]

Section 307 of the Trade and Tariff Act of 1984 focuses specifically on export performance requirements created by foreign countries. Such requirements are thought by many United States investors to be unreasonable. Section 307 requires the USTR to enter into consultations with any foreign country imposing export performance requirements in an effort to seek to alleviate them when they adversely the economic interests of the United States. If such consultations do not result in a settlement, the USTR is authorized to impose import restraints on the products or services of the country in question.[29] In one instance, for example, the USTR was able to successfully negotiate away export performance requirements maintained by the Taiwanese relative to automobiles.[30]

The Telecommunications Trade Act of 1988[31] focuses upon foreign market opportunities in the telecommunication field. It is integrated into Section 301 procedures and administrative determinations. In undertaking retaliation, however, the USTR is directed to target telecommunications industry exports to the U.S. unless other action would be more effective in opening up foreign export markets. Section 1374 of the 1988 Act requires the USTR to identify priority countries whose practices cause the greatest telecommunications trade barriers. South Korea and the European Union were so identified in 1989. Ensuing negotiations resulted in a

---

[27] See 52 Fed.Reg. 13412 (1987).
[28] See 52 Fed.Reg. 22693 (1987).
[29] See 19 U.S.C.A. § 2112(g)(3).
[30] See 51 Fed.Reg. 41558.
[31] Pub.L. 100–418.

market-opening telecommunications agreement with South Korea and the European Union.

In the fall of 1991, the USTR initiated a prominent investigation of restrictive trade practices of the People's Republic of China. This investigation was undertaken in part to mitigate Congressional frustration over President Bush's continued willingness to grant most-favored-nation tariff status to Chinese goods despite record U.S. trade deficits with the PRC (second only to Japan). The Section 301 investigation focused upon PRC import quotas, prohibitions and licensing procedures, and PRC technical barriers to trade (e.g., standards, testing and certification requirements). It also challenged the failure to publish PRC laws, regulations, judicial decisions and administrative rulings relating to import restraints. Additional discussions regarding PRC tariffs (ranging up to 200 percent) and import taxes were held. The main thrust of the proceeding was to open up China's markets to U.S. exports.

Since China was not a member of the GATT, and in spite of U.S. bilateral trade agreements with the PRC, the USTR proceeded with this investigation on an unfair practices' basis. This meant that no trade agreement dispute settlement procedures were triggered. In October of 1992 the United States and China signed a memorandum of understanding that narrowly avoided massive, unilateral Section 301 trade sanctions. The People's Republic agreed to phase out by the end of 1977 numerous nontariff trade barriers, including import licenses, quotas and bans as well as regulatory restraints. The removal of these barriers improved U.S. export possibilities for telecommunications equipment, airplanes, machinery, agricultural goods, electrical appliances, computers, auto parts and pharmaceuticals. Furthermore, China promised to undertake a series of significant tariff cuts.

China's import-substitution regulations and policies were eliminated. In particular, the PRC may not condition entry into its market upon technology transfers. All laws, regulations, policies and decrees dealing with China's import and export system will be published on a regular basis and no such rules can be enforced unless they have been made readily available to foreign traders and governments. The goal is complete "transparency" of PRC trade law and an end to the use of secret internal directives. For its part, the United States committed itself to full GATT/WTO membership for the PRC, which was finally realized in 2001.

§ 14.9　Text of Section 301

19 U.S.C. 2411

(a) Mandatory action

(1) If the United States Trade Representative determines under section 2414(a)(1) of this title that—

(A) the rights of the United States under any trade agreement are being denied; or

(B) an act, policy, or practice of a foreign country—

(i) violates, or is inconsistent with, the provisions of, or otherwise denies benefits to the United States under, any trade agreement, or

(ii) is unjustifiable and burdens or restricts United States commerce;

the Trade Representative shall take action authorized in subsection (c) of this section, subject to the specific direction, if any, of the President regarding any such action, and shall take all other appropriate and feasible action within the power of the President that the President may direct the Trade Representative to take under this subsection, to enforce such rights or to obtain the elimination of such act, policy, or practice. Actions may be taken that are within the power of the President with respect to trade in any goods or services, or with respect to any other area of pertinent relations with the foreign country.

(2) The Trade Representative is not required to take action under paragraph (1) in any case in which—

(A) the Dispute Settlement Body (as defined in section 3531(5) of this title) has adopted a report, or a ruling issued under the formal dispute settlement proceeding provided under any other trade agreement finds, that—

(i) the rights of the United States under a trade agreement are not being denied, or

(ii) the act, policy, or practice—

(I) is not a violation of, or inconsistent with, the rights of the United States, or

(II) does not deny, nullify, or impair benefits to the United States under any trade agreement; or

(B) the Trade Representative finds that—

(i) the foreign country is taking satisfactory measures to grant the rights of the United States under a trade agreement,

(ii) the foreign country has—

> **(I)** agreed to eliminate or phase out the act, policy, or practice, or

> **(II)** agreed to an imminent solution to the burden or restriction on United States commerce that is satisfactory to the Trade Representative,

(iii) it is impossible for the foreign country to achieve the results described in clause (i) or (ii), as appropriate, but the foreign country agrees to provide to the United States compensatory trade benefits that are satisfactory to the Trade Representative,

> **(iv)** in extraordinary cases, where the taking of action under this subsection would have an adverse impact on the United States economy substantially out of proportion to the benefits of such action, taking into account the impact of not taking such action on the credibility of the provisions of this subchapter, or

> **(v)** the taking of action under this subsection would cause serious harm to the national security of the United States.

(3) Any action taken under paragraph (1) to eliminate an act, policy, or practice shall be devised so as to affect goods or services of the foreign country in an amount that is equivalent in value to the burden or restriction being imposed by that country on United States commerce.

(b) Discretionary action

If the Trade Representative determines under section 2414(a)(1) of this title that—

(1) an act, policy, or practice of a foreign country is unreasonable or discriminatory and burdens or restricts United States commerce, and

(2) action by the United States is appropriate, the Trade Representative shall take all appropriate and feasible action authorized under subsection (c) of this section, subject to the specific direction, if any, of the President regarding any such action, and all other appropriate and feasible action within the power of the President that the President may direct the Trade Representative to take under this subsection, to obtain the elimination of that act, policy, or practice. Actions may be taken that are within the power of the President with respect to trade in any goods or services, or with respect to any other area of pertinent relations with the foreign country.

(c) Scope of authority

(1) For purposes of carrying out the provisions of subsection (a) or (b) of this section, the Trade Representative is authorized to—

(A) suspend, withdraw, or prevent the application of, benefits of trade agreement concessions to carry out a trade agreement with the foreign country referred to in such subsection;

(B) impose duties or other import restrictions on the goods of, and, notwithstanding any other provision of law, fees or restrictions on the services of, such foreign country for such time as the Trade Representative determines appropriate;

(C) in a case in which the act, policy, or practice also fails to meet the eligibility criteria for receiving duty-free treatment under subsections (b) and (c) of section 2462 of this title, subsections (b) and (c) of section 2702 of this title, or subsections (c) and (d) of section 3202 of this title, withdraw, limit, or suspend such treatment under such provisions, notwithstanding the provisions of subsection (a)(3) of this section; or

(D) enter into binding agreements with such foreign country that commit such foreign country to—

   (i) eliminate, or phase out, the act, policy, or practice that is the subject of the action to be taken under subsection (a) or (b) of this section,

   (ii) eliminate any burden or restriction on United States commerce resulting from such act, policy, or practice, or

   (iii) provide the United States with compensatory trade benefits that—

      (I) are satisfactory to the Trade Representative, and

      (II) meet the requirements of paragraph (4).

(2)

(A) Notwithstanding any other provision of law governing any service sector access authorization, and in addition to the authority conferred in paragraph (1), the Trade Representative may, for purposes of carrying out the provisions of subsection (a) or (b) of this section—

   (i) restrict, in the manner and to the extent the Trade Representative determines appropriate, the terms and conditions of any such authorization, or

   (ii) deny the issuance of any such authorization.

(B) Actions described in subparagraph (A) may only be taken under this section with respect to service sector access authorizations granted, or applications therefor pending, on or after the date on which—

   (i) a petition is filed under section 2412(a) of this title, or

   (ii) a determination to initiate an investigation is made by the Trade Representative under section 2412(b) of this title.

(C) Before the Trade Representative takes any action under this section involving the imposition of fees or other restrictions on the services of a foreign country, the Trade Representative shall, if the services involved are subject to regulation by any agency of the Federal Government or of any State, consult, as appropriate, with the head of the agency concerned.

(3) The actions the Trade Representative is authorized to take under subsection (a) or (b) of this section may be taken against any goods or economic sector—

(A) on a nondiscriminatory basis or solely against the foreign country described in such subsection, and

(B) without regard to whether or not such goods or economic secor were involved in the act, policy, or practice that is the subject of such action.

(4) Any trade agreement described in paragraph (1)(D)(iii) shall provide compensatory trade benefits that benefit the economic sector which includes the domestic industry that would benefit from the elimination of the act, policy, or practice that is the subject of the action to be taken under subsection (a) or (b) of this section, or benefit the economic sector as closely related as possible to such economic sector, unless—

(A) the provision of such trade benefits is not feasible, or

(B) trade benefits that benefit any other economic sector would be more satisfactory than such trade benefits.

(5) If the Trade Representative determines that actions to be taken under subsection (a) or (b) of this section are to be in the form of import restrictions, the Trade Representative shall—

(A) give preference to the imposition of duties over the imposition of other import restrictions, and

(B) if an import restriction other than a duty is imposed, consider substituting, on an incremental basis, an equivalent duty for such other import restriction.

(6) Any action taken by the Trade Representative under this section with respect to export targeting shall, to the extent possible, reflect the full benefit level of the export targeting to the beneficiary over the period during which the action taken has an effect.

(d) Definitions and special rules

For purposes of this subchapter—

(1) The term "commerce" includes, but is not limited to—

(A) services (including transfers of information) associated with international trade, whether or not such services are related to specific goods, and

(B) foreign direct investment by United States persons with implications for trade in goods or services.

(2) An act, policy, or practice of a foreign country that burdens or restricts United States commerce may include the provision, directly or indirectly, by that foreign country of subsidies for the construction of vessels used in the commercial transportation by water of goods between foreign countries and the United States.

(3)

(A) An act, policy, or practice is unreasonable if the act, policy, or practice, while not necessarily in violation of, or inconsistent with, the international legal rights of the United States, is otherwise unfair and inequitable.

(B) Acts, policies, and practices that are unreasonable include, but are not limited to, any act, policy, or practice, or any combination of acts, policies, or practices, which—

(i) denies fair and equitable—

(I) opportunities for the establishment of an enterprise,

(II) provision of adequate and effective protection of intellectual property rights notwithstanding the fact that the foreign country may be in compliance with the specific obligations of the Agreement on Trade-Related Aspects of Intellectual Property Rights referred to in section 3511(d)(15) of this title,

(III) nondiscriminatory market access opportunities for United States persons that rely upon intellectual property protection, or

(IV) market opportunities, including the toleration by a foreign government of systematic anticompetitive activities by enterprises or among enterprises in the foreign country that have the effect of restricting, on a basis that is inconsistent with commercial considerations, access of United States goods or services to a foreign market,

(ii) constitutes export targeting, or

(iii) constitutes a persistent pattern of conduct that—

(I) denies workers the right of association,

(II) denies workers the right to organize and bargain collectively,

(III) permits any form of forced or compulsory labor,

(IV) fails to provide a minimum age for the employment of children, or

(V) fails to provide standards for minimum wages, hours of work, and occupational safety and health of workers.

(C)

(i) Acts, policies, and practices of a foreign country described in subparagraph (B)(iii) shall not be treated as being unreasonable if the Trade Representative determines that—

(I) the foreign country has taken, or is taking, actions that demonstrate a significant and tangible overall advancement in providing throughout the foreign country (including any designated zone within the foreign country) the rights and other standards described in the subclauses of subparagraph (B)(iii), or

(II) such acts, policies, and practices are not inconsistent with the level of economic development of the foreign country.

(ii) The Trade Representative shall publish in the Federal Register any determination made under clause (i), together with a description of the facts on which such determination is based.

(D) For purposes of determining whether any act, policy, or practice is unreasonable, reciprocal opportunities in the United States for foreign nationals and firms shall be taken into account, to the extent appropriate.

(E) The term "export targeting" means any government plan or scheme consisting of a combination of coordinated actions (whether carried out severally or jointly) that are bestowed on a specific enterprise, industry, or group thereof, the effect of which is to assist the enterprise, industry, or group to become more competitive in the export of a class or kind of merchandise.

(F)

(i) For the purposes of subparagraph (B)(i)(II), adequate and effective protection of intellectual property rights includes adequate and effective means under the laws of the foreign country for persons who are not citizens or nationals of such country to secure, exercise, and enforce rights and enjoy commercial benefits relating to patents, trademarks, copyrights and related rights, mask works, trade secrets, and plant breeder's rights.

(ii) For purposes of subparagraph (B)(i)(IV), the denial of fair and equitable nondiscriminatory market access opportunities includes restrictions on market access related to the use, exploitation, or enjoyment of commercial benefits derived from exercising intellectual property rights in protected works or fixations or products embodying protected works.

(4)

(A) An act, policy, or practice is unjustifiable if the act, policy, or practice is in violation of, or inconsistent with, the international legal rights of the United States.

(B) Acts, policies, and practices that are unjustifiable include, but are not limited to, any act, policy, or practice described in subparagraph (A) which denies national or most-favored-nation treatment or the right of establishment or protection of intellectual property rights.

(5) Acts, policies, and practices that are discriminatory include, when appropriate, any act, policy, and practice which denies national or most-favored-nation treatment to United States goods, services, or investment.

(6) The term "service sector access authorization" means any license, permit, order, or other authorization, issued under the authority of Federal law, that permits a foreign supplier of services access to the United States market in a service sector concerned.

(7) The term "foreign country" includes any foreign instrumentality. Any possession or territory of a foreign country that is administered separately for customs purposes shall be treated as a separate foreign country.

(8) The term "Trade Representative" means the United States Trade Representative.

(9) The term "interested persons", only for purposes of sections 2412(a)(4)(B), 2414(b)(1)(A), 2416(c)(2), and 2417(a)(2) of this title, includes, but is not limited to, domestic firms and workers, representatives of consumer interests, United States product exporters, and any industrial user of any goods or services that may be affected by actions taken under subsection (a) or (b) of this section.

Part 4

PREFERENTIAL TRADE AGREEMENTS

Chapter 15

FREE TRADE AGREEMENTS AND CUSTOMS UNIONS

Table of Sections

For coverage of the European Union see Chapters 17–19. For coverage of NAFTA and Free Trade in the Americas, see Chapter 16. For coverage of U.S. FTAs generally, see Section 2.4.

§ 15.1   Free Trade Agreements and Customs Unions

There is a massive movement towards free trade agreements (FTAs) and customs unions (CUs) throughout the world, though not often of the consequence of that occurring in Europe and North America. Some of these developments are a competitive by-product of European Union and NAFTA integration. Others simply reflect the desire (but not always the political will) to capture the economic gains and international negotiating strength that such economic relations can bring. This is particularly true of attempts at free trade and customs unions in the developing world.

Over half of all world trade now occurs under free trade or customs union agreements. The United States has roughly 20 free trade agreements. U.S. FTAs, USTR negotiations and Congressional implementation acts under "fast track" procedures are reviewed in Section 2.4. The global explosion of FTA and CU agreements creates systemic risks for the World Trade Organization. It reports that nearly all of its members are partners in one or more regional or bilateral agreements. Here is a sampling of such agreements: Hong Kong–China, Japan-Singapore, Russia-CIS states, New Zealand–China, Mexico-Israel, Canada-Peru, EU–South Africa, Chile–South Korea, the South Asian Free Trade Area (India, Pakistan, Bangladesh, Nepal, Bhutan, Sri Lanka) . . . and the list goes on. At this stage, only Mongolia is without at least one FTA.

One reason for this proliferation may be doubts about the prospects of success for the Doha Round of WTO negotiations. GATT/WTO regulatory failures have also fueled this reality. Yet these "negatives" do not fully explain the FTA and CU feeding frenzy. A range of attractions are also at work. For example, FTAs and CUs often extend to subject matters beyond WTO competence. Foreign investment law is a prime example, and many such agreements serve as investment magnets. Government procurement, optional at the WTO level, is often included in free trade and customs union agreements. Competition policy and labor and environmental matters absent from the WTO are sometimes covered.

In addition, FTAs and CUs can reach beyond the scope of existing WTO agreements. Services are one "WTO-plus" area where this is clearly true. Intellectual property rights are also being "WTO-plussed" in free trade and customs union agreements. Whether this amounts to competitive trade liberalization or competitive trade imperialism is a provocative question.

Further, FTAs and CUs are politically and economically selective. In other words they avoid not only global most-favored-nation principles, but also domestically "sensitive" national politics and economics. For example, Singapore's absence of farm exports helped make it an ideal U.S. and Japanese free trade partner. The micro-sized economy of Chile contributed to its attraction as a free trade partner with Mexico, China, the European Union, the United States and others. U.S. free trade deals with Jordan, Bahrain and Oman fit economically in a similar fashion, not to mention national security objectives.

Like it or not, the "spaghetti-bowl" maze of FTAs and CUs is driven by powerful negative and positive forces. It is not only the preferred trade medium of today, but very likely the future. Already more than half of world trade is conducted under them. While international trade lawyers may celebrate full employment, it bears remembering that FTAs and CUs *are* discriminatory. They could render MFN the least favored status in world trade. Such an outcome would be especially harmful to the world's poorest nations, those with whom few WTO partners seek a bilateral agreement.

Degrees of Economic Integration

There is a continuum of sorts, a range of options to be considered when nations contemplate economic integration. In "free trade areas," tariffs, quotas, and other barriers to trade among participating states are reduced or removed while individual national trade barriers vis-à-vis third party states are retained. "Customs unions" not only remove trade barriers among participating states, but they also create common tariff and trade barriers for all participating states as regards third-party states. "Common markets" go further than customs unions by providing for the free movement of factors of production (capital, labor, enterprise, technology) among participating states.

"Economic communities" build on common markets by introducing some harmonization of basic national policies related to the economy of the community, e.g. transport, taxation, corporate behavior and structure, monetary matters and regional growth. Finally, "economic unions" embrace a more or less complete harmonization of national policies related to the economy of the union, e.g. company laws, commercial treaties, social welfare, currencies, and government subsidies. The difference between an economic community and an economic union relates to the number and importance of harmonized national policies.

Trade Creation and Trade Diversion

All such international economic integration agreements are inherently discriminatory in their trade impact. As nonuniversalized trade preferences, they tend to simultaneously *create trade* among participating states and *divert trade* between those states and the rest of the world. With free trade agreements, diversionary trade effects are usually not distinct because of the absence of a common trade wall against outsiders. Trade diversion nonetheless occurs.

"Rules of origin" in free trade area agreements keep third-party imports from seeking the lowest tariff or highest quota state and then exploiting trade advantages within an FTA. Under rules of origin, free trade areas are "free" only for goods substantially originating therein. This causes member state goods to be preferred over goods from other states. Rules of origin under a free trade agreement can be as trade diversionary as common external tariffs in customs unions.

§ 15.2   GATT Article 24

FTA and CU agreements are an exception to the core GATT/WTO principle of most-favored-nation trading. *See* Section 1.1. Article 24 of the GATT (reproduced in Section 15.9) attempts to manage the internal trade-creating and external trade-diverting effects of these agreements. Free trade area and custom union proposals must run the gauntlet of a formal GATT/WTO review procedure during which "binding" recommendations are possible to bring the proposals into conformity. Such recommendations might deal with Article 24 requirements for the elimination of internal tariffs and other restrictive regulations of commerce on "substantially all" products originating in a customs union or free trade area.

Or they might deal with Article 24 requirements that common external tariffs not be "on the whole higher or more restrictive" in effect than the general incidence of prior existing national tariffs. The broad purpose of Article 24, acknowledged therein, is to facilitate trade among the GATT contracting parties and not to raise trade barriers. Because they create common external tariffs, CU agreements, but not FTAs, create a duty to compensate other WTO member states. Prior to the WTO, GATT "working parties" conducted Article 24 review proceedings.

Early Regulatory Failure

It is through this review mechanism that most free trade and customs union agreements have passed *without* substantial modification. The GATT, not economic agreements, most often has given way. For example, during GATT review of the 1957 Treaty of Rome creating what we now call the European Union, many "violations" of the letter and spirit of Article 24 were cited. The derivation of the common external tariff by arithmetically averaging existing national tariffs was challenged as more restrictive of trade than previous arrangements. Such averaging on a given product fails to take account of differing national import volumes. If a product was faced originally with a lower than average national tariff and a larger than average national demand, the new average tariff is clearly more "restrictive" of imports than before. Averaging in high tariffs of countries of low demand quite plausibly created more restrictions on third-party trade. If so, the letter and spirit of Article 24 were breached.

Despite these and other arguments, the Treaty of Rome passed through GATT study and review committees without final resolution of its legal status under Article 24. Postponement of these issues became permanent. GATT attempts—through the lawyer-like conditions of Article 24 to maximize trade creation and minimize trade diversion—must be seen as generally inadequate. Treaty terms became negotiable demands that were not accepted.

Regulatory Reform: Interpreting Article 24

The early regulatory failure of Article 24 and the limited requirements of the Enabling Clause arguably created an incentive to reach free trade area and customs union agreements as a means to avoid MFN trade principles. In the 1960s, 1970s and into the 1980s, a goodly number of FTAs and CUs were established, especially in the developing world. Yet there was no avalanche of agreements, in part because of MFN successes in GATT tariff negotiating rounds. *See* Section 1.2. The turning point came when major delays and perceptions of possible failure in the Uruguay Round (1986–1994) accelerated this trend, most visibly the Canada-U.S. FTA of 1989 and NAFTA (1994).

The emergence, also, of export-driven (not import substituting) developing economies, such as Mexico and Chile, also contributed to this acceleration. Chile has free trade agreements with China, Korea, Costa Rica, El Salvador, Canada, Mexico, the United States, and the European Union among others. Mexico has free trade agreements with Japan, the European Union, Costa Rica, Guatemala, Honduras, Nicaragua, Colombia, Peru and Uruguay, among others.

The Uruguay Round, which created the World Trade Organization, presented an opportunity to come to grips with the regulatory failure of Article 24 and the implications of the Enabling Clause. Agreement was reached in 1994 on an "Understanding on the Interpretation of Article 24," which presently binds the roughly 150 member nations of the WTO. This Interpretation reaffirms that free trade area and customs union agreements *must* satisfy the provisions of Article 24, clarifies the manner in which before and after evaluations of common external tariffs are to be undertaken, limits in most cases interim agreements to 10 years, and details Article 24 notification, report and recommendation duties and processes.

Most importantly, the 1994 Understanding on Interpretation expressly permits invocation of standard WTO dispute settlement procedures (DSU) regarding any Article 24 matters. *See* Turkey-Textiles, WT/DS34/AB/R (1999) (Turkey's invocation of Article 24 customs union "defense" to Article 11 and 13 GATT quota violations rejected by Appellate Body; Turkey bears burden of proof of compliance with Article 24).

All that said, the 1994 Understanding did not come to grips with the systemic ambiguities that led to Article 24's early and ongoing regulatory failure.

§ 15.3   GATS Integrated Services Agreements

Since 1995, "economic integration agreements" (EIAs) covering services are permitted under Article 5 of the General Agreement on Trade in Services (GATS). Such agreements, which can be staged, must have "substantial sectoral coverage," eliminate "substantially" all discrimination in sectors subject to multilateral commitments, and not raise the "overall" level of barriers to trade in GATS services compared to before the EIA. EIAs involving developing nations are to be accorded "flexibility." Like GATT Article 24 customs unions, there is an Article 5 duty to compensate EIA nonparticipants.

Review of GATS Article 5 notifications is undertaken, when requested by the WTO Council for Trade in Services, by the Committee on Regional Trade Agreements (CRTA). Whereas CRTA examinations of GATT Article 24 agreements are required, such examinations are optional under GATS. Nevertheless, numerous Article 5 examinations have been conducted, including notably the services components of NAFTA, the EEC Treaty (1957) and EU Enlargement (2004), Japan's FTAs with Singapore, Mexico and Malaysia, China's FTAs with Hong Kong and Macau, and various U.S. bilaterals. None of these examinations have resulted in a final report on consistency with GATS Article 5. This pattern continues the GATT/WTO record of regulatory failure regarding economic integration agreements.

§ 15.4   Enabling Clause FTAs and CUs

Developing nations in Africa, the Caribbean, Central America, South America and Southeast Asia (among others) had free trade and customs union agreements in place as early as the 1960s. In 1979, under what is commonly called the Enabling Clause, the GATT parties decided to permit developing nations to enter into differential and more favorable bilateral, regional or global arrangements among themselves to reduce or eliminate tariffs and nontariff barriers applicable to trade in goods. Like Article 24, the Enabling Clause constitutes an exception to MFN trade principles. It has generally been construed to authorize third world free trade area and customs union agreements.

Whether the Enabling Clause was intended to take such agreements out of Article 24 and its requirements, or be construed in conjunction therewith, is unclear. However, the creation of alternative notification and review procedures for Enabling Clause arrangements suggests Article 24 is inapplicable.

Notification to GATT of Enabling Clause arrangements is mandatory. Since 1995, the WTO Committee on Trade and Development (CTD) is the forum where such notifications are reviewed, but in practice not examined in depth. Enabling Clause arrangements should be designed to promote the trade of developing countries and not raise external trade barriers or undue trade difficulties. Consultations with individual GATT members experiencing such difficulties must be undertaken, and these consultations may be expanded to all GATT members if requested.

Unlike GATT Article 24 and GATS Article 5, compensation to nonparticipants and formal reporting on the consistency with the Enabling Clause of developing nation arrangements are not anticipated. The ASEAN-China (2004), India–Sri Lanka (2002), and "revived" Economic Community of West African States (ECOWAS 2005) agreements illustrate notified but unexamined preferential arrangements sheltered by the Enabling Clause.

§ 15.5 WTO Review of FTA and CU Agreements

Article 24 of the GATT attempts to manage the internal trade-creating and external trade-diverting effects of FTAs and CUs. Under its terms, free trade area and custom union proposals should be notified "promptly," although most agreements have been notified after their conclusion. Once notified, such agreements should run the gauntlet of formal review and report procedures during which recommendations are possible to bring them into conformity with Article 24. Prior to the WTO, GATT "working parties" conducted these procedures. Since 1995, the WTO Committee on Regional Trade Agreements (CRTA) reviews Article 24 notifications.

The Transparency Mechanism of 2006

The post-Uruguay Round of regulatory failure put preferential trade arrangements on the Doha negotiating agenda. Special emphasis has been placed on "transparency" issues, i.e., notification and reporting duties. Surprisingly, in June 2006, agreement was reached on a "Transparency Mechanism for Regional Trade Agreements." This agreement has been provisionally implemented, although it is less than clear that it will bring about all required notifications and still retains the ex post facto nature of WTO regulatory review. Whether this Mechanism will solve the present regulatory gridlock is seriously problematic.

The Transparency Mechanism envisions multiple electronic filings and detailed data submissions by parties to FTAs and CUs, and substantial posting of such information on the WTO website. Announcement of negotiations should be "early," notification of agreements "as early as possible" but no later than after ratification and before application of preferential treatment between the parties. In addition, the separate 1994 WTO Agreement on Rules of Origin specifies transparency requirements, including a duty to notify the WTO Secretariat of preferential rules of origin.   Review by the WTO of FTAs and CUs should "normally" be concluded within a year of notification. The WTO Secretariat will prepare a "factual presentation" *primarily* based on information submitted by the parties, but if necessary from other sources. The Secretariat is admonished to "refrain from any value judgment, which appears true of the presentations reported to date on the WTO website." Most importantly, its factual presentation may not be used "as a basis for dispute settlement procedures" or "to create new rights and obligations for members." A general notice and comment period is prescribed. Subsequently, the CRTA and CTD are supposed, as a rule, to devote a single formal meeting to consider each notified agreement.

The WTO Transparency Mechanism in Action?

The failure to launch a new round of WTO negotiations in Seattle (1999), followed by delays and perceptions of possible failure in the Doha Round that commenced in 2001, has contributed to the feeding frenzy of CU and FTA agreements. Supported by provisional application of a Doha Round WTO transparency mechanism, hundreds of agreements have been notified to the WTO. A large additional number are believed *not* to have been notified. In general, most of the notified agreements are bilateral, not regional in character. Meanwhile, the WTO Regional Trade Agreements Committee, working by consensus, has been unable since 1995 to complete even one assessment of a bilateral agreement's conformity to GATT Article 24 or GATS Article 5. The same is true for WTO Committee on Trade and Development "review" of Enabling Clause arrangements.

It has been suggested that this record can be explained by the ambiguous relationship between Committee reports and WTO dispute settlement proceedings. For example, can such reports be used in evidence in WTO dispute proceedings? Can fact-finding by WTO Secretariat and information gathered for WTO regulatory purposes be similarly used? This "dispute settlement awareness" makes WTO members reluctant to provide information or agree on conclusions that could later be used or interpreted in DSU proceedings.

Decades later, the ineffectiveness of GATT/WTO supervision of free trade and customs union agreements continues. At best Article 24 exerts a marginal influence over their contents. Whether the extraordinary proliferation of preferential agreements undermines or supports WTO trade policies is hotly debated.

§ 15.6   Developing World FTAs and CUs

Africa

Several trade groups have been formed in Africa. In 1966 the central African countries of Cameroon, Central African Republic, Chad, Congo (Brazzaville) and Gabon formed the Economic and Customs Union of Central Africa (Union Douaniere et Économique de l'Afrique Centrale: UDEAC) to establish a common customs and tariff approach toward the rest of the world and to formulate a common foreign investment code. Implementation has proceeded very slowly. In 1967 Kenya, Tanzania and Uganda created the East African Community (EAC) in an attempt to harmonize customs and tariff practices among themselves and in relation to other countries. The practical effect of that Community has frequently been negated by political strife, but efforts are underway to revive it. In 1974 six French speaking West African nations formed the West African Economic Community (known by its French initials CEAO). This Community is a sub-group within and pacesetter for ECOWAS, the Economic Community of West African States.

ECOWAS was created in 1975 by Dahomey, Gambia, Ghana, Guinea, Guinea-Bissau, Ivory Coast, Liberia, Mali, Mauritania, Niger, Nigeria, Senegal, Sierra Leone, Togo and Upper Volta to coordinate economic development and cooperation. Some progress on liberalized industrial trade has been made and a Cooperation, Compensation and Development Fund established. During the 1980s the pace of regionalization quickened. ECOWAS countries agreed upon formulative policies for the Community, especially regarding air transport, communications, agriculture, freedom of movement between Member States, currency convertibility, and a common currency. ECOWAS (now the West African Economic and Monetary Union, WAEMU) and CARICOM have agreed upon policies and programs for mutual promotion of inter-Community trade.

In June of 1991, the Organization of African Unity (OAU) member states agreed to a Treaty Establishing the African Economic Community. This wide-ranging Treaty embraces 51

African nations, and includes a regional Court of Justice. In September of 1995, 12 southern African countries, with South Africa under Mandela participating for the first time, targeted free trade under the Southern African Development Community. A 26-member Common Market for Eastern and Southern Africa (COMESA) has also been launched.

Islamic World

Bahrain, Kuwait, Oman, Qatar, Saudi Arabia, and United Arab Emirates have formed the Gulf Cooperation Council (GCC) with objectives to establish freedom of movement, a regional armaments industry, common banking and financial systems, a unified currency policy, a customs union, a common foreign aid program, and a joint, international investment company, the Gulf Investment Corporation (capitalized in 1984 at two and one-half billion dollars).

The Council has already implemented trade and investment rules concerning tariffs on regional and imported goods, government contracts, communications, transportation, real estate investment, and freedom of movement of professionals. Progress has been made on a Uniform Commercial Code and a Commission for Commercial Arbitration of the Gulf states. In 1987, the GCC entered into negotiations with the EU which resulted in a major 1990 trade and cooperation agreement. In 2003, the non-Arab states of Iran, Pakistan, Turkey, Afghanistan and five Central Asian nations joined together in an Economic Cooperation Organization Trade Agreement (ECOTA). In 2004, Jordan, Egypt, Tunisia and Morocco concluded their Agadir free trade agreement.

Latin America and Caribbean

Other regional groups have been established in Latin America and the Caribbean. Since 1973, the Caribbean countries of Barbados, Belize, Dominica, Jamaica, Trinidad-Tobago, Grenada, St. Kitts-Nevis-Anguilla, St. Lucia, and St. Vincent have participated in the Caribbean Community (CARICOM), an outgrowth of the earlier Caribbean Free Trade Association. In 1958 Costa Rica, El Salvador, Guatemala, Honduras and Nicaragua formed the Central American Common Market (CACM), another victim of political strife, but still functioning in a limited way. Numerous countries in Latin America were members of the Latin American Free Trade Association (LAFTA) (1961) which had small success in reducing tariffs and developing the region through cooperative industrial sector programs. These programs allocated industrial production among the participating states.

The Grand Anse Declaration commits CARICOM to establishment of its own common market. The Latin American Integration Association (LAIA) (1981), the eleven member successor to LAFTA, is continuing arrangements for intra-community tariff concessions. They agreed to a 50 percent tariff cut on LAIA goods. Antigua, Dominica, Grenada, Montserrat, St. Kitts-Nevis, St. Lucia, St. Vincent and the Grenadines have formed the Organization of Eastern Caribbean States (OECS) in part "to establish common institutions which could serve to increase their bargaining power as regards third countries or groupings of countries". Some 37 nations signed the Association of Caribbean States agreement in 1994 with long-term economic integration goals.

Latin America became a central focus in the 1990s of economic integration. Mexico not only has a free trade agreement with the United States and Canada, it has also agreed to free trade with Colombia, Venezuela, Chile, Bolivia, Costa Rica, Nicaragua, Guatemala, Honduras, El Salvador, Peru and Uruguay. It has even negotiated free trade agreements with the European Union and EFTA (European Free Trade Assn) and Japan. Argentina, Brazil, Paraguay and Uruguay signed a treaty establishing the MERCOSUR (Southern Cone) common market in March of 1991 and Chile and Bolivia joined them as Associates in 1996. Venezuela under Chavez finally obtained membership in 2012. All of this activity occurs against the background of the Free Trade Area of the Americas (FTAA) initiative led by the United States.

ANCOM ("The Cartegena Agreement") was founded by Bolivia, Chile, Colombia, Ecuador, and Peru in 1969 primarily to counter the economic power of Argentina, Brazil and Mexico and to reduce dependency upon foreign capital and technology. Its Decision No. 24 regulating foreign investment and technology transfers was widely copied during the 1970s. A major boost came in 1973 with the addition of Venezuela, but some of the fragile dynamics of the regional grouping are illustrated by Chile's withdrawal in 1977, Bolivia's withdrawal in 1981 and resumption of membership barely four months later, and Peru's economic (but not political) withdrawal in 1991 and return in 1996.

In 2003 the ANCOM and MERCOSUR groups nominally agreed upon free trade, at least partly to counterbalance United States power in the FTAA negotiations. The United States, pursuing in turn a divide and conquer strategy, has been negotiating bilateral free trade agreements with all ANCOM members save Venezuela. *See* Section 16.3.

§ 15.7   The Association of Southeast Asian Nations (ASEAN)

Some interesting moves toward third world free trade and rule-making have been taken by the Association of Southeast Asian Nations (ASEAN). Its problems, failures and successes are representative of third world attempts at legal and economic integration. ASEAN has its genesis in the 1967 Bangkok Declaration, with common trade rules in various states of growth, implementation and retrenchment. ASEAN has internal tariff preferences, industrial development projects, "complementation schemes," and regional joint ventures, all discussed below.

An important juncture in the integration process is the point in time at which member countries of a regional group accept a supranational mechanism for enforcing the regime's law irrespective of national feelings and domestic law within a member country. The 1957 Treaty of Rome provided for a supranational European Court of Justice, which decided quickly upon a mandatory enforcement stance regarding national (Member State) compliance with regional law. ASEAN does not have a comparable enforcement mechanism. A vigorous administrator can also make regional law a reality. In Europe, the Commission frequently issues regulations and decisions which are binding within the territories of Member States. These rules are enforced through fines and penalties, and ultimately by the Court of Justice and European Court of First Instance. Violations are investigated and, if necessary, prosecuted by the Commission. *See* Section 19.4. In contrast, the ASEAN Secretary-General once remarked that ASEAN's Secretariat was "a postman collecting and distributing letters." The surrender of national sovereignty to ASEAN institutions has been a painfully slow process. That said, NAFTA provides an alternative example of achieving free trade without significantly surrendering national sovereignty to regional institutions.

ASEAN was formed in 1967 by Indonesia, Malaysia, the Philippines, Singapore and Thailand. Brunei joined in 1984, Vietnam in 1995. Laos and Myanmar(Burma) joined in 1997, and more recently Kampuchea (Cambodia) became a member. Rarely have such culturally, linguistically and geographically diverse nations attempted integration. The Bangkok Declaration establishing ASEAN as a cooperative association is a broadly worded document. Later proposals were made for a formal ASEAN treaty or convention, but were rejected as unnecessary. The Bangkok Declaration sets forth numerous regional, economic, cultural and social goals, including acceleration of economic growth, trade expansion and industrial collaboration.

The Bangkok Declaration establishes several mechanisms, but little supranational legal machinery, to implement its stated goals. An annual ASEAN Meeting of Foreign Ministers is scheduled on a rotational basis among the Member States. Special meetings are held "as required". The Declaration provides for a Standing Committee composed of the Foreign Minister of the State in which the next annual Ministerial Meeting is to be held, and includes the ambassadors of other ASEAN States accredited to that State. The Declaration also provides for "Ad Hoc Committees and Permanent Committees of specialists and officials on specific subjects". Each Member State is charged to set up a National Secretariat to administer ASEAN affairs within that Member State and to work with the Ministerial Meeting and the Standing Committee.

There have been relatively infrequent meetings of the ASEAN heads of government. This contrasts with the semiannual European "summits" that have kept that group moving forward along the path of integration. The third ASEAN summit was held in Manila in 1987. This summit produced an agreement for the promotion and protection of investments by ASEAN investors (national and most-favored-nation treatment rights are created), made revisions to the basic ASEAN joint venture agreement, and continued the gradual extension of regional tariff and nontariff trade preferences. Goods already covered by the ASEAN tariff scheme were given a 50 percent margin of preference. New items received a 25 percent preferential margin. The nontariff preferences generally co-opt GATT rules, e.g. regarding technical standards and customs valuation.

The fourth ASEAN summit in 1992 committed the parties to the creation of a free trade area within 15 years. Five years were cut from this schedule by agreement in 1994, but operational reality has eluded ASEAN free trade. In 2003, a "watershed" date for complete integration in an ASEAN Economic Community targeted 2020. In 2007, this target date was changed to 2015, a reflection of the fear that ASEAN risks being overwhelmed by the powerhouse economies of China, India and Japan.

§ 15.8　East Asian Integration

East Asia, ranging from Japan in the North to Indonesia in the South, enjoyed truly remarkable economic growth during the 1980s and 1990s. When the Asian financial crisis hit in 1997–98, the region took it on the chin economically, but bounced back quickly. United States and other foreign investors participated in this growth largely on a country-by-country basis. All signs are that rapid growth, especially in China, will continue.

East Asia, unlike Europe or NAFTA, has not developed a formal agreement with uniform trade, licensing and investment rules. Only recently has the APEC (Asia-Pacific Economic Cooperation) group even begun to address this idea. The APEC group is comprised of Asia-Pacific nations including the United States. Late in 1994 the APEC nations targeted free trade and investment for industrial countries by 2010 and developing countries by 2020. Nine industries were selected for initial trade liberalization efforts.

With the European Union and the North American Free Trade Area maturing rapidly, one provocative question is the future of Japan. It is not in the interests of any nation that Japan should feel economically isolated or threatened. Yet it is hard to imagine incorporating Japan into the NAFTA, though some have suggested this. To some degree, what appears to be happening is that regional integration in East Asia is growing along lines that follow Japanese investment and economic aid decisions. Japan now has "economic cooperation" agreements with ASEAN, Thailand, Malaysia, the Philippines, Indonesia, Vietnam, Switzerland, India and Brunei. It has also joined in the negotiation of a Transpacific Partnership Agreement (TPP) spearheaded by the United States and including Vietnam, Malaysia, Brunei, Singapore, Australia, New Zealand, Chile, Peru, Colombia, Mexico, and Canada. Some have seen in these well-advanced negotiations a "containment" of China strategy.

The role of China in all of this is critical. China and Japan are clearly rivals for economic leadership of the region. China is pushing for influence in the East Asian economic sphere. Hong Kong's return in 1997 and Macau in 1999 moved in this direction. Some commentators foresee, as a practical matter, the emergence of a powerful Southern China coastal economic zone embracing Hong Kong, Taiwan, Guangdong and Fujian.

China is cultivating trade and investment relations with Singapore, South Korea, Taiwan and, to a lesser extent, Japan. China also has free trade deals with Hong Kong, Chile, Costa Rica, Peru, Singapore, Pakistan, New Zealand and others. China's FTAs, however, often allow numerous exceptions in the form of "sensitive" sectors and subjects. ASEAN and China have a free trade agreement, achieved before that of Japan, and both countries have commenced negotiating a Regional Comprehensive Economic Partnership (RCEP) with the 10 ASEAN states, Australia, India, New Zealand and South Korea participating.

§ 15.9 Text of GATT Article 24

1. The provisions of this Agreement shall apply to the metropolitan customs territories of the contracting parties and to any other customs territories in respect of which this Agreement has been accepted under Article XXVI or is being applied under Article XXXIII or pursuant to the Protocol of Provisional Application. Each such customs territory shall, exclusively for the purposes of the territorial application of this Agreement, be treated as though it were a contracting party; *Provided* that the provisions of this paragraph shall not be construed to create any rights or obligations as between two or more customs territories in respect of which this Agreement has been accepted under Article XXVI or is being applied under Article XXXIII or pursuant to the Protocol of Provisional Application by a single contracting party.

2. For the purposes of this Agreement a customs territory shall be understood to mean any territory with respect to which separate tariffs or other regulations of commerce are maintained for a substantial part of the trade of such territory with other territories.

3. The provisions of this Agreement shall not be construed to prevent:

(*a*) Advantages accorded by any contracting party to adjacent countries in order to facilitate frontier traffic;

(*b*) Advantages accorded to the trade with the Free Territory of Trieste by countries contiguous to that territory, provided that such advantages are not in conflict with the Treaties of Peace arising out of the Second World War.

4. The contracting parties recognize the desirability of increasing freedom of trade by the development, through voluntary agreements, of closer integration between the economies of the countries parties to such agreements. They also recognize that the purpose of a customs union or of a free-trade area should be to facilitate trade between the constituent territories and not to raise barriers to the trade of other contracting parties with such territories.

5. Accordingly, the provisions of this Agreement shall not prevent, as between the territories of contracting parties, the formation of a customs union or of a free-trade area or the adoption of an interim agreement necessary for the formation of a customs union or of a free-trade area; *Provided* that:

(*a*) with respect to a customs union, or an interim agreement leading to a formation of a customs union, the duties and other regulations of commerce imposed at the institution of any such union or interim agreement in respect of trade with contracting parties not parties to such union or agreement shall not on the whole be higher or more restrictive than the general incidence of the duties and regulations of commerce applicable in the constituent territories prior to the formation of such union or the adoption of such interim agreement, as the case may be;

(b) with respect to a free-trade area, or an interim agreement leading to the formation of a free trade area, the duties and other regulations of commerce maintained in each of the constituent territories and applicable at the formation of such free-trade area or the adoption of such interim agreement to the trade of contracting parties not included in such area or not parties to such agreement shall not be higher or more restrictive than the corresponding duties and other regulations of commerce existing in the same constituent territories prior to the formation of the free-trade area, or interim agreement as the case may be; and

(c) any interim agreement referred to in subparagraphs (a) and (b) shall include a plan and schedule for the formation of such a customs union or of such a free-trade area within a reasonable length of time.

6. If, in fulfilling the requirements of subparagraph 5 (a), a contracting party proposes to increase any rate of duty inconsistently with the provisions of Article II, the procedure set forth in Article XXVIII shall apply. In providing for compensatory adjustment, due account shall be taken of the compensation already afforded by the reduction brought about in the corresponding duty of the other constituents of the union.

7. (a) Any contracting party deciding to enter into a customs union or free-trade area, or an interim agreement leading to the formation of such a union or area, shall promptly notify the CONTRACTING PARTIES and shall make available to them such information regarding the proposed union or area as will enable them to make such reports and recommendations to contracting parties as they may deem appropriate.

(b) If, after having studied the plan and schedule included in an interim agreement referred to in paragraph 5 in consultation with the parties to that agreement and taking due account of the information made available in accordance with the provisions of subparagraph (a), the CONTRACTING PARTIES find that such agreement is not likely to result in the formation of a customs union or of a free-trade area within the period contemplated by the parties to the agreement or that such period is not a reasonable one, the CONTRACTING PARTIES shall make recommendations to the parties to the agreement. The parties shall not maintain or put into force, as the case may be, such agreement if they are not prepared to modify it in accordance with these recommendations.

(*c*) Any substantial change in the plan or schedule referred to in paragraph 5 (c) shall be communicated to the CONTRACTING PARTIES, which may request the contracting parties concerned to consult with them if the change seems likely to jeopardize or delay unduly the formation of the customs union or of the free-trade area.

8. For the purposes of this Agreement:

(*a*) A customs union shall be understood to mean the substitution of a single customs territory for two or more customs territories, so that

(i) duties and other restrictive regulations of commerce (except, where necessary, those permitted under Articles XI, XII, XIII, XIV, XV and XX) are eliminated with respect to substantially all the trade between the constituent territories of the union or at least with respect to substantially all the trade in products originating in such territories, and,

(ii) subject to the provisions of paragraph 9, substantially the same duties and other regulations of commerce are applied by each of the members of the union to the trade of territories not included in the union;

(*b*) A free-trade area shall be understood to mean a group of two or more customs territories in which the duties and other restrictive regulations of commerce (except, where necessary, those permitted under Articles XI, XII, XIII, XIV, XV and XX) are eliminated on substantially all the trade between the constituent territories in products originating in such territories.

9. The preferences referred to in paragraph 2 of Article I shall not be affected by the formation of a customs union or of a free-trade area but may be eliminated or adjusted by means of negotiations with contracting parties affected.* This procedure of negotiations with affected contracting parties shall, in particular, apply to the elimination of preferences required to conform with the provisions of paragraph 8 (a)(i) and paragraph 8 (b).

10. The CONTRACTING PARTIES may by a two-thirds majority approve proposals which do not fully comply with the requirements of paragraphs 5 to 9 inclusive, provided that such proposals lead to the formation of a customs union or a free-trade area in the sense of this Article.

11. Taking into account the exceptional circumstances arising out of the establishment of India and Pakistan as independent States and recognizing the fact that they have long constituted an economic unit, the contracting parties agree that the provisions of this Agreement shall not prevent the two countries from entering into special arrangements with respect to the

trade between them, pending the establishment of their mutual trade relations on a definitive basis.*

12. Each contracting party shall take such reasonable measures as may be available to it to ensure observance of the provisions of this Agreement by the regional and local governments and authorities within its territories.

Text of ad Article XXIV

Ad Article XXIV: Paragraph 9

> It is understood that the provisions of Article I would require that, when a product which has been imported into the territory of a member of a customs union or free-trade area at a preferential rate of duty is re-exported to the territory of another member of such union or area, the latter member should collect a duty equal to the difference between the duty already paid and any higher duty that would be payable if the product were being imported directly into its territory.

Paragraph 11

> Measures adopted by India and Pakistan in order to carry out definitive trade arrangements between them, once they have been agreed upon, might depart from particular provisions of this Agreement, but these measures would in general be consistent with the objectives of the Agreement.

Chapter 16

NAFTA, FREE TRADE AND FOREIGN INVESTMENT IN THE AMERICAS

Table of Sections

For more extensive treatment of this material, see R.
Folsom, *NAFTA, Free Trade and Foreign Investment in the
Americas.*

---

§ 16.0 U.S. Free Trade Agreements

The United States has entered into a growing number of major
free trade agreements. The first was with Israel, enacted through
the United States–Israel Free Trade Area Implementation Act of

1985.[1] The Israeli-U.S. Agreement (IFTA) was fully implemented by January 1, 1995. The second was with Canada, and this agreement was adopted through the United States–Canada Free Trade Area Agreement Implementation Act of 1988.[2] The Canada-U.S. Agreement (CUSFTA) was fully implemented by January 1, 1998. The United States negotiated along with Canada and Mexico a three-way North American Free Trade Area Agreement (NAFTA). The NAFTA took effect January 1, 1994 with full implementation in nearly all areas by the year 2003. NAFTA was incorporated into United States law by the North American Free Trade Agreement Implementation Act of 1993.[3] Late in 2001, Jordan and the United States agreed on free trade. In 2003, the United States reached free trade agreements with Chile and Singapore, notably incorporating coverage of E-Commerce and digital products. Early in 2004, free trade between the United States and five Central American states (CAFTA) plus the Dominican Republic, and with Australia and Morocco, was agreed. More bilateral free trade deals have been struck with Bahrain, Oman and Peru, and additional agreements with Panama, Colombia and South Korea took effect in 2012. *See* Section 2.4.

These trade agreements provide new duty free import opportunities into the U.S. market. Unlike the Generalized System of Preferences (GSP) program and the Caribbean Basin Initiative,[4] these agreements are reciprocal. That is to say they open up foreign markets to United States exports on a duty free basis. In addition, they establish detailed rules targeting nontariff trade barriers (NTBs) among the parties.

§ 16.1   Canada-U.S. Free Trade, Cultural Industries Exclusion

The United States and Canada have the largest bilateral trading relationship in the world. As early as 1854, the Elgin-Marcy Treaty concluded a free trade agreement covering agriculture, resource and other primary products between the U.S. and Canadian provinces. Termination of this treaty in 1866 led to adoption of protectionist national trade policy in Canada. Canada made repeated (1891, 1896, 1911) unsuccessful attempts to negotiate bilateral trade agreements of various kinds with the United States. In the post-War era, Canada was an early participant in the GATT 1947. The GATT proved successful in

---

[1]   Public Law 99–47, 98 Stat. 3013, June 11, 1985.
[2]   Public Law 100–449, 102 Stat. 1851, 19 U.S.C.A. § 2112 Note.
[3]   Public Law 103–182, 107 Stat. 2057.
[4]   See Sections 2.10–2.19.

expanding U.S. and Canadian trade, but by the 1980s the pace of GATT had slowed and the significance of access to the U.S. market required attention.

Prior to the Canada-U.S. Free Trade Area Agreement (CUSFTA), about 70 percent of the trade between the two nations was already duty free. Tariffs on the remaining products averaged about five percent when entering the United States and about 10 percent when entering Canada. Annual trade between the two countries was valued at more than $200 billion U.S. dollars. This was more than three times U.S.-Japan trade. Roughly one-third of all Canada-U.S. trading concerns automotive goods, an industry still largely dominated by U.S.-based companies. Canada has continued to maintain a healthy trade surplus with the United States. Free trade between the United States and Canada is based upon reciprocity and can be terminated by either party with six months' notice.

CUSFTA became the blueprint around NAFTA was negotiated in the early 1990s. Many of its provisions were revised (notably on rules of origin), new coverage (such as land transport) was added, and a few sections of CUSFTA were carried over in full force. The most prominent of the carry-overs is the Canadian "cultural industries" exclusion from free trade and investment. No such exclusion applies as between Mexico and the United States. For Canada, it was a deal breaker, their top negotiating priority.

Canadian Cultural Industries Exclusion

Canada has a long history of supporting cultural industries through investment, financial, tax and other governmental acts. The free trade and foreign investment agreement between Canada and the United States excluded "cultural industries" from its scope, and this exclusion has been retained under NAFTA. The argument for this exclusion is not to keep American culture out of the market, but instead to assure a Canadian presence as well. Indeed, Canada maintains that it has neither attempted nor succeeded in keeping out American cultural products. That certainly seems right. Over 90 percent of Canada's movie screens and more than 80 percent of its news and TV broadcasts are U.S. controlled. Books of U.S. origin occupy 60 percent of all Canadian shelf space and U.S. magazines take 80 percent of the English-language market.

Cultural industries are defined in CUSFTA and NAFTA as those engaged in publishing, distributing or selling:

(1) Books, periodicals and newspapers (except their printing or typesetting);

(2) Films or videos; audio or video music recordings; or printed or machine readable music;

(3) Public radio communications;

(4) Radio, television and cable TV broadcasting; and

(5) Satellite programming and broadcasting network services (Article 2012).

One practical effect of securing the cultural industries exclusion was to insulate Canada's broadcasting regulations from regional scrutiny. In Canada, content requirements and airtime rules are an important means by which the Canadian Radio-Television and Telecommunications Commission (CRTC) restricts the amount of foreign broadcast material. Current broadcasting regulations employ a quota system mandating Canadian content for a minimum of 60 percent of all programming and 50 percent of prime time. Comparable quotas apply to films, broadcast TV, cable TV and satellite transmissions. "Canadian content" is calculated under a points system traditionally requiring that the producer be Canadian and that at least 6 of 10 key creative positions be filled by Canadians. In addition, most production and distribution expenses must be paid to Canadians.

The requirements for radio are similar and focus on the nationality of the composer and performer, and the location and performance of the selection. The government also provides subsidies and tax incentives for national broadcasting enterprises which have financial difficulty in complying with content quotas. Furthermore, investment regulations effectively limit U.S. ownership or control of Canadian cultural enterprises. For example, Canada refused to permit Borders to open a super-bookstore in Toronto even after securing a Canadian partner as a majority owner.

Ironically, although these economically driven rules ensure a national presence in broadcasting, they do not guarantee Canadian cultural content. Moreover, there is a thriving gray market for dishes aimed at U.S. satellites. More broadly, Internet streaming has undermined Canada's cultural industry trade restraints in ways that will likely avoid even the most determined regulator.

There are exceptions and qualifications to the general exclusion of Canadian cultural industries from CUSFTA and NAFTA free trade. Tariff reductions were specified under CUSFTA for film, cassettes, records, cameras, musical instruments and the like. Additional tariff reductions were agreed to in NAFTA. Responding to a United States complaint about Canadian cable TV "pirates," copyright royalties must be paid when U.S.-sourced free transmissions are retransmitted to the Canadian public by cable.

In addition, no alteration or non-simultaneous retransmission of such broadcasts is permitted without the permission of the copyright holder. Likewise, no retransmission of cable or pay TV can occur without such authorization. Occasionally, United States investors may acquire a Canadian cultural industry company by merger or acquisition. If ordered to divest, the U.S. investor must be paid open market value by Canada. Apart from these exceptions, the Canadian cultural industry exclusion covers the entire gamut of the NAFTA agreement. It applies goods, services, investment, intellectual property, and dispute settlement.

Cultural Industries Exclusion Disputes—U.S. Responses

Canada's cultural industry exception comes with a price. The United States can unilaterally implement retaliation for cultural industry protection. The U.S. can undertake "measures of equivalent commercial effect" against acts that would have been "inconsistent" with CUSFTA but for the cultural industries exclusion (Article 2005.2). There is no need to utilize CUSFTA's (now NAFTA's) dispute settlement procedures prior to retaliation, which can be anything except a violation of the free trade agreement. Each year the United States Trade Representative must identify new Canadian acts, policies and practices affecting cultural industries.

Both Canada and the United States have sought to minimize the potential for cultural industry disputes through negotiations. The "successful" resolution of the Country Music Television (CMT) dispute in 1995 is often cited as an example. CMT of Nashville had, in the absence of a Canadian competitor, been licensed as a Canadian cable TV distributor. When a competitor emerged, CMT's license was revoked by the CRTC. CMT then petitioned the USTR for Section 301 relief, and an investigation was commenced. Intergovernmental negotiations resulted in the creation of a partnership of the two competitors, which was then licensed by the CRTC.

Cultural industry disputes have also been diverted from CUSFTA by using the World Trade Organization as an alternative forum. In March of 1997, a WTO Dispute Settlement Panel ruled that Canada's taxes, import regulations and postal subsidies concerning magazines (and advertising) violated the GATT 1994 agreement (WT/DS31/R, 3–14–97). This longstanding dispute centered on *Sports Illustrated*. Canada was seeking to protect and ensure "Canadian issues" of periodicals and prevent the export of its advertising revenues. The United States overcame culturally-based Canadian policies by electing to pursue WTO remedies, although Canada's compliance was disputed. In May of 1999, a settlement was reached. United States publishers may now wholly-own Canadian magazines. In addition, Canada will permit U.S. split-run editions without Canadian editorial content. Such editions may contain Canadian advertisements not in excess of 12 percent by lineage (rising to 18 percent).

Professor Oliver Goodenough has thoughtfully analyzed Canada's preoccupation with culture. *See* 15 *Ariz. J. Int'l & Comp. Law* 203 (1998). He believes that the cultural industry exclusion reflects a weak national identity and that a principal purpose is to rally Canadians around their flag in a "recurring pageant of threat and defense." Professor Goodenough notes that the "war" against Hollywood is primarily protective of Anglophone Canada. Francophone Canada, with a healthy cultural identity, has already demonstrated resilience to U.S. and Anglophonic Canadian influences.

Reaching into the literature on "culture transmission theory," Professor Goodenough finds that most foreign influences will "bounce off" healthy cultures without government intervention or, at the very least, compartmentalize such influences in ways which separate them from hearth and home. He concludes that Canada is "defending the imaginary to death" and if it continues to press its cultural protection policies: "[I]t will indeed be to the death, a death brought about not by 'invasion' from the south, but by the incomparably better claims to culturally-based nationhood possessed by Francophone Quebec and by the First Nation Peoples. Rather than acting as a rallying cry for national preservation, cultural protection provides the intellectual basis for a break-up of Canada."

§ 16.2 Getting to NAFTA

NAFTA did not repeal the Canada–United States Free Trade Agreement. The United States and Canada have "suspended" their 1989 agreement. If NAFTA failed or either Canada or the United States withdrew from it, CUSFTA would come out of suspended animation and continue to bind the two countries.

The U.S. free trade agreement with Canada in 1989 was nothing less than path breaking; the most sophisticated free trade agreement in the world. For most Canadians and Americans, revising the design to include Mexico required considerably more effort and discomfort. The discomfort came from years of observing protectionist Mexican trade policies, uncontrolled national debt, corruption, and the sense, somehow, that Mexico just did not "fit." In the end, these perspectives were overcome.

Mexico under Presidents de la Madrid, Salinas, Zedillo, and Fox had been unobtrusively breaking down its trade barriers and reducing the role of government in its economy. More than half of the enterprises owned by the Mexican government a decade ago have been sold to private investors, and more are on the auction block. Tariffs have been slashed to a maximum of 20 percent and import licensing requirements widely removed. Export promotion, not import substitution, became the highest priority. Like the U.S. and Canada, Mexico (since 1986) participates in the General Agreement on Tariffs and Trade (GATT) and World Trade Organization (WTO). This brought it into the mainstream of the world trading community on a wide range of fronts, including participation in nearly the full range of the Uruguay Round WTO agreements.

Mexican debt, hopefully, promises to become a manageable problem, although the collapse of the peso in 1994 and its slide in 2008/09 cast doubt on this. One party rule has ended nationally and in several states, with signs of an ever more pluralistic democracy on the horizon. Admittedly, political and economic corruption still runs deep within Mexico, but the winds of change are blowing. Major prosecutions of leading police, union and business leaders are underway. Perhaps most significantly, the rapid privatization of the state-owned sector of the economy combined with increasing tolerance of international competition has reduced not only the need for government subsidies but also the opportunity for personal enrichment by public officials.

Presidents Bush and Salinas, and Prime Minister Mulroney, pushed hard in 1991 to open "fast track" negotiations for a free trade agreement. In 1992, these efforts reached fruition when a NAFTA agreement was signed by Canada, the United States and Mexico with a scheduled effective date of Jan. 1, 1994. President Bush submitted the agreement to Congress in December 1992.

President Clinton supported NAFTA generally, but initiated negotiations upon taking office for supplemental agreements on the environment and labor. This delayed consideration of the NAFTA agreement in Congress until the Fall of 1993. Ratification was considered under fast track procedures which essentially gave Congress 90 session days to either ratify or reject NAFTA without amendments. After a bruising national debate that fractured both Democrats and Republicans with each party doing its best to avoid Ross Perot's strident anti-NAFTA attacks, ratification was achieved in mid-November, just weeks before NAFTA's effective date. During this same period, Canada's Conservative Party suffered a devastating defeat at the polls. This defeat was partly a rejection by the Canadian people of the earlier ratification of NAFTA under Prime Minister Mulroney.

The United States is Mexico's largest trading partner, accounting for nearly 70 percent of all Mexican trade and more than 60 percent of its foreign direct investment. In contrast, trade with Mexico in 1994 totaled only 7 percent of all U.S. international trade. Those facts help explain why Mexico has been the major beneficiary of the NAFTA accord.

§ 16.3   The NAFTA Agreement in Outline—Goods, Rules of Origin

Although each partner affirmed its rights and obligations under the General Agreement on Tariffs and Trade (GATT), the NAFTA generally takes priority over other international agreements in the event of conflict. The NAFTA, for example, prevailed over the former Multi-Fiber Arrangement on trade in textiles. Certain exceptions to this general rule of supremacy apply; the trade provisions of the international agreements on endangered species, ozone-depletion and hazardous wastes notably take precedence over the NAFTA (subject to a duty to minimize conflicts). Unlike the GATT/WTO, the NAFTA makes a general duty of national treatment for goods binding on all states, provinces and local governments of the three countries.

Prior to NAFTA, Mexican tariffs on U.S. goods averaged about 10 percent; U.S. tariffs on Mexican imports averaged about 5 percent. Under NAFTA, Mexican tariffs were eliminated on all U.S. exports within ten years except for corn and beans which were subject to a fifteen-year transition. United States tariffs on peanuts, sugar and orange juice from Mexico also lasted 15 years. Immediate Mexican tariff removals under the "A" list covered about half the industrial products exported from the United States. Further tariff eliminations were made for the "B" list after 5 years, and will occur for the "C" list when the treaty matures in ten years. Accelerated tariff reduction may occur by bilateral accord. The existing Canada-U.S. tariff reduction schedule remained in place.

Escape clause rules and procedures are generally applicable to United States–Mexico trade under the NAFTA. These permit temporary trade relief against import surges subject to a right of compensation in the exporting nation. During the 10-year transition period, escape clause relief could be undertaken as a result of NAFTA tariff reductions only once per product for a maximum in most cases of 3 years. The relief was the "snap-back" to pre-NAFTA tariffs. After the transition period, escape clause measures may only be undertaken by mutual consent. If a global escape clause proceeding is pursued by one NAFTA partner, the others must be excluded unless their exports account for a substantial share of the imports in question (top five suppliers) and contribute importantly to the serious injury or threat thereof (rate of growth of NAFTA imports must not be appreciably lower than total imports).

Rules of Origin

Mexico has the highest average tariffs on imported goods, the U.S. has the lowest, and Canada falls in the middle. Since free trade in goods only applies to goods that originate in North America, non-originating goods are subject to the normal tariffs of Canada, Mexico and the United States. Origin determinations are thus critical to NAFTA traders. There are Uniform NAFTA Regulations governing rules of origin and customs procedures, including a common Certificate of Origin.

Article 401 of the NAFTA agreement starts with the primary rule that all goods wholly obtained or produced entirely inside NAFTA originate there. Canadian lumber, U.S. apples and Mexican oil provide examples. Such goods fall under NAFTA Preference Criterion A. Article 415 authorizes free trade in goods made from materials that "originate" exclusively within NAFTA, Preference Criterion C. Agricultural, timber and mining products almost always qualify as such. A laptop computer whose components all come from Mexico, Canada or the United States would qualify under Criterion C.

Article 401 adopts the change of tariff classification rule initiated in CUSFTA. *See* Chapter 2. Subject to various exceptions, goods produced in one or more of the three countries with non-originating materials may be freely traded when all such materials (excepting a *de minimis* amount) undergo a change in tariff classification based upon the Harmonized Tariff System (HTS). Ordinarily this requires a change at the HTS product classification level and is known as Preference Criterion B. This Criterion is the most commonly used of all NAFTA's rules of origin for goods. *See* Example 1 below and *Cummins v. United States*, 454 F.3d 1361 (Fed. Cir. 2006) (crankshafts from Brazil not Mexico, no change in tariff classification).

Meeting the change in tariff classification rule of origin is sometimes insufficient to allow free trading. Some goods must *also* contain a minimum "regional value content" (discussed below) to qualify under Preference Criterion B. For example, footwear, chemicals and automobiles fall in this category. There are fewer such content requirements under NAFTA than under CUSFTA. Electronics and machinery are generally exempt. See Example 2 below.

Article 401 also permits certain assembly goods that do not undergo a change in tariff classification to be freely traded if their regional value content is sufficient. This is NAFTA Preference Criterion D. For goods with very small non-originating content, NAFTA creates a *"de minimis"* rule of origin. Article 405 generally permits free trade in goods whose non-originating value is 7 percent or less. Such goods, in other words, are treated as originating in North America and may be freely traded.

Here are two U.S. Customs Service examples of goods that qualify for free trade under NAFTA Criterion B:

Example 1

Frozen pork meat (HTS heading 0203) is imported into the U.S. from Hungary and combined with spices imported from the Caribbean (HTS subheadings 0907–0910). Then, the spiced meat is mixed with cereals grown and produced in the U.S. to make fresh pork sausage (HTS heading 1601).

The Annex 401 rule of origin for HTS heading 1601 states:

"A change to heading 1601 through 1605 from any other chapter."

Since the frozen meat is classified in Chapter 2 and the spices are classified in Chapter 9, these non-NAFTA-originating materials meet the tariff shift requirement. Note that one does not need to consider whether the cereal meets the applicable tariff shift requirement, as the cereal is itself NAFTA-originating.

In conclusion, the fresh pork sausage is originating under NAFTA.

Example 2

A manufacturer purchases inexpensive textile watch straps made in Taiwan (HTS heading 9113), to be assembled with originating mechanical watch movements (HTS heading 9108) and originating cases (HTS heading 9112). The value of the straps is less than seven percent (7%) of the total cost of the final watch (HTS heading 9102).

The rule of origin under Annex 402 for HTS heading 9102 states:

"A change to heading 9101 through 9107 from any other chapter; A change to heading 9101 through 9107 from 9114, whether or not there is also a change from any other chapter, provided there is a regional value content of not less than:

a) 60 percent where the transaction value method is used, or

b) 50 percent where the net cost method is used."

Remember that only non-originating materials need to meet the required tariff shift requirement, and, in this case, the textile straps are the only non-originating component. As the value of the straps is less than seven percent (7%) of the total cost of the finished watch, the *de minimis* rule applies, and the finished watch is originating under NAFTA.

NAFTA Regional Value Content

Article 402 establishes NAFTA's "top down" regional content valuation methods. These methods represent a change from CUSFTA's "bottom up" measurement of value for purposes of determining the origin of goods. There are two NAFTA regional content valuation methods: transaction value and net cost value.

In most instances, the importer seeking to qualify goods for duty free treatment under NAFTA can elect between the transaction value or net cost methods. The net cost method is generally thought to be the more difficult rule of origin. For most transactions among related parties, the net cost method must be used. Manipulation of prices in transfers among corporate affiliates might otherwise take advantage of NAFTA's transaction value method. The net cost method must also be followed if Customs rules the transaction value method "unacceptable."

The NAFTA transaction value method follows the GATT Customs Valuation Code of 1979 to which Canada, Mexico and the United States adhere. This method starts with an analysis of the F.O.B. price paid, including generally commissions, transport costs to the point of direct shipment, royalties on the goods, and manufacturing proceeds upon resale. Profits are included in the transaction value method of establishing the origin of goods as part of the price paid. The value of non-originating materials is then subtracted to arrive at the regional value content of the goods expressed in percentage terms. Normally, this percentage must be at least 60 percent in order to free trade the goods under NAFTA.

The NAFTA net cost method starts with a product's net cost to determine its regional value content. The value of non-originating materials is then subtracted. For NAFTA purposes, net cost is defined as total cost less expenses of sales promotion, marketing, after-sales service, royalties, shipping and packing, non-allowable interest charges and other "excluded costs." There are three authorized methods of allocating costs in calculating net cost (Article 402.8). The producer gets to elect among these methods (provided the allocation of all costs is consistent with the Uniform NAFTA Regulations on Rules of Origin and Customs Procedures).

A regional content of 50 percent or more calculated on a net cost basis qualifies most goods for free trade under NAFTA. For light duty motor vehicles and their parts, a regional value content rising to 62.5 percent since 2002 is required. Other automotive goods must possess to 60 percent regional content since 2002. Automotive goods must be valued on a net cost basis.

The value of non-originating materials (VNM) is excluded under both methods when determining the NAFTA origin of goods. This value is usually based on transaction values. If necessary, alternative values as determined under the GATT Customs Valuation Code of 1979 are used. "Intermediate materials" fabricated by producers are generally treated as originating, a rule which benefits vertically integrated producers.

NAFTA embraces an "all or nothing" roll up approach to non-originating materials that resolves some of the disputes that emerged under CUSFTA. In sum, the value of non-originating materials in components used to produce a good that is North American in origin is excluded from the VNM calculation in assessing regional content. This means that for both the transaction value and net cost methods, these materials are excluded in the determination of non-originating value. However, a tracing requirement for automobiles is added. The value of non-originating automotive materials must be traced back through suppliers. In the United States, cumulation provisions allow free trade partners to use inputs from other countries with which the U.S. free trades and still qualify for preferential treatment.

Components that do not originate in NAFTA but possess some originating materials, on the other hand, are rolled down on the same all or nothing basis. In other words, these originating materials are included in the determination of non-originating value. However, a nonintegrated producer may "accumulate" such originating material when calculating the regional value content of finished goods.

A diagram of the transaction (TV) and net cost (NC) methods of calculating regional value content percentages is provided in Article 402 of the agreement. For these purposes VMC equals the value of non-originating material.

$$\text{Regional Value Content} = \frac{\text{TV–VNM}}{\text{TV}} \times 100$$

$$\text{Regional Value Content} = \frac{\text{NC–VNM}}{\text{NC}} \times 100$$

Rules of Origin, Textiles and Apparel

Like automobiles, textiles and apparel have unique rules of origin. Special production requirements are created that protect North American manufacturers. There is a "yarn forward" rule. This requires: (1) use of North American spun yarns; (2) to make North American fabrics; (3) that are cut and sewn into clothing in North America. Similarly, cotton and man-made fiber yarns have to be "fiber forwarded" for North American free trade.

These "triple transformation" rules of origin had a substantial impact. Initially, Mexican imports (heavily comprised of U.S. content) displaced East Asian apparel, though less so after 2001 when China joined the World Trade Organization. Furthermore, Mexico raised its tariffs on non-NAFTA textiles in the wake of its 1995 financial crisis, while continuing NAFTA tariff reductions. The margin of preferential access to Mexico for Canadian and United States textiles was thus magnified. Exports of U.S. textile components to Mexico have also been enhanced by greater allowance under NAFTA of maquiladora apparel sales inside Mexico. However, since 2005 when international textile and apparel quotas were eliminated by WTO agreement, Mexico has lost substantial market share to China and East Asia.

Silk, linen and other fabrics that are scarce in North America are exceptions from NAFTA's triple transformation rules, but must still be cut and sewn in North America. Textile products with less than 7 percent non-originating material measured by weight can also be freely traded. This amount is treated as *de minimis*. Some non-qualifying textiles and clothing may be preferentially traded under quotas within NAFTA. U.S. manufacturers have complained about Canadian exports of wool suits under preferential quotas.

Rules of Origin, Electronics

NAFTA created some unique rules of origin for consumer electronics products. These rules are based on changes in tariff classifications that contain particular components. For example, in order to qualify for free trade, traditional color television sets with screens over fourteen inches must contain a North American-made color picture tube. Since 1999, color television sets must also contain, among other things, North American amplifiers, tuners and power suppliers.

For a video cassette recorder to qualify for preferential treatment under NAFTA, it must contain a North American circuit board. For a microwave oven, all the major parts, except the magnetron, must be made in the North American countries. Computers must contain a North American motherboard. Traditional computer monitors, like color television sets, must contain a North American color picture tube to be considered NAFTA originating.

The initial impact of NAFTA on the electronics and computer industries has been significant. United States, Japanese and Korean investment in electronics production facilities in Mexico grew, especially in the manufacture of those components that convey NAFTA origin. Mexican purchases of U.S. electronic components and finished goods produced in maquiladoras went up substantially. However, since 2001, as with textiles, there has actually been some disinvestment from Mexico as firms move their electronics plants to China and other low cost Asian manufacturing centers. More significantly, almost all production of flat screen TVs and monitors is done in Asia, not Mexico. The NAFTA free trade incentive just simply did not overcome Asia's lower production costs.

§ 16.4 The NAFTA Agreement in Outline—Energy

Canada and Mexico are important sources of United States energy imports. With oil embargoes in mind, energy security was a major goal for the United States in negotiating NAFTA. Nevertheless, the United States was unable to obtain the same degree of energy security from Mexico that it secured from Canada. Under CUSFTA, Canada arguably promised in an energy crisis to maintain energy exports to the USA consistent with prior export levels. However, Canada unilaterally issued in 1993 a declaration interpreting CUSFTA as *not* requiring Canadian energy crisis exports at any given level or proportion.

Like cultural industries for Canada, energy was non-negotiable for Mexico. Chapter 6 of NAFTA deals with trade in energy and basic petrochemical goods. It opens with a most unusual sentence: "The Parties confirm their full respect for their Constitutions." This is an oblique reference to the revolutionary Mexican Constitution of 1917 that reserved ownership and development of natural resources to the state. Today this constitutional clause is most evident in

PEMEX, the state oil, gas and basic petrochemical monopoly. CFE, the state electricity monopoly, also embodies revolutionary state ownership principles. Both of these monopolies are currently undergoing internal Mexican reforms. In 1992, prior to NAFTA, the private sector was allowed to invest in electrical generation facilities provided the energy produced was self-consumed or sold to CFE.

NAFTA Annex 602.3 demonstrates what "full respect" for the Mexican Constitution means. In it, Mexico reserves to its state a lengthy list of strategic activities: Exploration, exploitation, and refining of crude oil and natural gas; production of artificial gas and basic petrochemicals; pipelines; foreign trade in and transport, storage and distribution of the same; virtually the entire supply of electricity to the public in Mexico; and nuclear energy.

No private Canadian, Mexican or United States investment is permitted in these areas. However, it should be noted that basic petrochemicals include ethane, propane, butanes, pentanes, hexanes, heptanes, carbon black feedstocks and napthas. Compared to past Mexican law, this is a narrow definition. NAFTA investors may participate in all secondary and non-reserved basic petrochemicals, but there has been a slowdown in privatization of such opportunities. Transportation, distribution and storage of natural gas were opened to private investors (including foreigners) in 1995 and several U.S. companies have successfully bid on such opportunities. In 1999, Mexico proposed major structural reforms of its electricity sector, including privatization of power companies. Amendments to Mexico's constitutional law will be required. At this writing, reform of Mexico's electricity sector is still pending.

Cross-border trade in energy services is possible only by permit of the Mexican government. Cross-border trade in natural gas and basic petrochemicals is similarly allowed with PEMEX through regulated supply contracts. In some cases, Mexico will permit performance clauses in energy service contracts. Mexico's traditional opposition to sharing oil and gas ownership rights in PEMEX drilling contracts continues.

Mexico has allowed 100 percent foreign ownership of new coal mines. Existing joint ventures can now become wholly-owned by NAFTA investors. Mexican tariffs on coal were completely removed at the outset. NAFTA nationals may own or operate electricity companies when the production is for the owner's use. Excess electricity must be sold to CFE at rates agreed upon by contract. Co-generation is another possibility when electricity is generated by industrial production. Once again, excess supplies go to CFE at agreed rates. Independent power production plants located in

Mexico can be owned and operated by NAFTA nationals, but CFE gets the electricity. This has been done by leasing foreign-owned plants to CFE. In the border region, CFE may contract to sell electricity to United States utilities.

NAFTA incorporates by reference the GATT 1947 provisions relating to quotas and other restraints on trade in energy and petrochemical goods. Presumably, this applies to GATT Articles XI, XX and XXI. As in other areas, this incorporation permits utilization of NAFTA dispute settlement.

In addition, other rights and obligations relating to energy goods are established by NAFTA. There is an express prohibition of import or export price controls that applies to all parties. In times of energy crises, Canadian (but not Mexican) restraints must be proportionate to past export/domestic utilization ratios. Crisis restraints may not push export prices higher than those charged domestically. And the normal channels of supply must be maintained. Mexico is also exempted from the NAFTA rules on restraining trade in energy goods for reasons of national security, but is required to adhere to the general NAFTA rules on national security trade restraints.

Energy export licensing is permissible under NAFTA. Export taxes and other charges can be used only if they apply to energy goods consumed domestically. The regulation of energy is subject to NAFTA's general national and most-favored treatment duties. The more specific rules of Chapter 6 on trade restraints and export taxes also apply. NAFTA nations must also "seek" to ensure that energy regulation does not disrupt contractual relationships "to the maximum extent practicable." They must provide for "orderly and equitable" implementation of regulatory measures.

§ 16.5   The NAFTA Agreement in Outline— Services

Cross-border NAFTA trade in services is subject to national treatment, including no less favorable treatment than that most favorably given at federal, state or local levels. No member state may require that a service provider establish or maintain a residence, local office or branch in its country as a condition to cross-border provision of services. However, a general standstill on existing discriminatory or limiting laws affecting cross-border services has been adopted. Mutual recognition of professional licenses is encouraged (notably for legal consultants and engineers), but not made automatic. All citizenship or permanent residency requirements for professional licensing have been eliminated.

Additionally, a NAFTA country may deny the benefits of the rules on cross-border provision of services if their source is in reality a third country without substantial business activities within the free trade area. For transport services, these benefits may be denied if the services are provided with equipment that is not registered within a NAFTA nation. Most air, maritime, basic telecommunications and social services are not covered by these rules, nor are those that are subject to special treatment elsewhere in the NAFTA (e.g. procurement, financing and energy). Even so, the NAFTA considerably broadens the types of services covered by free trade principles: accounting, advertising, architecture, broadcasting, commercial education, construction, consulting, enhanced telecommunications, engineering, environmental science, health care, land transport, legal, publishing and tourism.

Whereas the CUSFTA allowed free trade in services only for those sectors that were positively listed in the agreement, the NAFTA adopts a broader "negative listing" approach. All services sectors are subject to free trade principles unless the NAFTA specifies otherwise.

Foreign Legal Consultants

Mexico has a unified national licensing system for attorneys (Abogados). Canada licenses its attorneys (Barristers and Solicitors) on a provincial basis. The 50 states of the United States and the District of Columbia do likewise. While the traditional perception that business lawyers are not fungible is open to challenge in a regional economy, it is reasonable to conclude that the services of Canadian, Mexican and United States lawyers cannot generally be substituted. Professor James Smith has argued that United States and Mexican legal traditions, constitutions and political systems are so "markedly different" that legal training and law practice in one country is more likely to "hinder rather than aid" in understanding each other's legal systems. *See* 1 U.S.-Mexico L.J. 85 (1993) Certainly the different Civil and Common Law legal traditions and ethical rules found in Quebec, the rest of Canada (ROC), Mexico, and among the states of the United States support this conclusion. On balance the broad exclusion of legal services from NAFTA seems justified, though less so for international business attorneys.

Against this background, NAFTA sought an alternative to mutual licensing of lawyers based on their national certifications. This alternative, the licensing of "foreign legal consultants," proved agreeable. A number of U.S. states had already authorized licensing foreign legal consultants primarily in order to retain opportunities for U.S. lawyers practicing abroad, especially in France. New York, California, Florida, Texas, Alaska, Connecticut, the District of

Columbia, Georgia, Hawaii, Illinois, Michigan, New Jersey, Ohio, Oregon and Washington had done so prior to NAFTA. British Columbia, Ontario and Saskatchewan also licensed foreign legal consultants. Mexico had no experience with such licensure, but promised to do so under NAFTA for jurisdictions granting reciprocal rights to Mexican attorneys.

In Section B of Annex 1210.5, the NAFTA partners agreed to promote the licensing of foreign legal consultants. This, of course, is ultimately a decision for the states and provinces of the U.S. and Canada. It was also agreed that such consultants would be permitted to practice or give advice on the laws of their home jurisdiction. It is unclear whether this includes the right to practice "international law" as a foreign legal consultant. One could argue that since the law of NAFTA is by ratification or implementation part of the law of Canada, Mexico and the United States that foreign legal consultants should at a minimum be able to counsel on it. The issue of just what law a foreign legal consultant can practice has split U.S. states. Alaska, California, Connecticut, Florida, Georgia and Texas only permit foreign legal consultants to advise on the law of their home jurisdictions. Nearly all the other participating states follow the Model Rule of the American Bar Association which permits practice of law except that of the licensing state and the United States.

The Trucking Dispute

Unlike CUSFTA, the NAFTA creates a timetable for the removal of barriers to cross-border land transport services and the establishment of compatible technical, environmental and safety standards. This extends to bus, trucking, port and rail services. It should eliminate the historic need to switch trailers to Mexican transporters at the border. Cross-border truck deliveries in the border states were supposed to come on line late in 1995, but U.S. concerns about the standards of Mexican carriers and (one suspects) Teamsters Union influence have delayed this result. After 6 years, truckers were supposed to be able to move freely anywhere within NAFTA. In 2001, Mexico unanimously prevailed in a NAFTA arbitration panel on truck access to the United States.

President George W. Bush commenced a pilot cross-border trucking program, but funds for it were eliminated in the Obama economic stimulus bill (H.R. 1105). Mexico undertook, as permitted, retaliatory tariffs on selected U.S. goods. Finally, a settlement was reached in 2010 allowing certified Mexican trucks to role on U.S. highways. Mexico removed its retaliatory tariffs.

Telecommunications

Public telecommunications networks and services must be opened on reasonable and nondiscriminatory terms for firms and individuals who need the networks to conduct business, such as intracorporate communications or so-called enhanced telecommunications and information services. This means that cellular phone, data transmission, earth stations, fax, electronic mail, overlay networks and paging systems are open to Canadian and American investors. Many of them have tried to enter the Mexican market, but have been largely stymied by Telmex and Carlos Slim.

Each NAFTA country must ensure reasonable access and use of leased private lines, terminal equipment attachments, private circuit interconnects, switching, signaling and processing functions and user-choice of operating protocols. Conditions on access and use may only be imposed to safeguard the public responsibilities of network operators or to protect technical network integrity.

Rates for public telecommunications transport services should reflect economic costs and flat-rate pricing is required for leased circuits. However, cross-subsidization between public transport services is not prohibited, nor are monopoly providers of public networks or services. Such monopolies may not engage in anticompetitive conduct outside their monopoly areas with adverse affects on NAFTA nationals. Various rights of access to information on public networks and services are established, and the NAFTA limits the types of technical standards that can be imposed on the attachment of equipment to public networks.

Financial Services

Financial services provided by banking, insurance, securities and other firms are separately covered under the NAFTA. Trade in such services is generally subject to specific liberalization commitments and transition periods. Financial service providers, including non-NAFTA providers operating through subsidiaries in a NAFTA country, are entitled to establish themselves anywhere within NAFTA and service customers there (the right of "commercial presence"). Existing cross-border restraints on the provision of financial services were frozen and no new restraints may be imposed (subject to designated exceptions).

Providers of financial services in each NAFTA nation receive both national and most favored nation treatment. This includes equality of competitive opportunity, which is defined as avoidance of measures that disadvantage foreign providers relative to domestic providers. Various procedural transparency rules are established to facilitate the entry and equal opportunity of NAFTA providers of financial services. The host nation may legislate reasonable prudential requirements for such companies and, under limited circumstances, protect their balance of payments in ways which restrain financial providers.

The following are some of the more notable country-specific commitments on financial service made in the NAFTA:

United States—A grace period allowed Mexican banks already operating a securities firm in the U.S. to continue to do so until July of 1997.

Canada—The exemption granted U.S. companies under the Canada-U.S. FTA to hold more than 25 percent of the shares of a federally regulated Canadian financial institution was extended to Mexican firms, as was the suspension of Canada's 12 percent asset ceiling rules. Multiple branches may be opened in Canada without Ministry of Finance approval.

Mexico—Banking, securities and insurance companies from the U.S. and Canada are able to enter the Mexican market through subsidiaries and joint ventures (but not branches) subject to market share limits during a transition period that ended in the year 2000 (insurance) or 2004 (banking and securities). Finance companies are able to establish separate subsidiaries in Mexico to provide consumer, commercial, mortgage lending or credit card services, subject to a 3 percent aggregate asset limitation (which does not apply to lending by affiliates of automotive companies). Existing U.S. and Canadian insurers could expand their ownership rights to 100 percent in 1996. No equity or market share requirements apply for warehousing and bonding, foreign exchange and mutual fund management enterprises.

§ 16.6 The NAFTA Agreement in Outline—Foreign Investment

NAFTA's foreign investment law is extremely controversial and investor-state arbitrations have been increasingly and aggressively pursued. This is the "hot area" of NAFTA law.

NAFTA places special emphasis on relaxation of Mexico's foreign investment controls. These controls find their roots in the revolutionary 1917 Mexican Constitution and the nationalization of foreign oil and gas interests in 1937 as well as the widespread adoption of foreign investment control commissions throughout

Latin America during the 1970s. Under Mexican regulation of foreign investment since the 1940s, some industries were reserved for state ownership while others could only be owned by Mexicans. Foreigners were ordinarily allowed to invest in less sensitive industries, but often subject to mandatory joint venture requirements with majority Mexican ownership and "Calvo clause" rules limiting foreign investor dispute remedies to those available under Mexican law.

In 1973, Mexico promulgated an Investment Law that mandated more use of joint ventures if approved by the National Foreign Investment Commission. This Law was the most restrictive of its kind in Mexican history. By the 1980s, after years of mismanagement and corruption while awash in petroleum dollars, Mexico had a massive national debt problem. Foreign investment regulations issued by Presidential decree in 1989 shifted significantly towards allowance of wholly-owned subsidiaries. However, these regulations conflicted with the 1973 Investment Law. These uncertainties were finally resolved in 1993 as a direct consequence of NAFTA when Mexico adopted a new Law on Foreign Investment.

The 1993 Law is much more permissive of foreign investment without prior approval of by the Mexican Investment Commission. Although adopted on the eve of NAFTA, the 1993 Law opens many of the same doors to all investors, not just those from NAFTA. Investment opportunities based upon the NAFTA agreement that are not generally available include the suspension of many performance requirements, the phased removal of market share caps on financial services, and reduced thresholds triggering Investment Commission review. In addition, NAFTA investors are not subject to Mexico's mandatory joint venture rule, nor its "Calvo clause." Removal of these restrictions represents a major concession on the part of Mexico.

Acquisitions or sales of existing Mexican companies are generally subject to Commission review if exceeding $25 million U.S. This threshold increased to $150 million U.S. for NAFTA investors in 2003. For NAFTA investors, no permission from the National Commission is required to invest on a wholly-owned basis or acquire or sell Mexican companies whose values fall below this threshold.

NAFTA Investment Rights

In an unusual provision, Article 1112 subordinates all of Chapter 11 on investment to the rest of the NAFTA agreement. In other words, if there are inconsistencies between Chapter 11 and other parts of the NAFTA agreement, those other parts are supreme. That said, NAFTA provides investors and their investments with a number of important rights.

Canadian, Mexican and United States citizens, permanently resident aliens, and other designated persons are eligible to benefit from NAFTA's investment rules. In addition, most private and public, profit and nonprofit businesses "constituted or organized" under Canadian, Mexican or United States law also qualify. This coverage specifically includes businesses operating as corporations, partnerships, trusts, sole proprietorships, joint ventures and business associations.

Furthermore, in a notable change from CUSFTA, it is not necessary for such businesses to be owned or controlled by Canadian, Mexican or U.S. nationals or enterprises. As with services, this means that businesses owned by anyone which are "constituted or organized" inside NAFTA benefit from the agreement *provided* they carry on substantial business activities in North America. Thus Asians, Europeans and Latin Americans (for example) can invest in North America and benefit from NAFTA. See *Corn Syrup Sweeteners* below. Exceptions are made for NAFTA businesses owned or controlled by third parties from countries lacking diplomatic relations with or economically embargoed by Canada, Mexico or the United States.

Beneficiaries of NAFTA rights enjoy a broad definition of "investment." This definition includes most stocks, bonds, loans, and income, profit or asset interests. Real estate, tangible or intangible (intellectual) business property, turnkey or construction contracts, concessions, and licensing and franchising contracts are also generally included (Article 1139). However, under Annex III, each member state reserves certain economic activities to its state or domestic investors. Mexico has done so under its 1993 Foreign Investment Law. For purposes of Chapter 11, investment is defined so as to exclude claims to money arising solely from commercial contracts for the sale of goods or services, or trade financing, and claims for money that do not involve the interests noted above.

Treatment of Foreign Investors and Investments

The NAFTA agreement establishes a so-called "minimum standard of treatment" for NAFTA investors and investments which is "treatment in accordance with international law," including "fair and equitable treatment and full protection and security" (Article 1105.) For example, if losses occur due to armed conflict or civil strife, NAFTA investors and investments must be accorded nondiscriminatory treatment in response. An official NAFTA interpretative ruling indicates that Article 1105 embraces treatment in accordance with "customary" international law, a ruling intended to limit the scope of protection afforded to foreign investors. In addition, limiting definitions of "fair and equitable treatment" and "full protection and security" have been established in subsequent U.S free trade agreements. *See* Section 16.10.

Beyond this minimum, NAFTA investors and their investments are entitled to the better of national or most-favored-nation treatment from federal governments. Such treatment rights extend to establishing, acquiring, expanding, managing, conducting, operating, and selling or disposing of investments. From state or provincial governments, NAFTA investors and their investments are entitled to receive the most-favored treatment those governments grant their own investors and investments. Along these lines, United Parcel Service found Mexico lacking when it was initially limited to using smaller vans than Mexican competitors. UPS persuaded the United States to lodge a complaint under Chapter 20 (*see* Section 16.10) which led to intergovernmental consultations followed by NAFTA Commission mediation. These efforts lasted many months but eventually UPS got permission to use larger vans.

Article 1102 of NAFTA prohibits requiring minimum levels of equity holdings by nationals of the host government. Hence the historic bias in Mexican law towards mandatory_joint ventures is overcome by NAFTA. No investor can be forced on grounds of nationality to sell or dispose of a qualified investment. Mandatory appointment of senior managers on the basis of nationality is also contrary to NAFTA. However, it is permissible to require boards of directors and corporate committees with majorities from one nationality or residence, provided this does not materially impair the investor's ability to exercise control. Canadian law often makes such stipulations. Residency requirements are generally authorized if there is no impairment of the treaty rights of NAFTA investors.

Article 1106 of NAFTA prohibits various investment performance obligations, including tax-related measures, in a scope that surpasses the WTO Agreement on Trade-Related Investment Measures (TRIMS) (1995). Requirements relating to exports, domestic content, domestic purchases, trade balancing of foreign exchange inflows or earnings, import/export ratios, technology transfers, and regional or global sales exclusivity ("product mandates") are broadly prohibited. All other types of investment-related performance requirements, such as employment and research and development obligations, are not prohibited and therefore presumably lawful.

Article 1106.3 of NAFTA further prohibits conditioning the receipt or continued receipt of "an advantage" (e.g., a government subsidy or tax benefit) on compliance with requirements relating to domestic content, domestic purchases, domestic sales restraints or trade balancing. But "advantages" can be given when the requirements concern production location, provision of services, training or employing workers, constructing or expanding facilities, or carrying out research and development locally. By way of exception, domestic content or purchase requirements *and* advantages can be linked to investor compliance with: (1) Laws and regulations that are consistent with NAFTA; (2) laws necessary to protect human, animal or plant life or health; or (3) laws needed to conserve living or non-living exhaustible natural resources. However, such requirements cannot be applied arbitrarily or unjustifiably, and may not constitute a disguised restraint on trade or investment.

All monetary transfers relating to NAFTA investments are to be allowed "freely and without delay." (Article 1109) Such transfers must be possible in a "freely usable currency" at the market rate of exchange prevailing in spot transactions on the transfer date. For these purposes, monetary transfers specifically include profits, dividends, interest, capital gains, royalties, management, technical assistance and other fees, returns in kind, and funds derived from the investment. Sale or liquidation proceeds, contract payments, compensatory payments for expropriation and NAFTA dispute settlement payments are also encompassed.

Requiring investment-related monetary transfers or penalizing them is prohibited. However, such transfers can be controlled in an equitable, nondiscriminatory and good faith application of bankruptcy, insolvency, creditors' rights, securities, criminal, currency reporting and satisfaction of judgment laws. Whereas tax withholding was a justifiable basis for restricting monetary transfers under CUSFTA, this is not the case under NAFTA. Special restraints may arise in connection with balance of payments problems and taxation laws.

Expropriation

Article 1110 of NAFTA generally prohibits direct or indirect nationalization or expropriation of NAFTA investments. Measures "tantamount to" nationalization or expropriation, such as creeping expropriation or confiscatory taxation, are also prohibited. Expropriation, nationalization or tantamount measures may occur for public purposes on a nondiscriminatory basis in accordance with due process of law and NAFTA's "minimum level of treatment" (above). Post-NAFTA U.S. free trade agreements have expressly limited the possibility of succeeding with "indirect" regulatory taking expropriation claims. *See* Section 16.14.

Any authorized expropriation must result in payment of compensation without delay. The amount of payment must be equivalent to the fair market value of the investment immediately prior to expropriation. In valuing the investment, going concern value, asset value (including declared tax values of tangible property) and other appropriate factors must be considered. Payment must be made in a manner that is fully realizable, such as in a "G7" currency (U.S. dollars, Canadian dollars, EUROS, British pounds sterling, Japanese yen). Interest at a commercially reasonable rate must also be included. If payment is made in Mexican pesos, this amount must be calculated as of the expropriation date in a G7 currency plus interest.

Certain governmental acts are not treated as expropriations. For example, NAFTA specifies that nondiscriminatory measures of general application that impose costs on defaulting debtors are not tantamount to expropriation of a bond or loan *solely* for that reason. Compulsory licensing of intellectual property rights is not an expropriation. Revocation, limitation or creation of such rights as allowed by Chapter 17 of NAFTA is also deemed not an expropriation.

These provisions embody an historic change in Mexico's position on expropriation law. Without explicitly saying so, Mexico has essentially embraced the U.S. position that under "international law" expropriation of foreign investments requires "prompt, adequate and effective" compensation. Mexico had specifically rejected this standard in negotiating a settlement of its oil and gas (and land) expropriations in the 1930s. Down through the years Mexico adamantly clung to its view that compensation would only be paid according to Mexican law. For investors protected under NAFTA (which are not just Canadian and U.S. investors), Chapter 11 represents the dawn of a new era.

Exceptions and Reservations, The Environment

Annexes I–IV of the NAFTA agreement reveal a host of investment-related reservations and exceptions. Many pre-existing, non-conforming regulations were grandfathered though most (not including basic telecommunications, social services and maritime services) are subject to a standstill agreement intended to avoid relapses into greater protection. In contrast, regulations promoting investment "sensitive to environmental concerns" are expressly authorized. Mexico's tradition of assessing the environmental impact of foreign investments will therefore continue. There is also a formal recognition that creating exceptions to environmental laws to encourage NAFTA investors to establish, acquire, expand or retain their investments is inappropriate. However, NAFTA's Chapter 20 dispute settlement mechanism cannot be invoked concerning this "commitment." Only intergovernmental consultations are mandatory.

Other investment-related exceptions concern government procurement, subsidies, export promotion, foreign aid and preferential trade arrangements. These exceptions apply mostly to the rules on nondiscriminatory treatment and performance requirements. Most general exceptions to NAFTA, such as for Canadian cultural industries (*see* Section 16.1), also apply to its investment rules. The general national security exception, for example, allows the United States to block the acquisition of U.S. companies by foreigners (including Canadians and Mexicans) under FINSA ("Exon-Florio") regulations (50 U.S.C. App. § 2170).

§ 16.7 The NAFTA Agreement in Outline— Arbitration of Foreign Investor-State Disputes

NAFTA has created a highly innovative and increasingly controversial investment dispute settlement system. This system provides a way for foreign investors to challenge governmental and state enterprise acts and recover damages for violation of rights established in Chapter 11. Remarkably, investors may not only assert claims as individuals, but also on behalf of NAFTA enterprises they own or control directly or indirectly (Article 1117). This authorization avoids one of international law's most famous problems . . . "standing to sue" when the investor's only loss or damage is injury to its investment abroad. See *Belgium v. Spain (the "Barcelona Traction Case")*, 1970 Int'l Court of Justice 3 (preliminary objections).

Chapter 20 NAFTA dispute settlement does not apply to "investor-state disputes." Such disputes are instead subject to binding arbitration, another major concession on the part of Mexico which has always adhered to the "Calvo Doctrine." That doctrine (widely followed in Latin America) requires foreign investors to forego protection by their home governments, be treated as Mexican nationals, and pursue legal remedies exclusively in Mexico. *See* Article 27 of the Mexican Constitution.

Individual investors claiming that a government has breached NAFTA investment or state enterprise obligations, or that one of its monopolies has done so, commence the dispute resolution process. All claims are filed against the federal government even when it is state, provincial or local government action that is being challenged.

This can place Canada, Mexico and the United States in the awkward position of defending sub-central governmental acts. *See Metalclad* and *Loewen* below.

The investor must allege that the breach of NAFTA caused loss or damage. Such claims must be asserted no later than three years after the date when knowledge of the alleged breach and knowledge of the loss or damage was first acquired or should have been first acquired. However, decisions by the Canadian or Mexican foreign investment control commissions, national security actions, and Canadian cultural industry reservations cannot be the basis for such a claim. Moreover, a host of reservations and exceptions contained in Chapter 11B deny access to NAFTA's investor-state arbitration remedy. Even so, as outlined below, the number of claims being filed is rising, some claims are producing unexpected results, and the process itself is under dispute.

Before submitting a claim to arbitration, individual investors must give 90 days' advance notice to the host country. Such notice must include an explanation of the issues, their factual basis and remedies sought. Claimants must also consent in writing to arbitrate under the procedures established in the NAFTA agreement. They *must waive* in writing their rights to initiate or continue any other damages proceedings. See *Commerce Group Corp. v. El Salvador* (ICSID, 2011) (CAFTA-DR tribunal dismisses complaint due to pending litigation). Individual investors need not, however, waive their rights to injunctive, declaratory or other extraordinary relief (not involving damages). These remedies may not be awarded through NAFTA arbitration of investor-state disputes.

Arbitration Procedures, Appeals and Remedies

The NAFTA nations consented unconditionally in advance to the submission of investor claims to arbitration under NAFTA procedures. Furthermore, they agreed not to assert insurance payments or other investor indemnification rights as a defense, counterclaim, right of setoff or otherwise.

The investor submitting a claim to arbitration against a NAFTA state ordinarily can elect between the following arbitration rules:

(1) The ICSID Convention* if both member states adhere. (This is impossible at present since only the United States has ratified ICSID);

(2) The Additional Facility Rules of ICSID provided one member state (i.e., the United States) adheres to the ICSID Convention; or

(3) The U.N.-derived UNCITRAL Arbitration Rules.

NAFTA investor-state tribunals have three panelists. The investor and the state each choose one arbitrator. If possible, the third presiding panelist is chosen by agreement. The ICSID Secretary-General selects the presiding arbitrator if agreement is not reached within 90 days. That person is chosen from a consensus roster of acceptable names, but may not be a national from either side of the dispute.

Investor-state tribunals must decide the dispute in accordance with the NAFTA agreement and "applicable rules of international law." The responding state may raise defenses based upon reservations or exceptions contained in Annexes I–IV to the NAFTA agreement. In such instances, the NAFTA Commission (not the arbitration panel) will generally issue a binding ruling on the validity of such a defense. Defenses based upon permissible regulation of monetary transfers by financial institutions are generally decided by the NAFTA Financial Services Committee.

By agreement of the parties, the investor-state arbitration tribunal can obtain expert reports on factual issues concerning environmental, health, safety or other scientific matters. The tribunal may also order temporary relief measures to preserve rights or the full effectiveness of its jurisdiction. It may, for example, order the preservation of evidence. The tribunal cannot, however, order attachment or enjoin governmental regulations that are being challenged.

NAFTA investor-state tribunals are authorized to award investors or NAFTA enterprises actual *damages* and interest, or restitution of property, or both. At this writing, damages have been awarded against and paid by Canada and Mexico, but not the United States. See *Metalclad* and *S.D. Myers* below. If the award is to an enterprise, any person may *also* pursue relief under "applicable domestic law." If restitution is ordered, the responsible member state may provide monetary damages and interest instead. NAFTA tribunals can apportion legal fees between the parties at

---

*   The Convention on the Settlement of Investment Disputes between States and Nationals of Other States (1966). The Convention is administered through the World Bank in Washington, D.C. and has been ratified by over 150 nations.

their discretion. Such fees routinely run into hundreds of thousands, if not millions, of dollars. The costs of administering Chapter 11 tribunals, including generous fees for the arbitrators, often exceed $500,000. The losing party is typically required to pay these costs.

The award of the tribunal is binding on the parties, but subject to revision or annulment in the courts of the arbitration's situs. See *Metalclad* and *S.D. Myers* below. Absent agreement, the arbitrators determine situs. Professor Brower and others have argued that a standing appellate body not unlike that of the WTO would provide greater legitimacy and uniformity to Chapter 11 arbitrations. See 36 *Vanderbilt J. Transnational Law* 37 (2003).

Awards are specifically not "precedent" in future NAFTA arbitrations (Article 1136), yet routinely cited and argued in Chapter 11 proceedings and decisions. NAFTA investor-state arbitration awards are supposed to be honored. Should this not occur, the investor may seek enforcement of the award. NAFTA nations have agreed to provide the means for such enforcement. The NAFTA investor-state dispute settlement system meets the various requirements of the ICSID Convention, its Additional Facility Rules, the New York Convention on Recognition and Enforcement of Foreign Arbitral Awards (1958), and the Inter-American Convention on International Commercial Arbitration (1975).

Should it become necessary to judicially enforce an investor-state arbitration award, the New York Convention provides a likely recourse as all three nations adhere to it. However, U.S. courts have held the grounds for denying enforcement of NAFTA awards under the New York Convention limited strictly to its provisions. Thus, the longstanding U.S. doctrine of denying enforcement when arbitrators "manifestly disregard the law", a doctrine not incorporated in the New York Convention, was not applied in a NAFTA award enforcement proceeding. See *In re Arbitration between International Thunderbird Gaming Corp. v. United Mexican States,* 473 F.Supp.2d 80 (D.C.2007).

If there is no compliance with the award and enforcement proceedings fail, the investor's government may as a last recourse commence intergovernmental dispute settlement under Chapter 20 of NAFTA. This panel rules on whether noncompliance inconsistent with the NAFTA agreement has occurred and can recommend compliance. If compliance still does not follow, benefits granted under NAFTA to the noncomplying nation may be suspended.

Foreign Investor Claims against States under NAFTA

Investors have not hesitated to invoke the innovative investor-state arbitration procedures authorized under Section B of Chapter 11 of NAFTA. Since 2001, in an official Interpretation, Chapter 11 has been construed as not imposing a general duty of confidentiality. The NAFTA governments have therefore released all documents submitted to or issued by Chapter 11 arbitration tribunals. A particularly good collection of these materials can be found at www.naftaclaims.com. Moreover, since late 2003 open Chapter 11 hearings have become the rule, as have permissive procedures for non-party submissions (amicus curiae).

Many investors allege state action that is "tantamount to expropriation." This is a claim that Article 1110 authorizes and one which could be construed to fit many fact patterns. National treatment and the NAFTA minimum standard of treatment (see above) are also commonly disputed. Some examples of these disputes follow.

Metalclad. A prominent dispute involved Metalclad Corp. of California, which had acquired a hazardous waste site operated by a Mexican company in Guadalcazar, San Luis Potosi subject to various federal approvals, all of which were obtained. State and local opposition to opening the site after an expensive clean-up resulted in the denial of a building permit in a newly created "ecological zone." Metalclad claimed these acts were tantamount to expropriation, and denial of national and the NAFTA minimum standards of treatment. It sought $90 million in damages from the Mexican federal government, which despite having supported the Metalclad contract was obliged to defend the hostile local and state actions. Metalclad received an award of $16 million under NAFTA Chapter 11 in 2000. The arbitration was conducted under the ICSID Additional Facility rules.

Mexico instituted judicial proceedings to set aside the award in British Columbia, the arbitration's legal *situs*. Canada intervened in support of Mexico. The arbitrators had found the Mexican regulatory action a breach of NAFTA's minimum standard based on a lack of "transparency," and tantamount to expropriation without adequate compensation.

The British Columbia Supreme Court, ruling under the B.C. International Arbitration Act, agreed that the expropriation decision fell within the scope of the dispute submitted and was therefore valid. It rejected, however, the transparency decision as beyond the scope of the submission. The court found no transparency obligations in Chapter 11, and none as a matter of *customary* international law (which traditionally bars only "egregious," "outrageous" or "shocking" conduct). Mexico subsequently paid Metalclad approximately $16 million U.S., the first payment by a state to an investor under Chapter 11.

   Ethyl and Methanex. A second prominent dispute involved Ethyl Corp. of the USA, which claimed $250 million U.S. damages against the Canadian government as a consequence of 1997 federal legislation banning importation or interprovincial trade of the gasoline additive, MMT. Canada was the first country to ban MMT as a pollution and health hazard, although California has also done so. MMT is a manganese-based octane enhancer alleged to interfere with the proper functioning of catalytic converters. Ethyl Corp. is the sole producer of MMT in North America. Ethyl claimed that the new law was tantamount to expropriation, violated NAFTA's national treatment standards and constituted an unlawful Canadian-content performance requirement (because the ban would favor Canadian ethanol as a substitute for MMT).

   A dispute resolution panel under Canada's Agreement on Internal Trade struck down the interprovincial trade ban. In 1998, Canada withdrew its ban on MMT and paid $13 million to Ethyl Corp. Ethyl then withdrew its $250 million arbitration claim. Canada noted the current lack of scientific evidence documenting MMT harm, an apparent abandonment of the "precautionary principle." Environmentalists decried evidence of NAFTA's negative impact, and Europeans cited *Ethyl* as good reason to reject multilateral investment guarantee agreements in the OECD (Organization for Economic Cooperation and Development). Both groups believe Chapter 11 has created a privileged class of "super-citizens" who are a threat to state sovereignty.

   Methanex Corp. of Canada submitted a claim that was in some ways the reverse of *Ethyl*. Methanex claimed that California's ban of the MTBE gasoline additive (for which it makes feedstock) amounted to an expropriation of its business interests and violated its minimum treatment rights. It sought $970 million in damages and simultaneously filed a petition under the North American Environmental Cooperation Agreement asserting that California failed to enforce its gasoline storage regulations, which Methanex saw as the source of MTBE water pollution. In 2002, the *Methanex* panel working under the UNCITRAL Rules largely rejected the complaint on jurisdictional grounds, allowing a limited re-filing on the question of intentional injury. The *Methanex* panel notably ruled that it would accept NGO amicus briefs, in this instance from the International Institute for Sustainable Development. This position was subsequently ratified for all Chapter 11 arbitrations by the NAFTA Free Trade Commission in 2003.

Loewen. The Loewen Group of Canada was held liable by a jury in 1995 to $500 million in a Mississippi breach of a funeral home contract suit. The case was settled for $150 million after the Mississippi Supreme Court required posting a $625 million bond prior to appealing the jury's verdict, a sum in excess of Loewen's net worth. In 1998, Loewen filed a claim under NAFTA alleging discrimination, denial of the minimum NAFTA standard of treatment, and uncompensated expropriation. This claim, like that of Ethyl Corp., was destined for controversy. Among other things, it challenged the discretion of American juries in awarding punitive damages. Note that it does so in a forum that does not give the American Trial Lawyers Association an opportunity to respond.

In 2003, the *Loewen* panel, calling the Mississippi decision "a disgrace," nevertheless ruled heavily against the bankrupt funeral home giant because its status as a Canadian (versus U.S.) company entitled to NAFTA investor rights was in doubt. Watch for a re-run challenging American punitive damages in the future.

Pope and Talbot. Pope and Talbot, Inc. of Portland, Oregon claimed that the 1996 Softwood Lumber Agreement (see Chapter 2) violated the national treatment, most-favored-nation treatment, minimum treatment and performance requirements rules of NAFTA. The claim asserted that the company's British Columbia subsidiary was the victim of discrimination in that the Canadian export restraints required under that Agreement applied only to four Canadian provinces. Pope & Talbot sought $20 million in compensation from the Canadian government. Rejecting most of the claims, the *Pope and Talbot* panel found Canada did violate the NAFTA minimum standard of treatment in denying export authorization to the company's B.C. subsidiary.

Although the award was only about $460,000 U.S., the panel's reasoning set off fireworks. In its view, Article 1105 demanded something more than the level of treatment commanded by customary international law. "Fair and equitable treatment" and "full protection and security" were seen as "additive;" new and expansive norms created by NAFTA's novel investor protection regime.

The additive reading of *Pope & Talbot* was subsequently rejected by the British Columbia Supreme Court in *Metalclad* (above), and collectively negated by a binding interpretation of Article 1105 issued by the three NAFTA parties in 2001. This controversial, defensive interpretation "clarifies" that Article 1105 corresponds to and thus does not expand the *customary* international law standard of minimum treatment (see *Metalclad* above), and that a breach of a NAFTA obligation does not ipso facto constitute a breach of that Article.

S.D. Myers. S.D. Myers is an Ohio company specializing in hazardous waste management of PCBs. Its Canadian affiliate imported PCBs from Ontario, to the consternation of the only Canadian PCB remediation company, Chem-Security of Alberta. In 1995, Canada banned PCB exports, intentionally giving Chem-Security a monopoly. S.D. Myers asserted this export ban violated the national treatment, performance requirements, expropriation and fair and equitable treatment provisions of Chapter 11. The arbitrators found in favor of S.D. Myers on the national treatment and fair and equitable treatment claims, awarding over $6,000,000 CDN in damages. Canada appealed to the courts of Ontario, the situs of the arbitration, and lost. In Ontario, at least, considerable deference is given to arbitral decisions. Compare British Columbia in *Metalclad* below. Subsequently, S. D. Myers and Canada settled the dispute.

Mondev. Mondev is a Canadian company engaged in commercial real estate development. It pursued various claims against the City of Boston and the Boston Redevelopment Authority in the Massachusetts courts, which were denied on sovereign immunity grounds. Mondev then filed a Chapter 11 claim arguing primarily unfair and inequitable treatment in the Massachusetts courts.

In its complaint, Mondev directly challenged the 2001 Interpretation of Article 1105, arguing it was de facto an amendment of the NAFTA agreement. Mondev also argued that customary international law should be construed in light of conclusions reached under hundreds of bilateral investment treaties and modern judgments. The tribunal recognized that fair and equitable treatment had evolved by 1994 (NAFTA's effective date) beyond what is "egregious" or "outrageous," and that bad faith on the part of states need not be shown. It then ruled against Mondev's denial of justice claims.

Glamis. Glamis, a Canadian mining company, alleged that government regulations limiting the impact of open-pit mining and protecting indigenous peoples' religious sites made its *proposed* California gold mine unprofitable. Under Chapter 11, it asserted violations of the NAFTA rules against government acts tantamount to expropriation, and denial of fair and equitable treatment. In June of 2009, a Chapter 11 tribunal accepted, in principle, that "regulatory taking" measures could amount to "creeping expropriation." That said, the tribunal undertook a detailed accounting of Glamis' alleged losses and found the mine project still had a net positive value of $20 million U.S. Hence it concluded Glamis was not impacted sufficiently to support a NAFTA expropriation claim.

While the outcome once again allowed the United States to avoid paying Chapter 11 damages, the willingness of the tribunal to entertain a regulatory taking claim was controversial (to put it mildly) and once again raised concerns that foreign investors may have greater rights under NAFTA than U.S. investors possess under United States law.

Corn Syrup Sweeteners. Late in 2009, a third Chapter 11 tribunal ruled against Mexico concerning its 20% tax from 2002 to 2007 on the production and sale of soft drinks using High Fructose Corn Syrup (HFCS). This tax was imposed in the context of a trade dispute between the U.S. and Mexico over HFCS exports south of the border and Mexican sugar exports headed north. U.S. agribusiness giants Cargill, Corn Products International and Archer Daniels Midlands, along with British Tate and Lyle's U.S. subsidiary, successfully argued that the tax constituted a "performance requirement" in violation of NAFTA Article 1106. The Mexican government was ordered to pay a total of $170 million plus interest.

AbitibiBowater. In August 2010, the Canadian federal government agreed to pay $130 million CDN to settle a Chapter 11 claim by a U.S. pulp and paper multinational, AbitibiBowater (AB). In 2008, AB closed a longstanding mill in Newfoundland via bankruptcy, terminating 800 workers without severance. Newfoundland passed a law returning, without compensation, the company's water and timber rights to the crown, and expropriating with compensation AB lands, buildings and dams in the province. AB asserted NAFTA expropriation violations. This settlement, along with the *Glamis* decision (above), has raised concerns that resource-related NAFTA investor claims may increase. For example, a Brazilian company with a U.S. subsidiary received a $15 million settlement form Canada after alleging permit delays for rock quarrying.

Apotex. Apotex is a Canadian manufacturer of generic pharmaceuticals. It has filed at least three Chapter 11 claims against the United States. These filings challenge U.S. federal court decisions denying its efforts to obtain "patent certainty" for drugs (in order to allow its generic versions to proceed), FDA denial of approval for another Apotex generic drug, and FDA import inspection practices for drugs. All of these complaints were pending as of this writing.

Exxon/Mobil. Exxon/Mobil challenged Canadian Petroleum Board rules mandating fees to support R & D in Newfoundland and Labrador. Nearby, Exxon/Mobil has developed oil fields offshore. A Chapter 11 panel affirmed in 2012 that these fees amounted to NAFTA-prohibited "performance requirements." The amount of damages is as yet undetermined, and may be influenced by increased equity stakes the provinces have obtained in the oil fields.

Other NAFTA/CAFTA Claims of Note. Several U.S. companies have commenced Chapter 11 proceedings against Canada asserting that Ontario's requirement that that a percentage of its green energy program be locally sourced excludes and damages them. Another U.S. firm is seeking damages based on Quebec's moratorium on "fracking", the use of water and chemicals to release sub-surface oil and gas reserves. Eli Lilly has filed a claim for damages because Canadian courts have invalidated the patent on one of its drugs.

One of the largest banks in France, the convoluted owner via a Nevada corporation of a share in Dominican Republic electric utilities, argued expropriation claims against the Dominican Republic after scheduled electricity rates increases were delayed. A parallel claim was filed under the France-DR Bilateral Investment Treaty (BIT). After initial success under the BIT claim, the bank obtained a $26.5 million settlement of both claims from the DR. The U.S. investor in Guatemala's privatized railroad system collected over $11 million after a CAFTA panel ruled that Guatemala's moves to revoke its contract amounted to "unfair and inequitable treatment." Claims are also pending against Guatemala by privatized owners (mostly Spanish, with a U.S. minority investor) of its electricity distribution system. The U.S. investor challenges governmentally lowered rates.

Summary

These examples of investor-state claims under NAFTA and CAFTA represent only the tip of the iceberg. Lawyers have learned that U.S. FTAs can be used to challenge or threaten to challenge all sorts of existing or proposed government actions, particularly regulatory decisions. There is leverage in the broad investor rights, and in its mandatory arbitral procedures.

Whether, and if so in what form, they will be replicated in the proposed Free Trade Area of the Americas agreement is hotly contested. Already, mutations on the law of investor-state claims have appeared in the U.S.-Chile, U.S.-CAFTA and U.S.-

Panama/Peru/Colombia free trade agreements. *See* Section 16.14. These mutations are in part a response to Congressional concerns expressed in the Trade Promotion Authority (fast-track) Act of 2002 that Chapter 11 of NAFTA may accord "greater substantive rights" to foreigners with respect to investment protection than enjoyed by U.S. investors in the United States.

§ 16.8   The NAFTA Agreement in Outline— Intellectual Property

NAFTA mandates adequate and effective intellectual property rights in all countries, including national treatment and effective internal and external enforcement rights. Specific commitments are made for virtually all types of intellectual property, including patents, copyrights, trademarks, plant breeds, industrial designs, trade secrets, semiconductor chips (directly and in goods incorporating them) and geographical indicators. NAFTA was the first international agreement to address trade secrets, and many of its IP provisions influenced the content of the WTO TRIPs agreement.

General IP Obligations

Specific commitments on patents, copyrights, trademarks, trade secrets and other intellectual property rights are made in the NAFTA agreement. These are discussed individually below. NAFTA also contains some general intellectual property rights obligations. Many of these obligations have counterparts under the TRIPS agreement. For example, except for secondary use of sound recordings, there is a general rule of national treatment.

There is also a general duty to protect intellectual property adequately and effectively, as long as barriers to legitimate trade are not created. At a minimum, this duty necessitates adherence to NAFTA Chapter 17. This general duty also embraces adherence to the substantive provisions of: The Geneva Convention of Phonograms (1971); the Berne Convention for the Protection of Literary and Artistic Works (1971); the Paris Convention for the Protection of Industrial Property (1967); and the 1978 or 1991 versions of the International Convention for the Protection of New Varieties of Plants. Protecting intellectual property rights more extensively than these Conventions is expressly authorized.

The process of intellectual property rights enforcement is covered in detail under NAFTA. Speaking generally, these provisions require fair, equitable, and not unnecessarily complicated, costly or time-consuming enforcement procedures. Written notice, independent legal counsel, the opportunity to substantiate claims and present evidence, and protection of confidential information are stipulated for civil enforcement proceedings. Overly burdensome mandatory personal appearances cannot be imposed. Remedies to enjoin infringement (new to Mexico), prevent importation of infringing goods, and order payment for damages and litigation costs must exist. However, proof of knowing infringement or reasonable grounds for such knowledge is an acceptable criterion. Recovery of profits or liquidated damages must be available when copyright or sound recording infringement is involved. Disposition of infringing or counterfeit goods outside the ordinary channels of commerce or even by destruction is anticipated by NAFTA. All administrative intellectual property rights decisions must be reviewable by a court of law.

Counterfeiting

Criminal penalties are required under NAFTA for willful trademark counterfeiting or copyright piracy undertaken on a commercial scale. For United States law on point, see the Trademark Counterfeiting Act of 1984 (18 U.S.C. § 2320 et seq.) and Section 8.2. When the counterfeit or pirated goods come from outside the region, those affected must be given the opportunity to bar importation and possibly obtain their destruction or other satisfactory disposal.

Despite strong provisions in NAFTA to fight counterfeiting and promote protection of intellectual property, Mexico is seen by some as still not measuring up. Annual submissions by the International Intellectual Property Alliance to the USTR under Special 301 procedures (19 U.S.C. § 2242) document the ineffectiveness of Mexico's anti-piracy law enforcement. Hundreds of millions of dollars of fake CDs, DVDs, software and the like can be found in Mexican marketplaces and the amount is increasing. Prosecutions to combat counterfeiting have been limited. For example, some 2500 Mexican government raids in 1998 netted just 35 convictions with no fines in excess of $1,000.

Mexico's Customs Law of 1996 placed border controls in the hands of the Mexican Institute of Industrial Property (IMPI) for the first time. This Institute was created in 1993 specifically for the task of enforcing Mexican intellectual property rights. Unlike the U.S. Patent and Trademark Office, IMPI has the power to enforce patent owners' rights against actual and potential infringers. It can prevent any commercialization of an infringing product, including removal from the stream of commerce. Mexico also has had, since 1993, a multi-departmental Anti-Piracy Commission. In 1998, the U.S. and Mexico reached agreement on new measures to combat counterfeiting in Mexico. These include a national anti-piracy campaign, tax crimes against counterfeiters, expeditious search and seizure and arrest warrants, and increased administrative enforcement resources. These measures in a limited way have helped to stem counterfeit goods in Mexico.

Gray Market Trading

NAFTA leaves each member state free to adopt its own rules on gray market trading. The question that gray market trading poses for NAFTA is the same as has been debated for decades in Europe. Should national intellectual property rights be allowed to function as trade barriers inside the region? Europe, especially the European Court of Justice, has by and large said no. *See* Section 17.13. In the European Union, free trade interests usually trump national intellectual property rights. Under NAFTA, there is no clear answer. Chapter 17 takes pains to expand and protect national intellectual property rights, and specifically addresses the issue of counterfeiting, but not gray market trading. The relevant law of each NAFTA nation remains intact. *See* generally, Chapter 9.

Patents

Article 1709 of NAFTA assures the availability of patents "in all fields of technology." New products and processes resulting from an inventive step that are capable of industrial application are patentable. Patents for pharmaceuticals, computer software, microorganisms and microbiological processes, plant varieties and agricultural chemicals were specifically included under NAFTA and caused changes in Mexican law. In addition, protection for layout designs of semiconductor integrated circuits was provided by Article 1710. All patent rights must be granted without discrimination as to field of technology, country of origin, and importation or local production of the relevant products.

NAFTA specifically reserves the right to deny patents for diagnostic, therapeutic and surgical methods, transgenic plants and animals, and for essentially biological processes that produce plants or animals. If commercial exploitation might endanger public morality or "ordre public" (state security) no patents need be granted. Patent denials to protect human, animal or plant life or health, or to avoid serious injury to nature or the environment, are also justifiable under NAFTA.

It was agreed that patents in NAFTA nations would run either for 20 years from the date of the filing of the patent application, or 17 years from the grant of patent rights (the traditional U.S. approach). However, the subsequent TRIPS agreement stipulates a 20-year patent term from the date of filing. Canadian, Mexican and

United States patent laws now follow this rule. For pharmaceutical patents, effectively speaking, an additional five years of protection from generic competition is often achieved because NAFTA requires five years exclusivity for product approval test data. Under NAFTA, patent owners generally possess the right to prevent others from making, using or selling the invention without their consent. No mention is made of the right to block infringing or unauthorized imports. If the patent covers a process, this includes the right to prevent others from using, selling or *importing* products obtained directly from that process. Assignment or transfer of patents, and licensing contracts for their use and exploitation, are also expressly protected.

On the touchy subject of compulsory licensing, not authorized under U.S. law, governments may allow limited nonexclusive usage without the owner's authorization if the invention has not been used or exploited locally through production or importation. This is generally permissible only after reasonable attempts at securing a license. However, under emergency, competition law or public noncommercial circumstances, no prior attempt at securing a license is required. In all cases of compulsory licensing, there is a duty to adequately remunerate the patent owner. Significant changes in Canadian compulsory licensing of pharmaceuticals were made in 1993. These changes caused some pharmaceutical prices to rise in Canada.

Apart from compulsory licensing, NAFTA authorizes "limited exceptions" to exclusive patents rights. Such exceptions may not "unreasonably conflict" with the normal exploitation of the patent. Nor may they "unreasonably prejudice" the owner's "legitimate interests." It is not clear how this broad authorization will be construed or applied.

Copyrights

The NAFTA provisions on copyrights promote uniformity in North America. Canada, Mexico and the United States promised extensive protection of copyrights, sound recordings, program-carrying satellite signals and industrial designs. Copyrights are available on all works of original expression. These include books, articles, choreography, photographs, paintings, sculpture, films, videos, records, tapes, CDs and other traditionally copyrighted materials. In most instances, copyrights must be granted for at least 50 years. (The United States now grants 70-year copyrights.) Computer programs and data compilations which constitute intellectual creations are subject to copyrights. Article 1707 requires criminal sanctions for makers and sellers of unauthorized decoding devices, and civil sanctions for unauthorized receivers of satellite signals.

Copyright holders also receive the rights enumerated in the Berne Convention for the Protection of Literary and Artistic Works (1971). However, translation and reproduction licenses permitted by the Berne Convention are not allowed under NAFTA if these needs could be fulfilled voluntarily by the copyright holder but for national laws. In addition, Article 1704.2 specifically conveys to copyright holders:

(1) Control over importation of unauthorized copies;

(2) First public distribution rights over the work (whether by sale, rental or otherwise);

(3) Control over communication of the work to the public; and

(4) Control over commercial rental of computer programs.

If the original or a copy of a computer program is put on the market, this does not exhaust rental rights. Despite the specific reference to control over unauthorized imports in Article 1704.2, it is doubtful whether NAFTA can be construed so as to block free trade in copyrighted goods after their first sale in the United States, Canada or Mexico. The "first sale doctrine" limits an owner's rights to control copyrighted goods to their first sale or transfer. Thereafter, the goods can be freely exchanged. *See* Section 9.4.

Licensing and conveyance of copyrights, royalties and the like are freely transferable under NAFTA. Assignment of works of creation to employers by employees is also protected. However, Article 1705.5 somewhat vaguely allows limits or exceptions in "special cases" that do not conflict with "normal exploitation" of the work. Presumably, "fair use" of copyrighted material falls within this provision. These exceptions may not unreasonably prejudice the owner's legitimate interests.

Trademarks

Trademarks are found on most products, and service and other marks are commonly used. The pervasiveness of marks arguably makes them the most important of NAFTA's intellectual property provisions. Such marks help make markets work by signaling attributes, qualities, price levels and other relevant information. The NAFTA provisions on marks foster uniform law. They stop short, however, from establishing a regional trademark as the Europeans have done. *See* Section 17.14.

Canada, Mexico and the United States agreed to register trademarks, service marks, collective organizational marks and certification marks. All of these marks must be capable of distinguishing goods or services. Internationally "well-known" marks are given special protections against pirates. Whether a mark is "well-known" depends upon knowledge of it in the sector of the public normally dealing with the goods or services, including knowledge in the NAFTA country resulting from promotion of the mark there. A reasonable opportunity to petition to cancel trademark registrations must be granted. In contrast, a reasonable opportunity to oppose registration applications is not mandatory under NAFTA. The nature of the goods or services *per se* cannot justify a refusal to register.

To apply for protection, there is no requirement of prior usage on goods or services. However, if actual usage does not occur within 3 years, Chapter 17 provides that registration may be denied. Immoral, deceptive, scandalous and disparaging marks, and those that falsely suggest a connection with or contempt of persons, institutions, beliefs or national symbols can be denied registration. No registration of words in English, French or Spanish that generically designate goods or services is permitted. Registration of marks indicating geographic origin can be rejected if "deceptively misdescriptive". Trademark registrations must be valid for at least 10 years. They can be renewed indefinitely provided use is continuous. If circumstances beyond the owner's control justify non-use, registrations can be continued. For all these purposes, the NAFTA nations agreed that use is continued when undertaken by franchisees or licensees.

NAFTA trademark owners can prevent persons from using identical or "similar" signs on identical or similar goods or services if this would cause a "likelihood of confusion." However, the "fair use" of descriptive terms may be allowed. Mandatory use of a second "local" trademark (as Mexico once required) is banned. Mandatory use that reduces the function of trademarks as source indicators is also prohibited. Furthermore, compulsory licensing of trademarks is contrary to NAFTA, but contractual licensing and assignment of trademarks can be conditioned.

Trade Secrets

NAFTA was the first international agreement on trade secret protection. Its primary impact has been on Mexican law. At a minimum, each nation must ensure legal means to prevent trade secrets from being disclosed, acquired or used without consent "in a manner contrary to honest commercial practices" (Article 1711). Breach of contract, breach of confidence, and inducement to breach of contract are specifically listed as examples of dishonest commercial practices. Moreover, persons who acquire trade secrets knowing them to be the product of such practices, or who were grossly negligent in failing to know this, also engage in dishonest commercial practices. This is true even if they do not use the secrets in question. NAFTA does not mention, however, the practice of "reverse engineering". This practice is thought to be common and has been authoritatively endorsed by the U.S. Supreme Court. See *Kewanee Oil Co. v. Bicron Corp.*, 416 U.S. 470 (1974).

For NAFTA purposes, information is "secret" if it is not generally known or readily accessible to persons who normally deal with it, has commercial value because of its secrecy, and reasonable steps have been taken to keep it secret. This definition ought to cover, for example, the secret formula for making Coca-Cola. Nevertheless, trade secret holders may be required to produce evidence documenting the existence of the secret in order to secure protection. Release of such information to government authorities obviously involves risks that will need to be considered.

No NAFTA government may discourage or impede the voluntary licensing of trade secrets (often referred to as "know-how licensing"). Imposing excessive or discriminatory conditions on know-how licenses is prohibited. More specifically, in testing and licensing the sale of pharmaceutical and agricultural chemical products, there is a general duty to protect against disclosure of proprietary data.

In 1996, independently of NAFTA, the United States enacted the Economic Espionage Act, 18 U.S.C. § 1831 et seq. This Act creates criminal penalties for misappropriation of trade secrets. For these purposes, a "trade secret" is defined as "financial, business, scientific, technical, economic or engineering information" that the owner has taken reasonable measures to keep secret and whose "independent economic value derives from being closely held". All proceeds from the theft of trade secrets and all property used or intended for use in the misappropriation can be seized and forfeited.

§ 16.9 The NAFTA Agreement in Outline—Other Provisions

The provisions on temporary entry visas for business persons found in the CUSFTA are extended under the NAFTA. These entry rights cover business persons, traders, investors, intra-company transferees and 63 designated professionals. Installers, after-sales repair and maintenance staff and managers performing services under a warranty or other service contract incidental to the sale of equipment or machinery are included, as are sales representatives, buyers, market researchers and financial service providers. White collar business persons only need proof of citizenship and documentation of business purpose to work in another NAFTA country for up to 5 years. Canadian professionals have flooded into the United States under NAFTA visas. Apart from these provisions, no common market for the free movement of labor is undertaken.

NAFTA embraces a competition policy principally aimed at state enterprises and governmentally sanctioned monopolies, mostly found in Mexico. State owned or controlled businesses, at all levels of government, are required to act consistently with the NAFTA when exercising regulatory, administrative or governmental authority (e.g. when granting licenses). Governmentally-owned and privately-owned state-designated monopolies are obliged to follow commercial considerations in their transactions and avoid discrimination against goods or services of other NAFTA nations. Furthermore, each country must ensure that such monopolies do not use their positions to engage in anticompetitive practices in non-monopoly markets. Since each NAFTA nation must adopt laws against anticompetitive business practices and cooperate in their enforcement, Mexico has revived its historically weak "antitrust" laws. A consultative Trade and Competition Committee reviews competition policy issues under the NAFTA.

Other notable provisions in the NAFTA include a general duty of legal transparency, fairness and due process regarding all laws affecting traders and investors with independent administrative or judicial review of government action. Generalized exceptions to the agreement cover action to protect national security and national interests such as public morals, health, national treasures, natural resources, or to enforce laws against deceptive or anticompetitive practices, short of arbitrary discriminations or disguised restraints on trade. Balance of payments trade restraints are governed by the rules of the International Monetary Fund.

Taxation issues are subject to bilateral double taxation treaties, including a new one between Mexico and the United States. The "cultural industry" reservations secured by the CUSFTA now cover Canada and Mexico, but are not extended to Mexican-U.S. trade. A right of compensatory retaliation through measures of equivalent commercial effect is granted when invocation of these reservations would have violated the Canada-U.S. FTA but for the cultural industries proviso.

The NAFTA is not forever. Any country may withdraw on 6 months notice. Other countries or groups of countries may be admitted to the NAFTA if Canada, Mexico and the United States agree and domestic ratification follows. In December of 1994, Chile was invited to become the next member of the NAFTA. Negotiations stalled for want of U.S. Congressional fast track negotiating authority, and subsequent bilateral free trade agreements between Chile and each of the three NAFTA nations.

§ 16.10   Dispute Settlement Under NAFTA, Dumping and Subsidy Disputes

The institutional dispute settlement arrangements accompanying the NAFTA are minimal. A trilateral Trade Commission (with Secretariat) comprised of ministerial or cabinet-level officials meets at least annually to ensure effective joint management of the NAFTA is established. The various intergovernmental committees established for specific areas of coverage of the NAFTA (e.g. competition policy) to oversee much of the work of making the free trade area function. These committees operate on the basis of consensus, referring contentious issues to the Trade Commission.

Intergovernmental Disputes

Investment, dumping and subsidy, financial services, environmental, labor and standards disputes are subject to special dispute resolution procedures. A general NAFTA dispute settlement procedure is also established (Chapter 20). A right of consultation exists when one country's rights are thought to be affected. If consultations do not resolve the issue within 45 days, the complainant may convene a meeting of the Trade Commission. The Commission must seek to promptly settle the dispute and may use its good offices, mediation, conciliation or any other alternative means.

Absent resolution, the complaining country or countries ordinarily commence proceedings under the GATT/WTO or the NAFTA. Once selected, the chosen forum becomes exclusive. However, if the dispute concerns environmental, safety, health or conservation standards, or arises under specific environmental agreements, the responding nation may elect to have the dispute heard by a NAFTA panel. In the tuna labeling dispute, however, the United States was unable to get Mexico to withdraw its WTO complaint, and Mexico subsequently prevailed at the WTO. *See* Section 7.5.

NAFTA Chapters and WTO Agreements

The right of NAFTA governments to elect as between NAFTA and WTO remedies is limited by the substantive content of the NAFTA and WTO agreements. The NAFTA Chapters chart below indicates the closest parallel WTO agreements.

NAFTA	WTO AGREEMENTS
Chapter 3, Trade in Goods	General Agreement on Tariffs and Trade 1994, Agreement on Textiles and Clothing
Chapter 4, Rules of Origin	Agreement on Rules of Origin
Chapter 5, Customs Procedures	No parallel
Chapter 6, Energy and Basic Petrochemicals	No parallel
Chapter 7, Agriculture and SPS Measures	Agreement on Agriculture, Agreement on SPS Measures
Chapter 8, Emergency Action	Agreement on Safeguards
Chapter 9, Product and Service Standards	Agreement on Technical Barriers to Trade
Chapter 10, Procurement	Agreement on Government Procurement (optional)
Chapter 11, Investment	Agreement on Trade-Related Investment Measures (TRIMs)
Chapter 12, Cross-Border Trade in Services	General Agreement on Trade in Services (GATS)
Chapter 13, Enhanced Telecommunications	See GATS, Basic Telecommunications Covered
Chapter 14, Financial Services	See GATS
Chapter 15, Competition Policy, Monopolies and State Enterprises	No parallel, but see Understanding on Interpretation of GATT Article XVII
Chapter 16, Temporary Entry for Business Persons	No parallel
Chapter 17, Intellectual Property	Agreement on Trade-Related Aspects of Intellectual Property Rights (TRIPs)

Chapter 18, Administrative Provisions	Not applicable
Chapter 19, Antidumping and Countervailing Duty Dispute Settlement	No parallel, but see DSU and Agreement on Implementation of GATT Article VI
Chapter 20, Dispute Settlement	Understanding on Rules and Procedures Governing the Settlement of Disputes (DSU)
Chapter 21, Exceptions	See GATT Articles XX, XXI and Understanding on GATT Balance of Payments Provisions
Agreement on Environmental Cooperation	No parallel
Agreement on Labor Cooperation	No parallel

Chapter 20 Dispute Settlement Procedures

Dispute settlement procedures under NAFTA Chapter 20 involve nonbinding arbitration by five persons chosen in most cases from a trilaterally agreed roster of experts (not limited to NAFTA citizens), with a special roster established for disputes about financial services. A "reverse selection" process is used. The chair of the panel is first chosen by agreement or, failing agreement, by designation of one side selected by lot. The chair cannot be a citizen of the selecting side but must be a NAFTA national. Each side then selects two additional arbitrators who are citizens of the country or countries on the *other* side.

The Commission has approved rules of procedure including the opportunity for written submissions, rebuttals and at least one oral hearing. Expert advice on environmental and scientific matters may be given by special procedures accessing science boards. Strict time limits are created so as to keep the panel on track to a prompt resolution. Within 90 days an initial confidential report must be circulated, followed by 14 days for comment by the parties and 16 days for the final panel report to the Commission. There is no "appeal" in Chapter 20 disputes from the arbitrators' decision . . . whereas the WTO has its Appellate Body. *See* Section 1.14.

Early NAFTA Chapter 20 arbitrations concerned Canadian tariffication of agricultural quotas (upheld), U.S. escape clause relief from Mexican corn broom exports (rejected) and a successful

Mexican challenge of the U.S. failure to implement cross-border trucking. *See* Section 16.5. Once the Trade Commission receives a final arbitration panel report, the NAFTA requires the disputing nations to agree within 30 days on a resolution (normally by conforming to the panel's recommendations). If a mutually agreed resolution does not occur at this stage, the complaining country may retaliate by suspending the application of equivalent benefits under the NAFTA, which Mexico did during the trucking dispute. Any NAFTA country may invoke the arbitration panel process if it perceives that this retaliation is excessive.

When NAFTA interpretational issues are disputed before domestic tribunals or courts, the Trade Commission (if it can agree) can submit an interpretation to that body. In the absence of agreement within the Commission, any NAFTA country may intervene and submit its views as to the proper interpretation or application of the NAFTA to the national court or tribunal.

Dumping and Subsidy Disputes

The independent bi-national review panel mechanism established in the CUSFTA for dumping and subsidy duties was carried over into NAFTA, along with the extraordinary challenge procedure to deal with allegations about the integrity of the panel review process. Chapter 19 panels are substituted for traditional judicial review at the national level of administrative dumping and countervailing duty orders. NAFTA does, however, seek to "professionalize" the process by adding judges and retired judges to the roster of acceptable Chapter 19 panelists. The panelists under CUSFTA were more often lawyers, economists or academicians.

Each party to the dispute chooses two panelists (invariably from their home country). Each party may peremptorily reject without cause four panelist selections. The fifth panelist is chosen by agreement if that is possible, or by lot if not. The panel then selects its chair (who must be a lawyer) by majority vote or failing that by lot. This panel selection procedure differs significantly from the "reverse selection" process used in Chapter 20 disputes (above).

Mexico has undertaken major developments to its law in this area. The procedures and rules for such panels generally follow those found in the CUSFTA. They are limited to issues of the consistency of the national decisions with domestic law, and once again have been numerous. United States administrative AD and CVD determinations (mostly annual reviews of prior proceedings) have been reviewed by NAFTA Chapter 19 panels more often than Canadian or Mexican determinations. Goods from Mexico have been involved in the U.S. determinations more than twice as frequently as Canadian goods.

Leather apparel, porcelain-on-steel cookware, cement, oil country tubular goods and fresh cut flowers provide examples of U.S. imports from Mexico that have been the subject of Chapter 19 panel decisions. Live swine, concrete, color picture tubes and carbon steel imports from Canada have also been decided under Chapter 19. Nearly all of these decisions have concerned the imposition of U.S. antidumping duties. U.S. exports of synthetic baler twine, steel sheet, malt beverages and refined sugar to Canada, and flat coated steel, steel plate and polystyrene to Mexico, provide examples of Chapter 19 panel decisions reviewing Canadian and Mexican AD and CVD determinations.

The never ending CUSFTA and NAFTA *Softwood Lumber* dispute involving repeated U.S. CVD tariffs on Canadian exports allegedly subsidized by unfair "stumpage fees" continues. The second Softwood Lumber Settlement Agreement between the two countries is set to expire in 2015. The U.S. has taken several disputes under this settlement, as agreed, to the London Court of Arbitration.

Only three U.S.-requested extraordinary challenges to NAFTA Chapter 19 panel decisions have been raised. These challenges concerned Cement from Mexico (ECC–2000–1904–01), Magnesium from Canada (ECC–2003–1904–01) and Softwood Lumber from Canada (ECC–2004–1904–01). All of them were rejected by the Extraordinary Challenge Committees, and none were as provocative as the ECC under CUSFTA.

AD and CVD disputes may also be taken to the WTO by NAFTA governments. In other words, bi-national panels are not exclusive. The *Softwood Lumber* dispute, for example, resulted in conflicting WTO and panel rulings on domestic injury. While most NAFTA trade remedy disputes are resolved by bi-national panels, some have been settled with controversy. The "tomatoes dispute" provides a ready example.

Tomatoes Dumping Dispute

This dispute concerned Mexican exports of tomatoes at prices that were rapidly taking market share from U.S. growers. After failing to persuade the U.S. International Trade Commission to pursue escape clause relief, Florida growers alleged dumping by Mexican tomato producers early in 1996. This politically high profile petition eventually led to a "suspension agreement" between the U.S. Commerce Department and Mexican growers. The Department promised to suspend its antidumping probe (dumping at a 17.56 percent margin had been found) in return for a commitment by Mexican growers not to sell at less than a specified "reference price." This price was based on the lowest average import price in a recent period not involving dumping. It amounted in 1996 to 20.68 cents per pound. At that price, there was no limit on the volume of Mexican tomatoes that could be shipped to the U.S. market.

Critics from states like Arizona alleged "political blackmail" as the settlement came just days before the 1996 Presidential election vote. President Clinton carried Florida in 1996, something he had failed to do in 1992. In 2013, bowing to pressure from Florida growers, a revised, more restrictive suspension agreement was reached by the Obama administration shortly after his re-election to office. Thus a suspension agreement remains in force, raising prices and managing trade in a most remarkable manner. It has not, however, significantly slowed Mexico's market penetration. Prior to NAFTA, Mexican tomatoes held about 30 percent of the U.S. market. At this point, Mexican tomatoes enjoy at least a 65 percent U.S. market share.

§ 16.11   The Side Agreements on Labor and the Environment, Procedures and Proceedings

The NAFTA side agreements on labor (NAALC) and the environment (NAAEC) do not create additional substantive regional rules. Rather the side agreements basically create law enforcement mechanisms. The side agreements commit each country to creation of environmental and labor bodies that monitor compliance with the adequacy and the enforcement of *domestic* law. The Commission for Environmental Cooperation (CEC) (Montreal) and three National Administrative Offices (NAO) concerning labor matters are empowered to receive complaints. Negotiations to resolve complaints first ensue.

NAAEC Proceedings

In the absence of a negotiated solution, the NAAEC establishes five environmental dispute settlement mechanisms. *First*, the CEC Secretariat may report on almost any environmental matter. *Second*, the Secretariat may develop a factual record in trade-related law enforcement disputes. *Third*, the CEC Council can release that record to the public. *Fourth*, if there is a persistent pattern of failure to enforce environmental law, the Council will mediate and conciliate. *Fifth*, if such efforts fail, the Council can send the matter to arbitration and awards can be enforced by monetary penalties. No NAEEC dispute has ever gotten beyond Stage Three, release of a Factual record.

The Commission for Environmental Cooperation (CEC)

A trilateral Commission for Environmental Cooperation (CEC) was established under the NAAEC side agreement. The Commission's Environmental Council of Ministers is comprised of cabinet-level officers from each member state. The Council can discuss, recommend and settle environmental disputes publicly by consensus. The Commission's Secretariat (located in Montreal) investigates, reviews and reports with recommendations to the Council on environmental matters. The Executive Director of the Secretariat rotates every three years among the NAAEC countries. He or she chooses the staff of the Secretariat on the basis of "competence and integrity." However, "due regard" must be given to recruiting "equitable proportions" from each country (Article 11). The CEC Council of Ministers and Secretariat are advised, especially on technical and scientific matters, by a 15-person Joint Public Advisory Committee.

Under the NAAEC, each member state agreed to maintain "high" levels of environmental protection, but this commitment is not enforceable through NAAEC dispute settlement. Rather, NAAEC focuses on enforcement of the individual environmental protection standards of each nation. This focus, politically speaking, targeted Mexico. There was a widespread perception in the United States that Mexican enforcement of its environmental laws states was inadequate. It is perhaps ironic therefore that many of the complaints lodged under NAAEC to date have challenged Canadian and U.S. environmental law enforcement.

CEC Article 13 Reports

Article 13 authorizes the CEC Secretariat to issue reports on virtually any environmental matter not involving law enforcement. Notice of intent to issue such a report must first be given to the CEC Council of Ministers. If the Council objects by a two-thirds vote, no report can be undertaken. Nongovernmental organizations (NGOs) and others can and have petitioned for Article 13 reports by the Secretariat. For example, the two first Article 13 reports concerned long range transport of air pollutants and the death of 40,000 migratory birds at the Silva Reservoir in Guanajuato. The latter report determined that avian botulism was the cause of the deaths and fostered a clean-up and cooperative information exchanges.

A 2004 report on the effects of transgenic maize in Mexico was noticeably high profile. Other reports have concerned continental pollutant pathways, electricity and the environment, green building in North America, and sustainable freight transport. An Article 13 report concerned water use in the Fort Huachuca, Arizona region. It was undertaken at the initiative of the CEC Secretariat after an Article 14 complaint (below) concerning riparian areas for migratory birds as dismissed. (The Secretariat determined that preparation of a factual record was not warranted.) Thus Article 13 reports can serve as an alternative to direct challenges raised under Article 14.

Article 14 Citizen and NGO Submissions

The NAAEC, under Article 14, contains its own submission, response and dispute resolution process. "Whistleblower" complaints can be filed with the CEC Secretariat by any person or nongovernmental organization (NGO) concerning workplaces, enterprises or sectors that produce NAAEC—traded or NAAEC— competitive goods or services. Article 14 submissions must allege that a NAAEC nation is not "effectively enforcing" *its* environmental law. See SEM–97–005 (submission challenging Canada's ratification [but not implementation by statute] of Biodiversity Convention did not concern effective enforcement of *Canadian* law). SEM stands for Submissions on Enforcement Matters. Guidelines for such submissions have been issued by the CEC Secretariat. They can be found at the Secretariat's excellent web site, www.cec.org.

The Secretariat can dismiss Article 14 submissions on a variety of grounds. For example, the NAAEC agreement stipulates that no ineffective enforcement of environmental law exists when the action or inaction reflects a reasonable exercise of official discretion in investigatory, prosecutorial, regulatory or compliance matters. Furthermore, since "environmental law" is defined in NAAEC as excluding occupational safety and health laws, and laws that primarily manage the harvest or exploitation of natural resources, such complaints can also be dismissed. *See* SEM–98–002 (submission concerning Mexican commercial forestry dispute dismissed). The submission must "appear to be aimed at promoting enforcement rather than harassing industry." (Article 14(1)(d)). It must also be filed in a timely manner. *See* SEM–97–004 (submission filed three years after Canadian environmental decision not timely).

The CEC Secretariat determines if the submission merits a response from the nation whose environmental law enforcement practices are being challenged. Private remedies available under national law must have been pursued and pending administrative or judicial proceedings will keep the CEC from moving forward on the complaint. See *Canadian Wetlands* and *Canadian Fisheries Act* (CEC rejects citizen and NGO submissions) SEM–96–002 and 003.

Since the NAAEC requires extensive private access to environmental remedies, including the ability to file complaints with administrative authorities, access to administrative, quasi-judicial and judicial proceedings, and the right to sue for damages, mitigating relief and injunctions, exhausting national remedies first is a major prerequisite. In evaluating whether a submission merits a response, the Secretariat is also to be "guided" by whether the submission alleges "harm" to the complaining party. Proof of such harm is not mandatory, merely a relevant issue. Several of the Secretariat's early decisions suggest that it takes a liberal view of this "standing" question. See *Cozumel Pier*, SEM–96–001 (discussed below).

In addition, as the rejection by the Secretariat of the first two Article 14 submissions made clear, legislative actions that diminish environmental law enforcement cannot be challenged SEM–95–001 and 002. Thus complaints by various NGOs against the suspension of enforcement of the U.S. Endangered Species Act listing provisions and elimination of private remedies for U.S. timber salvage sales (both alleged to have been accomplished in appropriations bills) failed to proceed under Article 14.

CEC Factual Records

With or without a response from the member state alleged to be inadequately enforcing its law, the Secretariat must decide whether development of a factual record is warranted and inform the Council of its reasons. The Council must approve development of a factual record by a two-thirds vote. If there are past, pending, or possible national administrative or judicial proceedings, the Secretariat or Council are unlikely to allow this to occur. NAAEC governments are obliged to submit relevant information throughout the factual record process, but the Secretariat cannot enforce this obligation.

The third submission under Article 14 was made by Mexican NGOs alleging that the Mexican government had failed to conduct an environmental impact review before authorizing a cruise ship pier at Cozumel Island, SEM–96–001. The CEC Secretariat ruled that this complaint passed muster under Article 14 and compiled the first factual record under NAAEC, Factual Record No. 1 (1997). After summarizing the submission and Mexican response, the CEC "presented" facts with respect to the "matters raised in the submissions." In this record, the CEC adopts the role of a neutral finder of facts.

The second Factual Record concerned a submission that alleged that the Canadian government failed to enforce the Fisheries Act to ensure protection of fish and fish habitat in connection with hydroelectric dams in British Columbia, SEM–97–001. Subsequent Article 14 Factual Records have concerned Canadian enforcement of the Fisheries Act in the Arctic (Oldman River, SEM–97–006), logging rules in British Columbia (SEM–00–004), and mining in British Columbia (SEM–98–004).

Other Factual Records have covered U.S. law enforcement regarding migratory birds (SEM–99–002), Mexican enforcement of hazardous waste law in Tijuana (SEM–98–007), and Mexico City (SEM–03–004), shrimp farming regulations in Nayarit (SEM–98–006), wastewater river pollution in Sonora (SEM–97–002), pulp and paper mill pollution in Canada (SEM–02–003), Canadian migratory bird protection from logging (SEM–02–001), (SEM–04–006), access to environmental justice by Mexican Indigenous communities (Tarahumara, SEM–00–006), copper smelting pollution in Sonora, Mexico (Molymex II, SEM–00–005) pollution of Lake Chapala in Mexico (SEM–03–003), auto pollution in Quebec (SEM–04–007) and toxic pollutants in Montreal (SEM–03–005). All of these Records are available at www.cec.org.

NAALC Proceedings

The NAALC labor law enforcement system is a calibrated four-tier series of dispute resolution mechanisms. *First*, the NAOs may review and report on eleven designated labor law enforcement matters that correspond to the NAALC Labor Principles. *Second*, ministerial consultations may follow when recommended by the NAO. *Third*, an Evaluation Committee of Experts can report on trade-related mutually recognized labor law enforcement patterns of practice concerning eight of the NAALC Labor Principles (excluding strikes, union organizing and collective bargaining). *Fourth*, persistent patterns of failure to enforce occupational health and safety, child labor or minimum wage laws can be arbitrated and awards enforced by monetary penalties. No NAALC dispute has ever gotten beyond Stage Two, ministerial consultations.

Labor Law Enforcement Submissions—Union Organizing

Early U.S. organized labor submissions to the United States NAO alleged the firing by U.S. and Japanese maquiladora subsidiaries of Mexican workers due to union organizing activities, U.S. NAO Submission Nos. 940001, 2 and 3. Public hearings were held at which Mexican workers, their attorneys and U.S. union supporters gave testimony. Honeywell, General Electric and SONY boycotted these hearings. The NAO Report in the Honeywell and GE cases was generally uncertain as to the legality of the firings under Mexican law, particularly because some of the dismissed workers accepted severance pay which indemnified the employers. No ministerial consultations were recommended, but some employees were reinstated and both Honeywell and GE made it clear to their managers that they did not want a reoccurrence of these events.

With SONY, the NAO Report cited "serious questions" about the legality of the firings and recommended ministerial consultations. These consultations resulted in a series of workshops, conferences, studies and meetings (including SONY representatives) on union registration and certification (especially of independent unions) in Mexico. In due course, the U.S. Secretary of Labor requested a follow-up NAO report. This report put a positive spin on developments in Mexico concerning union organizing, a topic that NAALC does not allow to proceed to the next dispute settlement tier (an Evaluation Committee of Experts).

On the other side of the border, the Telephone Workers Union of Mexico (collaborating with the Communications Workers of America) (CWA) filed a submission with the Mexican NAO about worker dismissals and a plant closing at Sprint's La Conexion Familiar in San Francisco, OAN Mex. Submission No. 9501. Again, the allegation involved denial of labor's right to organize. The NLRB eventually ruled against Sprint and ordered rehiring of the workers. *See* 322 NLRB 774 (1996). On appeal, the D.C. Circuit found that the claim that plant was closed because of union organizing activities was not substantiated. *LCF, Inc. v. NLRB*, 129 F.3d 1276 (1997). The Mexican NAO has accepted submissions challenging U.S. labor law enforcement concerning workers in a solar panel plant in California, the Washington State apple industry, a Maine egg farm, migrant workers in New York, H–2B Visa workers, and the North Carolina ban on public sector collective bargaining, OAN Mex. Nos. 9801, 9802, 9803, 2001–01, 2003–1, 2005–01.

In the *Sprint* submission the Mexican NAO found "possible problems" in enforcement of U.S. labor law and recommended ministerial consultations. These consultations resulted in a public forum, a special report by the NAALC Commission on *Plant Closings and Labor Rights* (1997) in all three NAFTA nations, and monitoring of the pending NLRB proceeding based upon Sprint's actions. The report highlights widespread use of anti-union plant closing tactics in the United States (but not Canada or Mexico):

"U.S. labor law authorities actively prosecute unfair labor practice cases involving plant closings and threats of plant closing. They demonstrate a high level of success in litigation before the NLRB and the courts. However, despite this effective enforcement, the incidence of anti-union plant closings and threats of plant closing continues with some frequency. There appears to be significant variation in the types of statements employers are permitted to make about plant closings in connection with a union organizing effort.

The Secretariat examined all 89 federal appeals court decisions in cases involving plant closings and threats of plant closing published between 1986 and 1993. Of the cases, 70 arose in the context of a new union organizing campaign. Closings or partial closings prompted 32 cases, and 57 cases involved threats of closing. Courts of appeals upheld NLRB determinations that employers unlawfully closed or threatened to close plants in 84 of the 89 cases.

The Secretariat studied 319 decisions of the NLRB between 1990 and 1995 involving plant closings and the threats of closing. Of the total, 109 cases involved closings or partial closings, and 210 involved threats of closing. New union organizing campaigns in non-union workplaces were involved in 275 of these cases, while 44 involved existing unions. The NLRB found a violation by the employer in 283 of the 319 cases.

The Secretariat also looked at case files in two regional offices of the NLRB to determine the volume and disposition of cases that do not reach the level of a published determination by an adjudicator. Findings suggest that for every case that reaches a published decision, 10 cases are initiated at the regional office level. More than half of these are withdrawn or dismissed.

In more than 40 percent of cases where the regional office found merit in the charge, the NLRB General Counsel took the case to trial before an ALJ. This is 10 times the rate of enforcement in other cases of meritorious unfair labor practice charges against employers. These findings indicate that the NLRB takes plant closing cases very seriously and actively pursues them to a litigated conclusion. The General Counsel prevails in nearly 90 percent of such cases.

In the United States, resources were readily available to conduct survey research for information that could not be gleaned from administrative and judicial records. Union representatives surveyed reported what they believed to be plant closing threats occurring in half of the sampled union organizing campaigns during the 3-year period studied, with a higher incidence in industries more susceptible to closing such as manufacturing, trucking, and warehousing. Perceived plant closing threats were the largest single factor identified by respondents who decided to withdraw an election petition they had earlier filed, thus discontinuing the organizing campaign. When unions proceeded to an election, the overall union win rate where plant closing threats were reported to have occurred was 33 percent, compared with 47 percent in elections where no threats were reported to have taken place."

The fourth submission to the U.S. NAO was made by labor and human rights groups and a Mexican lawyers association. They claimed that an independent public sector Mexican union lost its representation rights to a rival union when the government merged the Fisheries Ministry into a larger Ministry of the Environment, Natural Resources and Fisheries, U.S. NAO Submission No. 9610 ("Pesca Union"). After a public hearing at which many testified, the NAO Report recommended ministerial consultations on the effect of International Labor Organization (ILO) Conventions (No. 87 was cited) on Mexican labor law, particularly the prohibition against more than one union in a governmental entity. The independent union subsequently had its registration restored by Mexican court order.

Another union organizing case came to the U.S. NAO in 1996, Submission No. 9602. The Communications Workers of America and its Mexican ally (the STRM) alleged that Taiwan-owned Maxi-Switch had a "protection contract" with a CTM union that was not employee approved. CTM is closely allied with the ruling PRI party. After scheduling public testimony, the complaint was withdrawn when registration was granted to a STRM-affiliated "independent" union in the Maxi-Switch maquiladora plant.

Other submissions accepted by the U.S. NAO concerning union organizing in Mexico have involved the Itapsa export processing plant in Ciudad de los Reyes (also filed with the Canadian NAO), and TAESA flight attendants, U.S. Submissions 9801 and 9901. A rare Canadian-oriented submission challenged Quebec law enforcement on union organizing at a McDonald's restaurant in St. Hubert, U.S. Submission 9803.

Perhaps the most bitter of all the union organizing complaints was that filed against Han Young, a Hyundai Corporation maquiladora making truck chassis in Tijuana, Mexico, U.S. NAO Submission No. 9702. Unions and labor groups from all three NAFTA nations alleged a brutal and blatant pattern of employer-CTM opposition to an independent union organizing effort. The U.S. NAO report documents threats, bribes, harassment, intimidation and dismissals. Moreover, the independent union's election victory was inexplicably nullified by the local Mexican labor Conciliation and Arbitration Board (CAB). At this point, with outrage and embarrassment evident in the NAO investigation, the Mexican federal and state governments intervened and negotiated a settlement allowing a second supervised election which the independents also won. The local CAB then delayed notifying the election results to Han Young which in turn refused to collectively bargain. Indeed, Han Young hired a large number of new workers just in time for the CTM to petition for a third union representation election.

For a complete review of NAO submissions and reports in all three countries, see www.dol.gov/ilab/programs/nao.

NAO Submission Strategies

One pattern that emerges in NAALC dispute settlement is the cross-border alliance of U.S. organized labor with Mexican labor groups, particularly those that are part of the "forista" movement for independent unions. Another factor of note is the absence of any need to exhaust national administrative remedies, which is required under the NAAEC. Indeed, there are essentially no "standing to complain" requirements under NAALC. The NAOs can investigate and report at their discretion.

One example of creative use of the NAALC involves double barrel submissions. In at least two instances, organized labor and NGOs have filed complaints with both available NAOs. In one case, the U.S. NAO and the Canada NAO received essentially the same submission concerning union organizing and occupational safety at an auto parts plant in Ciudad de los Reyes, Mexico, U.S. Submission No. 9703 and Canada Submission No. 98–1. Each NAO then proceeded to review and report on inadequate Mexican labor law enforcement. Both NAOs recommended Ministerial Consultations.

Likewise, in the Fall of 1998, a coalition of NGOs headed by a Yale Law School group filed submissions with the Canadian and Mexican NAOs alleging ineffective enforcement of U.S. minimum wage and overtime pay laws against employers of foreign nationals, Submission Nos. Canada 98–2 and Mexico 9804. These complaints challenged U.S. Labor Department reporting of suspected immigration violations to the U.S. Immigration and Naturalization Service. They alleged that such practices deter immigrant workers from filing wage and hour complaints under U.S. law. On the same day that the Mexican NAO accepted the submission (Nov. 23, 1998), the U.S. government announced that a Memorandum of Understanding had been signed with the intent of dealing with these issues.

After a flurry of NAO submissions during the first decade of NAALC, the numbers have dropped significantly. It appears that

NAALC as a labor law enforcement "remedy" is increasingly perceived to be not worth pursuing.

Pregnancy Discrimination in Mexico

As the number, scope and creativity of the submissions and reports continue to grow, NAALC appears to be more than the toothless tiger many have alleged it to be. For example, the U.S. NAO investigated allegations of widespread state-tolerated sex discrimination against pregnant women in maquiladora plants, Submission No. 9701. This complaint could have resulted (but did not) in a report by an Evaluation Committee of Experts (discussed above).

Human Rights Watch/Americas, the International Labor Rights Fund and the Association Nacional de Abogados Democraticos (the same complainants in the *Pesca Union* case above) filed this submission. They maintained that employers regularly used pregnancy tests to avoid the six weeks paid maternity leave required under Mexican law. The Mexican NAO challenged these complaints as beyond the scope of the NAALC, asserted that Mexican law adequately protects women from gender discrimination, and argued that there is no Mexican law against pre-employment pregnancy screening. The U.S. NAO hired an expert on Mexican labor law and gender issues and held public hearings in Brownsville, Texas at which workers and expert witnesses testified.

The NAO, in its report, reviewed Mexican constitutional and labor law, their enforcement bodies, the Alliance for Equality (the Mexican National Program for Women, 1995–2000), the Mexican Human Rights Commission and relevant international conventions. Post-employment pregnancy discrimination is clearly illegal in Mexico. On pre-employment law, one decision of note that emerged from the investigation was that of the Human Rights Commission for the Federal District which found pre-employment pregnancy screening a violation of Articles 4 and 5 of the Mexican Constitution. Here is the U.S. NAO analysis on point. Note especially its implications concerning the credibility of the Mexican NAO submissions in response to the complaint:

"[T]he Human Rights Commission for the Federal District offers a markedly different interpretation to that of the Mexican NAO on the legality of pre-employment pregnancy screening. The Commission found (1) that the federal agencies it investigated did, in fact, conduct pregnancy screening and, (2) this practice violated Mexico's Constitution.

The Mexican NAO has asserted that the recommendations of the Commission are not binding and do not establish jurisprudence. The enacting legislation for the Commission, however, imposes an obligation on the responding agencies to comply with the recommendations once they accept the findings of the report. Additionally, the Commission was created pursuant to the Mexican Constitution and implemented by Federal law. It is composed of prominent jurists, appointed by the President and confirmed by the legislature, and their recommendation, in this case, was complied with by Federal Government agencies. Further, though the case involved public sector agencies, in its recommendation the Commission made no distinction on the application of the appropriate constitutional guarantees between the public and private sectors.

The position of the Human Rights Commission on the legality of pregnancy screening is markedly different from that expressed by the Mexican NAO. Moreover, the *Alliance for Equality* recognized pregnancy screening as a problem and outlined a plan of action to address such discriminatory practices. That pregnancy screening occurs and is of concern is supported by information from companies conducting business in Mexico, women workers, and the submitters. It also appears that the intrusive nature of the questioning described in the submission goes beyond what is necessary to determine if an applicant for employment is pregnant.

An additional question is raised with regard to the lack of any legal procedure by which to bring cases of pre-employment gender discrimination. The Mexican NAO asserted that the FLL [Federal Labor Law] does not provide for the adjudication of cases involving pre-employment discrimination. CAB officials interviewed by HRW [Human Rights Watch] also indicated that the CABs had no jurisdiction over these cases as they involved issues that occurred prior to the establishment of the employment relationship. The Mexican NAO's position appears to go beyond the question of pre-employment pregnancy screening to also include the lack of a legal procedure for bringing any pre-employment discrimination issue. Since Mexican law clearly prohibits employers from discriminating in hiring for a variety of reasons, the Mexican NAO's response creates a question as to what process exists for bringing such pre-employment discrimination claims."

The NAO report issued in Submission No. 9701 recommended ministerial consultations. These resulted in a U.S.-Mexican agreement on an improved "action plan" to combat pregnancy discrimination in the workplace, though pregnancy discrimination at hiring is said to continue.

§ 16.12   Expanding NAFTA

When Canada and the United States agreed to free trade in 1989, there was no expectation of extension of that agreement to Mexico or any other country. The NAFTA agreement, on the other hand, specifically anticipates growth by accession. Article 2204 invites applications to join NAFTA by countries or groups of countries without regard to their geographic location or cultural background. This is unlike the European Union which only allows "European" nations to join. The NAFTA Free Trade Commission is authorized to negotiate the terms and conditions of any new memberships. The resulting accession agreement must be approved and ratified by each NAFTA nation. Practically speaking, as in the European Union, this means that current members can veto NAFTA applicants.

In December 1994, at the "Summit of the Americas" in Miami, Canada and Mexico joined the United States formally invited Chile to apply for NAFTA membership. This invitation went nowhere because Congress repeatedly refused to authorize "fast track" negotiations by President Clinton. Fast track negotiations provide assurance to all concerned that Congress would not be able to alter the terms and conditions of Chile's accession. Under fast track, Congress would have to approve or disapprove the agreement by majority vote. Apart from partisan politics, one thorny issue was whether there would be side agreements with Chile on labor and the environment.

Absent U.S. fast track authority, Chile, Canada and Mexico steered different courses. Mexico and Chile renegotiated and expanded their pre-NAFTA free trade agreement. Canada and Chile reached agreement in 1997 on free trade along with side agreements that are similar to NAAEC and NAALC. Chile in 1996 became a free trade associate of MERCOSUR, the Southern Cone common market of Brazil, Argentina, Paraguay and Uruguay. All these free trade commitments flowed partly from want of U.S. fast track authority. They had an impact on trade and investment patterns. Some U.S. companies with Canadian subsidiaries, for example, shifted production and exports to Canada in order to take advantage of Canada-Chile free trade. When fast track authority was finally renewed in 2002, a U.S.-Chile FTA was the first to be signed.

§ 16.13   Free Trade and Foreign Investment in the Americas

The United States "Enterprise for the Americas Initiative" (EAI) under elder President Bush raised hopes of economic integration throughout the Americas against a background of competitive regionalism in trade relations, especially between the European Union and North America. At the Americas Summit in Miami, President Clinton and 33 Latin American heads of state (only Fidel Castro was absent) renewed this hope by agreeing to commence negotiations on a Free Trade Area of the Americas (FTAA). The year 2005 was targeted at the Summit for creation of the FTAA.

Preparatory working groups have regularly met since 1995 to discuss the following topics: (1) Market Access; (2) Customs Procedures and Rules of Origin; (3) Investment; (4) Standards and Technical Barriers to Trade; (5) Sanitary and Phytosanitary Measures; (6) Subsidies, Antidumping and Countervailing Duties; (7) Smaller Economies; (8) Government Procurement; (9) Intellectual Property Rights; (10) Services; (11) Competition Policy; and (12) Dispute Settlement. It is expected that each of these areas would be covered in any FTAA agreement. Formal FTAA negotiations were delayed several times, particularly because of differences between Brazil-led MERCOSUR and U.S.-led NAFTA.

Divisions were particularly evident during the November 2003 FTAA ministerial meeting in Miami. Lowered expectations, known as FTAA-Lite, reflect U.S. refusal to budge on agricultural protection and trade remedies, and Brazilian refusal to fully embrace investment, intellectual property, services and procurement "free trade." Absent successful resolution of these issues in the WTO Doha Round negotiations, an unlikely prospect at this writing, FTAA-Lite, even with different levels of country commitments, seems unlikely.

The absence of fast track authority and the general perception that political support for free trade in the United States is weak has clearly slowed FTAA developments. MERCOSUR and Brazil in particular seized the opportunity to move towards South American free trade. At this point, MERCOSUR's trade associates include every South American nation. This puts it in a much better position to negotiate terms and conditions with the NAFTA/CAFTA bloc than individual countries or sub-groups within South America. Venezuela has led a socialist-style "Trade Treaty for the Peoples" with Cuba, Bolivia, Ecuador, Nicaragua, Honduras and others.

In 2002, a bipartisan Congress authorized President George W. Bush to negotiate free trade agreements on a fast track basis. *See* Section 2.4. This authorization expired in July of 2007. President Bush, following the pattern established by Canada and Mexico, rapidly concluded a bilateral U.S. free trade agreement with Chile, including coverage of the environment and labor.

The 2002 Congressional authorization of fast track free trade negotiations covered the FTAA. President George W. Bush sought such an agreement, while simultaneously negotiating U.S. free trade deals with five Central American states and the Dominican Republic (CAFTA–DR, finalized early in 2004), Peru (2007), Colombia (implemented by President Obama in 2012) and Panama (ditto, 2012). Such a "divide and conquer" strategy undermines Brazil's hopes for a united South/Central American negotiating front for the FTAA. It also reflects the reality of the United States playing catch up with Canada (which has free trade and foreign investment agreements with Chile, Colombia, Peru, and Costa Rica) and Mexico (which has numerous Latin American free trade agreements).

In 2013, Latin American U.S. trade allies formed the Pacific Alliance (Colombia, Peru, Chile and Mexico), which serves as a counterweight to MERCOSUR. At this writing, fast track authority might be renewed in 2014. With all three NAFTA nations participating in the Trans-Pacific Partnership (TPP) negotiations, the NAFTA accords could effectively be updated via the TPP.

§ 16.14   Post-NAFTA U.S. Agreements—Plus and Minus

United States free trade agreements since NAFTA have evolved substantively under a policy known as "competitive liberalization." For example, coverage of labor law has been narrowed to core ILO principles: The rights of association, organization and collective bargaining; acceptable work conditions regarding minimum wages, hours and occupational health and safety; minimum ages for employment of children and elimination of the worst forms of child labor; and a ban on forced or compulsory labor. Coverage of labor and environmental law enforcement is folded into the trade agreement (compare NAFTA's side agreements) and all remedies are intergovernmental (compare private and NGO "remedies" in the side agreements).

Other NAFTA-plus provisions have emerged. These are most evident regarding foreign investment and intellectual property. Regarding investor-state claims, for example, post-NAFTA U.S. free trade agreements insert the word "customary" before international law in defining the minimum standard of treatment to which foreign investors are entitled. This insertion tracks the official Interpretation issued in that regard under NAFTA. Further, the contested terms "fair and equitable treatment" and "full protection and security" do not require treatment in addition to or beyond that customary standard, and do not create additional substantive rights. This language is defined for the first time:

> "fair and equitable treatment" includes the obligation not to deny justice in criminal, civil, or administrative adjudicatory proceedings in accordance with the principle of due process embodied in the principal legal systems of the world; and

> "full protection and security" requires each Party to provide the level of police protection required under customary international law.

More significantly perhaps, starting with the U.S.—Chile FTA, these agreements contain an Annex restricting the scope of "indirect expropriation" claims:

> Except in rare circumstances, nondiscriminatory regulatory actions by a Party that are designed and applied to protect legitimate public welfare objectives, such as public health, safety and the environment, do not constitute indirect expropriations.

Hence the potential for succeeding with "regulatory takings" investor-state claims has been reduced. Moreover, the CAFTA-DR agreement anticipates creating an appellate body of some sort for investor-state arbitration decisions.

Regarding intellectual property, NAFTA—plus has moved into the Internet age. Protection of domain names, and adherence to the WIPO Internet treaties, are stipulated. E-commerce and free trade in digital products are embraced, copyrights extended to rights-management (encryption) and anti-circumvention (hacking) technology, protection against web music file sharing enhanced, and potential liability of Internet Service Providers detailed.

Less visibly, pharmaceutical patent owners obtain extensions of their patents to compensate for delays in the approval process, and greater control over their test data, making it harder for generic competition to emerge. They also gain "linkage," meaning local drug regulators must make sure generics are not patent-infringing before their release. In addition, adherence to the Patent Law Treaty (2000) and the Trademark Law Treaty (1994) is agreed.

Anti-counterfeiting laws are tightened, particularly regarding destruction of counterfeit goods.

Other NAFTA-plus changes push further along the path of free trade in services and comprehensive customs law administration rules. Antidumping and countervailing duty laws remain applicable, but appeals from administrative determinations are taken in national courts, not binational panels. Except for limited provisions in the Chile—U.S. agreement, business visas drop completely out of U.S. free trade agreements, a NAFTA—minus development.

In sum, the United States has generally used its leverage with smaller trade partners in the Americas to obtain more preferential treatment and expanded protection for its goods, services, technology and investors. It has given up relatively little in return, for example a modest increase in agricultural market openings. The net results substantively suggest that the NAFTA/MERCOSUR divide is deepening.

§ 16.15   Quebec and NAFTA

The Canadian Constitution of 1982 was adopted by an Act of the British Parliament. As such, the Act and Constitution of 1982 are thought to bind all Canadian provinces including Quebec. That province, however, has never formally ratified the Constitution of Canada. Since 1982 a series of negotiations have attempted to secure Quebec's ratification, and all have failed miserably.

In 1987, for example, the "Meech Lake Accord" was reached. This agreement recognized Quebec as a "distinct society" in Canada. What the practical consequences of this recognition would have been will never be known. Quebec's adherence to the Meech Lake Accord was nullified when Manitoba, New Brunswick and ultimately Newfoundland failed to ratify the Accord. A second set of negotiations led in 1992 to the Charlottetown Accord which also acknowledged Quebec as a distinct society with its French language, unique culture and Civil Law tradition. This time a national referendum was held and its defeat was overwhelming. Quebec, five English-speaking Canadian provinces, and the Yukon territory voted against the Charlottetown Accord.

The failure of these Accords moved Quebec towards separation from Canada. In 1994 and again in 2012, the Parti Quebecois came to power. It held a provincial referendum on separation in 1995. By the narrowest of margins, the people of Quebec rejected separation from Canada. Just exactly what "separation" would have meant was never entirely clear during the debate, perhaps deliberately so.

In 1998, Canada's Supreme Court ruled that Quebec could not "under the Constitution" withdraw unilaterally. To secede, Quebec would need to negotiate a constitutional amendment with the rest of Canada. The rest of Canada would, likewise, be obliged to enter into such negotiations if a "clear majority" of Quebec's voters approved a "clear question" on secession in a referendum. Subsequently, the Canadian Parliament legislated rules which will make it difficult for Quebec to separate, should it ever wish to do so. That prospect now seems more remote, particularly because the Parti Quebecois lost power in 2003, resumed then lost control at this writing.

If Quebec ever separates from Canada, this will raise fundamental issues about Quebec and NAFTA. Would Quebec be forced to negotiate for membership in NAFTA? If so, would English-speaking Canada veto its application? Might Quebec's relationship to Canada continue in some limited manner (such as for defense and international trade purposes) such that NAFTA is not an issue at all? Might Quebec automatically "succeed" to the NAFTA treaty, thus becoming a member without application? Customary international practice maintains existing treaties when nations sub-divide. This practice was applied to the Czech Republic, Slovakia, and various states of the former Yugoslavia. Thus custom suggests that fears in Quebec about losing NAFTA benefits are exaggerated.

§ 16.16 NAFTA/Free Trade and Foreign Investment in the Americas Timeline

1986	Canada-U.S. free trade negotiations commence. Mexico joins the GATT. Uruguay Round of GATT negotiations launched.
1989	CUSFTA enters into effect.
1991	Congress extends fast track authority to NAFTA and Uruguay Round, MERCOSUR created by Brazil, Argentina, Paraguay and Uruguay.
1992	NAFTA signed by Presidents Bush and Salinas, Prime Minister Mulroney.
1993 (August)	Side agreements on North American Labor and Environmental Cooperation concluded under President Clinton.

1993 (October)	Vice President Gore "defeats" Ross Perot in nationally televised NAFTA debate.
1993 (November)	U.S. Congress ratifies NAFTA and sides agreements.
1993 (December)	Uruguay Round agreements concluded.
1994 (Jan)	NAFTA enters into effect.
1994 (December)	Miami Summit supports creation by 2005 of a Free Trade Area of the Americas (FTAA).
1994–95	Mexican peso crashes, U.S. organizes rescue package.
1995	Uruguay Round agreements enter into effect. WTO created. Negotiations commence for Chile to join NAFTA. Quebec voters barely reject separation from Canada.
1997	Canada and Chile agree on free trade with side agreements. Mexico revises its free trade agreement with Chile.
1995–2002	Congress refuses to authorize fast track negotiations. Mexico agrees to free trade with Colombia, Venezuela, Costa Rica, Bolivia, Nicaragua, Guatemala, Honduras, El Salvador, Peru and Uruguay. Canada agrees to free trade with Costa Rica.
2002	Congress authorizes bilateral and FTAA fast track negotiations.
2003	U.S.-Chile agree on free trade.
2004	U.S.-CAFTA plus Dominican Republic agree on free trade.
2005	FTAA deadline is not met, CAFTA-DR agreement passes House of Representative by two votes.
2006/2007	Panama, Peru and Colombia agree on free trade with the U.S. Venezuela applies for

MERCOSUR membership, creates Peoples'
Trade Treaty (ALBA) with Cuba, Bolivia,
Nicaragua, and Ecuador.

2007 (July)	U.S. fast track authority expires.
2007 (October)	Costa Rican people barely approve CAFTA.
2008	U.S.-Peru and Canada-Peru FTAs take effect
2009–2012	U.S.-Panama and U.S.-Colombia FTAs stalled, then implemented in 2012. Venezuela joins MERCOSUR. Canada free trades with Colombia and Panama. Trans-Pacific Partnership (TPP) negotiations include U.S., Canada, Mexico and Chile and Peru, plus seven other countries.
2013	Mexico, Chile, Colombia and Peru commence "Pacific Alliance", Canada and EU sign Comprehensive Economic and Trade Agreement (CETA), U.S. and EU undertake Transatlantic Trade and Investment Partnership (TTIP) Negotiations

§ 16.17   Text of NAFTA Chapter 11 (Foreign Investment)

Article 1101: Scope and Coverage

1. This Chapter applies to measures adopted or maintained by a Party relating to: (a) investors of another Party; (b) investments of investors of another Party in the territory of the Party; and (c) with respect to Article 1106, all investments in the territory of the Party.

2. A Party has the right to perform exclusively the economic activities set out in Annex III and to refuse to permit the establishment of investment in such activities.

3. This Chapter does not apply to measures adopted or maintained by a Party to the extent that they are covered by Chapter Fourteen (Financial Services).

4. Nothing in this Chapter shall be construed to prevent a Party from providing a service or performing a function such as law enforcement, correctional services, income security or insurance, social security or

insurance, social welfare, public education, public training, health, and child care, in a manner that is not inconsistent with this Chapter.

Article 1102: National Treatment

1. Each Party shall accord to investors of another Party treatment no less favorable than that it accords, in like circumstances, to its own investors with respect to the establishment, acquisition, expansion, management, conduct, operation, and sale or other disposition of investments.

2. Each Party shall accord to investments of investors of another Party treatment no less favorable than that it accords, in like circumstances, to investments of its own investors with respect to the establishment, acquisition, expansion, management, conduct, operation, and sale or other disposition of investments.

3. The treatment accorded by a Party under paragraphs 1 and 2 means, with respect to a state or province, treatment no less favorable than the most favorable treatment accorded, in like circumstances, by that state or province to investors, and to investments of investors, of the Party of which it forms a part.

4. For greater certainty, no Party may: (a) impose on an investor of another Party a requirement that a minimum level of equity in an enterprise in the territory of the Party be held by its nationals, other than nominal qualifying shares for directors or incorporators of corporations; or (b) require an investor of another Party, by reason of its nationality, to sell or otherwise dispose of an investment in the territory of the Party.

Article 1103: Most-Favored-Nation Treatment

1. Each Party shall accord to investors of another Party treatment no less favorable than that it accords, in like circumstances, to investors of another Party or of a non-Party with respect to the establishment, acquisition, expansion, management, conduct, operation, and sale or other disposition of investments.

2. Each Party shall accord to investments of investors of another Party treatment no less favorable than that it accords, in like circumstances, to investments of investors of another Party or of a non-Party with respect to the establishment, acquisition, expansion, management, conduct, operation, and sale or other disposition of investments.

Article 1104: Standard of Treatment

Each Party shall accord to investors of another Party and to investments of investors of another Party the better of the treatment required by Articles 1102 and 1103.

Article 1105: Minimum Standard of Treatment

1. Each Party shall accord to investments of investors of another Party treatment in accordance with international law, including fair and equitable treatment and full protection and security.

2. Without prejudice to paragraph 1 and notwithstanding Article 1108(7)(b), each Party shall accord to investors of another Party, and to investments of investors of another Party, non-discriminatory treatment with respect to measures it adopts or maintains relating to losses suffered by investments in its territory owing to armed conflict or civil strife.

3. Paragraph 2 does not apply to existing measures relating to subsidies or grants that are inconsistent with Article 1102.

Article 1106: Performance Requirements

1. No Party may impose or enforce any of the following requirements, or enforce any commitment or undertaking, in connection with the establishment, acquisition, expansion, management, conduct or operation of an investment of an investor of a Party or of a non-Party in its territory:

(a) to export a given level or percentage of goods or services; (b) to achieve a given level or percentage of domestic content; (c) to purchase, use or accord a preference to goods produced or services provided in its territory, or to purchase goods or services from persons in its territory; (d) to relate in any way the volume or value of imports to the volume or value of exports or to the amount of foreign exchange inflows associated with such investment; (e) to restrict sales of goods or services in its territory that such investment produces or provides by relating such sales in any way to the volume or value of its exports or foreign exchange earnings; (f) to transfer technology, a production process or other proprietary knowledge to a person in its territory, except when the requirement is imposed or the 4 commitment or undertaking is enforced by a court, administrative tribunal or competition authority to remedy an alleged violation of competition laws or to act in a manner not inconsistent with other provisions of this Agreement; or (g) to act as the exclusive supplier of the goods it produces or services it provides to a specific region or world market.

2. A measure that requires an investment to use a technology to meet generally applicable health, safety or environmental requirements shall not be construed to be inconsistent with paragraph (1)(f). For greater certainty, Articles 1102 and 1103 apply to the measure.

3. No Party may condition the receipt or continued receipt of an advantage, in connection with an investment in its territory of an investor of a Party or of a non-Party, on compliance with any of the following requirements:

(a) to purchase, use or accord a preference to goods produced in its territory, or to purchase goods from producers in its territory; (b) to achieve a given level or percentage of domestic content; (c) to relate in any way the volume or value of imports to the volume or value of exports or to the amount of foreign exchange inflows associated with such investment; or (d) to restrict sales of goods or services in its territory that such investment produces or provides by relating such sales in any way to the volume or value of its exports or foreign exchange earnings.

4. Nothing in paragraph 3 shall be construed to prevent a Party from conditioning the receipt or continued receipt of an advantage, in connection with an investment in its territory of an investor of a Party or of a non-Party, on compliance with a requirement to locate production, provide a service, train or employ workers, construct or expand particular facilities, or carry out research and development, in its territory.

5. Paragraphs 1 and 3 do not apply to any requirement other than the requirements set out in those paragraphs.

6. Provided that such measures are not applied in an arbitrary or unjustifiable manner, or do not constitute a disguised restriction on international trade or investment, nothing in 5 paragraph 1(b) or (c) or 3(a) or (b) shall be construed to prevent any Party from adopting or maintaining measures, including environmental measures: (a) necessary to secure compliance with laws and regulations that are not inconsistent with the provisions of this Agreement; (b) necessary to protect human, animal or plant life or health; or (c) necessary for the conservation of living or non-living exhaustible natural resources.

Article 1107: Senior Management and Boards of Directors

1. No Party may require that an enterprise of that Party that is an investment of an investor of another Party appoint to senior management positions individuals of any particular nationality.

2. A Party may require that a majority of the board of directors, or any committee thereof, of an enterprise of that Party that is an investment of an investor of another Party, be of a particular nationality, or resident in the territory of the Party, provided that the requirement does not materially impair the ability of the investor to exercise control over its investment.

Article 1108: Reservations and Exceptions

1. Articles 1102, 1103, 1106 and 1107 do not apply to:

(a) any existing non-conforming measure that is maintained by (i) a Party at the federal level, as set out in its Schedule to Annex I or III, (ii) a state or province, for two years after the date of entry into force of this Agreement, and thereafter as set out by a Party in its Schedule to Annex I, in accordance with paragraph 2, or (iii) a local government;

(b) the continuation or prompt renewal of any non-conforming measure referred to in subparagraph (a); or

(c) an amendment to any non-conforming measure referred to in subparagraph (a) to the extent that the amendment does not decrease the conformity of the measure, as it existed immediately before the amendment, with Articles 1102, 1103, 1106 and 1107.

2. Each Party may set out in its Schedule to Annex I any existing non-conforming measure maintained by a state or province, not including a local government, within two years of the date of entry into force of this Agreement.

3. Articles 1102, 1103, 1106 and 1107 do not apply to any measure that a Party adopts or maintains with respect to sectors, subsectors or activities, as set out in its Schedule to Annex II.

4. No Party may, under any measure adopted after the date of entry into force of this Agreement and covered by its Schedule to Annex II, require an investor of another Party, by reason of its nationality, to sell or otherwise dispose of an investment existing at the time the measure becomes effective.

5. Articles 1102 and 1103 do not apply to any measure that is an exception to, or derogation from, the obligations under Article 1703 (Intellectual Property—National Treatment) as specifically provided for in that Article.

6. Article 1103 does not apply to treatment accorded by a Party pursuant to agreements, or with respect to sectors, set out in its Schedule to Annex IV.

7. Articles 1102, 1103 and 1107 do not apply to: (a) procurement by a Party or a state enterprise; or (b) subsidies or grants provided by a Party or a state enterprise, including government-supported loans, guarantees and insurance.

8. The provisions of: (a) Article 1106(1)(a), (b) and (c), and (3)(a) and (b) do not apply to qualification requirements for goods or services with respect to export promotion and foreign aid programs; (b) Article 1106(1)(b), (c), (f) and (g), and (3)(a) and (b) do not apply to procurement by a Party or a state enterprise; and (c) Article 1106(3)(a) and (b) do not apply to requirements imposed by an importing Party relating to the content of goods necessary to qualify for preferential tariffs or preferential quotas.

Article 1109: Transfers

1. Each Party shall permit all transfers relating to an investment of an investor of another Party in the territory of the Party to be made freely and without delay. Such transfers include:

(a) profits, dividends, interest, capital gains, royalty payments, management fees, technical assistance and other fees, returns in kind and other amounts derived from the investment; (b) proceeds from the sale of all or any part of the investment or from the partial or complete liquidation of the investment; (c) payments made under a contract entered into by the investor, or its investment, including payments made pursuant to a loan agreement; (d) payments made pursuant to Article 1110; and (e) payments arising under Section B.

2. Each Party shall permit transfers to be made in a freely usable currency at the market rate of exchange prevailing on the date of transfer with respect to spot transactions in the currency to be transferred.

3. No Party may require its investors to transfer, or penalize its investors that fail to transfer, the income, earnings, profits or other amounts derived from, or attributable to, investments in the territory of another Party.

4. Notwithstanding paragraphs 1 and 2, a Party may prevent a transfer through the equitable, non-discriminatory and good faith application of its laws relating to: (a) bankruptcy, insolvency or the protection of the rights of creditors; (b) issuing, trading or dealing in securities; (c) criminal or penal offenses; (d) reports of transfers of currency or other monetary instruments; or (e) ensuring the satisfaction of judgments in adjudicatory proceedings.

5. Paragraph 3 shall not be construed to prevent a Party from imposing any measure through the equitable, non-discriminatory and good faith application of its laws relating to the matters set out in subparagraphs (a) through (e) of paragraph 4.

6. Notwithstanding paragraph 1, a Party may restrict transfers of returns in kind in circumstances where it could otherwise restrict such transfers under this Agreement.

Article 1110: Expropriation and Compensation

1. No Party may directly or indirectly nationalize or expropriate an investment of an investor of another Party in its territory or take a measure tantamount to nationalization or expropriation of such an investment ("expropriation"), except: (a) for a public purpose; (b) on a non-discriminatory basis; (c) in accordance with due process of law and Article 1105(1); and (d) on payment of compensation in accordance with paragraphs 2 through 6.

2. Compensation shall be equivalent to the fair market value of the expropriated investment immediately before the expropriation took place ("date of expropriation"), and shall not reflect any change in value occurring because the intended expropriation had become known earlier. Valuation criteria shall include going concern value, asset value including declared

tax value of tangible property, and other criteria, as appropriate, to determine fair market value.

3. Compensation shall be paid without delay and be fully realizable.

4. If payment is made in a G7 currency, compensation shall include interest at a commercially reasonable rate for that currency from the date of expropriation until the date of actual payment.

5. If a Party elects to pay in a currency other than a G7 currency, the amount paid on the date of payment, if converted into a G7 currency at the market rate of exchange prevailing on that date, shall be no less than if the amount of compensation owed on the date of expropriation had been converted into that G7 currency at the market rate of exchange prevailing on that date, and interest had accrued at a commercially reasonable rate for that G7 currency from the date of expropriation until the date of payment.

6. On payment, compensation shall be freely transferable as provided in Article 1109.

7. This Article does not apply to the issuance of compulsory licenses granted in relation to intellectual property rights, or the revocation, limitation or creation of intellectual property rights, to the extent that such issuance, revocation, limitation or creation is consistent with Chapter Seventeen (Intellectual Property).

8. For purposes of this Article and for greater certainty, a non-discriminatory measure of general application shall not be considered a measure tantamount to an expropriation of a debt security or loan covered by this Chapter solely on the ground that the measure imposes costs on the debtor that cause it to default on the debt.

Article 1111: Special Formalities and Information Requirements

1. Nothing in Article 1102 shall be construed to prevent a Party from adopting or maintaining a measure that prescribes special formalities in connection with the establishment of investments by investors of another Party, such as a requirement that investors be residents of the Party or that investments be legally constituted under the laws or regulations of the Party, provided that such formalities do not materially impair the protections afforded by a Party to investors of another Party and investments of investors of another Party pursuant to this Chapter.

2. Notwithstanding Articles 1102 or 1103, a Party may require an investor of another Party, or its investment in its territory, to provide routine information concerning that investment solely for informational or statistical purposes. The Party shall protect such business information that is confidential from any disclosure that would prejudice the competitive position of the investor or the investment. Nothing in this paragraph shall be 10 construed to prevent a Party from otherwise obtaining or disclosing

information in connection with the equitable and good faith application of its law.

Article 1112: Relation to Other Chapters

1. In the event of any inconsistency between a provision of this Chapter and a provision of another Chapter, the provision of the other Chapter shall prevail to the extent of the inconsistency.

2. A requirement by a Party that a service provider of another Party post a bond or other form of financial security as a condition of providing a service into its territory does not of itself make this Chapter applicable to the provision of that cross-border service. This Chapter applies to that Party's treatment of the posted bond or financial security.

Article 1113: Denial of Benefits

1. A Party may deny the benefits of this Chapter to an investor of another Party that is an enterprise of such Party and to investments of such investor if investors of a non-Party own or control the enterprise and the denying Party: (a) does not maintain diplomatic relations with the non-Party; or (b) adopts or maintains measures with respect to the non-Party that prohibit transactions with the enterprise or that would be violated or circumvented if the benefits of this Chapter were accorded to the enterprise or to its investments.

2. Subject to prior notification and consultation in accordance with Articles 1803 (Notification and Provision of Information) and 2006 (Consultations), a Party may deny the benefits of this Chapter to an investor of another Party that is an enterprise of such Party and to investments of such investors if investors of a non-Party own or control the enterprise and the enterprise has no substantial business activities in the territory of the Party under whose law it is constituted or organized.

Article 1114: Environmental Measures

1. Nothing in this Chapter shall be construed to prevent a Party from adopting, maintaining or enforcing any measure otherwise consistent with this Chapter that it considers appropriate to ensure that investment activity in its territory is undertaken in a manner sensitive to environmental concerns.

2. The Parties recognize that it is inappropriate to encourage investment by relaxing domestic health, safety or environmental measures. Accordingly, a Party should not waive or otherwise derogate from, or offer to waive or otherwise derogate from, such measures as an encouragement for the establishment, acquisition, expansion or retention in its territory of an investment of an investor. If a Party considers that another Party has offered such an encouragement, it may request consultations with the other Party and the two Parties shall consult with a view to avoiding any such encouragement.

Section B—Settlement of Disputes between a Party and an Investor of Another Party

Article 1115: Purpose

Without prejudice to the rights and obligations of the Parties under Chapter Twenty (Institutional Arrangements and Dispute Settlement Procedures), this Section establishes a mechanism for the settlement of investment disputes that assures both equal treatment among investors of the Parties in accordance with the principle of international reciprocity and due process before an impartial tribunal.

Article 1116: Claim by an Investor of a Party on Its Own Behalf

1. An investor of a Party may submit to arbitration under this Section a claim that another Party has breached an obligation under: (a) Section A or Article 1503(2) (State Enterprises); or (b) Article 1502(3)(a) (Monopolies and State Enterprises) where the monopoly has acted in a manner inconsistent with the Party's obligations under Section A, and that the investor has incurred loss or damage by reason of, or arising out of, that breach.

2. An investor may not make a claim if more than three years have elapsed from the date on which the investor first acquired, or should have first acquired, knowledge of the alleged breach and knowledge that the investor has incurred loss or damage.

Article 1117: Claim by an Investor of a Party on Behalf of an Enterprise

1. An investor of a Party, on behalf of an enterprise of another Party that is a juridical person that the investor owns or controls directly or indirectly, may submit to arbitration under this Section a claim that the other Party has breached an obligation under:

(a) Section A or Article 1503(2) (State Enterprises); or (b) Article 1502(3)(a) (Monopolies and State Enterprises) where the monopoly has acted in a manner inconsistent with the Party's obligations under Section A, and that the enterprise has incurred loss or damage by reason of, or arising out of, that breach.

2. An investor may not make a claim on behalf of an enterprise described in paragraph 1 if more than three years have elapsed from the date on which the enterprise first acquired, or should have first acquired, knowledge of the alleged breach and knowledge that the enterprise has incurred loss or damage.

3. Where an investor makes a claim under this Article and the investor or a noncontrolling investor in the enterprise makes a claim under Article 1116 arising out of the same events that gave rise to the claim under this Article, and two or more of the claims are submitted to arbitration under Article 1120, the claims should be heard together by a

Tribunal established under Article 1126, unless the Tribunal finds that the interests of a disputing party would be prejudiced thereby.

4. An investment may not make a claim under this Section.

Article 1118: Settlement of a Claim through Consultation and Negotiation

The disputing parties should first attempt to settle a claim through consultation or negotiation.

Article 1119: Notice of Intent to Submit a Claim to Arbitration

The disputing investor shall deliver to the disputing Party written notice of its intention to submit a claim to arbitration at least 90 days before the claim is submitted, which notice shall specify: (a) the name and address of the disputing investor and, where a claim is made under Article 1117, the name and address of the enterprise; (b) the provisions of this Agreement alleged to have been breached and any other relevant provisions; (c) the issues and the factual basis for the claim; and (d) the relief sought and the approximate amount of damages claimed.

Article 1120: Submission of a Claim to Arbitration

1. Except as provided in Annex 1120.1, and provided that six months have elapsed since the events giving rise to a claim, a disputing investor may submit the claim to arbitration under: (a) the ICSID Convention, provided that both the disputing Party and the Party of the investor are parties to the Convention; (b) the Additional Facility Rules of ICSID, provided that either the disputing Party or the Party of the investor, but not both, is a party to the ICSID Convention; or (c) the UNCITRAL Arbitration Rules.

2. The applicable arbitration rules shall govern the arbitration except to the extent modified by this Section.

Article 1121: Conditions Precedent to Submission of a Claim to Arbitration

1. A disputing investor may submit a claim under Article 1116 to arbitration only if: (a) the investor consents to arbitration in accordance with the procedures set out in this Agreement; and (b) both the investor and an enterprise of another Party that is a juridical person that the investor owns or controls directly or indirectly, waive their right to initiate or continue before any administrative tribunal or court under the law of any Party any proceedings with respect to the measure of the disputing Party that is alleged to be a breach referred to in Article 1116, except for proceedings for injunctive, declaratory or other extraordinary relief, not involving the payment of damages, before an administrative tribunal or court under the law of the disputing Party.

2. A disputing investor may submit a claim under Article 1117 to arbitration only if both the investor and the enterprise: (a) consent to arbitration in accordance with the procedures set out in this Agreement;

and (b) waive their right to initiate or continue before any administrative tribunal or court under the law of any Party any proceedings with respect to the measure of the disputing Party that is alleged to be a breach referred to in Article 1117, except for proceedings for injunctive, declaratory or other extraordinary relief, not involving the payment of damages, before an administrative tribunal or court under the law of the disputing Party.

3. A consent and waiver required by this Article shall be in writing, shall be delivered to the disputing Party and shall be included in the submission of a claim to arbitration.

Article 1122: Consent to Arbitration

1. Each Party consents to the submission of a claim to arbitration in accordance with the procedures set out in this Agreement.

2. The consent given by paragraph 1 and the submission by a disputing investor of a claim to arbitration shall satisfy the requirement of: (a) Chapter II of the ICSID Convention (Jurisdiction of the Centre) and the Additional Facility Rules for written consent of the parties; (b) Article II of the New York Convention for an agreement in writing; and (c) Article I of the Inter-American Convention for an agreement.

Article 1123: Number of Arbitrators and Method of Appointment

Except in respect of a Tribunal established under Article 1126, and unless the disputing parties otherwise agree, the Tribunal shall comprise three arbitrators, one arbitrator appointed by each of the disputing parties and the third, who shall be the presiding arbitrator, appointed by agreement of the disputing parties.

Article 1124: Constitution of a Tribunal When a Party Fails to Appoint an Arbitrator or the Disputing Parties Are Unable to Agree on a Presiding Arbitrator

1. The Secretary-General shall serve as appointing authority for an arbitration under this Section.

2. If a Tribunal, other than a Tribunal established under Article 1126, has not been constituted within 90 days from the date that a claim is submitted to arbitration, the Secretary-General, on the request of either disputing party, shall appoint, in his discretion, the arbitrator or arbitrators not yet appointed, except that the presiding arbitrator shall be appointed in accordance with paragraph 3.

3. The Secretary-General shall appoint the presiding arbitrator from the roster of presiding arbitrators referred to in paragraph 4, provided that the presiding arbitrator shall not be a national of the disputing Party or a national of the Party of the disputing investor. In the event that no such presiding arbitrator is available to serve, the Secretary-General shall

appoint, from the ICSID Panel of Arbitrators, a presiding arbitrator who is not a national of any of the Parties.

4. On the date of entry into force of this Agreement, the Parties shall establish, and thereafter maintain, a roster of 45 presiding arbitrators meeting the qualifications of the Convention and rules referred to in Article 1120 and experienced in international law and investment matters. The roster members shall be appointed by consensus and without regard to nationality.

Article 1125: Agreement to Appointment of Arbitrators

For purposes of Article 39 of the ICSID Convention and Article 7 of Schedule C to the ICSID Additional Facility Rules, and without prejudice to an objection to an arbitrator based on Article 1124(3) or on a ground other than nationality:

(a) the disputing Party agrees to the appointment of each individual member of a Tribunal established under the ICSID Convention or the ICSID Additional Facility Rules;

(b) a disputing investor referred to in Article 1116 may submit a claim to arbitration, or continue a claim, under the ICSID Convention or the ICSID Additional Facility Rules, only on condition that the disputing investor agrees in writing to the appointment of each individual member of the Tribunal; and

(c) a disputing investor referred to in Article 1117(1) may submit a claim to arbitration, or continue a claim, under the ICSID Convention or the ICSID Additional Facility Rules, only on condition that the disputing investor and the enterprise agree in writing to the appointment of each individual member of the Tribunal.

Article 1126: Consolidation

1. A Tribunal established under this Article shall be established under the UNCITRAL Arbitration Rules and shall conduct its proceedings in accordance with those Rules, except as modified by this Section.

* * *

Article 1128: Participation by a Party

On written notice to the disputing parties, a Party may make submissions to a Tribunal on a question of interpretation of this Agreement.

Article 1129: Documents

1. A Party shall be entitled to receive from the disputing Party, at the cost of the requesting Party a copy of: (a) the evidence that has been tendered to the Tribunal; and (b) the written argument of the disputing

2. A Party receiving information pursuant to paragraph 1 shall treat the information as if it were a disputing Party.

Article 1130: Place of Arbitration

Unless the disputing parties agree otherwise, a Tribunal shall hold an arbitration in the territory of a Party that is a party to the New York Convention, selected in accordance with: (a) the ICSID Additional Facility Rules if the arbitration is under those Rules or the ICSID Convention; or (b) the UNCITRAL Arbitration Rules if the arbitration is under those Rules.

Article 1131: Governing Law

1. A Tribunal established under this Section shall decide the issues in dispute in accordance with this Agreement and applicable rules of international law.

2. An interpretation by the Commission of a provision of this Agreement shall be binding on a Tribunal established under this Section.

Article 1132: Interpretation of Annexes

1. Where a disputing Party asserts as a defense that the measure alleged to be a breach is within the scope of a reservation or exception set out in Annex I, Annex II, Annex III or Annex IV, on request of the disputing Party, the Tribunal shall request the interpretation of the Commission on the issue. The Commission, within 60 days of delivery of the request, shall submit in writing its interpretation to the Tribunal.

2. Further to Article 1131(2), a Commission interpretation submitted under paragraph 1 shall be binding on the Tribunal. If the Commission fails to submit an interpretation within 60 days, the Tribunal shall decide the issue.

Article 1133: Expert Reports

Without prejudice to the appointment of other kinds of experts where authorized by the applicable arbitration rules, a Tribunal, at the request of a disputing party or, unless the disputing parties disapprove, on its own initiative, may appoint one or more experts to report to it in writing on any factual issue concerning environmental, health, safety or other scientific matters raised by a disputing party in a proceeding, subject to such terms and conditions as the disputing parties may agree.

Article 1134: Interim Measures of Protection

A Tribunal may order an interim measure of protection to preserve the rights of a disputing party, or to ensure that the Tribunal's jurisdiction is made fully effective, including an order to preserve evidence in the possession or control of a disputing party or to protect the Tribunal's jurisdiction. A Tribunal may not order attachment or enjoin the application of the measure alleged to constitute a breach referred to in Article 1116 or 1117. For purposes of this paragraph, an order includes a recommendation.

Article 1135: Final Award

1. Where a Tribunal makes a final award against a Party, the Tribunal may award only: (a) monetary damages and any applicable interest; or (b) restitution of property, in which case the award shall provide that the disputing Party may pay monetary damages and any applicable interest in lieu of restitution.

2. Subject to paragraph 1, where a claim is made under Article 1117(1): (a) an award of restitution of property shall provide that restitution be made to the enterprise; (b) an award of monetary damages and any applicable interest shall provide that the sum be paid to the enterprise; and (c) the award shall provide that it is made without prejudice to any right that any person may have in the relief under applicable domestic law.

3. A Tribunal may not order a Party to pay punitive damages.

Article 1136: Finality and Enforcement of an Award

1. An award made by a Tribunal shall have no binding force except between the disputing parties and in respect of the particular case.

2. Subject to paragraph 3 and the applicable review procedure for an interim award, a disputing party shall abide by and comply with an award without delay.

3. A disputing party may not seek enforcement of a final award until: (a) in the case of a final award made under the ICSID Convention (i) 120 days have elapsed from the date the award was rendered and no disputing party has requested revision or annulment of the award, or (ii) revision or annulment proceedings have been completed; and (b) in the case of a final award under the ICSID Additional Facility Rules or the UNCITRAL Arbitration Rules (i) three months have elapsed from the date the award was rendered and no disputing party has commenced a proceeding to revise, set aside or annul the award, or (ii) a court has dismissed or allowed an application to revise, set aside or annul the award and there is no further appeal.

4. Each Party shall provide for the enforcement of an award in its territory.

5. If a disputing Party fails to abide by or comply with a final award, the Commission, on delivery of a request by a Party whose investor was a party to the arbitration, shall establish a panel under Article 2008 (Request for an Arbitral Panel). The requesting Party may seek in such proceedings: (a) a determination that the failure to abide by or comply with the final

award is inconsistent with the obligations of this Agreement; and (b) a recommendation that the Party abide by or comply with the final award.

6. A disputing investor may seek enforcement of an arbitration award under the ICSID Convention, the New York Convention or the Inter-American Convention regardless of whether proceedings have been taken under paragraph 5.

7. A claim that is submitted to arbitration under this Section shall be considered to arise out of a commercial relationship or transaction for purposes of Article I of the New York Convention and Article I of the Inter-American Convention.

* * *

Article 1138: Exclusions

1. Without prejudice to the applicability or non-applicability of the dispute settlement provisions of this Section or of Chapter Twenty (Institutional Arrangements and Dispute Settlement Procedures) to other actions taken by a Party pursuant to Article 2102 (National Security), a decision by a Party to prohibit or restrict the acquisition of an investment in its territory by an investor of another Party, or its investment, pursuant to that Article shall not be subject to such provisions.

2. The dispute settlement provisions of this Section and of Chapter Twenty shall not apply to the matters referred to in Annex 1138.2.

Article 1139: Definitions

For purposes of this Chapter:

disputing investor means an investor that makes a claim under Section B;

disputing parties means the disputing investor and the disputing Party;

disputing party means the disputing investor or the disputing Party;

disputing Party means a Party against which a claim is made under Section B;

enterprise means an "enterprise" as defined in Article 201, and a branch of an enterprise;

enterprise of a Party means an enterprise constituted or organized under the law of a Party, and a branch located in the territory of a Party and carrying out business activities there;

equity or debt securities includes voting and non-voting shares, bonds, convertible debentures, stock options and warrants;

G7 Currency means the currency of Canada, France, Germany, Italy, Japan, the United Kingdom of Great Britain and Northern Ireland or the United States;

ICSID means the International Centre for Settlement of Investment Disputes;

ICSID Convention means the Convention on the Settlement of Investment Disputes between States and Nationals of other States, done at Washington, March 18, 1965;

Inter-American Convention means the Inter-American Convention on International Commercial Arbitration, done at Panama, January 30, 1975;

investment means: (a) an enterprise; (b) an equity security of an enterprise; (c) a debt security of an enterprise (i) where the enterprise is an affiliate of the investor, or (ii) where the original maturity of the debt security is at least three years, but does not include a debt security, regardless of original maturity, of a state enterprise; (d) a loan to an enterprise (i) where the enterprise is an affiliate of the investor, or (ii) where the original maturity of the loan is at least three years, but does not include a loan, regardless of original maturity, to a state enterprise; (e) an interest in an enterprise that entitles the owner to share in income or profits of the enterprise; (f) an interest in an enterprise that entitles the owner to share in the assets of that enterprise on dissolution, other than a debt security or a loan excluded from subparagraph (c) or (d); (g) real estate or other property, tangible or intangible, acquired in the expectation or used for the purpose of economic benefit or other business purposes; and (h) interests arising from the commitment of capital or other resources in the territory of a Party to economic activity in such territory, such as under (i) contracts involving the presence of an investor's property in the territory of the Party, including turnkey or construction contracts, or concessions, or (ii) contracts where remuneration depends substantially on the production, revenues or profits of an enterprise;

but investment does not mean, (i) claims to money that arise solely from (i) commercial contracts for the sale of goods or services by a national or enterprise in the territory of a Party to an enterprise in the territory of another Party, or (ii) the extension of credit in connection with a commercial transaction, such as trade financing, other than a loan covered by subparagraph (d); or (j) any other claims to money, that do not involve the kinds of interests set out in subparagraphs (a) through (h);

investment of an investor of a Party means an investment owned or controlled directly or indirectly by an investor of such Party;

investor of a Party means a Party or state enterprise thereof, or a national or an enterprise of such Party, that seeks to make, is making or has made an investment;

investor of a non-Party means an investor other than an investor of a Party, that seeks to make, is making or has made an investment;

New York Convention means the United Nations Convention on the Recognition and Enforcement of Foreign Arbitral Awards, done at New York, June 10, 1958;

Secretary-General means the Secretary-General of ICSID;

transfers means transfers and international payments;

Tribunal means an arbitration tribunal established under Article 1120 or 1126; and

UNCITRAL Arbitration Rules means the arbitration rules of the United Nations Commission on International Trade Law, approved by the United Nations General Assembly on December 15, 1976.

Annex 1120.1—Submission of a Claim to Arbitration

Mexico

With respect to the submission of a claim to arbitration: (a) an investor of another Party may not allege that Mexico has breached an obligation under: (i) Section A or Article 1503(2) (State Enterprises), or (ii) Article 1502(3)(a) (Monopolies and State Enterprises) where the monopoly has acted in a manner inconsistent with the Party's obligations under Section A, both in an arbitration under this Section and in proceedings before a Mexican court or administrative tribunal; and

(b) where an enterprise of Mexico that is a juridical person that an investor of another Party owns or controls directly or indirectly alleges in proceedings before a Mexican court or administrative tribunal that Mexico has breached an obligation under: (i) Section A or Article 1503(2) (State Enterprises), or (ii) Article 1502(3)(a) (Monopolies and State Enterprises) where the monopoly has acted in a manner inconsistent with the Party's obligations under Section A, the investor may not allege the breach in an arbitration under this Section.

* * *

Annex 1138.2—Exclusions from Dispute Settlement

Canada

A decision by Canada following a review under the Investment Canada Act, with respect to whether or not to permit an acquisition that is subject to review, shall not be subject to the dispute settlement provisions of Section B or of Chapter Twenty (Institutional Arrangements and Dispute Settlement Procedures).

Mexico

A decision by the National Commission on Foreign Investment ("Comision Nacional de Inversiones Extranjeras") following a review pursuant to Annex I, page I–M–4, with respect to whether or not to permit an acquisition that is subject to review, shall not be subject to the dispute settlement provisions of Section B or of Chapter Twenty (Institutional Arrangements and Dispute Settlement Procedures).

Chapter 17

THE EU COMMON MARKET

Table of Sections

This chapter focuses upon the internal trade law of the European Union (EU), the world's largest common market. Chapter 18 deals with EU customs and international trade law, and Chapter 19 with business competition law governing EU trade restraints. For much more extensive coverage, see R. Folsom, *Principles of European Union Law*.

§ 17.0   Introduction

Traders with the European Union have a great interest in how well its common market works. Their basic goal is to sell into and in a regional (not a national) market. This chapter highlights the law governing free movement of goods, money and services within the EU. It also very selectively focuses upon the development of common policies of particular concern to foreign traders (with emphasis on U.S. interests). Space does not permit treatment of European law governing medical and food products, free movement of people, worker and professional rights, insurance, investment advisors, transportation, value-added and excise taxation, corporate taxation, subsidies, industrial and intellectual property, procurement, consumer protection, advertising, company law, the environment, energy, telecommunications, and agricultural and fisheries policy. All of these subjects are treated in R. Folsom's *Principles of European Union Law*.

§ 17.1 Timeline of European Union Integration

A timeline presenting major developments in European integration follows:

1948— Benelux Customs Union Treaty

1949— COMECON Treaty (Eastern Europe, Soviet Union)

1951— European Coal and Steel Community ("Treaty of Paris")

1957— European Economic Community (EEC) ("Treaty of Rome") European Atomic Energy Community Treaty (EURATOM)

1959— European Free Trade Area Treaty (EFTA)

1968— EEC Customs Union fully operative

1973— Britain and Denmark switch from EFTA to EEC; Ireland joins EEC; Remaining EFTA states sign industrial free trade treaties with EEC

1979— Direct elections to European Parliament

1981— Greece joins EEC

1983— Greenland "withdraws" from EEC

1986— Spain and Portugal join EEC, Portugal leaves EFTA

1987— Single European Act amends Treaty of Rome to initiate campaign for a Community without internal frontiers, qualified majority legislative voting commences in earnest

1990— East Germany merged into Community via reunification process

1991—   COMECON defunct; trade relations with Central Europe develop rapidly

1993—   Maastricht Treaty on European Union (EU) ratified and operational, EEC officially becomes EC

1994—   European Monetary Institute established

1995—   Austria, Finland, and Sweden join EU, Norway votes no again

1999—   Amsterdam Treaty ratified and operational

1999—   Common currency (EURO) managed by European Central Bank commences with 11 members

2003—   Treaty of Nice ratified and operational, draft Constitution for Europe released

2004—   Cyprus, Estonia, Slovenia, Poland, Hungary, the Czech Republic, Slovakia, Latvia, Lithuania, Malta join EU

2005—   Constitution for Europe overwhelmingly defeated in France, Netherlands

2007—   Accession of Bulgaria and, Romania, Reform Treaty proposed

2008—   Irish voters reject Reform Treaty

2009—   Irish voters approve Reform Treaty, which takes effect Dec. 1, 2009, EU Charter of Fundamental Rights becomes binding law, EU accedes to European Convention on Human Rights, Treaty of Rome becomes Convention on the Functioning of the European Union (TFEU)

2010—   Greece and Ireland bailed out, 1 trillion temporary EURO safety net created for financial crises

2011—   Portugal bailed out, EURO in crisis

2012—   Spanish and Italian banks bailed out, Greece bailed out again, EURO in extreme crisis, Treaty on Stability, Coordination and Governance (TSCG) adopted by 25 member states creating permanent European Stability Mechanism crisis loan fund and a Fiscal Compact with balanced budget rules, ECB agrees to buy unlimited short-term national bonds

2013—   Croatia joins EU, Cyprus bailed out, Canada and EU sign Comprehensive Economic and Trade Agreement (CETA), EU and U.S. commence negotiations on Transatlantic Trade and Investment Partnership (TTIP) agreement

2014—   Latvia joins EURO zone, ECB becomes chief regulator
             of major EURO zone banks

§ 17.2   The EU Common Market

Commenced in 1957, the European Economic Community of six
states (France, Germany, Italy, Belgium Luxembourg and the
Netherlands) became a full customs union with no internal tariffs
and a common external tariff in 1968. Thereafter it struggled with
creating a truly common market. The main problem was nontariff
trade barriers (NTBs), those seemingly endless national product,
health, environmental and safety regulations. Unlike tariffs (which
can always be paid), NTBs typically blocked or inhibited trade
between the ever increasing number of EU member states.

The campaign for a European Community "without internal
frontiers" was the product of Commission studies in the mid-1980s
which concluded that a hardening of the trade arteries of Europe
had occurred. The Community was perceived to be stagnating
relative to the advancing economies of North America and East
Asia. Various projections of the wealth that could be generated from
a truly common market for Western Europe suggested the need for
revitalization. A "white paper" drafted under the leadership of Lord
Cockfield of Britain and issued by the Commission in 1985 became
the blueprint for the campaign.

The Commission's white paper identified three types of
barriers to a Europe without internal frontiers—physical, technical
and fiscal. Physical barriers occur at the borders. For goods, they
include national trade quotas, health checks, agricultural monetary
compensation amount (MCA) charges, statistical collections and
transport controls. For people, physical barriers involve clearing
immigrations, security checks and customs. Technical barriers
mostly involve national standards and rules for goods, services,
capital and labor which operate to inhibit trade among the member
states. Boilers, railway, medical and surgical equipment, and
pharmaceuticals provide traditional examples of markets restrained
by technical trade barriers. Fiscal barriers centered on different
value-added and excise taxation levels and the corresponding need
for tax collections at the border. There were, for example, wide
value-added tax (VAT) differences on auto sales within the Common
Market.

The Commission (Cecchini Report) estimated that removal of
all of these barriers could save the Community upwards of 100
billion ECUs (European Currency Units, now EUROs) in direct
costs. In addition, another roughly 100 billion ECUs could be gained

as price reductions and increased efficiency and competition took hold. Overall, the Commission projected an increase in the Common Market's gross domestic product (GDP) of between 4.5 to 7 percent, a reduction in consumer prices of between 6 to 4.5 percent, 1.75 to 5 million new jobs, and enhanced public sector and external trade balances. These figures were thus said to represent "the costs of non-Europe."

Single European Act

Pushed by the Cecchini Report, major amendments to the Treaty of Rome (now the Treaty on the Functioning of the European Union, TFEU) were undertaken in the Single European Act (SEA), which became effective in 1987. Proposals originating in the Commission's 1985 white paper on a Europe without internal frontiers were embodied in the Single European Act. The SEA amendments not only expanded the competence of the European institutions, but also sought to accelerate the speed of integration by relying more heavily on qualified majority (not unanimous) voting principles in legislative decision-making.

The Single European Act envisioned the adoption of hundreds of new legislative measures designed to remove NTBs and fully integrate the Common Market by the end of 1992. Nearly all of these measures and more were adopted. Implementation at the national level proceeded more slowly, and even now remains a concern. By 1996, the Commission reported that the single market program had increased internal trade by 20–30%, added 1% in GDP growth annually, and generated over 900,000 jobs.

§ 17.3 EU Common Market—Free Movement of Goods

North American traders and investors should understand that the free movement of goods within Europe is based upon the creation of a customs union. Under this union, the member states have eliminated customs duties among themselves.[1] They have established a common customs tariff for their trade with the rest of the world. Quantitative restrictions (quotas) on trade between member states are also prohibited, except in emergency and other limited situations.[2] The right of free movement applies to goods that originate in the Common Market. It also applies to goods that have lawfully entered the EU by paying the common external tariff and meeting its external trade rules. Such goods are said to be in "free

---

[1]   Article 30, Treaty on the Functioning of the European Union (TFEU).

[2]   Articles 34–37, TFEU.

circulation."[3] This contrasts with NAFTA where the right of free circulation is limited to goods deemed originating in North America.

Measures of Equivalent Effect

The establishment of the customs union has been a major accomplishment, though not without difficulties. The member states not only committed themselves to the elimination of tariffs and quotas on internal trade, but also to the elimination of "measures of equivalent effect."[4] The elastic legal concept of measures of equivalent effect has been interpreted broadly by the European Court of Justice and the Commission to prohibit a wide range of trade restraints, such as administrative fees charged at borders which are the equivalent of import or export tariffs.[5] Charges of equivalent effect to a tariff must be distinguished from internal taxes that are applicable to imported and domestic goods. The latter must be levied in a nondiscriminatory and non-protective manner (Article 110, TFEU), while the former are prohibited entirely (Articles 28, 30). There has been a considerable amount of litigation over this distinction.[6]

The elasticity of the concept of measures of an equivalent effect is even more pronounced in the Court's judgment relating to quotas. This jurisprudence draws upon an early Commission directive (no longer applicable) of extraordinary scope.[7] In this directive, the Commission undertook a lengthy listing of practices that it considered illegal measures of effect equivalent to quotas. It is still occasionally referenced in Commission and Court of Justice decisions. Its focus is on national rules that discriminate against imports or simply restrain internal trade.

Cassis Formula

In a famous case, the Court of Justice ruled that Belgium could not block the importation of Scotch whiskey via France because of the absence of a British certificate of origin as required by Belgian customs law.[8] The Court of Justice held that any national rule directly or indirectly, actually or potentially capable of hindering

---

[3]   Articles 28–29, TFEU.

[4]   See especially Articles 30, 34 and 35, TFEU.

[5]   Rewe Zentralfinanz v. Landwirtschaftskammer Westfalen-Lippe (1973) Eur.Comm.Rep. 1039; Commission v. Italy (1969) Eur.Comm.Rep. 193. But see Commission v. Germany (1988) Eur.Comm.Rep. 5427.

[6]   See e.g. Industria Gomma, Articoli Vari v. Ente Nazionale ENCC (1975) Eur.Comm.Rep. 699.

[7]   Procureur du Roi v. Dassonville (1974) Eur.Comm.Rep. 837.

[8]   Commission Directive 70/50 on the Abolition of Measures which have an Effect Equivalent to Quantitative Restrictions, 1970 O.J. L13/29 (Special Edition) (I), p. 17.

internal trade is generally forbidden as a measure of equivalent effect to a quota. However, *if* European law has not developed appropriate rules in the area concerned (here designations of origin), the member states may enact "reasonable" and "proportional" (no broader than necessary) regulations to ensure that the public is not harmed.[9] This is often referred to as the "*Cassis* formula". Products meeting reasonable national criteria, the *Cassis* opinion continues, may be freely traded. This is the origin of the innovative "mutual reciprocity" principle used in significant parts of the legislative campaign for a Europe without frontiers.

The *Cassis* decision suggests use of a Rule of Reason analysis for national fiscal regulations, public health measures, laws governing the fairness of commercial transactions and consumer protection. Environmental protection and occupational safety laws of the member states have been similarly treated. Under this approach, for example, a Danish "bottle bill" requiring use of approved containers was therefore unreasonable.[10] However, the Danes' argument that a deposit and return system was environmentally necessary prevailed. This was a reasonable restraint on internal trade recognized by the Court under the *Cassis* formula for analyzing compelling state interests. Likewise, a Belgian law prohibiting the importation of general wastes from neighboring countries was found reasonable and not in breach of Community free trade principles.[11]

Under *Cassis*, national rules requiring country of origin or "foreign origin" labels have fallen as measures of effect equivalent to quotas.[12] So have various restrictive national procurement laws, including a "voluntary" campaign to "Buy Irish."[13] Minimum and maximum retail pricing controls can also run afoul of the Court's expansive interpretations.[14] Compulsory patent licensing can amount to a measure of equivalent effect nullified by operation of regional law. The U.K. could not compulsorily require

---

[9]   See the "Cassis de Dijon" case, Rewe Zentral AG v. Bundesmonopolverwaltung für Branntwein (1979) Eur.Comm.Rep. 649 (German *minimum* alcoholic beverage rule not reasonable).

[10]   Commission v. Denmark (1988) Eur.Comm.Rep. 4607.

[11]   Commission v. Belgium (1992) Eur.Comm.Rep. I–4431 (Case C–2/90).

[12]   Commission v. Ireland (1981) Eur.Comm.Rep. 1625; Commission v. United Kingdom (1985) Eur.Comm.Rep. 1202.

[13]   Commission v. Ireland (1988) Eur.Comm.Rep. 4929 (product standards); Commission v. Ireland (1982) Eur.Comm.Rep. 4005 (Buy Irish). But see Apple and Pear Development Council (1983) Eur.Comm.Rep. 4083 (permissible promotion of local agricultural products).

[14]   Re Ricardo Tasca (1976) Eur.Comm.Rep. 291; Openbaar Ministerie v. Van Tiggele (1978) Eur.Comm.Rep. 25.

manufacturing within its jurisdiction.[15] Member states may not impose linguistic labeling requirements so as to block trade and competition in foodstuffs. In this instance, a Belgian law requiring Dutch labels in Flemish areas was nullified as in conflict with the Treaty.[16] These cases vividly illustrate the extent to which litigants are invoking the TFEU and the *Cassis* formula in attempts at overcoming commercially restrictive national laws.

There are cases which suggest that "cultural interests" may justify national restrictions on European trade. For example, British, French and Belgian bans on Sunday retail trading have survived initial scrutiny under the *Cassis* formula.[17] French legislation prohibiting the sale or rental of cassettes within one year of a film's debut also survived such scrutiny.[18] And British prohibitions of sales of sex articles except by licensed sex shops are compatible.[19] National laws prohibiting sales below cost, when applied without discrimination as between imports and domestic products, are not considered to affect trade between the member states. In this remarkable decision signaling a jurisprudential retreat, the ECJ ruled that such laws may not be challenged under the traditional *Cassis* formula.[20] Deceptive trade practices laws ordinarily do not amount to "selling arrangements,"[21] but national laws regulating sales outlets[22] and advertising[23] may.

In recent years, member state regulations capable of being characterized as governing "marketing modalities" or "selling arrangements" have sought shelter under *Keck*. For example, the French prohibition of televised advertising (intended to favor printed media) of the distribution of goods escaped the rule of reason analysis of *Cassis* in this manner. Some commentators see in *Keck* and its progeny an unarticulated attempt by the Court to take

---

[15]   Commission v. United Kingdom (1992) Eur.Comm.Rep. I–0829 (Case C–30/90).

[16]   Piageme ASBL v. Peeters BVBA (1991) Eur.Comm.Rep. I–2971 (Case C–369/89).

[17]   Torfaen Borough Council v. B+Q PLC Ltd (1989) Eur.Comm.Rep. 3851; UDS v. Sidef Conforma & Ors (1991) Eur.Comm.Rep. 997 (Case C–312/89); Re Marchandise & Ors (1991) Eur.Comm.Rep. 1027 (Case C–332/89).

[18]   Cinéthéque SA v. Federation Nationale des Cinémas Francais (1985) Eur.Comm.Rep. 2605.

[19]   Quietlynn Ltd. v. Southend Borough Council (1990) 1 Eur.Comm.Rep. 3051.

[20]   See Re Keck & Mithouard (1993) Eur.Comm.Rep. 6097 (Cases C–267/91, C–268/91).

[21]   Verband Sozialer Wettbewerb v. Clinique Laboratories (1994) Eur.Comm.Rep. I–317.

[22]   Commission v. Greece (1995) Eur.Comm.Rep. I–1621.

[23]   Societe d'Importation Edouard Leclerc-Siplec v. TF1 Publicite (1995) Eur.Comm. I–179. *Compare* Konsumertombusmannen (KO) v. Gourmet International Products ABS, (GIP) (2001) Eur.Comm.Rep. I–6493.

subsidiarity seriously. Others are just baffled by its newly found tolerance for trade distorting national marketing laws. But the Court of Justice has poignantly refused to extend *Keck* to the marketing of services, and some commentators suggest *Keck* may be fading into obscurity.

The Court has made it clear that all of the Rule of Reason justifications for national regulatory laws are temporary. Adoption of Common Market legislation in any of these areas would eliminate national authority to regulate trading conditions under *Cassis* and (presumably) *Keck*.[24] These judicial mandates, none of which are specified in the TFEU, vividly illustrate the powers of the Court of Justice to expansively interpret the Treaty and rule on the validity under European law of national legislation affecting internal trade in goods.

§ 17.4 EU Common Market—Article 36 and the Problem of Nontariff Trade Barriers (NTBs)

As in the world community, the major trade barrier within Europe has become NTBs. To some extent, in the absence of a harmonizing directive completely occupying the field,[25] this is authorized. Article 36 TFEU permits national restraints on imports and exports justified on the grounds of:

(1) Public morality, public policy ("ordre public") or public security;

(2) The protection of health and life of humans, animals or plants;

(3) The protection of national treasures possessing artistic, historical or archeological value[26]; and

(4) The protection of industrial or commercial property.

Article 36 amounts, within certain limits, to an authorization of nontariff trade barriers among the member nations. This "public interest" authorization exists in addition to, but somewhat overlaps

---

[24] Oberkreisdirektor des Kreises Borken v. Moorman B.V. (1988) Eur.Comm.Rep. 4689.

[25] See Firma Eau de Cologne v. Provide (1989) Eur.Comm.Rep. 3891 and Pubblico Ministero v. Ratti (1979) Eur.Comm.Rep. 1629 (Article 36 preempted by directives). But see Article 114 TFEU regarding internal market directives where member states retain certain Article 36 prerogatives and cases allowing member states to "supplement" directives on the basis of genuine need, including Ministére Public v. Grunert (1980) Eur.Comm.Rep. 1827; In re Motte (1985) Eur.Comm.Rep. 3887; Ministére Public v. Muller (1986) Eur.Comm.Rep. 1511; Ministére Public v. Bellon (1990) Eur.Comm.Rep. 4683.

[26] See Council Directive 93/7 securing the right of return of national cultural treasures removed unlawfully after Dec. 31, 1992.

with, the Rule of Reason exception formulated in *Cassis* above. However, in a sentence much construed by the European Court of Justice, Article 36 continues with the following language: "Such prohibitions or restrictions shall not, however, constitute a means of arbitrary discrimination or a disguised restriction on trade between member states."

Case Law

In a wide range of decisions, the Court of Justice has interpreted Article 36 in a manner which generally limits the ability of member states to impose NTB barriers to internal trade. Britain, for example, may use its criminal law under the public morality exception to seize pornographic goods made in Holland that it outlaws,[27] but not inflatable sex dolls from Germany which could be lawfully produced in the United Kingdom.[28] Germany cannot stop the importation of beer (e.g., Heineken's from Holland) which fails to meet its purity standards.[29] This case makes wonderful reading as the Germans, seeking to invoke the public health exception of Article 36, argue all manner of ills that may befall their populace if free trade in beer is allowed. Equally interesting are the unsuccessful Italian health protection arguments against free trade in pasta made from common (not durum) wheat.[30]

But a state may obtain whatever information it requires from importers to evaluate public health risks associated with food products containing additives that are freely traded elsewhere in the Common Market. This does not mean that an importer of muesli bars to which vitamins have been added must prove the product healthful, rather that the member state seeking to bar the imports must have an objective reason for keeping them out of its market.[31] Assuming such a reason exists, the trade restraint may not be disproportionate to the public health goal.[32] A notable 2002 ECJ opinion invalidated a French public health ban on U.K. beef imports maintained after a Commission decision to return to free trade following the "mad cow" outbreak.[33]

---

[27]   Regina v. Henn and Darby (1979) Eur.Comm.Rep. 3795.

[28]   Conegate Ltd. v. H.M. Customs and Excise (1986) Eur.Comm.Rep. 1007.

[29]   Commission v. Germany (1987) Eur.Comm.Rep. 1227. But see Aragonesa de Publicidad Exterior SA (APESA) + Anor v. Departamento de Sanidad y Seguridad Social (1991) Eur.Comm.Rep. 4151 (Cases C–1/90 and C–176/90) (advertising ban applied to strong alcoholic beverages can be justified on public health grounds).

[30]   Re Drei Glocken GmbH and Criminal Proceedings against Zoni (1988) Eur.Comm.Rep. 4233, 4285.

[31]   Officer van Justitie v. Sandoz BV (1983) Eur.Comm.Rep. 2445.

[32]   Commission v. United Kingdom (UHT Milk) (1983) Eur.Comm.Rep. 203.

[33]   National Farmers' Union v. Secrétariat Général (2002) Eur.Comm.Rep. I–9079.

Public security measures adopted under Article 36 can include external as well as internal security. An unusual case under the public security exception contained in Article 36 involved Irish petroleum products' restraints.[34] The Irish argued that oil is an exceptional product always triggering national security interests. Less expansively, the Court acknowledged that maintaining minimum oil supplies did fall within the ambit of Article 36. The public policy exception under Article 36 has been construed along French lines (ordre public). Only genuine threats to fundamental societal interests are covered.[35] Consumer protection (though a legitimate rationale for trade restraints under *Cassis*), does not fall within the public policy exception.[36] Permitting environmental protesters to block the Brenner Pass for 30 hours is acceptable public policy in support of fundamental assembly and expression rights.[37]

§ 17.5 EU Common Market—Legislative Solutions to NTBs

Nontariff trade barrier problems were the principal focus of the campaign for a fully integrated Common Market. Many legislative acts have been adopted which target NTB trade problems. When possible, a common European standard is adopted. For example, legislation on auto pollution requirements adopts this methodology. Products meeting these standards may be freely traded in the Common Market. Traditionally, this approach (called "harmonization") has required the formation of a consensus as to the appropriate level of protection.

Once adopted, harmonized standards must be followed. This approach can be deceptive, however. Some harmonization directives contain a list of options from which member states may choose when implementing those directives. In practice, this leads to differentiated national laws on the same so-called harmonized subject. Furthermore, in certain areas (notably the environment and occupational health and safety), the TFEU expressly indicates that member states may adopt laws that are more demanding. The result is, again, less than complete harmonization.

Harmonization Principles

Many efforts at the harmonization of European environmental, health and safety, standards and certification, and related law have

---

[34]   Campus Oil Ltd. v. Minister for Industry and Energy (1984) Eur.Comm.Rep. 2727.

[35]   See Regina v. Thompson (1978) Eur.Comm.Rep. 2247 (coinage).

[36]   Kohl KG v. Ringelhan and Rennett SA (1984) Eur.Comm.Rep. 3651.

[37]   Schmidberger v. Austria (2003) Eur.Comm.Rep. I–5659 (Case C–112/00).

been undertaken. Nearly all of these are supposed to be based upon "high levels of protection."[38] Many have criticized what they see as the "least common denominator" results of harmonization of national laws under the campaign for a Europe without internal frontiers. One example involves the safety of toys. Directive 88/378 permits toys to be sold throughout the Common Market if they satisfy "essential requirements." These requirements are broadly worded in terms of flammability, toxicity, etc. There are two ways to meet these requirements: (1) produce a toy in accordance with CEN standards (drawn up by experts); or (2) produce a toy that otherwise meets the essential safety requirements. Local language labeling requirements necessary for purchaser comprehension have generally, though not always, been upheld.[39]

The least common denominator criticism may be even more appropriate to the second legislative methodology utilized in the internal market campaign. The second approach is based on the *Cassis* principle of mutual reciprocity. Under this "new" minimalist approach, European legislation requires member states to recognize the standards laws of other member states and deem them acceptable for purposes of the operation of the Common Market.[40]

However, major legislation has been adopted in the area of professional services.[41] By mutual recognition of higher education diplomas based upon at least three years of courses, virtually all professionals have now obtained legal rights to move freely in pursuit of their careers. This is a remarkable achievement.

§ 17.6   EU Common Market—Product Standards and Testing

An important part of the single market campaign against nontariff trade barriers (NTBs) of great interest to international business involves product testing and standards. More than half of the legislation involved in the single market campaign concerned such issues. Since 1969, there has been a standstill agreement among the member states to avoid the introduction of new technical barriers to trade. A 1983 directive requires member states to notify the Commission of proposed new technical regulations and product standards. The Commission can enjoin the introduction of such

---

[38]   Article 114, TFEU.

[39]   *See* Piageme & Orrs v. Peeters (1995) Eur.Comm.Rep. I–2955; Colim v. Bigg's Continent Noord (1999) Eur.Comm.Rep. I–3175.

[40]   See, e.g., Council Resolution on a New Approach to Technical Harmonization and Standards, 1985 O.J. C136/1.

[41]   See Council Directives, 89/48, 92/51, 2005/36.

national rules for up to one year if it believes that a regional standard should be developed.[42]

The goal was to move from national regulatory approvals to one unified system embodying essential requirements on health, safety, the environment and consumer protection. Goods that meet these essential requirements bear a "CE mark" and can be freely traded. Manufacturers self-certify their compliance with relevant European standards. Design and production process standards generally follow the ISO 9000 series on quality management and assurance. Firms must maintain a technical file documenting compliance and produce the file upon request by national authorities.

Standards Bodies

Private regional standards bodies have been playing a critical role in the development of this system. These include the European Committee for Standardization (CEN), the European Committee for Electrotechnical Standardization (CENELEC), and the European Telecommunications Standards Institute (ETSI). Groups like these have been officially delegated the responsibility for creating thousands of technical product standards. They have been turning out some 150 common standards each year. For example, directives on the safety of toys, construction products and electromagnetic compatibility have been issued.[43] These directives adopt the so-called "new approach" of setting broad standards at the regional level which if met guarantee access to every member state market.

Under the "old approach", which still applies to most standards for processed foods, motor vehicles, chemicals and pharmaceuticals, European legislation on standards is binding law. The technical specifications and testing protocols of these directives must be followed and (unlike the new approach) the member states may add requirements to them. Under either approach, goods meeting these standards will bear a CE mark. North American producers have frequently complained that their ability to be heard by European standards' bodies is limited. They have had little influence on product standards to which they must conform in order to sell freely in the Common Market.

Testing and Certification

Testing and certification of products has been another part of the single market campaign. The main concern of North American companies is that recognition be granted of U.S., Canadian and

---

42   Council Directive 83/169.
43   See Council Directives 88/378, 89/106 and 89/336.

Mexican tests. In the past, many North American exporters have had to have their goods retested for European purposes. The EU is generally committed to a resolution of such issues under what it calls a "global approach" to product standards and testing. This involves creation of a regional system for authorizing certification and testing under common rules and procedures.[44]

In negotiations undertaken as part of the Uruguay Round on revising the Standards Code of the GATT, the EU indicated its commitment to giving recognition to "equivalent technical regulations" of other nations, and to avoidance of unnecessary obstacles to trade. The Transatlantic Partnership dialogue between Europe and the United States has successfully achieved mutual recognition on a range of product standards and testing.

§ 17.7   EU Common Market—Products Liability

Products liability law is one field where the Union acted before the single market campaign to harmonize national rules. Prior to the EU products liability directive, the rules of law on products liability of the individual member states varied greatly. Traditional negligence liability with plaintiff's burden of proof was the rule in Italy, Portugal, Spain and Greece. A presumption of liability shifting the burden of proof to the defendant bordering on strict products liability governed in Germany, Denmark, the Netherlands, the United Kingdom and Ireland. Absolute strict liability, creating a presumption liability that could not be overcome, was the rule in France, Belgium and Luxembourg.

Strict Liability

Council Directive 85/374 established, for all member states, a regime of strict (no-fault) defective products liability. The injured person is required to prove damages, the defect and a causal relationship between defect and damage. The term "product" applies to "all movables, with the exception of primary agricultural products and games, even though incorporated into another movable or into an immovable" and specifically includes electricity. Both new and used products are covered. However, the evaluation of whether a product is defective takes place at the time when the "producer" has most recently put the product into circulation. Manufacturers of components are treated as such producers.

Producers also include manufacturers of finished products, suppliers of raw materials or component parts and persons who, by putting names, trademarks or other distinguishing features on products, present themselves as producers. Licensors are not

---

[44]   Council Resolution Dec. 21, 1989, O.J. C10 (Jan. 16, 1990).

generally treated as producers but their licensees are. Thus, department stores and commercial chains will be regarded as producers if they sell products manufactured by others under their own names without referring to actual origin. They will be jointly and severally liable with the actual producer. However, if a department store has had a product specially made under the designation "specially manufactured for . . . by . . . ," the department store should not be regarded as a "producer."

Any person who imports products into the Union for distribution in the course of business is deemed a producer. This rule only concerns persons who import products into the Union, not persons who import from one member state to another. The importer's intentions at the time of importation are crucial. If the product was originally imported in the course of business, the importer will be regarded as a producer even if the product is later dedicated to personal use. An importer who originally imported the product for personal use, but later decides to use the product commercially, does not become a producer. The burden of proof that the product is not imported in the course of business rests with the importer. Whether the doctrine of strict products liability applies to retailers is decided by each member state.

A product is defective "when it does not provide the safety which a person is entitled to expect." It is not the injured person's expectations that control, but rather the normal expectations of purchasers of such products. The reasonable expected use of the product is determined when evaluating defects of production, design or the lack of adequate warnings or instruction. The gravity of the potential injury, the probability of the occurrence of injury, and the consumer's awareness of the danger are analyzed to determine whether adequate warnings or instruction have been given.

Exceptions and Defenses

The exception for "primary agricultural products" includes fish products but excludes all products that "have undergone initial processing." The line between primary and initially processed products thus becomes quite important and will no doubt be subjected to judicial interpretation. Moreover, member states can elect to include primary agricultural products under their strict liability regime. Luxembourg appears to be the only nation to do so to date. The Products Liability Directive does not apply to services. However, if a defective product is used when rendering services, the producer may be held strictly liable for any damages. The person rendering services will only be liable if he or she has acted with negligence.

Strict liability is tempered by certain defenses, notably the "state-of-the-art" defense which excludes liability if the manufacturer could not have discovered the defect when the product was made. However, the member states have the option of omitting this defense, which (to date) only Luxembourg has done. The British version of this defense, implemented in the 1987 Consumer Protection Act, was unsuccessfully challenged as too broad by the Commission before the European Court of Justice.[45] Strict liability is also tempered in the award of damages by contributory negligence principles. The calculation and types of damages that may be recovered and damages caps are largely left to national law. Thus the award of "pain and suffering" or punitive damages is under member state control, as is the imposition of total limits on recovery. Germany, Greece and Portugal have set such total limits. A three-year statute of limitations ordinarily applies, and a ten-year absolute bar on liability is established in the Council directive on products liability.

For some EU nations, such as Ireland and Spain, this directive mandated a fundamental switch away from liability systems grounded entirely in negligence principles. France, on the other hand, considered the directive too generous to manufacturers. All three were pursued by the Commission for their implementation failures.[46] Nevertheless, Americans who have studied the painstaking manner in which strict products liability doctrine was crafted in state courts are often surprised by the sweeping implementation of comparable law in the European Union.

One explanation lies in the goal of free movement and a desire to equalize the risks of liability (and the insurance costs) that most often accompany the distribution of goods to the public. There is, also, greater acceptance in Europe of the need to compensate accident victims regardless of fault. Moreover, the absence of a well-financed plaintiff's bar, contingency legal fees, juries and rules that require each party to pay their own legal costs (*i.e.,* the loser generally pays in Europe) have made products liability litigation infrequent. These factors facilitated the passage of the products liability directive and its implementation by the member states. The Products Liability Directive has, with certain adaptations, been extended to the EFTA countries (excluding Switzerland and Liechtenstein) by virtue of its inclusion in the Annex to the European Economic Area Agreement which came into force on January 1, 1994.

---

[45]   Commission v. United Kingdom (1997) Eur.Comm.Rep. I–2649.

[46]   *See, e.g.,* Commission v. French Republic (2002) Eur.Comm.Rep. I–03827 (Case 52/00).

§ 17.8 EU Common Market—Consumer Protection

The European Union has had a consumer protection and information policy since 1975. Its consumer protection role was recognized in 1993 amendments to the TFEU.[47] The member states, however, may enact more stringent protective measures provided they are compatible with the Treaty.[48] In addition to products liability (above), EU law covers health and safety product labeling and manufacturing. Foodstuffs, cosmetics, detergents, vehicles, textiles, toys, dangerous substances, medicines, chemicals (the REACH regulations), fertilizers, pesticides and animal feed are some of the areas now governed by Union consumer protection law. There is, for example, a directive which fixes the maximum level of pesticide residues on fruits and vegetables.[49] The Commission operates an information exchange network on products that present grave and immediate danger to consumers. The source member state notifies the Commission of the hazard, and the Commission forwards this information to the other member states. Opinions of the European Food Safety Authority play a critical role in this regard.[50]

Dangerous Substances

All products dangerous to humans or the environment are subject to the Union's dangerous substances directives.[51] This includes explosives, flammable, toxic and carcinogenic substances. No such products are to be allowed on the market until after a review of their "for-seeable risks" and "unfavorable effects" by national authorities. Child-resistant packaging is ordinarily required as is labeling using a common "CE" black on orange-yellow symbol. Any special risks associated with the product and safety advice must be spelled out on the label. Dangerous substances meeting the terms and conditions of this directive may be freely traded within the Union, each nation relying on the authorities of all other EU countries to implement the directive as to manufacturers within their borders.

Product Safety

An EU product safety directive has also been adopted Council Directive 92/59 revised by Directive 2001/95 applies to all products

---

[47]   See Article 169, TFEU. But see VTB-VAB NV v. Total Belgium NV, (2009) Eur.Comm.Rep. ___ (Cases C–261/07 and C–299/07) (blanket Belgian law against "combined offers" invalid).

[48]   Id.

[49]   Council Directive 76/895 (amended by Directive 90/642).

[50]   See Pfizer Animal Health v. Council, (2002) Eur. Comm. Rep. II–3305.

[51]   Council Directive 67/548.

not subject to more specific Union law on safety. Suppliers may place only safe products on the market. A safe product does not present any risk, or only risks considered acceptable and consistent with a high standard of protection. In assessing the acceptability of risk, the product's intended or reasonably foreseeable use must be evaluated. The supplier must give the user sufficient information to assess acceptable risks and to monitor the safety of the product. Suppliers will be deemed to meet the general safety requirement if they comply with Union standards or (in their absence) member state safety requirements. The directive requires member states to have the power to impose sanctions for violations, including the power to ban products from the market, but it does not require that consumers be given a damages remedy for unsafe products.

Precautionary Principle

One consistent theme in EU consumer and environmental protection law is the "precautionary principle." Health, safety and environmental risks are often regulated in advance of a thorough scientific analysis of their significance. A "beef hormones" ban, for example, was the subject of longstanding World Trade Organization dispute with the United States, whose beef exports to the EU dropped significantly. Although the U.S. "won" this dispute, the precautionary principle not being recognized in WTO law, the ban continued despite retaliatory U.S. tariff sanctions against EU exports of cheese, ham, sweaters and other products. Finally, in 2009, settlement of the beef hormones dispute was accomplished. The U.S. removed its retaliatory tariffs, and the EU allowed more non-hormone U.S. beef into its market. Hormone treated beef from anywhere remains excluded from the European Union.

In an increasingly globalized world economy, EU product and service regulations frequently prevail as other jurisdictions and multinational firms adopt them. Obedience to precautionary principles is spreading, from International Accounting Standards to personal data privacy (see Section 17.17.

§ 17.9 EU Common Market—Agricultural Policy (CAP)

The TFEU establishes the basic principles governing what is perhaps the most controversial of all Union policies, the Common Agricultural Program (CAP). The inclusion of agricultural trade in the Treaty was a critical element to the politics of the Union and remains largely without precedent in other regional economic treaties throughout the world. For many reasons, including the desire for self-sufficiency in food and the protection of farmers, free trade in agricultural products is an extremely sensitive issue around the globe. The United States has been disputing agricultural trade with the EU for decades. When the Common Market was established in 1957, France and Italy had substantial farming communities, many of which were family based and politically powerful. Both countries envisioned that free trade in agricultural products could threaten the livelihoods of these people. The solution, as outlined in the Treaty, was to set up a "common organization of agricultural markets."

The objectives of the CAP include the increase of productivity, the maintenance of a fair standard of living for the agricultural community, the stabilization of markets, and the provision of consumer goods at reasonable prices. It has not proved possible to accommodate all of these objectives. Consumer interests have generally lost out to farmers' incomes and trading company profits. Target prices for some commodities (*e.g.,* sugar, dairy products and grain) are established and supported through Union market purchases at "intervention levels". "Variable import levies" (tariffs) are periodically changed to ensure that cheaper imports do not disrupt CAP prices. External protection of this type is also extended to meat and eggs. Fruit, vegetables and wine are subject to quality controls which limit their flow into the market. Wine and agricultural products are subject to regulated designations of origin,[52] Rioja wine from Spain[53] and Feta cheese from Greece,[54] for examples. Such regulations do not extend to generic food names, such as edam,[55] jenerver (gin)[56] and emmenthal,[57] which can be freely traded with proper labels indicating variations in product qualities.

Regulatory Controls

In recent years, perhaps the most controversial "common organization" has been for bananas. The Europeans import bananas under a complex quota system adopted in 1993 that favors former colonies and dependencies. Internally and externally those affected have gone bananas over this regulation. Several challenges originating from Germany failed before the European Court of Justice, but in the end the United States, Mexico, Ecuador, Guatemala and Honduras prevailed in the World Trade Organization. After suffering "authorized retaliation" in the form of

---

[52] Regulation 823/87 (wine) and Regulation 2081/92 (agricultural products).

[53] See Belgium v. Spain (2000) Eur.Comm.Rep. 23.

[54] See Denmark v. Commission (1999) Eur.Comm.Rep. I–1541.

[55] Ministere Public v. Deserbais (1988) Eur.Comm.Rep. 4907.

[56] Criminal proceedings against Miro BV (1985) Eur.Comm.Rep. 3731.

[57] Criminal proceedings against Guimont (2000) Eur.Comm.Rep. I–10663 (Dec. 5, 2000).

tariffs on EU exports, the Europeans adjusted their "common organization" for bananas by replacing its quotas with non-preferential tariffs. The European Agricultural Guidance and Guarantee Fund (better known by its French initials as FEOGA) channels the Union agricultural budget into export refunds, intervention purchases, storage, and structural adjustment. Agricultural policy regulations cannot discriminate against like or substitute products. But the bias towards producers, not consumers, in the CAP has been consistently upheld by the Court of Justice. [58]

Agricultural goods, like industrial products, can trigger free movement litigation. In one case, for example, the Court of Justice suggested that British animal health regulations were a disguised restraint on Union trade in poultry and eggs. [59] As with industrial goods, if the real aim is to block imports, such regulations are unlawful measures of equivalent effect to a quota. On the other hand, the United Kingdom could establish a Pear and Apple Development Council for purposes of technical advice, promotional campaigns (not intended to discourage competitive imports), and common quality standards for its members. But it could not impose a mandatory fee to finance such activities. [60]

Apart from variable tariff protection, CAP quality control regulations can serve to keep foreign agricultural products from entering the European Union market. For example, the ban on beef hormones adopted by qualified majority vote in the late 1980s stirred opposition internally. [61] In the United States, the beef hormones legislation was vehemently opposed by the White House, but accepted by the renegade Texas Department of Agriculture which offered as much hormone-free beef to the Union as it would buy. The Texas offer delighted the EU Commissioner on Agriculture who rarely has a U.S. ally and is said to have wired: "I accept."

A veritable maze of legislation and case law governs the CAP. For many years, special agricultural "monetary compensation amounts" (MCAs) have been collected at national borders, greatly contributing to the failure to achieve a Europe without internal trade frontiers. It was not until 1987 that firm arrangements were realized to dismantle the MCA system. In most years, the net effect

---

[58]   Germany v. Commission (1963) Eur.Comm.Rep. 131; Balkan-Import-Export GmbH v. Hauptzollamt Berlin-Packhof (1973) Eur.Comm.Rep. 1091 (CAP measures valid unless "obviously unreasonable" consumer prices produced). *See* Article 34(3), Treaty of Rome

[59]   Commission v. United Kingdom (1982) Eur.Comm.Rep. 2793 (Newcastle disease).

[60]   The Apple and Pear Development Council v. K.J. Lewis, Ltd. (1983) Eur.Comm.Rep. 4083.

[61]   United Kingdom v. Council (1988) Eur.Comm.Rep. 855.

of the CAP is to raise food prices in the EU substantially above world price levels. The CAP has meant that agriculture is heavily subsidized. Indeed, it continues to consume the lion's share of the Union budget and at times seems like a spending policy that is out of control.

The Common Agricultural Policy does include a variety of "structural" programs intended to reduce the size of the farm population, increase the efficiency of its production, and hold down prices. These programs have involved retirement incentives, land reallocations, and training for other occupations. There has been a gradual reduction in the number of EU farmers over the years. In 1988, the Council adopted rules designed ultimately to reduce agricultural expenditures by linking total expenditures to the Union's rate of economic growth, establishing automatic price cuts when production ceilings are reached, and creating land set-aside and early retirement programs for farmers.

France and Italy, in the early years of the EU, became major beneficiaries of CAP subsidies. West Germany, with a minimal agricultural sector, was the primary payor under the program. It, in turn, principally benefitted from the custom union provisions establishing free trade in industrial goods. Hence a basic tradeoff was established in 1957 by the Treaty of Rome. France and Italy would receive substantial agricultural subsidies out of the regional budget while West Germany gained access for its industrial goods to their markets. Germany now holds a 25 percent share of internal EU trade.

Britain, like Germany, sees itself as a net payor under the CAP. It has repeatedly been able to negotiate special compensatory adjustments as a consequence. Greece, Spain, Portugal and Ireland, on the other hand, looked forward eagerly to membership as a means to CAP subsidies. These countries, along with unified Germany, Austria, Sweden and Finland (whose agricultural subsidies were actually *reduced* upon joining the CAP), are often the least efficient producers of agricultural products. As such, they stand to lose the most if the CAP is substantially replaced by market forces.

International Ramifications

In the main like the United States, the European Union seems unable to stabilize the level of its agricultural subsidies. This results in overproduction ("butter mountains", "wine lakes") and frequent commodity trade wars. A significant amount of fraud to obtain CAP subsidy payments has occurred. In 1989, the House of Lords Select Committee on the European Community released a

scathing report on subsidy abuses entitled "Fraud against the
Community." Others legitimately farm marginal land with lots of
fertilizer. The excess produce is stored, used in social welfare
programs and frequently "dumped" in cheap sales abroad.

Despite its incredible cost, the CAP remains one of the political
and economic cornerstones of the Union. External protests from
North America notwithstanding, the CAP is unlikely to disappear.
The provocative question, much debated, is whether a mutually
satisfactory reduction in the level of North American and European
Union subsidies to agriculture can actually be achieved. In 1992 the
Council of Agricultural Ministers agreed as an internal matter to
cuts in support prices of 29 percent for cereals, 15 percent for beef
and 5 percent for butter. Farmers received direct payments
representing the income lost from the price cuts. Further price cuts
and direct payments were agreed in 1999. It was hoped that these
reductions would reduce EU export subsidies on agricultural goods
and international trade tensions. They also supported the argument
that the extraordinary level of European subsidization of
agriculture was simply not sustainable in cost or EU politics.

European Union agricultural trade restraints are of enormous
consequence to North American exporters. Equally significant are
EU "export refunds" on agricultural commodities, refunds that
affect the opportunities of North American exporters in other parts
of the world. The United States has consistently argued (at times
successfully) that these refunds violate the GATT rules on
subsidies, while at the same time increasing its own export
subsidies on agricultural goods. The result has been an agricultural
"trade war" between the U.S. and the EU. Each side has sought to
outspend the other on agricultural export subsidies in a market that
has been wonderful to buyers.

Major attempts at a resolution or at least diminishment of the
agricultural trade war were undertaken in the Uruguay Round of
GATT negotiations during the late 1980s and early 1990s. Late in
1992, both sides announced the resolution of a number of
longstanding subsidies' disputes (notably on oilseeds) and a
compromise on the contested Uruguay Round agricultural trade
issues. Agreement was reached on 20 percent mutual reduction in
internal farm supports and a 21 percent mutual reduction on export
subsidies measured on a volume basis over 6 years using a 1986–90
base period. After a year of French protests and further
negotiations, this agreement was formally incorporated into the
WTO accords. Under it, the Union has been gradually switching
from production and export subsidies to direct income support for
farmers and rural businesses. This decoupling of agricultural

subsidies from output has steadily progressed and is crucial to the long-term viability of the CAP.

Tensions between Europe and the United States on agricultural trade have of late diminished (though hardly disappeared), but repeated U.S. Farm Bills threaten to reignite them. The really big cost on the CAP horizon is enlargement of the European Union to include Hungary and Poland, among others. Each enlargement of the Union plugs more farmers into the extraordinary CAP subsidy system and the ten new members admitted in 2004 will gain full payments by 2013. The Amsterdam and Nice Treaties notably failed to resolve ongoing disputes over agricultural reform.

A last minute deal in 2002 capped costs at their 2006 level plus 1 percent a year starting in 2007. In theory this will force a gradual winding down of CAP subsidies. Significant efforts are being made to de-couple CAP subsidies from production levels, notably for cotton, tobacco and olive oil. Meanwhile, one wonders just how much longer European taxpayers will continue to pay for the CAP.

§ 17.10   EU Common Market—Professional Services

The freedom of nonresidents to provide services within other parts of the Common Market is another part of the foundations of the TFEU[62] The freedom to provide services implies a right to receive and pay for them by going to the country of their source.[63] Industrial, commercial, craft and professional services are included within this right, which is usually not dependent upon establishment in the country where the service is rendered.[64] In other words, the freedom to provide or receive services across borders entails a right of entry into another member state.

The Council has adopted a general program for the abolition of national restrictions on the freedom to provide services across borders. This freedom is subject to the same public policy, public security and public health exceptions applied to workers and the self-employed.[65] The Council's program has slowly been implemented by a series of legislative acts applicable to professional and nonprofessional services. As with the right of self-

---

[62]   Articles 56 and 57, TFEU.

[63]   Luisi and Carbone v. Ministero del Tesoro (1984) Eur.Comm.Rep. 377; Cowan v. Le Tresor Public (1989) Eur.Comm.Rep. 195 (British tourist entitled to French criminal injury compensation).

[64]   Commission v. Germany (1986) Eur.Comm.Rep. 3755; Ministère Public v. van Wesemael (1979) Eur.Comm.Rep. 35 (employment agencies).

[65]   Article 74, TFEU.

establishment, discrimination based upon the nationality or non-residence of the service provider is generally prohibited even if no implementing law has been adopted.[66]

In parallel with law developed in connection with the free movement of goods, the Court of Justice in *van Binsbergen* indicated that member governments may require providers of services from other states to adhere to professional public interest rules. These rules must be applied equally to all professionals operating in the nation, and only if necessary to ensure that the out-of-state professional does not escape them by reason of establishment elsewhere. In other words, if the professional rules (e.g., ethics) of the country in which the service provider is established are equivalent, then application of the rules of the country where the service is provided does not follow.

Legal Profession

Considerable difficulty has been encountered in lifting restrictions within member states on the freedom to provide legal services. For example, within the legal profession there may be only a small amount of training or required knowledge held in common by a "lawyer" from a civil law jurisdiction (*e.g.,* an avocat from France) and a "lawyer" from a common law jurisdiction (*e.g.,* a solicitor from England). As a result, the initial directive relating to lawyers' services took a delicate approach to the question of freedom to provide legal services and stops short of dealing with a right of establishment.[67] This 1977 directive allows a lawyer from one member state, under that lawyer's national title (*e.g.,* abogado, rechtsanwalt, barrister), to temporarily provide services in other member states.

This includes the right to appear in court without retaining local co-counsel unless representation by counsel is mandatory under national laws.[68] Once retained, a local lawyer need not actually conduct the litigation. It is sufficient that the local attorney is retained to "act in conjunction with" the proceedings.[69] But the EU legal services directive cannot be used so as to circumvent national rules on professional ethics, particularly where a dual

---

[66] Van Binsbergen v. Bestuur van de Bedrijfsvereniging voor de Metaalnijverheid (1974) Eur.Comm.Rep. 1299 (legal representation); Coenen v. Sociaal Economische Raad (1975) Eur.Comm.Rep. 1547 (insurance intermediary).

[67] *See* Council Directive 77/249.

[68] Commission v. Germany (1988) Eur.Comm.Rep. 1123.

[69] Commission v. France (1991) Eur.Comm.Rep. I–3591 (Case C–294/89).

nationality lawyer has been disbarred and then moves to another state.[70]

Right of Establishment for Lawyers

Directive 77/249 gave rise to lawyer identity cards issued under the auspices of *Commission Consultative des Barreaux Européens* (C.C.B.E.), which has been charged to propose a specific directive about a right of establishment for lawyers. However, the mutual recognition of diplomas accomplished in Council Directive 89/48 applies to lawyers.[71] The maximum adaptation or training period allowed under this directive is three years. In 1997, the long-awaited right of establishment directive was adopted.[72] It mirrors much of the prior law, but makes it easier (than under the diploma directive) to join the local bar after three years of practice under home country title in the host state. This permits, for example, a German lawyer to bypass diploma and bar exam requirements of other EU countries in less time than most local lawyers spend meeting those criteria. Requiring local bar association membership is permitted under EU law.[73]

The C.C.B.E. adopted a common Code of Conduct for lawyers in 1988. It is hoped that this Code will ultimately become binding in all member states. It seeks to harmonize rules of conduct on confidentiality, conflicts of interest, segregation of client funds and malpractice insurance. In other areas, the Code does not harmonize, but rather provides choice of law rules to resolve conflicting national approaches to advertising, contingent fees and membership on boards of directors. The host country rules in these areas will apply to lawyers providing services across borders under Directive 77/249. Home country rules apply as to fee arrangements.[74] Some EU jurisdictions (e.g., Germany) allow multi-professional practices, but a Dutch ban on practicing law in full partnership with accountants was upheld primarily because of the absence of strict codes of ethics for accountants.[75] In 2007, the

---

[70]   Gullung v. Conseil de l'Ordre des Avocats (Colmar) (1988) Eur.Comm.Rep. 111.

[71]   *See* Morgenbesser v. Consiglio dell'Ordine degli avvocati di Genova (2003) Eur.Comm.Rep. I–13467 (Case C–313/01) (French maitrisse en droit degree must be recognized in Italy which has no equivalent).

[72]   Council Directive 98/5. Unsuccessfully challenged in Luxembourg v. Parliament and Council (2000) Eur.Comm.Rep. I–9131.

[73]   Ebert v. Budapesti Ügyvédi Kamara (2011) Eur.Comm.Rep. ___ (Case C–359/09).

[74]   Cipolla v. Meloni (2006) Eur.Comm.Rep. I–I–11241 (Cases C–94/04, 202/04) (Mandatory Italian fee schedules).

[75]   Wouters v. The General Council of the Dutch Order of Advocates (2002) Eur.Comm.Rep. I–1577.

C.C.B.E. agreed upon a common set of post-degree legal training standards focused on outcomes not inputs.

Admission to the practice of law is still governed by the rules of the legal profession of each member state. Several European Court judgments have upheld the right of lawyer applicants to be free from discrimination on grounds of nationality, residence or retention of the right to practice in home jurisdictions.[76] For example, a Greek lawyer who had a doctorate in German law and had worked for some time advising on Greek and EU law in Munich was denied admission to the German bar. On appeal, the Court of Justice held that Article 59 obligates member states not to impede the movement of lawyers in the Union. The member state must compare an applicant's specific qualifications with those detailed by national law. Only if the applicant does not meet all the necessary qualifications may the host state require additional courses or training.[77]

Moreover, the ECJ has ruled that law graduates who have not trained or qualified in their home states may take aptitude tests to qualify or obtain training in other EU states[78] . . . a kind of "have law degree will travel" outcome. Once qualified as an attorney elsewhere within the EU, individuals may even return to their home state to take aptitude (not bar exam) tests for qualification.[79]

By joining the bar in another EU country, lawyers acquire the right to establish themselves in more than one nation. The multinational law firm, pioneered by Baker and McKenzie in the United States and duplicated in the United Kingdom, has relatively few counterparts on the continent practicing of European Union law. Slowly, however, attorneys from member states are establishing affiliations and sometimes partnerships which reflect and service the economic, political and social integration of Europe. These "European law firms" often compete with existing branches of United States and British multinational firms for the lucrative practice of EU law.

In professional fields, the real barrier to movement of people across borders is language. In some instances, linguistic requirements for jobs are lawful despite their negative impact on

---

[76] Reyners v. Belgium (1974) Eur.Comm.Rep. 631; Thieffry v. Conseil de l'Ordre des Avocats de Paris (1977) Eur.Comm.Rep. 765; Van Binsbergen v. Bestuur van de Bedrijfsvereniging voor de Metaalnijverheid (1974) Eur.Comm.Rep. 1299; Gebhard v. Consiglio Dell'Ordine Degli Avocati di Milano (1995) Eur.Comm.Rep. I–4165.

[77] Vlassopoulou v. Ministerum fuer Justiz, Bundes und Europaangelegenheiten, 1991 Eur.Comm.Rep. I–4087 (Case C–340/89).

[78] Morgenbesser v. Consiglio Dell'Ordine Degli Avvocati di Genova, 2003 Eur. Comm. Rep.I–13467.

[79] Koller, (2010) Eur. Comm. Rep. I–___ (Case C–118/09).

free movement rights.[80] As much as the Union may succeed in its campaign for truly establishing an integrated market, the language barriers within the EU will remain. Although younger generations are increasingly multilingual, a professional who cannot speak to his or her clients or students is unlikely to succeed in another member state.

Dual Nationals

National treatment and free movement rights have caused renewed interest by North Americans and others in becoming "dual nationals." Irish and Italian "laws of return" generally permit emigrants born in Europe *and* their children or grandchildren to obtain Irish and Italian citizenship. British subjects who are patrials may generally do likewise. German law on nationality applies to *descendants* of persons who were German citizens or German nationals, with a special preference for refugees of Nazism.

Although the U.S. government discourages dual citizenship status for Americans, the benefits of being an EU national under the TFEU makes this status quite attractive. Dual nationals with a member state citizenship may not be denied their Union rights to be employed, seek employment, conduct business, reside and provide services in another member state. For example, an Argentinian/Italian was entitled to reside and enter business in Spain.[81]

§ 17.11   EU Common Market—Single Passport Financial Services

Bankers, investment advisors and insurance companies long awaited the arrival of a truly common market. Their right of establishment in other member states has existed for some time. The right to provide services across borders without establishing local subsidiaries was forcefully reaffirmed by the Court of Justice in 1986.[82] This decision largely rejected a requirement that all insurers servicing the German market be located and established there.

Legislative initiatives undertaken in connection with the single market campaign created genuinely competitive cross-border European markets for banking, investment and insurance services. Licensing of insurance and investment service companies and banks

---

[80]   *See* Groener v. Minister for Education (1989) Eur.Comm.Rep. 3967. (Irish required for vocational teaching job); Haim v. Kassenzahrartzliche Vereinigung (2000) Eur.Comm.Rep. I-5123 (German required to practice dentistry).

[81]   Micheleitti & ORS v. Delegación del Gobierno en Cantabria (1992) Eur.Comm.Rep. I-4239 (Case C-369/90).

[82]   Commission v. Germany (1986) Eur.Comm.Rep. 3755.

meeting minimum capital, solvency ratio and other requirements as implemented in member state law is done on a "one-stop" ("single passport") home country basis. Banks, for example, cannot maintain individual equity positions in non-financial entities in excess of 15 percent of their capital funds, and the total value of such holdings cannot exceed 50 percent of those funds.[83] They can participate and service securities transactions and issues, financial leasing and trade for their own accounts. The proposed investment services directive requires home country supervision of the "good repute" and "suitability" of managers and controlling shareholders.

Member states must ordinarily recognize home country licenses and the principle of home country control. For example, Council Directive 89/646 ("the Second Banking Directive") employs the home country single license procedure to liberalize banking services throughout the region. However, host states retain the right to regulate a bank's liquidity and supervise it through monetary policy and in the name of the "general good." Similarly, no additional insurance permits or requirements may be imposed by host countries when large industrial risks (sophisticated purchasers) are involved. However, when the public at large is concerned (general risk), host country rules still apply.[84] Major auto and life insurance directives employing one-stop licensing principles were adopted in 1990.[85] The auto insurance directive reproduces the large versus general risk distinctions found in the Second Non-Life Insurance Directive. Host country controls over general risk auto insurance policies were retained until 1995. Host country permits are also required when life insurers from other member states actively solicit business.

Reciprocity and the United States

North Americans and others have been particularly concerned about certain features of the legislation mandating equivalent opportunities in foreign markets for European companies before outsiders may benefit from the liberalization of financial services within the Common Market. This rule is generally referred to as the "reciprocity requirement", but only applies to financial institutions newly established in the EU from 1993 onwards. There was a rush by non-member state bankers, investment advisors and insurers to get established in the EU before January 1, 1993 in order to qualify for home country licenses.

---

[83]   Council Directive 89/646.
[84]   Council Directive 88/357 ("the Second Non-Life Insurance Directive").
[85]   Council Directives 90/619 (life insurance) and 90/618 (auto insurance).

The reciprocity requirement gave the campaign for a Europe without internal frontiers the stigma of increasing the degree of external trade barriers. Many outsiders, in rhetoric which sometimes seems excessive, refer to the development of a "Fortress Europe" mentality and threat to world trading relations. U.S. state and federal laws governing banking, investment services and insurance are restrictive, and in no sense can it be said that a "one stop" license permits a financial company to operate throughout the United States. A consequence of European integration has arguably been reform of United States regulatory legislation. The U.S. has noticeably relaxed its rules on interstate banking and largely repealed the Depression-era Glass-Steagall Act limitations on universal banking.

§ 17.12   EU Common Market—The Broadcasting Directive

The European Union Council of Ministers laid the basis for a statutory framework for the free movement of audiovisual programs throughout the European Union with its "Television Without Frontiers" Broadcasting Directive 89/552. The Broadcasting Directive has been extended to the EFTA countries (with the exception of Liechtenstein and Switzerland). In short, each state must admit television broadcast from the others. The regulation of the control of the content of those broadcasts is generally left to home state control, subject to various harmonizing rules concerning rights of reply, protection of minors and advertising and sponsorship.

The Broadcasting Directive provides that "when practicable", broadcasters (many of which are government-owned) should reserve a majority of their time for programs of European (not just Union) origin. This is more restrictive than meets the eye because broadcast time devoted to news, sports events, games, advertising and teletext services is *excluded* when measuring compliance. Moreover, no member state may reduce the percentage of broadcast time allotted to European works from that which existed in 1988. France imposes a 40% rule. The rules of origin for television programs focus on producer citizenship and production costs, not cultural content. A work is "European" if it is made by producers in a member state, supervised and actually controlled by producers there or the contribution of EU co-producers to the cost is "preponderant".

The Broadcasting Directive, when first proposed, contained an absolute requirement of more than 50 percent European broadcasting content. Intense lobbying by the United States, a major exporter of films and TV shows to Europe, introduced the "when practicable" limitation. Nevertheless, the long term goal of broadcasting European television productions at least half the time is clearly stated. Many U.S. firms moved quickly into EU co-productions intended to qualify as European under the Broadcasting Directive. There is a view that the "as practicable" exception has been used (and abused) as a loophole.

U.S. Reaction

The Broadcasting Directive was one of the few early single market campaign laws to attract headlines in the United States. The entertainment industry is America's second largest source of export earnings after military products and technology. The broadcasting and the banking directives caused the United States business community to wake up and become proactive in the European Union. They have been supported by Congressional resolutions denouncing the Broadcasting Directive, and repeated statements by the United States Trade Representative (USTR) that it is the "enemy of free trade".

The USTR put the European Union on a "priority watch-list" of nations whose intellectual property practices are suspect by U.S. standards. This was done under the "Special 301" trade sanction provisions of Section 182 of the Trade Act of 1974. The USTR is monitoring national implementation of the Broadcasting Directive within the EU to determine whether, and to what degree, American programs are denied access. Since France, Italy, the United Kingdom, Spain and Portugal have already enacted broadcast quotas, and the Uruguay Round of the GATT did not produce an agreement on trade in media products, the potential for Section 301 retaliation and exacerbation of the dispute between the U.S. and the EU exists.

Most balanced observers note that the Broadcasting Directive, despite its economic production criteria, reflects the sense of cultural and English-language invasion that many Europeans (and Canadians) resent and associate with more than just television, *e.g.,* a McDonald's on every corner. Canada, for its part, obtained a "cultural industries" exclusion from NAFTA free trade. *See* R. Folsom, *NAFTA, Free Trade and Foreign Investment in the Americas,* Chapter 2. This exclusion allows it to maintain broadcasting quotas similar to those of the European Union, along with magazine, film, book and other media trade restraints. In practical terms, satellite TV and Internet streaming have overwhelmed the ability of these jurisdictions to effectively maintain local broadcast content rules. But don't expect the EU to repeal the Broadcasting Directive.

§ 17.13   EU Common Market—National Intellectual Property Rights as Trade Barriers

A truly remarkable body of case law has developed around the authority granted national governments in Article 36 to protect industrial or commercial property by restraining imports and exports. These cases run the full gamut from protection of trademarks and copyrights to protection of patents and know-how. There is a close link between this body of case law and that developed under Article 101 concerning restraints on competition. [86]

Internal trade restraints involving intellectual property arise out of the fact that such rights are nationally granted. Owners of intellectual property rights within the Union are free under most traditional law to block the unauthorized importation of goods into national markets. There is a strong tendency for national infringement lawsuits to serve as vehicles for the division of the Common Market. Although considerable energy has been spent by the Commission on developing Common Market patents that would provide an alternative to national intellectual property rights, these proposals have yet to be fully implemented. In 1993, the Council reached agreement on a Common Market trademark regime. And the Council adopted Directive 89/104, which seeks to harmonize member state laws governing trademarks. In the copyright field, several directives have harmonized European law, perhaps most importantly on copyrights for computer software (No. 91/250).

Exhaustion Doctrine

The European Court of Justice has addressed the problems under Article 36 and generally resolved against the exercise of national intellectual property rights in ways which inhibit free internal trade. In many of these decisions, the Court acknowledges the existence of the right to block trade in infringing goods, but holds that the *exercise* of that right is subordinate to the TFEU. The Court has also fashioned a doctrine which treats national intellectual property rights as having been *exhausted* once the goods to which they apply are freely sold on the market. One of the few exceptions to this doctrine is broadcast performing rights which the Court treats as incapable of exhaustion. [87] CDs embodying such rights are, however, subject to the exhaustion doctrine once released into the market. [88] Such goods often end up in the hands of third parties who then ship them into another member state.

---

[86]   See Chapter 18.

[87]   See Coditel v. Ciné Vog Films SA (1980) Eur.Comm.Rep. 881; (1982) Eur.Comm.Rep. 3381.

[88]   Musik-Vertrieb membran Gmbh v. GEMA (1981) Eur.Comm.Rep. 147.

The practical effect of many of the rulings of the Court of Justice is to remove the ability of the owners of the relevant intellectual property rights from successfully pursuing infringement actions in national courts. When intellectual property rights share a common origin and have been placed on goods by consent, as when a licensor authorizes their use in other countries, then infringement actions to protect against trade in the goods to which the rights apply are usually denied. It is only when intellectual property rights do not share a common origin or the requisite consent is absent that they stand a chance of being upheld so as to stop trade in infringing products.[89] Compulsory licensing of patents, for example, does not involve consensual marketing of products. Patent rights may therefore be used to block trade in goods produced under such a license.[90] But careful repackaging and resale of goods subject to a common trademark may occur against the objections of the owner of the mark.[91]

Centrafarm Case

An excellent example of the application of the judicial doctrine developed by the Court of Justice in the intellectual property field under Article 36 can be found in the *Centrafarm* case.[92] The United States pharmaceutical company, Sterling Drug, owned the British and Dutch patents and trademarks relating to "Negram." Subsidiaries of Sterling Drug in Britain and Holland had been respectively assigned the British and Dutch trademark rights to Negram. Owing in part to price controls in the UK, a substantial difference in cost for Negram emerged as between the two countries. Centrafarm was an independent Dutch importer of Negram from the UK and Germany. Sterling Drug and its subsidiaries brought infringement actions in the Dutch courts under their national patent and trademark rights seeking an injunction against Centrafarm's importation of Negram into The Netherlands.

The Court of Justice held that the intellectual property rights of Sterling Drug and its subsidiaries could not be exercised in a way which blocked trade in "parallel goods" (aka "gray market goods"). In the Court's view, the exception established in Article 36 for the protection of industrial and commercial property covers only those rights that were specifically intended to be conveyed by the grant of

---

[89]   See CNL-Sucal v. HAG (1990) Eur.Comm.Rep. 3711 (Case C–10/89) (wartime expropriation of trademark removes common origin).

[90]   Pharmon BV v. Hoechst AG (1985) Eur.Comm.Rep. 2281.

[91]   Hoffman-LaRoche & Co. AG v. Centrafarm Vertriebsgesellschaft Pharmazeutischer Erzeugnisse mgH (1978) Eur.Comm.Rep. 1132; Pfizer, Inc. v. Eurim-Pharm GmbH (1981) Eur.Comm.Rep. 2913.

[92]   Centrafarm BV and Adriaan de Peipjper v. Sterling Drug Inc. (1974) Eur.Comm.Rep. 1147.

national patents and trademarks. Blocking trade in parallel gray market goods after they have been put on the market with the consent of a common owner was not intended to be part of the package of benefits conveyed. If Sterling Drug succeeded, an arbitrary discrimination or disguised restriction on Union trade would be achieved in breach of the language which qualifies Article 36. Thus the European Court of Justice ruled in favor of the free movement of goods within the Common Market even when that negates clearly existing national intellectual property remedies. Only in the unusual situation where the intellectual property rights in question have been acquired by independent proprietors under different national laws may such rights inhibit internal trade.[93]

EU Intellectual Property Rights and Imports

While the goal of creation of the Common Market can override national intellectual property rights when internal trade is concerned, these rights apply fully to the importation of goods from outside the European Union.[94] North American exporters may therefore find entry into the EU challenged by infringement actions in national courts. This is notably true regarding trade in "gray market" or "parallel goods" (genuine goods traded across borders without authorization). The ECJ has ruled that the exhaustion doctrine that applies to free internal trade does **not** apply when goods are imported into the common market.[95] Levi Strauss, owner of British trademarks to Levi jeans, successfully cited this ruling to keep low-price (Made in the USA) Levi's out of the EU.[96]

§ 17.14   EU Common Market—Intellectual Property Rights

All of the European Union member states are parties to the Paris Convention on the Protection of Industrial Property (1883). The expression "industrial property" is now usually replaced by "intellectual property." This means that each of them grants national treatment rights to citizens of other member states regarding patents and trademarks. The Paris Convention also gives applicants a one year right of priority to apply in other states for

---

[93]   See Terrapin (Overseas) Ltd. v. Terranova Industrie CA Kapferer & Co. (1976) Eur.Comm.Rep. 1039; CNL-Sucal v. HAG (1990) Eur.Comm.Rep. 3711 (Case C–10/89).

[94]   See E.M.I. Records Ltd. v. CBS United Kingdom Ltd. (1976) Eur.Comm.Rep. 811 and Silhouette International v. Hartlauer, No. C–355/96 (July 16, 1998) (graymarket goods).

[95]   Silhouette International v. Hartlauer (1998) Eur.Comm.Rep. I–4799 (Case C–355/96).

[96]   Zino Davidoff SA v. A + G Imports Ltd. (2001) Eur.Comm.Rep. I–8691 (Cases C–414/99 to 416/99).

patent rights and a six months right of priority for trademark rights. These priority rights date from the initial home country application. Thus the Paris Convention achieved limited harmonization of EU patent and trademark law. Article 118 TFEU, added in 2009, authorizes the Council and Parliament acting via "co-decision" to create European intellectual property rights (IPR) and provide for uniform protection of IPR throughout the Union.

Patents and Designs

The 1973 European Patent Convention (EPC)[97] established the European Patent Office (EPO) in Munich. It allows applicants to simultaneously apply for national patent rights in any of the contracting countries. These include all of the EU nations, plus a number of other European states. In other words, the EPC is not part of European Union law. The applicant must meet the requirements for patentability established by the EPC. United States, Japanese and German applicants heavily use the EPC. Unlike the States, patents on business methods and software are ordinarily unavailable. For example, Amazon's "Buy now with 1-Click" patent was rejected in Europe. Challenges to patentability decisions by the EPO can be made within 9 months after granting of the patent. Thereafter, challenges must be made in national courts subject to national patent laws.

The EPC basically presents a one-stop opportunity to obtain a basket of national patents in Europe. It does not foreclose the option of individual national patent applications and it does not eliminate the expense of translation costs when EPC patents are validated by national authorities.

A long-proposed Community Patent Convention finally came into force in 2014 as the EU Unitary Patent (UP) regime. It is applicable in all EU member states save Spain and Italy, miffed by the omission of their languages as "official". The UP regime operates in French, German or English through its headquarters in Paris. It can issue or revoke a Common Market patent valid in any contracting state. Transfers and licenses for part of the Union are possible. The cost-saving UP is an alternative to (but not a replacement for) national patent and European Patent Convention rights. However, the UP requires its signatories to harmonize national patent laws to conform to Unitary Patent rules on infringement, litigation procedures, exhaustion of rights and other issues. New Unitary Patent Courts have been created in Luxembourg. By 2021 their centralized jurisdiction will govern

---

[97]   113 Int'l Legal Mats. 268 (1974).

infringement and validity disputes concerning national patents, European patents and Unified patents.

Biotechnology patents are mandated by Council Directive 98/44, provided industrial application is possible. The human body, its stem cells and genes are not patentable, nor are processes for cloning human beings or uses of human embryos for industrial or commercial purposes. Plant variety rights are established in Regulation 2100/94.

The protection of semiconductor topographies is regulated by Council Directive 87/54. This directive was adopted in response to U.S. requirements of reciprocity before EU nationals can obtain comparable U.S. rights under the Semiconductor Chip Protection Act of 1984. Topographies that are original ("not commonplace") are protected for ten years. This protection includes the right to prohibit reproduction of the topography and its commercial exploitation. But exclusivity is not preserved when reverse engineering occurs or a semiconductor product is put on the market by consent. The European Union has not signed the Washington Treaty on protection of microcircuits.

After years of debate, Council Directive 98/71 harmonized national rules on design rights, an area of intellectual property rights law with diverse coverage throughout the EU. Design rights are possible for jewelry, cars, furniture, consumer electronics, machinery, tools, spare auto parts and other products. Such rights last from five to 25 years, and may be used to preclude Common Market trade.[98]

Trademarks and Designations of Origin

Designations of origin are widely protected under EU law, especially regarding wine. Spain, for example, successfully sued Belgium to stop the bottling of bulk "Rioja" wine on origin grounds.[99] Other ECJ judgments have protected "Parma" ham and "Feta" cheese.[100] Late in 1993, the Council adopted a regulation creating "Community Trademarks." Businesses operating in the European Common Market may now elect to process applications for such marks through the Union's Trademark Office in Alicante, Spain using English, Italian, German, French or Spanish language. This presents a streamlined alternative to seeking national trademark registration, in each member state.

---

[98]   *See* Consorzio Italiano v. Regie Nationale des Usines Renau H (1988) Eur.Comm.Rep. 6039.

[99]   Belgium v. Spain (2000) Eur.Comm.Rep. I-3123.

[100]   Prosciutto di Parma v. Asda Stores (2003) Eur.Comm.Rep. I-5121; Denmark v. Commission (2005) Eur.Comm.Rep. I-9115 and Germany v. Commission (2005) Eur.Comm.Rep. I-9115 (Feta cheese).

Any words or symbols[101] capable of distinguishing goods or services can be registered even if exclusively descriptive.[102] Colors may also be distinctive. But the Lego brick was denied registration since its shape was necessary to obtain a technical result.[103] Trademarks may be opposed whenever there is likelihood of confusion,[104] prior national registrations of marks that have been genuinely used already exist, or on various disqualifying grounds (e.g., generic words).[105] EU Trademarks are valid for 10 years and may be renewed. Any failure to use a mark for 5 years can cause protection to be withdrawn. Hundreds of thousands of EU marks have been issued, many to U.S. businesses. There is a Board of Appeal within the Trademark Office, followed by what have been numerous appeals to the General Court.

In addition, the Council has adopted Directive 89/104. This directive seeks to harmonize some aspects of EU trademark law, but not trademark registration procedures. A summary of its highlights follows. The directive applies to individual trademarks, service marks, collective marks, and guarantee or certification marks. It does not cover trademark rights acquired through use, which is possible in Italy, Ireland and the United Kingdom. A trademark may consist of any "sign" capable of being represented graphically. This includes words, personal names, designs, letters, numerals, and the shape of goods or their packaging, provided that such signs are capable of distinguishing the goods or services of one firm from those of others. It may therefore include such things as musical jingles or screen layouts/user interfaces for computer programs (in each case to the extent that third party rights are not infringed).

Article 3 distinguishes between absolute grounds for refusal or invalidity of marks (*e.g.,* marks devoid of distinctive character,

---

[101]   *See* Proctor & Gamble v. OHIM (2000) Eur.Comm.Rep. II–00265 (Feb. 16, 2000) (shape of soap bar not registrable); Phillips Electronics NV v. Remington Consumer Products Ltd. (2002) Eur.Comm.Rep. I–5475 (3D shapes).

[102]   *See* Wrigley v. OHIM (2003) Eur.Comm.Rep. I–12447 (Case C–191/01) (Doublemint gum possibly registrable); Proctor + Gamble Co. v. OHIM (2001) Eur.Comm.Rep. I–6251 (Baby-Dry possibly registrable). *Compare* Best Buy Concepts v. OHIM (2003) Eur.Comm.Rep. II–02235 (Case T–220/01) (Best Buy rejected as descriptive mark); Eurcool Logistik GmbH v. OHIM (2002) Eur.Comm.Rep. II–00683 (Case T–34/00) (Lite not registrable).

[103]   Libertel Groep BV v. Benelux Merkenbureau (2003) Eur.Comm.Rep. I–03793 (Case C–104/01); Lego Juris A/S v. OHIM, (2010) Eur.Comm.Rep. ___ (c–48/09) (Lego brick not registrable).

[104]   *See* Sabel v. Puma (1997) Eur.Comm.Rep. I–6191; Lloyd v. Schuhfabrik Meyer v. Klijsen Handel (1999) Eur.Comm.Rep. I–3819 (reasonably well informed and reasonably observant consumer standard); Citigroup v. OHIM (2008) Eur.Comm.Rep. II–669 (CITI registration denied as free riding on CITIBANK)

[105]   *See* DVK v. OHIM (2000) Eur.Comm.Rep. II–00001 (Jan. 12, 2000).

contrary to public policy or accepted principles of morality) and relative grounds (*e.g.,* a sign of high symbolic value, particularly a religious symbol). Allowance is made for registered marks which acquire a distinctive character through use. Member states are also permitted to continue to refuse registration on grounds already in force prior to adoption of the directive. Article 4 provides that registration of a mark which is identical or confusingly similar to one registered nationally or as a regional trademark, or a well-known but unregistered mark, is not allowed.

A common set of infringement criteria are contemplated in Article 5 of the directive. These criteria include presentation of the use of registered trademarks on different classes of goods if detrimental to the distinctive character of the mark. Article 7 provides that the principle of the exhaustion of rights applies.[106] Licensing of marks for limited use or for limited areas is generally permissible. Article 9 states that where a proprietor for an earlier trademark has acquiesced for a period of five successive years to the use of a later trademark registered in good faith in that member state while being aware of such use, he or she is no longer entitled to apply for a declaration that the trademark is invalid or to oppose the use of the later trademark. This provision resembles adverse possession. Furthermore, trademark rights can be revoked if the owner has not put the mark to genuine use for five years absent valid reasons for non-use. Use of the mark on exported goods will meet the genuine use requirement.

Copyrights

In November of 1992, the Council adopted Directive 92/100 on minimum 50-year rental and lending rights for copyrighted works. This directive requires the member states to provide authors' and producers' rights to allow or prohibit the rental or lending of original or copied copyrighted works, such as records, videos or films. The concepts of "rental" and "lending" are broadly defined to include any "direct or indirect economic or commercial advantage." Libraries that loan such works to the public at charges which do not exceed operating costs are not deemed to have an "advantage" and therefore are not caught within Directive 92/100.

The member states may override a refusal to lend for cultural promotion and other activities provided they remunerate the rights' holder, but cannot override a refusal to rent. Even when there is an assignment of rental rights to record or film producers, the original holder retains an equitable right to remuneration that cannot be

---

[106] *See* Section 9.5 for a discussion of the principle of exhaustion of intellectual property rights.

waived. Performers and broadcasters obtain exclusive rights to authorize or deny the fixation of their works and their reproduction and distribution. When broadcasters use sound recordings, a mandatory remuneration scheme is triggered with the funds shared between the record producers and the performers. A number of exceptions to these exclusive rights may be granted, including private, reportorial, teaching, scientific and ephemeral use. In 1993, the ECJ ruled in a landmark case that Germany could not deny a British performer remedies against distribution of unauthorized CDs of a concert given in the United States. Such a denial was treated as a breach of the general principle of nondiscrimination on the basis of nationality created in the EEC Treaty.

Late in 1993, the Council adopted Directive 93/83 in order to harmonize copyright and related rights for satellite and cable TV transmissions. The primary goal is to insure payment for the holders of such rights. For satellites, commencing in 1995, broadcast rights must be obtained in the country of origin not destination. Prior contracts must be adapted to this rule by the end of 1999. For cable TV, broadcast rights must be negotiated through cooperative bodies representing various categories of rights holders. Unreasonable refusals by broadcasters to retransmit programs by cable were arbitrated until 2003.

The Council also adopted Directive 93/98 in order to harmonize the duration of copyrights and related rights (e.g. photographs and posthumous works). As from July 1, 1995, all works subject to copyright protection in the Union will last for 70 years after the death of the author. The term is 50 years for neighboring rights. For audiovisual and cinematic works, there was some dispute about who is "the author." Copyright protection for these works will extend for 70 years from the death of the last survivor of the following persons: the principal director, the author of the script, the author of the dialogue and the composer of the music. Directive 2001/84 harmonizes the law of monetary resale rights for artists ("droit de suite").

Directive 2001/29 draws upon the WIPO Copyright Treaty of 1996 and corresponds to the U.S. Digital Millennium Copyright Act of 1998. The Directive is Internet driven, and outlaws possession, making or providing all tools capable of circumventing technological measures intended to protect copyrighted material. In other words, "hackers" beware. Likewise, tampering with copyright management information (that is to say, encryption devices) is prohibited under Directive 2001/29. Remedies may vary among the member states, but must be "effective." Some EU members have enacted criminal sanctions, others have limited relief to damages.

§ 17.15   EU Common Market—Computer Software

One area of technology law of particular interest to U.S. firms has been legislated amidst controversy and a blitz of American lobbying. The Software Directive was the subject of fierce industry lobbying in 1990, the two opposing camps being ECIS (the European Committee for Interoperable Systems) which had a liberal "open systems" outlook on matters such as de-compilation/reverse-engineering, and SAGE (the Software Action Group for Europe) which represented the big manufacturers' interests in proprietary architectures by seeking copyright protection for interface specifications. The ECIS lobby largely prevailed.

Council Directive 91/250 (now 2009/24) requires member states to protect computer programs by copyright as literary works within the meaning of the Berne Convention of the Protection of Literary and Artistic Work. "Computer programs," although not specifically defined, are deemed to include preparatory design material. Protection applies to the expression of any form of a computer program. Ideas and principles which underlie any element of a computer program, including those which underlie its interfaces, are not protected. A computer program is protected if it is original in the sense that it is the author's own intellectual creation. This test for originality accords with the approach taken in the U.S. No other criteria (aesthetic or qualitative) are to be applied to determine its eligibility for protection.

Council Directive 91/250 rules on "de-compilation" (reverse engineering) for purposes of interoperability with an independently created program are liberal by U.S. standards. There is a specific right to "observe, study or test the functioning of the program in order to determine the ideas and principles that underlie any element of the program." However, de-compilation may not be used for the development, production and marketing of a substantially similar computer program. The directive takes no position on the patentability of computer software.

It has been suggested that the de-compilation provisions of the EU directive will change traditional software licensing clauses. The traditional clause "Licensee agrees not to cause or permit the reverse engineering, disassembly or de-compilation of the Licensed Program" will have to be redrafted to something like:

"Licensee shall not decompile the Licensed Program, except to the extent necessary to achieve interoperability of the Licensed Program with an independently created program, whenever the information necessary to achieve such interoperability has not been made readily available by Licensor to Licensee upon Licensee's written request. Such decompilation acts shall be restricted to the parts of the Licensed Program that are necessary to achieve interoperability. In no event may Licensee subcontract such decompilation to a third party without Licensor's prior written authorization."[107]

The same practitioner suggests that a clause more adapted to the spirit of the directive would be the following:

"Licensee shall not cause or permit de-compilation of the Licensed Program, except to the extent necessary to achieve interoperability of the Licensed Program with an independently created program, whenever the information necessary to achieve such interoperability has not been made readily available by Licensor to Licensee upon Licensee's written request. Such de-compilation acts shall be restricted to the parts of the Licensed Program that are necessary to achieve interoperability."[108]

§ 17.16   EU Common Market—E-Commerce Initiative[*]

E-commerce giants like Amazon and eBay have a special interest in EU electronic commerce law. The European Union began considering the advent of the "Information Society," and the need to establish a Pan-European information technology infrastructure with the 1994 white paper on "Growth, Competitiveness and Employment: the Challenges and Courses for Entering into the XXIst Century" prepared by former European Commission Vice-President Martin Bangemann. The Bangemann Report led to the establishment of an Information Society Project (now Promotion) Office within the EU,[109] and a series of actions plans to promote the Information Society in Europe.

These plans were intended to formulate strategies to change the existing regulatory and legal framework, technical infrastructure, and the cultural attitudes necessary to promote the Information Society. This led to the e-Europe Initiative to further accelerate the development of a European Information Society.[110]

---

[107] *See* Bertone, "The EEC Directive on Computer Software," in Folsom, Lake and Nanda (eds.), *European Community Law After 1992: A Practical Guide for Lawyers Outside the Common Market* (Kluwer, 1992).

[108] *Id.*

[*] I am indebted to Professor Andy Spanogle for his work on a prior version of this section.

[109] See "Europe's Way to the Information Society—An Action Plan," COM(94) 347 final, 19.07.1994.

[110] "eEurope—An Information Society for All," COM(99) 687 final, 8.12.1999.

The EU efforts to coherently address the impact of technology on European society as a whole results in a very different approach to many of the issues raised by E-Commerce than that seen in the United States for example. It is an approach which is inherently multinational, and characterized by a conscious effort to harmonize or approximate legal rules throughout the different member countries in the EU. At the same time it is an approach which also consciously seeks to identify and remove barriers to the development of E-Commerce and other Information Society services. Although only one aspect of the broader European Information Society initiative, legal measures related to E-Commerce are central to the various EU action plans.

These measures include the 1997 European Initiative on Electronic Commerce,[111] which focused on primarily on developing infrastructure and protecting consumers' economic and legal interests; the related 1997 Distance Selling Directive;[112] the 1999 Electronic Signature Directive;[113] and most recently the Electronic Commerce Directive in 2000.[114] There are also several other important measures aimed at particular issues, such as Privacy Directives,[115] which have a significant impact upon online transactions. *See* Section 17.17.

All this said, cross-border E-commerce within the Union is plagued by nontariff trade barriers and buy/sell national proclivities that run deep. Oddly, it is a U.S. online traders like Amazon, eBay and Apple that are the most active E-commerce merchants within the European Union.

§ 17.17   EU Common Market—Data Protection and E-Privacy

The European Convention on Human Rights provides that "everyone has the right to respect for his private and family life, his

---

[111] "A European Initiative on Electronic Commerce," COM(97) 157 final, 16.6.1997.

[112] Directive 1997/7/EC of the European Parliament and of the Council of 20 May 1997 on the Protection of Consumers in respect of Distance Contracts, *Official Journal L 144, 04/06/1997.*

[113] Directive 1999/93/EC of the European Parliament and of the Council of 13 December 1999 on a Community framework for Electronic Signatures, *Official Journal L 013, 19/01/2000.*

[114] Directive 2000/31/EC of the European Parliament and of the Council of 8 June 2000 on certain legal aspects of information society services, in particular electronic commerce, in the Internal Market, *Official Journal L 178, 17/07/2000.*

[115] Directive 95/46/EC of 24 October 1995 on the protection of individuals with regard to the processing of personal data and on the free movement of such data., *Official Journal L 281, 23.11.1995. See* Directive 2002/58 on privacy in electronic communications.

home and his correspondence". Article 16 TFEU recognizes that
"everyone" has a right to protection of personal data. The European
Union has adopted personal data protection directives that apply to
international electronic commerce. Council Directive 95/46 (effective
October 1998) requires each member EU state to protect the
processing of personal data.

Under this directive, any information relating to natural
persons must be secure, current, relevant and not excessive in
content. User location data is also protected. In most cases, personal
data may be processed only with the consent of the individual
involved. Processing data revealing racial or ethnic origin, political
opinions, religious beliefs, philosophical or ethical persuasion, and
health or sexual life is rarely permitted without written consent.
Posting phone numbers, working conditions and hobbies of persons
on an Internet page constitutes processing of personal data within
the Directive.[116]

Directive 2002/58 concerns privacy and personal data
protection in electronic communications including mobile, fixed and
Internet communications. The Directive contains a Union-wide ban
on sending spam to individuals as well as restraints on installing
"cookies" on personal computers without consent. Social networking
websites must offer privacy-friendly default settings, limit retention
of data on inactive users, delete abandoned accounts, allow
pseudonyms, and notify users that pictures should only be uploaded
by consent.

Individual Rights

Directive 95/46 guarantees individual access to processed
information and notice of its use. Individuals may object at any time
to the legitimacy of personal data processing. They may also
demand erasure without cost of personal data before it is disclosed
to or used by third parties for direct mail marketing. Data
processors are required to make extensive disclosures to individuals
and to governments. Such disclosure duties, for example, apply to
virtually all web sites that invite registration. National authorities
are empowered where appropriate to access, erase or block
information held by data processors. Private civil liability and
public penalty remedies are administered under member state laws,
which allow electronic commerce consumers to sue in their
countries of residence.

---

[116] Re Bodil Lindqvist (2003) Eur.Comm.Rep. I–12971 (Case C–101/01) (Swedish
criminal prosecution).

Data Transfers, U.S. Safe Harbors

Article 25 of Directive 95/46 mandates a prohibition against the transfer of personal data to non-member states (like those of North America) that fail to ensure an "adequate level of protection." Hence the adequacy of United States laws offering personal data protection is generally at issue. Exemptions from this scrutiny exist for "unambiguous" consent, when the data is necessary for contract performance between individuals and data processors (e.g., billing), the transfer is legally required or serves "important public interests," the transfer is necessary to protect the individual's "vital interests," or the transfer comes from an open, public register.

Practically speaking, Directive 95/46 governs most global businesses since it is difficult to segregate European Union data from that collected elsewhere. Online and offline data processors fall within its scope. The directive's impact has been felt, for example, in restrictive orders denying U.S. direct mail companies access to European mailing lists. More broadly, the European Commission and the U.S. Department of Commerce have sought to defuse the potentially explosive issue of the "adequacy" of U.S. law on personal data privacy. Early in 2000, agreement was reached to create a "safe harbor" for U.S. firms from EU data privacy litigation or prosecution.

To obtain such immunity, U.S. data processors and document storage companies can: (1) formally agree to be subject to regulatory oversight in a member EU state; (2) sign up with a U.S. self-regulating privacy group that is supervised by the U.S. Federal Trade Commission or the Department of Transportation; (3) demonstrate to European satisfaction that relevant U.S. laws are comparable to Directive 95/46; or (4) agree to refer privacy disputes to a European panel of data protection authorities. Financial services (including insurance) are not covered by these safe harbor provisions. The European Union has adopted standardized financial services contracts clauses that subject U.S. data processors to European jurisdiction and ensure compliance.[117]

A growing number of U.S. companies (Microsoft, Facebook and Google included) have signed up with self-regulatory privacy groups (such as BBBOnline) to obtain shelter from Directive 95/46. Some U.S. companies (e.g., Amazon.com) assert that they are in compliance. Others (e.g., DoubleClick.com) have selectively curtailed their use of "cookies" to track online users. A 2009 Directive requires consent before tracking user identities and habits via cookies. Yahoo was the first net provider to allow opting out of

---

[117] See, e.g., Decision 2004/915, (2004) O.J. L385/74.

such practices. Privacy rights "to be forgotten" by removing personal information from the Internet are being asserted in European courts. Some U.S. companies seem blissfully unaware of the scope and intensity of European Union data privacy law, which also impacts corporate E-data retention duties for existing and reasonably foreseeable litigation.

§ 17.18　The EURO

Preparing for the EURO: The European Monetary System

Capital movements legislation of the 1990s, combined with the various banking and investment services reforms and Maastricht amendments, promised to bring forth a remarkable new financial sector in the European Union. It also supported the EURO replacing national currencies. For Germany, with the strongest currency in the Union and memories of hyper-inflation between the two World Wars, supporting the EURO had to result in money "as good as the Deutschmark." A EURO Zone without Germany was a non-sequitur. In moving step-by-step toward monetary union, the member states created the European Monetary System (EMS). When the EMS was established in 1979, member states deposited 20 percent of their gold and dollar assets with the European Monetary Cooperation Fund in exchange for an equivalent amount of European Currency Units (ECUs). This fund was used as a non-cash means of settlement between central banks undertaking exchange rate support.

The legal basis for the European Monetary System and European Currency Units was substantially advanced by the Single European Act of 1987. This article committed the member states to further development of the EMS and ECU, recognized the cooperation of the central banks in management of the system, but specifically required further amendment of the Treaty if "institutional changes" were required. In other words, a common currency managed by a central bank system was *not* part of the campaign for a Europe without internal frontiers. Draft plans for such developments surfaced in the Commission using the U.S. Federal Reserve Board as a model. Britain, always concerned about losses of economic sovereignty, proposed an alternative known as the "hard ECU." This proposal would have retained the national currencies but added the hard ECU as competitor of each, letting the marketplace in most instances decide which currency it preferred.

In December of 1989, the European Council (outvoting Britain) approved a three stage approach to economic and monetary union (EMU). Stage One began July 1, 1990. Its focus was on expanding the power and influence of the Committee of Central Bank Governors over monetary affairs. This Committee was a kind of

EuroFed in embryo. It was primarily engaged in "multilateral surveillance." Stage One also sought greater economic policy coordination and convergence among the member states.

Stage Two anticipated the creation of a European Union central banking system, but functioned with the existing national currencies in the context of the EMS and ERM. Stage Two was a learning and transition period. In October of 1990, it was agreed (save Britain) that Stage Two would commence January 1, 1994. This deadline was actually met, and the European Monetary Institute was installed in Frankfurt. It was the precursor to the European Central Bank. Stage Three involved the replacement of the national currencies with a single currency, the EURO, managed by a European Central Bank. In December of 1991, agreement was reached at Maastricht to implement Stage Three no later than Jan. 1, 1999 with a minimum of seven states. Britain and Denmark reserved a right to opt out of Stage Three.

Admission to the EURO Zone

All member states wishing to join the EURO Zone in 1999 had to meet strict economic convergence criteria on inflation rates, government deficits, long-term interest rates and currency fluctuations. To join the third stage, a country was supposed to have an inflation rate not greater than 1.5 percent of the average of the three lowest member state rates, long-term interest rates no higher than 2 percent above the average of the three lowest, a budget deficit less than 3 percent of gross domestic product (GDP), a total public indebtedness of less than 60 percent of GDP, and no devaluation within the ERM during the prior two years. These criteria continue to govern admission of other member states into the EURO zone. One could argue they have been honored more in the breach than conformity.

The economic performance of member states in 1997 became the test for admission to the economic and monetary union. Since both France and Germany had trouble meeting the admissions criteria, this opened a window for much more marginal states such as Belgium, Italy and Spain to join immediately in 1999. Eleven of the then fifteen EU members commenced the EURO Zone. Greece subsequently in 2001 was deemed "qualified" for the EURO Zone based upon (as we now know) dubious financial data. As expected, Denmark, Britain and Sweden opted out of initial participation in the common currency. The Danes did so by voting No in a year 2000 national referendum. The Swedes voted similarly in 2003. By 2014, Slovenia, Malta, Estonia, Latvia, Cyprus and Slovakia had joined the EURO zone, for a total of 18 out of 28 member-states of the Union. The world financial crisis of 2008–09 initially increased the interest of some outside the EURO zone, notably Iceland, to partake of its relative stability. Denmark, Lithuania and Bulgaria pegged their national currencies to the EURO.

On January 1, 1999, the 11 original participating states fixed the exchange rates between the EURO and their national currencies. National notes and coins were removed from the market by July 2002 as the EURO was installed. The EURO has been used for most commercial banking, foreign exchange and public debt purposes since 1999. It has also been adopted (voluntarily) by the world's securities markets, and by Monaco, San Marino, the Vatican, Andorra, Montenegro and Kosovo.

The arrival of the EURO had important implications for the United States and the dollar. For decades, the dollar had been the world's leading currency, although its dominance has been declining since the early 1980s. Use of the Deutsche Mark and Yen in commercial and financial transactions, and in savings and reserves, had been steadily rising. The EURO was expected to continue the dollar's decline in all of these markets. It was certainly the hope of many Europeans that they have successfully created a rival to the dollar.

European Central Bank

It was also agreed at Maastricht that in the third stage the European Central Bank (ECB) and the European System of Central Banks (ECSB) would start operations. The ECB and ECSB are governed by an executive board of six persons appointed by the member states and the governors of the national central banks. The ECB and the ECSB are independent of any other European institution and in theory free from member state influence. Their primary responsibility is to maintain price stability, specifically keeping price inflation below two percent per year. In contrast, the U.S. Federal Reserve has two primary responsibilities: maximum employment and stable prices.

The main functions of the ECB and ECSB are: (1) define and implement regional monetary policy; (2) conduct foreign exchange operations; (3) hold and manage the official foreign reserves of the member states; and (4) supervise the payments systems. The ECB has the exclusive right to authorize the issue of bank notes within the Common Market and must set interest rates to principally achieve price stability. The Court of Justice may review the legality of ECB decisions.

Under the EURO's founding rules, the ECB worked closely with the Ecofin Council's broad guidelines for economic policy, such as keeping national budget deficits below 3 percent of GDP in all but exceptional circumstances (2 percent decline in annual GDP). If the Ecofin considered a national government's policy to be inconsistent with that of the region, it could recommend changes including budget cuts. If appropriate national action did not follow such a warning, the Ecofin could have required a government to disclose the relevant information with its bond issues, blocked European Investment Bank credits, mandated punitive interest-free deposits, or levied fines and penalties.

Regrettably, the fiscal enforcement system established when the EURO was created did not work. Sanctions for failure to comply with the 3 percent budget deficit rule were held unenforceable by the Court of Justice.[118] Since 1999, many EURO states have been under threat of sanctions for failure to comply with the 3 percent budget deficit rule, most notably Greece, Portugal, Spain, Italy and Ireland after the global financial meltdown of 2008–09. Yet no EURO Zone member state was ever sanctioned, suggesting this system for controlling national deficits is toothless. It has essentially been replaced by the 2012 Treaty on Stability, Coordination and Governance (TSCG, below).

Financial Bailouts

The global meltdown also caused financial markets to finally realize that national debt issued in EUROs by different Zone members came with different levels of risk. Interest rates rose on Greek, Portuguese, Irish and other bonds, while German and to a lesser extent French EURO bonds held firm. Despite a specific TFEU Article 125 prohibition against Union bailouts of member state governments, as the market-driven European financial crisis of 2010/11 demonstrated, bailouts of debt-ridden EURO zone members may occur. Joining with the IMF, a 110 billion EURO rescue package for Greece was organized over German laments. Fearing a cascade of financial crises in Spain, Portugal, Italy and Ireland, a 1 trillion EURO liquidity safety net (EFSF) was devised using EU-backed bonds, special purpose EU-guaranteed investment loans, and more IMF funds. In addition, the ECB for the first time began buying EURO zone national government bonds in the open market.

All this caused Germany to publicly re-think its traditional role as paymaster and proponent of the European Union and EURO. Clearly the EURO was not as good as the fondly remembered Deutschmark. Sure enough, Ireland tapped into this safety net for over 100 billion EUROs late in 2010 followed by Portugal in 2011. In 2012, massive loans to Spanish and Italian banks and their

---

[118] See *Commission v. Council* (2004) Eur.Comm.Rep. I–6649 (Case C–27/04).

governments staved off bailouts and moderated interest rates, and Greece was bailed out a second time. In 2013, Cyprus was bailed out under terms that for the first time "bailed in" bank creditors and uninsured depositors. These actions ran down the safety net and ECB resources.

Most private holders of Greek debt have been pushed into a renegotiated deal with roughly a 50% "haircut" in the value of their holdings. Since 2013, EU bailouts require sovereign bond holders to take losses under "collective action clauses" designed to keep individual investors from blocking restructured debt deals. Mandatory losses can be imposed when Euro-zone nations are deemed insolvent by the European Central Bank, the European Commission and the IMF, acting somewhat like a "bankruptcy court," and the Euro-zone finance ministers unanimously are in accord.

Treaty on Stability, Coordination and Governance (TSCG), ECB Bond Buying

In March of 2012, with market pressures and threats of a Greek default or exit from the EURO Zone escalating, 25 of the 27 EU members (minus Britain and the Czech Republic) adopted a Treaty on Stability, Coordination and Governance (TCSG) intended to provide a "permanent" solution to the EURO crisis. Only Ireland allowed its voters a referendum on this Treaty, which was negotiated outside the regular TFEU framework. The Irish, their bailout in progress, voted in favor of ratification by approximately a 60% margin. Importantly, ratification by the German Parliament was upheld by Germany's Constitutional Court under that country's "eternal democracy" clause. The TCSG has two principal components: The European Stability mechanism (ESM) and a "Fiscal Compact."

Effective in 2013, the ESM created a permanent 900 billion EURO loan fund, 27% of which is financed by Germany. Any increase in the ESM fund must be approved by the German Parliament. EURO Zone countries may apply for bailout loans conditioned upon fiscal and economic reforms. As a general rule, all EURO Zone national parliaments must approve of any ESM rescue package. Finland has indicated its approval may require loan collateral. The "Fiscal Compact" incorporates a "balanced budget" rule. "Automatic corrective measures" apply if excessive budgets are reached. The EU Commission monitors national budget deficits under a "European Semester" system that reviews over 100 economic indicators. Breach of the Compact can result in enforcement actions before the European Court of Justice with penalties payable to the ESM.

In addition, in 2012, the European Central Bank announced its willingness to buy unlimited, short-term national government bonds if an ESM rescue is secured by a EURO Zone member. Germany's revered Bundesbank openly opposed this announcement, which had the support of the Merkel government. Like ESM loans, such purchases will be conditioned upon fiscal and economic austerity commitments with the ECB serving as the regulator of Zone banks. The extent of the ECB's regulatory powers was much debated, though ECB licensing and penalty powers over major banks represented a regulatory base line. In 2012 as well, the ECB President announced that the Bank had the resources to do "whatever it takes" to protect the EURO. This "jawboning" helped calm market fears.

Thus there is a three-part attempt at "permanently" solving the EURO crisis: The ESM, Fiscal Compact and ECB bond buying. This attempt once again seeks to come to grips with systemic flaws that have haunted the EURO since its creation . . . can national spending policies be stabilized, coordinated and governed in support of a common currency? Since all EURO Zone countries are jointly liable for ESM and ECB monies, this amounts to a partial mutualization of national debt risk. It is not, however, as some have suggested is needed, EURO bonds backed by the EURO Zone. That said, the TGSG is certainly a step in that direction.

Chapter 18

EU CUSTOMS, INTERNATIONAL TRADE AND FOREIGN INVESTMENT LAW

Table of Sections

§ 18.0   Common Customs Code

Articles 206–207 of the Treaty on the Functioning of the European Union (TFEU) concern trade between the European Union and third countries. These articles vest in the European Union control over external commercial relations, a power completely absent from the NAFTA agreement. This is referred to as the Union's "common commercial policy," and it covers both imports and exports. Article 207 provides some illustrative examples of the wide scope of this policy, including tariffs, quotas, trade agreements, export controls, dumping and subsidies. For example, its common rules on exports[1] generally authorize free exportation of Union products, subject to security (oil and defense) and environmental exceptions. The Common Commercial Policy can

---

[1]   *See* Council Regulations 2603/69, 1934/82.

also involve the application of international boycott sanctions.[2] The 1993 Treaty on European Union added provisions intended to promote cooperation among the member states and the Union on aid to developing nations.[3]

The European Court of Justice has ruled that the member states cannot enact external commercial policy laws without "specific authorization."[4] In this field, the Union should be supreme. Operationally speaking, however, this is not always the case. This is illustrated by the following discussion of national import quotas, voluntary export restraints and "mixed" trade agreements. Surrendering national sovereignty over external commercial relations is a most sensitive area.

Customs Union

As regards customs law, which is invariably involved in any trade transaction with the Union, the relevant provisions are Articles 28–32 TFEU. The basic principle is that the EU is a customs union,[5] with a directly applicable[6] prohibition of national customs duties and measures having an equivalent effect on internal trade. The EU also has a common customs tariff. Thus, once goods have cleared customs in any member state they are released for "free circulation", moving throughout the Union without incurring any further tariffs or any other equivalent charges. Equivalent charges are understood to comprise any pecuniary charge, however small and whatever its designation and mode of application, which is imposed unilaterally on domestic or foreign goods by reason of the fact that they cross a frontier, and which is not a customs duty in the strict sense.[7] Hence products

---

[2]   Article 215, TFEU. *See* Bosphorus Hava Yollari Turizim Ve Ticaret AS v. Minister for Transport, Energy and Communication (1996) Eur.Comm.Rep. I–3953 (Serbia boycott).

[3]   *See* Articles 208–211, TFEU.

[4]   Criel and Schou v. Procureur de la République (1976) Eur.Comm.Rep. 1921.

[5]   *See* Article XXIV(8)(a) GATT 1994:

"A customs union shall be understood to mean the substitution of a single customs territory for two or more customs territories, so that

(i) duties and other restrictive regulations of commerce . . . are eliminated with respect to substantially all the trade between the constituent territories of the union or at last with respect to substantially all the trade in products originating in such territories, and

(ii) . . . , substantially the same duties and other regulations of commerce are applied by each of the member of the union to the trade of territories not included in the Union".

[6]   Van Gend & Loos v. Nederlandse administratie der belastingen (1963) Eur.Comm.Rep. 1, 13.

[7]   Commission v. Italy (1969) Eur.Comm.Rep. 193, 201.

originating in third countries enjoy the same status as goods originating in a member state for purposes of internal trade.

In addition, U.S. exporters to any of the member states will pay the same customs duties, regardless of the port of entry. This is different from NAFTA arrangements, which establish a free trade area[8] exclusively for products originating in NAFTA, with no common external tariff. Canada, Mexico and the U.S. have retained different tariff levels and law, and the right to pursue their own international trade agreements.

Common Customs Code

The customs law of the EU had been dispersed and shattered in some 25 individual directives and regulations. In a major codification effort all these texts were consolidated and further developed in a Common Customs Code which entered into force on Jan. 1, 1994.[9] This Code includes coverage of customs clearance procedures, customs warehouses and free trade zones, duty free entry for processing and re-export (inward processing arrangement), duty free entry of components of Union origin that have been processed abroad (outward processing arrangement), classification, valuation, origin, payment and customs' bonds. Judicial review of decisions of the national customs authorities must be allowed by a national court capable of referring questions of EU law to the European Court of Justice under Article 267 TFEU.[10] The EU follows the 1999 Kyoto Convention on modernized customs procedures.

§ 18.1 EU Customs Law: Tariffs, Classification, Valuation, Origin and Quotas

Tariffs

The Common Customs Tariff (CCT), now called the Combined Nomenclature (CN), has been steadily reduced over the years as a result of the GATT/WTO tariff Rounds. After the Tokyo Round (1978), EU tariffs on manufactured goods dropped on average to about 8 percent.[11] Under the Uruguay Round WTO regime[12] it

---

[8]   *See* Article XXIV(8)(b) GATT 1994.

"A free-trade area shall be understood to mean a group of two or more customs territories in which the duties and other restrictive regulations of commerce . . . are eliminated on substantially all the trade between the constituent territories in products originating in such territories."

[9]   Council Regulation 2913/92, O.J. L 302/1 (October 19, 1992); implementing provisions have been promulgated by Commission Regulation 2454/93, O.J. L 253/1 (October 11, 1993) as amended last by Commission Regulation 2193/94, O.J. L 235/6 (September 9, 1994).

[10]   Article 243, Common Customs Code.

[11]   *See* Council Regulation 2658/87 (Schedule of Customs Duties).

dropped even further: On aggregate the weighted average Union tariff on industrial products was cut from 6.8 to 4.1 percent, a reduction of 37 percent. In some sectors (construction equipment, medical and pharmaceutical equipment, furniture, steel, agricultural equipment, paper, toys, beer and spirits) duties will disappear entirely. Even so, most imported goods enjoy more preferential tariff status under various EU trade agreements and programs. See the coverage of the GSP, Lomé/Cotonou Convention and Mediterranean Policy below.

Member states may not alter the common customs tariff by unilaterally imposing additional duties.[13] The CN is supplemented by tariff rate quotas, tariff preferences, antidumping and other special duties, all of which are reported in the "Taric." All of these duties are established by EU law, but it is the member states that apply the rules and collect Union tariffs. These revenues are forwarded by the national customs' services to the Commission less a 10 percent administrative charge. Litigation concerning European Union customs law therefore tends to originate in national tribunals as importers dispute classification, valuation and origin issues. These EU law issues are then typically referenced to the Court of Justice for resolution under Article 234.

The Combined Nomenclature details a tariff schedule that makes two fundamental distinctions. Goods admitted into the Common Market are subject to either "Autonomous" or "Conventional" duties. The Autonomous Duties represent the original 1968 CCT tariffs and are higher than the Conventional Duties which are the Union's current most-favored-nation (MFN) tariffs as negotiated within the GATT/WTO. For most exports to the EU, including nearly all those from the United States and Canada, the MFN rates of duty are applied. The various duty free entry programs to which the Union subscribes[14] will almost never apply to goods originating in either Canada or the United States. Mexican exports, in contrast, benefit from the EU-Mexico free trade agreement (2000).

New members are usually phased into the EU customs union rules and tariffs over a transitional period. Portugal and Spain, for example, were only fully aligned at the end of 1992. The member states that joined the Union in 1995, however, were immediately

---

[12]   Agreement establishing the World Trade Organization, Annex 1A (Multilateral Agreements on Trade in Goods) No. 1 (General Agreement on Tariffs and Trade 1994) Schedule LXXX (European Communities).

[13]   Sociaal Fonds voor de Diamant Arbeiders v. NG Indiamex (1973) Eur.Comm.Rep. 1609.

[14]   See Sections 18.2, 18.9, 18.10.

integrated into the customs union. The ten new members joining in 2004 and Romania and Bulgaria (2007) will be phased into the customs union over an extended period of years.

The common customs law of the European Union also includes regulations targeting counterfeit goods. Such goods may not be imported into the Union, nor freely circulated within it. They are subject to seizure by national customs authorities. The definition of counterfeit goods contained in this regulation refers to goods bearing marks without authorization. Thus the regulation does not apply to trade in "gray market goods" (those produced abroad under license). The Union also operates a computerized, encoded data network known as the Customs Information System (CIS) to help combat fraud and illegal trading (especially in drugs). Customs officials at all points of entry and exit may communicate with each other, central authorities and the Commission.

Classification

In its customs classification system,[15] the European Union follows the International Convention on the Harmonized Commodity Description and Coding System[16] created by the Customs Cooperation Council. Well over 100 countries representing more than 80 percent of world trade adhere to this system. This generally corresponds to the classifications found in the Harmonized Tariff System (HTS) adopted by the United States in 1988. Starting in 1993, the Union instituted a binding tariff classification system based upon mutual recognition of classification decisions made by national customs authorities. Whenever an importer requests and obtains such a binding tariff information ("BTI"; Articles 11–12 Common Customs Code), it applies to imports of the same product in all other member states. This process reduces the number of divergent tariff classifications, particularly regarding trade sensitive textiles and electronics. That said, EU classification decisions regarding "art" versus "goods" have proven controversial and costly not only as to tariffs, but also VAT taxation.[17]

Nevertheless there are recurrent instances where despite the general obligation to interpret the Combined Nomenclature uniformly the national authorities stick to their traditional views.[18] This results in products being classified differently depending on

---

[15]   Council Regulations 1445/72, 2658/87.

[16]   Council Decision 87/369, O.J. L 198/1 (July 20, 1987).

[17]   *See* EU Regulation No. 731/2010 (light sculptures treated as fixtures increasing VAT from 5 to 20%).

[18]   *See, e.g.,* Peacock AG v. Hauptzollamt Paderborn (2000) Eur.Comm.Rep. I–08947 (Oct. 19, 2000).

the member state where the release for free circulation is applied
for. It is advisable, therefore, to check whether a particular product
should not be imported via another member state when problems
arise due to an unfavorable interpretation of the Combined
Nomenclature by a national customs administration. The purpose of
a binding tariff information is not just that if presented upon import
the customs authorities are bound by it, but also that there may not
be any post-clearance recovery of duties in case of an incorrect
classification or a change of classification. Thus the BTI, if used,
offers substantial protection for an importer. It is issued upon
request and is subject to judicial review by the competent judicial
authorities of the member state[19].

Valuation

The valuation of goods for purposes of assessing the CN is
presently done according to the GATT/WTO Customs Valuation
Code.[20] This means that in most instances arms-length transaction
value is the basis for tariff assessments, subject to various
adjustments.[21] One notable difference between EU and U.S.
implementation of the Valuation Code concerns international
freight and insurance charges. Unlike the United States, the Union
includes such charges in the customs value of goods subject to its
common external tariff. Purchasing agents' commission are not
included in customs values for purposes of collecting the common
external tariff[22] nor are export permit or quota charges[23]
(irrespective of whether the quota is traded legally[24] and unless the
charges concern quotas obtained from third parties[25]), weighing
charges,[26] and separately invoiced intra-Union transport charges.[27]

---

[19]   Article 243, Common Customs Code.

[20]   Articles 28–36, Common Customs Code; the Customs Valuation Code was
revised during the Uruguay Round Negotiations.

[21]   *See* Hauptzollamt Hamburg-Ericus v. Van Houten International GmbH (1986)
Eur.Comm.Rep. 447 (Costs of weighing imports on arrival excluded from transaction
value); Hauptzollamt Schweinfurt v. Mainfrucht Obstverwertung (1985)
Eur.Comm.Rep. 3909 (Costs of internal EC transport that are separately invoiced
excluded).

[22]   Hauptzollamt Karlstruhe v. Gerbr Hepp & Co Kg (1991) Eur.Comm.Rep. 4319
(Case 299/90); Hans Sommer GmbH & Co. KG v. Hauptzollamt Bremen (2000)
Eur.Comm.Rep. I–08989 (Oct. 19, 2000).

[23]   Ospig Texilgesellschaft KG W. Ahlers v. Hauptzollamt Bremen-Ost (1984)
Eur.Comm.Rep. 609; Malt (1990) Eur.Comm.Rep. 1482.

[24]   Ospig Textil-Gesellschaft W. Ahlers GmbH & Co. KG v. Hauptzollamt Bremen-
Freihafen (1994) Eur.Comm.Rep. I–1963 (Case C–29/93).

[25]   Klaus Thierschmidt GmbH v. Hauptzollamt Essen (1994) I–3905 (Case
C–340/93).

[26]   Hauptzollamt Hamburg-Ericus v. Van Houten International GmbH (1986)
Eur.Comm.Rep. 447.

[27]   Hauptzollamt Schweinfurt v. Mainfrucht Obstverwertung (1985)
Eur.Comm.Rep. 3909.

A leading case discusses when computer software is part of the value of imported "goods" subject to the common customs tariff.[28]

Careful analysis of European Union law and an appropriate structuring of export transactions is particularly required with regard to customs value questions concerning licensing fees. Article 32(1)(c) Common Customs Code provides that such fees have to be added to the price paid or payable if the buyer must pay them as a condition of sale of the imported goods and to the extent that they are not yet included in the price. This means that, e.g. in the case of fees paid in respect of the right to use a trademark, such fee may only be added to the price if

—The goods are resold in the same state or after minor processing,

—The goods are marketed under the trademark, and

—The buyer is not free to obtain the goods from other suppliers unrelated to the seller.[29]

In cases where the licensing fees do not have to be added to the price it is essential that the fees are invoiced separately.

Origin

As a general matter, the Union determines the origin of goods in accordance with the 1973 Kyoto Convention[30], which has not been ratified by the United States. According to the Common Customs Code a product originates either in the country where it was wholly obtained or produced[31] or—in case of a production process involving raw materials or semi-finished products from various countries—where the last, substantial, economically justified processing or working took place in an enterprise equipped for that purpose and resulting in the manufacture of a new product or representing an import stage of manufacture.[32]

This is usually the case where a change in the tariff heading occurs, i.e. where the finished product is to be classified in another heading of the Combined Nomenclature as compared to the classification of the raw materials or of the semi-finished products. A process is "economically justified" if it adds value or provides

---

[28]   *See* Brown Boveri & CIE AG v. Hauptzollamt Mannheim (1991) Eur.Comm.Rep. 1884 (Case C–79/89); *see now* Article 167, Commission Regulation 2913/92.

[29]   Article 159, Commission Regulation 2913/92.

[30]   Council Decision 75/199, O.J. L 100/1 (April 21, 1975) and O.J. L 166/1 (April 21, 1977).

[31]   Article 23, Common Customs Code.

[32]   Article 24, Common Customs Code.

commercial advantages. A process or operation is "substantial," for these purposes, only if the resulting product has its own properties and composition.[33] Cleaning, grinding, grading, and packaging a raw material do not meet this standard.[34] If the change in tariff heading approach to origin is insufficient, a "value added" analysis is pursued. This analysis focuses on the value added to the product in the claimed country of origin. Ten percent is insufficient to confer country of origin status.[35]

Specific "rules of origin" exist for semiconductors,[36] photocopiers,[37] radio and television receivers,[38] tape recorders,[39] and ball bearings[40] as well as a number of other products.[41] Most of these specific rules of origin relate to EU dumping law.[42] Rules of origin are critical to duty free or preferential entry of goods from Cotonou Convention, Mediterranean Basin or GSP developing nations as well as from EFTA countries or countries of Central and Eastern Europe.[43] Generally speaking, the rules of origin associated with these programs focus on changes in tariff headings as the determining factor. But many unique product-specific rules of origin are also created, and these often stress value added approaches. The most generous of these rules of origin apply to Cotonou exports to the EU where, for example, any Union contribution may be counted as from a Cotonou nation for purposes of value added calculations, so-called cumulation.

Special rules of origin and EU content requirements apply to high-technology products like printed circuit boards, integrated circuits and the like. These rules often have the purpose and effect of transferring technology and production to the European Union. Processed EFTA exports originate therein, and may be freely traded to the EU under rules that emphasize a change in tariff heading. The many variations on the origin of goods contained in Union law

---

[33] Gesellschaft für Überseehandel v. Handelskammer Hamburg (1977) Eur.Comm.Rep. 41.

[34] *Id.*

[35] Brother International GmbH v. Hauptzollamt Giessen (1989) Eur.Comm.Rep. 4253.

[36] Council Regulation 288/89.

[37] Council Regulation 2071/89.

[38] Council Regulation 2632/70.

[39] Council Regulation 861/71.

[40] Council Regulation 1836/78.

[41] Eggs (Council Regulation 2448/90), spare parts (Council Regulation 37/70), meat and meat products (Council Regulation 3620/90), clothing, shoes and textiles (Council Regulation 1365/91), ceramics (Council Regulation 2025/73) and grape juice (Council Regulation 2883/90).

[42] *See* Section 18.5.

[43] *See* Sections 18.2, 18.9 and 18.10.

and EU trade agreements make these rules particularly complex. A product from one country that fails to meet one of the specialized or preferential rules of origin governing such entry into the Common Market will be judged under the general rule of origin discussed above.

Quotas

Until the completion of the internal market on January 1, 1993 a complicated system of import quotas for individual member states existed for various products, notably for automobiles from Japan as well as bananas. The elimination of controls at the Union's internal borders necessitated a harmonization of all European Union import and customs quotas. Regrettably this has not always resulted in a liberalized access to the EU market, but in a number of cases the Union has introduced new regimes which make it more difficult to export to the European Union. A particularly prominent example is the Common Market Organization for bananas,[44] which although incompatible with the GATT according to the findings of GATT/WTO panels, was upheld by the European Court of Justice.[45] It resulted in a discriminatory foreclosure of the Union market for Latin American bananas which before could be imported freely into Germany and the Benelux countries. Since the exporters of bananas most adversely affected by the EU regime of trade restraints are U.S. multinationals, the United States was authorized by the WTO to retaliate against EU exports and did so by imposing substantial tariffs. Ecuador and other banana producers were authorized by the WTO to "cross-retaliate" by not paying intellectual property royalties to EU parties. This remarkable remedy was never, but its authorization generated in 2001 a settlement of the "bananas dispute". The EU replaced its quotas with a non-preferential tariff scheme.

For coverage of U.S. Customs law on classification, valuation and origin, see Chapter 3.

§ 18.2   EU Generalized Tariff Preferences (GSP)

The European Union participates in the generalized system of tariff preferences (GSP) initiated within the GATT to give duty free access to industrial markets for selected goods coming from the developing world. This policy is implemented in the common customs tariff regulations.[46] The Central European countries were added to the Union's GSP list for the interim period between the

---

[44]   Council Regulation 404/93 and Commission Regulation 1442/93.

[45]   Germany v. Council (1994) Eur.Comm.Rep. I–4973 (Case C–280/93).

[46]   *See* O.J. 1993 C–169/1.

collapse of the Communist regimes and the entry into force of the free trade and economic association agreements concluded with the EU.[47] The countries of the former USSR are GSP beneficiaries until any free-trade agreement with them comes into force, and provided they undertake to open their markets to developing-country exports.

Approximately 150 non-European developing nations now benefit from the GSP trade preferences of the EU, including China. Goods from the Four Dragons of East Asia (South Korea, Taiwan, Hong Kong and Singapore) still qualify. South Korean goods were disqualified between 1987 and 1991 because of inadequate intellectual property protection in that nation. In contrast, the Four Dragons were "graduated" (*i.e.,* no longer treated as developing nations) out of the United States' GSP program in 1989. Burma was suspended from the EU program in 1997 for human rights concerns, but is now eligible. In 2001, the EU began phasing in complete duty free access for the world's poorest 49 countries, a program known as "Everything But Arms". Special duty free preferences have been granted to developing countries that combat illegal drug production. Pakistan received this status, over strenuous objections by India before the World Trade Organization. The WTO Appellate Body rejected the EU scheme in 2004 as discriminatory, and in breach of the Enabling Clause. WT/DS246/AB/R (April 20, 2004). Subsequent EU amendments continued special duty free tariff status for countries implementing 27 international conventions related to human and labor rights, the environment and good governance (including drug trafficking). Pakistan remains ineligible for special treatment.

The European Union system of generalized tariff preferences is selectively applied when about 130 "sensitive products" are involved. In other words, there are limitations (quotas and tariff ceilings) on duty free access to the Common Market if the goods compete with Union manufacturers. However, these GSP limitations do not apply to products already receiving duty free access under the Cotonou Convention or the Union's Mediterranean Policy.[48] Thus, nations that are covered by the latter trade rules still obtain some margin of preference over other third world GSP beneficiaries.

A solidarity mechanism was introduced in 1995 and is applicable in exceptional circumstances: Beneficiary countries whose exports of products covered by the GSP in a given sector exceed 25 percent of all beneficiaries' exports of those products in

---

[47]   GSP status has also been granted to the successor states of former Yugoslavia.

[48]   *See* Sections 18.9, 18.10.

that sector will be excluded from GSP entitlement for that sector irrespective of their level of development.[49] In addition sector/country graduation was introduced on the basis of relative specialization (ratio of a beneficiary country's share of total Union imports in a given sector), coupled with a development weighing (development index, combining a country's per capita income and the level of its exports as compared with those of the Union). Both mechanisms were phased in gradually to keep within the framework of overall neutrality. Preferences for Hong Kong, Singapore, South Korea and the Gulf Cooperation Council (GCC) states[50] were limited to half the margin applied in 1995. In no case may the application of both mechanisms result in a more favorable level of preferential access than that applied in 1993. For sensitive products, lists limit the preferential duty to 80 percent, respectively 40 percent of the most-favored nation (MFN) duty.

For coverage of the U.S. GSP program, see Sections 2.10–2.16.

§ 18.3   EU Safeguard Proceedings and Voluntary Trade Restraints

European Union commercial policy regulations establish common rules for imports and exports. These rules authorize "escape clause" (safeguard) measures to curb exports in the face of shortages, or to curb surging imports that threaten serious injury to similar EU products.[51] Special rules apply to escape clause proceedings when the imports are from state-trading countries.[52] European Union escape clause law on imports is derived from Article XIX of the GATT and the WTO Safeguards Agreement (1994). The counterparts in U.S. law are found in Sections 201 and 406 of the Trade Act of 1974.[53] Use of escape clause relief triggers a duty to compensate WTO trade partners.

The protective measures authorized by the EU escape clause regulations may include tariffs, quotas, and more controversially, agreements with exporting nations to voluntarily control the flow of certain goods into the Union *or* particular EU nations. Such "voluntary export restraints" (VERs) have been used by the Union on consumer electronics, machine tools, food products and steel imports. The Union itself has "voluntarily" restrained the export of steel to the United States. After much effort, and adherence to the WTO escape clause agreement, Europe has greatly reduced its

---

[49]   Commission Document COM (94) 337 final of September 19, 1994.
[50]   Saudi Arabia, Qatar, United Arab Emirates, Kuwait, Bahrain.
[51]   Council Regulation 3285/94.
[52]   *Id.*
[53]   319 U.S.C.A. " 2261, 2436.

dependence upon VERs as a means of protection against import competition. Europe has generally refrained from frequent invocation of escape clause relief.

For coverage of U.S. Safeguards law, see Chapter 6.

§ 18.4 EU Foreign Country Trade Barriers

Another area of the Common Commercial Policy was commenced in 1984 in response to efforts (ultimately withdrawn) by the Reagan Administration at limiting participation of European licensees of United States technology in the Siberian natural gas pipeline project. This was sometimes called the "new commercial policy" and is now embodied in the Trade Barriers Regulation No. 3286/94. It covers situations not subject to escape clause, dumping or subsidy proceedings.[54] Regulation 3286/94 concerns "obstacles to trade" by foreign *countries* and roughly approximates Section 301 of the U.S. Trade Act of 1974.[55]

When countries engage in practices that are incompatible with international agreement (e.g., the GATT/WTO agreements), adversely affect a petitioner's trade and it is in the Union's interest to take action, the EU may undertake international dispute settlement procedures and (possibly) retaliatory measures. The latter can include raising tariffs, suspending trade concessions or imposing quotas. Private parties can file "market access" complaints with the Commission to initiate examination of alleged obstacles to trade. Negative decisions by the Commission may be appealed to the Court of Justice.[56]

§ 18.5 EU Antidumping Duties

Another part of the Common Commercial Policy concerns unfair trading practices applied to goods *exported* to the Union. The two most important areas of law here concern dumping and subsidies.[57] Unlike NAFTA, the European Union has eliminated antidumping and countervailing duties internally among its members. Similar rules apply to unfair shipping services used to bring goods to the Union.[58] In recent years, European Union use of antidumping proceedings to protect its market has risen substantially. EU companies with at least 25% of their market sector must support a dumping complaint. Nearly half of these proceedings involve goods from nonmarket economy states (NMEs).

---

[54] *See* Sections 18.3–18.6.
[55] 19 U.S.C.A. § 2411. *See* Chapter 14.
[56] FEDIOL v. Commission (1989) Eur.Comm.Rep. 1781.
[57] Council Regulations 384/94 and 3284/96.
[58] Council Regulation 4057/86.

Apart from NMEs, Chinese, Japanese and United States exports have most frequently been involved in Union antidumping proceedings. Many of these proceedings are settled by promises of the exporters to raise prices and refrain from "dumping." The standing of most exporters and complainants to challenge EU dumping decisions has been affirmed by the European Court.[59] Such persons would otherwise lack any possible judicial remedy. Importers, on the other hand, have remedies in the national courts of the member states and are therefore generally unable to challenge EU dumping decisions directly before the European Court.[60] However, importers who are end-users of the product in question and seriously affected by the antidumping duties may challenge antidumping determinations under Article 230.[61]

Dumping involves selling abroad at a price that is less than the price used to sell the same goods at home (the "normal" or "fair" value). To be unlawful, dumping must threaten or cause material injury to an industry in the export market, the market where prices are lower. Dumping is recognized by most of the trading world as an unfair practice (akin to price discrimination as an antitrust offense). Dumping is the subject of a special GATT/WTO code which establishes the basic parameters for determining when dumping exists, what constitutes material injury and the remedy of antidumping tariffs.[62] Such tariffs can amount to the margin of the dump, *i.e.,* the difference in the price charged at home and (say) the European Union.

Dumping Determinations

"Normal value" under Union dumping law is first defined as the comparable price actually paid or payable in the ordinary course of trade for the like product intended for consumption in the exporting country or country of origin. The Commission usually considers all sales made in the period under investigation (typically 12 months). It requires that the domestic sales exceed 5 percent of the export sales in order to be considered to be representative and this threshold has been upheld by the European Court of Justice.[63] However, only sales made in the ordinary course of business enter

---

[59] Allied Corp. v. Commission (1984) Eur.Comm.Rep. 1005 (named exporters may challenge imposition of dumping duties); Timex Corp. v. Council and Commission (1985) Eur.Comm.Rep. 849 (complainant may challenge antidumping decisions).

[60] Alusuisse Italia v. Council and Commission (1982) Eur.Comm.Rep. 3463.

[61] Extramet v. Council (1991) Eur.Comm.Rep. 2527 (Case C–49/88); Nashua Corp. v. Commission (1990) 1 Eur.Comm.Rep. 719.

[62] *See* the Agreement on Implementation of Article VI of the GATT (1979) (Antidumping Code) and the Agreement on Implementation of Article VI of the General Agreement on Tariffs and Trade 1994 (WTO Antidumping Code).

[63] Goldstar v. Council (1992) Eur.Comm.Rep. I–677.

into the calculation. Transactions between related or compensated parties may not be considered in the ordinary course of trade unless the Commission believes they are comparable to arms-length dealings. Sales below cost, for example, are regularly excluded from the Commission's determination of normal value and may trigger "constructed value" determinations if they exceed 20 percent of the sales under consideration.

If there are no sales of the like product in the ordinary course of trade on the domestic market of the exporting country or such sales are inadequate to permit a proper comparison, the Commission turns to (1) the "comparable price" of the product as exported to another surrogate country or (2) its constructed value. The constructed value methodology is often used on Chinese imports. It involves calculation of production costs plus a reasonable profit. The costs of production include materials, components and manufacturing costs, as well as sales, administrative and other general expenses. The Commission need not follow the exporter's accountings in making these calculations, but must give priority to the records kept by the producers/exporters and to actual data in determining costs. In addition the Commission makes adjustments for start-up operations. A profit margin of 10 percent is used.

If the goods are from nonmarket economies, a status some Central and East European countries have finally escaped, the Commission has three options for determining normal value. These are utilization of a price derived from the sale of a like product in a market country, a constructed value price based on the costs of a producer in a market country or (if needed) the price actually paid in the Union adjusted to include a reasonable profit margin. The choice of the "market economy third country" for purposes of normal value determination has to be based on sufficient reasons and objections of parties to the investigation have to be taken into account if they are substantiated. The failure to take them into consideration will result in the quashing of the Regulation imposing antidumping duties by the European Court of Justice[64].

Once a normal value for the goods is established by the Commission, the export price is determined. This is defined as the price actually paid or payable for the product sold for export to the Union. Relatively speaking, this calculation is less controversial except when the producer sells through its own subsidiary. In such cases the Commission practice has been to calculate the export price on the basis of the price at which the good is first resold to an independent buyer, and deductions (adjustments) are made both for

---

[64]   Nölle v. Hauptzollamt Bremen-Freihafen (1991) Eur.Comm.Rep. 5163.

direct and indirect expenses. The normal value, however, is adjusted only for costs which are directly related to the sales. As a result, the export price is necessarily inferior to the normal value. This asymmetrical approach has repeatedly been upheld by the European Court of Justice[65]. In addition, certain adjustments must be made to the normal value and export prices so calculated. These adjustments reflect differences in physical attributes, import charges, indirect taxes and selling expenses. The object of making these adjustments is to arrive at comparable "ex-factory" price calculations.

The EU dumping margin is the difference between the adjusted normal value and the adjusted export price. It is established by the Union institutions by comparing a weighted average normal value with individual export transactions,[66] thus excluding so called negative dumping margins, i.e. the effect of export sales above the normal value upon the calculation of a weighted average export price. This dumping margin ultimately determines the maximum extra duty the EU importer must pay provided there also is material injury to an EU industry and the Commission decides that imposing the duty would be in the Union's interest. This "public interest" determination typically pits EU consumer interests against industrial interests. The manufacturers usually win out, but occasionally the consumers' interest in lower-priced imports prevails.[67]

EU antidumping proceedings have of late become politicized. Actual imposition of antidumping duties requires a majority vote of the member states, for example the 13–12 vote in 2006 in favor of duties on Asian shoes, vigorously opposed by EU retailers. After much debate, a decision to remove these duties in 2010 was reversed by another bare majority in the Council of Ministers.[68] In 2013, imposition of antidumping duties on Chinese solar panels survived considerable opposition.

Dumping Duties

A *de minimis* dumping margin of 2 percent is required to establish injury. Similarly if the volume of imports is less than 3 percent of imports of the like product the investigation has to be

---

[65]   Nippon Seiko v. Council (1987) Eur.Comm.Rep. 1923; Canon and others v. Council (1988) Eur.Comm.Rep. 5731; Matsushita Electric v. Council (1992) Eur.Comm.Rep. I–1409; Matsushita Electric Industrial Co. Ltd. (1993) I–04981 (Case C–104/90).

[66]   Upheld by the European Court of Justice in NTN Tokyo (1987) Eur.Comm.Rep. 1854.

[67]   *See* Commission Dec. May 22, 1990 O.J. L138/48 (May 31, 1990) (photo albums).

[68]   Re Chinese Shoes, (2010) Eur.Comm.Rep. ___ (Case T–401/06).

terminated immediately—unless countries which individually account for less than 3 percent of these imports collectively account for more than 7 percent. This may entice producers in the future to direct complaints against as many countries as possible. The precise amount of the antidumping duty is supposed to represent only that which is necessary to remove the injury. European Union dumping duties are imposed prospectively, applying in most cases to all future imports during the next five years.

The EU authorities have a wide discretion to impose different forms of duty. These may be:

(a)   A specific duty (i.e. fixed amount per unit of product imported);

(b)   An ad valorem duty; or

(c)   A minimum floor price (i.e. if the exporter sells below the minimum price, the difference between such a price and the minimum price is collected as duty).

In theory, the minimum price approach should be the most appropriate since the object is to eliminate the injury caused by dumping, not to punish the dumpers. In fact, ad valorem duties are the most common as they are more difficult to evade and much easier to administer, particularly when there is a range of types of the dumped product. Ad valorem duties are chosen because the payment of duties cannot be avoided simply by the exporter raising ex-factory export prices so that the imports are no longer dumped (though the importer may be able to claim a refund or seek to have the duty reviewed in such circumstances). The Antidumping Regulation contains specific anti-absorption provisions which prevent the exporter from bearing the duty by reducing export prices so that the retail price is unaffected. If this occurs, the Union authorities may impose an additional duty, to compensate for the amount borne by the exporter.

Undertakings or commitments are commonly offered by exporters during the course of anti-dumping investigations. Indeed more than half of the investigations commenced by the Commission are resolved in this way. To be acceptable, the effect of the undertaking must be that either the dumping margin or the injurious effect of it is eliminated. An undertaking usually involves an upward revision of prices, though exceptionally an undertaking to limit exports may be accepted. In deciding whether to accept an undertaking, the previous violation of an enterprise may also be taken into account. However, as indicated above in the section on duties, the acceptance of undertakings can also be subject to political considerations; for instance, several years ago the Council of Ministers rejected a Commission proposal that a procedure be terminated in this way in the light of the then prevailing trading relations with Japan. Although the Commission may suggest undertakings, the fact that they are not offered may not prejudice the case; but if dumping continues, the Commission may treat that as evidence that a threat of injury is more likely to lead to material injury.

Investigations

The antidumping investigation will cover a period of not less than six months immediately prior to the initiation of the proceeding and will normally be concluded either by termination or definitive action within one year. Some cases, however, take very much longer. In the course of an investigation, the Commission may seek all necessary information from, and examine and verify the records of importers, exporters, traders, agents, producers, trade associations and organizations. Investigations in third countries can take place only if the firms concerned consent and their government has been notified and does not object. The member states may send officials to assist in such investigations. Within the Union, the Commission will obtain assistance from the member states, in particular to carry out checks and inspections of importers, traders and EU producers. Although the Commission does not have the power to obtain the information it requires if an enterprise, within or outside the Union, does not wish to cooperate, findings will be made on the basis of the facts available. Hence anti-dumping duties may be imposed on producers who refuse to cooperate on the basis of the allegations set forth in the complaint[69] or on the basis of the dumping found against other producers and at the highest rate imposed on those other producers[70] or even higher.[71]

As part of the investigation, the Commission will send questionnaires to producers/exporters, importers and Union producers known to it. The normal time period in which to respond to the questionnaire is 37 days but an extension can be requested. The purpose of the questionnaires is to collect all the necessary information to determine normal value, export price and adjustments in order to enable a comparison to be made. In addition, some information relating to injury will be gleaned from the questionnaires. Apart from the questionnaire, the most

---

[69] Video cassette recorders originating in Korea and Japan, O.J. L 57/55 (27.2.1989); Compact disk players originating in Japan and Korea; O.J. L 13/21 (16.1.1990).

[70] Large electrolytic aluminum capacitors originating in Japan, O.J. L 152/22 (June 4, 1992).

[71] Electronic weighing scales originating in Singapore and Korea, O.J. L 112/20 (May 6, 1993).

important step in an anti-dumping proceeding will be the verification visit by Commission officials to the company, which usually takes two to three days. The aim is to compare the answers on the questionnaire with the company's books to ensure that the information supplied is both correct and complete. Answers may be rejected if the officials are not satisfied that they are consistent with the business records. It is important for the company to be able to show how each figure in the questionnaire was arrived at, and all materials used in the preparation of the answers should be kept.

All information obtained or received by the Commission can be used solely for the purpose for which it was requested. It cannot be passed to other Commission departments, such as the Directorate-General for Competition.[72] Confidential treatment can be requested with an indication why the information is confidential, and a non-confidential summary, or statement of reasons why the information is not susceptible to summary, should be provided. This summary is intended for supply to other parties to the proceedings. Failure to submit a summary, where summary is possible, or the unwarranted claiming of confidentiality coupled with an unwillingness to authorize disclosure in generalized or summary form, will result in the information being disregarded. Even in the absence of a request for confidentiality, information will be treated as confidential if its disclosure is likely to have a significantly adverse effect on the supplier or the source of the information.

Judicial Review

Since March 1994 the Court of First Instance (CFI) (now General Court) has had jurisdiction over antidumping matters and the European Court of Justice is only competent to hear appeals against the GC judgments. The Court of Justice had restricted its control to manifest errors of appraisal and abuse of power. It had thus granted the Union institutions an extremely wide margin of discretion. The reasoning underlying this approach was that the imposition of antidumping duties involves a difficult appraisal of complex economic issues. Finally it should be mentioned that successful litigation before the European Court in antidumping matters opens the way to a claim for damages under Article 340(2) TFEU.[73]

---

[72]   But see for limits of confidentiality provisions the caselaw relating to the confidentiality rule in Regulation 17 on competition law infringement investigations, Dirección General de Defensa de la Competencia v. Asociación Española de Banca Privada and others (1992) Eur.Comm.Rep. I-4785; Samenwerkende Elektriciteitsproductiebedrijven NV v. Commission (1994) I-01911 (Case C-36/92).
[73]   Case T-167/94 (formerly Case C-326/93), Nölle v. EEC.

Critiques

Although much of the EU law on antidumping duties is consistent with the GATT/WTO code, and therefore generally conforms to United States law on the subject,[74] some interesting twists have been applied. One of the most controversial is the so-called "screwdriver plant regulation" aimed mostly at Japanese exporters.[75] These exporters, when faced with antidumping duties on top of the common customs tariff, began to assemble consumer electronics and other products inside the Union using Japanese made components plus a screwdriver. The net effect of the Union's regulatory response is to re-impose dumping duties on these products unless at least 40 percent of the components originate outside the source country (Japan). Similar results have been achieved in certain cases when the Japanese export goods assembled in United States to the EU.[76] In the photocopiers case, the goods had actually qualified as American for purposes of U.S. procurement rules. This origin was rejected by the European Union. The Japanese successfully challenged the screwdriver regulation within the GATT.[77] The Union has indicated that its anti-circumvention rules will remain in effect.

Some have asserted that the European Union employs a double standard when calculating export prices and normal values for dumping law purposes. They claim that the EU has cloaked itself in the technical obscurity of the law so as to systematically inflate normal values and deflate export prices, thereby causing more dumping to be found. Use of asymmetrical methods to reach these determinations has been upheld by the European Court.[78] Additional criticism has been levied against the Commission's refusal to disclose the information upon which it relies in making critical dumping law decisions.[79] Consumer groups have not traditionally been granted access to non-confidential files accumulated by the Commission in antidumping proceedings.[80]

---

[74]   19 U.S.C.A. § 1673.

[75]   *See* Council Regulation 1761/87 and Article 13(10) of Regulation 4057/86.

[76]   *See* Council Regulation 3205/88 (photocopiers) (assembly does not involve a substantial operation or process so as to alter origin of goods). *Accord,* Brother International GmbH v. Hauptzollamt Giessen (1989) Eur.Comm.Rep. 4253 (Case 26/88) (suggesting typewriters assembled in Taiwan originate from Japan unless assembly causes the use to which components are put to become definite and the goods to be given their specific qualities).

[77]   GATT Basic Instruments and Selected Documents (B.I.S.D.) 37S/132 (1991).

[78]   Miniature Bearings, Nippon Seiko v. Council (1987) Eur.Comm.Rep. 1923.

[79]   *See* Al-Jubail Fertilizer Co. v. Council (1991) Eur.Comm.Rep. 3187 (Case C–49/88).

[80]   BEUC v. Commission (1991) Eur.Comm.Rep. 5709 (Case C–170/89).

However, by amendment,[81] consumers and consumer organizations have been granted the right to inspect all non-confidential information made available to the Commission by any party to an investigation.

For coverage of U.S. antidumping law, see Chapter 4.

§ 18.6 EU Countervailing Duties

The internal trade problems associated with member state "aids" (subsidies) to enterprises located inside the EU have already been discussed in connection with the Union's competition policy.[82] Many of the same problems re-emerge in the Common Commercial Policy. This time, however, the source of the subsidies is governments located *outside* the Common Market. Many subsidies, especially export subsidies, are treated as an unfair trading practice under the GATT/WTO. As with dumping, there is a separate code which creates the ground rules in this area.[83] This code (as revised after the Uruguay Round) is implemented as a matter of Common Commercial Policy by the EU and therefore parallels similar law in the United States.[84]

The types of "subsidies" subject to "countervailing duties" are in dispute internationally. European Union regulations illustrate what constitutes a countervailable subsidy.[85] Certain domestic manufacturing, production, and transportation subsidies can also be countervailed if they (like export subsidies) threaten material injury to an EU industry. The European Court of Justice has said that the concept of a countervailable subsidy presupposes the grant of an economic advantage through a charge on the public account.[86] For a domestic subsidy to be countervailable, it must have "sectoral specificity" (seek to grant an advantage only to certain firms). For an export subsidy to be countervailable, it must specifically benefit the imported product.[87] As with dumping proceedings, the Commission makes these judgments provisionally and the Council renders final judgment (issued as a customs regulation). The amount of the extra duty corresponds to the amount of the subsidy.

---

[81]   Article 2(8) Council Regulation 521/94.

[82]   *See* Chapter 19.

[83]   *See* the Agreement on Interpretation and Application of Articles VI, XVI and XXIII of the GATT (1979) (Subsidies Code). Substantial amendments to this code under the Uruguay Round of GATT negotiations were undertaken, resulting in the 1994 WTO Subsidies Code. EU law conforms to this new Subsidies Code.

[84]   19 U.S.C.A. § 1671.

[85]   Council Regulation 2026/97.

[86]   FEDIOL v. Commission (1988) Eur.Comm.Rep. 4193.

[87]   *Id.*

Relatively few external subsidy proceedings have been pursued under Union law.

For coverage of U.S. subsidies and CVD law, see Chapter 5.

§ 18.7   EU Trade Relations . . . with the United States, Japan and China

United States / EU Trade

Trade between the United States and the European Union is voluminous, roughly in balance and increasingly fractious. While the focal point in recent years has been agricultural trade, especially the problem of export subsidies and nontariff trade barriers (notably Europe's banana quotas, beef hormone bans and freeze on GMO approvals) there are many contentious issues. For example, Airbus subsidies have been said to threaten Boeing and vice-versa, disputes that are pending at the WTO. The single market legislative campaign led to fears concerning the erection of a "Fortress Europe" in banking, insurance, broadcasting and other areas. There is a general concern in North America that Europe is turning inward and protective. A particularly contentious issue has been the field of public procurement, notably the provision of the Utilities Directive[88] which provides for a preference of tenders for supplies which contain less than 50 percent materials originating outside the Union. The dispute between the United States and the European Union was settled in negotiations which led to the conclusion of two agreements[89].

The Union, for its part, has begun imitating the United States' practice of issuing annual reports voicing *its* objections to U.S. trade barriers and unfair practices. Extraterritorial U.S. jurisdiction has been a constant complaint, including the Helms-Burton Cuban LIBERTAD and Iran-Libya Sanctions Act. *See* Chapter 11. These reports have also targeted Section 301 of the Trade Act of 1974.[90] The U.S. invoked Section 301 in trade disputes with the EU over the use of animal hormones and EU regulation of oil seeds. The European Union perceives Section 301 to be a unilateral retaliatory mechanism that runs counter to multilateral resolution of trade disputes through the GATT/WTO. This perception has not stopped the Union from partially duplicating this mechanism in EU law

---

[88]   Article 36, Council Directive 93/38, O.J. L 199/84 (Aug. 9, 1993).

[89]   Council Decision 93/394, O.J. L 125/54 (May 20, 1993), the Memorandum of Understanding is published in O.J. L 125/2 (May 20, 1993); Commission proposal for a Council Decision concerning the conclusion of an Agreement in the form of an exchange of letters, O.J. C 291/4 (October 19, 1994).

[90]   19 U.S.C.A. § 2411 as amended. See Chapter 14.

protections against "illicit commercial practices."[91] Nevertheless, since the United States has been taking the bulk of its trade disputes to the WTO under its Dispute Settlement Understanding, the Europeans have less to complain about on this score. An EU challenge to Section 301 before the WTO was rejected in recognition of the U.S. commitment not to employ Section 301 when WTO remedies can be pursued.

Another issue that has been prominently and regularly mentioned is the problem (from the EU perspective) of the diversity of state and local regulation of procurement, product standards, the environment, financial services and taxation. U.S. critics of Europe's legislative diversity could not have said it better. Recent reports by the EU on U.S. trade practices identified major areas of complaint: unilateral U.S. trade legislation; extraterritorial trade law; national security restraints; Buy American policies; import fees, quotas and paperwork; agricultural export subsidies; tax rules on transfer pricing, autos and unitary income taxation; selectively high tariffs; the multiplicity of product standards; services; intellectual property rights; and investment. Perhaps both sides are headed for stronger central government regulation of trade-impacting measures.[92] Each has a lot at stake in trade with the other. The tough question is whether the World Trade Organization dispute resolution procedures can be made to work so as to preserve mutually beneficial trade relations between the Union and North America.

Trade relations between the EU and the U.S. have improved in limited ways under the Transatlantic Economic Partnership Program (1995). A 20-year dispute on wine production and labeling practices, for example, was finally resolved, and starting in 2009 there is agreement on use of International Financial Reporting Standards, replacing U.S. Generally Accepted Accounting Principles. Common standards for electric cars have been developed. In 2013, faced with recessionary economies and the rising economic tide of Asia, the EU and the United States started negotiations on a Transatlantic Trade and Investment Partnership Agreement.

Nevertheless, deep underlying conflicts remain, especially regarding cultural goods (TV shows, films), agriculture, GMOs, airplane subsidies, and procurement. It is this author's view that NAFTA and the EU are competing with good reason for possession of the world's largest market. Larger markets bring greater

---

[91]   *See* Section 18.4.

[92]   *See especially* the discussion of EU product standards and liability law in Section 17.7.

leverage in intergovernmental trade negotiations, economies of scale, improved "terms of trade" (pay less for imports, receive more for exports), and enhanced abilities to exercise global economic leadership. And so the struggle for market power is likely to continue.

Japan/China/EU Trade

The European Union's trade relations with Japan and China are less voluminous, less in balance and (at least superficially) less fractious than with the United States. Japan and China run an annual surplus in its trade with the EU, but the amount is much smaller than the huge surplus they accumulate in trading with the States. Many Europeans speak quietly and with determination about their intent to avoid the "United States example" in their trade relations with Japan and China. Less quietly, some national governments imposed rigorous quotas on the importation of Japanese autos and instituted demanding local content requirements for Japanese cars assembled in Europe. The Union, for its part, has frequently invoked antidumping proceedings against Japanese and especially Chinese goods. It has demonstrated a willingness to create arcane rules of origin that promote its interests at the expense of Japan and China. At the GATT/WTO level, however, Japan and the EU share common concerns about retaining their agricultural support systems. These concerns place them in opposition to the U.S. and others who seek to liberalize world trade in agricultural products.

§ 18.8   EU Trade and Foreign Investment Agreements

Article 218 TFEU establishes the procedures used in the negotiation of most trade agreements with the European Union. Basically, the Commission proposes and then receives authorization from the Council to open negotiations with third countries or within an international organization. When the Commission reaches tentative agreement, conclusion or ratification must take place in the Council. If the Commission alone concludes an agreement, the European Court of Justice will declare void the act whereby the Commission sought to conclude the agreement.[93] The Council votes by qualified majority on Common Commercial Policy agreements.[94] These include most GATT/WTO agreements.

---

[93]   France v. Commission (1994) Eur.Comm.Rep. I–3641 (Case C–327/91) (Agreement between the Commission and the United States regarding the application of their competition laws).

[94]   Article 218(2), TFEU.

The Council votes unanimously on association agreements[95] and on international agreements undertaken via Article 352 (*e.g.,* environmental conventions prior to 1987). The 1993 Treaty on European Union amended Article 218 to provide that the Council must also vote unanimously on international agreements covering areas where an unanimous vote is required to adopt internal EU rules.[96] Parliament's role in international agreements was expanded by the TEU and the Reform Treaty of 2009. Its assent must now be obtained for virtually all EU trade and foreign investment agreements. The Council is also authorized to take emergency measures to cut off or reduce trading with other nations for common foreign or security policy reasons.[97]

An opinion of the European Court as to the compatibility with the TFEU of the proposed agreement and the procedures used to reach it may be obtained in advance at the request of the Commission, Council or a member state. There are no public proceedings when such opinions are sought. Use of this advance ruling procedure may forestall judicial review at a later date of the compatibility of Union agreements with the Treaty.[98] This lesson was vividly made when the Court of Justice rejected the final draft of the 1991 European Economic Area Agreement between the EU and EFTA because it considered the provisions on judicial control incompatible with the authority of the Union's legal order.[99] This rejection sent the Agreement back for renegotiation and a new set of dispute settlement procedures which subsequently met with ECJ approval.[100]

Trade agreements and other international treaties of the European Union are subject to judicial review by the Court of Justice as "acts" of its institutions.[101] Moreover, such agreements are binding on the member states which must ensure their full implementation.[102] When the European Court holds international agreements of the Union to be "directly effective" EU law, individuals may rely upon them in national litigation.[103] The direct effects doctrine has led to cases where citizens end up enforcing the

---

[95]   *See* Section 18.9.

[96]   *See* Section 18.6.

[97]   *See* Article 215 TFEU.

[98]   *See* ECJ Opinion 1/75 (1975) Eur.Comm.Rep. 1355 (Local Cost Standards).

[99]   ECJ Opinion 1/91 (1991) Eur.Comm.Rep. 6079.

[100]   ECJ Opinion 1/92 (1992) Eur.Comm.Rep. 2821.

[101]   *See* Articles 263, 265 and 267, TFEU; an example of a decision declaring void the act whereby the Commission sought to conclude an agreement is Case C–327/91, France v. Commission (1994) Eur.Comm.Rep. I–364.

[102]   Article 218(2), TFEU.

[103]   See R. Folsom, *Principles of European Union Law*, Chapter 3.

trade agreements of the EU despite contrary law of their own or other member state governments.[104]

ERTA and WTO Agreements Cases

Article 220 TFEU gives the Commission the power to represent the Union within the General Agreement on Tariffs and Trade (GATT)/WTO. This representation affords EU nations much more bargaining power over tariffs and other trade issues with Canada, the United States, and Japan than they ever had individually. The exact extent and delimitation of the Union competences and the competences of the member states were disputed. With regard to the many Uruguay Round agreements, therefore, the European Commission requested the European Court of Justice to render an opinion to determine whether the Union was competent to conclude the Agreement establishing the World Trade Organization (WTO), in particular as regards the Agreement on Trade in Services (GATS), the Agreement on Trade-Related Aspects of Intellectual Property Rights, including trade in counterfeit goods (TRIPS), and with respect to products and/or services falling within the ECSC and EURATOM Treaties. This WTO Agreements opinion is discussed below.

Article 207 TFEU conveys the power to enter into international commitments to the European Union. This is the case by implication even when there is no express Treaty authorization to enter into international agreements necessary to achieve internal Common Market objectives.[105] A prominent decision of the European Court holds the scope of the Union's trade agreements power to be coextensive with all *effective* surrenders of national sovereignty accomplished under the Treaty.[106] Thus, if an internal economic policy matter is governed by existing EU law, the external aspects of that policy are (either expressly or *by implication*) exclusively within the Union's competence. More recently, the Court of Justice revisited the *ERTA* doctrine in an opinion reviewing the Uruguay Round trade agreements. The European Community had long represented the member states in the GATT and exclusively negotiated these agreements. But the General Agreement on Trade in Services (GATS) and the Agreement on Trade-Related Aspects of Intellectual Property (TRIPS) raised special concerns since the

---

[104]   Bresciani v. Amministrazione della Finanze (1976) Eur.Comm.Rep. 129 (Yaoundé Conventions); Hauptzollamt Mainz v. Kupferberg (1982) Eur.Comm.Rep. 3641 (EC–Portugal Free Trade Agreement); Eurim-Pharm GmbH v. Bundesgesundheitsamt (1993) Eur.Comm.Rep. I–03723 (Case C–207/91).

[105]   ECJ Opinion 1/76 (1977) Eur.Comm.Rep. 741 (Inland Waterways).

[106]   Commission v. Council (1971) Eur.Comm.Rep. 263 (the "*ERTA*" decision).

Treaty and *ERTA* were ambiguous as to whether the Union or the member states or both had the power to conclude these agreements.

The Court of Justice, in the complex *WTO Agreements* opinion, ruled that the Union had exclusive power regarding trade in goods agreements (including agriculture) based on Article 207 TFEU authorizing the Common Commercial Policy. While the cross-frontier supply of services not involving movement of persons also fell under Article 207, all other aspects of the GATS did not. Regarding TRIPS, only the provisions dealing with counterfeit goods came under the Community's exclusive Article 207 authority. Noting that the effective surrender of national sovereignty over intellectual property is not (yet) total and that internal trade in services is not "inextricably linked" to external relations, the Court ruled the competence to conclude GATS and TRIPs was jointly shared by the Community and the member states. Likewise, they share a duty to cooperate within the WTO in the administration of these agreements and disputes relating to them.[107] Under the Lisbon Treaty of 2009, trade in services, trade-related intellectual property rights, and notably foreign direct investment became exclusive EU competences.[108]

Member State Involvement

Article 351 TFEU indicates that most treaties the member states reached prior to joining the EU continue to be valid even if they impact on areas now governed by Union law. Many bilateral treaties of Friendship, Commerce and Navigation fall within this category despite their impact on immigration, employment and investment opportunities. For example, such a dispute between Germany and the Commission concerned the compatibility of the preference-provision in the Utilities Directive[109] for supply contracts with the German-American Treaty of Friendship and Commerce of 1953.[110] Member states are required to take all appropriate steps (*e.g.*, upon renewal) to eliminate any incompatibilities between national trade and investment agreements and the Treaty.[111] Whether prior treaties can be invoked so as to negate or fail to fulfill Treaty obligations is unclear.[112]

---

[107]   Opinion 1/94 (1994) Eur.Comm.Rep. I–5267 (WTO).

[108]   See Daiichi Sankyo Co v. DEMO Anonimous, (2013) Eur. Comm. Rep. ___ (Case C–414/11) (TRIPs is now exclusive EU competence).

[109]   Article 36, Council Directive 93/38, O.J. L 199/84 (August 9, 1993).

[110]   Germany in EC row over US sanctions, Financial Times of 12./13.6.1993; EC hopes Bonn row will fade, Financial Times of 14.6.1993.

[111]   *See generally* Kramer et al. (1976) Eur.Comm.Rep. 1279 (North Atlantic Fisheries); Council Decision 91/167.

[112]   Compare Re Van Wesemael (1979) Eur.Comm.Rep. 35 (International Labor Organization Convention no ground for member state failure to apply Union law) and

As a rule, member states may *not* negotiate trade treaties in EU-occupied fields. They may do so on a transitional basis in areas where the Union lacks authority or (less clearly) has not effectively implemented its authority. For example, in the early 1970s the EU had not developed an effective overall energy policy, although it clearly had competence in the coal and nuclear fields. Thus, the International Energy Agreement achieved through the Organization for Economic Cooperation and Development (OECD) in 1975 after the first oil shocks is not an EU agreement. In contrast, the Union clearly had competence in the field of export credits. OECD arrangements in this area are exclusively the province of the Union with no residual or parallel authority in the member states.[113] Likewise, in 2002 the ECJ ruled that bilateral "open skies" aviation agreement between eight individual member states and the United States were illegal incursions into an exclusively EU domain. A United States–European Union open skies agreement followed in 2008.

The *ERTA* and to a lesser degree the *WTO* decisions of the European Court, combined with the expanding competence of the Union, leaves less and less room for national governments to enter into trade agreements. Several ECJ decisions suggest that the Union's external authority parallels its internal powers even if it has not effectively implemented those powers.[114] However, recognizing the sensitivities involved, "mixed agreements" negotiated by the Commission (acting on a Council mandate) and representatives of the member states are frequently used. Both the Union and the member states are signatories to such accords. This has been done with the "association agreements" authorized by Article 217 TFEU, certain of the WTO Codes, the Ozone Layer Convention and the Law of the Sea Convention.

The Court of Justice has upheld the validity of mixed international agreements and procedures, but suggested that absent special circumstances their use should not occur when the Union's exclusive jurisdiction over external affairs is fully involved.[115] In other words, mixed procedures should be followed only when the competence to enter into and implement international agreements is in fact shared between the Union and

---

Ministre Public & Anor v. Levy (1993) Eur.Comm.Rep. I–04287 (Case C–158/91) (ILO Convention may take precedence over Community directive on night work by women).

[113]   ECJ Opinion 1/75 (1975) Eur.Comm.Rep. 1355 (Local Cost Standards).

[114]   Kramer et al. (1976) Eur.Comm.Rep. 1279 (North Atlantic Fisheries); ECJ Opinion 1/76 (1977) Eur.Comm.Rep. 741 (Inland Waterways).

[115]   ECJ Opinion 1/78 (1979) Eur.Comm.Rep. 2871 (Natural Rubber Agreement).

its member states.[116] The Treaty of Nice (2003) makes it clear that trade agreements relating to cultural and audiovisual services, educational services, and social and human health services are shared competences. The Reform Treaty (2009) contains a lengthy list of shared competences that are found at Article 4(2) TFEU.

The Reform Treaty also clarified that Common Commercial Policy matters are an exclusive EU competence, as are the customs union, business competition rules, EURO zone monetary policy, and marine biology conservation policies. Article 3 TFEU further indicates that the Union has exclusive competence to conclude international agreements provided for by EU legislative act, necessary to enable the EU to exercise its internal powers, or where concluding an international agreement may affect common rules or alter their scope. In all of these areas, therefore, trade agreements can only be concluded by the European Union.

Free Trade Agreements and Foreign Investment Treaties

Very significantly, Mexico and the European Union reached a *free trade* agreement in 2000. Mexico, with its NAFTA membership, thus becomes a production center with duty free access to the world's two largest consumer markets. The Union has been aggressively pursuing other free trade agreements. South Africa, Peru, Colombia, Central America (6 nations), Chile and South Korea have signed on. One notable feature of these agreements is the inclusion of a Human Rights and Democracy Clause backed up by potential trade sanctions. Vietnam, India, ASEAN, MERCOSUR and the Gulf Council may follow. Early in 2013, the European Union and the United States commenced Transatlantic Trade and Investment Partnership negotiations. Late in 2013, Canada and the EU concluded a Comprehensive Economic and Trade Agreement (CETA) that includes intellectual property and foreign investment. Ratification by the EU Parliament and member states, and the Canadian Parliament and provinces is underway.

Foreign investment has traditionally been governed by the national laws of the member states. Hundreds of Bilateral Investment Treaties (BITs) have been negotiated between member states and other, largely developing nations. Germany, for example, has over 100 BITs, and France nearly as many. Since the Reform Treaty of 2009, foreign investment law has become an exclusive competence of the European Union. It is expected that all national BITs will in time be replaced by EU BITs, much as has already been done concerning international aviation agreements. In 2013, the EU

---

[116]   *See* Opinion 2/91 (Convention No. 170 of the ILO).

Council authorized the Commission to commence BIT negotiations with China.

In addition, the European Union has a host of other trading and cooperation agreements. These include agreements with Sri Lanka, Pakistan, Bangladesh, India, China, the ASEAN group (Thailand, Singapore, Malaysia, The Philippines, Vietnam, Cambodia, Laos, Myanmar, Brunei, and Indonesia), the Andean Pact (Bolivia, Colombia, Ecuador, Peru), Argentina, Uruguay, Brazil and Mexico. In 1990, a Cooperation Agreement was signed with the countries of the Gulf Cooperation Council (GCC): Kuwait, Saudi Arabia, Oman, Bahrain, Qatar and the United Arab Emirates.

§ 18.9   EU Association Agreements, Mediterranean Policy, Central and Eastern Europe

Association Agreements

Article 217 TFEU authorizes the Union to conclude association agreements with other nations, regional groups and international organizations. The Council must act unanimously in adopting association agreements. Since the Single European Act of 1987, association agreements also require Parliamentary assent (which it threatened to withhold from renewal of the Israeli-EU association agreement unless better treatment of Palestinian exports to the Union is achieved). The network of trade relations established by association agreements covers much of the globe. Those who are "associated" with the EU usually receive trade and aid preferences which, as a practical matter, discriminate against non-associates. Arguments about the illegality of such discrimination within the GATT/WTO and elsewhere have typically not prevailed.

Article 217 indicates that association agreements involve "*reciprocal* rights and obligations, common action and special procedures" (emphasis added). The reciprocity requirement mirrors GATT law on non-preferential trading and free trade area agreements.[117] European Union association agreements usually establish wide-ranging but hardly reciprocal trade and economic links. Greece for many years prior to membership was an EU associate. Turkey has been an associate since 1963. These two agreements illustrate the use of association agreements to convey high levels of financial, technical and commercial aid as a preliminary to membership. Turkey now has a customs union with Europe. Another type of association agreement links the remaining EFTA nations with the European Union. These agreements

---

[117]   *See* Section 15.2.

originally provided for industrial free trade and symbolize an historic reconciliation of the EU (then EEC) and EFTA trading alliances in 1973. A much broader European Economic Area agreement now governs EU-EFTA trade relations.[118]

Relations between the Union and the EFTA states—with the exception of Switzerland—were put on a new footing with the entry into force of the Agreement on the European Economic Area[119] in 1994. The EEA establishes a free trade area larger than NAFTA[120] and, in addition, provides that the four fundamental freedoms of the internal market of the Union (free movement of goods, persons, services and capital) as well as the competition rules and certain horizontal policies (social policy, consumer protection, environment, statistics and company law) are applied throughout the EEA area.[121] The EFTA states had to adopt the "acquis communautaire", *i.e.* the established EU law in all these areas. A special EFTA Surveillance Authority was set up with powers similar to those of the Commission, and also an EFTA Court, resembling the European Court of Justice. However, the EEA Agreement did not create a customs union, thus there is no common external customs tariff. Excluded are also such sensitive subjects like agriculture, fisheries and economic and monetary policy. The lasting importance of the EEA Agreement is difficult to assess since several EFTA countries joined the EU in 1995,[122] and it now applies only to Norway, Iceland and Lichtenstein.

Mediterranean Policy

Still another type of association agreement involves pursuit of what the EU refers to as its "Mediterranean Policy." This policy acknowledges the geographic proximity and importance of Mediterranean basin nations to the Union. The Mediterranean is viewed as a European sphere of influence. Most of these association agreements grant trade preferences (including substantial duty free EU entry) and economic aid to Mediterranean nations *without* requiring reciprocal, preferential access for Union goods. Agreements of this type have been concluded with Algeria, Morocco, Tunisia, Egypt, Jordan, Lebanon, Syria, Israel, the former Yugoslavia, Malta and Cyprus. These agreements are not at all uniform. They may be asymmetrical free trade agreements with the

---

[118]   See R. Folsom, *Principles of European Union Law*, Chapter 1.

[119]   O.J. L 1/3 (January 3, 1994).

[120]   See R. Folsom, *NAFTA, Free Trade and Foreign Investment in the Americas.*

[121]   The EEA area in 1994 comprised the EU and Austria, Finland, Iceland, Norway, Sweden and Liechtenstein.

[122]   Finland, Sweden and Austria have done so. This leaves only Iceland, Norway and Liechtenstein as parties to the EEA.

final goal of a customs union (Malta, Cyprus), or without such goal (Israel, Maghreb countries) or simple cooperation agreements (e.g. Egypt). In 1995, Europe and these partners declared an intent to create a Mediterranean industrial free trade zone by 2010. Since then, EU trade agreements in the Mediterranean basin have moved significantly towards reciprocal trade preferences.

Central and Eastern Europe

Because the former Soviet Union and its European satellites refused for many years to even recognize the European Community (now Union), some bilateral trade and cooperation agreements between those nations and the member states continue in place. It was not until 1988 that official relations between the Union and COMECON were initiated. As more democracy has taken hold, first generation trade and aid ("Partnership and Cooperation") agreements were concluded by the EU with Hungary, Poland, the Czech and Slovak Federal Republic, Bulgaria and nearly every other Central European nation. Similar agreements were concluded with the Baltic states, Slovenia, Albania, Russia, Ukraine and other former Soviet nations.

The Union advanced to second generation "association agreements" with some of these countries. These are known as "Europe Agreements." They anticipate substantial adoption of EU law on product standards, the environment, competition, telecommunications, financial services, broadcasting, and a host of other areas. Free movement of workers is not provided. Free trading will emerge over a ten-year period with special protocols on sensitive products like steel, textiles and agricultural goods. More fundamentally, these agreements are clearly focused on the eventual incorporation of these countries into the Union, as many did in 2005 along with Romania and Bulgaria in 2007.

With respect to the former USSR, the basis of the relationship between the EU and the Commonwealth of Independent States initially was the Trade and Cooperation Agreement of 1989 concluded with the Soviet Union. This agreement has been replaced by bilateral Partnership and Cooperation Agreements. The negotiations with Ukraine were concluded in March 1994, with Kazakhstan and Kyrgyzstan in May 1994, with Russia in June 1994, and with Moldova in July 1994. These new agreements laid down the framework for future commercial and economic cooperation and created a new legal basis for the development of trade and investment links. For example, the agreement with Russia on trade and trade-related issues removed all quotas and other quantitative restrictions on Russian exports to the European Union, with the exception of certain textile and steel products. In

2004, responding to the admission of 10 new EU member states, Russia and the European Union concluded a Partnership agreement. Customs duties on cargo shipments between Russia its Kaliningrad enclave on the Baltic Sea are dropped, tariffs generally lowered, Russian steel quotas increased and EU antidumping duties relaxed. The European Union has also promised to guarantee language rights for the Russian-speaking minorities in Estonia and Latvia.

Russia has become increasingly concerned with the eastern drift of EU memberships. It is organizing its own Eurasian Economic Union to counterbalance EU expansion. Belarus, Kazakhstan and Armenia have signed on. Ukraine, Moldova and Georgia, on the other hand, are expected to become EU associates and eventually members.

§ 18.10   EU Lomé/Cotonou Conventions, Economic Partnership Agreements

The 1957 Treaty of Rome, in a section entitled the "association of overseas territories and countries," was intended to preserve the special trading and development preferences that came with "colonial" status. France, Belgium, Italy and The Netherlands still had a substantial number of these relationships. Article 200 TFEU completely abolished (after a transitional period) tariffs on goods coming from associated overseas territories and countries. There is no duty on the part of these regions to reciprocate with duty free access to their markets for EU goods. Although some territories continue to exist (*e.g.*, French territories like Polynesia, New Caledonia, Guadeloupe, Martinique, etc.), most of the once associated overseas colonies are now independent nations. This is true as well for most of the former colonies of Britain, Denmark, Portugal and Spain.

As independence arrived throughout Asia, Africa and elsewhere, new conventions of association were employed by the EU as a form of developmental assistance. The first of these were the Yaoundé Conventions (1964 and 1971) with newly independent French-speaking African states. These conventions were in theory free trade agreements, but the African states could block almost any EU export and the Union in turn could protect itself from agricultural imports that threatened its Common Agricultural Policy. A healthy amount of financial and technical aid from the Union was thrown into the bargain.

Participating ACP States

When Britain joined in 1973, it naturally wished to preserve as many of the Commonwealth trade preferences as it could. The Yaoundé Conventions were already in place favoring former French colonies south of the Sahara. The compromise was the creation of a new convention, the first Lomé Convention (1975), to expand the Yaoundé principles to developing Caribbean and Pacific as well as English-speaking African nations. The fourth Lomé Convention (1990) governed trade and aid between the EU and a large number of African, Caribbean and Pacific (ACP) states. Lomé IV was replaced in 2000 by the Cotonou Agreement, which will operate for 20 years. The Cotonou nations presently include: Angola, Antigua & Barbuda, Bahamas, Barbados, Belize, Benin, Botswana, Burkina Faso, Burundi, Cameroon, Cape Verde, Central African Republic, Chad, Comoros, Congo, Djibouti, Dominica, Dominican Republic, Equatorial Guinea, Eritrea, Ethiopia, Fiji, Gabon, Gambia, Ghana, Grenada, Guinea, Guinea Bissau, Guyana, Haiti, Ivory Coast, Jamaica, Kenya, Kiribati, Lesotho, Liberia, Madagascar, Malawi, Mali, Mauritania, Mauritius, Mozambique, Namibia, Niger, Nigeria, Niue, Palau, Papua New Guinea, Rwanda, St. Christopher & Nevis, St. Lucia, St. Vincent & The Grenadines, Samoa, Sao Tomé & Principe, Senegal, Seychelles, Sierra Leone, Solomon Islands, Somalia, South Africa, Sudan, Suriname, Swaziland, Tanzania, Togo, Tonga, Trinidad & Tobago, Tuvalu, Uganda, Vanuatu, Zambia and Zimbabwe.

Perhaps the most important feature of this lengthy listing is the developing nations that are *not* Cotonou Convention participants. Unless they fall within the Union's Mediterranean Policy, they are apt to perceive the Lomé/Cotonou Conventions as highly discriminatory against their exports and economic interests.

Contents

Unlike the Yaoundé Conventions, the Lomé Conventions did not create (even in theory) reciprocal free trading relationships. While the Lomé states retained substantial duty free access to the Common Market, the Union obtained no comparable benefit. The Lomé nations did promise not to discriminate in trading among EU countries and to grant EU member states most-favored-nation benefits. This meant, in practice, that they were free to block imports from the EU whenever desired. This one-sided relationship was continued temporarily under the Cotonou Agreement through 2008. Thereafter six regionally organized economic partnership agreements mutually embracing free trade were established, to be fully implemented by 2020. It is hoped that each region will internally adopt free trade principles. A variety of "development" preferences are also granted by the Union in the Cotonou Convention. These include expensive purchasing obligations on sugar, for example. There is no free movement of persons as between the ACP states and the Union. However, whenever such persons are lawfully resident and working in the other's territories, they must be given national treatment rights.

Most significantly, the Cotonou nations now participate in two innovative EU mechanisms designed to stabilize their agricultural and mineral commodity export earnings. These programs are known as STABEX and MINEX (also known as SYSMIN). STABEX covers (*inter alia*) ground nuts, cocoa, coffee, cotton, coconut, palm, rawhides, leather and wood products, and tea. MINEX deals with copper, phosphates, bauxite, alumina, manganese, iron ore, and tin. These programs are an acknowledgement of the economic dependence of many Lomé nations on commodity exports for very large portions of their hard currency earnings.

Some have argued vigorously that STABEX and MINEX perpetuate rather than relieve this dependence. Both programs provide loans and grants in aid to Lomé nations who have experienced significant declines in export earnings because of falling commodity prices, crop failures and the like. The greater the dependency and decline, the larger the EU financial transfers. These sums are not, for the most part, tied to reinvestment in the commodity sectors causing their payment, nor to the purchase of Union products or technology. In a world where most development aid is tied (*i.e.*, must usually be spent on the donor's products or projects), STABEX and MINEX represent a different approach. Many Latin American nations have lobbied the United States to create similar mechanisms for their commodities.

The Lomé IV Convention (1990) added several new features carried over under the Cotonou Agreement (2000). The European Union now financially supports structural adjustments in ACP states, including remedies for balance of payments difficulties, debt burdens, budget deficits, and public enterprises. Cultural and social cooperation, trade in services, and environmental issues are also addressed. For example, an agreement not to ship toxic and radioactive waste was reached. The Convention builds upon earlier provisions by specifying protected human rights such as equal treatment, civil and political liberty, and economic, social and cultural rights. Financial support from the EU is given to ACP nations that promote human rights and has been withheld after military coups.

The one-way nature of ACP trade benefits is inconsistent with WTO obligations. The EU has therefore undertaken to negotiate two-way "Economic Partnership Agreements" with six groupings of ACP states. The first such EPA was finalized in 2008 with 13 Caribbean nations. Duties on nearly all European exports will be phased out by 2033, trade in services is eased, and procurement as well as investment rules are established.

§ 18.11   Duty Free Access to the EU Common Market

The end-game so far as exporters to the European Union are concerned is unlimited duty free access. Except for raw materials, few North American exports will qualify for such treatment. However, subsidiaries based in developing or EFTA nations may achieve this goal. This is possible because of the Union's adherence to the GSP program, its Mediterranean basin trade agreements, the Lomé/Cotonou Conventions, and the EEA Agreement with certain EFTA countries. It may also be possible to ship goods produced in Central and East European nations duty free into the EU under the "second generation" trade agreements. All of these topics have been previously discussed. There are, of course, exceptions and controls (quotas, NTBs) that may apply under these programs. Nevertheless, the Common Market is so lucrative that careful study of its external trade rules is warranted.

Such studies can realize unusually advantageous trade situations. For example, many developing nations are Lomé Convention participants or GSP beneficiaries. The goods of some of these nations are also entitled to duty free access to the United States market under the U.S. version of the GSP program,[123] the Caribbean Basin Economic Recovery Act (1983),[124] the Andean Trade Preference Act (1991) or various U.S. free trade agreements. *See* Chapters 2 and 16. A producer strategically located in such a nation (*e.g.*, Jamaica) can have the best of both worlds, duty free access to the European Union and the United States. The same applies for Israel which not only has a free-trade agreement with the Union but also with the United States. Since 2000, this ideal outcome is most importantly available via Mexico, which is a member of NAFTA and has a free trade agreement with the European Union. Canada seems close to a free trade deal with the EU. And, in 2013, the U.S. commenced negotiations with the EU on a Transatlantic Trade and Investment Partnership Agreement.

---

[123]   19 U.S.C.A. § 2461.
[124]   19 U.S.C.A. § 2701.

Chapter 19

EU BUSINESS COMPETITION (ANTITRUST) LAW

Table of Sections

The material that follows highlights EU Business Competition Law's impact on international trade. Broader and more detailed coverage can be found in R. Folsom, *Principles of European Union Law*, Chapter 7.

§ 19.1   Introduction

The primary purpose of competition policy (called antitrust law and policy in the States) in the European Union is preservation of the trade and other benefits of economic integration. The removal of governmental trade barriers unaccompanied by measures to ensure that businesses do not recreate those barriers would be an incomplete effort. For example, competing enterprises might agree to geographically allocate markets to each other, making the elimination of national tariffs and quotas by the Treaty on the Functioning of the European Union (TFEU) irrelevant. Similarly, a dominant enterprise in one state might tie up all important distributors or purchasers of its goods through long-term exclusive dealing contracts. The result could make entry into that market by another business exceedingly difficult. By assisting in the formation and maintenance of an economic union, business competition law is an important component in EU competition policy. It prevents enterprise behavior from becoming a substantial nontariff trade barrier to economic integration. In contrast, coverage of competition law and policy under NAFTA is cosmetic and devoid of institutional force.

The secondary purpose of European Union competition policy is not unique to regional integration. This purpose is the attainment of the economic benefits generally thought to accrue in any economy organized on a competitive basis. These benefits are many. Perhaps most important of all, an economy characterized by competitive enterprise answers the questions of economic organization by maximizing the market desires of its human constituents. A genuinely competitive market is responsive to individual choice in a way that acknowledges and promotes diversity. Competition among businesses protects the public interest in having its cumulative demand for goods and services provided at the lowest possible prices and with the greatest possible degree of response to public tastes. It is in this sense that a competitive economy is said to be guided by the principle of "consumer welfare or consumer sovereignty." When, for example, EU law prevents competing enterprises from fixing prices for their goods or prevents a dominant enterprise from charging monopoly prices at the consumers' expense, such law helps to realize the economic benefits of competition within the Euro-economy.

The Maastricht Treaty on European Union added provisions to the TFEU focused specifically on industrial competitiveness. The Union will promote a system of open and competitive markets by accelerating structural change, encouraging enterprise initiatives, fostering business cooperation and supporting innovation, research and development. However, Article 173 indicates that this authority may not result in "any measure which could lead to a distortion of competition."

§ 19.2 Article 101—Restraints of Trade

Article 101(1) TFEU deals with concerted business practices, business agreements and trade association decisions. Such business activities are deemed incompatible with the Common Market and are prohibited when they have the potential to affect trade between member states *and* have the object or effect of preventing, restricting or distorting competition *within* the Union. The focus of Article 101(1) is thus on cartels. By way of example, Article 101(1) lists certain prohibited activities:

(1)   The fixing of prices or trading conditions;

(2)   The limitation of production, markets, technical development or investment;

(3)   The sharing of markets or sources of supply;

(4)   The application of unequal terms to equivalent transactions, creating competitive disadvantages; and

(5)   The conditioning of a contract on the acceptance of commercially unrelated additional supplies (tying arrangements).

Article 101(1) has been used to review and challenge a wide range of anticompetitive business activities, some of which are not listed above. These activities include joint buying,[1] joint selling,[2] joint ventures and strategic alliances,[3] and data exchanges[4] among horizontal competitors. They also include an even wider range of activities between vertically related suppliers, manufacturers and franchisee/licensee/distributors.[5]

Void Agreements

Article 101(2) voids agreements and decisions prohibited by Article 101(1). Thus the prohibitions of Article 101(1) against anticompetitive activity are absolute and immediately effective under 101(2) without prior judicial or administrative action. The open-ended text of Article 101(1) gives considerable leeway for interpretation and enforcement purposes. It has, for example, been interpreted to cover nonbinding "gentlemen's agreements."[6] Trade association "recommendations" influencing competition are caught.[7] It also generates considerable uncertainty as to the validity of many

---

[1]   *See Intergroup (SPAR)* Commission Decision 75/482, O.J. L 212/23 (Aug. 9, 1975).

[2]   *See* Kali & Salz AG v. Commission (1975) Eur.Comm.Rep. 499.

[3]   *See AEG/Alcatel*, Commission Decision 90/46, O.J. L. 32/16 (Feb. 3, 1990); *Elopak*, Commission Decision 90/410, O.J. L 209/15 (Aug. 8, 1990); European Night Services v. Commission (1998) Eur.Comm.Rep. II–3141.

[4]   *See* John Deere Ltd. v. Commission (1998) Eur.Comm.Rep. I–3111.

[5]   *See* Sections 19.6, 19.7, and 19.9.

[6]   ACF Chemiefarma v. Commission (1970) Eur.Comm.Rep. 661.

[7]   Verband der Sachversicherer v. Commission (1987) Eur.Comm.Rep. 405; Re ANSEAU–NAVEWA (1983) Eur.Comm.Rep. 3369.

business agreements, since full market analyses of their competitive and trade impact are often required.[8]

Exemptions

Article 101(3) permits Article 101(1) to be declared inapplicable when agreements, decisions, concerted practices or classes thereof:

(1) Contribute to the improvement of the production or distribution of goods, or to the promotion of technical or economic progress; while

(2) Reserving to consumers an equitable share of the resulting benefits; and neither

(3) Impose any restrictions not indispensable to objectives 1 and 2 (*i.e.,* least restrictive means must be used);[9] nor

(4) Make it possible for the businesses concerned to substantially eliminate competition.

The prohibitions of Article 101(1) may be tempered by "declarations of inapplicability" (exemptions) only when the circumstances of Article 101(3) are present. As befits exemptions from broad prohibitions, the terms of 101(3) are more narrow and specific. Article 101(3) and Article 101(1) legal issues are often considered simultaneously in the process of analyzing the market impact of restrictive agreements, decisions and concerted practices. The overall net result resembles the "rule of reason" approach found in United States antitrust law.[10] Since May 1, 2004, Article 101(3) is directly effective law, opening up the possibility of its application by national courts and authorities as well as the Commission.

§ 19.3   Commission Investigations, Attorney-Client Privilege, Shared Prosecutorial Powers

In March of 1962 the Council of Ministers adopted Regulation 17 on the basis of proposals from the Commission. Regulation 17 was the major piece of secondary law under Articles 81 and 82 (now 101 and 102 TFEU). Effective May 1, 2004, Regulation 17 was replaced by Regulation 1/ 2003. These regulations establish the scheme of enforcement for competition law. The Commission, for the most part its Competition Directorate-General, acquires a wide range of powers.

---

8   *See* Section 19.3.

9   Grundig, O.J. 1994 L 20/15, 21.

10   See Peeters, The Rule of Reason Revisited: Prohibition on Restraints of Competition in the Sherman Act and the EEC Treaty, 37 Am.J.Comp.L. 521 (1989).

Commission Investigations

The regulations confer investigatory powers in the Commission to conduct general studies into economic sectors and to review the affairs of individual businesses and trade associations. The Commission may investigate in response to a complaint or upon its own initiative. These powers are particularly significant because (except in the case of mergers) notification of restrictive agreements, decisions and practices to the Commission, although at times beneficial, is not mandatory. The Commission may request all information *it* considers necessary, and examine and make copies of record books and business documents. The Commission decides upon whether the information it obtains in competition law investigations and proceedings contains "business secrets" and whether to release that information.[11] There is some suggestion that release may be obtained by plaintiffs before national courts in civil actions for damages caused by cartel activities.[12] However, the Court of Justice has ruled that the Commission must give the information source notice and an opportunity to challenge these decisions.[13]

In conducting its investigations, the Commission may ask for verbal explanations on the spot and have access to and seal off business premises. One author refers to these powers as "dawn raids and other nightmares." Nevertheless, the Court of Justice has affirmed this right of hostile access.[14] Effective May 1, 2004, subject to the issuance of a local court warrant, this right of access extends to private homes, motor vehicles and other personal property of corporate directors, managers and staff. In these matters the Commission acts on its own authority. It must, however, inform member states prior to taking such steps and may request their assistance. The member states must render assistance when businesses fail to comply with competition law investigations conducted by the Commission. Although the Commission may require production of all necessary information in its competition law investigations, it may not force firms to answer questions which could lead to actual admissions of infringement.[15] Information

---

[11] *See* Samenwerkende lektriciteits-produktiebedrijven NV v. Commission (1994) Eur.Comm.Rep. I–01911 (Case C–36/92).

[12] Pfleiderer v. Bundeskartellamt, (2011) Eur. Comm. Rep. ___ (Case C–360/09).

[13] AKZO Chemie BV v. Commission (1986) Eur.Comm.Rep. 1965.

[14] Hoeschst v. Commission (1987) Eur.Comm.Rep. 1549; Dow Chemical Nederland BV v. Commission (1987) Eur.Comm.Rep. 4367; NV Samenwerkende lectriciteits-produktiebedrijven (SEP) v. Commission (1991) Eur.Comm.Rep. II 649 (Case T–39/90).

[15] Orkem v. Commission (1989) Eur.Comm.Rep. 3283. However, this principle does not necessarily apply to civil proceedings before the courts of the member states.

provided to the Commission as part of an EU competition law investigation may not generally be used by member states to commence enforcement proceedings under their own competition laws.[16]

Businesses involved in the Commission's investigatory process have limited rights to notice and hearing.[17] They do not have access to the Commission's files. Any failure on the part of an enterprise to provide information requested by the Commission or to submit to its investigation can result in the imposition of considerable fines and penalties. For example, the Belgian and French subsidiaries of the Japanese electrical and electronic group, Matsushita, were fined by the Commission for supplying it with false information about whether Matsushita recommended retail prices for its products. These sanctions are civil in nature and run against the corporation, not its directors or management.

The Commission has been increasing the use of its investigatory powers. Several procedural requirements for Commission investigations and hearings have been discussed by the Court of Justice. One notable Court decision upheld the authority of the Commission to conduct searches of corporate offices without notice or warrant when it has reason to believe that pertinent evidence may be lost.[18] Another notable decision permitted a Swiss "whistle blower" who once worked for Hoffmann–La Roche (a defendant in EU competition law proceedings) to sue the Union in tort for disclosure of his identity as an informant.[19]

Attorney-Client Privileges

Written communications with external lawyers licensed in an EU member state undertaken for defense purposes are confidential and need not be disclosed.[20] Written communications with in-house lawyers are *not* exempt from disclosure, nor are communications with external *non*-EU counsel.[21] Thus communications with North

---

Otto, (1993) Eur.Comm.Rep. I-05683 (Case No. C-60/92). In such cases, the right against self-incrimination depends on national law.

[16]   Dirección General de Defensa de la Competencia (DGDC) v. Asociación Espaola de Banca Privada (AEB) & ORS (1992) Eur.Comm.Rep. I-4785 (Case C-67/91).

[17]   Commission Regulation 99/63. *See generally* Hoffmann–La Roche v. Commission (1979) Eur.Comm.Rep. 461.

[18]   Re National Panasonic (1980) Eur.Comm.Rep. 2033.

[19]   Adams v. Commission (1985) Eur.Comm.Rep. 3539.

[20]   AM & S Europe Ltd. v. Commission (1982) Eur.Comm.Rep. 1575. *Accord*, Akzo Nobel Chemicals Ltd v. Commission, (2007) Eur.Comm.Rep. II-3523 (documents) and Akzo Nobel v. Commission, (2009) Eur.Comm.Rep. ___ (emails received in EU subject to EU rules); Akzo Nobel Chemicals Ltd. v. Akcros, (2010) Eur. Comm. Rep. ___ (C-48/09) (internal company communications with in-house lawyers).

[21]   *Id.*

American attorneys (who are not also EU licensed attorneys) are generally discoverable. For example, shortly after the *AM & S* decision, the Commission obtained in-house counsel documents from John Deere, Inc., a Belgian subsidiary of the United States multinational. These documents were drafted as advice to management on how to avoid EU competition liability for export prohibition restraints. They were used by the Commission to justify the finding of an intentional Article 101 violation and a fine of 2 million EUROs.[22] United States attorneys have followed these developments with amazement and trepidation. Disclaimers of possible non-confidentiality are one option to consider in dealing with clients on EU law matters. At a minimum, U.S. attorneys ought to advise their clients that the usual rules on attorney-client privilege may not apply and always consider involving a U.S. attorney throughout.

Shared Powers

Regulation 17 and Regulation 1 envision significant cooperation between European Union and national authorities in the field of competition law. Effective May 1, 2004, enforcement of Articles 101 and 102 is shared with the competition agencies and national courts of the member states. A new European Competition Network has been established to facilitate cooperative law enforcement and minimize divergent application of competition law principles, with the Commission to act as final arbiter on substantive matters. The principal reason for this sharing of enforcement duties is to allow the Commission to focus its energies on price fixing, cartel arrangements and other serious violations of Articles 101 and 102.

The Commission is not under an affirmative duty to carry out an investigation when a complaint is submitted to it.[23] The Court of First Instance (now the General Court) ruled that the Commission can refuse to pursue a competition law complaint if an adequate remedy is available from a national court.[24] This decision supports the Commission's customary practice of decentralized "subsidiarity" in the competition law field. Of course, subsidiarity carries with it the potential for the inconsistent application of the competition rules. The ECJ has construed the power of national courts to enforce EU competition law narrowly. Since May 1, 2004, national courts may ask the Commission for support regarding Article 101 or 102, with the Commission and national authorities empowered to

---

[22]   John Deere O.J. 1985 L. 35/58. Accord, AKZO Nobel Chemicals v. Commission, (EC Commission) T-125/03, T-253/03.

[23]   BEUC v. Commission, (2000) Eur.Comm.Rep. II-00101.

[24]   Automec SRL v. Commission (1992) Eur.Comm.Rep. II-367.

file opinions with the national courts. Moreover, in all cases affecting member state trade, Regulation 1/2003 permits the Commission to issue *ex ante* binding decisions determining that a particular agreement or practice does not infringe European competition law. Such decisions would preclude different results at the national level. For an example of arguably different results in analogous situations, an example which casts doubt on Regulation 1 cooperation, see *Intrepreneur Pub Co CPC v. Crehan.*[25] The Commission has taken to regularly monitoring decisions of national competition law authorities and courts involving Articles 101 and 102.

§ 19.4   Commission Prosecutions, Immunity and Sanctions

Enforcement Procedures

In addition to its investigatory powers, the Commission determines when violations of the competition law provisions of Article 101 or 102 occur. This is the source of the Commission's power to render enforcement decisions. A regulation limits the time period in which the Commission may render a decision in competition law cases to five years. All Commission decisions, including enforcement decisions and decisions to investigate, fine or penalize must be published and are subject to judicial review. Since 1989, most of these appeals are heard by the General Court. During interim periods, the Commission has the power to order measures indispensable to its functions.[26] Interim relief should be granted when there is prima facie evidence of an Article 101 or 102 violation and an urgent need to prevent serious and irreparable private damage (or intolerable damage to the public interest).[27]

Any measures the Commission takes must, however, be temporary and conservatory in nature, restricted to what is required in the given situation, and take into account the legitimate interests of the enterprise which is the subject of the interim measures.[28] La Cinq, a private television service twice denied membership in the European Broadcasting Union, successfully met these criteria. The General Court rebuked the Commission's refusal to grant provisional Article 102 protection.[29] Before deciding that a competition law breach has occurred, the Commission issues a

---

[25]   2006 U.K. House of Lords 38 (July 19, 2006) reviewed at 32 Eur. Law Rev. 260 (April 2007).

[26]   Camera Care v. Commission (1980) Eur.Comm.Rep. 119.

[27]   Sea Containers v. Stena Sealink, O.J. L 15 (1994) 8, 15 point 56.

[28]   *Id.*

[29]   La Cinq v. Commission (1992) Eur.Comm.Rep. II-1.

statement of "objections."[30] This statement must reveal which facts the Commission intends to rely upon in reaching a decision that a violation has occurred and be worded with sufficient clarity to enable the parties to know what conduct is being objected to.[31]

A hearing can then be requested by the alleged violator(s) or any interested person.[32] These hearings are conducted in private, with separate reviews of complainants and witnesses. The Commission must disclose only those non-confidential documents in its file upon which it intends to rely and are necessary to prepare an adequate defense.[33] The parties generally receive, along with the statement of objections, a list of all the documents in the Commission's possession with an indication of the documents or parts of documents to which they may have access. Among the documents generally regarded as confidential, and therefore inaccessible, are internal Commission documents such as memoranda, drafts and other working papers.[34] After the hearing, the Commission consults with the Advisory Committee on Restrictive Practices and Monopolies, which is composed of one civil servant expert from each member state. The results of this consultation are not made public. Having consulted the Committee, the Commission is then free to render an enforcement decision.

Sanctions and Immunity

In its enforcement decision, the Commission may require businesses to "cease and desist" their infringing activities. The Commission may not, at least in an Article 101 proceeding, require a violator to contract with the complainant.[35] In practice, this power has sufficed to permit the Commission to order infringing enterprises to come up with their own remedial solutions. However, the Commission may not, at least in Article 101 proceedings, require a violator to contract with the complainant. Daily penalties may be imposed to compel adherence to the order to cease and desist. Commission decisions on violations of Articles 101 and 102 are also accompanied by a capacity to substantially fine any intentionally or negligently infringing enterprise. Fines may be based on up to 30 percent of annual sales, multiplied by the number of years of infringement. When appeals are lodged against Commission decisions imposing fines and penalties, payment is

---

[30]   Regulation 99/63, Article 2(4).

[31]   AEG v. Commission (1983) Eur.Comm.Rep. 3151.

[32]   Regulation 99/63, Article 7.

[33]   VBVB and VBBB v. Commission (1984) Eur.Comm.Rep. 19.

[34]   23rd Report on Competition Policy (1994) point 353.

[35]   Automec SRL v. Commission (1992) Eur.Comm.Rep. II–367. *Compare* Article 86 Case law on refusals to deal by dominant firms in Section 7.20.

suspended but interest is charged and a bank guarantee for the amounts concerned must be provided.[36]

In the early years, fines and penalties actually levied by the Commission were few, relatively small in amount, and frequently reduced on appeal to the Court of Justice. As EU competition law doctrine has become clearer, these trends have all been reversed. In its more recent decisions, the Court has upheld substantial fines and penalties imposed by the Commission in competition law proceedings and recognized their deterrent value.[37] The trend towards larger fines has been confirmed by the Commission in recent cases, with immunity or reduced fines granted to firms that "confess" first, or early, in EU competition law proceedings. The Commission has imposed substantial fines on cartels in the chemicals industry,[38] the carton industry[39] and the steel industry.[40]

In 2001, the Commission imposed competition law fines of more than 850 million Euros on European companies for conspiring to fix prices and divide up the vitamins market. Fines against other cartels have ratcheted up since Regulation 1 took effect in 2004, hitting *inter alia* producers of industrial bags, copper fittings, fasteners, hydrogen peroxide, acrylic glass, car glass, synthetic rubber, gas insulated switches, and lifts and escalators. Challenges to EU cartel fines based on the EU Fundamental Freedoms Charter and the European Convention on Human Rights are pending.

More recently, the Commission has granted total immunity to the first cartel participant to confess and provide material evidence. The second participant to "provide significant value" to an investigation can secure a 30 to 50 percent reduction in fines. Third and subsequent confessors may receive lesser reductions. Hence, there are strong incentives to be first in the confessional queue. U.S. chip maker Micron Technology, for example, escaped all fines by being the whistle blower on a global price-fixing chip cartel.

Any complete picture of the development of Article 101 must include the Commission's informal negotiations as well as its decisions to prosecute, exempt or clear infringing activities. Compliance with Articles 101 and 102 is often achieved short of a formal Commission decision. Word of informal file-closings is occasionally revealed. In *Re Eurofima,* for example, the Commission terminated proceedings without issuing a decision. In the process of

---

[36]   Hasselblad v. Commission (1982) Eur.Comm.Rep. 1555.

[37]   *See* Musique Diffusion Française SA v. Commission (1983) Eur.Comm.Rep. 1825.

[38]   PVC, O.J. 1994 L 239/14.

[39]   Cartonboard, O.J. 1994 L 243/1.

[40]   Steel Beams, O.J. 1994 L 116/1.

responding to complaints from suppliers, the Commission was able to secure termination of infringing conduct from Eurofima, the most important buyer of railway rolling stock in the Union. Eurofima also undertook to continue to comply with EU competition law. The Commission announced these results in a press release.[41]

§ 19.5 Group Exemptions and Notices

The Commission received an onslaught of negative clearance requests and Article 101(3) notifications in 1962 when Regulation 17 took effect. The vast majority of the business activities involved in this deluge were in the distribution and licensing areas. As a result, the Commission sought and obtained authorization in 1965 from the Council to formulate, for limited time periods, group "declarations of inapplicability" under Article 101(3).[42] These are commonly known as "group or block exemptions." The Council granted this authorization, noting that Article 101(3) allows "classes" of exempt agreements. Group exemptions invite businesses to conform their agreements and behavior to their terms and conditions. In other words, group exemptions rely upon confidential business self-regulation.

Another important indication of permissible business practices are the various notices and guidelines which the Commission has issued. However, in contrast to the group exemptions, these notices are mere policy declarations and have no legally binding effect on the national courts or the European courts. Nonetheless, the notices provide an important indication of the Commission's policy toward certain practices and it is unlikely that the Commission will impose fines on businesses which have relied in good faith on the pronouncements of the Commission in one of its notices.[43] Competition law notices issued by the Commission have concerned agreements of "minor" importance,[44] horizontal cooperation agreements,[45] exclusive agency contracts,[46] and technology sharing agreements among small and medium-sized businesses.[47] Many business agreements are drafted with the details of these group exemption regulations and policy notices in mind.

---

[41]   (1973) Common Mkt.L.Rep. D217.

[42]   Regulation 19/65.

[43]   In fact, the Commission may be estopped from imposing fines in such cases. *See* Miller v. Commission (1978) Eur.Comm.Rep. 131, 158.

[44]   1986 Official Journal C231/2, revised O.J. C 368/07 (Dec. 22, 2001).

[45]   2011 Official Journal C11/1.

[46]   1962 Official Journal 2921.

[47]   1979 Official Journal C1/2.

After a number of test enforcement decisions and definitive rulings by the Court of Justice, the Commission issued Regulation 67 in 1967. It became the first of a series of group exemptions from Article 101(1). Group exemptions now exist for vertical restraints (including distribution and franchise agreements),[48] vehicle distribution and servicing agreements,[49] production specialization agreements among small firms,[50] research and development agreements among small firms,[51] and technology transfer agreements.[52] In addition there are a number of group exemptions which are directed at specific sectors of the economy. These include most notably the insurance sector[53] and the transport sector.[54]

§ 19.6 EU Commercial Agent and Distribution Agreements, Vertical Restraints Regulation

Commercial Agents

Council Directive 86/653 coordinates member state laws regarding self-employed commercial agents. This directive was inspired by existing French and German law. In Denmark and Britain new legislation was required for its implementation. From a United States perspective, the directive is remarkably protective of the agent. It is particularly significant because many North American firms first do business in Europe through commercial agents. The directive defines a commercial agent as a "self-employed intermediary who has continuing authority to negotiate the purchase or sale of goods on behalf of another person (the principal), or to negotiate and conclude such transactions on behalf of and in the name of that principal."

Directive 86/653 establishes various rights and obligations for commercial agents and principals, e.g., the agent's duty to comply with reasonable instructions and the principal's duty to act in good faith. In the absence of an agreed compensation, customary local practices prevail (and if none, reasonable remuneration). Compensation may apparently be by commission or salary. Compensation rights before and after the effective period of the agency contract are specified. Directive 86/653 also establishes when the agent's commission becomes due and payable, as well as the conditions under which it is extinguishable. For example, the

---

[48]   Regulation 2790/99. See Section 19.6.
[49]   Regulation 461/2010.
[50]   Regulation 1218/2010.
[51]   Regulation 1217/2010.
[52]   Regulation 772/2004. See Section 19.7.
[53]   Regulation 3932/92, replaced by Regulation 358/2003.
[54]   Regulation 1617/93; Regulation 83/91.

agent is entitled to a compensation on all transactions in which he or she participated. Moreover, transactions that have been concluded during the term of the agreement with third parties the agent previously procured as customers for the principal fall within this rule. The agent is also entitled to compensation on transactions with customers located in his or her area of responsibility or for whom the agent is an exclusive representative.

Termination Rights

An important element concerns the notice and termination rights of the agent. Agency agreements for fixed periods of time that continue to be performed by both parties upon expiration become contracts for an indefinite period. Minimum termination notice requirements of one month per year of service up to three years, and optional notice requirements up to six months for six years are created. The member states must provide for either a right of indemnification or for damages compensation, which must be claimed within one year of termination. The agency agreement cannot waive or otherwise "derogate" these rights. The indemnity cannot exceed one year's remuneration but does not foreclose damages. The indemnity is payable if the agent has brought in new customers or increased volumes with existing customers to the substantial continuing benefit of the principal and is equitable in light of all circumstances.

The right to damages as a result of termination occurs when the agent is deprived of commissions which would have been earned upon proper performance to the substantial benefit of the principal. The agent may also seek damages relief when termination blocks amortization of the costs and expenses incurred on advice of the principal while performing under the agency contract. The death of the agent triggers these indemnity or compensation rights. They are also payable if the agent must terminate the contract because of age, infirmity or illness causing an inability to reasonably continue service. If an agency agreement chooses non-EU law to govern its terms, this choice of law will not override the agent's mandatory damages remedies.[55] No indemnity or damages may be had under specified circumstances, including when the agent is in default justifying immediate termination under national law. "Restraint of trade" clauses (covenants not to compete) are permissible upon termination to the extent that they are limited to two years, the goods in question and the geographic area and/or customers of the agent. Such clauses can be made a pre-condition to the payment of an indemnity.

---

[55] Ingmar GB v. Eaton Leonard Technologies, 2000 Eur.Comm.Rep. I–9305 (Nov. 9, 2000) (California choice of law clause).

Competition Law Applicability

A 1962 Commission Notice announced that agreements with "commercial agents" were outside Article 101(1) TFEU.[56] The theory behind exempting commercial agents from EU antitrust law was their "auxiliary function" on behalf of principals who were subject to the law. In *Flemish Travel Agents,*[57] however, the European Court of Justice ruled that the relationship between suppliers and independent commercial agents could present competitive implications under the Treaty. The 1962 Notice defines "commercial agents" as those who undertake for a specified territory to negotiate or conclude transactions on behalf of an enterprise either in their own name or in the name of that enterprise. The key to distinguishing agents from independent traders who are subject to Article 101 is whether the intermediary assumes any risk in the transaction, including nonpayment, title to a considerable inventory of products, liability for substantial services to customers, or control over prices or terms of sale. This definition of "commercial agents" has been somewhat narrowed by case law.[58]

In December 1990, the Commission released a draft of a new notice on commercial agency agreements. Under it, the Commission distinguishes between "integrated" agents dependent on the supplier and not generally subject to Article 101, and more independent "un-integrated" agents. An agent is "integrated" if he or she generally devotes at least one-third of the time to the principal and does not handle competing products. Certain restrictions apply even to integrated agents. For example, absolute bans on transactions with customers or suppliers outside designated territories may be prohibited. Nonintegrated agents are generally treated as independent traders subject to full review under Article 101.

Distribution Agreements

Regulation 67/67 was replaced in 1983 by Regulation 1983/83 (exclusive distribution) and Regulation 1984/83 (exclusive purchasing).[59] Exclusive dealing agreements ordinarily involve restrictions on manufacturers or suppliers and independent distributors of goods. These restraints concern persons the manufacturer may supply, to whom the manufacturer or distributor may sell, and from whom the distributor may acquire the goods or

---

[56]   1962 Official Journal 2921; *see* Section 19.1.

[57]   1987 Eur.Comm.Rep. 3801.

[58]   *See* Cooperative Vereniging "Suiker Unie" V.A. v. Commission, 1975 Eur.Comm.Rep. 1663.

[59]   *See* Delimitis v. Henninger Bräu (1991) Eur.Comm.Rep. I-935 (234/89) (Regulation 1984/83 applied extensively to beer-supply agreements).

similar goods. Exclusive dealing agreements should be distinguished from agency or consignment agreements where title and most risk remain with the manufacturer until the goods are sold by their retail agents to consumers. The announced EU policy position is that competition law will not require a manufacturer to compete with its agents.[60] Territorial exclusivity in genuine retail agency agreements is therefore legal.[61]

Regulation 67 and its successors may be seen as an excellent example of Commission efforts to employ and develop competition law under Article 81 (now 101 TFEU) to serve the goal of economic integration. The formation of absolute territorial trade barriers, similar in impact to national tariffs and quotas that existed prior to the creation of the Common Market, would negate some of the economic benefits of increased trade and economic integration. Yet to prohibit exclusive dealing entirely would deter Common Market sales by national manufacturers. Hence, distributive competition among goods for sale within the EU is encouraged by permitting exclusive dealing agreements between manufacturers and independent distributors *and* by insuring that competition as between exclusive dealers in the same goods is also preserved.

It is only *absolute* territorial exclusive dealing that precludes benefit from the group exemption. It is precluded whether achieved by the exercise of national patent, copyright or trademark rights, or simply by contractual restraints between manufacturers and their exclusive dealers. For example, when territorial protection for distributors is obtained by making slight changes to a product's content, this constitutes an Article 101 violation. Manufacturers and distributors may not seek product approvals which effectively divide up the common market in this manner.[62] Pharmaceutical distribution agreements have been given somewhat wider leeway to restrict the cross-border sale of drugs given differing government price caps.[63]

According to the Commission, vertical agreements must therefore be examined on two levels:

Firstly, the exclusive nature of a contractual relationship between a producer and a distributor is viewed as

---

[60] Notice on exclusive agency contracts made with commercial agents, O.J.1962, 2921.

[61] *But see* Re Pittsburgh Corning Europe (1973) Common Mkt.L.Rep. D2; Commission Announcement on Exclusive Agency Contracts Made with Commercial Agents, O.J. 1962, 2921.

[62] *See* Zera Montedison/Hinkins Staehler, O.J. 1993 L 272/28.

[63] *See* Sot. Lelos v. GlaxoSmithKline, 2008 Eur Comm. Rep I–7139 and GlaxoSmithKline v. Commission, 2006 Eur. Comm. Rep. II–02969.

restricting competition, since it limits the parties' freedom of action on the territory covered. Secondly, the agreement may normally be exempted under Article 101(3) of the Treaty if it does not contain any provisions that create absolute territorial protection for the distributor or, at any rate, does not objectively have such an effect.[64]

Export bans applied by manufacturers to their EU distributors have attracted sizeable fines and penalties under Article 101.[65] This outcome fosters intra-brand competition in ways which have largely been abandoned under United States antitrust law.[66]

Selective Distribution

Another form of distribution which is of practical importance is selective distribution. Although, in contrast to exclusive distribution and exclusive supply agreements, the Commission has not adopted a block exemption for selective distribution agreements,[67] there are certain rules which arise from the Commission's decisions and the case law. A selective distribution system exists where a supplier limits the number of approved distributors of its products based on particular criteria. Whether such a system infringes Article 101(1) depends largely on the criteria used and the justification for not supplying to certain distributors.

Generally, a selective distribution system will not infringe Article 101(1) if it is based on qualitative criteria, these criteria are objectively applied so that any qualifying distributor is admitted to the system, and it does not include any provisions which are likely to prohibit parallel imports.[68] A selective distribution system based on quantitative criteria, on the other hand, will likely infringe Article 101(1)[69] or if the nature of the products is such that a

---

[64]   23rd Report on Competition Policy (1994) point 212.

[65]   *See, e.g.,* John Deere & Co., 28 O.J. 1985 L 35/58 (fined two million ECU for violation of Article 81(1) for imposing, accepting or practicing bans on the export of its products by dealers or distributors to other member states); Sperry New Holland, a Division of Sperry Corp., 28 O.J. 1985 L 376/21 (fined 750,000 ECU for violation of Article 101(1) for imposing, accepting or practicing a ban on export of SNH products by dealers of distributors to other member states).

[66]   *Compare* Continental T.V., Inc. v. GTE Sylvania Inc., 433 U.S. 36, 97 S.Ct. 2549, 53 L.Ed.2d 568 (1977); Business Electronics Corp. v. Sharp Electronics Corp., 485 U.S. 717, 108 S.Ct. 1515, 99 L.Ed.2d 808 (1988).

[67]   The Commission however adopted in 1985 a block exemption applicable to selective distribution systems in the automobile sector, now as amended Regulation 1400/2002.

[68]   *See* Metro v. Commission, (1977) Eur.Comm.Rep. 1875; AEG v. Commission, (1983) Eur.Comm.Rep. 3151; Hasselblad v. Commission, (1984) Eur.Comm.Rep. 883; Grundig's distribution system, O.J.1994 L 20/15.

[69]   Ford v. Commission, (1985) Eur.Comm.Rep. 2725; Vichy v. Commission, (1992) Eur.Comm.Rep. II–415; Omega, O.J.1970 L 242/22.

selective distribution system is not necessary.[70] In addition, any particular restraints imposed on the distributors should be examined because they could individually infringe Article 101(1).

For example, in the *Grundig* decision, the Commission stated that while the selective distribution system established by Grundig did not in itself infringe Article 101(1), but certain obligations imposed on the dealers did. This included the requirement that retailers carry as complete a selection of the relevant Grundig range as is necessary for the size of the specialized shop or specialized department and keep adequate stocks of a representative selection of the relevant range, and the requirement that wholesalers carry and stock as far as possible the whole Grundig range.[71]

If the selective distribution system infringes Article 101(1), it will often qualify for an exemption under Article 101(3) unless it includes absolute territorial protection, restricts parallel imports or is used to control prices. The Commission is aware that selective distribution systems can improve the distribution of the goods and that the consumer benefits from the resulting provision of specialist sales and after-sales services. Thus, the Commission is generally receptive to arguments that additional obligations such as those imposed by Grundig are indispensable to the system and therefore exempt under Article 101(3).[72]

Vertical Restraints Regulation

The group exemptions for exclusive dealing, exclusive purchasing and franchise agreements were replaced in 2000 by Regulation 2790/99, known as the vertical restraints regulation. It was accompanied by lengthy vertical restraints guidelines. This regulation and its guidelines are more economic and less formalistic than the predecessors. The efficiency enhancing qualities of intra-brand vertical restraints are recognized. Supply, distribution (including selective distribution) and franchise agreements of firms with less than 30 percent market shares are generally exempt; this is known as a "safe harbor." Companies whose market shares exceed 30 percent may or may not be exempt, depending upon the results of individual competition law reviews. Since 2004, these may be undertaken by the Commission, national competition authorities and national courts. In either case, no vertical agreements containing so-called "hard core restraints" are exempt. These restraints concern primarily resale price maintenance, territorial

---

[70]   Ideal Standard distribution system, O.J.1985 L 20/38; Grohe distribution system, O.J.1985 L 19/17.

[71]   Grundig's distribution system, O.J.1994 L 20/15, 21 point 35.

[72]   Grundig's distribution system, O.J.1994 L 20/15, 21.

and customer protection leading to market allocation, and in most instances exclusive dealing covenants that last more than five years.

In 2010, a new Vertical Restraints Regulation 330/10 (with accompanying Guidelines) was issued. Its content is similar to that of 1999. Restrictions on the use of the Internet by distributors with at least one "brick-and-mortar" store are treated as hard core restraints. For example, distributors cannot be required to reroute Internet customers outside their territories to local dealers. Nor can they be forced to pay higher prices for online sales ("dual pricing"), or be limited in the amount sales made via the Internet, although a minimum amount of offline sales can be stipulated. Generally speaking, distributors may sell anywhere in the EU in response to customer demand ("passive sales"). Restraints on "actively" soliciting sales outside designated distributor territories, including by email or banner web advertising, are permissible. *Both* supplier and distributor must have less than 30% market shares to qualify for the 2010 "safe harbor."

§ 19.7   EU Patent Licensing Agreements, Technology Transfer Regulation

In its seminal 1982 *Maize Seed* judgment, the Court of Justice addressed patent license restrictions under the Union's competition rules.[73] The Commission waited for this judgment before publishing the 1984 group exemption under Article 101(3) for patent licensing agreements. In this case, a research institute financed by the French government (INRA) bred varieties of basic seeds. In 1960, INRA assigned to Kurt Eisele plant breeder's rights for maize seed in the Federal Republic of Germany. Eisele agreed to apply for registration of these rights in accordance with German law. In 1965, a formal agreement was executed by the parties. This agreement consisted of five relevant clauses.

Clause 1 gave Eisele the exclusive rights to "organize" sales of six identified varieties of maize seed propagated from basic seeds provided by INRA. This enabled Eisele to exercise control over distribution outlets. Eisele undertook not to deal in maize varieties other than those provided by INRA. Clause 2 required Eisele to place no restriction on the supply of seed to technically suitable distributors except for rationing in conditions of shortage. The prices charged to the distributors by Eisele were fixed in consultation with INRA, according to a specified formula. Clause 3 obligated Eisele to import from France for sale in Germany at least

---

[73]   Nungesser v. Commission (1982) Eur.Comm.Rep. 2015.

two-thirds of that territory's requirements for the registered varieties. This restricted Eisele's own production and sale to only one-third of the German market. Clause 4 concerned the protection by Eisele of INRA's proprietary rights, including its trademark, from infringement and granted Eisele the power to take any action to that end. Clause 5 contained a promise by INRA that no exports to Germany of the relevant varieties would take place otherwise than through the agency of Eisele. This meant that INRA would ensure that its French marketing organization would prevent the relevant varieties from being exported to Germany to parallel importers.

In September 1972, it became apparent that dealers in France were selling the licensed varieties of maize seed directly to German traders who were marketing the products in breach of the breeder's rights claimed by Eisele. This resulted in an action by Eisele in the German courts against one of the traders. The parties reached a court approved settlement under which the French trader promised to refrain from offering for sale without permission any variety of maize seed within the rights held by Eisele, and to pay a fine. In February 1974, another breach took place, this time advertising in the German press by a French dealer. In response to threats of legal proceedings, this dealer lodged a complaint with the Commission alleging breach of the competition rules.

The Commission considered both the agreement and the settlement to infringe Article 101(1) because they granted an exclusive license and provided absolute territorial protection. The Court of Justice reversed the Commission with respect to exclusivity, but upheld the Commission with respect to absolute territorial protection. The Court drew a distinction between "open" licenses which do not necessarily fall under Article 101(1), and "closed" licenses which do so.

Open license agreements are those which do not involve third parties. In *Maize Seed,* the obligation upon INRA or those deriving rights through INRA to refrain from producing or selling the relevant seeds in Germany was treated as an open license term. The Court held such clauses necessary to the dissemination of new technology inasmuch as potential licensees might otherwise be deterred from accepting the risk of cultivating and marketing new products. The Court defined closed licenses as those involving third parties. Thus, the obligation upon INRA or those deriving rights through INRA to prevent third parties from exporting the seeds into Germany without authorization, Eisele's concurrent use of his exclusive contractual rights, and his breeder's rights, to prevent all imports into Germany or exports to other member states were invalid under Article 101(1).

Patent Licensing Regulation

The Commission adopted in 1984 a patent licensing group exemption regulation under Article 101(3).[74] It acknowledged that patent licensing improves the production of goods and promotes technical progress by allowing licensees to operate with the latest technology. The Commission also believed that patent licensing increases both the number of production facilities and the quantity and quality of goods in the Common Market. Much of its focus concerned territorial restrictions in patent licensing agreements. Specifically, the following clauses were permitted:

(1) Restraints on licensors granting rights to other licensees or exploiting the patent in the designated territory during the life of the patent;

(2) Restraints on licensee exploitation of the invention in other EU countries to the extent the licensor has parallel patent rights;[75]

(3) Restraints on licensee manufacture, use or active selling of the product in territories licensed to others, to the extent the licensor has parallel patent rights;

(4) Restraints on licensees intended to keep them from actively or passively selling the product in territories licensed to others for five years after the product is first put on the market, to the extent the licensor has parallel patents; and

(5) Restraints on licensees mandating use of the licensor's trademark on the product.

The distinction between active and passive selling was and remains critical. "Active selling" involves sending agents to call on customers, advertising or creating an office or distribution depot in an EU country other than the licensed territory. "Passive selling" involves responding to unsolicited requests to purchase products from customers outside the licensed territory. Similar regulations governed know-how licensing.[76]

---

[74]   Commission Regulation 2349/84 as amended by Regulation 151/93, O.J. 1993 L 21/8.

[75]   Parallel patents are defined in the regulation as covering the same invention such that the licensor could bring an infringement action against unauthorized activities.

[76]   Commission Regulation 2349/84 and 556/89. *See* Section 19.8.

Transfer of Technology Regulation 240/96

In 1996 the Commission enacted Regulation 240/96 on the application of Article 101(3) to transfer technology agreements. The intention of this Regulation was to combine the existing patent and know-how block exemptions into a single regulation covering technology transfer agreements, and to simplify and harmonize the rules for patent and know-how licensing. It contained detailed lists of permitted, permissible and prohibited clauses.

Regulation 240/96 stated that Article 101(1) of the Treaty did not apply to "pure patent and know-how licensing agreements and missed patent and know-how licensing agreements," as well as to agreements with ancillary provisions relating to intellectual property other than patents, when only two undertakings are parties and when one or more of eight listed obligations were included. These were obligations of limitation, such as not to license other undertakings to exploit the technology. There were time limits (5 years patents/10 years know-how) for the exemption of these eight obligations in certain situations. Article 1 was known as the White List. Article 2 allowed technology transfers even when certain clauses existed (17 were listed). These clauses were considered generally not restrictive of competition. There were various obligations on the licensee, such as not divulging know-how communicated by the licensor. Article 2 was known as the Permissible List.

Article 3 of Regulation 240/96 designated that Articles 1 and 2(2) did not apply when any one of seven obligations were present, such as restricting a party in the determination of prices, competition restrictions, limitations on production quantity, licensee improvement grant-back requirements, etc. Article 3 was known as the Black List. Article 4 carried the scope of the exemption provided for in Articles 1 and 2 to certain other restrictive agreements which were notified to the Commission and received no Commission opposition. Article 4 was known as the Gray List. Regulation 240/96, according to Article 5, did not apply to four classes of agreements, such as most agreements within a joint venture. But under Article 5 it did apply to three forms of agreements, including where the licensor is itself a licensee of the technology and was authorized to grant sub-licenses.

The Commission retained power to withdraw benefits of the Regulation 240/96 if in a specific case the exempted agreement was incompatible with the conditions of Article 101(3). Final articles provided some definitions, a list of what were deemed patents, preservation of confidentiality of information, and the repeal of the two regulations combined in this regulation.

Transfer of Technology Regulation 772/2004

The detailed regulation of technology transfer agreement clauses contained in Regulation 240/96 was replaced by Regulation 772/2004, which applies to patent, know-how and software copyright licensing. The new Regulation distinguishes agreements between those of "competing" and "noncompeting" parties, the latter being treated less strictly than the former. Parties are deemed "competing" if they compete (without infringing each other's IP rights) in either the relevant technology or product market, determined in each instance by what buyers regard as substitutes.[77] If the competing parties have a *combined* market share of 20 percent or less, their licensing agreements are covered by group exemption under Regulation 772/2004.[78] Noncompeting parties, on the other hand, benefit from the group exemption so long as their *individual* market shares do not exceed 30 percent.[79] Agreements initially covered by Regulation 772/2004 that subsequently exceed the "safe harbor" thresholds noted above lose their exemption subject to a two-year grace period.[80] Outside these exemptions, a "rule of reason" approach applies.

Inclusion of certain "hardcore restraints" causes license agreement to lose their group exemption. For competing parties, such restraints include price fixing,[81] output limitations on both parties,[82] limits on the licensee's ability to exploit its own technology,[83] and allocation of markets or competitors (subject to exceptions).[84] Specifically, restraints on active and passive selling by the licensee in a territory reserved for the licensor are allowed, as are active (but not passive) selling restraints by licensees in territories of other licensees.[85] Licensing agreements between noncompeting parties may not contain the "hardcore" restraint of maximum price fixing.[86] Active selling restrictions on licensees can be utilized, along with passive selling restraints in territories reserved to the licensor or (for two years) another licensee.[87] For

---

[77]   Regulation 772/2004, Article 1(1)j.

[78]   *Id.*, Article 3(1).

[79]   *Id.*, Article 3(2).

[80]   *Id.*, Article 8(2).

[81]   *Id.*, Article 4(1)(a).

[82]   *Id.*, Article 4(1)(b).

[83]   *Id.*, Article 4(1)(d).

[84]   *Id.*, Article 4(1)(c).

[85]   *Id.*, Article 4(1)(c)(iv) and (v).

[86]   *Id.*, Article 4(2)(a).

[87]   *Id.*, Article 4(2)(b).

these purposes, the competitive status of the parties is decided at the outset of the agreement.[88]

Other license terms deemed "excluded restrictions" also cause a loss of exemption.[89] Such clauses include: (1) mandatory grant-backs or assignments of severable improvements by licensees, excepting nonexclusive license-backs;[90] (2) no-challenges by the licensee of the licensor's intellectual property rights, subject to the licensor's right to terminate upon challenge;[91] and (3) for noncompeting parties, restraints on the licensee's ability to exploit its own technology or either party's ability to carry out research and development (unless indispensable to prevent disclosure of the licensed Know-how).[92]

In all cases, exemption under Regulation 772/2004 may be withdrawn where in any particular case an agreement has effects that are incompatible with Article 101(3).[93]

§ 19.8   EU Know-how Licensing Agreements

Prior to the 1996 technology transfer regulation (above), there were two group exemptions which applied to know-how licensing agreements. Commission Regulation 2349/84 applied to agreements combining patent and know-how licenses. However, provisions concerning know-how in such mixed agreements were only covered by the group exemption in so far as the licensed patents were necessary for achieving the objects of the licensed technology and as long as at least one of the licensed patents remained in force. In such cases, the "mixed agreement" could qualify for an exemption under Regulation 556/89.

Regulation 556/89 applied to bilateral, pure know-how licensing agreements, bilateral mixed agreements not falling under Regulation 2349/84 and bilateral, pure know-how licensing or mixed agreements containing ancillary provisions relating to trademarks and other intellectual property rights.[94] The concept of know-how was broadly conceived in this regulation to include "a body of technical information that is secret, substantial and identified in any appropriate form."[95] "Secret" meant that the know-how package as a body was not generally known or easily accessible. Each

---

[88]   *Id.*, Article 4(3).

[89]   *Id.*, Article 5.

[90]   *Id.*, Article 5(1)(a).

[91]   *Id.*, Article 5(1)(b) and (c).

[92]   *Id.*, Article 5(2).

[93]   *Id.*, Article 6.

[94]   Art. 1(1) of Regulation 556/89.

[95]   Art. 1(7)1 of Regulation 556/89.

individual component of the know-how did not have to be unknown or unobtainable. "Substantial" meant that the know-how includes important information regarding a manufacturing process, a product or service, or for their development. It excluded information which is trivial. The know-how also had to be useful. Such information was useful if it could be expected to improve the competitive position of the licensee.

These approaches, along with the focus on active and passive territorial sales restraints discussed above regarding patent licenses, have largely been retained in Regulations 240/96 and 772/2004. The latter group exemption now regulates both patent licensing and know-how licensing agreements. Its content is detailed in Section 19.7.

§ 19.9   EU Franchise Agreements

The Pronuptia Case

Prior to its landmark decision in *Pronuptia,*[96] the Commission had never sought to apply Article 101 to franchise agreements. *Pronuptia* arose from the refusal of a franchisee to pay license fees to the franchisor. The distribution of the Pronuptia brand wedding attire in the Federal Republic of Germany was handled by shops operated by the German franchisor and by independent retailers through franchise agreements with that franchisor. The franchisee had obtained franchises for three areas (Hamburg, Oldenburg and Hannover). The franchisor granted exclusive rights to market and advertise under the name of "Pronuptia de Paris" in these specific territories. The franchisor promised not to open any shops or provide any goods or services to another person in those territories. The franchisor also agreed to assist the franchisee with business strategies and profitability.

The franchisee agreed to assume all the risk of opening a franchise as an independent retailer. The franchisee also agreed to the following: (1) To sell Pronuptia goods only in the store specified in the contract and to decorate and design the shop according to the franchisor's instructions; (2) to purchase 80 percent of wedding related attire and a proportion of evening dresses from the franchisor, and to purchase the rest of such merchandise only from sellers approved by the franchisor; (3) to pay a one-time entrance fee for exclusive rights to the specified territory and a yearly royalty fee of 10 percent of the total sales of Pronuptia and all other products; (4) to advertise only with the franchisor's approval in a

---

[96] Pronuptia de Paris GmbH v. Pronuptia de Paris Irmgard Schillgallis (1986) Eur.Comm.Rep. 353.

method which would enhance the international reputation of the franchise; (5) to make the sale of bridal fashions the franchisee's main business purpose; (6) to consider the retail price recommendations of the franchisor; (7) to refrain from competing directly or indirectly during the contract period or for one year afterward with any Pronuptia store; and (8) to obtain the franchisor's prior approval before assigning the rights and obligations arising under the contract to a third party.

In due course, the case was referred to the European Court of Justice. The Court's judgment concentrates on the crucial issue of whether franchise agreements come within Article 101. The Court draws a preliminary distinction between "distribution" franchises such as Pronuptia as opposed to "service" and "production" franchises. The Court concludes that a franchising system as such does not interfere with competition. Consequently, clauses essential to enable franchising to function are not prohibited. Thus, the franchisor can communicate know-how or assistance and help franchisees apply its methods. The franchisor can take reasonable steps to keep its know-how or assistance from becoming available to competitors. Location clauses forbidding the franchisee during the contract, or for a reasonable time thereafter, from opening a store with a similar or identical object in an area where it might compete with another member of the franchise network were necessary for distribution franchises and therefore permissible. The obligation of the franchisee not to sell a licensed store without prior consent of the franchisor was similarly allowable.

Clauses necessary to preserve the identity and reputation of the franchise network, such as decorations and use of trademarks, were upheld. The reputation and identity of the network may also justify a clause requiring the franchisee to sell only products supplied by the franchisor or by approved sources, at least if it would be too expensive to monitor the quality of the stock otherwise. Nevertheless, each franchisee must be allowed to buy from other franchisees. The requirement of uniformity may also justify advertisement approvals by the franchisor, but the franchisee must be allowed to set and advertise resale prices. The Court rejected the view that clauses tending to divide the Common Market between franchisor and franchisee or between franchisees are always necessary to protect the know-how or the identity and the reputation of the network. The location clause in *Pronuptia* was seen as potentially supporting exclusive territories. In combination, location clauses and exclusive territories may divide markets and so restrict competition within the network. Even if a potential franchisee would not take the risk of joining the network by making its own investment because it could not expect a profitable business due to the absence of protection from competition from other franchisees, that consideration (in the Court's view) could be taken into account only under an Article 101(3) individual exemption. The Commission, in fact, ultimately granted such an exemption to Pronuptia.[97]

Franchising Regulation

The Commission, following the European Court of Justice in *Pronuptia*,[98] adopted a group exemption regulation for franchise agreements under Article 101(3).[99] Regulation 4087/88 required each franchisee to identify itself as an independent enterprise apart from the trademark/service mark/trade name owner. This disclosure could avoid joint and several franchisor liability for the provision by franchisees of defective goods or services. Regulation 4087/88 defined a "franchise" as a package of industrial or intellectual property rights relating to trademarks, trade names, signs, utility models, designs, copyrights, know-how or patents exploited for the resale of goods or the provision of services to customers.[100] "Franchise agreements" were defined as those in which the franchisor grants the franchisee, in exchange for direct or indirect financial consideration, the right to exploit a franchise so as to market specified types of goods and/or services.[101] A "master franchise agreement" involved the right to exploit a franchise by concluding franchising agreements with third parties.[102]

Vertical Restraints Regulation

Starting with these basics, Regulation 4087/88 proceeded to detail permitted and prohibited clauses in EU franchise agreements. . . . This approach remained in force until 2000, when Regulation 2790/99 (the "vertical restraints" group exemption) took over franchise agreements, along with exclusive dealing and other distribution agreements. Regulation 2790/99 is accompanied by lengthy vertical restraints guidelines. This regulation and its guidelines are more economic and less formalistic than the predecessors. Supply and distribution agreements of firms with less than 30 percent market shares are generally exempt; this is known as a "safe harbor." Companies whose market shares exceed 30 percent may or may not be exempt, depending upon the results of individual competition law reviews. In either case, no vertical

---

[97]   Re Pronuptia, 30 O.J.Eur.Comm. 39 (L13/1987).

[98]   Pronuptia de Paris GmbH v. Pronuptia de Paris Irmgard Schillgallis (1986) Eur.Comm.Rep. 353.

[99]   Regulation 4087/88.

[100]   *Id.*, Article 1(3)(a).

[101]   *Id.*, Article 1(3)(b).

[102]   *Id.*, Article 1(3)(c).

agreements containing so-called "hard core restraints" are exempt. These restraints concern primarily resale price maintenance, territorial and customer protection leading to market allocations, and in most instances exclusive dealing covenants that last more than five years. In 2010, a new Vertical Restraints Regulation 330/10 was issued. Its content is similar to that of 1999, except that restrictions on the use of the Internet by distributors are treated as a hard-core restraints. *See* Section 19.6.

§ 19.10   Article 102—Abuse of Dominant Positions

Article 102 is primarily of consequence to foreign investors operating in the EU common market. Since it is of less significance to international traders, minimal coverage of it is presented in this book. Considerably more material exploring Article 102 can be found in R. Folsom, *Principles of European Union Law,* Chapter 7.

Article 102 TFEU prohibits abuse by one or more undertakings of a dominant position within a substantial part of the Common Market insofar as the abuse may affect trade between member states. The existence of a dominant position is not prohibited by European law. Only its abuse is proscribed. Although both Articles 101 and 102 may be applied to the same business practices,[103] they constitute two independent legal instruments addressing different legal situations.[104] Whereas Article 101 is directed at trade restraints of competition through agreement or concerted practices between undertakings, Article 102 is concerned with restrictive practices arising from the position of the undertaking regardless of the existence of an agreement or concerted practice between undertakings.[105] However, fines for the same conduct under both Articles 101 and 102 will not be permitted by the ECJ.[106]

Article 102 differs fundamentally from Article 101 in other respects. There are no provisions to declare abuses automatically void, or to permit any exemptions from its prohibitions. Thus, under the administrative frameworks of Regulation 17 and Regulation 1, no individual or group exemptions can be granted by the Commission for Article 102. The absence of exemptions means that there has been little incentive for dominant firms to notify their abuses to the Commission. Regulations 17 and 1 grant the Commission the same powers with reference to Article 102 as it

---

[103] Ahmed Saeed Flugreisen v. Zentrale zur Bekämpfung unlauteren Wettbewerbs, (1989) Eur.Comm.Rep. 803, 849 para. 37.

[104] Tetra Pak Rausing v. Commission (1990) Eur.Comm.Rep. II–309, II–356 para. 22.

[105] *Id.*

[106] ACF Chemiefarma v. Commission (1970) Eur.Comm.Rep. 661.

possesses under Article 101 to obtain information, investigate corporate affairs, render infringement decisions, and fine or penalize offenders.

§ 19.11   National Litigation and Remedies for EU Competition Law Violations

Direct Effect

As primary Union law, Articles 101 and 102 are directly effective in the member states.[107] All regulations, for example, the various group exemption regulations discussed above, are directly applicable law in member states. Directly applicable EU provisions give individuals and enterprises within member states the immediate right to rely on Union law. This means that they may raise competition law issues in private litigation before national courts and tribunals.[108] Indeed, under the supremacy doctrine, they may rely on such law to challenge contradictory national law.[109] The directly effective nature of Articles 101 and 102 and the numerous EU regulations in this area helps to explain the pervasive impact that competition law has had in European business life.

Role of National Courts, Nullification, Damages

Article 101(2) renders agreements which infringe Article 101(1) (or parts thereof) null and void. Since this is a directly effective Treaty provision, the national courts ordinarily enjoin such agreements. This assumes of course that the agreement is not group exempted by the Commission under Article 101(3), which under the 2004 modernization rules can also be applied individually by national authorities and courts.[110] National courts and tribunals may request advice from *the Commission*.[111] Such requests may seek procedural as well as substantive advice. For example, the national courts may inquire whether a case or investigation into the same dispute is pending before the Commission, and how long the Commission will take before acting. They may also consult with the Commission on points of law, e.g. whether the necessary impact on EU trade is present and whether the contested agreement is eligible for an individual exemption under Article 101(3).

---

[107]   Bosch v. de Geus (1962) Common Mkt.L.Rep. 1; Belgische Radio en Televisie v. SABAM (1974) Eur.Comm.Rep. 51.

[108]   *See* R. Folsom, *Principles of European Union Law*, Chapter 3.

[109]   Id., Chapter 2.

[110]   Id., Chapter 3.

[111]   *See* Commission Press Release IP/92/1107 (Dec. 23, 1992) and Regulation 1/2003.

National courts can also obtain statistics, market studies and economic analyses from the Commission. All of this information and advice is intended to encourage national courts to efficiently and correctly apply Articles 101 and 102 to disputes coming before them. It is part of a broad policy of decentralized EU competition law enforcement designed to leave the Commission free to pursue cases of major importance.[112] National courts need not refer EU competition law questions to the Commission. They may simply rely upon their own analysis of the various group exemption regulations,[113] guidelines and policy notices issued by the Commission under Article 101(3). They may also rely on existing ECJ, GC and Commission case law.

If the agreement violates European Union competition law, it is up to the national courts to determine the consequences of the nullification of agreements by Article 101(2).[114] This could possibly include an award of damages and legal costs. The right to bring such actions in national courts has been affirmed by the European Court of Justice.[115] Article 102 does not contain a provision that is comparable to Article 101(2). Thus the private legal remedies available when a dominant firm abuses its position must be determined strictly under national law. In Britain, for example, the House of Lords suggested that Article 102 creates "statutory duties," the breach of which permits the recovery of damages under torts principles.[116]

§ 19.12 The Extraterritorial Reach of EU Business Competition Law

There is a question about the extent to which the competition rules of the European Union extend to activity anywhere in the world, including activity occurring entirely or partly within the territorial limits of the United States or Canada. Decisions by the Commission and the Court of Justice suggest that the territorial reach of Articles 101 and 102 is expanding and may extend to almost any international business transaction.

---

[112] *See* Commission Notice clarifying the application of Community competition law by national courts, 1993 O.J. C239/6.

[113] *See* Section 19.5.

[114] Société de vente de Ciments Bétons v. Kerpen + Kerpen (1983) Eur.Comm.Rep. 4173.

[115] Courage v. Crehan, (2001) Eur.Comm.Rep. I–6297 (Case C–453/99); Manfred: Joined Cases C295/04, 207–298/04.

[116] Garden Cottage Foods Ltd. v. Milk Marketing Board (1983) 2 All Eng.Rep. 770, 1984 A.C. 130. For additional discussion *see* Hoskins, Garden Cottage Revisited: The Availability of Damages in the National Courts for Breaches of the EEC Competition Rules, 6 E.C.L.R. 257 (1992).

For an agreement to be incompatible with the Common Market and prohibited under Article 101(1), it must be "likely to affect trade between Member States" and have the object or effect of impairing "competition within the Common Market." These requirements amount to an "effects test" for extraterritorial application of Article 101. This test is similar to that which operates under the Sherman Act of the United States.

Extraterritorial Application

The Court has repeatedly held that the fact that one of the parties to an agreement is domiciled in a third country does not preclude the applicability of Article 101(1).[117] Swiss and British chemical companies, for example, argued that the Commission was not competent to impose competition law fines for acts committed in Switzerland and Britain (before joining the EU) by enterprises domiciled outside the Union even if the acts had effects within the Common Market.[118] Nevertheless, the Court held those companies in violation of Article 101 because they owned subsidiary companies within the Community and controlled their behavior. The foreign parent and its EU subsidiaries were treated as a "single enterprise" for purposes of service of process, judgment, and collection of fines and penalties. In doing so, the Court observed that the fact that a subsidiary company has its own legal personality does not rule out the possibility that its conduct is attributable to the parent company.

The Court has extended its reasoning to the extraterritorial application of Article 102.[119] A United States parent company, for example, was held potentially liable for acquisitions by its EC subsidiary which affected market conditions within the Community.[120] In another decision, the Court held that a Maryland company's refusal to sell its product to a competitor of its affiliate company within the Union was a result of united "single enterprise" action.[121] It proceeded to state that extraterritorial conduct merely having "repercussions on competitive structures" in the Common Market fell within the parameters of Article 102. The Court ordered Commercial Solvents, through its Italian affiliate, to supply the competitor at reasonable prices.

---

[117]   Ahlström v. Commission (1988) Eur.Comm.Rep. 5193; Zinc Producers v. Commission (1984) Eur.Comm.Rep. 1679.

[118]   *See* ICI v. Commission (1972) Eur.Comm.Rep. 619.

[119]   For a discussion of the extraterritorial reach of the Merger Control Regulation, *see* Montag, Common Market Merger Control of Third-Country Enterprises, Comparative Law Yearbook of International Business 47 (1991).

[120]   *See* Europemballage Corp. and Continental Can Co., Inc. v. Commission (1973) Eur.Comm.Rep. 215.

[121]   *See* Commercial Solvents Corp. v. Commission (1974) Eur.Comm.Rep. 223.

Wood Pulp Case

In 1988, the Court of Justice widened the extraterritorial reach of Article 101 in a case where wood pulp producers from the U.S., Canada, Sweden and Finland were fined for price fixing activities affecting EU trade and competition. These firms did not have substantial operations within the Union. They were primarily exporters to the Common Market. This decision's utilization of a place of implementation "effects test" is quite similar to that used under the Sherman Act.[122] And the reliance by the U.S. exporters upon a traditional Webb–Pomerene cartel exemption from United States antitrust law carried no weight in the European Union. The Court has also affirmed the extraterritorial reach of Articles 101 and 102 to airfares in and out of the Union,[123] and the EU Mergers Regulation clearly applies to firms located outside the Common Market.

§ 19.13   EU and U.S. Jurisdictional Effects Tests, Blocking Statutes

It may be a substantial jump to predict that Articles 101 and 102 bear upon a business transaction done in the United States or another non-EU country which merely inures to the competitive disadvantage of a company located within the Common Market. Yet in one of the *Dyestuffs* cases as early as 1969 the Commission took the position that:

> The rules of competition of the Treaty are therefore applicable to all restrictions on competition that produce within the Common Market effects to which Article 101, paragraph 1, applies. There is therefore no need to examine whether the enterprises that originated such restraints of competition have their head office within or outside of the Union.[124]

Although the Court's disposition of the *Dyestuffs* cases did not endorse such reasoning, the Commission has reasserted its "effects test" in subsequent arguments. The Commission's approach merits close consideration if only because the initiation of an Article 101 or 102 inquiry can generate local overhead costs for those involved in EU business transactions. That courts in the United States have also used an "effects test" in connection with the question of the

---

[122]   Woodpulp Producers v. Commission (1988) Eur.Comm.Rep. 5193.

[123]   Ahmed Saeed Flugreisen v. Zentrale zur Bekämpfung unlauteren Wettbewerbs (1989) Eur.Comm.Rep. 803.

[124]   Commission v. I.C.I., 8 Common Mkt.L.Rep. 494 (1969).

extraterritoriality of American antitrust laws increases the potential for uncertainty and costs in international transactions.[125]

U.S. Extraterritorial Antitrust

United States courts have long asserted the right to apply the Sherman Antitrust Act to foreign commerce affecting the United States market.[126] In some cases, this approach has been tempered to allow consideration of the interests of comity and foreign countries in the outcome.[127] Sherman Act amendments adopted in 1984 stress the "direct, substantial and reasonably foreseeable" nature of effects on American foreign commerce as a prerequisite to antitrust jurisdiction. Nevertheless, the potential for conflict in this field is enormous. For example, a multinational enterprise (MNE) headquartered in the U.S. but doing business in Europe could be constrained by United States antitrust law from fixing prices, yet permitted by EU competition law under Article 101(3) to do exactly that.

Assuming that the price fixing in question has effects in both markets, what course of action is to be followed? There is no easy answer. When the MNE is located within a country other than one of the member states of the EU or the United States, but engages in activity having effects within those markets, the problem potential of extraterritoriality may be even more acute. Reconciling a conflict of antitrust laws applied extraterritorially by these two jurisdictions could become a flashpoint in international business transactions.

The problem becomes all the more apparent when one considers the increasing influence of international trade policy on the application of antitrust laws. For example, the U.S. Department of Justice has indicated that it will take enforcement action against conduct occurring overseas that restrains exports, regardless of whether or not there is direct harm to U.S. consumers, where it is clear that the conduct has a direct, substantial and reasonably foreseeable effect on exports of goods and services from the United States, the conduct infringes U.S. antitrust laws, and the U.S. courts have jurisdiction over the foreign persons or corporations engaged in such conduct.[128] Although the application of this policy

---

[125]   *See generally* Spencer Weber Waller, International Trade and U.S. Antitrust Law (Supp. 1994).

[126]   *See especially* United States v. Aluminum Co. of America, 148 F.2d 416 (2d Cir. 1945) (L. Hand, J.); Hartford Fire Insurance Co. v. California, 509 U.S. 764, 113 S.Ct. 2891, 125 L.Ed.2d 612 (1993).

[127]   *See especially* Timberlane Lumber Co. v. Bank of America, 549 F.2d 597 (9th Cir. 1976); *Compare* Laker Airways Ltd. v. Sabena, Belgian World Airlines, 731 F.2d 909 (D.C. Cir. 1984); Hartford Fire Insurance Co. v. California, 509 U.S. 764, 113 S.Ct. 2891, 125 L.Ed.2d 612 (1993).

[128]   Dept. of Justice press release (3 April 1992).

has not created any significant problems,[129] the influence of international trade policy on the application of antitrust law does carry the potential of becoming a major issue in relations with foreign countries.

Blocking Statutes

In the case of antitrust judgments emanating from United States courts, most notably the "Uranium Cartel" treble damages litigation of the late 1970s,[130] many nations consider the flashpoint already reached. At least nine nations (Australia, Canada, France, Germany, Netherlands, New Zealand, Philippines, South Africa, and the United Kingdom) have taken retaliatory action by enacting "blocking statutes." In addition, the 41 Commonwealth nations have resolved general support for a position similar to that of the United Kingdom.

The United Kingdom blocking statute is the Protection of Trading Interests Act of 1980.[131] This Act (without specifying American antitrust law) makes it difficult to depose witnesses, obtain documents or enforce multiple liability judgments extraterritorially in the U.K. Violation of the 1980 Act may result in criminal penalties. Furthermore, under the "claw-back" provision of the Act, parties with outstanding multiple liabilities in foreign jurisdictions (e.g., United States treble damages defendants) may recoup the punitive element of such awards in Britain against assets of the successful plaintiff. The British Act invites other nations to adopt claw-back provisions by offering claw-back reciprocity. United States attorneys confronted with a blocking statute need to understand that multiple liability judgments combined with contingency fee arrangements are virtually unknown elsewhere.

Policy Debate

The extensive array of pre-trial discovery mechanisms allowed in U.S. civil litigation rarely, if ever, have a counterpart in foreign law. Discovery subpoenas originating in American litigation are often "shocking" to many foreign defendants. And the U.S. Supreme Court has ruled that use of letters rogatory under the Hague Convention[132] is not obligatory.[133] It is the blocking of discovery that

---

[129]   See United States v. Pilkington, 7 Trade Reg.Rep. (CCH) ¶ 50,758 (1994); United States v. MCI Communications, 7 Trade Reg.Rep. (CCH) ¶ 50,761 (1994).

[130]   See In re Uranium Antitrust Litigation (Westinghouse Electric Corp.) v. Rio Algom Limited, 617 F.2d 1248 (7th Cir. 1980).

[131]   Reprinted in 21 I.L.M. 834 (1982).

[132]   Hague Convention on the Taking of Evidence Abroad in Civil or Commercial Matters, 23 U.S.T. 2555, T.A.I.S. No. 7444.

potentially most threatens the extraterritorial application of United States laws, especially antitrust. Since United States courts may sanction parties who in bad faith fail to respond to discovery requests, foreign defendants requesting help from their home governments under blocking statutes are especially at risk. On the other hand, good faith efforts to modify or work around discovery blockades may favor foreign defendants. Such defendants are often caught in a "no win" situation. Either way they will be penalized.

Reasons advanced to support an extraterritorial application of United States antitrust laws are founded on the idea that some extraterritorial extension is necessary to prevent their circumvention by multinational corporations which have the business sagacity to ensure that anticompetitive transactions are consummated beyond the territorial borders of the United States. An extraterritorial extension of antitrust laws can help to protect the export opportunities of domestic firms. Extraterritorial application of the antitrust laws can also help to ensure that the American consumer receives the benefit of competing imports, which in turn may spur complacent domestic industries. The effect of foreign auto imports on the car manufacturers in the United States may be cited as an example. In an increasingly internationalized world, extraterritorial antitrust may merely reflect economic reality.

On the other hand, the British argue that American extraterritoriality permits the U.S. to unjustifiably "mold the international economic and trading world to its own image." In particular, the U.S. "effects" doctrine creates legal uncertainty for international traders, and U.S. courts pay little attention to the competing policies (interests) of other concerned governments. As the House of Lords has stated: "It is axiomatic that in anti-trust matters the policy of one state may be to defend what it is the policy of another state to attack."[134] The British also argue, not without some support, that customary international law does not permit extraterritorial application of national laws.[135] In making this argument, the British have a convenient way of forgetting about the extraterritorial scope of Articles 101 and 102, which are now part of

---

[133] Société Nationale Industrielle Aérospatiale v. U.S. District Court, 482 U.S. 522, 107 S.Ct. 2542, 96 L.Ed.2d 461 (1987).

[134] Westinghouse Electric Corp. V. Rio Tinto Zinc Corp., 2 W.L.R. 81 (1978).

[135] See arguments presented by the British government in Hartford Fire Insurance Co. v. California discussed in Reuland, Hartford Fire Insurance Co., Comity and the Extraterritorial Reach of United States Antitrust Laws, 29 Tex.Int'l L.J. 159 (1994) and Brief of the Government of the United Kingdom of Great Britain and Northern Ireland as Amicus Curiae in Société Nationale Industrielle Aérospatiale v. U.S. District Ct., reprinted in 25 I.L.M. 1557 (1986).

their law. Moreover, in a curious reversal of roles illustrating the extremes of the debate, the British government applied the Protection of Trading Interests Act to block the pursuit of treble damages in *United States* courts by the liquidator of Laker Airways against British Airways and other defendants. A House of Lords decision reversed this ban but retained government restrictions on discovery related to the case.[136]

§ 19.14   United States–European Union Cooperation on Antitrust

U.S. Antitrust Cooperation Agreements

Some evidence of international antitrust cooperation is contained in a 1967 recommendation of the OECD which provides for notification of antitrust actions, exchanges of information to the extent that the disclosure is domestically permissible, and where practical, coordination of antitrust enforcement.[137] The OECD resolution served as a model for the 1972 "Antitrust Notification and Consultation Procedure" between Canada and the United States. Following the "Uranium Cartel" litigation, Australia, and the United States reached an Agreement on Cooperation in Antitrust Matters (1982) to minimize jurisdictional conflicts.[138] Australia has taken the position that United States courts are not a proper institution to balance interests of concerned countries within the context of private antitrust litigation.

The Agreement on Cooperation provides that when the Government of Australia is concerned with private antitrust proceedings pending in a United States court, the Government of Australia may request the Government of the United States to participate in the litigation. The United States must report to the court on the substance and outcome of consultations with Australia on the matter concerned. In this way, Australia's views and interests in the litigation and its potential outcome are made known to the court. The court is not required to defer to those views, or even to openly consider them. It merely receives the "report." Australia, in turn, has indicated a willingness to be more receptive to discovery requests in U.S. antitrust litigation and to consult before invoking its blocking statute.

Similar arrangements were made in the Memorandum of Understanding between the U.S. and Canada with Respect to the

---

[136]   British Airways Board v. Laker Airways, 3 W.L.R. 413 (1984).

[137]   In 1986, the OECD issued a similar Recommendation Concerning Cooperation Between Member States on Restrictive Business Practices Affecting International Trade, reprinted in 25 I.L.M. 1629 (1986).

[138]   Reprinted in 21 I.L.M. 702 (1982).

Application of National Antitrust Laws (1984). No such agreement has been reached with the United Kingdom, with whom the extraterritoriality issue remains contentious, a fact which has led some to wonder whether the United States ought to have its own blocking statute against extraterritorial EU competition law. However, an antitrust cooperation agreement seems more appropriate, and late in 1991 the European Union and the United States reached such an agreement.[139] Comparable agreements between the EU and Canada, and the EU and Japan have been concluded.

EU-U.S. Cooperation, Microsoft

The U.S.-EU accord commits the parties to notify each other of imminent enforcement action, to share relevant information and consult on potential policy changes. An innovative feature is the inclusion of "comity" principles, each side promising to take the other's interests and requests into account when considering antitrust prosecutions. The agreement has had a significant effect on mergers of firms doing business in North America and the Union. Each side has agreed to notify and consult with the other regarding antitrust matters, including mergers and acquisitions, that "may affect important interests."

In its first six months of operation, about 45 notifications were exchanged between the Commission, the U.S. Federal Trade Commission, and the Antitrust Division of the U.S. Justice Department. A large portion of these notifications concerned international mergers and acquisitions. Since both the EU and the U.S. have premerger notification systems, the exchange of such information has increased rapidly. In the first year after the cooperation agreement, U.S. antitrust enforcers sent 37 such notifications to the European Commission and received 15 in return. About 20 percent of all the mergers reviewed by the Commission under its competition law were simultaneously being reviewed by U.S. antitrust authorities, but cooperative review can result in conflicting decisions.

The agreement was prominently used to jointly negotiate a 1994 settlement on restrictive practices of the Microsoft Corporation. Since the Commission has traditionally permitted U.S. lawyers to appear before it on competition law matters, the FTC announced on the same day as the signing of the US-EU antitrust

---

[139]   Because the Court of Justice held that the Cooperation Agreement with the United States was void since the Commission did not have the requisite authority to enter into such an agreement, France v. Commission (1994) Eur.Comm.Rep. I–03641 (Case No. C–327/91), the Commission has recently asked the Council to expressly approve the Agreement.

cooperation agreement that EU lawyers would be permitted to appear before it on a reciprocal basis.

In the public prosecutions of Microsoft focused on Windows as a monopoly, the United States settlement reached in 2001 is less demanding than the Commission judgment of 2004 which also requires an unbundling of media playback capabilities. This example reaffirms that transatlantic antitrust "cooperation" need not necessarily result in similar outcomes. In 2007, the General Court broadly confirmed the Commission's 2004 decision. Shortly thereafter, Microsoft settled the prosecution by altering its operating systems' licensing arrangements to favor "open source" software developers (e.g., Linux). Prior to settlement, Microsoft had been fined, including daily noncompliance penalties, in excess of 2 billion Euros.

By 2008, the Commission was investigating Microsoft's bundling of its web browser with Windows, and the compatibility of its Office software with rival programs. A quick settlement "unbundled" web browsers on Windows . . . there are now a dozen or more choices. But in 2013, the Commission fined Microsoft over 500 million Euros for breach of this settlement agreement.

Other U.S. technology firms have been under the EU competition law microscope: Qualcomm, Intel, IBM, Google and Apple included. In 2009, the Commission fined Intel 1.06 billion Euros for abusing its dominant position in microprocessors for PCs. Intel's price discounts and loyalty rebates were the center of this proceeding.

§ 19.15 Text of TFEU Articles 101 and 102

Article 101

1. The following shall be prohibited as incompatible with the internal market: all agreements between undertakings, decisions by associations of undertakings and concerted practices which may affect trade between Member States and which have as their object or effect the prevention, restriction or distortion of competition within the internal market, and in particular those which:

(a) directly or indirectly fix purchase or selling prices or any other trading conditions;

(b) limit or control production, markets, technical development, or investment;

(c) share markets or sources of supply;

(d) apply dissimilar conditions to equivalent transactions with other trading parties, thereby placing them at a competitive disadvantage;

(e) make the conclusion of contracts subject to acceptance by the other parties of supplementary obligations which, by their nature or according to commercial usage, have no connection with the subject of such contracts.

2. Any agreements or decisions prohibited pursuant to this Article shall be automatically void.

3. The provisions of paragraph 1 may, however, be declared inapplicable in the case of:

- any agreement or category of agreements between undertakings,

- any decision or category of decisions by associations of undertakings,

- any concerted practice or category of concerted practices,

which contributes to improving the production or distribution of goods or to promoting technical or economic progress, while allowing consumers a fair share of the resulting benefit, and which does not:

(a) impose on the undertakings concerned restrictions which are not indispensable to the attainment of these objectives;

(b) afford such undertakings the possibility of eliminating competition in respect of a substantial part of the products in question.

Article 102

Any abuse by one or more undertakings of a dominant position within the internal market or in a substantial part of it shall be prohibited as incompatible with the internal market in so far as it may affect trade between Member States.

Such abuse may, in particular, consist in:

(a) directly or indirectly imposing unfair purchase or selling prices or other unfair trading conditions;

(b) limiting production, markets or technical development to the prejudice of consumers;

(c) applying dissimilar conditions to equivalent transactions with other trading parties, thereby placing them at a competitive disadvantage;

(d) making the conclusion of contracts subject to acceptance by the other parties of supplementary obligations which, by their nature or according to commercial usage, have no connection with the subject of such contracts.

Part 5

ADDITIONAL INTERNATIONAL TRADE LAW TOPICS

Chapter 20

TECHNOLOGY TRANSFERS ACROSS BORDERS

Table of Sections

This chapter concerns the lawful transfer of technology across borders. In 2010, the United States paid over $33 billion in technology royalties and license fees, receiving that year over $89 billion. Japan is the only other country to have received more than it paid in technology transfer monies. Singapore, Canada, South Korea and China paid substantially more for technology than they received in 2010.

A vast amount of technology is transferred illegally around the world by pirates and counterfeiters. That subject is covered in Chapter 8.

§ 20.1　Franchising Abroad

Franchising constitutes a rapidly expanding form of doing business abroad. Most franchisors have established fairly standard contracts and business formulae which are utilized in their home markets, and receive counsel on the myriad of laws relevant to their domestic business operations. Approaches to developing, defining and managing franchise relationships that have worked domestically may not work abroad. For example, agreements authorizing development of multiple locations within a given territory and, possibly, subfranchising by a master franchisee are often used overseas while infrequent in the United States.

International franchising confronts the attorney with the need to research and evaluate a broad range of foreign laws which may apply in any particular jurisdiction. Such laws tend to focus on placing equity and control in the hands of local individuals and on regulating the franchise agreement to benefit the franchisees. In addition, counsel should be sensitive to the cultural impact of foreign franchising. For example, the appearance of a franchise building or trademark symbol may conflict in a foreign setting with traditional architectural forms (such as in European cities) or nationalist feelings hostile to the appearance of foreign trademarks on franchised products (such as in India or Mexico). Cultural conflicts can diminish the value of international franchises. To anticipate and solve legal and cultural problems, foreign counsel is often chosen to assist in the task of franchising abroad.

This chapter explores some of the concerns a franchisor or prospective franchisee may encounter in opting for, negotiating, drafting or enforcing an international franchise agreement. Although patents, copyrights and trademarks may all be involved in international franchising, trademark licensing is at the core of most international franchise agreements. Many rightly consider franchising to be a U.S. invention, but foreigners have rapidly been developing international franchising systems. Thus, while the primary focus in this chapter is on the problems of United States franchisors who intend to go abroad, additional coverage is given to United States law relevant to franchising.

§ 20.2   International Trademark Protection

Virtually all countries offer some legal protection to trademarks, even when they do not have trademark registration systems. Trademark rights derived from the use of marks on goods in commerce have long been recognized at common law and remain so today in countries as diverse as the United States and the United Arab Emirates. The latter nation, for example, had no trademark registration law in 1986, but this did not prevent McDonald's from obtaining an injunction against a local business using its famous name and golden arches without authorization.[1] However, obtaining

---

[1]   Case No. 823/85. See 76 Trademark Reports 356 (1986).

international trademark protection normally involves separate registration under the law of each nation. Over three million trademarks are registered around the globe each year.

In the United States, trademarks are protected at common law and by state and federal registrations. Federal registration is permitted by the U.S. Trademark Office for all marks capable of distinguishing the goods on which they appear from other goods.[2] Unless the mark falls within a category of forbidden registrations (e.g., those that offend socialist morality in the People's Republic of China), a mark becomes valid for a term of years following registration.

In some countries (like the U.S. prior to 1989), marks must be used on goods before registration. In others, use is not required and speculative registration of marks can occur. It is said that ESSO was obliged to purchase trademark rights from such a speculator when it switched to EXXON in its search for the perfect global trademark. Since 1989, United States law has allowed applications when there is a bona fide intent to use a trademark within 12 months and, if there is good cause for the delay in actual usage, up to 24 additional months.[3] Such filings in effect reserve the mark for the applicant. The emphasis on bona fide intent and good cause represent an attempt to control any speculative use of U.S. trademark registrations.

The scope of trademark protection may differ substantially from country to country. Under U.S. federal trademark law, injunctions, damages and seizures of goods by customs officials may follow infringement. Other jurisdictions may provide similar remedies on their law books, but offer little practical enforcement. Thus, trademark registration is no guarantee against trademark piracy. A pair of blue jeans labeled "Levi Strauss made in San Francisco" may have been counterfeited in Israel or Paraguay without the knowledge or consent of Levi Strauss and in spite of its trademark registrations in those countries. Trademark counterfeiting is not just a third world problem, as any visitor to a United States "flea market" can tell. Congress created criminal offenses and private treble damages remedies for the first time in the Trademark Counterfeiting Act of 1984.

In many countries trademarks (appearing on goods) may be distinguished from "service marks" used by providers of services (e.g., the Law Store), "trade names" (business names), "collective marks" (marks used by a group or organization), and "certificate

---

[2]   15 U.S.C.A. § 1052.

[3]   15 U.S.C.A. § 1051(b).

marks" (marks which certify a certain quality, origin, or other fact). Although national trademark schemes differ, it can be said generally that a valid trademark (e.g., a mark not "canceled," "renounced," "abandoned," "waived" or "generic") will be protected against infringing use. A trademark can be valid in one country (ASPIRIN brand tablets in Canada), but invalid because generic in another (BAYER brand aspirin in the United States).

Unlike patents and copyrights, trademarks may be renewed in perpetuity. A valid mark may be licensed, perhaps to a "registered user" or it may be assigned, in some cases only with the sale of the goodwill of a business. A growing example of international licensing of trademarks can be found in franchise agreements taken abroad. And national trademark law sometimes accompanies international licensing. The principal U.S. trademark law, the Lanham Act of 1946, has been construed to apply extraterritorially (much like the Sherman Antitrust Act) to foreign licensees engaging in deceptive practices.[4] Foreigners who seek a registration may be required to prove a prior and valid "home registration," and a new registration in another country may not have an existence "independent" of the continuing validity of the home country registration. Foreigners are often assisted in their registration efforts by international and regional trademark treaties.

The WTO TRIPs Agreement (see Section 1.11) supports common approaches to trademark rights, including recognition of service marks, a ban on linking foreign marks with local marks, a prohibition of compulsory trademark licensing, and general re-affirmation of the Paris Convention (see Section 20.8).

§ 20.3   Quality Controls in Franchising

Because franchising links trademarks with business attributes, there is a broad duty in the law for the franchisor to maintain quality controls over the franchisee, particularly in the business format franchise system. Any failure of the franchisor to maintain such quality controls could cause the trademark in question to be abandoned and lost to the franchisor.[5] In order to maintain adequate quality controls, the franchisor must typically police the operations of the franchisee.[6]

Broadly speaking, the duty to maintain quality controls arises because a trademark is a source symbol. The public is entitled to

---

[4]   See especially Scotch Whiskey Association v. Barton Distilling Co., 489 F.2d 809 (7th Cir.1973).

[5]   See, e.g., Yamamoto & Co. v. Victor United, Inc., 219 U.S.P.Q. 968 (C.D.Cal.1982).

[6]   See Dawn Donut Co. v. Hart's Food Stores, Inc., 267 F.2d 358 (2d Cir.1959).

rely upon that source symbol in making its purchasing decisions so as to obtain consistent product quality and attributes. International franchisors operating at a distance from their franchisees must be especially concerned with quality controls. On the other hand, excessive control or the public appearance of such control may give rise to an agency relationship between the franchisor and the franchisee. Such a relationship could be used to establish franchisor liability for franchisee conduct, including international product and other tort liabilities.[7] It may be possible to minimize these risks through disclaimer or indemnification clauses in the franchise agreement.

§ 20.4   Copyright Protection in Franchising

Although franchising primarily focuses upon trademarks and trademark licensing, the use of copyrights frequently parallels such activity. For example, the designs and logos of the franchisor may be copyrighted, and certainly its instruction manual and other such written communications to franchisees should be copyrighted. These copyrights benefit in many countries from the Universal Copyright Convention (UCC) of 1952 and the Berne Convention of 1886. The United States now adheres to both of these conventions. Under the UCC, copyright holders receive national treatment, translation rights (subject to compulsory license) and other benefits. This convention will excuse any national registration requirement provided a notice of a claim of copyright is adequately given. However, in the United States, a reservation was made such that registration of foreign copyrights is required if the only convention under which foreigners are seeking such protection is the Universal Copyright Convention of 1952.

If the foreigner comes from a nation which adheres to the Berne Convention, national treatment and a release from U.S. registration formalities is obtained. The Berne Convention permits local copyright protection independent of protection granted in the country of origin and does not require copyright notice. Prior to 1987, most United States copyright holders acquired Berne Convention benefits by simultaneously publishing their works in Canada, a member country. Since 1987 the United States has ratified the Berne Convention, including an ambiguous adherence to its provisions on "moral rights" (rights of "integrity" and "paternity") for artists and authors. This has the practical effect of eliminating registration requirements for foreign copyright holders.

---

[7]   See Hanson, The Franchising Dilemma: Franchisor Liability for Actions of a Local Franchisee, 19 N.C.Central L.J. 190 (1991).

It also extends United States copyright relations to approximately 25 new nations.

§ 20.5   Protection of Franchise Trade Secrets

Franchise formulae often involve utilization of trade secrets. This may range from recipes and cooking techniques to customer lists, pricing formulas, market data or bookkeeping procedures. It is extremely difficult to protect such trade secrets under United States law. The first problem arises from the concept of what is a trade secret. Generally speaking, abstract ideas or business practices which do not involve an element of novelty are not considered trade secrets.[8] Even if franchise trade secrets are involved, maintaining such secrets can be difficult given the wide number of persons who may have access to the confidential information. Even though the franchisees may promise to maintain such secrets, once released into the business public there may not be an effective way to recapture the secret or remedy the harm.[9]

The duty not to disclose trade secrets should be extended to employees of the franchisee. This can be done by permitting dissemination only on a need-to-know basis. However, it may be impossible not to permit certain employees from the knowledge of cooking procedures or recipes, for example. Once again the remedies and efforts to recapture the secret are likely to be inadequate.[10] Terminated employees and terminated franchisees are another fertile source of the loss of trade secrets. Tort remedies employing misappropriation theories may prevent the utilization or disclosure by such persons of trade secrets where there is a possibility of competition with the franchisor.[11] Damages are generally viewed as an inadequate remedy in the trade secret field because the harm of the loss of the secret is irreparable. *See* Section 20.14.

§ 20.6   The Franchise Agreement, U.S. Franchising

International franchising raises a host of legal issues under intellectual property, antitrust, tax, licensing and other laws. The significance of these issues is magnified by the rapid growth of international franchising. Hundreds of U.S. companies have, in total, tens of thousands of foreign franchises. Nearly 70 percent of these franchisors started in Canada, with Japan and Britain

---

[8]   See Kewanee Oil Co. v. Bicron Corp., 416 U.S. 470, 94 S.Ct. 1879, 40 L.Ed.2d 315 (1974).

[9]   See Smith v. Dravo Corp., 203 F.2d 369 (7th Cir.1953).

[10]   See Shatterproof Glass Corp. v. Guardian Glass Co., 322 F.Supp. 854 (E.D.Mich.1970) *affirmed* 462 F.2d 1115 (6th Cir.1972).

[11]   See FMC Corp. v. Taiwan Tainan Giant Industrial Co., 730 F.2d 61 (2d Cir.1984).

following. Some United States investors have found franchising the least risky and most popular way to enter Eastern Europe. But franchising is not just a United States export. Many foreign franchisors have entered the U.S. market.

Most franchisors have standard contracts which are used in their home markets and receive counsel on the myriad of laws relevant to their business operations. Such contracts need to be revised and adapted to international franchising without significantly altering the franchisor's successful business formula. Franchise fees and royalties must be specified, the provision of services, training, and control by the franchisor detailed, the term and area of the franchise negotiated ("master franchises" conveying rights in an entire country or region are common in international franchise agreements), accounting procedures agreed upon, business standards and advertising selected, insurance obtained, taxes and other liabilities allocated, default and dispute settlement procedures decided. At the heart of all franchise agreements lies a trademark licensing clause conveying local trademark rights of the franchisor to the franchisee in return for royalty payments.

Franchising is an important sector in the United States economy. Thousands of franchisors have created and administer franchise systems throughout the nation. U.S. franchisees number in the hundreds of thousands. These franchisees are typically independent business persons, and their local franchise outlets employ millions of people. It has been estimated that approximately one-third of all retail sales in the United States take place through franchised outlets. Just as U.S. franchisors have found franchising particularly effective for market penetration abroad, Canadian, European and Japanese companies are increasingly penetrating the U.S. market through franchising.

Franchising is a business technique that permits rapid and flexible penetration of markets, growth and capital development. In the United States, there are traditional distinctions between product franchises and business format franchises. Product franchises involve manufacturers who actually produce the goods that are distributed through franchise agreements. For example, ice cream stores, soft drink bottling companies and gasoline retailers are often the subject of product franchises. Business format franchises are more common. These do not involve the manufacture by the franchisor of the product being sold by the franchisee. More typically, the franchisor licenses intellectual property rights in conjunction with a particular "formula for success" of the business. Fast food establishments, hotels, and a variety of service franchises are examples of business format franchising.

U.S. regulation of franchise relationships occurs at both the federal and state levels of government. Such regulation can be as specific as the Federal Trade Commission Franchising Rule and state franchise disclosure duties, or as amorphous as the ever present dangers of state and federal antitrust law.

§ 20.7   Regulation of International Franchising

Were franchising unaffected by regulation, the attorney's role would be limited to negotiation and drafting of the agreement. But international franchising is increasingly regulated by home and host jurisdictions, including regional groups like the European Union (EU). In third world countries, especially Latin America, technology transfer laws aimed principally at international patent and know-how licensing also regulate franchise agreements. These laws benefit franchisees and further development policies, e.g., the conservation of hard currencies by control of royalty levels. In 1986, the European Court of Justice issued a major opinion on the legality of franchise agreements under EU competition law.[12] This decision indicates that Union law can depart significantly from leading United States antitrust law on market division arrangements for distributors.[13]   The EU first implemented a comprehensive regulation on franchise agreements in 1988.[14]

There is often a perception of being invaded culturally that follows franchising. Local laws sometimes respond to the cultural impact of foreign franchises, but this did not stop McDonald's from opening in Moscow with great success. In India and Mexico, nationalist feelings hostile to the appearance of foreign trademarks on franchised products have produced laws intended to remove such usage. For example, the Mexican Law of Inventions and Trademarks (1976) (repealed 1987) anticipated requiring use of culturally Mexican marks in addition to marks of foreign origin. Dual marks are now voluntary in Mexico and prohibited by NAFTA. Other nations require local materials (olive oil in the Mediterranean) to be substituted. This could, for example, alter the formula for success (and value) of fast food franchises. Still others (e.g., Alberta, Canada) mandate extensive disclosures by franchisors in a registered prospectus before agreements may be

---

[12]   Pronuptia de Paris GmbH v. Pronuptia de Paris Irmgard Schillgallis (1986) Eur.Comm.Rep. 353. See Section 19.9.

[13]   Compare Continental T.V., Inc. v. GTE Sylvania Inc., 433 U.S. 36, 97 S.Ct. 2549, 53 L.Ed.2d 568 (1977) (location clauses not per se illegal); American Motor Inns, Inc. v. Holiday Inns, Inc., 521 F.2d 1230 (3d Cir.1975) (allocation of franchisor/franchisee towns and territories *per se* illegal).

[14]   Commission Regulation No. 4087/88, replaced by Regulation 2790/99, and replaced again by Regulation 330/10, discussed in Section 19.9.

completed. Disclosure violations can trigger a range of franchisee remedies: recision, injunctions and damages. Such laws are also found in many of the states of the United States.

Franchise advertising must conform to local law. For example, regulations in the People's Republic of China prohibit ads which "have reactionary . . . content." Antitrust and tax law are important in international franchising. Double taxation treaties, for example, will affect the level of taxation of royalties. Antitrust law will temper purchasing requirements of the franchisor, lest unlawful "tying arrangements" be undertaken. Tying arrangements involve coercion of franchisees to take supplies from the franchisor or designated sources as part of the franchise.

Such arrangements must, by definition, involve two products: the tying and tied products. They are subject to a complex and not entirely consistent body of case law under the U.S. Sherman Antitrust Act, Articles 101 and 102 of the TFEU and other laws. *See* Chapter 19. For example, one leading United States antitrust case treats the trademark licenses as a separate tying product and the requirement of the purchase by franchisees of non-essential cooking equipment and paper products unlawful.[15] Another case permits franchisors to require franchisees to purchase "core products" (e.g., chicken) subject to detailed specifications, or from a designated list of approved sources.[16] Sometimes the "core product" and the trademark license are treated as a single product incapable of being tied in violation of the law.[17] Still another leading case suggests that anything comprising the franchisor's "formula for success" may possibly be tied in the franchise contract.[18] This may be notably lawful if there was full pre-contract disclosure by the franchisor.

§ 20.8   The Paris Convention as Applied to Trademarks

The premium placed on priority of use of a trademark is reflected in several international trademark treaties. These include the 1883 Paris Convention for the Protection of Industrial Property, the 1957 Arrangement of Nice Concerning the International Classification of Goods and Services, and the 1973 Trademark

---

[15]   Siegel v. Chicken Delight, Inc., 448 F.2d 43 (9th Cir.1971), *cert. denied* 405 U.S. 955, 92 S.Ct. 1172, 31 L.Ed.2d 232 (1972).

[16]   Kentucky Fried Chicken Corp. v. Diversified Packaging Corp., 549 F.2d 368 (5th Cir.1977).

[17]   Krehl v. Baskin-Robbins Ice Cream Co., 664 F.2d 1348 (9th Cir.1982) (franchisees must buy Baskin-Robbins ice cream).

[18]   Principe v. McDonald's Corp., 631 F.2d 303 (4th Cir.1980), *cert. denied* 451 U.S. 970, 101 S.Ct. 2047, 68 L.Ed.2d 349 (1981) (franchisees required to lease land and buildings from McDonald's).

Registration Treaty. The treaties of widest international application are the Paris Convention and the Arrangement of Nice, to which the United States is a signatory. The International Bureau of the World Intellectual Property Organization (WIPO) in Geneva plays a central role in the administration of arrangements contemplated by these agreements.

The Paris Convention reflects an effort to internationalize some trademark rules. In addition to extending the nondiscriminatory principal of national treatment and providing for a right of priority of six months for trademarks, the Convention mitigates the frequent national requirement that foreigners seeking trademark registration prove a pre-existing, valid and continuing home registration. This makes it easier to obtain foreign trademark registration, avoids the possibility that a lapse in registration at home will cause all foreign registrations to become invalid, and allows registration abroad of entirely different (and perhaps culturally adapted) marks. The Paris Convention right of priority eliminates the need to simultaneously file for trademark protection around the globe. Filings abroad that are undertaken within six months of the home country filing for trademark registration will take priority. Paris Convention parties may, however, reject trademark applications if they infringe existing marks, lack distinctive character, offend public morality or order, or may deceive the public . . .

The Paris Convention has in excess of 170 member nations. Since the Convention provides that any domestic trademark registration filing gives rise to priority in all Paris Convention countries, this means that foreign marks registered in countries that do not require use of the mark on an actual product can be obtained in the United States. In other words, foreign trademarks that are not used are entitled under the Paris Convention to U.S. trademark registration. Since 1988, the foreign applicant must state a bona fide intention to use the mark in commerce, but actual use is not required prior to registration.[19]

The Paris Convention also deals with unregistered trademarks. Article 6bis requires the member nations to refuse to register, to cancel an existing registration or to prohibit the use of a trademark which is considered by the trademark registration authorities of that country to be "well known" and owned by a person entitled to the benefits of the Paris Convention. This provision concerns what are called "famous marks" and prevents their infringement even if there has been no local registration of the mark. This is a

---

[19]   15 U.S.C.A. § 1126(e).

remarkable development because it effectively creates trademark rights without registration. It has, for example, been successfully invoked in the People's Republic of China in order to protect against infringing use of Walt Disney and other well-known trademarks. In protecting such marks, China sided with the interpretation of the Paris Convention that marks that are well-known internationally deserve protection, even if not well known locally.

§ 20.9   The Nice Agreement on Trademark Classification

The Nice Agreement addresses the question of registration by "class" or "classification" of goods. In order to simplify internal administrative procedures relating to marks, many countries classify and thereby identify goods (and sometimes services) which have the same or similar attributes. An applicant seeking registration of a mark often is required to specify the class or classes to which the product mark belongs. However, not all countries have the same classification system and some lack any such system. Article 1 of the Nice Agreement adopts, for the purposes of the registration of marks, a single classification system for goods and services. This has brought order out of chaos in the field.

§ 20.10   International Trademark Registration Treaties

The 1973 Vienna Trademark Registration Treaty (to which the United States is a signatory) contemplates an international filing and examination scheme like that in force for patents under the Patent Cooperation Treaty of 1970. *See* Section 20.13. This treaty has not yet been fully implemented, but holds out the promise of reduced costs and greater uniformity when obtaining international trademark protection. The 1994 Trademark Law Treaty substantially harmonized trademark registration procedures.

Numerous European and Mediterranean countries are parties to the 1891 Madrid Agreement for International Registration of Marks. Since 2002, the United States has joined in the Madrid Protocol of 1989. This agreement permits international filings to obtain national trademark rights and is administered by WIPO. German, French and U.S. filers are the greatest users of the Madrid Protocol, often seeking Chinese, EU or Russian registrations.

A Common Market trademark can now be obtained in the European Union, an alternative to national trademark registrations and the "principle of territoriality" underlying IP laws. *See* Section 17.14.

§ 20.11   Patents and Know-how

The following sections concern the most common form of lawful international technology transfer—patent and know-how licensing. Before any patent licensing can take place, patents must be acquired in all countries in which the owner hopes there will be persons interested in purchasing the technology. Even in countries where the owner has no such hope, patent rights may still be obtained so as to foreclose future unlicensed competitors.

Licensing is a middle ground alternative to exporting from the owner's home country and direct investment in host markets. It can often produce, with relatively little cost, immediate positive cash flows. After a brief introduction to patents and know-how, the main themes of are standard licensing contract terms and the regulation of international licensing agreements.

§ 20.12   Protecting Patents

For the most part, patents are granted to inventors according to national law. Thus, patents represent *territorial* grants of exclusive rights. The inventor receives Canadian patents, United States patents, Mexican patents, and so on. There are relatively few jurisdictions without some form of patent protection. However, legally protected intellectual property in one country may not be protected similarly in another country. For example, third world nations sometimes *refuse* to grant patents on pharmaceuticals. These countries often assert that their public health needs require such a policy. Thailand has been one such country and unlicensed "generics" have been a growth industry there. Similarly, most European countries do not grant patents on medical and surgical therapeutic techniques for reasons of public policy.

Nominal patent protection in some developing nations may lack effective forms of relief—giving the appearance but not the reality of legal rights. Since international patent protection is expensive to obtain, some holders take a chance and limit their applications to those markets where they foresee demand or competition for their product. Nevertheless, U.S. nationals continue to receive tens of thousands of patents in other countries. But the reverse is also increasingly true. Residents of foreign countries now receive over 50 percent of the patents issued under United States law. In many countries, persons who deal with the issuance and protection of patents are called patent agents. In the United States, patent practice is a specialized branch of the legal profession. Obtaining international patent protection often involves retaining the services of specialists in each country.

What constitutes a "patent" and how it is protected in any country depends upon domestic law. In the United States, a patent issued by the U.S. Patent Office grants the right for 20 years to exclude everyone from making, using or selling the patented invention without the permission of the patentee.[20] The United States traditionally granted patents to the "first to invent," not (as in many other countries) the "first to file." The U.S. has switched to first to file rules. Moreover, foreign patent applications are now considered part of the prior art in reviewing novelty issues regardless of their language. Patent infringement can result in injunctive and damages relief in the U.S. courts. "Exclusion orders" against foreign-made patent infringing goods are also available. Such orders are frequently issued by the International Trade Commission under Section 337 of the Tariff Act of 1930, and are enforced by the U.S. Customs Service. *See* Chapter 8.

A U.S. patent thus provides a short-term legal, but not necessarily economic, monopoly. For example, the exclusive legal rights conveyed by the patents held by Xerox on its photocopying machines have not given it a monopoly in the marketplace. There are many other producers of non-infringing photocopy machines with whom Xerox competes.

There are basically two types of patent systems in the world community, registration and examination. Some countries (e.g., France) grant a patent upon "registration" accompanied by appropriate documents and fees, without making an inquiry about the patentability of the invention. The validity of such a patent grant is most difficult to gauge until a time comes to defend the patent against alleged infringement in an appropriate tribunal. In other countries, the patent grant is made following a careful "examination" of the prior art and statutory criteria on patentability or a "deferred examination" is made following public notice given to permit an "opposition." The odds are increased that the validity of such a patent will be sustained in the face of an alleged infringement.

The United States and Germany have examination systems. To obtain U.S. patents, applicants must demonstrate to the satisfaction of the Patent and Trademark Office that their inventions are novel, useful and nonobvious. Nevertheless, a significant number of U.S. patents have been subsequently held invalid in the courts and the Patent Office has frequently been criticized for a lax approach to issuance of patents. Much of this growth is centered in high-tech industries, including computer software and business methods

---

[20]   35 U.S.C.A. § 154.

patents. The U.S. has also been criticized for sometimes allowing patents on "traditional knowledge" (e.g., Mexican Enola Beans) found primarily in the developing world.

The terms of a patent grant vary from country to country. For example, local law may provide for "confirmation," "importation," "introduction" or "revalidation" patents (which serve to extend limited protection to patents already existing in another country). "Inventor's certificates" and rewards are granted in some socialist countries where private ownership of the means of production is discouraged. The state owns the invention. This was the case in China, for example, but inventors now may obtain patents and exclusive private rights under the 1984 Patent Law. Some countries, such as Britain, require that a patent be "worked" (commercially applied) within a designated period of time. This requirement is so important that the British mandate a "compulsory license" to local persons if a patent is deemed unworked. Many developing nations have similar provisions in their patent laws . . . the owner must use it or lose it.

§ 20.13   International Acquisition of Patents

The principal treaties regarding patents are the 1970 Patent Cooperation Treaty and the 1883 Paris Convention for the Protection of Industrial Property, frequently revised and amended. To some extent, the Paris Convention also deals with trademarks, service marks, trade names, industrial designs, and unfair competition. Other recent treaties dealing with patents are the European Patent Convention (designed to permit offices at Munich and The Hague to issue patents of all countries party to the treaty), the European Union Unitary Patent (designed to create a single patent valid throughout most of the EU). *See* Section 17.14.

Paris Convention

The Paris Convention,[21] to which over 170 countries including the U.S. are parties, remains the basic international agreement dealing with treatment of foreigners under national patent laws. It is administered by the International Bureau of the World Intellectual Property Organization (WIPO) at Geneva. The "right of national treatment" (Article 2) prohibits discrimination against foreign holders of local patents and trademarks. Thus, for example, an American granted a Canadian patent must receive the same legal rights and remedies accorded Canadian nationals. Furthermore, important "rights of priority" are granted to patent holders provided they file in foreign jurisdictions within twelve

---

[21]   21 U.S.T. 1583, T.I.A.S. No. 6295, 828 U.N.T.S. 305 (Stockholm revision).

months of their home country patent applications. But such rights conceivably may not overcome prior filings in "first to file" jurisdictions, now including the United States.

Patent applications in foreign jurisdictions are not dependent upon success in the home country: Patentability criteria vary from country to country. Nevertheless, the Paris Convention obviates the need to file simultaneously in every country where intellectual property protection is sought. If an inventor elects not to obtain patent protection in other countries, anyone may make, use or sell the invention in that territory. The Paris Convention does not attempt to reduce the need for individual patent applications in all jurisdictions where patent protection is sought. Nor does it alter the various domestic criteria on patentability. It does anticipate compulsory licensing of patents that are not "worked" within three years of their grant.

Patent Cooperation Treaty

The Patent Cooperation Treaty (PCT),[22] to which about 140 countries including the U.S. are parties, is designed to achieve greater uniformity and less cost in the international patent filing process, and in the examination of prior art. Instead of filing patent applications individually in each nation, filings under the PCT are done in selected countries. The national patent offices of Japan, Sweden, the former Soviet Union and the United States have been designated International Searching Authorities (ISA), as have the European Patent Offices at Munich and The Hague. The international application, together with the international search report, is communicated by an ISA to each national patent office where protection is sought. Nothing in this Treaty limits the freedom of each nation to establish substantive conditions of patentability and determine infringement remedies.

However, the Patent Cooperation Treaty also provides that the applicant may arrange for an international preliminary examination in order to formulate a nonbinding opinion on whether the claimed invention is novel, involves an inventive step (non-obvious) and is industrially applicable. In a country without sophisticated search facilities, the report of the international preliminary examination may largely determine whether a patent will be granted. For this reason alone, the Patent Cooperation Treaty may generate considerable uniformity in world patent law. In 1986 the United States ratified the PCT provisions on preliminary examination reports, thereby supporting such uniformity. China, Japan and South Korea now account for more

---

[22]   28 U.S.T. 7645, T.I.A.S. No. 8733.

than the largest number of PCT applications, with Germany and the United States declining in utilization.

§ 20.14   Protecting Know-how and Trade Secrets

Know-how is commercially valuable knowledge. It may or may not be a trade secret, and may or may not be patentable. Though often technical or scientific, e.g., engineering services, know-how can also be more general in character. Marketing and management skills as well as simply business advice can constitute know-how. If someone is willing to pay for the information, it can be sold or licensed internationally.

Legal protection for know-how varies from country to country and is, at best, limited. Unlike patents, copyrights and trademarks, you cannot by registration obtain exclusive legal rights to know-how. Knowledge, like the air we breathe, is a public good. Once released in the community, know-how can generally be used by anyone and is almost impossible to retrieve. In the absence of exclusive legal rights, preserving the confidentiality of know-how becomes an important business strategy. If everyone knows it, who will pay for it? If your competitors have access to the knowledge, your market position is at risk. It is for these reasons that only a few people on earth ever know the Coca Cola formula, which is perhaps the world's best kept know-how.

In the United States, the Economic Espionage Act of 1996 creates *criminal* penalties for misappropriation of trade secrets on goods or services for the benefit of foreign governments or anyone. For these purposes, a "trade secret" is defined as "financial, business, scientific, technical, economic or engineering information" that the owner has taken reasonable measures to keep secret and whose "independent economic value derives from being closely held." In addition to criminal fines, forfeitures and jail terms, the Act authorizes seizure of all proceeds from the theft of trade secrets as well as property used or intended for use in the misappropriation (e.g., buildings and capital equipment). The number of criminal prosecutions under this statute is rising, notably regarding theft of software code, hybrid technologies, military technology, and pharmaceutical and chemical formulae.

Protecting know-how is mostly a function of contract, tort and trade secrets law. NAFTA was the first international agreement to require recognition and protection of trade secrets. *See* Section 16.8. Comparable provisions followed in the WTO TRIPs agreement. *See* Section 1.11. Employers will surround their critical know-how with employees bound by contract to confidentiality. But some valuable knowledge leaks from or moves with these employees, e.g., when a disgruntled retired or ex-employee sells or goes public with the know-how. The remedies at law or in equity for breach of contract are unlikely to render the employer whole. Neither is tort relief likely to be sufficient since most employees are essentially judgment proof, although they may be of more use if a competitor induced the breach of contract. Likewise, even though genuine trade secrets are protected by criminal statutes in a few jurisdictions, persuading the prosecutor to take up your business problem is not easy and criminal penalties will not recoup the trade secrets (though they may make the revelation of others less likely in the future).

Despite all of these legal hazards, even when certain know-how is patentable, a desire to prolong the commercial exploitation of that knowledge may result in no patent registrations. The international chemicals industry, for example, is said to prefer trade secrets to public disclosure and patent rights with time limitations. Licensing or selling such know-how around the globe is risky, but lucrative.

§ 20.15 International Patent and Know-how Licensing

This section concerns the most common form of lawful international technology transfer-patent and know-how licensing. Before any patent licensing can take place, patents must be acquired in all countries in which the owner hopes there will be persons interested in purchasing the technology. Even in countries where the owner has no such hope, patent rights may still be obtained so as to foreclose future unlicensed competitors. Licensing is a middle ground alternative to exporting from the owner's home country and direct investment in host markets. It can often produce, with relatively little cost, immediate positive cash flows.

International patent and know-how licensing is the most critical form of technology transfer to third world development. From the owner's standpoint, it presents an alternative to and sometimes a first step towards foreign investment. Such licensing involves a transfer of patent rights or know-how (commercially valuable knowledge, often falling short of a patentable invention) in return for payments, usually termed royalties. Unlike foreign investment, licensing does not have to involve a capital investment in a host jurisdiction and may be tax-advantaged. However, licensing of patents and know-how is not without legal risks.

From the licensee's standpoint, and the perspective of its government, there is the risk that the licensed technology may be old or obsolete, not "state of the art." Goods produced under old technology will be hard to export and convey a certain "second class" status. On the other hand, older more labor intensive technologies may actually be sought (as sometimes done by the PRC) in the early stages of development. Excessive royalties may threaten the economic viability of the licensee and drain hard currencies from the country. The licensee typically is not in a sufficiently powerful position to bargain away restrictive features of standard international licenses. For all these reasons, and more, third world countries frequently regulate patent and know-how licensing agreements. Such law is found in the Brazilian Normative Act No. 17 (1976) and the Mexican Technology Transfer Law (1982) (repealed 1991), among others. Royalty levels will be limited, certain clauses prohibited (e.g., export restraints, resale price maintenance, mandatory gran backs to the licensor of improvements), and the desirability of the technology evaluated.

Regulation of licensing is not limited to the developing world. The European Union extensively regulates patent and know-how licensing. *See* Sections 19.7 and 19.8. In the United States, there is a less direct form of licensing regulation via antitrust law.

The licensor also faces legal risks. The flow of royalty payments may be stopped, suspended or reduced by currency exchange regulations. The taxation of the royalties, if not governed by double taxation treaties, may be confiscatory. The licensee may abscond with the technology or facilitate "gray market" goods (see Chapter 9) which eventually compete for sales in markets exclusively intended for the licensor. In the end, patents expire and become part of the world domain. At that point, unless the technology is somehow tied to a protected trade secret, the licensee has effectively purchased the technology and becomes an independent competitor (though not necessarily an effective competitor if the licensor has made new technological advances).

Licensing is a kind of partnership. If the licensee succeeds, the licensor's royalties (often based on sales volumes) will increase and a continuing partnership through succeeding generations of technology may evolve. If not, the dispute settlement provisions of the agreement may be called upon as either party withdraws from the partnership. Licensing of patents and know-how often is combined with, indeed essential to, foreign investments. A foreign subsidiary or joint venture will need technical assistance and know-how to commence operations. When this occurs, the licensing terms are usually a part of the basic joint venture or investment agreement. Licensing may also be combined with a trade agreement, as where the licensor ships necessary supplies to the licensee, joint venturer, or subsidiary. Such supply agreements have sometimes been used to overcome royalty limitations through a form of "transfer pricing," the practice of marking up or down the price of goods so as to allocate revenues to preferred parties and jurisdictions (e.g., tax havens).

§ 20.16   Technology Transfer Agreements

The process of transferring technology involves an agreement which outlines the relationship between the transferor and the transferee. The extent to which the agreement is detailed may depend upon the character of the transferee.

Subsidiary or affiliate as transferee. Even when the technology is transferred to a wholly owned subsidiary in a foreign nation, there is almost always some agreement, at the very least for tax purposes. The corporate structure using a parent and subsidiary (the latter being an entity incorporated under the laws of the foreign host nation) demands that the separate nature of the two entities be maintained. If not, the parent may be held responsible for the debts of the subsidiary under veil piercing theory. Consequently, the transfer of technology from a parent to a subsidiary should be at arms-length to avoid transfer pricing allegations and represented by a written agreement. But if the parent is convinced that there is little likelihood that the subsidiary's management will adversely affect the value of the technology, or produce poor quality goods using the technology, there are likely to be fewer provisions in the agreement than where the transferee is an independent entity, unrelated to the transferor.

Independent transferee. When the agreement is to transfer technology to an entity which is not part of the transferor's corporate structure, such as a subsidiary or affiliate, there will be a sense that more detail ought to appear in the technology agreement. For example, disputes will not be settled "within" the company, as they may when the transfer of technology is to a subsidiary, but by judicial or arbitral tribunals. A transfer within a corporate structure is usually easily worked out, but a transfer to an independent transferee may involve considerable negotiation of many details.

§ 20.17   Regulation of Technology Transfers (TT)

When transfer of technology rules do not exist in the recipient country, the technology transfer agreement is the conclusion of the bargaining of the two parties. The agreement will not be public; it will not be registered. But in some nations, especially developing nations and nonmarket economy nations, the government may be involved in the determination and regulation of the technology transfer agreement. Typically, without approval from a technology transfer commission, the TT agreement is void and unenforceable.

In such jurisdictions, the parties end up negotiating terms for their agreement that are acceptable to the TT Commission.

Developing World Technology Transfer Regulations

During the 1970s a number of developing nations enacted transfer of technology laws. In Latin America, Decision No. 24 of the ANCOM group pioneered the use of regulatory TT Commissions. The ANCOM approach spread like wildfire throughout Latin America. The laws were adopted both as part of the general attempt to control foreign investment and technology transfers, but also to preserve scarce hard currency at a time of severe balance of payment problems. The developing nations viewed technology transfer agreements as an area where there were serious abuses, and believed that their laws would adequately address these issues.[23] The principal abuses were thought to include the following:

1. Transfer of obsolete technology;

2. Excessive price paid for the technology;

3. Limitations on use of new developments by the transferee by grant back provisions;

4. Little research performed by the transferee;

5. Too much intervention by the transferor in transferee activities;

6. Limitations on where the transferee may market the product;

7. Requirements for components be purchased from the transferor which are available locally or could be obtained from other foreign sources more cheaply;

8. Inadequate training of transferee's personnel to do jobs performed by personnel of the transferor;

9. Transfer of technology which has adequate domestic substitutes and is therefore not needed;

10. Too long a duration of the agreement; and

11. Application of foreign law and use of foreign tribunals for dispute resolution.

These do not establish an exclusive list. Some nations had different reasons for wishing to more closely govern technology transfers. But

---

[23] See Radway, Antitrust, Technology Transfers and Joint Ventures in Latin American Development, 15 Lawyer Am. 47 (1983).

these reasons provide an outline of what areas transfer of technology laws in the 1970s attempted to govern.

The result of these restrictive laws was the transfer of less technology, and of technology less valuable to the source. It was often older technology over which the company was willing to relinquish some control. The bureaucracies established to register and approve or disapprove the agreements were often staffed with persons who knew little about technology, less about international business, but who possessed all of the inefficiency and incompetence of many government agencies. The laws did not bring in more technology, but less. The consequence was that they did not serve the purpose of helping the balance of payments. Furthermore, the nations which adopted strict rules regulating the transfer of technology often did not have laws which protected intellectual property.

In the 1980s and 1990s, some of these restrictive laws were dismantled, whether by formal repeal or replacement by more transfer encouraging and intellectual property protecting laws, or by a relaxed interpretation of the laws and a general automatic approval of what the transferor and transferee agreed upon. Mexico, for example, eliminated its Technology Transfer Commission in 1991. Ironically, some technology agreements which were used in the 1960s before the enactment of the strict laws, and which became unusable after such enactments, are now once again being used in the developing world, but regulated in the European Union. *See* Section 19.7. However, a substantial number of "technology transfer" control laws remain in force in Latin America, notably Brazil.

§ 20.18 The WTO TRIPs Agreement, EU and NAFTA Coverage

Obtaining protection of intellectual property rights around the world, and the transfer of those rights freely or under compulsory license, is significantly influenced by the WTO Trade-Related Intellectual Property Rights (TRIPs) agreement. *See* Section 1.11. For coverage of intellectual property rights and transfers in Europe, see Sections 17.13, 17.14 and 19.7–19.9. For NAFTA coverage, see Section 16.8.

Chapter 21

INTERNATIONAL COMMERCIAL ARBITRATION

Table of Sections

For coverage of arbitration of numerous foreign "investor-state" disputes under NAFTA, see Section 16.10.

---

§ 21.0   Introduction

Dispute resolution in international trade transactions ranges from friendly consultations to litigation everywhere. In between, nonbinding conciliation and mediation do their best at facilitating a compromise, an approach common to Asia. In between also lies international commercial arbitration, a binding alternative to days in court. The volume of international commercial arbitration has grown enormously in recent decades, particularly in the Americas, Europe and the Middle East.

One variation of a *forum* selection clause is one that chooses no court at all, but selects an alternate dispute resolution mechanism, such as an arbitration tribunal. For a long time, the courts of many nations resisted validating such clauses, holding that they deprived the parties of due process of law (a reaction one might expect toward a competitor). For example, England was slow to adopt arbitration anywhere near to its current use, largely due to the belief that adversaries were entitled to their day in court. Legislatures were far more sympathetic to allowing arbitration, and around the early years of the last century began to enact statutes validating arbitration clauses. The issue now is firmly settled.

In addition to arbitration, there are many even less formal alternate dispute resolution mechanisms. The mini-trial, for example, comes in a variety of packages, each with a different impact on resolution of the dispute. It can be nonbinding if used with a "neutral advisor"; it can be semi-binding if its results are admissible in later judicial proceedings; or it can be binding before a court appointed master.[1]

§ 21.1 Why Arbitrate?

The growth of international commercial arbitration is in part a retreat from the vicissitudes and uncertainties of international business litigation. More positively, international commercial arbitration offers predictability, confidentiality and neutrality as a forum (who knows which court you otherwise may end up in) and the potential for specialized expertise (most judges have relatively little experience in applying international or foreign law). International commercial arbitration also allows the parties to select and shape the procedures and costs of dispute resolution. That said, international commercial arbitration procedures are often informal and not laden with legal rights. To quote Judge Learned Hand:

> Arbitration may or may not be a desirable substitute for trials in courts; as to that the parties must decide in each instance. But when they have adopted it, they must be content with its informalities; they may not hedge it about with those procedural limitations which it is precisely its purpose to avoid. They must content themselves with looser approximations to the enforcement of their rights than those that the law accords them, when they resort to its machinery.[2]

One of the most attractive attributes of international commercial arbitration is the enforceability in national courts of arbitral awards under the 1958 U.N. Convention on Recognition and Enforcement of Arbitral Awards, commonly called the New

---

[1]   For a review of the variety of such alternative dispute resolution mechanisms, see Nelson, "Alternatives to Litigation of International Disputes," 23 *Int'l Lawyer* 187 (1989).

[2]   American Almond Products Co. v. Consolidated Pecan Sales Co., Inc., 144 F.2d 448, 451 (2d Cir.1944).

York Convention.[3] Roughly 150 nations participate in the New York Convention. There is no comparable convention for the enforcement of court judgments, although lengthy negotiations took place around the end of the last century for the adoption of a Hague Convention on Jurisdiction and Enforcement of Judgments, it was not concluded. Only a less encompassing 2005 Convention on Choice of Court Agreements was concluded, but it has not been successful in attracting signatories.

Other less encompassing agreements governing aspects of arbitration exist, one of the more important to the United States being the Inter-American Convention on International Commercial Arbitration, commonly called the Panama Convention.[4] That 1975 Convention renders arbitral awards enforceable in Latin America. It has attracted nineteen members, nearly all the nations of Latin America with the exception of Cuba.

Another major advantage of international commercial arbitration is the support of legal regimes that give arbitration agreements dispositive effects. In the United States, for example, the Federal Arbitration Act provides a level of legal security unknown to international business litigation. Many countries have similar statutes, thus avoiding issues of subject matter and personal jurisdiction, *forum non conveniens,* and the like.[5] Professor Park has noted that, excepting New York, there are no statutory frameworks supporting court selection clauses at the state or federal level.[6] In worst case scenarios, parties selecting a court to resolve their disputes may end up with a court that refuses to hear the case.

One of the least attractive attributes of international commercial arbitration is the minimal availability of pre-trial provisional remedies.[7] In addition, many arbitrators focus on splitting the differences between the parties, not the vindication of legal rights which in courts might result in "winner takes all." But such extreme results could permanently disrupt otherwise longstanding and mutually beneficial business relationships.

---

[3]   U.N. Convention on Recognition and Enforcement of Arbitral Awards (1958), 21 U.S.T. 2517, 330 U.N.T.S. 38.

[4]   Inter-American Convention on International Commercial Arbitration of 1975, 14 I.L.M. 336 (1975).

[5]   See Park, "When and Why Arbitration Matters" in Hartwell (ed.), The Commercial Way of Justice (1997); Richards v. Lloyd's of London, 107 F.3d 1422 (9th Cir.1997) *reversed* 135 F.3d 1289 (9th Cir.1998).

[6]   Park, "Bridging the Gap in Forum Selection: Harmonizing Arbitration and Court Selection," 8 Transnat'l Law & Contemp. Probs. 19 (Spring 1998).

[7]   See Borden, Inc. v. Meiji Milk Products Co., 919 F.2d 822 (2d Cir.1990), *cert. denied*, 500 U.S. 953, 111 S.Ct. 2259, 114 L.Ed.2d 712 (1991).

Perhaps, therefore, "splitting the baby" through arbitration really is the optimal outcome, even when the split is not equal.

Clearly international commercial arbitration has its pros and cons. Regardless of which way you would like to see the balance tipped, the use of arbitral dispute resolution methods is. One distinguished set of authors believes that this trend is hardly surprising. Here is their analysis of why:

> "Trade and investment across state lines is on the rise, and parties from different jurisdictions who engage in such activity frequently seek the comparative neutrality of a non-state tribunal to resolve their differences. Parties to a transaction from different states may be reluctant to submit to the jurisdiction of the courts of the other. This reluctance may arise from lack of enthusiasm about operating in another language, or according to the procedures and, insofar as it infiltrates procedure, the substantive law of another state. In some circumstances, one party may fear that the courts of the other may have a preference for their own nationals, may share a dislike of a particular foreign nationality or may, in cases involving very large amounts of money, lean toward finding in favor of their national because of the consequences for their national economy and political system. Where one of the parties is a state or state agency, a non-state party may prefer arbitration to submitting a dispute to the courts of the other contracting party. Arbitration may thus serve to "equalize" the non-state entity by transferring the dispute to a setting which may be designed to minimize or ignore the sovereign character of one of the parties rather more than would a national court.
>
> Arbitration may also be utilized because the various national laws which might be relevant have not developed enough to treat problems raised in a pioneer industry. Thus issues regarding intellectual property rights in computer software of companies from different states may be submitted to arbitration as a way of resolving a dispute by shaping new law on the matter. In some circumstances potential litigants may also seek out arbitration because it is touted as more rapid, private and cheaper than domestic adjudication, though many of these characteristics of international commercial arbitration may be relative and sometimes overstated.
>
> International commercial arbitration is also on the increase because many national court systems not only

help international arbitration but appear anxious to externalize a larger amount of the disputes that are formally within their jurisdiction. The willingness of national courts to compel parties who have made prior commitments to engage in private arbitration and then to enforce the awards that ensue, subject only to limited judicial review, increases the likelihood that parties will resort to that mode of dispute resolution.[8]

§ 21.2 Types and Places of International Commercial Arbitrations

There are two distinct types of international commercial arbitrations: ad hoc and institutional. Ad hoc arbitrations involve selection by the parties of the arbitrators and rules governing the arbitration. The classic formula involves each side choosing one arbitrator who in turn agree upon a third arbitrator. The ad hoc arbitration panel selects its procedural rules (such as the UNCITRAL Arbitration Rules). Ad hoc arbitration can be agreed upon in advance or, quite literally, selected ad hoc as disputes arise.

Institutional arbitration involves selection of a specific arbitration center or "court," often accompanied by its own rules of arbitration. Institutional arbitration is in a sense pre-packaged, and the parties need only "plug in" to the arbitration system of their choice. There are numerous competing centers of arbitration, each busy marketing its desirability to the world business community. Some centers are longstanding and busy, such as the International Chamber of Commerce "Court of Arbitration" in Paris which has its own Rules of Arbitration. Other centers are more recent in time and still struggling for clientele, such as the Commercial Arbitration and Mediation Center for the Americas, the Kuala Lumpur Regional Arbitration Center, and the Cairo Regional Center for International Arbitration.

Proceedings conducted in "arbitration friendly" seats (jurisdictions) such as London, New York, Paris, Stockholm, Hong Kong and Singapore (but not this author's home state of California) allow considerable freedom to choose home-country lawyers, what procedures to follow, which language to use, where to meet, pursue class arbitrations, and face minimal mandatory legal provisions (see Section 21.3). Moreover, the seat or legal situs of the arbitration may influence the degree to which courts interject themselves before, during or after the proceedings, and facilitate enforcement of the award under the New York Convention (see Section 21.7).

---

[8]   W. Michael Reisman, W. Laurence Craig, William W. Park & Jan Paulsson, International Commercial Arbitration (Foundation Press 1997).

Ad hoc arbitration presupposes a certain amount of goodwill and flexibility between the parties. It can be speedy and less costly than institutional arbitration. The latter, on the other hand, offers ease of incorporation in an international business agreement, supervisory services, a stable of experienced arbitrators and a fixed fee schedule. The institutional environment is professional, a quality that sometimes can get lost in ad hoc arbitrations. Awards from well-established arbitration centers (including default awards) are more likely to be favorably recognized in the courts if enforcement is needed. Many institutional arbitration centers now also offer "fast track" or "mini" services to the international business community.

Uncertainty about identity of the country and the court in which a dispute may be heard, about procedural and substantive rules to be applied, about the degree of publicity to be given the proceedings and the judgment, about the time needed to settle a dispute, and about the efficacy which may be given to a resulting judgment all have combined to make arbitration the preferred mechanism for solving international commercial disputes. Some Western European countries long have been accustomed to arbitration (e.g., see English Arbitration Act of 1889 and English Arbitration Act of 1950, as amended by Arbitration Act of 1979); the London Court of Arbitration, a private arbitration institution, has existed since 1892. The United States has had a Federal Arbitration Act since 1947.[9]

Arbitration in international commercial contracts is favored by the People's Republic of China, if mediation and conciliation fails, either through the Chinese International Economic and Trade Arbitration Commission (CIETAC) or the Chinese Maritime Arbitration Commission (MAC). Most of the nations of the former Soviet Union also favor arbitration, and have organizations similar to the Chinese CIETAC and MAC. In terms of volume, CIETAC is now the world's largest arbitration center.

The Japan Commercial Arbitration Association has been active since 1953. Virtually all countries in Africa have arbitration statutes. Latin America, historically disadvantaged in many arbitral awards, increasingly is accepting arbitration. For example, the 1975 Inter-American Convention on International Commercial Arbitration[10] provides, in part, that "The Governments of the Member States of the Organization of American States . . . have agreed that . . . an agreement in which parties undertake to submit to arbitral decision any differences . . . with respect to a commercial

---

9   9 U.S.C.A. § 1 et seq.
10   See 14 Int'l Legal Mat. 336.

transaction is valid." The 1979 Inter-American Convention on Extraterritorial Validity of Foreign Judgments and Arbitral Awards expands upon the scope of the 1975 Convention.

§ 21.3　Mandatory Law

Almost all jurisdictions have enacted law they consider "mandatory," *i.e.* public law that private parties cannot avoid by contract. Exactly where the line is drawn between mandatory and non-mandatory law is crucial to ICA.

Many lower U.S. federal courts had held that "mandatory laws" could not be the subject matter of arbitration because of the public interest indicated by the legislative intent underlying the enactment of mandatory law and the public policy favoring judicial enforcement of such law. However, the Supreme Court has rejected that doctrine. In *Scherk v. Alberto-Culver Co.*[11], the Court held that Securities and Exchange Commission law issues arising out of an international contract are subject to arbitration under the Federal Arbitration Act *(9 U.S.C.A.* § 1 et seq.) despite the public interest in protecting the United States investment climate. In *Mitsubishi Motors Corp. v. Soler Chrysler-Plymouth, Inc.*[12], the Court held that antitrust claims arising out of an international transaction were arbitrable, despite the public interest in a competitive national economy, and the legislative pronouncements favoring enforcement by private parties.

In *Vimar Seguros y Reaseguros, S.A. v. M/V Sky Reefer*,[13] claims that the foreign arbitrators would not apply the United States mandatory COGSA bill of lading law were rejected on the ground that the U.S. could "review" the arbitral award at the award-enforcement stage. That power may, however, be very narrow under the 1958 United Nation's Convention on the Recognition and Enforcement of Foreign Arbitral Awards (the New York Convention). *See* Section 21.7.

In both *Mitsubishi Motors* and *M/V Sky Reefer*, the Court determined that issues arising out of international transactions involving U.S. mandatory law were arbitrable. However, in *dictum* at the end of the *Mitsubishi* opinion, the Court stated that U.S. courts would have a second chance at the enforcement stage to

---

[11]　417 U.S. 506, 94 S.Ct. 2449, 41 L.Ed.2d 270 (1974).

[12]　473 U.S. 614, 105 S.Ct. 3346, 87 L.Ed.2d 444 (1985). The Ninth, Eleventh and First Circuits have held on the basis of *Mitsubishi* that private antitrust claims are arbitrable. See Seacoast Motors of Salisbury, Inc. v. DaimlerChrysler Motors Corp., 271 F.3d 6 (1st Cir. 2001), *cert. denied* 535 U.S. 1054, 122 S.Ct. 1911, 152 L.Ed.2d 821 (2002).

[13]　515 U.S. 528, 115 S.Ct. 2322, 132 L.Ed.2d 462 (1995).

examine whether the arbitral tribunal "took cognizance of the antitrust claims and actually decided them." Similar language can be found in *M/V Sky Reefer* regarding COGSA claims. It would seem to be difficult to fit any such examination by the U.S. courts properly into the structure of the New York Convention. It is not clear whether *Mitsubishi* invites the U.S. courts merely to examine whether the arbitrators state that they considered the antitrust issues, or further invites them to examine whether the arbitrators considered these issues *correctly* (review on the merits). The former can be evaded by a mechanical phrase; the latter can harm the arbitral process, especially if the parties have chosen non-U.S. law to govern their agreement.

In either case, arbitrators' enforcement of U.S. antitrust laws may not be to the standards of U.S. courts, and the status of recognition and enforcement of arbitral awards involving antitrust issues is not yet clear. Under the New York Convention, a mere "misunderstanding," or error in interpretation, of a mandatory law by an arbitral tribunal has generally not been held to "contravene public policy." The cases are split as to whether even a "manifest disregard" of United States law constitutes such a violation of public policy. Awards have been upheld which violate the U.S. Vessel Owner's Limitation of Liability Act, previously considered mandatory law. Thus, it is not certain, under the New York Convention, that United States courts retain the review powers assumed by the *Mitsubishi* and *M/V Sky Reefer* Courts to be available at the "award-enforcement stage" of the proceedings.

§ 21.4   International Arbitral Rules and Laws: UNICITRAL

The factors considered above are incorporated in Model International Commercial Arbitration Rules[14] issued in 1976 by the United Nations Commission on International Trade Law (UNCITRAL) following ten years of study. They were revised in 2010. The UNCITRAL Rules are intended to be acceptable in all legal systems and in all parts of the world. Rapidly developing countries favor the Rules because of the care with which they have been drafted, and because UNCITRAL was one forum for developing arbitration rules in which their concerns would be heard. The Arbitral Institute of the Stockholm Chamber of Commerce has been willing to work with the UNCITRAL Rules, as has the London Court of Arbitration. The Iran–United States Claims Tribunal has used the UNCITRAL Rules in dealing with claims arising out of the confrontation between the two countries in

---

[14]   See 15 Int'l Legal Mat. 701 (1978).

1980. Unlike the Stockholm Chamber of Commerce Rules, the UNCITRAL Rules are not identified with any national or international arbitration organization.

Among other things, UNCITRAL rules provide that an "appointing authority" shall be chosen by the parties or, if they fail to agree upon that point, shall be chosen by the Secretary-General of the Permanent Court of Arbitration at The Hague (comprised of a body of persons prepared to act as arbitrators if requested). The UNCITRAL rules also cover notice requirements, representation of the parties, challenges of arbitrators, evidence, hearings, the place of arbitration, language, statements of claims and defenses, pleas to the arbitrator's jurisdiction, provisional remedies, experts, default, rule waivers, the form and effect of the award, applicable law, settlement, interpretation of the award and costs. In 2012, UNCITRAL issued a pre-release of its "Recommendations to assist arbitral institutions and other interested bodies with regard to arbitration under the UNCITRAL Arbitration Rules as revised in 2010." They will replace recommendations issued in 1982.

In addition to its 1976 Model Arbitration Rules, UNCITRAL also promulgated a 1985 Model Law on International Commercial Arbitration, amended in 2006.[15] While the Model Rules are directed to potential or actual disputing parties, the Model Law is directed to states. The Model Law, or legislation based on the Model Law, has been enacted in more than sixty nations. It has also been enacted as state law by several states of the U.S., including California, Connecticut, Florida, Illinois, Louisiana, Oregon, and Texas. There seems to be no competing federal law which would pre-empt the application of these enactments. Additionally, China has not adopted the law, but both Hong Kong and Macao have. Similarly, the United Kingdom has not adopted the law, but both Bermuda and Scotland have.

Under the UNCITRAL Model Law, submission to arbitration may be *ad hoc* for a particular dispute, but is accomplished most often in advance of the dispute by a general submission clause within a contract. Under Article 8 of the Model Law, an agreement to arbitrate is specifically enforceable.

Although no specific language will guarantee the success of an arbitral submission, UNCITRAL recommends the following model submission clause:

> Any dispute, controversy or claim arising out of or relating
> to this contract, or the breach, termination or invalidity

---

[15]   www.uncitral.org. See Lowry, Critical Documents Sourcebook Ann. 345 (1991).

thereof, shall be settled by arbitration in accordance with
the UNCITRAL Arbitration Rules as at present in force.

§ 21.5 International Arbitration Rules: ICSID

Some of the same issues discussed immediately above are also
incorporated in the text of the Arbitration Rules adopted under the
1966 Convention on the Settlement of Investment Disputes
Between States and Nationals of Other States (TIAS 6090), to
which over 140 countries are parties. The Convention was
implemented in the United States by 22 U.S.C. § 1650 and § 1650a.
An arbitral money award, rendered pursuant to the Convention, is
entitled to the same full faith and credit in the United States as a
final judgment of a court of general jurisdiction in a State of the
United States.[16]

The 1966 Convention provided for the establishment of an
International Center for the Settlement of Investment Disputes
(ICSID), as a non-financial organ of the World Bank (the
International Bank for Reconstruction and Development). ICSID is
designed to serve as a forum for both conciliation and arbitration of
disputes between private investors and host governments. It
provides an institutional framework within which arbitrators,
selected by the disputing parties from an ICSID Panel of
Arbitrators or from elsewhere, conduct arbitration in accordance
with ICSID Rules of Procedure for Arbitration Proceedings.
Arbitrations are held in Washington D.C. unless agreed otherwise.

Under the 1966 Convention (Article 25), ICSID's jurisdiction
extends only "to any legal dispute arising directly out of an
investment, between a Contracting State or . . . any subdivision . . .
and a national of another Contracting State, which the parties to
the dispute consent in writing to submit to the Centre. Where the
parties have given their consent, either in respect of future disputes
or in respect of existing disputes, no party may withdraw its
consent unilaterally." Thus, ICSID is an attempt to institutionalize
dispute resolution between States and non-State investors. It
therefore always presents a "mixed" arbitration.

If one party questions such jurisdiction (predicated upon
disputes arising "directly out of" an investment, between a
Contracting Party and the national of another, and written consent
to submission), the issue may be decided by the arbitration tribunal
(Rule 41). A party may seek annulment of any award by an appeal
to an ad hoc committee of persons drawn by the Administrative
Council of ICSID from the Panel of Arbitrators under the

---

[16]   22 U.S.C.A. § 1650a.

Convention (Article 52). Annulment is available only if the Tribunal was not properly constituted, exceeded its powers, seriously departed from a fundamental procedural rule, failed to state the reasons for its award, or included a member who practiced corruption.

The Convention's 1966 jurisdictional limitations have prompted the ICSID Administrative Counsel to establish an Additional Facility for conducting conciliations and arbitrations for disputes which do not arise directly out of an investment and for investment disputes in which one party is not a Contracting State to the Convention or the national of a Contracting State. The Additional Facility is intended for use by parties having long-term relationships of special economic importance to the State party to the dispute and which involve the commitment of substantial resources on the part of either party. The Facility is not designed to service disputes which fall within the 1966 Convention or which are "ordinary commercial transaction" disputes. ICSID's Secretary General must give advance approval of an agreement contemplating use of the Additional Facility. Because the Additional Facility operates outside the scope of the 1966 Convention, the Facility has its own arbitration Rules.

The ICSID Arbitration Rules have become adopted for use in most NAFTA Chapter 11 investor-state arbitrations and, more recently, in CAFTA-DR Chapter 10 investor-state arbitrations. *See* Section 16.7.

§ 21.6   ICC and LCIA Arbitral Rules and Clauses

Many parties use the Rules of the Court of Arbitration of the International Chamber of Commerce (ICC) at Paris or of one of its national committees, such as the international commercial panel of the American Arbitration Association. The ICC Rules are modern, most recently updated in 2012, and often used in international arbitration. Some 13,000 arbitrations have been administered by the ICC.[17]

Although the ICC International Court of Arbitration is not a court in the judicial meaning of that label, its primary role is to administer arbitrations. The Court does not itself resolve disputes, such function being that of independent arbitral tribunals appointed under the ICC Rules, a major goal of the Court is to see that arbitral awards are enforceable at law.

---

[17]   See W. Laurence Craig, William W. Park and Jan Paulsson, International Chamber of Commerce Arbitration (3rd Edition, 2000).

The London Court of International Arbitration (LCIA), with roots to 1883, is another leading global forum for dispute resolution using arbitration, although it also is active in mediation. The London Court has its own rules and procedures. Its hourly rates are often less expensive than the ICC's percentage of the amount in controversy fees.

The Court of Arbitration of the ICC in Paris recommends use of the following model clause for the adoption of its rules:

> All disputes arising in connection with the present contract shall be finally settled under the Rules of Conciliation and Arbitration of the International Chamber of Commerce by one or more arbitrators appointed in accordance with the said Rules.

Parties who wish to refer any dispute to the equally active London Court of International Arbitration may use the following model clause:

> The validity, construction and performance of this contract (agreement) shall be governed by the laws of England and any dispute that may arise out of or in connection with this contract (agreement), including its validity, construction and performance, shall be determined by arbitration under the Rules of the London Court of International Arbitration at the date hereof, which Rules with respect to matters not regulated by them, incorporate the UNCITRAL Arbitration Rules. The parties agree that service of any notices in reference to such arbitration at their addresses as given in this contract (agreement) (or as subsequently varied in writing by them) shall be valid and sufficient.

§ 21.7 Enforcement of Arbitral Awards: The New York Convention

Arbitration is only as useful as its decisions are recognized and enforced. Perhaps no other instrument has been more important to the success of international arbitration than the New York Convention.

In approximately 150 countries, the enforcement of arbitral awards is facilitated by the 1958 United Nations Convention on the Recognition and Enforcement of Foreign Arbitral Awards (the "New York Convention").[18] "[T]he principal purpose underlying American

---

[18]   21 U.S.T. 2518, T.I.A.S. No. 6997, 330 U.N.T.S. 38, implemented in the United States by 9 U.S.C.A. §§ 201–208. www.newyorkconvention1958.org.

. . . implementation . . . was to encourage the recognition and enforcement of commercial arbitration agreements in international contracts and to unify the standards by which agreements to arbitrate are observed and arbitral awards are enforced in the signatory countries."[19] In an abbreviated procedure, under the Federal Arbitration Act (FAA) enactment of the New York Convention, federal district courts entertain motions to confirm or to challenge a foreign award. For these purposes, awards between U.S. citizens may be treated as foreign based upon performance or property located abroad. *See* Section 21.9 for the text of the New York Convention and its FAA enactment.

The New York Convention commits the courts in each Contracting State to recognize and enforce arbitration clauses and written arbitration agreements for the resolution of international commercial disputes between parties having a "defined legal relationship." Where the court finds an arbitral clause or agreement, it "*shall* . . . refer the parties to arbitration, unless it finds that the said agreement is null and void, inoperative, or incapable of being performed" (emphasis added).[20] This amounts to a judicial duty to compel arbitration absent contract deficiencies. The New York Convention also commits the courts in each Contracting State to recognize and enforce (under local procedural rules) the awards of arbitral tribunals under such clauses or agreements, and also sets forth the limited grounds under which recognition and enforcement may be refused. Under the New York Convention, grounds for refusal to enforce include:

(1) Incapacity or invalidity of the agreement containing the arbitration clause "under the law applicable to" a party to the agreement,

(2) Lack of proper notice of the arbitration proceedings, the appointment of the arbitrator or other reasons denying an adequate opportunity to present a defense,

(3) Failure of the arbitral award to restrict itself to the terms of the submission to arbitration, or decision of matters not within the scope of that submission,

(4) Composition of the arbitral tribunal not according to the arbitration agreement or applicable law, and

(5) Non-finality or the setting aside or suspension of the arbitral award by authorities in the country where the

---

[19]   Scherk v. Alberto-Culver Co., 417 U.S. 506, 520 n. 15, 94 S.Ct. 2449, 41 L.Ed.2d 270 (1974).

[20]   Article II(3).

award was rendered, or by authorities of the country under whose law the award was made.[21]

In addition to these grounds for refusal, recognition or enforcement may also be refused if it would be contrary to the public policy of the country in which enforcement is sought, or if the subject matter of the dispute cannot be settled by arbitration under the law of that country.[22] Courts in the United States have taken the position that the "public policy limitation on the New York Convention is to be construed narrowly [and] to be applied only where enforcement would violate the forum state's most basic notions of morality and justice."[23] Recourse to other limitations of the Convention, in order to defeat its applicability, has been greeted with judicial caution in the absence of violation of basic U.S. notions of morality and justice.[24] However, the Second Circuit has held that the doctrine of *forum non conveniens* applies in arbitral award confirmation proceedings under the New York Convention.[25]

Whether the N.Y. Convention applies generally turns upon where the award was or will be made, not the citizenship of the parties.[26] A growing number of courts in developing nations are issuing injunctions against arbitration proceedings before they commence. Many of these injunctions seem deliberately intended to protect local companies. Parties who proceed to arbitrate after such an injunction has been issued do so at their peril. Subsequent enforcement of the award under the New York Convention in the enjoining nation will almost certainly be voided on grounds of public policy. Hence enforcement can only proceed in non-enjoining jurisdictions, assuming that their public policy permits this.

§ 21.8   International Arbitration Agreements, Arbitrators and Awards Under U.S. Law

International arbitration agreements, traditionally called *compromis,* come in a variety of forms. Many arbitration centers sponsor model clauses that can be incorporated into business agreements. The New York Convention obliges courts of participating nations, upon request, to refer disputes to arbitration

---

[21]   Article V.

[22]   *Id.*

[23]   Fotochrome, Inc. v. Copal Co., Ltd., 517 F.2d 512 (2d Cir.1975).

[24]   Parsons & Whittemore Overseas Co., Inc. v. Societe Generale De L'Industrie Du Papier (RAKTA), 508 F.2d 969 (2d Cir.1974).

[25]   In re Monegasque de Reassurances S.A.M. v. Nak Naftogaz of Ukraine, 311 F.3d 488 (2d Cir.2002).

[26]   See Ministry of Defense of the Islamic Republic of Iran v. Gould Inc., 887 F.2d 1357 (9th Cir.1989), *cert. denied*, 494 U.S. 1016, 110 S.Ct. 1319, 108 L.Ed.2d 494 (1990).

unless the agreement is "null and void, inoperative or incapable of being performed."[27] The existence and validity of an arbitration agreement must be proved, and can be litigated before the arbitration takes place.

Article II(2) of the New York Convention requires states to recognize written arbitration agreements *signed* by the parties "or contained in an exchange of letters or telegrams." In most jurisdictions exchanges of fax, email and the like embracing arbitration will also be recognized. However, arbitration clauses in unsigned purchase orders do not amount to a written agreement to arbitrate.[28] Pre-arbitration litigation often revolves around motions to compel arbitration.[29] If no such motion is made, and a court judgment is rendered (even by default), the right to arbitrate may be waived.[30] Delays in triggering arbitration or invocation of litigation rights may constitute a waiver of arbitration rights.[31]

Whether a valid agreement to arbitrate exists depends on the specifics of the arbitration clause, not the entire business agreement. The arbitration clause is severable, and issues of validity (such as fraud in the inducement of the arbitration clause and unconscionability) are directed to it.[32] Many courts will stretch the limits of the New York Convention in order to uphold an arbitration clause.[33] When there is a battle of forms, the same judicial bias towards arbitration is often found.[34] But, in most cases, the disputes must "arise under" the business transaction to be arbitrable,[35] legal claims falling outside the transaction remain in court.[36]

The closure or misdescription of an arbitration center designated in the agreement (e.g., the New York Chamber of

---

[27]   Article II(3).

[28]   Kahn Lucas Lancaster, Inc. v. Lark Int'l Ltd., 186 F.3d 210 (2d Cir.1999).

[29]   See, e.g., Tennessee Imports, Inc. v. P.P. Filippi & Prix Italia, S.R.L., 745 F.Supp. 1314 (M.D.Tenn.1990).

[30]   See Menorah Insurance Co. v. INX Reinsurance Corp., 72 F.3d 218 (1st Cir.1995).

[31]   See O.J. Distributing, Inc. v. Hornell Brewing Co., 340 F.3d 345 (6th Cir.2003); Colón v. R. K. Grace & Co., 358 F.3d 1 (1st Cir.2003).

[32]   Prima Paint Corp. v. Flood & Conklin Mfg. Co., 388 U.S. 395, 87 S.Ct. 1801, 18 L.Ed.2d 1270 (1967). See Republic of Nicaragua v. Standard Fruit Co., 937 F.2d 469 (9th Cir.1991). See also Hunt v. Up North Plastics, Inc., 980 F.Supp. 1046 (D.Minn.1997), *cert. denied*, 503 U.S. 919, 112 S.Ct. 1294, 117 L.Ed.2d 516 (1992).

[33]   See Sphere Drake Insurance PLC v. Marine Towing, Inc., 16 F.3d 666 (5th Cir.1994), *cert. denied* 513 U.S. 871, 115 S.Ct. 195, 130 L.Ed.2d 127 (1994) (absence of signature to standard insurance policy contract no barrier to arbitration).

[34]   See I.T.A.D. Associates, Inc. v. Podar Bros., 636 F.2d 75 (4th Cir.1981).

[35]   See Mediterranean Enterprises, Inc. v. Ssangyong Corp., 708 F.2d 1458 (9th Cir.1983).

[36]   Id. See Coors Brewing Co. v. Molson Breweries, 51 F.3d 1511 (10th Cir.1995).

Commerce) is no barrier to arbitration. A substitute arbitrator will be appointed by the court if the parties cannot agree.[37] The U.S. Supreme Court has held that arbitrators are subject to "requirements of impartiality" and must "disclose to the parties any dealings that might create an impression of possible bias."[38] That said, most U.S. courts are loathed to intrude or vacate an arbitration award on disclosure grounds.[39]

There is a split of opinion as to whether the implied ground of "manifest disregard of the law" bars enforcement of an arbitral award in U.S. courts under the New York Convention. The Second Circuit believes so[40] while the Eleventh and D.C. Circuits say no.[41] Article V of the New York Convention does not recognize manifest disregard of the law as a basis for denial of enforcement.

Another issue concerning the New York Convention is whether to adjourn U.S. enforcement proceedings if parallel proceedings to vacate the award have been commenced in the country of arbitration. Despite the risks of forum shopping and delay, the Second Circuit indicated that adjournment can be appropriate, depending upon the circumstances.[42] The Second Circuit has also denied use of 28 U.S.C. § 1782 to obtain compulsory non-party discovery in private commercial arbitrations. The issue was whether the I.C.C. in Paris constituted a "tribunal" within the scope of that statute.[43]

Cases in the United States have pointed out that parties cannot refer a dispute to a court while an arbitration is in

---

[37]   See Astra Footwear Industry v. Harwyn International, Inc., 442 F.Supp. 907 (S.D.N.Y.1978).

[38]   Commonwealth Coatings Corp. v. Continental Casualty Co., 393 U.S. 145, 89 S.Ct. 337, 21 L.Ed.2d 301 (1968).

[39]   See Andros Compania Maritima v. Marc Rich & Co., 579 F.2d 691 (2d Cir. 1978).

[40]   Yusuf Ahmed Alghanim & Sons v. Toys 'R' Us, Inc., 126 F.3d 15 (2d Cir.1997), cert. denied 522 U.S. 1111, 118 S.Ct. 1042, 140 L.Ed.2d 107 (1998); Westerbeke Corp. v. Daihatsu Motor Co., Ltd., 304 F.3d 200 (2d Cir.2000); Duferco International Steel Trading v. T. Klaveness Shipping, 333 F.3d 383 (2d Cir.2003); Hardy v. Walsh Manning Securities, LLC, 341 F.3d 126 (2d Cir.2003). In view of Hall Street Associates, LLC v. Mattel, Inc., 552 U.S. 576, 128 S.Ct. 1396 (2008), doubt exists as to the current view in the Second Circuit. The Hall decision has been criticized in subsequent lower federal court decisions. See, e.g., Robert Lewis Rosen Assoc., Ltd. v. Webb, 566 F.Supp2d 228 (S.D.N.Y. 2008); F. Hoffman-LaRoche Ltd. v. Qiagen Gaithersburg, Inc., 2010 WL 3184228 (S.D.,N.Y. 2010).

[41]   Industrial Risk Insurers v. M.A.N. Gutehoffnungshutte GmbH, 141 F.3d 1434 (11th Cir.1998), cert.denied 525 U.S. 1068, 119 S.Ct. 797, 142 L.Ed.2d 659 (1999). Accord, In re Arbitration between Int'l Thunderbird Gaming Corp. v. United Mexican States, 473 F. Supp.2d 80 (D.C. Cir. 2007).

[42]   Europcar Italia, S.p.A. v. Maiellano Tours, Inc., 156 F.3d 310 (2d Cir.1998).

[43]   National Broadcasting Co. v. Bear Stearns & Co., 165 F.3d 184 (2d Cir.1999).

progress[44] or block enforcement of an award in the United States in reliance upon the fact that the award, although binding in the country where rendered, is under appeal there.[45] Interim orders of arbitrators, such as records disclosures, may be enforceable "awards" under the N.Y. Convention.[46] After the arbitration is concluded, a party may not be able to block enforcement of the award in reliance upon the United States Foreign Sovereign Immunities Act[47], but a court may decline to enforce in reliance upon the Act of State Doctrine.[48] U.S.bankruptcy courts may enjoin international arbitration agreements.[49]

One court granted enforcement, under the Convention, of a New York award rendered in favor of a non-citizen claimant against a non-citizen defendant.[50] Awards entirely between U.S. citizens are not subject to the New York Convention unless they concern property located abroad, envisage performance or enforcement abroad, or have some other reasonable relation with foreign state(s).[51]

When arbitral awards are annulled at their *situs*, courts in enforcing jurisdictions have taken different positions on the enforceability of the award. French courts enforced an improperly vacated award to the detriment of the claimant who had prevailed in a second arbitration.[52] A U.S. federal district court refused to honor the clearly legitimate annulment of an arbitral award by an Egyptian court because the parties had agreed not to appeal the award.[53] The Second Circuit, on the other hand, recognized the annulment of two arbitral awards vacated by a Nigerian court and refused enforcement.[54] The latter approach seems more consistent

---

[44]   Siderius, Inc. v. Compania de Acero del Pacifico, S.A., 453 F.Supp. 22 (S.D.N.Y.1978).

[45]   Fertilizer Corp. of India v. IDI Management, Inc., 517 F.Supp. 948 (S.D.Ohio 1981).

[46]   See Publicis Communication v. True North Communications, Inc. 206 F.3d 725 (7th Cir.2000).

[47]   See Ipitrade International, S.A. v. Federal Republic of Nigeria, 465 F.Supp. 824 (D.D.C.1978) and Creighton Ltd. v. Government of Qatar, 181 F.3d 118 (D.C.Cir.1999).

[48]   Libyan American Oil Co. v. Socialist People's, etc., 482 F.Supp. 1175 (D.D.C.1980).

[49]   In re US Lines, 197 F3d 631 (2d Cir 1999); In re White Mountain Mining Co., LLC, 403 F3d 164 (4th Cir 2005).

[50]   Bergesen v. Joseph Muller Corp., 548 F.Supp. 650 (S.D.N.Y.1982).

[51]   9 U.S.C. § 202 (1994).

[52]   Hilmarton v. OTV, 1997 Rev. Arb. 376, note Ph. Fouchard discussed in Park, "Duty and Discretion in International Arbitration," 93 Am. J. Int'l Law 805 (1999).

[53]   Chromalloy Aeroservices v. Egypt, 939 F.Supp. 907 (D.D.C.1996). Accord, In re COMMISA, ___ F.Supp. ___ (S.D.N.Y. Aug. 27, 2013) (award annulled in Mexico arbitral seat enforced).

[54]   Baker Marine (Nig.) Ltd. v. Chevron (Nig.) Ltd., 191 F.3d 194 (2d Cir.1999).

with the terms of Article V(e) of the New York Convention regarding awards that have been set aside or suspended in their source country. *See* Section 21.7.

The U.S. Supreme Court has repeatedly affirmed that arbitrators have jurisdiction to decide their own jurisdiction (compétence-compétence).[55] The Court has indicated that questions of the arbitrability of disputes may be arbitrated, but only if the parties have manifested a *clear* willingness to be bound by arbitration on such issues.[56] Silence or ambiguity should favor judicial review of arbitrability issues.[57] Arbitration clauses that adopt the UNITRAL Rules meet the requirement of clarity to arbitrate arbitrability because Article 21 conveys jurisdictional issues to the tribunal.[58]

U.S. courts are split on whether contract parties may alter the scope of judicial review of arbitration awards. Three Circuits reject expansion of statutory or common law review standards.[59] The Ninth and Tenth Circuits permit contractual expansion of judicial review standards.[60] Attempts at *narrowing* statutory standards are likely to be rejected.[61]

§ 21.9   Text of the New York Convention (NYC) and Federal Arbitration Act Enactment of the NYC

Public Law 91–368, Approved July 31, 1970,
9 U.S.C. §§ 201–208, 84 Stat. 692

§ 201.   Enforcement of Convention

The Convention on the Recognition and Enforcement of Foreign Arbitral Awards of June 10, 1958, shall be enforced in United States courts in accordance with this chapter.

---

[55]   See, e.g., Howsam v. Dean Witter Reynolds, Inc., 537 U.S. 79, 123 S.Ct. 588, 154 L.Ed.2d 491 (2002); Pacificare Health Systems, Inc. v. Book, 538 U.S. 401, 123 S.Ct. 1531, 155 L.Ed.2d 578 (2003).

[56]   First Options of Chicago, Inc. v. Kaplan, 514 U.S. 938, 115 S.Ct. 1920, 131 L.Ed.2d 985 (1995).

[57]   *Id.*

[58]   Wal-Mart Stores, Inc. v. PT Multipolar Corp., 202 F.3d 280 (9th Cir.1999) (unpublished).

[59]   See Roadway Package System, Inc. v. Kayser, 257 F.3d 287 (3d Cir.2001); Syncor Int'l Corp. v. McLeland, 120 F.3d 262 (4th Cir.1997), *cert. denied*, 522 U.S. 1110, 118 S.Ct. 1039, 140 L.Ed.2d 105 (1998); Gateway Techn., Inc. v. MCI Telecomm. Corp., 64 F.3d 993 (5th Cir.1995).

[60]   See Kyocera Corp. v. Prudential-Bache Trade Services, Inc., 341 F.3d 987 (9th Cir.2003), *cert. dismissed*, 540 U.S. 1098, 124 S.Ct. 980, 157 L.Ed.2d 810 (2004); Bowen v. Amoco Pipeline Co., 254 F.3d 925 (10th Cir.2001).

[61]   See Hoeft v. MVL Group, Inc., 343 F.3d 57 (2d Cir.2003).

CONVENTION ON THE RECOGNITION AND ENFORCEMENT OF FOREIGN ARBITRAL AWARDS

Article I

1.   This Convention shall apply to the recognition and enforcement of arbitral awards made in the territory of a State other than the State where the recognition and enforcement of such awards are sought, and arising out of differences between persons, whether physical or legal. It shall also apply to arbitral awards not considered as domestic awards in the State where their recognition and enforcement are sought.

2.   The term "arbitral awards" shall include not only awards made by arbitrators appointed for each case but also those made by permanent arbitral bodies to which the parties have submitted.

3.   When signing, ratifying or acceding to this Convention, or notifying extension under article X hereof, any State may on the basis of reciprocity declare that it will apply the Convention to the recognition and enforcement of awards made only in the territory of another Contracting State. It may also declare that it will apply the Convention only to differences arising out of legal relationships, whether contractual or not, which are considered as commercial under the national law of the State making such declaration.

Article II

1.   Each Contracting State shall recognize an agreement in writing under which the parties undertake to submit to arbitration all or any differences which have arisen or which may arise between them in respect of a defined legal relationship, whether contractual or not, concerning a subject matter capable of settlement by arbitration.

2.   The term "agreement in writing" shall include an arbitral clause in a contract or an arbitration agreement, signed by the parties or contained in an exchange of letters or telegrams.

3.   The court of a Contracting State, when seized of an action in a matter in respect of which the parties have made an agreement within the meaning of this article, shall, at the request of one of the parties, refer the parties to arbitration, unless it finds that the said agreement is null and void, inoperative or incapable of being performed.

Article III

Each Contracting State shall recognize arbitral awards as binding and enforce them in accordance with the rules of procedure of the territory where the award is relied upon, under the conditions laid down in the following articles. There shall not be imposed substantially more onerous conditions or higher fees or charges on the recognition or enforcement of arbitral awards to which this Convention applies than are imposed on the recognition or enforcement of domestic arbitral awards.

Article IV

1.   To obtain the recognition and enforcement mentioned in the preceding article, the party applying for recognition and enforcement shall, at the time of the application, supply:

(a) The duly authenticated original award or a duly certified copy thereof;

(b) The original agreement referred to in article II or a duly certified copy thereof.

2.   If the said award or agreement is not made in an official language of the country in which the award is relied upon, the party applying for recognition and enforcement of the award shall produce a translation of these documents into such language. The translation shall be certified by an official or sworn translator or by a diplomatic or consular agent.

Article V

1.   Recognition and enforcement of the award may be refused, at the request of the party against whom it is invoked, only if that party furnishes to the competent authority where the recognition and enforcement is sought, proof that:

(a) The parties to the agreement referred to in article II were, under the law applicable to them, under some incapacity, or the said agreement is not valid under the law to which the parties have subjected it or, failing any indication thereon, under the law of the country where the award was made; or

(b) The party against whom the award is invoked was not given proper notice of the appointment of the arbitrator or of the arbitration proceedings or was otherwise unable to present his case; or

(c) The award deals with a difference not contemplated by or not falling within the terms of the submission to arbitration, or it contains decisions on matters beyond the scope of the submission to arbitration, provided that, if the decisions on matters submitted to arbitration can be separated from those not so submitted, that part of the award which contain decisions on matters submitted to arbitration may be recognized and enforced; or

(d) The composition of the arbitral authority or the arbitral procedure was not in accordance with the agreement of the parties, or, failing such agreement, was not in accordance with the law of the country where the arbitration took place; or

(e) The award has not yet become binding on the parties, or has been set aside or suspended by a competent authority of the country in which, or under the law of which, that award was made.

2.   Recognition and enforcement of an arbitral award may also be refused if the competent authority in the country where recognition and enforcement is sought finds that:

(a) The subject matter of the difference is not capable of settlement by arbitration under the law of that country; or

(b) The recognition or enforcement of the award would be contrary to the public policy of that country.

Article VI

If an application for the setting aside or suspension of the award has been made to a competent authority referred to in article V(1)(e), the authority before which the award is sought to be relied upon may, if it considers it proper, adjourn the decision on the enforcement of the award and may also, on the application of the party claiming enforcement of the award, order the other party to give suitable security.

* * *

Article XIV

A Contracting State shall not be entitled to avail itself of the present Convention against other Contracting States except to the extent that it is itself bound to apply the Convention.

* * *

Article XVI

1.   This Convention, of which the Chinese, English, French, Russian and Spanish texts shall be equally authentic, shall be deposited in the archives of the United Nations.

2.   The Secretary-General of the United Nations shall transmit a certified copy of this Convention to the States contemplated in article VIII.

Done at New York June 10, 1958: entered into force for the United States December 29, 1970, subject to declarations.*

Appendix

Federal Arbitration Act Provisions Enacting New York Convention 9 U.S.C. §§ 201–208

§ 202.   Agreement or Award Falling Under the Convention

An arbitration agreement or arbitral award arising out of a legal relationship, whether contractual or not, which is considered as commercial, including a transaction, contract, or agreement described in section 2 of this title, falls under the Convention. An agreement or award arising out of such a relationship which is entirely between citizens of the United States shall be deemed not to fall under the Convention unless that

---

*   The United States of America will apply the Convention, on the basis of reciprocity, to the recognition and enforcement of only those awards made in the territory of another Contracting State.

The United States of America will apply the Convention only to differences arising out of legal relationships, whether contractual or not, which are considered as commercial under the national law of the United States.

The Convention applies to all of the territories for the international relations of which the United States of America is responsible.

relationship involves property located abroad, envisages performance or enforcement abroad, or has some other reasonable relation with one or more foreign states. For the purpose of this section a corporation is a citizen of the United States if it is incorporated or has its principal place of business in the United States.

§ 203.   Jurisdiction; Amount in Controversy

An action or proceeding falling under the Convention shall be deemed to arise under the laws and treaties of the United States. The district courts of the United States (including the courts enumerated in section 460 of title 28) shall have original jurisdiction over such an action or proceeding, regardless of the amount in controversy.

§ 204.   Venue

An action or proceeding over which the district courts have jurisdiction pursuant to section 203 of this title may be brought in any such court in which save for the arbitration agreement an action or proceeding with respect to the controversy between the parties could be brought, or in such court for the district and division which embraces the place designated in the agreement as the place of arbitration if such place is within the United States.

§ 205.   Removal of Cases From State Courts

Where the subject matter of an action or proceeding pending in a State court relates to an arbitration agreement or award falling under the Convention, the defendant or the defendants may, at any time before the trial thereof, remove such action or proceeding to the district court of the United States for the district and division embracing the place where the action or proceeding is pending. The procedure for removal of causes otherwise provided by law shall apply, except that the ground for removal provided in this section need not appear on the face of the complaint but may be shown in the petition for removal. For the purposes of Chapter 1 of this title any action or proceeding removed under this section shall be deemed to have been brought in the district court to which it is removed.

§ 206.   Order to Compel Arbitration; Appointment of Arbitrators

A court having jurisdiction under this chapter may direct that arbitration be held in accordance with the agreement at any place therein provided for, whether that place is within or without the United States. Such court may also appoint arbitrators in accordance with the provisions of the agreement.

§ 207.   Award   of   Arbitrators;   Confirmation;   Jurisdiction; Proceeding

Within three years after an arbitral award falling under the Convention is made, any party to the arbitration may apply to any court having jurisdiction under this chapter for an order confirming the award as against any other party to the arbitration. The court shall confirm the award unless it finds one of the grounds for refusal or deferral of recognition or enforcement of the award specified in the said Convention.

§ 208.   Chapter 1; Residual Application

Chapter 1 applies to actions and proceedings brought under this chapter to the extent that that chapter is not in conflict with this chapter or the Convention as ratified by the United States.

Appendix

DOCUMENTS APPENDIX

Table of Sections

Sec.

1. General Agreement on Tariffs and Trade (GATT)

(Selected Provisions) (as amended)

The following provisions are selected sections from the General Agreement on Tariffs and Trade as enacted in 1947 and as amended and in force in 1994, when the Uruguay Round proposals were enacted. The original GATT 1947 is reproduced in 55 U.N.T.S. 194. It is also reproduced in the GATT Documents, "Basic Instruments and Selected Documents", also referred to as B.I.S.D. B.I.S.D. also includes the GATT as amended and in force in 1994.

Notes and supplementary provisions have been included at the end of each Article and Paragraph to which they apply.

Table of Contents

701

THE GENERAL AGREEMENT ON TARIFFS AND TRADE

The Governments of the Commonwealth of Australia, the Kingdom of Belgium, the United States of Brazil, Burma, Canada, Ceylon, the Republic of Chile, the Republic of China, the Republic of Cuba, the Czechoslovak Republic, the French Republic, India, Lebanon, the Grand-Duchy of Luxemburg, the Kingdom of the Netherlands, New Zealand, the Kingdom of Norway, Pakistan, Southern Rhodesia, Syria, the Union of South Africa, the United Kingdom of Great Britain and Northern Ireland, and the United States of America:

Recognizing that their relations in the field of trade and economic endeavour should be conducted with a view to raising standards of living, ensuring full employment and a large and steadily growing volume of real income and effective demand, developing the full use of the resources of the world and expanding the production and exchange of goods,

Being desirous of contributing to these objectives by entering into reciprocal and mutually advantageous arrangements directed to the substantial reduction of tariffs and other barriers to trade and to the elimination of discriminatory treatment in international commerce,

Have through their Representatives agreed as follows:

PART I

ARTICLE I. GENERAL MOST-FAVOURED-NATION TREATMENT

1. With respect to customs duties and charges of any kind imposed on or in connection with importation or exportation or imposed on the international transfer of payments for imports or exports, and with respect to the method of levying such duties and charges, and with respect to all rules and formalities in connection with importation and exportation, and with respect to all matters referred to in paragraphs 2 and 4 of Article III, any advantage, favour, privilege or immunity granted by any contracting party to any product originating in or destined for any other country shall

be accorded immediately and unconditionally to the like product originating in or destined for the territories of all other contracting parties.

Ad *Article I*

Paragraph 1

The obligations incorporated in paragraph 1 of Article I by reference to paragraphs 2 and 4 of Article III and those incorporated in paragraph 2(b) of Article II by reference to Article VI shall be considered as falling within Part II for the purposes of the Protocol of Provisional Application.

The cross-references, in the paragraph immediately above and in paragraph 1 of Article I, to paragraphs 2 and 4 of Article III shall only apply after Article III has been modified by the entry into force of the amendment provided for in the Protocol Modifying Part II and Article XXVI of the General Agreement on Tariffs and Trade, dated September 14, 1948.

---

2.   The provisions of paragraph 1 of this Article shall not require the elimination of any preferences in respect of import duties or charges which do not exceed the levels provided for in paragraph 4 of this Article and which fall within the following descriptions:

(a) Preferences in force exclusively between two or more of the territories listed in Annex A, subject to the conditions set forth therein;

* * *

ARTICLE II.   SCHEDULES OF CONCESSIONS

1.   (a) Each contracting party shall accord to the commerce of the other contracting parties treatment no less favourable than that provided for in the appropriate Part of the appropriate Schedule annexed to this Agreement.

(b) The products described in Part I of the Schedule relating to any contracting party, which are the products of territories of other contracting parties, shall, on their importation into the territory to which the Schedule relates, and subject to the terms, conditions or qualifications set forth in that Schedule, be exempt from ordinary customs duties in excess of those set forth and provided for therein. Such products shall also be exempt from all other duties or charges of any kind imposed on or in connection with importation in excess of those imposed on the date of this Agreement or those directly and mandatorily required to be imposed thereafter by legislation in force in the importing territory on that date.

(c) The products described in Part II of the Schedule relating to any contracting party which are the products of territories entitled under Article I to receive preferential treatment upon importation into the territory to which the Schedule relates shall, on their importation into such territory, and subject to the terms, conditions or qualifications set forth in that Schedule, be exempt from ordinary customs duties in excess of those set forth and provided for in Part II of that Schedule. Such products shall also be exempt from all other duties or charges of any kind imposed on or in connection with importation in excess of those imposed on the date of this Agreement or those directly and mandatorily required to be imposed thereafter by legislation in force in the importing territory on that date. Nothing in this Article shall prevent any contracting party from maintaining its requirements existing on the date of this Agreement as to the eligibility of goods for entry at preferential rates of duty.

2. Nothing in this Article shall prevent any contracting party from imposing at any time on the importation of any product:

(a) a charge equivalent to an internal tax imposed consistently with the provisions of paragraph 2 of Article III in respect of the like domestic product or in respect of an article from which the imported product has been manufactured or produced in whole or in part;

Ad *Article II*

Paragraph 2(a)

The cross-reference, in paragraph 2(a) of Article II, to paragraph 2 of Article III shall only apply after Article III has been modified by the entry into force of the amendment provided for in the Protocol Modifying Part II and Article XXVI of the General Agreement on Tariffs and Trade, dated September 14, 1948.

(b) any anti-dumping or countervailing duty applied consistently with the provisions of Article VI;

Ad *Article II*

Paragraph 2(b)

See the note relating to paragraph 1 of Article I.

(c) fees or other charges commensurate with the cost of services rendered.

3.   No contracting party shall alter its method of determining dutiable value or of converting currencies so as to impair the value of any of the concessions provided for in the appropriate Schedule annexed to this Agreement.

4.   If any contracting party establishes, maintains or authorizes, formally or in effect, a monopoly of the importation of any product described in the appropriate Schedule annexed to this Agreement, such monopoly shall not, except as provided for in that Schedule or as otherwise agreed between the parties which initially negotiated the concession, operate so as to afford protection on the average in excess of the amount of protection provided for in that Schedule. The provisions of this paragraph shall not limit the use by contracting parties of any form of assistance to domestic producers permitted by other provisions of this Agreement.

Ad *Article II*

Paragraph 4

Except where otherwise specifically agreed between the contracting parties which initially negotiated the concession, the provisions of this paragraph will be applied in the light of the provisions of Article 31 of the Havana Charter.

---

5.   If any contracting party considers that a product is not receiving from another contracting party the treatment which the first contracting party believes to have been contemplated by a concession provided for in the appropriate Schedule annexed to this Agreement, it shall bring the matter directly to the attention of the other contracting party. If the latter agrees that the treatment contemplated was that claimed by the first contracting party, but declares that such treatment cannot be accorded because a court or other proper authority has ruled to the effect that the product involved cannot be classified under the tariff laws of such contracting party so as to permit the treatment contemplated in this Agreement, the two contracting parties, together with any other contracting parties substantially interested, shall enter promptly into further negotiations with a view to a compensatory adjustment of the matter.

* * *

PART II

ARTICLE III. NATIONAL TREATMENT ON INTERNAL TAXATION AND REGULATION

Ad Article III

Any internal tax or other internal charge, or any law, regulation or requirement of the kind referred to in paragraph 1 which applies to an imported product and to the like domestic product and is collected or enforced in the case of the imported product at the time or point of importation, is nevertheless to be regarded as an internal tax or other internal charge, or a law, regulation or requirement of the kind referred to in paragraph 1, and is accordingly subject to the provisions of Article III.

---

1. The contracting parties recognize that internal taxes and other internal charges, and laws, regulations and requirements affecting the internal sale, offering for sale, purchase, transportation, distribution or use of products, and internal quantitative regulations requiring the mixture, processing or use of products in specified amounts or proportions, should not be applied to imported or domestic products so as to afford protection to domestic production.

Ad Article III

Paragraph 1

The application of paragraph 1 to internal taxes imposed by local governments and authorities within the territory of a contracting party is subject to the provisions of the final paragraph of Article XXIV. The term "reasonable measures" in the last-mentioned paragraph would not require, for example, the repeal of existing national legislation authorizing local governments to impose internal taxes which, although technically inconsistent with the letter of Article III, are not in fact inconsistent with its spirit, if such repeal would result in a serious financial hardship for the local governments or authorities concerned. With regard to taxation by local governments or authorities which is inconsistent with both the letter and spirit of Article III, the term "reasonable measures" would permit a contracting party to eliminate the inconsistent taxation gradually over a transition period, if abrupt action would create serious administrative and financial difficulties.

---

2.   The products of the territory of any contracting party imported into the territory of any other contracting party shall not be subject, directly or indirectly, to internal taxes or other internal charges of any kind in excess of those applied, directly or indirectly, to like domestic products. Moreover, no contracting party shall otherwise apply internal taxes or other internal charges to imported or domestic products in a manner contrary to the principles set forth in paragraph 1.

Ad *Article III*

Paragraph 2

A tax conforming to the requirements of the first sentence of paragraph 2 would be considered to be inconsistent with the provisions of the second sentence only in cases where competition was involved between, on the one hand, the taxed product and, on the other hand, a directly competitive or substitutable product which was not similarly taxed.

---

3.   With respect to any existing internal tax which is inconsistent with the provisions of paragraph 2, but which is specifically authorized under a trade agreement, in force on April 10, 1947, in which the import duty on the taxed product is bound against increase, the contracting party imposing the tax shall be free to postpone the application of the provisions of paragraph 2 to such tax until such time as it can obtain release from the obligations of such trade agreement in order to permit the increase of such duty to the extent necessary to compensate for the elimination of the protective element of the tax.

4.   The products of the territory of any contracting party imported into the territory of any other contracting party shall be accorded treatment no less favourable than that accorded to like products of national origin in respect of all laws, regulations and requirements affecting their internal sale, offering for sale, purchase, transportation, distribution or use. The provisions of this paragraph shall not prevent the application of differential internal transportation charges which are based exclusively on the economic operation of the means of transport and not on the nationality of the product.

5.   No contracting party shall establish or maintain any internal quantitative regulation relating to the mixture, processing or use of products in specified amounts or proportions which requires, directly or indirectly, that any specified amount or proportion of any product which is the subject of the regulation must be supplied from domestic sources. Moreover, no contracting party shall otherwise apply internal quantitative regulations in a manner contrary to the principles set forth in paragraph 1.

Ad *Article III*

Paragraph 5

Regulations consistent with the provisions of the first sentence of paragraph 5 shall not be considered to be contrary to the provisions of the second sentence in any case in which all of the products subject to the regulations are produced domestically in substantial quantities. A regulation cannot be justified as being consistent with the provisions of the second sentence on the ground that the proportion or amount allocated to each of the products which are the subject of the regulation constitutes an equitable relationship between imported and domestic products.

---

* * *

8. (a) The provisions of this Article shall not apply to laws, regulations or requirements governing the procurement by governmental agencies of products purchased for governmental purposes and not with a view to commercial resale or with a view to use in the production of goods for commercial sale.

(b) The provisions of this Article shall not prevent the payment of subsidies exclusively to domestic producers, including payments to domestic producers derived from the proceeds of internal taxes or charges applied consistently with the provisions of this Article and subsidies effected through governmental purchases of domestic products.

9. The contracting parties recognize that internal maximum price control measures, even though conforming to the other provisions of this Article, can have effects prejudicial to the interests of contracting parties supplying imported products. Accordingly, contracting parties applying such measures shall take account of the interests of exporting contracting parties with a view to avoiding to the fullest practicable extent such prejudicial effects.

* * *

ARTICLE IV.   SPECIAL PROVISIONS RELATING TO CINEMATOGRAPH FILMS

* * *

ARTICLE V.   FREEDOM OF TRANSIT

* * *

ARTICLE VI.   ANTI-DUMPING AND COUNTERVAILING DUTIES

1. The contracting parties recognize that dumping, by which products of one country are introduced into the commerce of another country at less than the normal value of the products, is to be condemned if

it causes or threatens material injury to an established industry in the territory of a contracting party or materially retards the establishment of a domestic industry. For the purposes of this Article, a product is to be considered as being introduced into the commerce of an importing country at less than its normal value, if the price of the product exported from one country to another

(a) is less than the comparable price, in the ordinary course of trade, for the like product when destined for consumption in the exporting country, or,

(b) in the absence of such domestic price, is less than either

(i) the highest comparable price for the like product for export to any third country in the ordinary course of trade, or

(ii) the cost of production of the product in the country of origin plus a reasonable addition for selling cost and profit.

Due allowance shall be made in each case for differences in conditions and terms of sale, for differences in taxation, and for other differences affecting price comparability.

———————

Ad *Article VI*

Paragraph 1

1.   Hidden dumping by associated houses (that is, the sale by an importer at a price below that corresponding to the price invoiced by an exporter with whom the importer is associated, and also below the price in the exporting country) constitutes a form of price dumping with respect to which the margin of dumping may be calculated on the basis of the price at which the goods are resold by the importer.

2.   It is recognized that, in the case of imports from a country which has a complete or substantially complete monopoly of its trade and where all domestic prices are fixed by the State, special difficulties may exist in determining price comparability for the purposes of paragraph 1, and in such cases importing contracting parties may find it necessary to take into account the possibility that a strict comparison with domestic prices in such a country may not always be appropriate.

———————

2.   In order to offset or prevent dumping, a contracting party may levy on any dumped product an anti-dumping duty not greater in amount than the margin of dumping in respect of such product. For the purposes of

this Article, the margin of dumping is the price difference determined in accordance with the provisions of paragraph 1.

3. No countervailing duty shall be levied on any product of the territory of any contracting party imported into the territory of another contracting party in excess of an amount equal to the estimated bounty or subsidy determined to have been granted, directly or indirectly, on the manufacture, production or export of such product in the country of origin or exportation, including any special subsidy to the transportation of a particular product. The term "countervailing duty" shall be understood to mean a special duty levied for the purpose of offsetting any bounty or subsidy bestowed, directly or indirectly, upon the manufacture, production or export of any merchandise.

Ad *Article VI*

Paragraphs 2 and 3

1. As in many other cases in customs administration, a contracting party may require reasonable security (bond or cash deposit) for the payment of anti-dumping or countervailing duty pending final determination of the facts in any case of suspected dumping or subsidization.

2. Multiple currency practices can in certain circumstances constitute a subsidy to exports which may be met by countervailing duties under paragraph 3 or can constitute a form of dumping by means of a partial depreciation of a country's currency which may be met by action under paragraph 2. By "multiple currency practices" is meant practices by governments or sanctioned by governments.

---

4. No product of the territory of any contracting party imported into the territory of any other contracting party shall be subject to anti-dumping or countervailing duty by reason of the exemption of such product from duties or taxes borne by the like product when destined for consumption in the country of origin or exportation, or by reason of the refund of such duties or taxes.

5. No product of the territory of any contracting party imported into the territory of any other contracting party shall be subject to both anti-dumping and countervailing duties to compensate for the same situation of dumping or export subsidization.

6. (a) No contracting party shall levy any anti-dumping or countervailing duty on the importation of any product of the territory of another contracting party unless it determines that the effect of the dumping or subsidization, as the case may be, is such as to cause or threaten material injury to an established domestic industry, or is such as to retard materially the establishment of a domestic industry.

(b) The CONTRACTING PARTIES may waive the requirement of subparagraph (a) of this paragraph so as to permit a contracting party to levy an anti-dumping or countervailing duty on the importation of any product for the purpose of offsetting dumping or subsidization which causes or threatens material injury to an industry in the territory of another contracting party exporting the product concerned to the territory of the importing contracting party. The CONTRACTING PARTIES shall waive the requirements of sub-paragraph (a) of this paragraph, so as to permit the levying of a countervailing duty, in cases in which they find that a subsidy is causing or threatening material injury to an industry in the territory of another contracting party exporting the product concerned to the territory of the importing contracting party.

Ad *Article VI*

Paragraph 6(b)

Waivers under the provisions of this sub-paragraph shall be granted only on application by the contracting party proposing to levy an anti-dumping or countervailing duty, as the case may be.

(c) In exceptional circumstances, however, where delay might cause damage which would be difficult to repair, a contracting party may levy a countervailing duty for the purpose referred to in subparagraph (b) of this paragraph without the prior approval of the CONTRACTING PARTIES; *Provided* that such action shall be reported immediately to the CONTRACTING PARTIES and that the countervailing duty shall be withdrawn promptly if the CONTRACTING PARTIES disapprove.

7.   A system for the stabilization of the domestic price or of the return to domestic producers of a primary commodity, independently of the movements of export prices, which results at times in the sale of the commodity for export at a price lower than the comparable price charged for the like commodity to buyers in the domestic market, shall be presumed not to result in material injury within the meaning of paragraph 6 if it is determined by consultation among the contracting parties substantially interested in the commodity concerned that:

(a) the system has also resulted in the sale of the commodity for export at a price higher than the comparable price charged for the like commodity to buyers in the domestic market, and

(b) the system is so operated, either because of the effective regulation of production, or otherwise, as not to stimulate exports unduly or otherwise seriously prejudice the interests of other contracting parties.

ARTICLE VII. VALUATION FOR CUSTOMS PURPOSES

1. The contracting parties recognize the validity of the general principles of valuation set forth in the following paragraphs of this Article, and they undertake to give effect to such principles, in respect of all products subject to duties or other charges or restrictions on importation and exportation based upon or regulated in any manner by value. Moreover, they shall, upon a request by another contracting party review the operation of any of their laws or regulations relating to value for customs purposes in the light of these principles. The CONTRACTING PARTIES may request from contracting parties reports on steps taken by them in pursuance of the provisions of this Article.

Ad Article VII

Paragraph 1

The expression "or other charges" is not to be regarded as including internal taxes or equivalent charges imposed on or in connexion with imported products.

---

2. (a) The value for customs purposes of imported merchandise should be based on the actual value of the imported merchandise on which duty is assessed, or of like merchandise, and should not be based on the value of merchandise of national origin or on arbitrary or fictitious values.

(b) "Actual value" should be the price at which, at a time and place determined by the legislation of the country of importation, such or like merchandise is sold or offered for sale in the ordinary course of trade under fully competitive conditions. To the extent to which the price of such or like merchandise is governed by the quantity in a particular transaction, the price to be considered should uniformly be related to either (i) comparable quantities, or (ii) quantities not less favourable to importers than those in which the greater volume of the merchandise is sold in the trade between the countries of exportation and importation.

(c) When the actual value is not ascertainable in accordance with sub-paragraph (b) of this paragraph, the value for customs purposes should be based on the nearest ascertainable equivalent of such value.

Ad *Article VII*

Paragraph 2

1.   It would be in conformity with Article VII to presume that "actual value" may be represented by the invoice price, plus any non-included charges for legitimate costs which are proper elements of "actual value" and plus any abnormal discount or other reduction from the ordinary competitive price.

2.   It would be in conformity with Article VII, paragraph 2(b), for a contracting party to construe the phrase "in the ordinary course of trade * * * under fully competitive conditions", as excluding any transaction wherein the buyer and seller are not independent of each other and price is not the sole consideration.

3.   The standard of "fully competitive conditions" permits a contracting party to exclude from consideration prices involving special discounts limited to exclusive agents.

4.   The wording of sub-paragraphs (a) and (b) permits a contracting party to determine the value for customs purposes uniformly either (1) on the basis of a particular exporter's prices of the imported merchandise, or (2) on the basis of the general price level of like merchandise.

---

3.   The value for customs purposes of any imported product should not include the amount of any internal tax, applicable within the country of origin or export, from which the imported product has been exempted or has been or will be relieved by means of refund.

4.   (a) Except as otherwise provided for in this paragraph, where it is necessary for the purposes of paragraph 2 of this Article for a contracting party to convert into its own currency a price expressed in the currency of another country, the conversion rate of exchange to be used shall be based, for each currency involved, on the par value as established pursuant to the Articles of Agreement of the International Monetary Fund or on the rate of exchange recognized by the Fund, or on the par value established in accordance with a special exchange agreement entered into pursuant to Article XV of this Agreement.

(b) Where no such established par value and no such recognized rate of exchange exist, the conversion rate shall reflect effectively the current value of such currency in commercial transactions.

(c) The CONTRACTING PARTIES, in agreement with the International Monetary Fund, shall formulate rules governing the conversion by contracting parties of any foreign currency in respect of which multiple rates of exchange are maintained consistently with the Articles of Agreement of the International Monetary Fund. Any contracting party may apply such rules in respect of such foreign currencies for the purposes of paragraph 2 of this Article as an alternative to the use of par values. Until such rules are adopted by the CONTRACTING PARTIES, any contracting party may employ, in respect of any such foreign currency, rules of conversion for the purposes of paragraph 2 of this Article which are designed to reflect effectively the value of such foreign currency in commercial transactions.

(d) Nothing in this paragraph shall be construed to require any contracting party to alter the method of converting currencies for customs purposes which is applicable in its territory on the date of this Agreement, if such alteration would have the effect of increasing generally the amounts of duty payable.

5.   The bases and methods for determining the value of products subject to duties or other charges or restrictions based upon or regulated in any manner by value should be stable and should be given sufficient publicity to enable traders to estimate, with a reasonable degree of certainty, the value for customs purposes.

ARTICLE VIII.   FEES AND FORMALITIES CONNECTED WITH IMPORTATION AND EXPORTATION

1.   (a) All fees and charges of whatever character (other than import and export duties and other than taxes within the purview of Article III) imposed by contracting parties on or in connexion with importation or exportation shall be limited in amount to the approximate cost of services rendered and shall not represent an indirect protection to domestic products or a taxation of imports or exports for fiscal purposes.

* * *

ARTICLE IX.   MARKS OF ORIGIN

1.   Each contracting party shall accord to the products of the territories of other contracting parties treatment with regard to marking requirements no less favourable than the treatment accorded to like products of any third country.

2.   The contracting parties recognize that, in adopting and enforcing laws and regulations relating to marks of origin, the difficulties and inconveniences which such measures may cause to the commerce and industry of exporting countries should be reduced to a minimum, due regard being had to the necessity of protecting consumers against fraudulent or misleading indications.

3.   Whenever it is administratively practicable to do so, contracting parties should permit required marks of origin to be affixed at the time of importation.

4.   The laws and regulations of contracting parties relating to the marking of imported products shall be such as to permit compliance without seriously damaging the products, or materially reducing their value, or unreasonably increasing their cost.

5.   As a general rule, no special duty or penalty should be imposed by any contracting party for failure to comply with marking requirements prior to importation unless corrective marking is unreasonably delayed or deceptive marks have been affixed or the required marking has been intentionally omitted.

6.   The contracting parties shall co-operate with each other with a view to preventing the use of trade names in such manner as to misrepresent the true origin of a product, to the detriment of such distinctive regional or geographical names of products of the territory of a contracting party as are protected by its legislation. Each contracting party shall accord full and sympathetic consideration to such requests or representations as may be made by any other contracting party regarding the application of the undertaking set forth in the preceding sentence to names of products which have been communicated to it by the other contracting party.

ARTICLE X. PUBLICATION AND ADMINISTRATION OF TRADE REGULATIONS (omitted)

* * *

ARTICLE XI.   GENERAL ELIMINATION OF QUANTITATIVE RESTRICTIONS

Ad *Articles XI, XII, XIII, XIV and XVIII*

Throughout Articles XI, XII, XIII, XIV and XVIII, the terms "import restrictions" or "export restrictions" include restrictions made effective through state-trading operations.

---

1.   No prohibitions or restrictions other than duties, taxes or other charges, whether made effective through quotas, import or export licenses or other measures, shall be instituted or maintained by any contracting party on the importation of any product of the territory of any other contracting party or on the exportation or sale for export of any product destined for the territory of any other contracting party.

2.   The provisions of paragraph 1 of this Article shall not extend to the following:

(a) Export prohibitions or restrictions temporarily applied to prevent or relieve critical shortages of foodstuffs or other products essential to the exporting contracting party;

(b) Import and export prohibitions or restrictions necessary to the application of standards or regulations for the classification, grading or marketing of commodities in international trade;

(c) Import restrictions on any agricultural or fisheries product, imported in any form, necessary to the enforcement of governmental measures which operate:

(i) to restrict the quantities of the like domestic product permitted to be marketed or produced, or, if there is no substantial domestic production of the like product, of a domestic product for which the imported product can be directly substituted; or

(ii) to remove a temporary surplus of the like domestic product, or, if there is no substantial domestic production of the like product, of a domestic product for which the imported product can be directly substituted, by making the surplus available to certain groups of domestic consumers free of charge or at prices below the current market level; or

(iii) to restrict the quantities permitted to be produced of any animal product the production of which is directly dependent, wholly or mainly, on the imported commodity, if the domestic production of that commodity is relatively negligible.

Ad *Article XI*

Paragraph 2(c)

The term "in any form" in this paragraph covers the same products when in an early stage of processing and still perishable, which compete directly with the fresh product and if freely imported would tend to make the restriction on the fresh product ineffective.

Any contracting party applying restrictions on the importation of any product pursuant to sub-paragraph (c) of this paragraph shall give public notice of the total quantity or value of the product permitted to be imported during a specified future period and of any change in such quantity or value. Moreover, any restrictions applied under (i) above shall not be such as will reduce the total of imports relative to the total of domestic production, as compared with the proportion which might reasonably be expected to rule between the two in the absence of restrictions. In determining this proportion, the contracting party shall pay due regard to the proportion prevailing during a previous representative period and to any special factors which may have affected or may be affecting the trade in the product concerned.

Ad *Article XI*

Paragraph 2, last sub-paragraph

The term "special factors" includes changes in relative productive efficiency as between domestic and foreign producers, or as between different foreign producers, but not changes artificially brought about by means not permitted under the Agreement.

———————

ARTICLE XII. RESTRICTIONS TO SAFEGUARD THE BALANCE OF PAYMENTS

———————

Ad *Articles XI, XII, XIII, XIV and XVIII*

Throughout Articles XI, XII, XIII, XIV and XVIII, the terms "import restrictions" or "export restrictions" include restrictions made effective through state-trading operations.

———————

Ad *Article XII*

The CONTRACTING PARTIES shall make provision for the utmost secrecy in the conduct of any consultation under the provisions of this Article.

———————

1.   Notwithstanding the provisions of paragraph 1 of Article XI, any contracting party, in order to safeguard its external financial position and its balance of payments, may restrict the quantity or value of merchandise permitted to be imported, subject to the provisions of the following paragraphs of this Article.

2.   (a) Import restrictions instituted, maintained or intensified by a contracting party under this Article shall not exceed those necessary:

(i) to forestall the imminent threat of, or to stop, a serious decline in its monetary reserves, or

(ii) in the case of a contracting party with very low monetary reserves, to achieve a reasonable rate of increase in its reserves.

Due regard shall be paid in either case to any special factors which may be affecting the reserves of such contracting party or its need for reserves, including, where special external credits or other resources are available to it, the need to provide for the appropriate use of such credits or resources.

(b) Contracting parties applying restrictions under sub-paragraph (a) of this paragraph shall progressively relax them as such conditions improve, maintaining them only to the extent that the conditions specified in that sub-paragraph still justify their application. They shall eliminate the restrictions when conditions would no longer justify their institution or maintenance under that sub-paragraph.

3. (a) Contracting parties undertake, in carrying out their domestic policies, to pay due regard to the need for maintaining or restoring equilibrium in their balance of payments on a sound and lasting basis and to the desirability of avoiding an uneconomic employment of productive resources. They recognize that, in order to achieve these ends, it is desirable so far as possible to adopt measures which expand rather than contract international trade.

(b) Contracting parties applying restrictions under this Article may determine the incidence of the restrictions on imports of different products or classes of products in such a way as to give priority to the importation of those products which are more essential.

(c) Contracting parties applying restrictions under this Article undertake:

(i) to avoid unnecessary damage to the commercial or economic interests of any other contracting party;

Ad *Article XII*

Paragraph 3(c)(i)

Contracting parties applying restrictions shall endeavour to avoid causing serious prejudice to exports of a commodity on which the economy of a contracting party is largely dependent.

(ii) not to apply restrictions so as to prevent unreasonably the importation of any description of goods in minimum commercial quantities the exclusion of which would impair regular channels of trade; and

(iii) not to apply restrictions which would prevent the importation of commercial samples or prevent compliance with patent, trade mark, copyright, or similar procedures.

(d) The contracting parties recognize that, as a result of domestic policies directed towards the achievement and maintenance of full and productive employment or towards the development of economic resources, a contracting party may experience a high level of demand for imports involving a threat to its monetary reserves of the sort referred to in paragraph 2(a) of this Article. Accordingly, a contracting party otherwise complying with the provisions of this Article shall not be required to withdraw or modify restrictions on the ground that a change in those policies would render unnecessary restrictions which it is applying under this Article.

4.   (a) Any contracting party applying new restrictions or raising the general level of its existing restrictions by a substantial intensification of the measures applied under this Article shall immediately after instituting or intensifying such restrictions (or, in circumstances in which prior consultation is practicable, before doing so) consult with the CONTRACTING PARTIES as to the nature of its balance of payments difficulties, alternative corrective measures which may be available, and the possible effect of the restrictions on the economies of other contracting parties.

(b) On a date to be determined by them, the CONTRACTING PARTIES shall review all restrictions still applied under this Article on that date. Beginning one year after that date, contracting parties applying import restrictions under this Article shall enter into consultations of the type provided for in sub-paragraph (a) of this paragraph with the CONTRACTING PARTIES annually.

Ad *Article XII*

Paragraph 4(b)

It is agreed that the date shall be within ninety days after the entry into force of the amendments of this Article effected by the Protocol Amending the Preamble and Parts II and III of this Agreement. However, should the CONTRACTING PARTIES find that conditions were not suitable for the application of the provisions of this sub-paragraph at the time envisaged, they may determine a later date; Provided that such date is not more than thirty days after such time as the obligations of Article VIII, Sections 2, 3 and 4, of the Articles of Agreement of the International Monetary Fund become applicable to contracting parties, members of the Fund, the combined foreign trade of which constitutes at least fifty per centum of the aggregate foreign trade of all contracting parties.

(c)(i) If, in the course of consultations with a contracting party under sub-paragraph (a) or (b) above, the CONTRACTING PARTIES find that the restrictions are not consistent with the provisions of this Article or with those of Article XIII (subject to the provisions of Article XIV), they shall indicate the nature of the inconsistency and may advise that the restrictions be suitably modified.

(ii) If, however, as a result of the consultations, the CONTRACTING PARTIES determine that the restrictions are being applied in a manner involving an inconsistency of a serious nature with the provisions of this Article or with those of Article XIII (subject to the provisions of Article XIV) and that damage to the trade of any contracting party is caused or threatened thereby, they shall so inform the contracting party applying the restrictions and shall make appropriate recommendations for securing conformity with such provisions within a specified period of time. If such contracting party does not comply with these recommendations within the specified period, the CONTRACTING PARTIES may release any contracting party the trade of which is adversely affected by the restrictions from such obligations under this Agreement towards the contracting party applying the restrictions as they determine to be appropriate in the circumstances.

(d) The CONTRACTING PARTIES shall invite any contracting party which is applying restrictions under this Article to enter into consultations with them at the request of any contracting party which can establish a *prima facie* case that the restrictions are inconsistent with the provisions of this Article or with those of Article XIII (subject to the provisions of Article XIV) and that its trade is adversely affected thereby. However, no such invitation shall be issued unless the CONTRACTING PARTIES have ascertained that direct discussions between the contracting parties concerned have not been successful. If, as a result of the consultations with the CONTRACTING PARTIES, no agreement is reached and they determine that the restrictions are being applied inconsistently with such provisions, and that damage to the trade of the contracting party initiating the procedure is caused or threatened thereby, they shall recommend the withdrawal or modification of the restrictions. If the restrictions are not withdrawn or modified within such time as the CONTRACTING PARTIES may prescribe, they may release the contracting party initiating the procedure from such obligations under this Agreement towards the contracting party applying the restrictions as they determine to be appropriate in the circumstances.

(e) In proceeding under this paragraph, the CONTRACTING PARTIES shall have due regard to any special external factors adversely affecting the export trade of the contracting party applying restrictions.

Ad *Article XII*

Paragraph 4(e)

It is agreed that paragraph 4(e) does not add any new criteria for the imposition or maintenance of quantitative restrictions for balance of payments reasons. It is solely intended to ensure that all external factors such as changes in the terms of trade, quantitative restrictions, excessive tariffs and subsidies, which may be contributing to the balance of payments difficulties of the contracting party applying restrictions, will be fully taken into account.

————

(f) Determinations under this paragraph shall be rendered expeditiously and, if possible, within sixty days of the initiation of the consultations.

5. If there is a persistent and widespread application of import restrictions under this Article, indicating the existence of a general disequilibrium which is restricting international trade, the CONTRACTING PARTIES shall initiate discussions to consider whether other measures might be taken, either by those contracting parties the balances of payments of which are under pressure or by those the balances of payments of which are tending to be exceptionally favourable, or by any appropriate intergovernmental organization, to remove the underlying causes of the disequilibrium. On the invitation of the CONTRACTING PARTIES, contracting parties shall participate in such discussions.

ARTICLE XIII.   NON-DISCRIMINATORY ADMINISTRATION OF QUANTITATIVE RESTRICTIONS

————

Ad *Articles XI, XII, XIII, XIV and XVIII*

Throughout Articles XI, XII, XIII, XIV and XVIII, the terms "import restrictions" or "export restrictions" include restrictions made effective through state-trading operations.

————

1. No prohibition or restriction shall be applied by any contracting party on the importation of any product of the territory of any other contracting party or on the exportation of any product destined for the territory of any other contracting party, unless the importation of the like product of all third countries or the exportation of the like product to all third countries is similarly prohibited or restricted.

2. In applying import restrictions to any product, contracting parties shall aim at a distribution of trade in such product approaching as closely as possible the shares which the various contracting parties might

be expected to obtain in the absence of such restrictions, and to this end shall observe the following provisions:

(a) Wherever practicable, quotas representing the total amount of permitted imports (whether allocated among supplying countries or not) shall be fixed, and notice given of their amount in accordance with paragraph 3(b) of this Article;

(b) In cases in which quotas are not practicable, the restrictions may be applied by means of import licences or permits without a quota;

(c) Contracting parties shall not, except for purposes of operating quotas allocated in accordance with sub-paragraph (d) of this paragraph, require that import licences or permits be utilized for the importation of the product concerned from a particular country or source;

(d) In cases in which a quota is allocated among supplying countries, the contracting party applying the restrictions may seek agreement with respect to the allocation of shares in the quota with all other contracting parties having a substantial interest in supplying the product concerned. In cases in which this method is not reasonably practicable, the contracting party concerned shall allot to contracting parties having a substantial interest in supplying the product shares based upon the proportions, supplied by such contracting parties during a previous representative period, of the total quantity or value of imports of the product, due account being taken of any special factors which may have affected or may be affecting the trade in the product. No conditions or formalities shall be imposed which would prevent any contracting party from utilizing fully the share of any such total quantity or value which has been allotted to it, subject to importation being made without any prescribed period to which the quota may relate.

Ad *Article XIII*

Paragraph 2(d)

No mention was made of "commercial considerations" as a rule for the allocation of quotas because it was considered that its application by governmental authorities might not always be practicable. Moreover, in cases where it is practicable, a contracting party could apply these considerations in the process of seeking agreement, consistently with the general rule laid down in the opening sentence of paragraph 2.

---

3.   (a) In cases in which import licences are issued in connection with import restrictions, the contracting party applying the restrictions shall provide, upon the request of any contracting party having an interest in the trade in the product concerned, all relevant information concerning the administration of the restrictions, the import licences granted over a recent period and the distribution of such licences among supplying countries; *Provided* that there shall be no obligation to supply information as to the names of importing or supplying enterprises.

(b) In the case of import restrictions involving the fixing of quotas, the contracting party applying the restrictions shall give public notice of the total quantity or value of the product or products which will be permitted to be imported during a specified future period and of any change in such quantity or value. Any supplies of the product in question which were *en route* at the time at which public notice was given shall not be excluded from entry; *Provided* that they may be counted so far as practicable, against the quantity permitted to be imported in the period in question, and also, where necessary, against the quantities permitted to be imported in the next following period or periods; and *Provided* further that if any contracting party customarily exempts from such restrictions products entered for consumption or withdrawn from warehouse for consumption during a period of thirty days after the day of such public notice, such practice shall be considered full compliance with this sub-paragraph.

(c) In the case of quotas allocated among supplying countries, the contracting party applying the restrictions shall promptly inform all other contracting parties having an interest in supplying the product concerned of the shares in the quota currently allocated, by quantity or value, to the various supplying countries and shall give public notice thereof.

4.   With regard to restrictions applied in accordance with paragraph 2(d) of this Article or under paragraph 2(c) of Article XI, the selection of a representative period for any product and the appraisal of any special factors affecting the trade in the product shall be made initially by the contracting party applying the restriction; *Provided* that such contracting party shall, upon the request of any other contracting party having a substantial interest in supplying that product or upon the request of the CONTRACTING PARTIES, consult promptly with the other contracting party or the CONTRACTING PARTIES regarding the need for an adjustment of the proportion determined or of the base period selected, or for the reappraisal of the special factors involved, or for the elimination of conditions, formalities or any other provisions established unilaterally relating to the allocation of an adequate quota or its unrestricted utilization.

Ad *Article XIII*

Paragraph 4

See note relating to "special factors" in connexion with the last subparagraph of paragraph 2 of Article XI.

———————

5.   The provisions of this Article shall apply to any tariff quota instituted or maintained by any contracting party, and, in so far as applicable, the principles of this Article shall also extend to export restrictions.

———————

ARTICLE XIV.   EXCEPTIONS TO THE RULE OF NONDISCRIMINATION

———————

Ad *Articles XI, XII, XIII, XIV and XVIII*

Throughout Articles XI, XII, XIII, XIV and XVIII, the terms "import restrictions" or "export restrictions" include restrictions made effective through state-trading operations.

———————

1.   A contracting party which applies restrictions under Article XII or under Section B of Article XVIII may, in the application of such restrictions, deviate from the provisions of Article XIII in a manner having equivalent effect to restrictions on payments and transfers for current international transactions which that contracting party may at that time apply under Article VIII or XIV of the Articles of Agreement of the International Monetary Fund, or under analogous provisions of a special exchange agreement entered into pursuant to paragraph 6 of Article XV.

———————

Ad *Article XIV*

Paragraph 1

The provisions of this paragraph shall not be so construed as to preclude full consideration by the CONTRACTING PARTIES, in the consultations provided for in paragraph 4 of Article XII and in paragraph 12 of Article XVIII, of the nature, effects and reasons for discrimination in the field of import restrictions.

———————

2.   A contracting party which is applying import restrictions under Article XII or under Section B of Article XVIII may, with the consent of the CONTRACTING PARTIES, temporarily deviate from the provisions of Article XIII in respect of a small part of its external trade where the benefits to the contracting party or contracting parties concerned substantially outweigh any injury which may result to the trade of other contracting parties.

Ad *Article XIV*

Paragraph 2

One of the situations contemplated in paragraph 2 is that of a contracting party holding balances acquired as a result of current transactions which it finds itself unable to use without a measure of discrimination.

----

3.   The provisions of Article XIII shall not preclude a group of territories having a common quota in the International Monetary Fund from applying against imports from other countries, but not among themselves, restrictions in accordance with the provisions of Article XII or of Section B of Article XVIII on condition that such restrictions are in all other respects consistent with the provisions of Article XIII.

4.   A contracting party applying import restrictions under Article XII or under Section B of Article XVIII shall not be precluded by Articles XI to XV or Section B of Article XVIII of this Agreement from applying measures to direct its exports in such a manner as to increase its earnings of currencies which it can use without deviation from the provisions of Article XIII.

5.   A contracting party shall not be precluded by Articles XI to XV, inclusive, or by Section B of Article XVIII, of this Agreement from applying quantitative restrictions:

(a) having equivalent effect to exchange restrictions authorized under Section 3(*b*) of Article VII of the Articles of Agreement of the International Monetary Fund, or

(b) under the preferential arrangements provided for in Annex A of this Agreement, pending the outcome of the negotiations referred to therein.

ARTICLE XV.   EXCHANGE ARRANGEMENTS

1.   The CONTRACTING PARTIES shall seek co-operation with the International Monetary Fund to the end that the CONTRACTING PARTIES and the Fund may pursue a co-ordinated policy with regard to exchange questions within the jurisdiction of the Fund and questions of

quantitative restrictions and other trade measures within the jurisdiction of the CONTRACTING PARTIES.

* * *

ARTICLE XVI.   SUBSIDIES

Ad *Article XVI*

The exemption of an exported product from duties or taxes borne by the like product when destined for domestic consumption, or the remission of such duties or taxes in amounts not in excess of those which have accrued, shall not be deemed to be a subsidy.

Section A—Subsidies in General

1.   If any contracting party grants or maintains any subsidy, including any form of income or price support, which operates directly or indirectly to increase exports of any product from, or to reduce imports of any product into, its territory, it shall notify the CONTRACTING PARTIES in writing of the extent and nature of the subsidization, of the estimated effect of the subsidization on the quantity of the affected product or products imported into or exported from its territory and of the circumstances making the subsidization necessary. In any case, in which it is determined that serious prejudice to the interests of any other contracting party is caused or threatened by any such subsidization, the contracting party granting the subsidy shall, upon request, discuss with the other contracting party or parties concerned, or with the CONTRACTING PARTIES, the possibility of limiting the subsidization.

Section B—Additional Provisions on Export Subsidies

Ad *Article XVI*

Section B

1.   Nothing in Section B shall preclude the use by a contracting party of multiple rates of exchange in accordance with the Articles of Agreement of the International Monetary Fund.

2.   For the purposes of Section B, a "primary product" is understood to be any product of farm, forest or fishery, or any mineral, in its natural form or which has undergone such processing as is customarily required to prepare it for marketing in substantial volume in international trade.

2. The contracting parties recognize that the granting by a contracting party of a subsidy on the export of any product may have harmful effects for other contracting parties, both importing and exporting, may cause undue disturbance to their normal commercial interests, and may hinder the achievement of the objectives of this Agreement.

3. Accordingly, contracting parties should seek to avoid the use of subsidies on the export of primary products. If, however, a contracting party grants directly or indirectly any form of subsidy which operates to increase the export of any primary product from its territory, such subsidy shall not be applied in a manner which results in that contracting party having more than an equitable share of world export trade in that product, account being taken of the shares of the contracting parties in such trade in the product during a previous representative period, and any special factors which may have affected or may be affecting such trade in the product.

Ad *Article XVI*

Paragraph 3

1. The fact that a contracting party has not exported the product in question during the previous representative period would not in itself preclude that contracting party from establishing its right to obtain a share of the trade in the product concerned.

2. A system for the stabilization of the domestic price or of the return to domestic producers of a primary product independently of the movements of export prices, which results at times in the sale of the product for export at a price lower than the comparable price charged for the like product to buyers in the domestic market, shall be considered not to involve a subsidy on exports within the meaning of paragraph 3 if the CONTRACTING PARTIES determine that:

(a) the system has also resulted, or is so designed as to result, in the sale of the product for export at a price higher than the comparable price charged for the like product to buyers in the domestic market; and

(b) the system is so operated, or is designed so to operate, either because of the effective regulation of production or otherwise, as not to stipulate exports unduly or otherwise seriously to prejudice the interests of other contracting parties.

Notwithstanding such determination by the CONTRACTING PARTIES, operations under such a system shall be subject to the provisions of paragraph 3 where they are wholly or partly financed out of government funds in addition to the funds collected from producers in respect of the product concerned.

---

4.   Further, as from 1 January 1958 or the earliest practicable date thereafter, contracting parties shall cease to grant either directly or indirectly any form of subsidy on the export of any product other than a primary product which subsidy results in the sale of such product for export at a price lower than the comparable price charged for the like product to buyers in the domestic market. Until 31 December 1957 no contracting party shall extend the scope of any such subsidization beyond that existing on 1 January 1955 by the introduction of new, or the extension of existing, subsidies.

Ad *Article XVI*

Paragraph 4

The intention of paragraph 4 is that the contracting parties should seek before the end of 1957 to reach agreement to abolish all remaining subsidies as from 1 January 1958; or, failing this, to reach agreement to extend the application of the standstill until the earliest date thereafter by which they can expect to reach such agreement.

---

5.   The CONTRACTING PARTIES shall review the operation of the provisions of this Article from time to time with a view to examining its effectiveness, in the light of actual experience, in promoting the objectives of this Agreement and avoiding subsidization seriously prejudicial to the trade or interests of contracting parties.

ARTICLE XVII. STATE TRADING ENTERPRISES

1.   (a) Each contracting party undertakes that if it establishes or maintains a State enterprise, wherever located, or grants to any enterprise, formally or in effect, exclusive or special privileges, such enterprise shall, in its purchases or sales involving either imports or exports, act in a manner consistent with the general principles of nondiscriminatory treatment prescribed in this Agreement for governmental measures affecting imports or exports by private traders.

Ad *Article XVII*

Paragraph 1

The operations of Marketing Boards, which are established by contracting parties and are engaged in purchasing or selling, are subject to the provisions of sub-paragraphs (a) and (b).

The activities of Marketing Boards which are established by contracting parties and which do not purchase or sell but lay down regulations covering private trade are governed by the relevant Articles of this Agreement.

The charging by a state enterprise of different prices for its sales of a product in different markets is not precluded by the provisions of this Article, provided that such different prices are charged for commercial reasons, to meet conditions of supply and demand in export markets.

Paragraph 1(a)

Governmental measures imposed to ensure standards of quality and efficiency in the operation of external trade, or privileges granted for the exploitation of national natural resources but which do not empower the government to exercise control over the trading activities of the enterprise in question, do not constitute "exclusive or special privileges".

(b) The provisions of sub-paragraph (a) of this paragraph shall be understood to require that such enterprises shall, having due regard to the other provisions of this Agreement, make any such purchases or sales solely in accordance with commercial considerations, including price, quality, availability, marketability, transportation and other conditions of purchase or sale, and shall afford the enterprises of the other contracting parties adequate opportunity, in accordance with customary business practice, to compete for participation in such purchases or sales.

Ad *Article XVII*

Paragraph 1(b)

A country receiving a "tied loan" is free to take this loan into account as a "commercial consideration" when purchasing requirements abroad.

(c) No contracting party shall prevent any enterprise (whether or not an enterprise described in sub-paragraph (a) of this paragraph) under its jurisdiction from acting in accordance with the principles of sub-paragraphs (a) and (b) of this paragraph.

2. The provisions of paragraph 1 of this Article shall not apply to imports of products for immediate or ultimate consumption in governmental use and not otherwise for resale or use in the production of goods for sale. With respect to such imports, each contracting party shall

accord to the trade of the other contracting parties fair and equitable treatment.

Ad *Article XVII*

Paragraph 2

The term "goods" is limited to products as understood in commercial practice, and is not intended to include the purchase or sale of services.

---

3. The contracting parties recognize that enterprises of the kind described in paragraph 1(a) of this Article might be operated so as to create serious obstacles to trade; thus negotiations on a reciprocal and mutually advantageous basis designed to limit or reduce such obstacles are of importance to the expansion of international trade.

Ad *Article XVII*

Paragraph 3

Negotiations which contracting parties agree to conduct under this paragraph may be directed towards the reduction of duties and other charges on imports and exports or towards the conclusion of any other mutually satisfactory arrangement consistent with the provisions of this Agreement. (See paragraph 4 of Article II and the note to that paragraph.)

---

4. (a) Contracting parties shall notify the CONTRACTING PARTIES of the products which are imported into or exported from their territories by enterprises of the kind described in paragraph 1(a) of this Article.

(b) A contracting party establishing, maintaining or authorizing an import monopoly of a product, which is not the subject of a concession under Article II, shall, on the request of another contracting party having a substantial trade in the product concerned, inform the CONTRACTING PARTIES of the import mark-up on the product during a recent representative period, or, when it is not possible to do so, of the price charged on the resale of the product.

Ad *Article XVII*

Paragraph 4(b)

The term "import mark-up" in this paragraph shall represent the margin by which the price charged by the import monopoly for the imported product (exclusive of internal taxes within the purview of Article III, transportation, distribution, and other expenses incident to the purchase, sale or further processing, and a reasonable margin of profit) exceeds the landed cost.

(c) The CONTRACTING PARTIES may, at the request of a contracting party which has reason to believe that its interests under this Agreement are being adversely affected by the operations of an enterprise of the kind described in paragraph 1(a), request the contracting party establishing, maintaining or authorizing such enterprise to supply information about its operations related to the carrying out of the provisions of this Agreement.

(d) The provisions of this paragraph shall not require any contracting party to disclose confidential information which would impede law enforcement or otherwise be contrary to the public interest or would prejudice the legitimate commercial interests of particular enterprises.

ARTICLE XVIII. GOVERNMENTAL ASSISTANCE TO ECONOMIC DEVELOPMENT

Ad *Articles XI, XII, XIII, XIV and XVIII*

Throughout Articles XI, XII, XIII, XIV and XVIII, the terms "import restrictions" or "export restrictions" include restrictions made effective through state-trading operations.

Ad *Article XVIII*

The CONTRACTING PARTIES and the contracting parties concerned shall preserve the utmost secrecy in respect of matters arising under this Article.

---

1.   The contracting parties recognize that the attainment of the objectives of this Agreement will be facilitated by the progressive development of their economies, particularly of those contracting parties

the economies of which can only support low standards of living and are in the early stages of development.

―――――――――

Ad *Article XVIII*

Paragraphs 1 and 4

1.   When they consider whether the economy of a contracting party "can only support low standards of living", the CONTRACTING PARTIES shall take into consideration the normal position of that economy and shall not base their determination on exceptional circumstances such as those which may result from the temporary existence of exceptionally favourable conditions for the staple export product or products of such contracting party.

2.   The phrase "in the early stages of development" is not meant to apply only to contracting parties which have just started their economic development, but also to contracting parties the economics of which are undergoing a process of industrialization to correct an excessive dependence on primary production.

―――――――――

2.   The contracting parties recognize further that it may be necessary for those contracting parties, in order to implement programmes and policies of economic development designed to raise the general standard of living of their people, to take protective or other measures affecting imports, and that such measures are justified in so far as they facilitate the attainment of the objectives of this Agreement. They agree, therefore, that those contracting parties should enjoy additional facilities to enable them (a) to maintain sufficient flexibility in their tariff structure to be able to grant the tariff protection required for the establishment of a particular industry and (b) to apply quantitative restrictions for balance of payments purposes in a manner which takes full account of the continued high level of demand for imports likely to be generated by their programmes of economic development.

―――――――――

Ad *Article XVIII*

Paragraphs 2, 3, 7, 13 and 22

The reference to the establishment of particular industries shall apply not only to the establishment of a new industry, but also to the establishment of a new branch of production in an existing industry and to the substantial transformation of an existing industry, and to the substantial expansion of an existing industry supplying a relatively small proportion of the domestic demand. It shall also cover the reconstruction of an industry destroyed or substantially damaged as a result of hostilities or natural disasters.

---

3.   The contracting parties recognize finally that, with those additional facilities which are provided for in Sections A and B of this Article, the provisions of this Agreement would normally be sufficient to enable contracting parties to meet the requirements of their economic development. They agree, however, that there may be circumstances where no measure consistent with those provisions is practicable to permit a contracting party in the process of economic development to grant the governmental assistance required to promote the establishment of particular industries with a view to raising the general standard of living of its people. Special procedures are laid down in Sections C and D of this Article to deal with those cases.*

4.   (a) Consequently, a contracting party the economy of which can only support low standards of living and is in the early stages of development shall be free to deviate temporarily from the provisions of the other Articles of this Agreement, as provided in Sections A, B and C of this Article.**

(b) A contracting party the economy of which is in the process of development, but which does not come within the scope of subparagraph (a) above, may submit applications to the CONTRACTING PARTIES under Section D of this Article.

5.   The contracting parties recognize that the export earnings of contracting parties, the economies of which are of the type described in paragraph 4(a) and (b) above and which depend on exports of a small number of primary commodities, may be seriously reduced by a decline in the sale of such commodities. Accordingly, when the exports of primary commodities by such a contracting party are seriously affected by measures taken by another contracting party, it may have resort to the consultation provisions of Article XXII of this Agreement.

* * *

ARTICLE XIX.   EMERGENCY ACTION ON IMPORTS OF PARTICULAR PRODUCTS

1.   (a) If, as a result of unforeseen developments and of the effect of the obligations incurred by a contracting party under this Agreement, including tariff concessions, any product is being imported into the territory of that contracting party in such increased quantities and under such conditions as to cause or threaten serious injury to domestic producers in that territory of like or directly competitive products, the contracting party shall be free, in respect of such product, and to the extent and for such time as may be necessary to prevent or remedy such injury, to suspend the obligation in whole or in part or to withdraw or modify the concession.

---

*   See addition to Paragraph 2.
**   See addition to Paragraph 1.

(b) If any product, which is the subject of a concession with respect to a preference, is being imported into the territory of a contracting party in the circumstances set forth in sub-paragraph (a) of this paragraph, so as to cause or threaten serious injury to domestic producers of like or directly competitive products in the territory of a contracting party which receives or received such preference, the importing contracting party shall be free, if that other contracting party so requests, to suspend the relevant obligation in whole or in part or to withdraw or modify the concession in respect of the product, to the extent and for such time as may be necessary to prevent or remedy such injury.

2.   Before any contracting party shall take action pursuant to the provisions of paragraph 1 of this Article, it shall give notice in writing to the CONTRACTING PARTIES as far in advance as may be practicable and shall afford the CONTRACTING PARTIES and those contracting parties having a substantial interest as exporters of the product concerned an opportunity to consult with it in respect of the proposed action. When such notice is given in relation to a concession with respect to a preference, the notice shall name the contracting party which has requested the action. In critical circumstances, where delay would cause damage which it would be difficult to repair, action under paragraph 1 of this Article may be taken provisionally without prior consultation, on the condition that consultation shall be effected immediately after taking such action.

3.   (a) If agreement among the interested contracting parties with respect to the action is not reached, the contracting party which proposes to take or continue the action shall, nevertheless, be free to do so, and if such action is taken or continued, the affected contracting parties shall then be free, not later than ninety days after such action is taken, to suspend, upon the expiration of thirty days from the day on which written notice of such suspension is received by the CONTRACTING PARTIES, the application to the trade of the contracting party taking such action, or, in the case envisaged in paragraph 1(b) of this Article, to the trade of the contracting party requesting such action, of such substantially equivalent concessions or other obligations under this Agreement the suspension of which the CONTRACTING PARTIES do not disapprove.

(b) Notwithstanding the provisions of sub-paragraph (a) of this paragraph, where action is taken under paragraph 2 of this Article without prior consultation and causes or threatens serious injury in the territory of a contracting party to the domestic producers of products affected by the action, that contracting party shall, where delay would cause damage difficult to repair, be free to suspend, upon the taking of the action and throughout the period of consultation, such concessions or other obligations as may be necessary to prevent or remedy the injury.

ARTICLE XX.   GENERAL EXCEPTIONS

Subject to the requirement that such measures are not applied in a manner which would constitute a means of arbitrary or unjustifiable discrimination between countries where the same conditions prevail, or a disguised restriction on international trade, nothing in this Agreement shall be construed to prevent the adoption or enforcement by any contracting party of measures:

(a) necessary to protect public morals;

(b) necessary to protect human, animal or plant life or health;

(c) relating to the importation or exportation of gold or silver;

(d) necessary to secure compliance with laws or regulations which are not inconsistent with the provisions of this Agreement, including those relating to customs enforcement, the enforcement of monopolies operated under paragraph 4 of Article II and Article XVII, the protection of patents, trade marks and copyrights, and the prevention of deceptive practices;

(e) relating to the products of prison labour;

(f) imposed for the protection of national treasures of artistic, historic or archaeological value;

(g) relating to the conservation of exhaustible natural resources if such measures are made effective in conjunction with restrictions on domestic production or consumption;

(h) undertaken in pursuance of obligations under any intergovernmental commodity agreement which conforms to criteria submitted to the CONTRACTING PARTIES and not disapproved by them or which is itself so submitted and not so disapproved;

Ad *Article XX*

Sub-paragraph (h)

The exception provided for in this sub-paragraph extends to any commodity agreement which conforms to the principles approved by the Economic and Social Council in its resolution 30(IV) of 28 March 1947.

(i) involving restrictions on exports of domestic materials necessary to ensure essential quantities of such materials to a domestic processing industry during periods when the domestic price of such materials is held below the world price as part of a governmental stabilization plan; *Provided* that such restrictions shall not operate to increase the exports of or the protection afforded to such domestic industry, and shall not depart from the provisions of this Agreement relating to non-discrimination;

(j) essential to the acquisition or distribution of products in general or local short supply; *Provided* that any such measures shall be consistent with the principle that all contracting parties are entitled to an equitable share of the international supply of such products, and that any such measures, which are inconsistent with the other provisions of this Agreement shall be discontinued as soon as the conditions giving rise to them have ceased to exist. The CONTRACTING PARTIES shall review the need for this sub-paragraph not later than 30 June 1960.

ARTICLE XXI.   SECURITY EXCEPTIONS

Nothing in this Agreement shall be construed

(a) to require any contracting party to furnish any information the disclosure of which it considers contrary to its essential security interests; or

(b) to prevent any contracting party from taking any action which it considers necessary for the protection of its essential security interests

(i) relating to fissionable materials or the materials from which they are derived;

(ii) relating to the traffic in arms, ammunition and implements of war and to such traffic in other goods and materials as is carried on directly or indirectly for the purpose of supplying a military establishment;

(iii) taken in time of war or other emergency in international relations; or

(c) to prevent any contracting party from taking any action in pursuance of its obligations under the United Nations Charter for the maintenance of international peace and security.

ARTICLE XXII.   CONSULTATION

1.   Each contracting party shall accord sympathetic consideration to, and shall afford adequate opportunity for consultation regarding, such representations as may be made by another contracting party with respect to any matter affecting the operation of this Agreement.

2.   The CONTRACTING PARTIES may, at the request of a contracting party, consult with any contracting party or parties in respect of any matter for which it has not been possible to find a satisfactory solution through consultation under paragraph 1.

ARTICLE XXIII.   NULLIFICATION OR IMPAIRMENT

1.   If any contracting party should consider that any benefit accruing to it directly or indirectly under this Agreement is being nullified or impaired or that the attainment of any objective of the Agreement is being impeded as the result of

(a) the failure of another contracting party to carry out its obligations under this Agreement, or

(b) the application by another contracting party of any measure, whether or not it conflicts with the provisions of this Agreement, or

(c) the existence of any other situation,

the contracting party may, with a view to the satisfactory adjustment of the matter, make written representations or proposals to the other contracting party or parties which it considers to be concerned. Any contracting party thus approached shall give sympathetic consideration to the representations or proposals made to it.

2.   If no satisfactory adjustment is effected between the contracting parties concerned within a reasonable time, or if the difficulty is of the type described in paragraph 1(c) of this Article, the matter may be referred to the CONTRACTING PARTIES. The CONTRACTING PARTIES shall promptly investigate any matter so referred to them and shall make appropriate recommendations to the contracting parties which they consider to be concerned, or give a ruling on the matter, as appropriate. The CONTRACTING PARTIES may consult with contracting parties, with the Economic and Social Council of the United Nations and with any appropriate inter-governmental organization in cases where they consider such consultation necessary. If the CONTRACTING PARTIES consider that the circumstances are serious enough to justify such action, they may authorize a contracting party or parties to suspend the application to any other contracting party or parties of such concessions or other obligations under this Agreement as they determine to be appropriate in the circumstances. If the application to any contracting party of any concession or other obligation is in fact suspended, that contracting party shall then be free, not later than sixty days after such action is taken, to give written notice to the Executive Secretary to the CONTRACTING PARTIES of its intention to withdraw from this Agreement and such withdrawal shall take effect upon the sixtieth day following the day on which such notice is received by him.

PART III

ARTICLE XXIV. TERRITORIAL APPLICATION—FRONTIER TRAFFIC—CUSTOMS UNIONS AND FREE-TRADE AREAS

1.   The provisions of this Agreement shall apply to the metropolitan customs territories of the contracting parties and to any other customs territories in respect of which this Agreement has been accepted under Article XXVI or is being applied under Article XXXIII or pursuant to the Protocol of Provisional Application. Each such customs territory shall, exclusively for the purposes of the territorial application of this Agreement, be treated as though it were a contracting party; *Provided* that the provisions of this paragraph shall not be construed to create any rights or obligations as between two or more customs territories in respect of which this Agreement has been accepted under Article XXVI or is being applied under Article XXXIII or pursuant to the Protocol of Provisional Application by a single contracting party.

2. For the purposes of this Agreement a customs territory shall be understood to mean any territory with respect to which separate tariffs or other regulations of commerce are maintained for a substantial part of the trade of such territory with other territories.

3. The provisions of this Agreement shall not be construed to prevent:

(a) Advantages accorded by any contracting party to adjacent countries in order to facilitate frontier traffic;

(b) Advantages accorded to the trade with the Free Territory of Trieste by countries contiguous to that territory, provided that such advantages are not in conflict with the Treaties of Peace arising out of the Second World War.

4. The contracting parties recognize the desirability of increasing freedom of trade by the development, through voluntary agreements, of closer integration between the economies of the countries parties to such agreements. They also recognize that the purpose of a customs union or of a free-trade area should be to facilitate trade between the constituent territories and not to raise barriers to the trade of other contracting parties with such territories.

5. Accordingly, the provisions of this Agreement shall not prevent, as between the territories of contracting parties, the formation of a customs union or of a free-trade area or the adoption of an interim agreement necessary for the formation of a customs union or of a free-trade area; *Provided* that:

(a) with respect to a customs union, or an interim agreement leading to the formation of a customs union, the duties and other regulations of commerce imposed at the institution of any such union or interim agreement in respect of trade with contracting parties not parties to such union or agreement shall not on the whole be higher or more restrictive than the general incidence of the duties and regulations of commerce applicable in the constituent territories prior to the formation of such union or the adoption of such interim agreement, as the case may be;

(b) with respect to a free-trade area, or an interim agreement leading to the formation of a free-trade area, the duties and other regulations of commerce maintained in each of the constituent territories and applicable at the formation of such free-trade area or the adoption of such interim agreement to the trade of contracting parties not included in such area or not parties to such agreement shall not be higher or more restrictive than the corresponding duties and other regulations of commerce existing in the same constituent territories prior to the formation of the free-trade area, or interim agreement, as the case may be; and

(c) any interim agreement referred to in sub-paragraphs (a) and (b) shall include a plan and schedule for the formation of such a customs union or of such a free-trade area within a reasonable length of time.

6.   If, in fulfilling the requirements of sub-paragraph 5(a), a contracting party proposes to increase any rate of duty inconsistently with the provisions of Article II, the procedure set forth in Article XXXVIII shall apply. In providing for compensatory adjustment, due account shall be taken of the compensation already afforded by the reductions brought about in the corresponding duty of the other constituents of the union.

7.   (a) Any contracting party deciding to enter into a customs union or free-trade area, or an interim agreement leading to the formation of such a union or area, shall promptly notify the CONTRACTING PARTIES and shall make available to them such information regarding the proposed union or area as will enable them to make such reports and recommendations to contracting parties as they may deem appropriate.

(b) If, after having studied the plan and schedule included in an interim agreement referred to in paragraph 5 in consultation with the parties to that agreement and taking due account of the information made available in accordance with the provisions of sub-paragraph (a), the CONTRACTING PARTIES find that such agreement is not likely to result in the formation of a customs union or of a free-trade area within the period contemplated by the parties to the agreement or that such period is not a reasonable one, the CONTRACTING PARTIES shall make recommendations to the parties to the agreement. The parties shall not maintain or put into force, as the case may be, such agreement if they are not prepared to modify it in accordance with these recommendations.

(c) Any substantial change in the plan or schedule referred to in paragraph 5(c) shall be communicated to the CONTRACTING PARTIES, which may request the contracting parties concerned to consult with them if the change seems likely to jeopardize or delay unduly the formation of the customs union or of the free-trade area.

8.   For the purposes of this Agreement:

(a) A customs union shall be understood to mean the substitution of a single customs territory for two or more customs territories, so that

(i) duties and other restrictive regulations of commerce (except, where necessary, those permitted under Articles XI, XII, XIII, XIV, XV and XX) are eliminated with respect to substantially all the trade between the constituent territories of the union or at least with respect to substantially all the trade in products originating in such territories, and,

(ii) subject to the provisions of paragraph 9, substantially the same duties and other regulations of commerce are applied by each of the members of the union to the trade of territories not included in the union;

(b) A free-trade area shall be understood to mean a group of two or more customs territories in which the duties and other restrictive regulations of commerce (except, where necessary, those permitted under Articles XI, XII, XIII, XIV, XV and XX) are eliminated on substantially all the trade between the constituent territories in products originating in such territories.

9.   The preferences referred to in paragraph 2 of Article I shall not be affected by the formation of a customs union or of a free-trade area but may be eliminated or adjusted by means of negotiations with contracting parties affected. This procedure of negotiations with affected contracting parties shall, in particular, apply to the elimination of preferences required to conform with the provisions of paragraph 8(a)(i) and paragraph 8(b).

Ad *Article XXIV*

Paragraph 9

It is understood that the provisions of Article I would require that, when a product which has been imported into the territory of a member of a customs union or free-trade area at a preferential rate of duty is re-exported to the territory of another member of such union or area, the latter member should collect a duty equal to the difference between the duty already paid and any higher duty that would be payable if the product were being imported directly into its territory.

---

10.   The CONTRACTING PARTIES may by a two-thirds majority approve proposals which do not fully comply with the requirements of paragraphs 5 to 9 inclusive, provided that such proposals lead to the formation of a customs union or a free-trade area in the sense of this Article.

11.   Taking into account the exceptional circumstances arising out of the establishment of India and Pakistan as independent States and recognizing the fact that they have long constituted an economic unit, the contracting parties agree that the provisions of this Agreement shall not prevent the two countries from entering into special arrangements with respect to the trade between them, pending the establishment of their mutual trade relations on a definitive basis.

Ad *Article XXIV*

Paragraph 11

Measures adopted by India and Pakistan in order to carry out definitive trade arrangements between them, once they have been agreed upon, might depart from particular provisions of this Agreement, but these measures would in general be consistent with the objectives of the Agreement.

---

12.   Each contracting party shall take such reasonable measures as may be available to it to ensure observance of the provisions of this Agreement by the regional and local governments and authorities within its territory.

ARTICLE XXV.   JOINT ACTION BY THE CONTRACTING PARTIES

Article XXV

Joint Action by the Contracting Parties

1.   Representatives of the contracting parties shall meet from time to time for the purpose of giving effect to those provisions of this Agreement which involve joint action and, generally, with a view to facilitating the operation and furthering the objectives of this Agreement. Wherever reference is made in this Agreement to the contracting parties acting jointly they are designated as the CONTRACTING PARTIES.

2.   The Secretary-General of the United Nations is requested to convene the first meeting of the CONTRACTING PARTIES, which shall take place not later than March 1, 1948.

3.   Each contracting party shall be entitled to have one vote at all meetings of the CONTRACTING PARTIES.

4.   Except as otherwise provided for in this Agreement, decisions of the CONTRACTING PARTIES shall be taken by a majority of the votes cast.

5.   In exceptional circumstances not elsewhere provided for in this Agreement, the CONTRACTING PARTIES may waive an obligation imposed upon a contracting party by this Agreement; *Provided* that any such decision shall be approved by a two-thirds majority of the votes cast and that such majority shall comprise more than half of the contracting parties. The CONTRACTING PARTIES may also by such a vote

(i) define certain categories of exceptional circumstances to which other voting requirements shall apply for the waiver of obligations, and

(ii) prescribe such criteria as may be necessary for the application of this paragraph.

* * *

ARTICLE XXVI. ACCEPTANCE, ENTRY INTO FORCE AND REGISTRATION

1.   The date of this Agreement shall be 30 October 1947.

2.   This Agreement shall be open for acceptance by any contracting party which, on 1 March 1955, was a contracting party or was negotiating with a view to accession to this Agreement.

3.   This Agreement, done in a single English original and in a single French original, both texts authentic, shall be deposited with the Secretary-General of the United Nations, who shall furnish certified copies thereof to all interested governments.

* * *

6.   This Agreement shall enter into force, as among the governments which have accepted it, on the thirtieth day following the day on which instruments of acceptance have been deposited with the Executive Secretary* to the CONTRACTING PARTIES on behalf of governments named in Annex H, the territories of which account for 85 per centum of the total external trade of the territories of such governments, computed in accordance with the applicable column of percentages set forth therein. The instrument of acceptance of each other government shall take effect on the thirtieth day following the day on which such instrument has been deposited.

7.   The United Nations is authorized to effect registration of this Agreement as soon as it enters into force.

ARTICLE XXVII. WITHHOLDING OR WITHDRAWAL OF CONCESSIONS

Any contracting party shall at any time be free to withhold or to withdraw in whole or in part any concession, provided for in the appropriate Schedule annexed to this Agreement, in respect of which such contracting party determines that it was initially negotiated with a government which has not become, or has ceased to be, a contracting party. A contracting party taking such action shall notify the CONTRACTING PARTIES and, upon request, consult with contracting parties which have a substantial interest in the product concerned.

ARTICLE XXVIII.   MODIFICATION OF SCHEDULES

Modification of Schedules

1.   On the first day of each three-year period, the first period beginning on 1 January 1958 (or on the first day of any other period* that may be specified by the CONTRACTING PARTIES by two-thirds of the votes cast) a contracting party (hereafter in this Article referred to as the "applicant contracting party") may, by negotiations and agreement with any contracting party with which such concession was initially negotiated

---

*   Now referred to as Director-General.

and with any other contracting party determined by the CONTRACTING PARTIES to have a principal supplying interest* (which two preceding categories of contracting parties, together with the applicant contracting party, are in this Article hereinafter referred to as the "contracting parties primarily concerned"), and subject to consultation with any other contracting party determined by the CONTRACTING PARTIES to have a substantial interest* in such concession, modify or withdraw a concession* included in the appropriate Schedule annexed to this Agreement.

2. In such negotiations and agreement, which may include provision for compensatory adjustment with respect to other products, the contracting parties concerned shall endeavour to maintain a general level of reciprocal and mutually advantageous concessions not less favourable to trade than that provided for in this Agreement prior to such negotiations.

3. (a) If agreement between the contracting parties primarily concerned cannot be reached before 1 January 1958 or before the expiration of a period envisaged in paragraph 1 of this Article, the contracting party which proposes to modify or withdraw the concession shall, nevertheless, be free to do so and if such action is taken any contracting party with which such concession was initially negotiated, any contracting party determined under paragraph 1 to have a principal supplying interest and any contracting party determined under paragraph 1 to have a substantial interest shall then be free not later than six months after such action is taken, to withdraw, upon the expiration of thirty days from the day on which written notice of such withdrawal is received by the CONTRACTING PARTIES, substantially equivalent concessions initially negotiated with the applicant contracting party.

(b) If agreement between the contracting parties primarily concerned is reached but any other contracting party determined under paragraph 1 of this Article to have a substantial interest is not satisfied, such other contracting party shall be free, not later than six months after action under such agreement is taken, to withdraw, upon the expiration of thirty days from the day on which written notice of such withdrawal is received by the CONTRACTING PARTIES, substantially equivalent concessions initially negotiated with the applicant contracting party.

4. The CONTRACTING PARTIES may, at any time, in special circumstances, authorize* a contracting party to enter into negotiations for modification or withdrawal of a concession included in the appropriate Schedule annexed to this Agreement subject to the following procedures and conditions:

(a) Such negotiations* and any related consultations shall be conducted in accordance with the provisions of paragraphs 1 and 2 of this Article.

(b) If agreement between the contracting parties primarily concerned is reached in the negotiations, the provisions of paragraph 3(b) of this Article shall apply.

(*c*) If agreement between the contracting parties primarily concerned is not reached within a period of sixty days* after negotiations have been authorized, or within such longer period as the CONTRACTING PARTIES may have prescribed, the applicant contracting party may refer the matter to the CONTRACTING PARTIES.

(*d*) Upon such reference, the CONTRACTING PARTIES shall promptly examine the matter and submit their views to the contracting parties primarily concerned with the aim of achieving a settlement. If a settlement is reached, the provisions of paragraph 3(*b*) shall apply as if agreement between the contracting parties primarily concerned had been reached. If no settlement is reached between the contracting parties primarily concerned, the applicant contracting party shall be free to modify or withdraw the concession, unless the CONTRACTING PARTIES determine that the applicant contracting party has unreasonably failed to offer adequate compensation.* If such action is taken, any contracting party with which the concession was initially negotiated, any contracting party determined under paragraph 4(*a*) to have a principal supplying interest and any contracting party determined under paragraph 4(*a*) to have a substantial interest, shall be free, not later than six months after such action is taken, to modify or withdraw, upon the expiration of thirty days from the day on which written notice of such withdrawal is received by the CONTRACTING PARTIES, substantially equivalent concessions initially negotiated with the applicant contracting party.

5. Before 1 January 1958 and before the end of any period envisaged in paragraph 1 a contracting party may elect by notifying the CONTRACTING PARTIES to reserve the right, for the duration of the next period, to modify the appropriate Schedule in accordance with the procedures of paragraphs 1 to 3. If a contracting party so elects, other contracting parties shall have the right, during the same period, to modify or withdraw, in accordance with the same procedures, concessions initially negotiated with that contracting party.

ARTICLE XXVIII bis. TARIFF NEGOTIATIONS

1. The contracting parties recognize that customs duties often constitute serious obstacles to trade; thus negotiations on a reciprocal and mutually advantageous basis, directed to the substantial reduction of the general level of tariffs and other charges on imports and exports and in particular to the reduction of such high tariffs as discourage the importation even of minimum quantities, and conducted with due regard to the objectives of this Agreement and the varying needs of individual contracting parties, are of great importance to the expansion of

international trade. The CONTRACTING PARTIES may therefore sponsor such negotiations from time to time.

2.   (a) Negotiations under this Article may be carried out on a selective product-by-product basis or by the application of such multilateral procedures as may be accepted by the contracting parties concerned. Such negotiations may be directed towards the reduction of duties, the binding of duties at then existing levels or undertakings that individual duties or the average duties on specified categories of products shall not exceed specified levels. The binding against increase of low duties or of duty-free treatment shall, in principle, be recognized as a concession equivalent in value to the reduction of high duties.

(b) The contracting parties recognize that in general the success of multilateral negotiations would depend on the participation of all contracting parties which conduct a substantial proportion of their external trade with one another.

3.   Negotiations shall be conducted on a basis which affords adequate opportunity to take into account:

(a) the needs of individual contracting parties and individual industries;

(b) the needs of less-developed countries for a more flexible use of tariff protection to assist their economic development and the special needs of these countries to maintain tariffs for revenue purposes; and

(c) all other relevant circumstances, including the fiscal, developmental, strategic and other needs of the contracting parties concerned.

Ad *Article XXVIII bis*

Paragraph 3

It is understood that the reference to fiscal needs would include the revenue aspect of duties and particularly duties imposed primarily for revenue purposes or duties imposed on products which can be substituted for products subject to revenue duties to prevent the avoidance of such duties.

ARTICLE XXIX.   THE RELATION OF THIS AGREEMENT TO THE HAVANA CHARTER (omitted)

* * *

ARTICLE XXX.   AMENDMENTS

1.   Except where provision for modification is made elsewhere in this Agreement, amendments to the provisions of Part I of this Agreement

or to the provisions of Article XXIX or of this Article shall become effective upon acceptance by all the contracting parties, and other amendments to this Agreement shall become effective, in respect of those contracting parties which accept them, upon acceptance by two-thirds of the contracting parties and thereafter for each other contracting party upon acceptance by it.

2. Any contracting party accepting an amendment to this Agreement shall deposit an instrument of acceptance with the Secretary-General of the United Nations within such period as the CONTRACTING PARTIES may specify. The CONTRACTING PARTIES may decide that any amendment made effective under this Article is of such a nature that any contracting party which has not accepted it within a period specified by the CONTRACTING PARTIES shall be free to withdrawn from this Agreement, or to remain a contracting party with the consent of the CONTRACTING PARTIES.

ARTICLE XXXI. WITHDRAWAL

Without prejudice to the provisions of paragraph 12 of Article XVIII, of Article XXIII or of paragraph 2 of Article XXX, any contracting party may withdraw from this Agreement, or may separately withdraw on behalf of any of the separate customs territories for which it has international responsibility and which at the time possesses full autonomy in the conduct of its external commercial relations and of the other matters provided for in this Agreement. The withdrawal shall take effect upon the expiration of six months from the day on which written notice of withdrawal is received by the Secretary-General of the United Nations.

ARTICLE XXXII. CONTRACTING PARTIES

1. The contracting parties to this Agreement shall be understood to mean those governments which are applying the provisions of this Agreement under Article XXVI or XXXIII or pursuant to the Protocol of Provisional Application.

2. At any time after the entry into force of this Agreement pursuant to paragraph 6 of Article XXVI, those contracting parties which have accepted this Agreement pursuant to paragraph 4 of Article XXVI may decide that any contracting party which has not so accepted it shall cease to be a contracting party.

ARTICLE XXXIII. ACCESSION

A government not party to this Agreement, or a government acting on behalf of a separate customs territory possessing full autonomy in the conduct of its external commercial relations and of the other matters provided for in this Agreement, may accede to this Agreement, on its own behalf or on behalf of that territory, on terms to be agreed between such government and the CONTRACTING PARTIES. Decisions of the CONTRACTING PARTIES under this paragraph shall be taken by a two-thirds majority.

ARTICLE XXXIV.   ANNEXES

The annexes to this Agreement are hereby made an integral part of this Agreement.

ARTICLE XXXV. NON-APPLICATION OF THE AGREEMENT BETWEEN PARTICULAR CONTRACTING PARTIES

1.   This Agreement, or alternatively Article II of this Agreement, shall not apply as between any contracting party and any other contracting party if:

(a) the two contracting parties have not entered into tariff negotiations with each other, and

(b) either of the contracting parties, at the time either becomes a contracting party, does not consent to such application.

2.   The CONTRACTING PARTIES may review the operation of this Article in particular cases at the request of any contracting party and make appropriate recommendations.

PART IV.   TRADE AND DEVELOPMENT

Ad *Part IV*

The words "developed contracting parties" and the words "less-developed contracting parties," as used in Part IV are to be understood to refer to developed and less-developed countries which are parties to the General Agreement on Tariffs and Trade.

ARTICLE XXXVI.   PRINCIPLES AND OBJECTIVES

1.   The contracting parties,

(a) recalling that the basic objectives of this Agreement include the raising of standards of living and the progressive development of the economies of all contracting parties, and considering that the attainment of these objectives is particularly urgent for less-developed contracting parties;

(b) considering that export earnings of the less-developed contracting parties can play a vital part in their economic development and that the extent of this contribution depends on the prices paid by the less-developed contracting parties for essential imports, the volume of their exports, and the prices received for these exports;

(c) noting, that there is a wide gap between standards of living in less-developed countries and in other countries;

(d) recognizing that individual and joint action is essential to further the development of the economies of less-developed contracting parties and to bring about a rapid advance in the standards of living in these countries;

(e) recognizing that international trade as a means of achieving economic and social advancement should be governed by such rules and procedures—and measures in conformity with such rules and procedures—as are consistent with the objectives set forth in this Article;

(f) noting that the CONTRACTING PARTIES may enable less-developed contracting parties to use special measures to promote their trade and development;

agree as follows.

Ad *Article XXXVI*

Paragraph 1

This Article is based upon the objectives set forth in Article I as it will be amended by Section A of paragraph 1 of the Protocol Amending Part I and Articles XXIX and XXX when that Protocol enters into force.[1]

---

2.   There is need for a rapid and sustained expansion of the export earnings of the less-developed contracting parties.

3.   There is need for positive efforts designed to ensure that less-developed contracting parties secure a share in the growth in international trade commensurate with the needs of their economic development.

4.   Given the continued dependence of many less-developed contracting parties on the exportation of a limited range of primary products, there is need to provide in the largest possible measure more favourable and acceptable conditions of access to world markets for these products, and wherever appropriate to devise measures designed to stabilize and improve conditions of world markets in these products, including in particular measures designed to attain stable, equitable and remunerative prices, thus permitting an expansion of world trade and demand and a dynamic and steady growth of the real export earnings of these countries so as to provide them with expanding resources for their economic development.

---

[1]   This Protocol was abandoned on January 1, 1968.

Ad *Article XXXVI*

Paragraph 4

The term "primary products" includes agricultural products, vide paragraph 2 of the note ad Article XVI, Section B.

---

5. The rapid expansion of the economies of the less-developed contracting parties will be facilitated by a diversification of the structure of their economies and the avoidance of an excessive dependence on the export of primary products. There is, therefore, need for increased access in the largest possible measure to markets under favourable conditions for processed and manufactured products currently or potentially of particular export interest to less-developed contracting parties.

Ad *Article XXXVI*

Paragraph 5

A diversification programme would generally include the intensification of activities for the processing of primary products and the development of manufacturing industries, taking into account the situation of the particular contracting party and the world outlook for production and consumption of different commodities.

---

6. Because of the chronic deficiency in the export proceeds and other foreign exchange earnings of less-developed contracting parties, there are important inter-relationships between trade and financial assistance to development. There is, therefore, need for close and continuing collaboration between the CONTRACTING PARTIES and the international lending agencies so that they can contribute most effectively to alleviating the burdens these less-developed contracting parties assume in the interest of their economic development.

7. There is need for appropriate collaboration between the CONTRACTING PARTIES, other intergovernmental bodies and the organs and agencies of the United Nations system, whose activities relate to the trade and economic development of less-developed countries.

8. The developed contracting parties do not expect reciprocity for commitments made by them in trade negotiations to reduce or remove tariffs and other barriers to the trade of less-developed contracting parties.

Ad *Article XXXVI*

Paragraph 8

It is understood that the phrase "do not expect reciprocity" means, in accordance with the objectives set forth in this Article, that the less-developed contracting parties should not be expected, in the course of trade negotiations, to make contributions which are inconsistent with their individual development, financial and trade needs, taking into consideration past trade developments.

This paragraph would apply in the event of action under Section A of Article XVII, Article XXVIII, Article XXVIII bis (Article XXIX after the amendment set forth in Section A of paragraph 1 of the Protocol Amending Part I and Articles XXIX and XXX shall have become effective), Article XXXIII, or any other procedure under this Agreement.

---

9.   The adoption of measures to give effect to these principles and objectives shall be a matter of conscious and purposeful effort on the part of the contracting parties both individually and jointly.

ARTICLE XXXVII.   COMMITMENTS

1.   The developed contracting parties shall to the fullest extent possible—that is, except when compelling reasons, which may include legal reasons, make it impossible—give effect to the following provisions:

> (a) accord high priority to the reduction and elimination of barriers to products currently or potentially of particular export interest to less-developed contracting parties, including customs duties and other restrictions which differentiate unreasonably between such products in their primary and in their processed forms;

Ad *Article XXXVII*

Paragraph 1(a)

This paragraph would apply in the event of negotiations for reduction or elimination of tariffs or other restrictive regulations of commerce under Articles XXVIII, XXVIII bis (XXIX after the amendment set forth in Section A of paragraph 1 of the Protocol Amending Part I and Articles XXIX and XXX shall have become effective[1]), and Article XXXIII, as well as in connexion with other action to effect such reduction or elimination which contracting parties may be able to undertake.

---

[1]   This Protocol was abandoned on January 1, 1968.

(b) refrain from introducing, or increasing the incidence of, customs duties or non-tariff import barriers on products currently or potentially of particular export interest to less-developed contracting parties; and

(c)(i) refrain from imposing new fiscal measures, and

(ii) in any adjustments of fiscal policy accord high priority to the reduction and elimination of fiscal measures, which would hamper, or which hamper, significantly the growth of consumption of primary products, in raw or processed form, wholly or mainly produced in the territories of less-developed contracting parties, and which are applied specifically to those products.

2.   (a) Whenever it is considered that effect is not being given to any of the provisions of sub-paragraph (a), (b) or (c) of paragraph 1, the matter shall be reported to the CONTRACTING PARTIES either by the contracting party not so giving effect to the relevant provisions or by any other interested contracting party.

(b)(i) The CONTRACTING PARTIES shall, if requested so to do by any interested contracting party, and without prejudice to any bilateral consultations that may be undertaken, consult with the contracting party concerned and all interested contracting parties with respect to the matter with a view to reaching solutions satisfactory to all contracting parties concerned in order to further the objectives set forth in Article XXXVI. In the course of these consultations, the reasons given in cases where effect was not being given to the provisions of subparagraph (a), (b) or (c) of paragraph 1 shall be examined.

(ii) As the implementation of the provisions of sub-paragraph (a), (b) or (c) of paragraph 1 by individual contracting parties may in some cases be more readily achieved where action is taken jointly with other developed contracting parties, such consultation might, where appropriate, be directed towards this end.

(iii) The consultations by the CONTRACTING PARTIES might also, in appropriate cases, be directed towards agreement on joint action designed to further the objectives of this Agreement as envisaged in paragraph 1 of Article XXV.

3.   The developed contracting parties shall:

(a) make every effort, in cases where a government directly or indirectly determines the resale price of products wholly or mainly produced in the territories of less-developed contracting parties, to maintain trade margins at equitable levels;

(b) give active consideration to the adoption of other measures designed to provide greater scope for the development of imports from less-developed contracting parties and collaborate in appropriate international action to this end;

Ad *Article XXXVII*

Paragraph 3(b)

The other measures referred to in this paragraph might include steps to promote domestic structural changes, to encourage the consumption of particular products, or to introduce measures of trade promotion.

(c) have special regard to the trade interests of less-developed contracting parties when considering the application of other measures permitted under this Agreement to meet particular problems and explore all possibilities of constructive remedies before applying such measures where they would affect essential interests of those contracting parties.

4. Less-developed contracting parties agree to take appropriate action in implementation of the provisions of Part IV for the benefit of the trade of other less-developed contracting parties, in so far as such action is consistent with their individual present and future development, financial and trade needs taking into account past trade developments as well as the trade interests of less-developed contracting parties as a whole.

5. In the implementation of the commitments set forth in paragraphs 1 to 4 each contracting party shall afford to any other interested contracting party or contracting parties full and prompt opportunity for consultations under the normal procedures of this Agreement with respect to any matter or difficulty which may arise.

ARTICLE XXXVIII.   JOINT ACTION (omitted)

* * *

ANNEX A

LIST OF TERRITORIES REFERRED TO IN PARAGRAPH 2(A) OF ARTICLE I

United Kingdom of Great Britain and Northern Ireland

Dependent territories of the United Kingdom of Great Britain and Northern Ireland

Canada

Commonwealth of Australia

Dependent territories of the Commonwealth of Australia

New Zealand

Dependent territories of New Zealand

Union of South Africa including South West Africa

Ireland

India (as of April 10, 1947)

Newfoundland

Southern Rhodesia

Burma

Ceylon

Certain of the territories listed above have two or more preferential rates in force for certain products. Any such territory may, by agreement with the other contracting parties which are principal suppliers of such products at the most-favoured-nation rate, substitute for such preferential rates a single preferential rate which shall not on the whole be less favourable to suppliers at the most-favoured-nation rate than the preferences in force prior to such substitution.

The imposition of an equivalent margin of tariff preference to replace a margin of preference in an internal tax existing on April 10, 1947 exclusively between two or more of the territories listed in this Annex or to replace the preferential quantitative arrangements described in the following paragraph, shall not be deemed to constitute an increase in a margin of tariff preference.

The preferential arrangements referred to in paragraph 5(b) of Article XIV are those existing in the United Kingdom on April 10, 1947, under contractual agreements with the Governments of Canada, Australia and New Zealand, in respect of chilled and frozen beef and veal, frozen mutton and lamb, chilled and frozen pork, and bacon. It is the intention, without prejudice to any action taken under subparagraph (h) of Article XX, that these arrangements shall be eliminated or replaced by tariff preferences, and that negotiations to this end shall take place as soon as practicable among the countries substantially concerned or involved.

The film hire tax in force in New Zealand on April 10, 1947, shall, for the purposes of this Agreement, be treated as a customs duty under Article I. The renters' film quota in force in New Zealand on April 10, 1947, shall, for the purposes of this Agreement, be treated as a screen quota under Article IV.

The Dominions of India and Pakistan have not been mentioned separately in the above list since they had not come into existence as such on the base date of April 10, 1947.

* * *

ANNEX H

Percentage Shares of Total External Trade to be Used for the Purpose of Making the Determination Referred to in Article XXVI

(based on the average of 1949–1953)

If, prior to the accession of the Government of Japan to the General Agreement, the present Agreement has been accepted by contracting parties the external trade of which under column I accounts for the percentage of such trade specified in paragraph 6 of Article XXVI, column I shall be applicable for the purposes of that paragraph. If the present Agreement has not been so accepted prior to the accession of the Government of Japan, column II shall be applicable for the purposes of that paragraph.

	Column I (Contracting parties on 1 March 1955)	*Column II* (Contracting parties on 1 March 1955 and Japan)
Australia	3.1	3.0
Austria	0.9	0.8
Belgium-Luxemburg	4.3	4.2
Brazil	2.5	2.4
Burma	0.3	0.3
Canada	6.7	6.5
Ceylon	0.5	0.5
Chile	0.6	0.6
Cuba	1.1	1.1
Czechoslovakia	1.4	1.4
Denmark	1.4	1.4
Dominican Republic	0.1	0.1
Finland	1.0	1.0
France	8.7	8.5
Germany, Federal Republic of	5.3	5.2
Greece	0.4	0.4
Haiti	0.1	0.1

	Column I	*Column II*
	(Contracting parties on 1 March 1955)	(Contracting parties on 1 March 1955 and Japan)
India	2.4	2.4
Indonesia	1.3	1.3
Italy	2.9	2.8
Netherlands, Kingdom of the	4.7	4.6
New Zealand	1.0	1.0
Nicaragua	0.1	0.1
Norway	1.1	1.1
Pakistan	0.9	0.8
Peru	0.4	0.4
Rhodesia and Nyasaland	0.6	0.6
Sweden	2.5	2.4
Turkey	0.6	0.6
Union of South Africa	1.8	1.8
United Kingdom	20.3	19.8
United States of America	20.6	20.1
Uruguay	0.4	0.4
Japan	—	2.3
	100.0	100.0

Note: These percentages have been computed taking into account the trade of all territories in respect of which the General Agreement on Tariffs and Trade is applied.

2. Agreement Establishing the World Trade Organization (WTO)

(Selected Provisions)

The *Parties* to this Agreement,

Recognizing that their relations in the field of trade and economic endeavour should be conducted with a view to raising standards of living, ensuring full employment and a large and steadily growing volume of real income and effective demand, and expanding the production of and trade in goods and services, while allowing for the optimal use of the world's resources in accordance with the objective of sustainable development, seeking both to protect and preserve the environment and to enhance the means for doing so in a manner consistent with their respective needs and concerns at different levels of economic development,

Recognizing further that there is need for positive efforts designed to ensure that developing countries, and especially the least developed among them, secure a share in the growth in international trade commensurate with the needs of their economic development,

Being desirous of contributing to these objectives by entering into reciprocal and mutually advantageous arrangements directed to the substantial reduction of tariffs and other barriers to trade and to the elimination of discriminatory treatment in international trade relations,

Resolved, therefore, to develop an integrated, more viable and durable multilateral trading system encompassing the General Agreement on Tariffs and Trade, the results of past trade liberalization efforts, and all of the results of the Uruguay Round of Multilateral Trade Negotiations,

Determined to preserve the basic principles and to further the objectives underlying this multilateral trading system,

Agree as follows:

Article I

Establishment of the Organization

The World Trade Organization (hereinafter referred to as "the WTO") is hereby established.

Article II

Scope of the WTO

1.   The WTO shall provide the common institutional framework for the conduct of trade relations among its Members in matters related to the agreements and associated legal instruments included in the Annexes to this Agreement.

2.   The agreements and associated legal instruments included in Annexes 1, 2 and 3 (hereinafter referred to as "Multilateral Trade Agreements") are integral parts of this Agreement, binding on all Members.

3.   The agreements and associated legal instruments included in Annex 4 (hereinafter referred to as "Plurilateral Trade Agreements") are also part of this Agreement for those Members that have accepted them, and are binding on those Members. The Plurilateral Trade Agreements do not create either obligations or rights for Members that have not accepted them.

4.   The General Agreement on Tariffs and Trade 1994 as specified in Annex 1A (hereinafter referred to as "GATT 1994") is legally distinct from the General Agreement on Tariffs and Trade, dated 30 October 1947, annexed to the Final Act Adopted at the Conclusion of the Second Session of the Preparatory Committee of the United Nations Conference on Trade and Employment, as subsequently rectified, amended or modified (hereinafter referred to as "GATT 1947").

Article III

Functions of the WTO

1.   The WTO shall facilitate the implementation, administration and operation, and further the objectives, of this Agreement and of the Multilateral Trade Agreements, and shall also provide the framework for the implementation, administration and operation of the Plurilateral Trade Agreements.

2.   The WTO shall provide the forum for negotiations among its Members concerning their multilateral trade relations in matters dealt with under the agreements in the Annexes to this Agreement. The WTO may also provide a forum for further negotiations among its Members concerning their multilateral trade relations, and a framework for the implementation of the results of such negotiations, as may be decided by the Ministerial Conference.

3.   The WTO shall administer the Understanding on Rules and Procedures Governing the Settlement of Disputes (hereinafter referred to as the "Dispute Settlement Understanding" or "DSU") in Annex 2 to this Agreement.

4.   The WTO shall administer the Trade Policy Review Mechanism (hereinafter referred to as the "TPRM") provided for in Annex 3 to this Agreement.

5.   With a view to achieving greater coherence in global economic policymaking, the WTO shall cooperate, as appropriate, with the International Monetary Fund and with the International Bank for Reconstruction and Development and its affiliated agencies.

Article IV

Structure of the WTO

1.   There shall be a Ministerial Conference composed of representatives of all the Members, which shall meet at least once every two years. The Ministerial Conference shall carry out the functions of the WTO and take actions necessary to this effect. The Ministerial Conference shall have the authority to take decisions on all matters under any of the

Multilateral Trade Agreements, if so requested by a Member, in accordance with the specific requirements for decision-making in this Agreement and in the relevant Multilateral Trade Agreement.

2. There shall be a General Council composed of representatives of all the Members, which shall meet as appropriate. In the intervals between meetings of the Ministerial Conference, its functions shall be conducted by the General Council. The General Council shall also carry out the functions assigned to it by this Agreement. The General Council shall establish its rules of procedure and approve the rules of procedure for the Committees provided for in paragraph 7.

3. The General Council shall convene as appropriate to discharge the responsibilities of the Dispute Settlement Body provided for in the Dispute Settlement Understanding. The Dispute Settlement Body may have its own chairman and shall establish such rules of procedure as it deems necessary for the fulfilment of those responsibilities.

4. The General Council shall convene as appropriate to discharge the responsibilities of the Trade Policy Review Body provided for in the TPRM. The Trade Policy Review Body may have its own chairman and shall establish such rules of procedure as it deems necessary for the fulfilment of those responsibilities.

5. There shall be a Council for Trade in Goods, a Council for Trade in Services and a Council for Trade-Related Aspects of Intellectual Property Rights (hereinafter referred to as the "Council for TRIPS"), which shall operate under the general guidance of the General Council. The Council for Trade in Goods shall oversee the functioning of the Multilateral Trade Agreements in Annex 1A. The Council for Trade in Services shall oversee the functioning of the General Agreement on Trade in Services (hereinafter referred to as "GATS"). The Council for TRIPS shall oversee the functioning of the Agreement on Trade-Related Aspects of Intellectual Property Rights (hereinafter referred to as the "Agreement on TRIPS"). These Councils shall carry out the functions assigned to them by their respective agreements and by the General Council. They shall establish their respective rules of procedure subject to the approval of the General Council. Membership in these Councils shall be open to representatives of all Members. These Councils shall meet as necessary to carry out their functions.

* * *

Article V

Relations With Other Organizations

* * *

Article VI

The Secretariat

* * *

Article VII

Budget and Contributions

* * *

Article VIII

Status of the WTO

* * *

Article IX

Decision-Making

1.   The WTO shall continue the practice of decision-making by consensus followed under GATT 1947.[1] Except as otherwise provided, where a decision cannot be arrived at by consensus, the matter at issue shall be decided by voting. At meetings of the Ministerial Conference and the General Council, each Member of the WTO shall have one vote. Where the European Communities exercise their right to vote, they shall have a number of votes equal to the number of their member States[2] which are Members of the WTO. Decisions of the Ministerial Conference and the General Council shall be taken by a majority of the votes cast, unless otherwise provided in this Agreement or in the relevant Multilateral Trade Agreement.[3]

2.   The Ministerial Conference and the General Council shall have the exclusive authority to adopt interpretations of this Agreement and of the Multilateral Trade Agreements. In the case of an interpretation of a Multilateral Trade Agreement in Annex 1, they shall exercise their authority on the basis of a recommendation by the Council overseeing the functioning of that Agreement. The decision to adopt an interpretation shall be taken by a three-fourths majority of the Members. This paragraph

---

[1]   The body concerned shall be deemed to have decided by consensus on a matter submitted for its consideration, if no Member, present at the meeting when the decision is taken, formally objects to the proposed decision.

[2]   The number of votes of the European Communities and their member States shall in no case exceed the number of the member States of the European Communities.

[3]   Decisions by the General Council when convened as the Dispute Settlement Body shall be taken only in accordance with the provisions of paragraph 4 of Article 2 of the Dispute Settlement Understanding.

shall not be used in a manner that would undermine the amendment provisions in Article X.

3. In exceptional circumstances, the Ministerial Conference may decide to waive an obligation imposed on a Member by this Agreement or any of the Multilateral Trade Agreements, provided that any such decision shall be taken by three fourths[4] of the Members unless otherwise provided for in this paragraph.

(a) A request for a waiver concerning this Agreement shall be submitted to the Ministerial Conference for consideration pursuant to the practice of decision-making by consensus. The Ministerial Conference shall establish a time-period, which shall not exceed 90 days, to consider the request. If consensus is not reached during the time-period, any decision to grant a waiver shall be taken by three fourths of the Members.

(b) A request for a waiver concerning the Multilateral Trade Agreements in Annexes 1A or 1B or 1C and their annexes shall be submitted initially to the Council for Trade in Goods, the Council for Trade in Services or the Council for TRIPS, respectively, for consideration during a time-period which shall not exceed 90 days. At the end of the time-period, the relevant Council shall submit a report to the Ministerial Conference.

4. A decision by the Ministerial Conference granting a waiver shall state the exceptional circumstances justifying the decision, the terms and conditions governing the application of the waiver, and the date on which the waiver shall terminate. Any waiver granted for a period of more than one year shall be reviewed by the Ministerial Conference not later than one year after it is granted, and thereafter annually until the waiver terminates. In each review, the Ministerial Conference shall examine whether the exceptional circumstances justifying the waiver still exist and whether the terms and conditions attached to the waiver have been met. The Ministerial Conference, on the basis of the annual review, may extend, modify or terminate the waiver.

5. Decisions under a Plurilateral Trade Agreement, including any decisions on interpretations and waivers, shall be governed by the provisions of that Agreement.

Article X

Amendment

1. Any Member of the WTO may initiate a proposal to amend the provisions of this Agreement or the Multilateral Trade Agreements in Annex 1 by submitting such proposal to the Ministerial Conference. The Councils listed in paragraph 5 of Article IV may also submit to the Ministerial Conference proposals to amend the provisions of the

---

[4] A decision to grant a waiver in respect of any obligation subject to a transition period or a period for staged implementation that the requesting Member has not performed by the end of the relevant period shall be taken only by consensus.

corresponding Multilateral Trade Agreements in Annex 1 the functioning of which they oversee. Unless the Ministerial Conference decides on a longer period, for a period of 90 days after the proposal has been tabled formally at the Ministerial Conference any decision by the Ministerial Conference to submit the proposed amendment to the Members for acceptance shall be taken by consensus. Unless the provisions of paragraphs 2, 5 or 6 apply, that decision shall specify whether the provisions of paragraphs 3 or 4 shall apply. If consensus is reached, the Ministerial Conference shall forthwith submit the proposed amendment to the Members for acceptance. If consensus is not reached at a meeting of the Ministerial Conference within the established period, the Ministerial Conference shall decide by a two-thirds majority of the Members whether to submit the proposed amendment to the Members for acceptance. Except as provided in paragraphs 2, 5 and 6, the provisions of paragraph 3 shall apply to the proposed amendment, unless the Ministerial Conference decides by a three-fourths majority of the Members that the provisions of paragraph 4 shall apply.

2.   Amendments to the provisions of this Article and to the provisions of the following Articles shall take effect only upon acceptance by all Members:

Article IX of this Agreement;

Articles I and II of GATT 1994;

Article II:1 of GATS;

Article 4 of the Agreement on TRIPS.

3.   Amendments to provisions of this Agreement, or of the Multilateral Trade Agreements in Annexes 1A and 1C, other than those listed in paragraphs 2 and 6, of a nature that would alter the rights and obligations of the Members, shall take effect for the Members that have accepted them upon acceptance by two thirds of the Members and thereafter for each other Member upon acceptance by it. The Ministerial Conference may decide by a three-fourths majority of the Members that any amendment made effective under this paragraph is of such a nature that any Member which has not accepted it within a period specified by the Ministerial Conference in each case shall be free to withdraw from the WTO or to remain a Member with the consent of the Ministerial Conference.

4.   Amendments to provisions of this Agreement or of the Multilateral Trade Agreements in Annexes 1A and 1C, other than those listed in paragraphs 2 and 6, of a nature that would not alter the rights and obligations of the Members, shall take effect for all Members upon acceptance by two thirds of the Members.

5.   Except as provided in paragraph 2 above, amendments to Parts I, II and III of GATS and the respective annexes shall take effect for the Members that have accepted them upon acceptance by two thirds of the Members and thereafter for each Member upon acceptance by it. The Ministerial Conference may decide by a three-fourths majority of the

Members that any amendment made effective under the preceding provision is of such a nature that any Member which has not accepted it within a period specified by the Ministerial Conference in each case shall be free to withdraw from the WTO or to remain a Member with the consent of the Ministerial Conference. Amendments to Parts IV, V and VI of GATS and the respective annexes shall take effect for all Members upon acceptance by two thirds of the Members.

6.　Notwithstanding the other provisions of this Article, amendments to the Agreement on TRIPS meeting the requirements of paragraph 2 of Article 71 thereof may be adopted by the Ministerial Conference without further formal acceptance process.

7.　Any Member accepting an amendment to this Agreement or to a Multilateral Trade Agreement in Annex 1 shall deposit an instrument of acceptance with the Director-General of the WTO within the period of acceptance specified by the Ministerial Conference.

8.　Any Member of the WTO may initiate a proposal to amend the provisions of the Multilateral Trade Agreements in Annexes 2 and 3 by submitting such proposal to the Ministerial Conference. The decision to approve amendments to the Multilateral Trade Agreement in Annex 2 shall be made by consensus and these amendments shall take effect for all Members upon approval by the Ministerial Conference. Decisions to approve amendments to the Multilateral Trade Agreement in Annex 3 shall take effect for all Members upon approval by the Ministerial Conference.

9.　The Ministerial Conference, upon the request of the Members parties to a trade agreement, may decide exclusively by consensus to add that agreement to Annex 4. The Ministerial Conference, upon the request of the Members parties to a Plurilateral Trade Agreement, may decide to delete that Agreement from Annex 4.

10.　Amendments to a Plurilateral Trade Agreement shall be governed by the provisions of that Agreement.

Article XI

Original Membership

1.　The contracting parties to GATT 1947 as of the date of entry into force of this Agreement, and the European Communities, which accept this Agreement and the Multilateral Trade Agreements and for which Schedules of Concessions and Commitments are annexed to GATT 1994 and for which Schedules of Specific Commitments are annexed to GATS shall become original Members of the WTO.

2.　The least-developed countries recognized as such by the United Nations will only be required to undertake commitments and concessions to the extent consistent with their individual development, financial and trade needs or their administrative and institutional capabilities.

Article XII

Accession

1.   Any State or separate customs territory possessing full autonomy in the conduct of its external commercial relations and of the other matters provided for in this Agreement and the Multilateral Trade Agreements may accede to this Agreement, on terms to be agreed between it and the WTO. Such accession shall apply to this Agreement and the Multilateral Trade Agreements annexed thereto.

2.   Decisions on accession shall be taken by the Ministerial Conference. The Ministerial Conference shall approve the agreement on the terms of accession by a two-thirds majority of the Members of the WTO.

3.   Accession to a Plurilateral Trade Agreement shall be governed by the provisions of that Agreement.

Article XIII

Non-Application of Multilateral Trade Agreements Between Particular Members

1.   This Agreement and the Multilateral Trade Agreements in Annexes 1 and 2 shall not apply as between any Member and any other Member if either of the Members, at the time either becomes a Member, does not consent to such application.

2.   Paragraph 1 may be invoked between original Members of the WTO which were contracting parties to GATT 1947 only where Article XXXV of that Agreement had been invoked earlier and was effective as between those contracting parties at the time of entry into force for them of this Agreement.

3.   Paragraph 1 shall apply between a Member and another Member which has acceded under Article XII only if the Member not consenting to the application has so notified the Ministerial Conference before the approval of the agreement on the terms of accession by the Ministerial Conference.

4.   The Ministerial Conference may review the operation of this Article in particular cases at the request of any Member and make appropriate recommendations.

5.   Non-application of a Plurilateral Trade Agreement between parties to that Agreement shall be governed by the provisions of that Agreement.

Article XIV

Acceptance, Entry into Force and Deposit

1.   This Agreement shall be open for acceptance, by signature or otherwise, by contracting parties to GATT 1947, and the European Communities, which are eligible to become original Members of the WTO in accordance with Article XI of this Agreement. Such acceptance shall apply to this Agreement and the Multilateral Trade Agreements annexed hereto.

This Agreement and the Multilateral Trade Agreements annexed hereto shall enter into force on the date determined by Ministers in accordance with paragraph 3 of the Final Act Embodying the Results of the Uruguay Round of Multilateral Trade Negotiations and shall remain open for acceptance for a period of two years following that date unless the Ministers decide otherwise. An acceptance following the entry into force of this Agreement shall enter into force on the 30th day following the date of such acceptance.

2.　　A Member which accepts this Agreement after its entry into force shall implement those concessions and obligations in the Multilateral Trade Agreements that are to be implemented over a period of time starting with the entry into force of this Agreement as if it had accepted this Agreement on the date of its entry into force.

3.　　Until the entry into force of this Agreement, the text of this Agreement and the Multilateral Trade Agreements shall be deposited with the Director-General to the CONTRACTING PARTIES to GATT 1947. The Director-General shall promptly furnish a certified true copy of this Agreement and the Multilateral Trade Agreements, and a notification of each acceptance thereof, to each government and the European Communities having accepted this Agreement. This Agreement and the Multilateral Trade Agreements, and any amendments thereto, shall, upon the entry into force of this Agreement, be deposited with the Director-General of the WTO.

4.　　The acceptance and entry into force of a Plurilateral Trade Agreement shall be governed by the provisions of that Agreement. Such Agreements shall be deposited with the Director-General to the CONTRACTING PARTIES to GATT 1947. Upon the entry into force of this Agreement, such Agreements shall be deposited with the Director-General of the WTO.

Article XV

Withdrawal

1.　　Any Member may withdraw from this Agreement. Such withdrawal shall apply both to this Agreement and the Multilateral Trade Agreements and shall take effect upon the expiration of six months from the date on which written notice of withdrawal is received by the Director-General of the WTO.

2.　　Withdrawal from a Plurilateral Trade Agreement shall be governed by the provisions of that Agreement.

Article XVI

Miscellaneous Provisions

1.　　Except as otherwise provided under this Agreement or the Multilateral Trade Agreements, the WTO shall be guided by the decisions, procedures and customary practices followed by the CONTRACTING PARTIES to GATT 1947 and the bodies established in the framework of GATT 1947.

2.   To the extent practicable, the Secretariat of GATT 1947 shall become the Secretariat of the WTO, and the Director-General to the CONTRACTING PARTIES to GATT 1947, until such time as the Ministerial Conference has appointed a Director-General in accordance with paragraph 2 of Article VI of this Agreement, shall serve as Director-General of the WTO.

3.   In the event of a conflict between a provision of this Agreement and a provision of any of the Multilateral Trade Agreements, the provision of this Agreement shall prevail to the extent of the conflict.

4.   Each Member shall ensure the conformity of its laws, regulations and administrative procedures with its obligations as provided in the annexed Agreements.

5.   No reservations may be made in respect of any provision of this Agreement. Reservations in respect of any of the provisions of the Multilateral Trade Agreements may only be made to the extent provided for in those Agreements. Reservations in respect of a provision of a Plurilateral Trade Agreement shall be governed by the provisions of that Agreement.

6.   This Agreement shall be registered in accordance with the provisions of Article 102 of the Charter of the United Nations.

DONE at Marrakesh this fifteenth day of April one thousand nine hundred and ninety-four, in a single copy, in the English, French and Spanish languages, each text being authentic.

DONE at Marrakesh this fifteenth day of April one thousand nine hundred and ninety-four, in a single copy, in the English, French and Spanish languages, each text being authentic.

Explanatory Notes:

The terms "country" or "countries" as used in this Agreement and the Multilateral Trade Agreements are to be understood to include any separate customs territory Member of the WTO.

In the case of a separate customs territory Member of the WTO, where an expression in this Agreement and the Multilateral Trade Agreements is qualified by the term "national", such expression shall be read as pertaining to that customs territory, unless otherwise specified.

LIST OF ANNEXES

ANNEX 1

ANNEX 1A: Multilateral Agreements on Trade in Goods

General Agreement on Tariffs and Trade 1994

Agreement on Agriculture

Agreement on the Application of Sanitary and Phytosanitary Measures

Agreement on Textiles and Clothing

Agreement on Technical Barriers to Trade

Agreement on Trade-Related Investment Measures

Agreement on Implementation of Article VI of the General Agreement on Tariffs and Trade 1994

Agreement on Implementation of Article VII of the General Agreement on Tariffs and Trade 1994

Agreement on Preshipment Inspection

Agreement on Rules of Origin

Agreement on Import Licensing Procedures

Agreement on Subsidies and Countervailing Measures

Agreement on Safeguards

ANNEX 1B: General Agreement on Trade in Services and Annexes

ANNEX 1C: Agreement on Trade-Related Aspects of Intellectual Property Rights

ANNEX 2

Understanding on Rules and Procedures Governing the Settlement of Disputes

ANNEX 3

Trade Policy Review Mechanism

ANNEX 4

Plurilateral Trade Agreements

Agreement on Trade in Civil Aircraft

Agreement on Government Procurement

International Dairy Agreement

International Bovine Meat Agreement

ANNEX 1A

MULTILATERAL AGREEMENTS ON TRADE IN GOODS

General interpretative note to Annex 1A:

In the event of conflict between a provision of the General Agreement on Tariffs and Trade 1994 and a provision of another agreement in Annex 1A to the Agreement Establishing the World Trade Organization (referred to in the agreements in Annex 1A as the "WTO Agreement"), the provision of the other agreement shall prevail to the extent of the conflict.

3. Decision on Measures in Favour of Least-Developed Countries

(Selected Provisions)

Recognizing the plight of the least-developed countries and the need to ensure their effective participation in the world trading system, and to take further measures to improve their trading opportunities;

Recognizing the specific needs of the least-developed countries in the area of market access where continued preferential access remains an essential means for improving their trading opportunities;

Reaffirming their commitment to implement fully the provisions concerning the least-developed countries contained in paragraphs 2(*d*.), 6 and 8 of the Decision of 28 November 1979 on Differential and More Favourable Treatment, Reciprocity and Fuller Participation of Developing Countries;

Having regard to the commitment of the participants as set out in Section B(vii) of Part I of the Punta del Este Ministerial Declaration;

1.   *Decide* that, if not already provided for in the instruments negotiated in the course of the Uruguay Round, notwithstanding their acceptance of these instruments, the least-developed countries, and for so long as they remain in that category, while complying with the general rules set out in the aforesaid instruments, will only be required to undertake commitments and concessions to the extent consistent with their individual development, financial and trade needs, or their administrative and institutional capabilities. The least-developed countries shall be given additional time of one year from 15 April 1994 to submit their schedules as required in Article XI of the Agreement Establishing the World Trade Organization.

2.   *Agree* that:

(i) Expeditious implementation of all special and differential measures taken in favour of least-developed countries including those taken within the context of the Uruguay Round shall be ensured through, *inter alia,* regular reviews.

(ii) To the extent possible, MFN concessions on tariff and non-tariff measures agreed in the Uruguay Round on products of export interest to the least-developed countries may be implemented autonomously, in advance and without staging. Consideration shall be given to further improve GSP and other schemes for products of particular export interest to least-developed countries.

(iii) The rules set out in the various agreements and instruments and the transitional provisions in the Uruguay Round should be applied in a flexible and supportive manner for the least-developed countries. To this effect, sympathetic consideration shall be given to specific and motivated concerns raised by the least-developed countries in the appropriate Councils and Committees.

(iv) In the application of import relief measures and other measures referred to in paragraph 3(c) of Article XXXVII of GATT 1947 and the corresponding provision of GATT 1994, special consideration shall be given to the export interests of least-developed countries.

(v) Least-developed countries shall be accorded substantially increased technical assistance in the development, strengthening and diversification of their production and export bases including those of services, as well as in trade promotion, to enable them to maximize the benefits from liberalized access to markets.

3. *Agree* to keep under review the specific needs of the least-developed countries and to continue to seek the adoption of positive measures which facilitate the expansion of trading opportunities in favour of these countries.

4. WTO Understanding on Rules and Procedures Governing the Settlement of Disputes (DSU)

(Annex 2 to the Agreement Establishing the World Trade Organization)

(Selected Provisions)

Article 1

Coverage and Application

1.   The rules and procedures of this Understanding shall apply to disputes brought pursuant to the consultation and dispute settlement provisions of the agreements listed in Appendix 1 to this Understanding (referred to in this Understanding as the "covered agreements"). The rules and procedures of this Understanding shall also apply to consultations and the settlement of disputes between Members concerning their rights and obligations under the provisions of the Agreement Establishing the World Trade Organization (referred to in this Understanding as the "WTO Agreement") and of this Understanding taken in isolation or in combination with any other covered agreement.

2.   The rules and procedures of this Understanding shall apply subject to such special or additional rules and procedures on dispute settlement contained in the covered agreements as are identified in Appendix 2 to this Understanding. To the extent that there is a difference between the rules and procedures of this Understanding and the special or additional rules and procedures set forth in Appendix 2, the special or additional rules and procedures in Appendix 2 shall prevail. In disputes involving rules and procedures under more than one covered agreement, if there is a conflict between special or additional rules and procedures of such agreements under review, and where the parties to the dispute cannot agree on rules and procedures within 20 days of the establishment of the panel, the Chairman of the Dispute Settlement Body provided for in paragraph 1 of Article 2 (referred to in this Understanding as the "DSB"), in consultation with the parties to the dispute, shall determine the rules and procedures to be followed within 10 days after a request by either Member. The Chairman shall be guided by the principle that special or additional rules and procedures should be used where possible, and the rules and procedures set out in this Understanding should be used to the extent necessary to avoid conflict.

Article 2

Administration

1.   The Dispute Settlement Body is hereby established to administer these rules and procedures and, except as otherwise provided in a covered agreement, the consultation and dispute settlement provisions of the covered agreements. Accordingly, the DSB shall have the authority to establish panels, adopt panel and Appellate Body reports, maintain surveillance of implementation of rulings and recommendations, and

authorize suspension of concessions and other obligations under the covered agreements. With respect to disputes arising under a covered agreement which is a Plurilateral Trade Agreement, the term "Member" as used herein shall refer only to those Members that are parties to the relevant Plurilateral Trade Agreement. Where the DSB administers the dispute settlement provisions of a Plurilateral Trade Agreement, only those Members that are parties to that Agreement may participate in decisions or actions taken by the DSB with respect to that dispute.

2.   The DSB shall inform the relevant WTO Councils and Committees of any developments in disputes related to provisions of the respective covered agreements.

3.   The DSB shall meet as often as necessary to carry out its functions within the time-frames provided in this Understanding.

4.   Where the rules and procedures of this Understanding provide for the DSB to take a decision, it shall do so by consensus.[1]

Article 3

General Provisions

1.   Members affirm their adherence to the principles for the management of disputes heretofore applied under Articles XXII and XXIII of GATT 1947, and the rules and procedures as further elaborated and modified herein.

2.   The dispute settlement system of the WTO is a central element in providing security and predictability to the multilateral trading system. The Members recognize that it serves to preserve the rights and obligations of Members under the covered agreements, and to clarify the existing provisions of those agreements in accordance with customary rules of interpretation of public international law. Recommendations and rulings of the DSB cannot add to or diminish the rights and obligations provided in the covered agreements.

3.   The prompt settlement of situations in which a Member considers that any benefits accruing to it directly or indirectly under the covered agreements are being impaired by measures taken by another Member is essential to the effective functioning of the WTO and the maintenance of a proper balance between the rights and obligations of Members.

4.   Recommendations or rulings made by the DSB shall be aimed at achieving a satisfactory settlement of the matter in accordance with the rights and obligations under this Understanding and under the covered agreements.

5.   All solutions to matters formally raised under the consultation and dispute settlement provisions of the covered agreements, including arbitration awards, shall be consistent with those agreements and shall not

---

[1]   The DSB shall be deemed to have decided by consensus on a matter submitted for its consideration, if no Member, present at the meeting of the DSB when the decision is taken, formally objects to the proposed decision.

nullify or impair benefits accruing to any Member under those agreements, nor impede the attainment of any objective of those agreements.

6.   Mutually agreed solutions to matters formally raised under the consultation and dispute settlement provisions of the covered agreements shall be notified to the DSB and the relevant Councils and Committees, where any Member may raise any point relating thereto.

7.   Before bringing a case, a Member shall exercise its judgment as to whether action under these procedures would be fruitful. The aim of the dispute settlement mechanism is to secure a positive solution to a dispute. A solution mutually acceptable to the parties to a dispute and consistent with the covered agreements is clearly to be preferred. In the absence of a mutually agreed solution, the first objective of the dispute settlement mechanism is usually to secure the withdrawal of the measures concerned if these are found to be inconsistent with the provisions of any of the covered agreements. The provision of compensation should be resorted to only if the immediate withdrawal of the measure is impracticable and as a temporary measure pending the withdrawal of the measure which is inconsistent with a covered agreement. The last resort which this Understanding provides to the Member invoking the dispute settlement procedures is the possibility of suspending the application of concessions or other obligations under the covered agreements on a discriminatory basis vis-á-vis the other Member, subject to authorization by the DSB of such measures.

8.   In cases where there is an infringement of the obligations assumed under a covered agreement, the action is considered *prima facie* to constitute a case of nullification or impairment. This means that there is normally a presumption that a breach of the rules has an adverse impact on other Members parties to that covered agreement, and in such cases, it shall be up to the Member against whom the complaint has been brought to rebut the charge.

9.   The provisions of this Understanding are without prejudice to the rights of Members to seek authoritative interpretation of provisions of a covered agreement through decision-making under the WTO Agreement or a covered agreement which is a Plurilateral Trade Agreement.

10.   It is understood that requests for conciliation and the use of the dispute settlement procedures should not be intended or considered as contentious acts and that, if a dispute arises, all Members will engage in these procedures in good faith in an effort to resolve the dispute. It is also understood that complaints and counter-complaints in regard to distinct matters should not be linked.

11.   This Understanding shall be applied only with respect to new requests for consultations under the consultation provisions of the covered agreements made on or after the date of entry into force of the WTO Agreement. With respect to disputes for which the request for consultations was made under GATT 1947 or under any other predecessor agreement to the covered agreements before the date of entry into force of the WTO Agreement, the relevant dispute settlement rules and procedures in effect

immediately prior to the date of entry into force of the WTO Agreement shall continue to apply.[2]

12. Notwithstanding paragraph 11, if a complaint based on any of the covered agreements is brought by a developing country Member against a developed country Member, the complaining party shall have the right to invoke, as an alternative to the provisions contained in Articles 4, 5, 6 and 12 of this Understanding, the corresponding provisions of the Decision of 5 April 1966 (BISD 14S/18), except that where the Panel considers that the time-frame provided for in paragraph 7 of that Decision is insufficient to provide its report and with the agreement of the complaining party, that time-frame may be extended. To the extent that there is a difference between the rules and procedures of Articles 4, 5, 6 and 12 and the corresponding rules and procedures of the Decision, the latter shall prevail.

Article 4

Consultations

1. Members affirm their resolve to strengthen and improve the effectiveness of the consultation procedures employed by Members.

2. Each Member undertakes to accord sympathetic consideration to and afford adequate opportunity for consultation regarding any representations made by another Member concerning measures affecting the operation of any covered agreement taken within the territory of the former.[3]

3. If a request for consultations is made pursuant to a covered agreement, the Member to which the request is made shall, unless otherwise mutually agreed, reply to the request within 10 days after the date of its receipt and shall enter into consultations in good faith within a period of no more than 30 days after the date of receipt of the request, with a view to reaching a mutually satisfactory solution. If the Member does not respond within 10 days after the date of receipt of the request, or does not enter into consultations within a period of no more than 30 days, or a period otherwise mutually agreed, after the date of receipt of the request, then the Member that requested the holding of consultations may proceed directly to request the establishment of a panel.

4. All such requests for consultations shall be notified to the DSB and the relevant Councils and Committees by the Member which requests consultations. Any request for consultations shall be submitted in writing and shall give the reasons for the request, including identification of the measures at issue and an indication of the legal basis for the complaint.

5. In the course of consultations in accordance with the provisions of a covered agreement, before resorting to further action under this

---

[2]   This paragraph shall also be applied to disputes on which panel reports have not been adopted or fully implemented.

[3]   Where the provisions of any other covered agreement concerning measures taken by regional or local governments or authorities within the territory of a Member contain provisions different from the provisions of this paragraph, the provisions of such other covered agreement shall prevail.

Understanding, Members should attempt to obtain satisfactory adjustment of the matter.

6.   Consultations shall be confidential, and without prejudice to the rights of any Member in any further proceedings.

7.   If the consultations fail to settle a dispute within 60 days after the date of receipt of the request for consultations, the complaining party may request the establishment of a panel. The complaining party may request a panel during the 60-day period if the consulting parties jointly consider that consultations have failed to settle the dispute.

8.   In cases of urgency, including those which concern perishable goods, Members shall enter into consultations within a period of no more than 10 days after the date of receipt of the request. If the consultations have failed to settle the dispute within a period of 20 days after the date of receipt of the request, the complaining party may request the establishment of a panel.

9.   In cases of urgency, including those which concern perishable goods, the parties to the dispute, panels and the Appellate Body shall make every effort to accelerate the proceedings to the greatest extent possible.

10.   During consultations Members should give special attention to the particular problems and interests of developing country Members.

11.   Whenever a Member other than the consulting Members considers that it has a substantial trade interest in consultations being held pursuant to paragraph 1 of Article XXII of GATT 1994, paragraph 1 of Article XXII of GATS, or the corresponding provisions in other covered agreements,[4] such Member may notify the consulting Members and the DSB, within 10 days after the date of the circulation of the request for consultations under said Article, of its desire to be joined in the consultations. Such Member shall be joined in the consultations, provided that the Member to which the request for consultations was addressed agrees that the claim of substantial interest is well-founded. In that event they shall so inform the DSB. If the request to be joined in the consultations is not accepted, the applicant Member shall be free to request consultations under paragraph 1 of Article XXII or paragraph 1 of Article XXIII of GATT 1994, paragraph 1 of Article XXII or paragraph 1 of Article

---

4   The corresponding consultation provisions in the covered agreements are listed hereunder: Agreement on Agriculture, Article 19; Agreement on the Application of Sanitary and Phytosanitary Measures, paragraph 1 of Article 11; Agreement on Textiles and Clothing, paragraph 4 of Article 8; Agreement on Technical Barriers to Trade, paragraph 1 of Article 14; Agreement on Trade-Related Investment Measures, Article 8; Agreement on Implementation of Article VI of GATT 1994, paragraph 2 of Article 17; Agreement on Implementation of Article VII of GATT 1994, paragraph 2 of Article 19; Agreement on Preshipment Inspection, Article 7; Agreement on Rules of Origin, Article 7; Agreement on Import Licensing Procedures, Article 6; Agreement on Subsidies and Countervailing Measures, Article 30; Agreement on Safeguards, Article 14; Agreement on Trade-Related Aspects of Intellectual Property Rights, Article 64.1; and any corresponding consultation provisions in Plurilateral Trade Agreements as determined by the competent bodies of each Agreement and as notified to the DSB.

XXIII of GATS, or the corresponding provisions in other covered agreements.

Article 5

Good Offices, Conciliation and Mediation

1.   Good offices, conciliation and mediation are procedures that are undertaken voluntarily if the parties to the dispute so agree.

2.   Proceedings involving good offices, conciliation and mediation, and in particular positions taken by the parties to the dispute during these proceedings, shall be confidential, and without prejudice to the rights of either party in any further proceedings under these procedures.

3.   Good offices, conciliation or mediation may be requested at any time by any party to a dispute. They may begin at any time and be terminated at any time. Once procedures for good offices, conciliation or mediation are terminated, a complaining party may then proceed with a request for the establishment of a panel.

4.   When good offices, conciliation or mediation are entered into within 60 days after the date of receipt of a request for consultations, the complaining party must allow a period of 60 days after the date of receipt of the request for consultations before requesting the establishment of a panel. The complaining party may request the establishment of a panel during the 60-day period if the parties to the dispute jointly consider that the good offices, conciliation or mediation process has failed to settle the dispute.

5.   If the parties to a dispute agree, procedures for good offices, conciliation or mediation may continue while the panel process proceeds.

6.   The Director-General may, acting in an *ex officio* capacity, offer good offices, conciliation or mediation with the view to assisting Members to settle a dispute.

Article 6

Establishment of Panels

1.   If the complaining party so requests, a panel shall be established at the latest at the DSB meeting following that at which the request first appears as an item on the DSB's agenda, unless at that meeting the DSB decides by consensus not to establish a panel.[5]

2.   The request for the establishment of a panel shall be made in writing. It shall indicate whether consultations were held, identify the specific measures at issue and provide a brief summary of the legal basis of the complaint sufficient to present the problem clearly. In case the applicant requests the establishment of a panel with other than standard terms of reference, the written request shall include the proposed text of special terms of reference.

---

[5]   If the complaining party so requests, a meeting of the DSB shall be convened for this purpose within 15 days of the request, provided that at least 10 days' advance notice of the meeting is given.

Article 7

Terms of Reference of Panels

1.   Panels shall have the following terms of reference unless the parties to the dispute agree otherwise within 20 days from the establishment of the panel:

> "To examine, in the light of the relevant provisions in (name of the covered agreement(s) cited by the parties to the dispute), the matter referred to the DSB by (name of party) in document ... and to make such findings as will assist the DSB in making the recommendations or in giving the rulings provided for in that/those agreement(s)."

2.   Panels shall address the relevant provisions in any covered agreement or agreements cited by the parties to the dispute.

3.   In establishing a panel, the DSB may authorize its Chairman to draw up the terms of reference of the panel in consultation with the parties to the dispute, subject to the provisions of paragraph 1. The terms of reference thus drawn up shall be circulated to all Members. If other than standard terms of reference are agreed upon, any Member may raise any point relating thereto in the DSB.

Article 8

Composition of Panels

1.   Panels shall be composed of well-qualified governmental and/or non-governmental individuals, including persons who have served on or presented a case to a panel, served as a representative of a Member or of a contracting party to GATT 1947 or as a representative to the Council or Committee of any covered agreement or its predecessor agreement, or in the Secretariat, taught or published on international trade law or policy, or served as a senior trade policy official of a Member.

2.   Panel members should be selected with a view to ensuring the independence of the members, a sufficiently diverse background and a wide spectrum of experience.

3.   Citizens of Members whose governments[6] are parties to the dispute or third parties as defined in paragraph 2 of Article 10 shall not serve on a panel concerned with that dispute, unless the parties to the dispute agree otherwise.

4.   To assist in the selection of panelists, the Secretariat shall maintain an indicative list of governmental and non-governmental individuals possessing the qualifications outlined in paragraph 1, from which panelists may be drawn as appropriate. That list shall include the roster of non-governmental panelists established on 30 November 1984 (BISD 31S/9), and other rosters and indicative lists established under any

---

[6]   In the case where customs unions or common markets are parties to a dispute, this provision applies to citizens of all member countries of the customs unions or common markets.

of the covered agreements, and shall retain the names of persons on those rosters and indicative lists at the time of entry into force of the WTO Agreement. Members may periodically suggest names of governmental and non-governmental individuals for inclusion on the indicative list, providing relevant information on their knowledge of international trade and of the sectors or subject matter of the covered agreements, and those names shall be added to the list upon approval by the DSB. For each of the individuals on the list, the list shall indicate specific areas of experience or expertise of the individuals in the sectors or subject matter of the covered agreements.

5.   Panels shall be composed of three panelists unless the parties to the dispute agree, within 10 days from the establishment of the panel, to a panel composed of five panelists. Members shall be informed promptly of the composition of the panel.

6.   The Secretariat shall propose nominations for the panel to the parties to the dispute. The parties to the dispute shall not oppose nominations except for compelling reasons.

7.   If there is no agreement on the panelists within 20 days after the date of the establishment of a panel, at the request of either party, the Director-General, in consultation with the Chairman of the DSB and the Chairman of the relevant Council or Committee, shall determine the composition of the panel by appointing the panelists whom the Director-General considers most appropriate in accordance with any relevant special or additional rules or procedures of the covered agreement or covered agreements which are at issue in the dispute, after consulting with the parties to the dispute. The Chairman of the DSB shall inform the Members of the composition of the panel thus formed no later than 10 days after the date the Chairman receives such a request.

8.   Members shall undertake, as a general rule, to permit their officials to serve as panelists.

9.   Panelists shall serve in their individual capacities and not as government representatives, nor as representatives of any organization. Members shall therefore not give them instructions nor seek to influence them as individuals with regard to matters before a panel.

10.   When a dispute is between a developing country Member and a developed country Member the panel shall, if the developing country Member so requests, include at least one panelist from a developing country Member.

11.   Panelists' expenses, including travel and subsistence allowance, shall be met from the WTO budget in accordance with criteria to be adopted by the General Council, based on recommendations of the Committee on Budget, Finance and Administration.

Article 9

Procedures for Multiple Complainants

1.   Where more than one Member requests the establishment of a panel related to the same matter, a single panel may be established to

examine these complaints taking into account the rights of all Members concerned. A single panel should be established to examine such complaints whenever feasible.

2.   The single panel shall organize its examination and present its findings to the DSB in such a manner that the rights which the parties to the dispute would have enjoyed had separate panels examined the complaints are in no way impaired. If one of the parties to the dispute so requests, the panel shall submit separate reports on the dispute concerned. The written submissions by each of the complainants shall be made available to the other complainants, and each complainant shall have the right to be present when any one of the other complainants presents its views to the panel.

3.   If more than one panel is established to examine the complaints related to the same manner, to the greatest extent possible the same persons shall serve as panelists on each of the separate panels and the timetable for the panel process in such disputes shall be harmonized.

Article 10

Third Parties

1.   The interests of the parties to a dispute and those of other Members under a covered agreement at issue in the dispute shall be fully taken into account during the panel process.

2.   Any Member having a substantial interest in a matter before a panel and having notified its interest to the DSB (referred to in this Understanding as a "third party") shall have an opportunity to be heard by the panel and to make written submissions to the panel. These submissions shall also be given to the parties to the dispute and shall be reflected in the panel report.

3.   Third parties shall receive the submissions of the parties to the dispute [at] the first meeting of the panel.

4.   If a third party considers that a measure already the subject of a panel proceeding nullifies or impairs benefits accruing to it under any covered agreement, that Member may have recourse to normal dispute settlement procedures under this Understanding. Such a dispute shall be referred to the original panel wherever possible.

Article 11

Function of Panels

The function of panels is to assist the DSB in discharging its responsibilities under this Understanding and the covered agreements. Accordingly, a panel should make an objective assessment of the matter before it, including an objective assessment of the facts of the case and the applicability of and conformity with the relevant covered agreements, and make such other findings as will assist the DSB in making the recommendations or in giving the rulings provided for in the covered agreements. Panels should consult regularly with the parties to the dispute and give them adequate opportunity to develop a mutually satisfactory solution.

Article 12

Panel Procedures

1. Panels shall follow the Working Procedures in Appendix 3 unless the panel decides otherwise after consulting the parties to the dispute.

2. Panel procedures should provide sufficient flexibility so as to ensure high-quality panel reports, while not unduly delaying the panel process.

3. After consulting the parties to the dispute, the panelists shall, as soon as practicable and whenever possible within one week after the composition and terms of reference of the panel have been agreed upon, fix the timetable for the panel process, taking into account the provisions of paragraph 9 of Article 4, if relevant.

4. In determining the timetable for the panel process, the panel shall provide sufficient time for the parties to the dispute to prepare their submissions.

5. Panels should set precise deadlines for written submissions by the parties and the parties should respect those deadlines.

6. Each party to the dispute shall deposit its written submissions with the Secretariat for immediate transmission to the panel and to the other party or parties to the dispute. The complaining party shall submit its first submission in advance of the responding party's first submission unless the panel decides, in fixing the timetable referred to in paragraph 3 and after consultations with the parties to the dispute, that the parties should submit their first submissions simultaneously. When there are sequential arrangements for the deposit of first submissions, the panel shall establish a firm time-period for receipt of the responding party's submission. Any subsequent written submissions shall be submitted simultaneously.

7. Where the parties to the dispute have failed to develop a mutually satisfactory solution, the panel shall submit its findings in the form of a written report to the DSB. In such cases, the report of a panel shall set out the findings of fact, the applicability of relevant provisions and the basic rationale behind any findings and recommendations that it makes. Where a settlement of the matter among the parties to the dispute has been found, the report of the panel shall be confined to a brief description of the case and to reporting that a solution has been reached.

8. In order to make the procedures more efficient, the period in which the panel shall conduct its examination, from the date that the composition and terms of reference of the panel have been agreed upon until the date the final report is issued to the parties to the dispute, shall, as a general rule, not exceed six months. In cases of urgency, including those relating to perishable goods, the panel shall aim to issue its report to the parties to the dispute within three months.

9.   When the panel considers that it cannot issue its report within six months, or within three months in cases of urgency, it shall inform the DSB in writing of the reasons for the delay together with an estimate of the period within which it will issue its report. In no case should the period from the establishment of the panel to the circulation of the report to the Members exceed nine months.

10.   In the context of consultations involving a measure taken by a developing country Member, the parties may agree to extend the periods established in paragraphs 7 and 8 of Article 4. If, after the relevant period has elapsed, the consulting parties cannot agree that the consultations have concluded, the Chairman of the DSB shall decide, after consultation with the parties, whether to extend the relevant period and, if so, for how long. In addition, in examining a complaint against a developing country Member, the panel shall accord sufficient time for the developing country Member to prepare and present its argumentation. The provisions of paragraph 1 of Article 20 and paragraph 4 of Article 21 are not affected by any action pursuant to this paragraph.

11.   Where one or more of the parties is a developing country Member, the panel's report shall explicitly indicate the form in which account has been taken of relevant provisions on differential and more-favourable treatment for developing country Members that form part of the covered agreements which have been raised by the developing country Member in the course of the dispute settlement procedures.

12.   The panel may suspend its work at any time at the request of the complaining party for a period not to exceed 12 months. In the event of such a suspension, the time-frames set out in paragraphs 8 and 9 of this Article, paragraph 1 of Article 20, and paragraph 4 of Article 21 shall be extended by the amount of time that the work was suspended. If the work of the panel has been suspended for more than 12 months, the authority for establishment of the panel shall lapse.

Article 13

Right to Seek Information

1.   Each panel shall have the right to seek information and technical advice from any individual or body which it deems appropriate. However, before a panel seeks such information or advice from any individual or body within the jurisdiction of a Member it shall inform the authorities of that Member. A Member should respond promptly and fully to any request by a panel for such information as the panel considers necessary and appropriate. Confidential information which is provided shall not be revealed without formal authorization from the individual, body, or authorities of the Member providing the information.

2.   Panels may seek information from any relevant source and may consult experts to obtain their opinion on certain aspects of the matter. With respect to a factual issue concerning a scientific or other technical matter raised by a party to a dispute, a panel may request an advisory

report in writing from an expert review group. Rules for the establishment of such a group and its procedures are set forth in Appendix 4.

Article 14

Confidentiality

1.   Panel deliberations shall be confidential.

2.   The reports of panels shall be drafted without the presence of the parties to the dispute in the light of the information provided and the statements made.

3.   Opinions expressed in the panel report by individual panelists shall be anonymous.

Article 15

Interim Review Stage

1.   Following the consideration of rebuttal submissions and oral arguments, the panel shall issue the descriptive (factual and argument) sections of its draft report to the parties to the dispute. Within a period of time set by the panel, the parties shall submit their comments in writing.

2.   Following the expiration of the set period of time for receipt of comments from the parties to the dispute, the panel shall issue an interim report to the parties, including both the descriptive sections and the panel's findings and conclusions. Within a period of time set by the panel, a party may submit a written request for the panel to review precise aspects of the interim report prior to circulation of the final report to the Members. At the request of a party, the panel shall hold a further meeting with the parties on the issues identified in the written comments. If no comments are received from any party within the comment period, the interim report shall be considered the final panel report and circulated promptly to the Members.

3.   The findings of the final panel report shall include a discussion of the arguments made at the interim review stage. The interim review stage shall be conducted within the time-period set out in paragraph 8 of Article 12.

Article 16

Adoption of Panel Reports

1.   In order to provide sufficient time for the Members to consider panel reports, the reports shall not be considered for adoption by the DSB until 20 days after the date they have been circulated to the Members.

2.   Members having objections to a panel report shall give written reasons to explain their objections for circulation at least 10 days prior to the DSB meeting at which the panel report will be considered.

3.   The parties to a dispute shall have the right to participate fully in the consideration of the panel report by the DSB, and their views shall be fully recorded.

4.   Within 60 days after the date of circulation of a panel report to the Members, the report shall be adopted at a DSB meeting[7] unless a party to the dispute formally notifies the DSB of its decision to appeal or the DSB decides by consensus not to adopt the report. If a party has notified its decision to appeal, the report by the panel shall not be considered for adoption by the DSB until after completion of the appeal. This adoption procedure is without prejudice to the right of Members to express their views on a panel report.

Article 17

Appellate Review

Standing Appellate Body

1.   A standing Appellate Body shall be established by the DSB. The Appellate Body shall hear appeals from panel cases. It shall be composed of seven persons, three of whom shall serve on any one case. Persons serving on the Appellate Body shall serve in rotation. Such rotation shall be determined in the working procedures of the Appellate Body.

2.   The DSB shall appoint persons to serve on the Appellate Body for a four-year term, and each person may be reappointed once. However, the terms of three of the seven persons appointed immediately after the entry into force of the WTO Agreement shall expire at the end of two years, to be determined by lot. Vacancies shall be filled as they arise. A person appointed to replace a person whose term of office has not expired shall hold office for the remainder of the predecessor's term.

3.   The Appellate Body shall comprise persons of recognized authority, with demonstrated expertise in law, international trade and the subject matter of the covered agreements generally. They shall be unaffiliated with any government. The Appellate Body membership shall be broadly representative of membership in the WTO. All persons serving on the Appellate Body shall be available at all times and on short notice, and shall stay abreast of dispute settlement activities and other relevant activities of the WTO. They shall not participate in the consideration of any disputes that would create a direct or indirect conflict of interest.

4.   Only parties to the dispute, not third parties, may appeal a panel report. Third parties which have notified the DSB of a substantial interest in the matter pursuant to paragraph 2 of Article 10 may make written submissions to, and be given an opportunity to be heard by, the Appellate Body.

5.   As a general rule, the proceedings shall not exceed 60 days from the date a party to the dispute formally notifies its decision to appeal to the date the Appellate Body circulates its report. In fixing its timetable the Appellate Body shall take into account the provisions of paragraph 9 of Article 4, if relevant. When the Appellate Body considers that it cannot

---

[7]   If a meeting of the DSB is not scheduled within this period at a time that enables the requirements of paragraphs 1 and 4 of Article 16 to be met, a meeting of the DSB shall be held for this purpose.

provide its report within 60 days, it shall inform the DSB in writing of the reasons for the delay together with an estimate of the period within which it will submit its report. In no case shall the proceedings exceed 90 days.

6. An appeal shall be limited to issues of law covered in the panel report and legal interpretations developed by the panel.

7. The Appellate Body shall be provided with appropriate administrative and legal support as it requires.

8. The expenses of persons serving on the Appellate Body, including travel and subsistence allowance, shall be met from the WTO budget in accordance with criteria to be adopted by the General Council, based on recommendations of the Committee on Budget, Finance and Administration.

Procedures for Appellate Review

9. Working procedures shall be drawn up by the Appellate Body in consultation with the Chairman of the DSB and the Director-General, and communicated to the Members for their information.

10. The proceedings of the Appellate Body shall be confidential. The reports of the Appellate Body shall be drafted without the presence of the parties to the dispute and in the light of the information provided and the statements made.

11. Opinions expressed in the Appellate Body report by individuals serving on the Appellate Body shall be anonymous.

12. The Appellate Body shall address each of the issues raised in accordance with paragraph 6 during the appellate proceeding.

13. The Appellate Body may uphold, modify or reverse the legal findings and conclusions of the panel.

Adoption of Appellate Body Reports

14. An Appellate Body report shall be adopted by the DSB and unconditionally accepted by the parties to the dispute unless the DSB decides by consensus not to adopt the Appellate Body report within 30 days following its circulation to the Members.[8] This adoption procedure is without prejudice to the right of Members to express their views on an Appellate Body report.

Article 18

Communications With the Panel or Appellate Body

1. There shall be no *ex parte* communications with the panel or Appellate Body concerning matters under consideration by the panel or Appellate Body.

2. Written submissions to the panel or the Appellate Body shall be treated as confidential, but shall be made available to the parties to the

---

[8] If a meeting of the DSB is not scheduled during this period, such a meeting of the DSB shall be held for this purpose.

dispute. Nothing in this Understanding shall preclude a party to a dispute from disclosing statements of its own positions to the public. Members shall treat as confidential information submitted by another Member to the panel or the Appellate Body which that Member has designated as confidential. A party to a dispute shall also, upon request of a Member, provide a non-confidential summary of the information contained in its written submissions that could be disclosed to the public.

Article 19

Panel and Appellate Body Recommendations

    1.   Where a panel or the Appellate Body concludes that a measure is inconsistent with a covered agreement, it shall recommend that the Member concerned[9] bring the measure into conformity with that agreement.[10] In addition to its recommendations, the panel or Appellate Body may suggest ways in which the Member concerned could implement the recommendations.

    2.   In accordance with paragraph 2 of Article 3, in their findings and recommendations, the panel and Appellate Body cannot add to or diminish the rights and obligations provided in the covered agreements.

Article 20

Time-frame for DSB Decisions

    Unless otherwise agreed to by the parties to the dispute, the period from the date of establishment of the panel by the DSB until the date the DSB considers the panel or appellate report for adoption shall as a general rule not exceed nine months where the panel report is not appealed or 12 months where the report is appealed. Where either the panel or the Appellate Body has acted, pursuant to paragraph 9 of Article 12 or paragraph 5 of Article 17, to extend the time for providing its report, the additional time taken shall be added to the above periods.

Article 21

Surveillance of Implementation of Recommendations and Rulings

    1.   Prompt compliance with recommendations or rulings of the DSB is essential in order to ensure effective resolution of disputes to the benefit of all Members.

    2.   Particular attention should be paid to matters affecting the interests of developing country Members with respect to measures which have been subject to dispute settlement.

    3.   At a DSB meeting held within 30 days[11] after the date of adoption of the panel or Appellate Body report, the Member concerned shall

---

[9]   The "Member concerned" is the party to the dispute to which the panel or Appellate Body recommendations are directed.

[10]   With respect to recommendations in cases not involving a violation of GATT 1994 or any other covered agreement, see Article 26.

[11]   If a meeting of the DSB is not scheduled during this period, such a meeting of the DSB shall be held for this purpose.

inform the DSB of its intentions in respect of implementation of the recommendations and rulings of the DSB. If it is impracticable to comply immediately with the recommendations and rulings, the Member concerned shall have a reasonable period of time in which to do so. The reasonable period of time shall be:

(a) the period of time proposed by the Member concerned, provided that such period is approved by the DSB; or, in the absence of such approval,

(b) a period of time mutually agreed by the parties to the dispute within 45 days after the date of adoption of the recommendations and rulings; or, in the absence of such agreement,

(c) a period of time determined through binding arbitration within 90 days after the date of adoption of the recommendations and rulings.[12] In such arbitration, a guideline for the arbitrator[13] should be that the reasonable period of time to implement panel or Appellate Body recommendations should not exceed 15 months from the date of adoption of a panel or Appellate Body report. However, that time may be shorter or longer, depending upon the particular circumstances.

4. Except where the panel or the Appellate Body has extended, pursuant to paragraph 9 of Article 12 or paragraph 5 of Article 17, the time of providing its report, the period from the date of establishment of the panel by the DSB until the date of determination of the reasonable period of time shall not exceed 15 months unless the parties to the dispute agree otherwise. Where either the panel or the Appellate Body has acted to extend the time of providing its report, the additional time taken shall be added to the 15-month period; provided that unless the parties to the dispute agree that there are exceptional circumstances, the total time shall not exceed 18 months.

5. Where there is disagreement as to the existence or consistency with a covered agreement of measures taken to comply with the recommendations and rulings such dispute shall be decided through recourse to these dispute settlement procedures, including wherever possible resort to the original panel. The panel shall circulate its report within 90 days after the date of referral of the matter to it. When the panel considers that it cannot provide its report within this time frame, it shall inform the DSB in writing of the reasons for the delay together with an estimate of the period within which it will submit its report.

6. The DSB shall keep under surveillance the implementation of adopted recommendations or rulings. The issue of implementation of the recommendations or rulings may be raised at the DSB by any Member at

---

[12] If the parties cannot agree on an arbitrator within ten days after referring the matter to arbitration, the arbitrator shall be appointed by the Director-General within ten days, after consulting the parties.

[13] The expression "arbitrator" shall be interpreted as referring either to an individual or a group.

any time following their adoption. Unless the DSB decides otherwise, the issue of implementation of the recommendations or rulings shall be placed on the agenda of the DSB meeting after six months following the date of establishment of the reasonable period of time pursuant to paragraph 3 and shall remain on the DSB's agenda until the issue is resolved. At least 10 days prior to each such DSB meeting, the Member concerned shall provide the DSB with a status report in writing of its progress in the implementation of the recommendations or rulings.

7.   If the matter is one which has been raised by a developing country Member, the DSB shall consider what further action it might take which would be appropriate to the circumstances.

8.   If the case is one brought by a developing country Member, in considering what appropriate action might be taken, the DSB shall take into account not only the trade coverage of measures complained of, but also their impact on the economy of developing country Members concerned.

Article 22

Compensation and the Suspension of Concessions

1.   Compensation and the suspension of concessions or other obligations are temporary measures available in the event that the recommendations and rulings are not implemented within a reasonable period of time. However, neither compensation nor the suspension of concessions or other obligations is preferred to full implementation of a recommendation to bring a measure into conformity with the covered agreements. Compensation is voluntary and, if granted, shall be consistent with the covered agreements.

2.   If the Member concerned fails to bring the measure found to be inconsistent with a covered agreement into compliance therewith or otherwise comply with the recommendations and rulings within the reasonable period of time determined pursuant to paragraph 3 of Article 21, such Member shall, if so requested, and no later than the expiry of the reasonable period of time, enter into negotiations with any party having invoked the dispute settlement procedures, with a view to developing mutually acceptable compensation. If no satisfactory compensation has been agreed within 20 days after the date of expiry of the reasonable period of time, any party having invoked the dispute settlement procedures may request authorization from the DSB to suspend the application to the Member concerned of concessions or other obligations under the covered agreements.

3.   In considering what concessions or other obligations to suspend, the complaining party shall apply the following principles and procedures:

(a) the general principle is that the complaining party should first seek to suspend concessions or other obligations with respect to the same sector(s) as that in which the panel or Appellate Body has found a violation or other nullification or impairment;

(b) if that party considers that it is not practicable or effective to suspend concessions or other obligations with respect to the same sector(s), it may seek to suspend concessions or other obligations in other sectors under the same agreement;

(c) if that party considers that it is not practicable or effective to suspend concessions or other obligations with respect to other sectors under the same agreement, and that the circumstances are serious enough, it may seek to suspend concessions or other obligations under another covered agreement;

(d) in applying the above principles, that party shall take into account:

(i) the trade in the sector or under the agreement under which the panel or Appellate Body has found a violation or other nullification or impairment, and the importance of such trade to that party;

(ii) the broader economic elements related to the nullification or impairment and the broader economic consequences of the suspension of concessions or other obligations;

(e) if that party decides to request authorization to suspend concessions or other obligations pursuant to subparagraphs (b) or (c), it shall state the reasons therefor in its request. At the same time as the request is forwarded to the DSB, it also shall be forwarded to the relevant Councils and also, in the case of a request pursuant to subparagraph (b), the relevant sectoral bodies;

(f) for purposes of this paragraph, "sector" means:

(i) with respect to goods, all goods;

(ii) with respect to services, a principal sector as identified in the current "Services Sectoral Classification List" which identifies such sectors,[14]

(iii) with respect to trade-related intellectual property rights, each of the categories of intellectual property rights covered in Section 1, or Section 2, or Section 3, or Section 4, or Section 5, or Section 6, or Section 7 of Part II, or the obligations under Part III, or Part IV of the Agreement on TRIPS;

(g) for purposes of this paragraph, "agreement" means:

(i) with respect to goods, the agreements listed in Annex 1A of the WTO Agreement, taken as a whole as well as the Plurilateral Trade Agreements in so far as the

---

[14]   The list in document MTN.GNS/W/120 identifies eleven sectors.

relevant parties to the dispute are parties to these agreements;

   (ii) with respect to services, the GATS;

   (iii) with respect to intellectual property rights, the Agreement on TRIPS.

   4.   The level of the suspension of concessions or other obligations authorized by the DSB shall be equivalent to the level of the nullification or impairment.

   5.   The DSB shall not authorize suspension of concessions or other obligations if a covered agreement prohibits such suspension.

   6.   When the situation described in paragraph 2 occurs, the DSB, upon request, shall grant authorization to suspend concessions or other obligations within 30 days of the expiry of the reasonable period of time unless the DSB decides by consensus to reject the request. However, if the Member concerned objects to the level of suspension proposed, or claims that the principles and procedures set forth in paragraph 3 have not been followed where a complaining party has requested authorization to suspend concessions or other obligations pursuant to paragraph 3(b) or (c), the matter shall be referred to arbitration. Such arbitration shall be carried out by the original panel, if members are available, or by an arbitrator[15] appointed by the Director-General and shall be completed within 60 days after the date of expiry of the reasonable period of time. Concessions or other obligations shall not be suspended during the course of the arbitration.

   7.   The arbitrator[16] acting pursuant to paragraph 6 shall not examine the nature of the concessions or other obligations to be suspended but shall determine whether the level of such suspension is equivalent to the level of nullification or impairment. The arbitrator may also determine if the proposed suspension of concessions or other obligations is allowed under the covered agreement. However, if the matter referred to arbitration includes a claim that the principles and procedures set forth in paragraph 3 have not been followed, the arbitrator shall examine that claim. In the event the arbitrator determines that those principles and procedures have not been followed, the complaining party shall apply them consistent with paragraph 3. The parties shall accept the arbitrator's decision as final and the parties concerned shall not seek a second arbitration. The DSB shall be informed promptly of the decision of the arbitrator and shall upon request, grant authorization to suspend concessions or other obligations where the request is consistent with the decision of the arbitrator, unless the DSB decides by consensus to reject the request.

---

   [15]   The expression "arbitrator" shall be interpreted as referring either to an individual or a group.

   [16]   The expression "arbitrator" shall be interpreted as referring either to an individual or a group or to the members of the original panel when serving in the capacity of arbitrator.

8. The suspension of concessions or other obligations shall be temporary and shall only be applied until such time as the measure found to be inconsistent with a covered agreement has been removed, or the Member that must implement recommendations or rulings provides a solution to the nullification or impairment of benefits, or a mutually satisfactory solution is reached. In accordance with paragraph 6 of Article 21, the DSB shall continue to keep under surveillance the implementation of adopted recommendations or rulings, including those cases where compensation has been provided or concessions or other obligations have been suspended but the recommendations to bring a measure into conformity with the covered agreements have not been implemented.

9. The dispute settlement provisions of the covered agreements may be invoked in respect of measures affecting their observance taken by regional or local governments or authorities within the territory of a Member. When the DSB has ruled that a provision of a covered agreement has not been observed, the responsible Member shall take such reasonable measures as may be available to it to ensure its observance. The provisions of the covered agreements and this Understanding relating to compensation and suspension of concessions or other obligations apply in cases where it has not been possible to secure such observance.[17]

Article 23

Strengthening of the Multilateral System

1. When Members seek the redress of a violation of obligations or other nullification or impairment of benefits under the covered agreements or an impediment to the attainment of any objective of the covered agreements, they shall have recourse to, and abide by, the rules and procedures of this Understanding.

2. In such cases, Members shall:

(a) not make a determination to the effect that a violation has occurred, that benefits have been nullified or impaired or that the attainment of any objective of the covered agreements has been impeded, except through recourse to dispute settlement in accordance with the rules and procedures of this Understanding, and shall make any such determination consistent with the findings contained in the panel or Appellate Body report adopted by the DSB or an arbitration award rendered under this Understanding;

(b) follow the procedures set forth in Article 21 to determine the reasonable period of time for the Member concerned to implement the recommendations and rulings; and

(c) follow the procedures set forth in Article 22 to determine the level of suspension of concessions or other obligations and

---

[17] Where the provisions of any covered agreement concerning measures taken by regional or local governments or authorities within the territory of a Member contain provisions different from the provisions of this paragraph, the provisions of such covered agreement shall prevail.

obtain DSB authorization in accordance with those procedures before suspending concessions or other obligations under the covered agreements in response to the failure of the Member concerned to implement the recommendations and rulings within that reasonable period of time.

Article 24

Special Procedures Involving Least-Developed Country Members

1. At all stages of the determination of the causes of a dispute and of dispute settlement procedures involving a least-developed country Member, particular consideration shall be given to the special situation of least-developed country Members. In this regard, Members shall exercise due restraint in raising matters under these procedures involving a least-developed country Member. If nullification or impairment is found to result from a measure taken by a least-developed country Member, complaining parties shall exercise due restraint in asking for compensation or seeking authorization to suspend the application of concessions or other obligations pursuant to these procedures.

2. In dispute settlement cases involving a least-developed country Member, where a satisfactory solution has not been found in the course of consultations the Director-General or the Chairman of the DSB shall, upon request by a least-developed country Member offer their good offices, conciliation and mediation with a view to assisting the parties to settle the dispute, before a request for a panel is made. The Director-General or the Chairman of the DSB, in providing the above assistance, may consult any source which either deems appropriate.

Article 25

Arbitration

1. Expeditious arbitration within the WTO as an alternative means of dispute settlement can facilitate the solution of certain disputes that concern issues that are clearly defined by both parties.

2. Except as otherwise provided in this Understanding, resort to arbitration shall be subject to mutual agreement of the parties which shall agree on the procedures to be followed. Agreements to resort to arbitration shall be notified to all Members sufficiently in advance of the actual commencement of the arbitration process.

3. Other Members may become party to an arbitration proceeding only upon the agreement of the parties which have agreed to have recourse to arbitration. The parties to the proceeding shall agree to abide by the arbitration award. Arbitration awards shall be notified to the DSB and the Council or Committee of any relevant agreement where any Member may raise any point relating thereto.

4. Articles 21 and 22 of this Understanding shall apply *mutatis mutandis* to arbitration awards.

Article 26

1. *Non-Violation Complaints of the Type Described in Paragraph 1(b) of Article XXIII of GATT 1994*

Where the provisions of paragraph 1(b) of Article XXIII of GATT 1994 are applicable to a covered agreement, a panel or the Appellate Body may only make rulings and recommendations where a party to the dispute considers that any benefit accruing to it directly or indirectly under the relevant covered agreement is being nullified or impaired or the attainment of any objective of that Agreement is being impeded as a result of the application by a Member of any measure, whether or not it conflicts with the provisions of that Agreement. Where and to the extent that such party considers and a panel or the Appellate Body determines that a case concerns a measure that does not conflict with the provisions of a covered agreement to which the provisions of paragraph 1(b) of Article XXIII of GATT 1994 are applicable, the procedures in this Understanding shall apply, subject to the following:

(a) the complaining party shall present a detailed justification in support of any complaint relating to a measure which does not conflict with the relevant covered agreement;

(b) where a measure has been found to nullify or impair benefits under, or impede the attainment of objectives, of the relevant covered agreement without violation thereof, there is no obligation to withdraw the measure. However, in such cases, the panel or the Appellate Body shall recommend that the Member concerned make a mutually satisfactory adjustment;

(c) notwithstanding the provisions of Article 21, the arbitration provided for in paragraph 3 of Article 21, upon request of either party, may include a determination of the level of benefits which have been nullified or impaired, and may also suggest ways and means of reaching a mutually satisfactory adjustment; such suggestions shall not be binding upon the parties to the dispute;

(d) notwithstanding the provisions of paragraph 1 of Article 22, compensation may be part of a mutually satisfactory adjustment as final settlement of the dispute.

2. *Complaints of the Type Described in Paragraph 1(c) of Article XXIII of GATT 1994*

Where the provisions of paragraph 1(c) of Article XXIII of GATT 1994 are applicable to a covered agreement, a panel may only make rulings and recommendations where a party considers that any benefit accruing to it directly or indirectly under the relevant covered agreement is being nullified or impaired or the attainment of any objective of that Agreement is being impeded as a result of the existence of any situation other than those to which the provisions of paragraphs 1(a) and 1(b) of Article XXIII of GATT 1994 are applicable. Where and to the extent that such party considers and a panel determines that the matter is covered by this paragraph, the procedures of this Understanding shall apply only up to and including the point in the proceedings where the panel report has been circulated to the Members. The dispute settlement rules and procedures contained in the Decision of 12 April 1989 (BISD 36S/61–67) shall apply to consideration for adoption, and surveillance and implementation of recommendations and rulings. The following shall also apply:

(a) the complaining party shall present a detailed justification in support of any argument made with respect to issues covered under this paragraph;

(b) in cases involving matters covered by this paragraph, if a panel finds that cases also involve dispute settlement matters other than those covered by this paragraph, the panel shall circulate a report to the DSB addressing any such matters and a separate report on matters falling under this paragraph.

Article 27

Responsibilities of the Secretariat

1.   The Secretariat shall have the responsibility of assisting panels, especially on the legal, historical and procedural aspects of the matters dealt with, and of providing secretarial and technical support.

2.   While the Secretariat assists Members in respect of dispute settlement at their request, there may also be a need to provide additional legal advice and assistance in respect of dispute settlement to developing country Members. To this end, the Secretariat shall make available a qualified legal expert from the WTO technical cooperation services to any developing country Member which so requests. This expert shall assist the developing country Member in a manner ensuring the continued impartiality of the Secretariat.

3.   The Secretariat shall conduct special training courses for interested Members concerning these dispute settlement procedures and practices so as to enable Members' experts to be better informed in this regard.

APPENDIX 1

AGREEMENTS COVERED BY THE UNDERSTANDING

(A)   Agreement Establishing the World Trade Organization

(B)   Multilateral Trade Agreements

Annex 1A: Multilateral Agreements on Trade in Goods

Annex 1B: General Agreement on Trade in Services

Annex 1C: Agreement on Trade-Related Aspects of Intellectual Property Rights

Annex 2:   Understanding on Rules and Procedures Governing the Settlement of Disputes

(C)   Plurilateral Trade Agreements

     Annex 4:   Agreement on Trade in Civil Aircraft

                    Agreement on Government Procurement

                    International Dairy Agreement

                    International Bovine Meat Agreement

The applicability of this Understanding to the Plurilateral Trade Agreements shall be subject to the adoption of a decision by the parties to each agreement setting out the terms for the application of the Understanding to the individual agreement, including any special or additional rules or procedures for inclusion in Appendix 2, as notified to the DSB.

APPENDIX 2

SPECIAL OR ADDITIONAL RULES AND PROCEDURES CONTAINED IN THE COVERED AGREEMENTS

Agreement	*Rules and Procedures*
Agreement on the Application of Sanitary and Phytosanitary Measures	11.2
Agreement on Textiles and Clothing	2.14, 2.21, 4.4, 5.2, 5.4, 5.6, 6.9, 6.10, 6.11, 8.1 through 8.12
Agreement on Technical Barriers to Trade	14.2 through 14.4, Annex 2
Agreement on Implementation of Article VI of GATT 1994	17.4 through 17.7
Agreement on Implementation of Article VII of GATT 1994	19.3 through 19.5, Annex II.2(f), 3, 9, 21
Agreement on Subsidies and Countervailing Measures	4.2 through 4.12, 6.6, 7.2 through 7.10, 8.5, footnote 35, 24.4, 27.7, Annex V
General Agreement on Trade in Services	XXII:3, XXIII:3
Annex on Financial Services	4
Annex on Air Transport Services	4
Decision on Certain Dispute Settlement Procedures for the GATS	1 through 5

The list of rules and procedures in this Appendix includes provisions where only a part of the provision may be relevant in this context.

Any special or additional rules or procedures in the Plurilateral Trade Agreements as determined by the competent bodies of each agreement and as notified to the DSB.

* * *

5.   WTO Agreement on Technical Barriers to Trade (TBT Standards Code)

(Selected Provisions)

Article 1

General Provisions

1.1   General   terms   for   standardization   and   procedures   for assessment of conformity shall normally have the meaning given to them by definitions adopted within the United Nations system and by international standardizing bodies taking into account their context and in the light of the object and purpose of this Agreement.

1.2   However, for the purposes of this Agreement the meaning of the terms given in Annex 1 applies.

1.3   All products, including industrial and agricultural products, shall be subject to the provisions of this Agreement.

1.4   Purchasing specifications prepared by governmental bodies for production or consumption requirements of governmental bodies are not subject to the provisions of this Agreement but are addressed in the Agreement on Government Procurement, according to its coverage.

1.5   The provisions of this Agreement do not apply to sanitary and phytosanitary measures as defined in Annex A of the Agreement on the Application of Sanitary and Phytosanitary Measures.

1.6   All references in this Agreement to technical regulations, standards and conformity assessment procedures shall be construed to include any amendments thereto and any additions to the rules or the product coverage thereof, except amendments and additions of an insignificant nature.

TECHNICAL REGULATIONS AND STANDARDS

Article 2

Preparation, Adoption and Application of Technical Regulations by Central Government Bodies

With respect to their central government bodies:

2.1   Members shall ensure that in respect of technical regulations, products imported from the territory of any Member shall be accorded treatment no less favourable than that accorded to like products of national origin and to like products originating in any other country.

2.2   Members shall ensure that technical regulations are not prepared, adopted or applied with a view to or with the effect of creating unnecessary obstacles to international trade. For this purpose, technical regulations shall not be more trade-restrictive than necessary to fulfil a legitimate objective, taking account of the risks non-fulfilment would create. Such legitimate objectives are, *inter alia*: national security requirements; the prevention of deceptive practices; protection of human health or safety, animal or plant life or health, or the environment. In assessing such risks, relevant elements of consideration are, *inter alia*: available scientific and technical information, related processing technology or intended end-uses of products.

2.3 Technical regulations shall not be maintained if the circumstances or objectives giving rise to their adoption no longer exist or if the changed circumstances or objectives can be addressed in a less trade-restrictive manner.

2.4 Where technical regulations are required and relevant international standards exist or their completion is imminent, Members shall use them, or the relevant parts of them, as a basis for their technical regulations except when such international standards or relevant parts would be an ineffective or inappropriate means for the fulfilment of the legitimate objectives pursued, for instance because of fundamental climatic or geographical factors or fundamental technological problems.

2.5 A Member preparing, adopting or applying a technical regulation which may have a significant effect on trade of other Members shall, upon the request of another Member, explain the justification for that technical regulation in terms of the provisions of paragraphs 2 to 4. Whenever a technical regulation is prepared, adopted or applied for one of the legitimate objectives explicitly mentioned in paragraph 2, and is in accordance with relevant international standards, it shall be rebuttably presumed not to create an unnecessary obstacle to international trade.

* * *

2.7 Members shall give positive consideration to accepting as equivalent technical regulations of other Members, even if these regulations differ from their own, provided they are satisfied that these regulations adequately fulfil the objectives of their own regulations.

2.8 Wherever appropriate, Members shall specify technical regulations based on product requirements in terms of performance rather than design or descriptive characteristics.

2.9 Whenever a relevant international standard does not exist or the technical content of a proposed technical regulation is not in accordance with the technical content of relevant international standards, and if the technical regulation may have a significant effect on trade of other Members, Members shall:

2.9.1 publish a notice in a publication at an early appropriate stage, in such a manner as to enable interested parties in other Members to become acquainted with it, that they propose to introduce a particular technical regulation;

2.9.2 notify other Members through the Secretariat of the products to be covered by the proposed technical regulation, together with a brief indication of its objective and rationale. Such notifications shall take place at an early appropriate stage, when amendments can still be introduced and comments taken into account;

2.9.3   upon request, provide to other Members particulars or copies of the proposed technical regulation and, whenever possible, identify the parts which in substance deviate from relevant international standards;

2.9.4   without discrimination, allow reasonable time for other Members to make comments in writing, discuss these comments upon request, and take these written comments and the results of these discussions into account.

* * *

Article 3

Preparation, Adoption and Application of Technical Regulations by Local Government Bodies and Non-Governmental Bodies

With respect to their local government and non-governmental bodies within their territories:

3.1   Members shall take such reasonable measures as may be available to them to ensure compliance by such bodies with the provisions of Article 2, with the exception of the obligation to notify as referred to in paragraphs 9.2 and 10.1 of Article 2.

3.2   Members shall ensure that the technical regulations of local governments on the level directly below that of the central government in Members are notified in accordance with the provisions of paragraphs 9.2 and 10.1 of Article 2, noting that notification shall not be required for technical regulations the technical content of which is substantially the same as that of previously notified technical regulations of central government bodies of the Member concerned.

3.3   Members may require contact with other Members, including the notifications, provision of information, comments and discussions referred to in paragraphs 9 and 10 of Article 2, to take place through the central government.

3.4   Members shall not take measures which require or encourage local government bodies or non-governmental bodies within their territories to act in a manner inconsistent with the provisions of Article 2.

3.5   Members are fully responsible under this Agreement for the observance of all provisions of Article 2. Members shall formulate and implement positive measures and mechanisms in support of the observance of the provisions of Article 2 by other than central government bodies.

Article 4

Preparation, Adoption and Application of Standards

4.1   Members shall ensure that their central government standardizing bodies accept and comply with the Code of Good Practice for the Preparation, Adoption and Application of Standards in Annex 3 to this

Agreement (referred to in this Agreement as the "Code of Good Practice"). They shall take such reasonable measures as may be available to them to ensure that local government and non-governmental standardizing bodies within their territories, as well as regional standardizing bodies of which they or one or more bodies within their territories are members, accept and comply with this Code of Good Practice. In addition, Members shall not take measures which have the effect of, directly or indirectly, requiring or encouraging such standardizing bodies to act in a manner inconsistent with the Code of Good Practice. The obligations of Members with respect to compliance of standardizing bodies with the provisions of the Code of Good Practice shall apply irrespective of whether or not a standardizing body has accepted the Code of Good Practice.

4.2 Standardizing bodies that have accepted and are complying with the Code of Good Practice shall be acknowledged by the Members as complying with the principles of this Agreement.

CONFORMITY WITH TECHNICAL REGULATIONS AND STANDARDS

Article 5

Procedures for Assessment of Conformity by Central Government Bodies

5.1 Members shall ensure that, in cases where a positive assurance of conformity with technical regulations or standards is required, their central government bodies apply the following provisions to products originating in the territories of other Members:

5.1.1 conformity assessment procedures are prepared, adopted and applied so as to grant access for suppliers of like products originating in the territories of other Members under conditions no less favourable than those accorded to suppliers of like products of national origin or originating in any other country, in a comparable situation; access entails suppliers' right to an assessment of conformity under the rules of the procedure, including, when foreseen by this procedure, the possibility to have conformity assessment activities undertaken at the site of facilities and to receive the mark of the system;

5.1.2 conformity assessment procedures are not prepared, adopted or applied with a view to or with the effect of creating unnecessary obstacles to international trade. This means, *inter alia,* that conformity assessment procedures shall not be more strict or be applied more strictly than is necessary to give the importing Member adequate confidence that products conform with the applicable technical regulations or standards, taking account of the risks non-conformity would create.

* * *

5.4 In cases where a positive assurance is required that products conform with technical regulations or standards, and relevant guides or recommendations issued by international standardizing bodies exist or their completion is imminent, Members shall ensure that central government bodies use them, or the relevant parts of them, as a basis for their conformity assessment procedures, except where, as duly explained upon request, such guides or recommendations or relevant parts are inappropriate for the Members concerned, for, *inter alia,* such reasons as: national security requirements; the prevention of deceptive practices; protection of human health or safety, animal or plant life or health, or the environment; fundamental climatic or other geographical factors; fundamental technological or infrastructural problems.

* * *

5.6 Whenever a relevant guide or recommendation issued by an international standardizing body does not exist or the technical content of a proposed conformity assessment procedure is not in accordance with relevant guides and recommendations issued by international standardizing bodies, and if the conformity assessment procedure may have a significant effect on trade of other Members, Members shall:

5.6.1 publish a notice in a publication at an early appropriate stage, in such a manner as to enable interested parties in other Members to become acquainted with it, that they propose to introduce a particular conformity assessment procedure;

5.6.2 notify other Members through the Secretariat of the products to be covered by the proposed conformity assessment procedure, together with a brief indication of its objective and rationale. Such notifications shall take place at an early appropriate stage, when amendments can still be introduced and comments taken into account;

5.6.3 upon request, provide to other Members particulars or copies of the proposed procedure and, whenever possible, identify the parts which in substance deviate from relevant guides or recommendations issued by international standardizing bodies;

5.6.4 without discrimination, allow reasonable time for other Members to make comments in writing, discuss these comments upon request, and take these written comments and the results of these discussions into account.

* * *

Article 6

Recognition of Conformity Assessment by Central Government Bodies

With respect to their central government bodies:

6.1 Without prejudice to the provisions of paragraphs 3 and 4, Members shall ensure, whenever possible, that results of conformity assessment procedures in other Members are accepted, even when those procedures differ from their own, provided they are satisfied that those procedures offer an assurance of conformity with applicable technical regulations or standards equivalent to their own procedures. It is recognized that prior consultations may be necessary in order to arrive at a mutually satisfactory understanding regarding, in particular:

6.1.1 adequate and enduring technical competence of the relevant conformity assessment bodies in the exporting Member, so that confidence in the continued reliability of their conformity assessment results can exist; in this regard, verified compliance, for instance through accreditation, with relevant guides or recommendations issued by international standardizing bodies shall be taken into account as an indication of adequate technical competence;

6.1.2 limitation of the acceptance of conformity assessment results to those produced by designated bodies in the exporting Member.

* * *

Article 7

Procedures for Assessment of Conformity by Local Government Bodies

With respect to their local government bodies within their territories:

7.1 Members shall take such reasonable measures as may be available to them to ensure compliance by such bodies with the provisions of Articles 5 and 6, with the exception of the obligation to notify as referred to in paragraphs 6.2 and 7.1 of Article 5.

7.2 Members shall ensure that the conformity assessment procedures of local governments on the level directly below that of the central government in Members are notified in accordance with the provisions of paragraphs 6.2 and 7.1 of Article 5, noting that notifications shall not be required for conformity assessment procedures the technical content of which is substantially the same as that of previously notified conformity assessment procedures of central government bodies of the Members concerned.

7.3 Members may require contact with other Members, including the notifications, provision of information, comments and discussions referred to in paragraphs 6 and 7 of Article 5, to take place through the central government.

7.4 Members shall not take measures which require or encourage local government bodies within their territories to act in a manner inconsistent with the provisions of Articles 5 and 6.

7.5 Members are fully responsible under this Agreement for the observance of all provisions of Articles 5 and 6. Members shall formulate and implement positive measures and mechanisms in support of the observance of the provisions of Articles 5 and 6 by other than central government bodies.

Article 12

Special and Differential Treatment of Developing Country Members

12.1 Members shall provide differential and more favourable treatment to developing country Members to this Agreement, through the following provisions as well as through the relevant provisions of other Articles of this Agreement.

12.2 Members shall give particular attention to the provisions of this Agreement concerning developing country Members' rights and obligations and shall take into account the special development, financial and trade needs of developing country Members in the implementation of this Agreement, both nationally and in the operation of this Agreement's institutional arrangements.

12.3 Members shall, in the preparation and application of technical regulations, standards and conformity assessment procedures, take account of the special development, financial and trade needs of developing country Members, with a view to ensuring that such technical regulations, standards and conformity assessment procedures do not create unnecessary obstacles to exports from developing country Members.

12.4 Members recognize that, although international standards, guides or recommendations may exist, in their particular technological and socio-economic conditions, developing country Members adopt certain technical regulations, standards or conformity assessment procedures aimed at preserving indigenous technology and production methods and processes compatible with their development needs. Members therefore recognize that developing country Members should not be expected to use international standards as a basis for their technical regulations or standards, including test methods, which are not appropriate to their development, financial and trade needs.

* * *

Article 14

Consultation and Dispute Settlement

14.1 Consultations and the settlement of disputes with respect to any matter affecting the operation of this Agreement shall take place under the auspices of the Dispute Settlement Body and shall follow, *mutatis mutandis,* the provisions of Articles XXII and XXIII of GATT 1994, as elaborated and applied by the Dispute Settlement Understanding.

* * *

14.4 The dispute settlement provisions set out above can be invoked in cases where a Member considers that another Member has not achieved satisfactory results under Articles 3, 4, 7, 8 and 9 and its trade interests are significantly affected. In this respect, such results shall be equivalent to those as if the body in question were a Member.

FINAL PROVISIONS

Article 15

Final Provisions

Reservations

15.1 Reservations may not be entered in respect of any of the provisions of this Agreement without the consent of the other Members.

Review

15.2 Each Member shall, promptly after the date on which the WTO Agreement enters into force for it, inform the Committee of measures in existence or taken to ensure the implementation and administration of this Agreement. Any changes of such measures thereafter shall also be notified to the Committee.

15.3 The Committee shall review annually the implementation and operation of this Agreement taking into account the objectives thereof.

15.4 Not later than the end of the third year from the date of entry into force of the WTO Agreement and at the end of each three-year period thereafter, the Committee shall review the operation and implementation of this Agreement, including the provisions relating to transparency, with a view to recommending an adjustment of the rights and obligations of this Agreement where necessary to ensure mutual economic advantage and balance of rights and obligations, without prejudice to the provisions of Article 12. Having regard, *inter alia,* to the experience gained in the implementation of the Agreement, the Committee shall, where appropriate, submit proposals for amendments to the text of this Agreement to the Council for Trade in Goods.

Annexes

15.5 The annexes to this Agreement constitute an integral part thereof.

ANNEX 1

TERMS AND THEIR DEFINITIONS FOR THE PURPOSE OF THIS AGREEMENT

The terms presented in the sixth edition of the ISO/IEC Guide 2: 1991, General Terms and Their Definitions Concerning Standardization and Related Activities, shall, when used in this Agreement, have the same meaning as given in the definitions in the said Guide taking into account that services are excluded from the coverage of this Agreement.

For the purpose of this Agreement, however, the following definitions shall apply:

1. *Technical regulation*

Document which lays down product characteristics or their related processes and production methods, including the applicable administrative provisions, with which compliance is mandatory. It may also include or deal exclusively with terminology, symbols, packaging, marking or labelling requirements as they apply to a product, process or production method.

Explanatory note

The definition in ISO/IEC Guide 2 is not self-contained, but based on the so-called "building block" system.

2.   *Standard*

Document approved by a recognized body, that provides, for common and repeated use, rules, guidelines or characteristics for products or related processes and production methods, with which compliance is not mandatory. It may also include or deal exclusively with terminology, symbols, packaging, marking or labelling requirements as they apply to a product, process or production method.

Explanatory note

The terms as defined in ISO/IEC Guide 2 cover products, processes and services. This Agreement deals only with technical regulations, standards and conformity assessment procedures related to products or processes and production methods. Standards as defined by ISO/IEC Guide 2 may be mandatory or voluntary. For the purpose of this Agreement standards are defined as voluntary and technical regulations as mandatory documents. Standards prepared by the international standardization community are based on consensus. This Agreement covers also documents that are not based on consensus.

3.   *Conformity assessment procedures*

Any procedure used, directly or indirectly, to determine that relevant requirements in technical regulations or standards are fulfilled.

Explanatory note

Conformity assessment procedures include, *inter alia,* procedures for sampling, testing and inspection; evaluation, verification and assurance of conformity; registration, accreditation and approval as well as their combinations.

4.   *International body or system*

Body or system whose membership is open to the relevant bodies of at least all Members.

5.   *Regional body or system*

Body or system whose membership is open to the relevant bodies of only some of the Members.

6.   *Central government body*

Central government, its ministries and departments or any body subject to the control of the central government in respect of the activity in question.

Explanatory note

In the case of the European Communities the provisions governing central government bodies apply. However, regional bodies or conformity assessment systems may be established within the European Communities, and in such cases would be subject to the provisions of this Agreement on regional bodies or conformity assessment systems.

7. *Local government body*

Government other than a central government (e.g. states, provinces, Länder, cantons, municipalities, etc.), its ministries or departments or any body subject to the control of such a government in respect of the activity in question.

8. *Non-governmental body*

Body other than a central government body or a local government body, including a non-governmental body which has legal power to enforce a technical regulation.

ANNEX 3

CODE OF GOOD PRACTICE FOR THE PREPARATION, ADOPTION AND APPLICATION OF STANDARDS

General Provisions

A. For the purposes of this Code the definitions in Annex 1 of this Agreement shall apply.

B. This Code is open to acceptance by any standardizing body within the territory of a Member of the WTO, whether a central government body, a local government body, or a non-governmental body; to any governmental regional standardizing body one or more members of which are Members of the WTO; and to any non-governmental regional standardizing body one or more members of which are situated within the territory of a Member of the WTO (referred to in this Code collectively as "standardizing bodies" and individually as "the standardizing body").

C. Standardizing bodies that have accepted or withdrawn from this Code shall notify this fact to the ISO/IEC Information Centre in Geneva. The notification shall include the name and address of the body concerned and the scope of its current and expected standardization activities. The notification may be sent either directly to the ISO/IEC Information Centre, or through the national member body of ISO/IEC or, preferably, through the relevant national member or international affiliate of ISONET, as appropriate.

SUBSTANTIVE PROVISIONS

D. In respect of standards, the standardizing body shall accord treatment to products originating in the territory of any other Member of the WTO no less favourable than that accorded to like products of national origin and to like products originating in any other country.

E. The standardizing body shall ensure that standards are not prepared, adopted or applied with a view to, or with the effect of, creating unnecessary obstacles to international trade.

F. Where international standards exist or their completion is imminent, the standardizing body shall use them, or the relevant parts of them, as a basis for the standards it develops, except where such international standards or relevant parts would be ineffective or inappropriate, for instance, because of an insufficient level of protection or fundamental climatic or geographical factors or fundamental technological problems.

G. With a view to harmonizing standards on as wide a basis as possible, the standardizing body shall, in an appropriate way, play a full part, within the limits of its resources, in the preparation by relevant international standardizing bodies of international standards regarding subject matter for which it either has adopted, or expects to adopt, standards. For standardizing bodies within the territory of a Member, participation in a particular international standardization activity shall, whenever possible, take place through one delegation representing all standardizing bodies in the territory that have adopted, or expect to adopt, standards for the subject matter to which the international standardization activity relates.

H. The standardizing body within the territory of a Member shall make every effort to avoid duplication of, or overlap with, the work of other standardizing bodies in the national territory or with the work of relevant international or regional standardizing bodies. They shall also make every effort to achieve a national consensus on the standards they develop. Likewise the regional standardizing body shall make every effort to avoid duplication of, or overlap with, the work of relevant international standardizing bodies.

I. Wherever appropriate, the standardizing body shall specify standards based on product requirements in terms of performance rather than design or descriptive characteristics.

J. At least once every six months, the standardizing body shall publish a work programme containing its name and address, the standards it is currently preparing and the standards which it has adopted in the preceding period. A standard is under preparation from the moment a decision has been taken to develop a standard until that standard has been adopted. The titles of specific draft standards shall, upon request, be provided in English, French or Spanish. A notice of the existence of the work programme shall be published in a national or, as the case may be, regional publication of standardization activities.

The work programme shall for each standard indicate, in accordance with any ISONET rules, the classification relevant to the subject matter, the stage attained in the standard's development, and the references of any international standards taken as a basis. No later than at the time of publication of its work programme, the standardizing body shall notify the existence thereof to the ISO/IEC Information Centre in Geneva.

* * *

N.   The standardizing body shall take into account, in the further processing of the standard, the comments received during the period for commenting. Comments received through standardizing bodies that have accepted this Code of Good Practice shall, if so requested, be replied to as promptly as possible. The reply shall include an explanation why a deviation from relevant international standards is necessary.

* * *

Q.   The standardizing body shall afford sympathetic consideration to, and adequate opportunity for, consultation regarding representations with respect to the operation of this Code presented by standardizing bodies that have accepted this Code of Good Practice. It shall make an objective effort to solve any complaints.

6.   WTO Agreement on the Application of Sanitary and Phytosanitary Measures (SPS Code)

(Selected provisions)

Article 1

General Provisions

1.   This Agreement applies to all sanitary and phytosanitary measures which may, directly or indirectly, affect international trade. Such measures shall be developed and applied in accordance with the provisions of this Agreement.

2.   For the purposes of this Agreement, the definitions provided in Annex A shall apply.

3.   The annexes are an integral part of this Agreement.

4.   Nothing in this Agreement shall affect the rights of Members under the Agreement on Technical Barriers to Trade with respect to measures not within the scope of this Agreement.

Article 2

Basic Rights and Obligations

1.   Members have the right to take sanitary and phytosanitary measures necessary for the protection of human, animal or plant life or health, provided that such measures are not inconsistent with the provisions of this Agreement.

2.   Members shall ensure that any sanitary or phytosanitary measure is applied only to the extent necessary to protect human, animal or plant life or health, is based on scientific principles and is not maintained without sufficient scientific evidence, except as provided for in paragraph 7 of Article 5.

3.   Members shall ensure that their sanitary and phytosanitary measures do not arbitrarily or unjustifiably discriminate between Members where identical or similar conditions prevail, including between their own territory and that of other Members. Sanitary and phytosanitary measures shall not be applied in a manner which would constitute a disguised restriction on international trade.

4.   Sanitary or phytosanitary measures which conform to the relevant provisions of this Agreement shall be presumed to be in accordance with the obligations of the Members under the provisions of GATT 1994 which relate to the use of sanitary or phytosanitary measures, in particular the provisions of Article XX(b).

Article 3

Harmonization

1.   To harmonize sanitary and phytosanitary measures on as wide a basis as possible, Members shall base their sanitary or phytosanitary

measures on international standards, guidelines or recommendations, where they exist, except as otherwise provided for in this Agreement, and in particular in paragraph 3.

2.   Sanitary or phytosanitary measures which conform to international standards, guidelines or recommendations shall be deemed to be necessary to protect human, animal or plant life or health, and presumed to be consistent with the relevant provisions of this Agreement and of GATT 1994.

3.   Members may introduce or maintain sanitary or phytosanitary measures which result in a higher level of sanitary or phytosanitary protection than would be achieved by measures based on the relevant international standards, guidelines or recommendations, if there is a scientific justification, or as a consequence of the level of sanitary or phytosanitary protection a Member determines to be appropriate in accordance with the relevant provisions of paragraphs 1 through 8 of Article 5.[2] Notwithstanding the above, all measures which result in a level of sanitary or phytosanitary protection different from that which would be achieved by measures based on international standards, guidelines or recommendations shall not be inconsistent with any other provision of this Agreement.

* * *

5.   The Committee on Sanitary and Phytosanitary Measures provided for in paragraphs 1 and 4 of Article 12 (referred to in this Agreement as the "Committee") shall develop a procedure to monitor the process of international harmonization and coordinate efforts in this regard with the relevant international organizations.

Article 4

Equivalence

1.   Members shall accept the sanitary or phytosanitary measures of other Members as equivalent, even if these measures differ from their own or from those used by other Members trading in the same product, if the exporting Member objectively demonstrates to the importing Member that its measures achieve the importing Member's appropriate level of sanitary or phytosanitary protection. For this purpose, reasonable access shall be given, upon request, to the importing Member for inspection, testing and other relevant procedures.

---

[2]   For the purposes of paragraph 3 of Article 3, there is a scientific justification if, on the basis of an examination and evaluation of available scientific information in conformity with the relevant provisions of this Agreement, a Member determines that the relevant international standards, guidelines or recommendations are not sufficient to achieve its appropriate level of sanitary or phytosanitary protection.

* * *

Article 5

Assessment of Risk and Determination of the Appropriate Level of
Sanitary or Phytosanitary Protection

1.   Members shall ensure that their sanitary or phytosanitary measures are based on an assessment, as appropriate to the circumstances, of the risks to human, animal or plant life or health, taking into account risk assessment techniques developed by the relevant international organizations.

2.   In the assessment of risks, Members shall take into account available scientific evidence; relevant processes and production methods; relevant inspection, sampling and testing methods; prevalence of specific diseases or pests; existence of pest- or disease-free areas; relevant ecological and environmental conditions; and quarantine or other treatment.

3.   In assessing the risk to animal or plant life or health and determining the measure to be applied for achieving the appropriate level of sanitary or phytosanitary protection from such risk, Members shall take into account as relevant economic factors: the potential damage in terms of loss of production or sales in the event of the entry, establishment or spread of a pest or disease; the costs of control or eradication in the territory of the importing Member; and the relative cost-effectiveness of alternative approaches to limiting risks.

4.   Members should, when determining the appropriate level of sanitary or phytosanitary protection, take into account the objective of minimizing negative trade effects.

5.   With the objective of achieving consistency in the application of the concept of appropriate level of sanitary or phytosanitary protection against risks to human life or health, or to animal and plant life or health, each Member shall avoid arbitrary or unjustifiable distinctions in the levels it considers to be appropriate in different situations, if such distinctions result in discrimination or a disguised restriction on international trade. Members shall cooperate in the Committee, in accordance with paragraphs 1, 2 and 3 of Article 12, to develop guidelines to further the practical implementation of this provision. In developing the guidelines, the Committee shall take into account all relevant factors, including the exceptional character of human health risks to which people voluntarily expose themselves.

6.   Without prejudice to paragraph 2 of Article 3, when establishing or maintaining sanitary or phytosanitary measures to achieve the appropriate level of sanitary or phytosanitary protection, Members shall ensure that such measures are not more trade-restrictive than required to achieve their appropriate level of sanitary or phytosanitary protection, taking into account technical and economic feasibility.[3]

---

[3]   For purposes of paragraph 6 of Article 5, a measure is not more trade-restrictive than required unless there is another measure, reasonably available

7. In cases where relevant scientific evidence is insufficient, a Member may provisionally adopt sanitary or phytosanitary measures on the basis of available pertinent information, including that from the relevant international organizations as well as from sanitary or phytosanitary measures applied by other Members. In such circumstances, Members shall seek to obtain the additional information necessary for a more objective assessment of risk and review the sanitary or phytosanitary measure accordingly within a reasonable period of time.

8. When a Member has reason to believe that a specific sanitary or phytosanitary measure introduced or maintained by another Member is constraining, or has the potential to constrain, its exports and the measure is not based on the relevant international standards, guidelines or recommendations, or such standards, guidelines or recommendations do not exist, an explanation of the reasons for such sanitary or phytosanitary measure may be requested and shall be provided by the Member maintaining the measure.

Article 6

Adaptation to Regional Conditions, Including Pest- or Disease-Free Areas and Areas of Low Pest or Disease Prevalence

1. Members shall ensure that their sanitary or phytosanitary measures are adapted to the sanitary or phytosanitary characteristics of the area—whether all of a country, part of a country, or all or parts of several countries—from which the product originated and to which the product is destined. In assessing the sanitary or phytosanitary characteristics of a region, Members shall take into account, *inter alia,* the level of prevalence of specific diseases or pests, the existence of eradication or control programmes, and appropriate criteria or guidelines which may be developed by the relevant international organizations.

2. Members shall, in particular, recognize the concepts of pest- or disease-free areas and areas of low pest or disease prevalence. Determination of such areas shall be based on factors such as geography, ecosystems, epidemiological surveillance, and the effectiveness of sanitary or phytosanitary controls.

* * *

Article 7

Transparency

Members shall notify changes in their sanitary or phytosanitary measures and shall provide information on their sanitary or phytosanitary measures in accordance with the provisions of Annex B.

---

taking into account technical and economic feasibility, that achieves the appropriate level of sanitary or phytosanitary protection and is significantly less restrictive to trade.

Article 8

Control, Inspection and Approval Procedures

Members shall observe the provisions of Annex C in the operation of control, inspection and approval procedures, including national systems for approving the use of additives or for establishing tolerances for contaminants in foods, beverages or feedstuffs, and otherwise ensure that their procedures are not inconsistent with the provisions of this Agreement.

Article 9

Technical Assistance

1.   Members agree to facilitate the provision of technical assistance to other Members, especially developing country Members, either bilaterally or through the appropriate international organizations. Such assistance may be, *inter alia,* in the areas of processing technologies, research and infrastructure, including in the establishment of national regulatory bodies, and may take the form of advice, credits, donations and grants, including for the purpose of seeking technical expertise, training and equipment to allow such countries to adjust to, and comply with, sanitary or phytosanitary measures necessary to achieve the appropriate level of sanitary or phytosanitary protection in their export markets.

2.   Where substantial investments are required in order for an exporting developing country Member to fulfil the sanitary or phytosanitary requirements of an importing Member, the latter shall consider providing such technical assistance as will permit the developing country Member to maintain and expand its market access opportunities for the product involved.

Article 10

Special and Differential Treatment

1.   In the preparation and application of sanitary or phytosanitary measures, Members shall take account of the special needs of developing country Members, and in particular of the least-developed country Members.

2.   Where the appropriate level of sanitary or phytosanitary protection allows scope for the phased introduction of new sanitary or phytosanitary measures, longer time-frames for compliance should be accorded on products of interest to developing country Members so as to maintain opportunities for their exports.

3.   With a view to ensuring that developing country Members are able to comply with the provisions of this Agreement, the Committee is enabled to grant to such countries, upon request, specified, time-limited exceptions in whole or in part from obligations under this Agreement, taking into account their financial, trade and development needs.

* * *

Article 11

Consultations and Dispute Settlement

1.   The provisions of Articles XXII and XXIII of GATT 1994 as elaborated and applied by the Dispute Settlement Understanding shall apply to consultations and the settlement of disputes under this Agreement, except as otherwise specifically provided herein.

* * *

Article 12

Administration

1.   A Committee on Sanitary and Phytosanitary Measures is hereby established to provide a regular forum for consultations. It shall carry out the functions necessary to implement the provisions of this Agreement and the furtherance of its objectives, in particular with respect to harmonization. The Committee shall reach its decisions by consensus.

2.   The Committee shall encourage and facilitate ad hoc consultations or negotiations among Members on specific sanitary or phytosanitary issues. The Committee shall encourage the use of international standards, guidelines or recommendations by all Members and, in this regard, shall sponsor technical consultation and study with the objective of increasing coordination and integration between international and national systems and approaches for approving the use of food additives or for establishing tolerances for contaminants in foods, beverages or feedstuffs.

3.   The Committee shall maintain close contact with the relevant international organizations in the field of sanitary and phytosanitary protection, especially with the Codex Alimentarius Commission, the International Office of Epizootics, and the Secretariat of the International Plant Protection Convention, with the objective of securing the best available scientific and technical advice for the administration of this Agreement and in order to ensure that unnecessary duplication of effort is avoided.

4.   The Committee shall develop a procedure to monitor the process of international harmonization and the use of international standards, guidelines or recommendations. For this purpose, the Committee should, in conjunction with the relevant international organizations, establish a list of international standards, guidelines or recommendations relating to sanitary or phytosanitary measures which the Committee determines to have a major trade impact. The list should include an indication by Members of those international standards, guidelines or recommendations which they apply as conditions for import or on the basis of which imported products conforming to these standards can enjoy access to their markets. For those cases in which a Member does not apply an international standard, guideline or recommendation as a condition for import, the Member should provide an indication of the reason therefor, and, in

particular, whether it considers that the standard is not stringent enough
to provide the appropriate level of sanitary or phytosanitary protection. If a
Member revises its position, following its indication of the use of a
standard, guideline or recommendation as a condition for import, it should
provide an explanation for its change and so inform the Secretariat as well
as the relevant international organizations, unless such notification and
explanation is given according to the procedures of Annex B.

* * *

7.   The Committee shall review the operation and implementation of
this Agreement three years after the date of entry into force of the WTO
Agreement, and thereafter as the need arises. Where appropriate, the
Committee may submit to the Council for Trade in Goods proposals to
amend the text of this Agreement having regard, *inter alia,* to the
experience gained in its implementation.

Article 13

Implementation

Members are fully responsible under this Agreement for the
observance of all obligations set forth herein. Members shall formulate and
implement positive measures and mechanisms in support of the observance
of the provisions of this Agreement by other than central government
bodies. Members shall take such reasonable measures as may be available
to them to ensure that non-governmental entities within their territories,
as well as regional bodies in which relevant entities within their territories
are members, comply with the relevant provisions of this Agreement. In
addition, Members shall not take measures which have the effect of,
directly or indirectly, requiring or encouraging such regional or non-
governmental entities, or local governmental bodies, to act in a manner
inconsistent with the provisions of this Agreement. Members shall ensure
that they rely on the services of non-governmental entities for
implementing sanitary or phytosanitary measures only if these entities
comply with the provisions of this Agreement.

Article 14

Final Provisions

The least-developed country Members may delay application of the
provisions of this Agreement for a period of five years following the date of
entry into force of the WTO Agreement with respect to their sanitary or
phytosanitary measures affecting importation or imported products. Other
developing country Members may delay application of the provisions of this
Agreement, other than paragraph 8 of Article 5 and Article 7, for two years
following the date of entry into force of the WTO Agreement with respect to
their existing sanitary or phytosanitary measures affecting importation or
imported products, where such application is prevented by a lack of
technical expertise, technical infrastructure or resources.

ANNEX A

DEFINITIONS

1.   Sanitary or phytosanitary measure—Any measure applied:

(a) to protect animal or plant life or health within the territory of the Member from risks arising from the entry, establishment or spread of pests, diseases, disease-carrying organisms or disease-causing organisms;

(b) to protect human or animal life or health within the territory of the Member from risks arising from additives, contaminants, toxins or disease-causing organisms in foods, beverages or feedstuffs;

(c) to protect human life or health within the territory of the Member from risks arising from diseases carried by animals, plants or products thereof, or from the entry, establishment or spread of pests; or

(d) to prevent or limit other damage within the territory of the Member from the entry, establishment or spread of pests.

Sanitary or phytosanitary measures include all relevant laws, decrees, regulations, requirements and procedures including, *inter alia,* end product criteria; processes and production methods; testing, inspection, certification and approval procedures; quarantine treatments including relevant requirements associated with the transport of animals or plants, or with the materials necessary for their survival during transport; provisions on relevant statistical methods, sampling procedures and methods of risk assessment; and packaging and labelling requirements directly related to food safety.

2.   *Harmonization*—The establishment, recognition and application of common sanitary and phytosanitary measures by different Members.

3.   *International standards, guidelines and recommendations*

(a) for food safety, the standards, guidelines and recommendations established by the Codex Alimentarius Commission relating to food additives, veterinary drug and pesticide residues, contaminants, methods of analysis and sampling, and codes and guidelines of hygienic practice;

(b) for animal health and zoonoses, the standards, guidelines and recommendations developed under the auspices of the International Office of Epizootics;

(c) for plant health, the international standards, guidelines and recommendations developed under the auspices of the Secretariat of the International Plant Protection Convention in cooperation with regional organizations operating within the framework of the International Plant Protection Convention; and

(d) for matters not covered by the above organizations, appropriate standards, guidelines and recommendations promulgated by other relevant international organizations open for membership to all Members, as identified by the Committee.

4. *Risk assessment*—The evaluation of the likelihood of entry, establishment or spread of a pest or disease within the territory of an importing Member according to the sanitary or phytosanitary measures which might be applied, and of the associated potential biological and economic consequences; or the evaluation of the potential for adverse effects on human or animal health arising from the presence of additives, contaminants, toxins or disease-causing organisms in food, beverages or feedstuffs.

5. *Appropriate level of sanitary or phytosanitary protection*—The level of protection deemed appropriate by the Member establishing a sanitary or phytosanitary measure to protect human, animal or plant life or health within its territory.

NOTE: Many Members otherwise refer to this concept as the "acceptable level of risk".

ANNEX B

TRANSPARENCY OF SANITARY AND PHYTOSANITARY REGULATIONS

Notification procedures

5. Whenever an international standard, guideline or recommendation does not exist or the content of a proposed sanitary or phytosanitary regulation is not substantially the same as the content of an international standard, guideline or recommendation, and if the regulation may have a significant effect on trade of other Members, Members shall:

(a) publish a notice at an early stage in such a manner as to enable interested Members to become acquainted with the proposal to introduce a particular regulation;

(b) notify other Members, through the Secretariat, of the products to be covered by the regulation together with a brief indication of the objective and rationale of the proposed regulation. Such notifications shall take place at an early stage, when amendments can still be introduced and comments taken into account;

(c) provide upon request to other Members copies of the proposed regulation and, whenever possible, identify the parts which in substance deviate from international standards, guidelines or recommendations;

(d) without discrimination, allow reasonable time for other Members to make comments in writing, discuss these comments upon request, and take the comments and the results of the discussions into account.

6. However, where urgent problems of health protection arise or threaten to arise for a Member, that Member may omit such of the steps

enumerated in paragraph 5 of this Annex as it finds necessary, provided that the Member:

(a) immediately notifies other Members, through the Secretariat, of the particular regulation and the products covered, with a brief indication of the objective and the rationale of the regulation, including the nature of the urgent problem(s);

(b) provides, upon request, copies of the regulation to other Members;

(c) allows other Members to make comments in writing, discusses these comments upon request, and takes the comments and the results of the discussions into account.

7. WTO Agreement on Trade-Related Aspects of Intellectual Property Rights (TRIPs)

(Selected Provisions)

Table of Contents

AGREEMENT ON TRADE-RELATED ASPECTS OF INTELLECTUAL PROPERTY RIGHTS

Members,

Desiring to reduce distortions and impediments to international trade, and taking into account the need to promote effective and adequate protection of intellectual property rights, and to ensure that measures and procedures to enforce intellectual property rights do not themselves become barriers to legitimate trade;

Recognizing, to this end, the need for new rules and disciplines concerning:

>   (a) the applicability of the basic principles of GATT 1994 and of relevant international intellectual property agreements or conventions;

>   (b) the provision of adequate standards and principles concerning the availability, scope and use of trade-related intellectual property rights;

>   (c) the provision of effective and appropriate means for the enforcement of trade-related intellectual property rights, taking into account differences in national legal systems;

>   (d) the provision of effective and expeditious procedures for the multilateral prevention and settlement of disputes between governments; and

>   (e) transitional arrangements aiming at the fullest participation in the results of the negotiations;

Recognizing the need for a multilateral framework of principles, rules and disciplines dealing with international trade in counterfeit goods;

Recognizing that intellectual property rights are private rights;

Recognizing the underlying public policy objectives of national systems for the protection of intellectual property, including developmental and technological objectives;

Recognizing also the special needs of the least-developed country Members in respect of maximum flexibility in the domestic implementation of laws and regulations in order to enable them to create a sound and viable technological base;

Emphasizing the importance of reducing tensions by reaching strengthened commitments to resolve disputes on trade-related intellectual property issues through multilateral procedures;

Desiring to establish a mutually supportive relationship between the WTO and the World Intellectual Property Organization (referred to in this Agreement as "WIPO") as well as other relevant international organizations;

Hereby agree as follows:

PART I

GENERAL PROVISIONS AND BASIC PRINCIPLES

Article 1

Nature and Scope of Obligations

1.   Members shall give effect to the provisions of this Agreement. Members may, but shall not be obliged to, implement in their law more extensive protection than is required by this Agreement, provided that such protection does not contravene the provisions of this Agreement. Members shall be free to determine the appropriate method of implementing the provisions of this Agreement within their own legal system and practice.

2.   For the purposes of this Agreement, the term "intellectual property" refers to all categories of intellectual property that are the subject of Sections 1 through 7 of Part II.

3.   Members shall accord the treatment provided for in this Agreement to the nationals of other Members.[1] In respect of the relevant intellectual property right, the nationals of other Members shall be understood as those natural or legal persons that would meet the criteria for eligibility for protection provided for in the Paris Convention (1967), the Berne Convention (1971), the Rome Convention and the Treaty on Intellectual Property in Respect of Integrated Circuits, were all Members of the WTO members of those conventions.[2] Any Member availing itself of the possibilities provided in paragraph 3 of Article 5 or paragraph 2 of Article 6 of the Rome Convention shall make a notification as foreseen in those provisions to the Council for Trade-Related Aspects of Intellectual Property Rights (the "Council for TRIPS").

Article 2

Intellectual Property Conventions

1.   In respect of Parts II, III and IV of this Agreement, Members shall comply with Articles 1 through 12, and Article 19, of the Paris Convention (1967).

---

[1]   When "nationals" are referred to in this Agreement, they shall be deemed, in the case of a separate customs territory Member of the WTO, to mean persons, natural or legal, who are domiciled or who have a real and effective industrial or commercial establishment in that customs territory.

[2]   In this Agreement, "Paris Convention" refers to the Paris Convention for the Protection of Industrial Property; "Paris Convention (1967)" refers to the Stockholm Act of this Convention of 14 July 1967. "Berne Convention" refers to the Berne Convention for the Protection of Literary and Artistic Works; "Berne Convention (1971)" refers to the Paris Act of this Convention of 24 July 1971. "Rome Convention" refers to the International Convention for the Protection of Performers, Producers of Phonograms and Broadcasting Organizations, adopted at Rome on 26 October 1961. "Treaty on Intellectual Property in Respect of Integrated Circuits" (IPIC Treaty) refers to the Treaty on Intellectual Property in Respect of Integrated Circuits, adopted at Washington on 26 May 1989. "WTO Agreement" refers to the Agreement Establishing the WTO.

2.   Nothing in Parts I to IV of this Agreement shall derogate from existing obligations that Members may have to each other under the Paris Convention, the Berne Convention, the Rome Convention and the Treaty on Intellectual Property in Respect of Integrated Circuits.

Article 3

National Treatment

1.   Each Member shall accord to the nationals of other Members treatment no less favourable than that it accords to its own nationals with regard to the protection[3] of intellectual property, subject to the exceptions already provided in, respectively, the Paris Convention (1967), the Berne Convention (1971), the Rome Convention or the Treaty on Intellectual Property in Respect of Integrated Circuits. In respect of performers, producers of phonograms and broadcasting organizations, this obligation only applies in respect of the rights provided under this Agreement. Any Member availing itself of the possibilities provided in Article 6 of the Berne Convention (1971) or paragraph 1(b) of Article 16 of the Rome Convention shall make a notification as foreseen in those provisions to the Council for TRIPS.

2.   Members may avail themselves of the exceptions permitted under paragraph 1 in relation to judicial and administrative procedures, including the designation of an address for service or the appointment of an agent within the jurisdiction of a Member, only where such exceptions are necessary to secure compliance with laws and regulations which are not inconsistent with the provisions of this Agreement and where such practices are not applied in a manner which would constitute a disguised restriction on trade.

Article 4

Most-Favoured-Nation Treatment

With regard to the protection of intellectual property, any advantage, favour, privilege or immunity granted by a Member to the nationals of any other country shall be accorded immediately and unconditionally to the nationals of all other Members. Exempted from this obligation are any advantage, favour, privilege or immunity accorded by a Member:

    (a) deriving from international agreements on judicial assistance or law enforcement of a general nature and not particularly confined to the protection of intellectual property;

    (b) granted in accordance with the provisions of the Berne Convention (1971) or the Rome Convention authorizing that the treatment accorded be a function not of national treatment but of the treatment accorded in another country;

---

[3]   For the purposes of Articles 3 and 4, "protection" shall include matters affecting the availability, acquisition, scope, maintenance and enforcement of intellectual property rights as well as those matters affecting the use of intellectual property rights specifically addressed in this Agreement.

(c) in respect of the rights of performers, producers of phonograms and broadcasting organizations not provided under this Agreement;

(d) deriving from international agreements related to the protection of intellectual property which entered into force prior to the entry into force of the WTO Agreement, provided that such agreements are notified to the Council for TRIPS and do not constitute an arbitrary or unjustifiable discrimination against nationals of other Members.

Article 5

Multilateral Agreements on Acquisition or Maintenance of Protection

The obligations under Articles 3 and 4 do not apply to procedures provided in multilateral agreements concluded under the auspices of WIPO relating to the acquisition or maintenance of intellectual property rights.

Article 6

Exhaustion

For the purposes of dispute settlement under this Agreement, subject to the provisions of Articles 3 and 4 nothing in this Agreement shall be used to address the issue of the exhaustion of intellectual property rights.

Article 7

Objectives

The protection and enforcement of intellectual property rights should contribute to the promotion of technological innovation and to the transfer and dissemination of technology, to the mutual advantage of producers and users of technological knowledge and in a manner conducive to social and economic welfare, and to a balance of rights and obligations.

Article 8

Principles

1.   Members may, in formulating or amending their laws and regulations, adopt measures necessary to protect public health and nutrition, and to promote the public interest in sectors of vital importance to their socio-economic and technological development, provided that such measures are consistent with the provisions of this Agreement.

2.   Appropriate measures, provided that they are consistent with the provisions of this Agreement, may be needed to prevent the abuse of intellectual property rights by right holders or the resort to practices which unreasonably restrain trade or adversely affect the international transfer of technology.

PART II

STANDARDS CONCERNING THE AVAILABILITY, SCOPE AND USE OF INTELLECTUAL PROPERTY RIGHTS
SECTION 1: COPYRIGHT AND RELATED RIGHTS

Article 9

Relation to the Berne Convention

1.   Members shall comply with Articles 1 through 21 of the Berne Convention (1971) and the Appendix thereto. However, Members shall not have rights or obligations under this Agreement in respect of the rights conferred under Article 6 *bis* of that Convention or of the rights derived therefrom.

2.   Copyright protection shall extend to expressions and not to ideas, procedures, methods of operation or mathematical concepts as such.

Article 10

Computer Programs and Compilations of Data

1.   Computer programs, whether in source or object code, shall be protected as literary works under the Berne Convention (1971).

2.   Compilations of data or other material, whether in machine readable or other form, which by reason of the selection or arrangement of their contents constitute intellectual creations shall be protected as such. Such protection, which shall not extend to the data or material itself, shall be without prejudice to any copyright subsisting in the data or material itself.

Article 11

Rental Rights

In respect of at least computer programs and cinematographic works, a Member shall provide authors and their successors in title the right to authorize or to prohibit the commercial rental to the public of originals or copies of their copyright works. A Member shall be excepted from this obligation in respect of cinematographic works unless such rental has led to widespread copying of such works which is materially impairing the exclusive right of reproduction conferred in that Member on authors and their successors in title. In respect of computer programs, this obligation does not apply to rentals where the program itself is not the essential object of the rental.

Article 12

Term of Protection

Whenever the term of protection of a work, other than a photographic work or a work of applied art, is calculated on a basis other than the life of a natural person, such term shall be no less than 50 years from the end of the calendar year of authorized publication, or, failing such authorized publication within 50 years from the making of the work, 50 years from the end of the calendar year of making.

Article 13

Limitations and Exceptions

Members shall confine limitations or exceptions to exclusive rights to certain special cases which do not conflict with a normal exploitation of the work and do not unreasonably prejudice the legitimate interests of the right holder.

Article 14

Protection of Performers, Producers of Phonograms (Sound Recordings) and Broadcasting Organizations

1.   In respect of a fixation of their performance on a phonogram, performers shall have the possibility of preventing the following acts when undertaken without their authorization: the fixation of their unfixed performance and the reproduction of such fixation. Performers shall also have the possibility of preventing the following acts when undertaken without their authorization: the broadcasting by wireless means and the communication to the public of their live performance.

2.   Producers of phonograms shall enjoy the right to authorize or prohibit the direct or indirect reproduction of their phonograms.

3.   Broadcasting organizations shall have the right to prohibit the following acts when undertaken without their authorization: the fixation, the reproduction of fixations, and the rebroadcasting by wireless means of broadcasts, as well as the communication to the public of television broadcasts of the same. Where Members do not grant such rights to broadcasting organizations, they shall provide owners of copyright in the subject matter of broadcasts with the possibility of preventing the above acts, subject to the provisions of the Berne Convention (1971).

4.   The provisions of Article 11 in respect of computer programs shall apply *mutatis mutandis* to producers of phonograms and any other right holders in phonograms as determined in a Member's law. If on 15 April 1994 a Member has in force a system of equitable remuneration of right holders in respect of the rental of phonograms, it may maintain such system provided that the commercial rental of phonograms is not giving rise to the material impairment of the exclusive rights of reproduction of right holders.

5.   The term of the protection available under this Agreement to performers and producers of phonograms shall last at least until the end of a period of 50 years computed from the end of the calendar year in which the fixation was made or the performance took place. The term of protection granted pursuant to paragraph 3 shall last for at least 20 years from the end of the calendar year in which the broadcast took place.

6.   Any Member may, in relation to the rights conferred under paragraphs 1, 2 and 3, provide for conditions, limitations, exceptions and reservations to the extent permitted by the Rome Convention. However, the provisions of Article 18 of the Berne Convention (1971) shall also apply,

mutatis mutandis, to the rights of performers and producers of phonograms in phonograms.

SECTION 2: TRADEMARKS

Article 15

Protectable Subject Matter

1.   Any sign, or any combination of signs, capable of distinguishing the goods or services of one undertaking from those of other undertakings, shall be capable of constituting a trademark. Such signs, in particular words including personal names, letters, numerals, figurative elements and combinations of colours as well as any combination of such signs, shall be eligible for registration as trademarks. Where signs are not inherently capable of distinguishing the relevant goods or services, Members may make registrability depend on distinctiveness acquired through use. Members may require, as a condition of registration, that signs be visually perceptible.

2.   Paragraph 1 shall not be understood to prevent a Member from denying registration of a trademark on other grounds, provided that they do not derogate from the provisions of the Paris Convention (1967).

3.   Members may make registrability depend on use. However, actual use of a trademark shall not be a condition for filing an application for registration. An application shall not be refused solely on the ground that intended use has not taken place before the expiry of a period of three years from the date of application.

4.   The nature of the goods or services to which a trademark is to be applied shall in no case form an obstacle to registration of the trademark.

5.   Members shall publish each trademark either before it is registered or promptly after it is registered and shall afford a reasonable opportunity for petitions to cancel the registration. In addition, Members may afford an opportunity for the registration of a trademark to be opposed.

Article 16

Rights Conferred

1.   The owner of a registered trademark shall have the exclusive right to prevent all third parties not having the owner's consent from using in the course of trade identical or similar signs for goods or services which are identical or similar to those in respect of which the trademark is registered where such use would result in a likelihood of confusion. In case of the use of an identical sign for identical goods or services, a likelihood of confusion shall be presumed. The rights described above shall not prejudice any existing prior rights, nor shall they affect the possibility of Members making rights available on the basis of use.

2.   Article 6 *bis* of the Paris Convention (1967) shall apply, *mutatis mutandis,* to services. In determining whether a trademark is well-known, Members shall take account of the knowledge of the trademark in the

relevant sector of the public, including knowledge in the Member concerned which has been obtained as a result of the promotion of the trademark.

3.   Article 6 *bis* of the Paris Convention (1967) shall apply, *mutatis mutandis,* to goods or services which are not similar to those in respect of which a trademark is registered, provided that use of that trademark in relation to those goods or services would indicate a connection between those goods or services and the owner of the registered trademark and provided that the interests of the owner of the registered trademark are likely to be damaged by such use.

Article 17

Exceptions

Members may provide limited exceptions to the rights conferred by a trademark, such as fair use of descriptive terms, provided that such exceptions take account of the legitimate interests of the owner of the trademark and of third parties.

Article 18

Term of Protection

Initial registration, and each renewal of registration, of a trademark shall be for a term of no less than seven years. The registration of a trademark shall be renewable indefinitely.

Article 19

Requirement of Use

1.   If use is required to maintain a registration, the registration may be cancelled only after an uninterrupted period of at least three years of non-use, unless valid reasons based on the existence of obstacles to such use are shown by the trademark owner. Circumstances arising independently of the will of the owner of the trademark which constitute an obstacle to the use of the trademark, such as import restrictions on or other government requirements for goods or services protected by the trademark, shall be recognized as valid reasons for non-use.

2.   When subject to the control of its owner, use of a trademark by another person shall be recognized as use of the trademark for the purpose of maintaining the registration.

Article 20

Other Requirements

The use of a trademark in the course of trade shall not be unjustifiably encumbered by special requirements, such as use with another trademark, use in a special form or use in a manner detrimental to its capability to distinguish the goods or services of one undertaking from those of other undertakings. This will not preclude a requirement prescribing the use of the trademark identifying the undertaking producing the goods or services along with, but without linking it to, the trademark distinguishing the specific goods or services in question of that undertaking.

Article 21

Licensing and Assignment

Members may determine conditions on the licensing and assignment of trademarks, it being understood that the compulsory licensing of trademarks shall not be permitted and that the owner of a registered trademark shall have the right to assign the trademark with or without the transfer of the business to which the trademark belongs.

SECTION 3.GEOGRAPHICAL INDICATIONS (omitted)

* * *

SECTION 4:INDUSTRIAL DESIGNS (omitted)

* * *

Requirements for Protection

SECTION 5:PATENTS

Article 27

Patentable Subject Matter

1.   Subject to the provisions of paragraphs 2 and 3, patents shall be available for any inventions, whether products or processes, in all fields of technology, provided that they are new, involve an inventive step and are capable of industrial application.[5] Subject to paragraph 4 of Article 65, paragraph 8 of Article 70 and paragraph 3 of this Article, patents shall be available and patent rights enjoyable without discrimination as to the place of invention, the field of technology and whether products are imported or locally produced.

2.   Members may exclude from patentability inventions, the prevention within their territory of the commercial exploitation of which is necessary to protect *ordre public* or morality, including to protect human, animal or plant life or health or to avoid serious prejudice to the environment, provided that such exclusion is not made merely because the exploitation is prohibited by their law.

3.   Members may also exclude from patentability:

(a) diagnostic, therapeutic and surgical methods for the treatment of humans or animals;

(b) plants and animals other than micro-organisms, and essentially biological processes for the production of plants or animals other than non-biological and microbiological processes. However, Members shall provide for the protection of plant varieties either by patents or by an effective *sui generis* system or by any combination thereof. The provisions of this subparagraph

---

[5]   For the purposes of this Article, the terms "inventive step" and "capable of industrial application" may be deemed by a Member to be synonymous with the terms "non-obvious" and "useful" respectively.

shall be reviewed four years after the date of entry into force of the WTO Agreement.

Article 28

Rights Conferred

1.   A patent shall confer on its owner the following exclusive rights:

(a) where the subject matter of a patent is a product, to prevent third parties not having the owner's consent from the acts of: making, using, offering for sale, selling, or importing[6] for these purposes that product;

(b) where the subject matter of a patent is a process, to prevent third parties not having the owner's consent from the act of using the process, and from the acts of: using, offering for sale, selling, or importing for these purposes at least the product obtained directly by that process.

2.   Patent owners shall also have the right to assign, or transfer by succession, the patent and to conclude licensing contracts.

Article 29

Conditions on Patent Applicants

1. Members shall require that an applicant for a patent shall disclose the invention in a manner sufficiently clear and complete for the invention to be carried out by a person skilled in the art and may require the applicant to indicate the best mode for carrying out the invention known to the inventor at the filing date or, where priority is claimed, at the priority date of the application.

2. Members may require an applicant for a patent to provide information concerning the applicant's corresponding foreign applications and grants.

Article 30

Exceptions to Rights Conferred

Members may provide limited exceptions to the exclusive rights conferred by a patent, provided that such exceptions do not unreasonably conflict with a normal exploitation of the patent and do not unreasonably prejudice the legitimate interests of the patent owner, taking account of the legitimate interests of third parties.

Article 31

Other Use Without Authorization of the Right Holder

Where the law of a Member allows for other use[7] of the subject matter of a patent without the authorization of the right holder, including use by

---

[6]   This right, like all other rights conferred under this Agreement in respect of the use, sale, importation or other distribution of goods, is subject to the provisions of Article 6.

[7]   "Other use" refers to other than that allowed under Article 30.

the government or third parties authorized by the government, the following provisions shall be respected:

(a) authorization of such use shall be considered on its individual merits;

(b) such use may only be permitted if, prior to such use, the proposed user has made efforts to obtain authorization from the right holder on reasonable commercial terms and conditions and that such efforts have not been successful within a reasonable period of time. This requirement may be waived by a Member in the case of a national emergency or other circumstances of extreme urgency or in cases of public non-commercial use. In situations of national emergency or other circumstances of extreme urgency, the right holder shall, nevertheless, be notified as soon as reasonably practicable. In the case of public non-commercial use, where the government or contractor, without making a patent search, knows or has demonstrable grounds to know that a valid patent is or will be used by or for the government, the right holder shall be informed promptly;

(c) the scope and duration of such use shall be limited to the purpose for which it was authorized, and in the case of semi-conductor technology shall only be for public non-commercial use or to remedy a practice determined after judicial or administrative process to be anti-competitive;

(d) such use shall be non-exclusive;

(e) such use shall be non-assignable, except with that part of the enterprise or goodwill which enjoys such use;

(f) any such use shall be authorized predominantly for the supply of the domestic market of the Member authorizing such use;

(g) authorization for such use shall be liable, subject to adequate protection of the legitimate interests of the persons so authorized, to be terminated if and when the circumstances which led to it cease to exist and are unlikely to recur. The competent authority shall have the authority to review, upon motivated request, the continued existence of these circumstances;

(h) the right holder shall be paid adequate remuneration in the circumstances of each case, taking into account the economic value of the authorization;

(i) the legal validity of any decision relating to the authorization of such use shall be subject to judicial review or other independent review by a distinct higher authority in that Member;

(j) any decision relating to the remuneration provided in respect of such use shall be subject to judicial review or other independent review by a distinct higher authority in that Member;

(k) Members are not obliged to apply the conditions set forth in subparagraphs (b) and (f) where such use is permitted to remedy a practice determined after judicial or administrative process to be anti-competitive. The need to correct anti-competitive practices may be taken into account in determining the amount of remuneration in such cases. Competent authorities shall have the authority to refuse termination of authorization if and when the conditions which led to such authorization are likely to recur;

(*l*) where such use is authorized to permit the exploitation of a patent ("the second patent") which cannot be exploited without infringing another patent ("the first patent"), the following additional conditions shall apply:

    (i) the invention claimed in the second patent shall involve an important technical advance of considerable economic significance in relation to the invention claimed in the first patent;

    (ii) the owner of the first patent shall be entitled to a cross-licence on reasonable terms to use the invention claimed in the second patent; and

    (iii) the use authorized in respect of the first patent shall be non-assignable except with the assignment of the second patent.

Article 32

Revocation / Forfeiture

An opportunity for judicial review of any decision to revoke or forfeit a patent shall be available.

Article 33

Term of Protection

The term of protection available shall not end before the expiration of a period of twenty years counted from the filing date.[8]

Article 34

Process Patents: Burden of Proof

1. For the purposes of civil proceedings in respect of the infringement of the rights of the owner referred to in paragraph 1(b) of Article 28, if the subject matter of a patent is a process for obtaining a product, the judicial authorities shall have the authority to order the defendant to prove that the process to obtain an identical product is

---

[8]   It is understood that those Members which do not have a system of original grant may provide that the term of protection shall be computed from the filing date in the system of original grant.

different from the patented process. Therefore, Members shall provide, in at least one of the following circumstances, that any identical product when produced without the consent of the patent owner shall, in the absence of proof to the contrary, be deemed to have been obtained by the patented process:

    (a) if the product obtained by the patented process is new;

    (b) if there is a substantial likelihood that the identical product was made by the process and the owner of the patent has been unable through reasonable efforts to determine the process actually used.

    2.   Any Member shall be free to provide that the burden of proof indicated in paragraph 1 shall be on the alleged infringer only if the condition referred to in subparagraph (a) is fulfilled or only if the condition referred to in subparagraph (b) is fulfilled.

    3.   In the adduction of proof to the contrary, the legitimate interests of defendants in protecting their manufacturing and business secrets shall be taken into account.

SECTION 6: LAYOUT-DESIGNS (TOPOGRAPHIES) OF INTEGRATED CIRCUITS (omitted)

* * *

SECTION 7: PROTECTION OF UNDISCLOSED INFORMATION

Article 39

    1.   In the course of ensuring effective protection against unfair competition as provided in Article 10 *bis* of the Paris Convention (1967), Members shall protect undisclosed information in accordance with paragraph 2 and data submitted to governments or governmental agencies in accordance with paragraph 3.

    2.   Natural and legal persons shall have the possibility of preventing information lawfully within their control from being disclosed to, acquired by, or used by others without their consent in a manner contrary to honest commercial practices[10] so long as such information:

    (a) is secret in the sense that it is not, as a body or in the precise configuration and assembly of its components, generally known among or readily accessible to persons within the circles that normally deal with the kind of information in question;

    (b) has commercial value because it is secret; and

    (c) has been subject to reasonable steps under the circumstances, by the person lawfully in control of the information, to keep it secret.

---

    [10]   For the purpose of this provision, "a manner contrary to honest commercial practices" shall mean at least practices such as breach of contract, breach of confidence and inducement to breach, and includes the acquisition of undisclosed information by third parties who knew, or were grossly negligent in failing to know, that such practices were involved in the acquisition.

3. Members, when requiring, as a condition of approving the marketing of pharmaceutical or of agricultural chemical products which utilize new chemical entities, the submission of undisclosed test or other data, the origination of which involves a considerable effort, shall protect such data against unfair commercial use. In addition, Members shall protect such data against disclosure, except where necessary to protect the public, or unless steps are taken to ensure that the data are protected against unfair commercial use.

SECTION 8: CONTROL OF ANTI-COMPETITIVE PRACTICES IN CONTRACTUAL LICENSES

Article 40

1. Members agree that some licensing practices or conditions pertaining to intellectual property rights which restrain competition may have adverse effects on trade and may impede the transfer and dissemination of technology.

2. Nothing in this Agreement shall prevent Members from specifying in their legislation licensing practices or conditions that may in particular cases constitute an abuse of intellectual property rights having an adverse effect on competition in the relevant market. As provided above, a Member may adopt, consistently with the other provisions of this Agreement, appropriate measures to prevent or control such practices, which may include for example exclusive grantback conditions, conditions preventing challenges to validity and coercive package licensing, in the light of the relevant laws and regulations of that Member.

3. Each Member shall enter, upon request, into consultations with any other Member which has cause to believe that an intellectual property right owner that is a national or domiciliary of the Member to which the request for consultations has been addressed is undertaking practices in violation of the requesting Member's laws and regulations on the subject matter of this Section, and which wishes to secure compliance with such legislation, without prejudice to any action under the law and to the full freedom of an ultimate decision of either Member. The Member addressed shall accord full and sympathetic consideration to, and shall afford adequate opportunity for, consultations with the requesting Member, and shall cooperate through supply of publicly available non-confidential information of relevance to the matter in question and of other information available to the Member, subject to domestic law and to the conclusion of mutually satisfactory agreements concerning the safeguarding of its confidentiality by the requesting Member.

4. A Member whose nationals or domiciliaries are subject to proceedings in another Member concerning alleged violation of that other Member's laws and regulations on the subject matter of this Section shall, upon request, be granted an opportunity for consultations by the other Member under the same conditions as those foreseen in paragraph 3.

PART III

ENFORCEMENT OF INTELLECTUAL PROPERTY RIGHTS

SECTION 1: GENERAL OBLIGATIONS

Article 41

1.   Members shall ensure that enforcement procedures as specified in this Part are available under their law so as to permit effective action against any act of infringement of intellectual property rights covered by this Agreement, including expeditious remedies to prevent infringements and remedies which constitute a deterrent to further infringements. These procedures shall be applied in such a manner as to avoid the creation of barriers to legitimate trade and to provide for safeguards against their abuse.

2.   Procedures concerning the enforcement of intellectual property rights shall be fair and equitable. They shall not be unnecessarily complicated or costly, or entail unreasonable time-limits or unwarranted delays.

3.   Decisions on the merits of a case shall preferably be in writing and reasoned. They shall be made available at least to the parties to the proceeding without undue delay. Decisions on the merits of a case shall be based only on evidence in respect of which parties were offered the opportunity to be heard.

4.   Parties to a proceeding shall have an opportunity for review by a judicial authority of final administrative decisions and, subject to jurisdictional provisions in a Member's law concerning the importance of a case, of at least the legal aspects of initial judicial decisions on the merits of a case. However, there shall be no obligation to provide an opportunity for review of acquittals in criminal cases.

5.   It is understood that this Part does not create any obligation to put in place a judicial system for the enforcement of intellectual property rights distinct from that for the enforcement of law in general, nor does it affect the capacity of Members to enforce their law in general. Nothing in this Part creates any obligation with respect to the distribution of resources as between enforcement of intellectual property rights and the enforcement of law in general.

SECTION 2: CIVIL AND ADMINISTRATIVE PROCEDURES
AND REMEDIES

Article 42

Fair and Equitable Procedures

Members shall make available to right holders[11] civil judicial procedures concerning the enforcement of any intellectual property right covered by this Agreement. Defendants shall have the right to written

---

[11]   For the purpose of this Part, the term "right holder" includes federations and associations having legal standing to assert such rights.

notice which is timely and contains sufficient detail, including the basis of the claims. Parties shall be allowed to be represented by independent legal counsel, and procedures shall not impose overly burdensome requirements concerning mandatory personal appearances. All parties to such procedures shall be duly entitled to substantiate their claims and to present all relevant evidence. The procedure shall provide a means to identify and protect confidential information, unless this would be contrary to existing constitutional requirements.

Article 43

Evidence

1.   The judicial authorities shall have the authority, where a party has presented reasonably available evidence sufficient to support its claims and has specified evidence relevant to substantiation of its claims which lies in the control of the opposing party, to order that this evidence be produced by the opposing party, subject in appropriate cases to conditions which ensure the protection of confidential information.

2.   In cases in which a party to a proceeding voluntarily and without good reason refuses access to, or otherwise does not provide necessary information within a reasonable period, or significantly impedes a procedure relating to an enforcement action, a Member may accord judicial authorities the authority to make preliminary and final determinations, affirmative or negative, on the basis of the information presented to them, including the complaint or the allegation presented by the party adversely affected by the denial of access to information, subject to providing the parties an opportunity to be heard on the allegations or evidence.

Article 44

Injunctions

1.   The judicial authorities shall have the authority to order a party to desist from an infringement, *inter alia* to prevent the entry into the channels of commerce in their jurisdiction of imported goods that involve the infringement of an intellectual property right, immediately after customs clearance of such goods. Members are not obliged to accord such authority in respect of protected subject matter acquired or ordered by a person prior to knowing or having reasonable grounds to know that dealing in such subject matter would entail the infringement of an intellectual property right.

2.   Notwithstanding the other provisions of this Part and provided that the provisions of Part II specifically addressing use by governments, or by third parties authorized by a government, without the authorization of the right holder are complied with, Members may limit the remedies available against such use to payment of remuneration in accordance with subparagraph (h) of Article 31. In other cases, the remedies under this Part shall apply or, where these remedies are inconsistent with a Member's law, declaratory judgments and adequate compensation shall be available.

Article 45

Damages

1.   The judicial authorities shall have the authority to order the infringer to pay the right holder damages adequate to compensate for the injury the right holder has suffered because of an infringement of that person's intellectual property right by an infringer who knowingly, or with reasonable grounds to know, engaged in infringing activity.

2.   The judicial authorities shall also have the authority to order the infringer to pay the right holder expenses, which may include appropriate attorney's fees. In appropriate cases, Members may authorize the judicial authorities to order recovery of profits and/or payment of pre-established damages even where the infringer did not knowingly, or with reasonable grounds to know, engage in infringing activity.

Article 46

Other Remedies

In order to create an effective deterrent to infringement, the judicial authorities shall have the authority to order that goods that they have found to be infringing be, without compensation of any sort, disposed of outside the channels of commerce in such a manner as to avoid any harm caused to the right holder, or, unless this would be contrary to existing constitutional requirements, destroyed. The judicial authorities shall also have the authority to order that materials and implements the predominant use of which has been in the creation of the infringing goods be, without compensation of any sort, disposed of outside the channels of commerce in such a manner as to minimize the risks of further infringements. In considering such requests, the need for proportionality between the seriousness of the infringement and the remedies ordered as well as the interests of third parties shall be taken into account. In regard to counterfeit trademark goods, the simple removal of the trademark unlawfully affixed shall not be sufficient, other than in exceptional cases, to permit release of the goods into the channels of commerce.

Article 47

Right of Information

Members may provide that the judicial authorities shall have the authority, unless this would be out of proportion to the seriousness of the infringement, to order the infringer to inform the right holder of the identity of third persons involved in the production and distribution of the infringing goods or services and of their channels of distribution.

Article 48

Indemnification of the Defendant

1.   The judicial authorities shall have the authority to order a party at whose request measures were taken and who has abused enforcement procedures to provide to a party wrongfully enjoined or restrained adequate compensation for the injury suffered because of such abuse. The judicial

authorities shall also have the authority to order the applicant to pay the defendant expenses, which may include appropriate attorney's fees.

2. In respect of the administration of any law pertaining to the protection or enforcement of intellectual property rights, Members shall only exempt both public authorities and officials from liability to appropriate remedial measures where actions are taken or intended in good faith in the course of the administration of that law.

Article 49

Administrative Procedures

To the extent that any civil remedy can be ordered as a result of administrative procedures on the merits of a case, such procedures shall conform to principles equivalent in substance to those set forth in this Section.

SECTION 3: PROVISIONAL MEASURES

Article 50

1. The judicial authorities shall have the authority to order prompt and effective provisional measures:

(a) to prevent an infringement of any intellectual property right from occurring, and in particular to prevent the entry into the channels of commerce in their jurisdiction of goods, including imported goods immediately after customs clearance;

(b) to preserve relevant evidence in regard to the alleged infringement.

2. The judicial authorities shall have the authority to adopt provisional measures *inaudita altera parte* where appropriate, in particular where any delay is likely to cause irreparable harm to the right holder, or where there is a demonstrable risk of evidence being destroyed.

3. The judicial authorities shall have the authority to require the applicant to provide any reasonably available evidence in order to satisfy themselves with a sufficient degree of certainty that the applicant is the right holder and that the applicant's right is being infringed or that such infringement is imminent, and to order the applicant to provide a security or equivalent assurance sufficient to protect the defendant and to prevent abuse.

4. Where provisional measures have been adopted *inaudita altera parte,* the parties affected shall be given notice, without delay after the execution of the measures at the latest. A review, including a right to be heard, shall take place upon request of the defendant with a view to deciding, within a reasonable period after the notification of the measures, whether these measures shall be modified, revoked or confirmed.

5. The applicant may be required to supply other information necessary for the identification of the goods concerned by the authority that will execute the provisional measures.

6.   Without prejudice to paragraph 4, provisional measures taken on the basis of paragraphs 1 and 2 shall, upon request by the defendant, be revoked or otherwise cease to have effect, if proceedings leading to a decision on the merits of the case are not initiated within a reasonable period, to be determined by the judicial authority ordering the measures where a Member's law so permits or, in the absence of such a determination, not to exceed 20 working days or 31 calendar days, whichever is the longer.

7.   Where the provisional measures are revoked or where they lapse due to any act or omission by the applicant, or where it is subsequently found that there has been no infringement or threat of infringement of an intellectual property right, the judicial authorities shall have the authority to order the applicant, upon request of the defendant, to provide the defendant appropriate compensation for any injury caused by these measures.

8.   To the extent that any provisional measure can be ordered as a result of administrative procedures, such procedures shall conform to principles equivalent in substance to those set forth in this Section.

SECTION 4: SPECIAL REQUIREMENTS RELATED TO BORDER MEASURES[12]

Article 51

Suspension of Release by Customs Authorities

Members shall, in conformity with the provisions set out below, adopt procedures[13] to enable a right holder, who has valid grounds for suspecting that the importation of counterfeit trademark or pirated copyright goods[14] may take place, to lodge an application in writing with competent authorities, administrative or judicial, for the suspension by the customs authorities of the release into free circulation of such goods. Members may enable such an application to be made in respect of goods which involve other infringements of intellectual property rights, provided that the

---

[12]   Where a Member has dismantled substantially all controls over movement of goods across its border with another Member with which it forms part of a customs union, it shall not be required to apply the provisions of this Section at that border.

[13]   It is understood that there shall be no obligation to apply such procedures to imports of goods put on the market in another country by or with the consent of the right holder, or to goods in transit.

[14]   For the purposes of this Agreement:

(a) "counterfeit trademark goods" shall mean any goods, including packaging, bearing without authorization a trademark which is identical to the trademark validly registered in respect of such goods, or which cannot be distinguished in its essential aspects from such a trademark, and which thereby infringes the rights of the owner of the trademark in question under the law of the country of importation;

(b) "pirated copyright goods" shall mean any goods which are copies made without the consent of the right holder or person duly authorized by the right holder in the country of production and which are made directly or indirectly from an article where the making of that copy would have constituted an infringement of a copyright or a related right under the law of the country of importation.

requirements of this Section are met. Members may also provide for corresponding procedures concerning the suspension by the customs authorities of the release of infringing goods destined for exportation from their territories.

Article 52

Application

Any right holder initiating the procedures under Article 51 shall be required to provide adequate evidence to satisfy the competent authorities that, under the laws of the country of importation, there is *prima facie* an infringement of the right holder's intellectual property right and to supply a sufficiently detailed description of the goods to make them readily recognizable by the customs authorities. The competent authorities shall inform the applicant within a reasonable period whether they have accepted the application and, where determined by the competent authorities, the period for which the customs authorities will take action.

Article 53

Security or Equivalent Assurance

1.   The competent authorities shall have the authority to require an applicant to provide a security or equivalent assurance sufficient to protect the defendant and the competent authorities and to prevent abuse. Such security or equivalent assurance shall not unreasonably deter recourse to these procedures.

2.   Where pursuant to an application under this Section the release of goods involving industrial designs, patents, layout-designs or undisclosed information into free circulation has been suspended by customs authorities on the basis of a decision other than by a judicial or other independent authority, and the period provided for in Article 55 has expired without the granting of provisional relief by the duly empowered authority, and provided that all other conditions for importation have been complied with, the owner, importer, or consignee of such goods shall be entitled to their release on the posting of a security in an amount sufficient to protect the right holder for any infringement. Payment of such security shall not prejudice any other remedy available to the right holder, it being understood that the security shall be released if the right holder fails to pursue the right of action within a reasonable period of time.

Article 54

Notice of Suspension

The importer and the applicant shall be promptly notified of the suspension of the release of goods according to Article 51.

Article 55

Duration of Suspension

If, within a period not exceeding 10 working days after the applicant has been served notice of the suspension, the customs authorities have not been informed that proceedings leading to a decision on the merits of the case have been initiated by a party other than the defendant, or that the duly empowered authority has taken provisional measures prolonging the suspension of the release of the goods, the goods shall be released, provided that all other conditions for importation or exportation have been complied with; in appropriate cases, this time-limit may be extended by another 10 working days. If proceedings leading to a decision on the merits of the case have been initiated, a review, including a right to be heard, shall take place upon request of the defendant with a view to deciding, within a reasonable period, whether these measures shall be modified, revoked or confirmed. Notwithstanding the above, where the suspension of the release of goods is carried out or continued in accordance with a provisional judicial measure, the provisions of paragraph 6 of Article 50 shall apply.

Article 56

Indemnification of the Importer and of the Owner of the Goods

Relevant authorities shall have the authority to order the applicant to pay the importer, the consignee and the owner of the goods appropriate compensation for any injury caused to them through the wrongful detention of goods or through the detention of goods released pursuant to Article 55.

Article 57

Right of Inspection and Information

Without prejudice to the protection of confidential information, Members shall provide the competent authorities the authority to give the right holder sufficient opportunity to have any goods detained by the customs authorities inspected in order to substantiate the right holder's claims. The competent authorities shall also have authority to give the importer an equivalent opportunity to have any such goods inspected. Where a positive determination has been made on the merits of a case, Members may provide the competent authorities the authority to inform the right holder of the names and addresses of the consignor, the importer and the consignee and of the quantity of the goods in question.

Article 58

Ex Officio Action

Where Members require competent authorities to act upon their own initiative and to suspend the release of goods in respect of which they have acquired *prima facie* evidence that an intellectual property right is being infringed:

(a) the competent authorities may at any time seek from the right holder any information that may assist them to exercise these powers;

(b) the importer and the right holder shall be promptly notified of the suspension. Where the importer has lodged an appeal against the suspension with the competent authorities, the suspension shall be subject to the conditions, *mutatis mutandis,* set out at Article 55;

(c) Members shall only exempt both public authorities and officials from liability to appropriate remedial measures where actions are taken or intended in good faith.

Article 59

Remedies

Without prejudice to other rights of action open to the right holder and subject to the right of the defendant to seek review by a judicial authority, competent authorities shall have the authority to order the destruction or disposal of infringing goods in accordance with the principles set out in Article 46. In regard to counterfeit trademark goods, the authorities shall not allow the re-exportation of the infringing goods in an unaltered state or subject them to a different customs procedure, other than in exceptional circumstances.

Article 60

De Minimis Imports

Members may exclude from the application of the above provisions small quantities of goods of a non-commercial nature contained in travellers' personal luggage or sent in small consignments.

SECTION 5: CRIMINAL PROCEDURES

Article 61

Members shall provide for criminal procedures and penalties to be applied at least in cases of wilful trademark counterfeiting or copyright piracy on a commercial scale. Remedies available shall include imprisonment and/or monetary fines sufficient to provide a deterrent, consistently with the level of penalties applied for crimes of a corresponding gravity. In appropriate cases, remedies available shall also include the seizure, forfeiture and destruction of the infringing goods and of any materials and implements the predominant use of which has been in the commission of the offence. Members may provide for criminal procedures and penalties to be applied in other cases of infringement of intellectual property rights, in particular where they are committed wilfully and on a commercial scale.

PART IV

ACQUISITION AND MAINTENANCE OF INTELLECTUAL PROPERTY RIGHTS AND RELATED *INTER-PARTES* PROCEDURES

Article 62

1.   Members may require, as a condition of the acquisition or maintenance of the intellectual property rights provided for under Sections 2 through 6 of Part II, compliance with reasonable procedures and formalities. Such procedures and formalities shall be consistent with the provisions of this Agreement.

2. Where the acquisition of an intellectual property right is subject to the right being granted or registered, Members shall ensure that the procedures for grant or registration, subject to compliance with the substantive conditions for acquisition of the right, permit the granting or registration of the right within a reasonable period of time so as to avoid unwarranted curtailment of the period of protection.

3. Article 4 of the Paris Convention (1967) shall apply *mutatis mutandis* to service marks.

4. Procedures concerning the acquisition or maintenance of intellectual property rights and, where a Member's law provides for such procedures, administrative revocation and *inter partes* procedures such as opposition, revocation and cancellation, shall be governed by the general principles set out in paragraphs 2 and 3 of Article 41.

5. Final administrative decisions in any of the procedures referred to under paragraph 4 shall be subject to review by a judicial or quasi-judicial authority. However, there shall be no obligation to provide an opportunity for such review of decisions in cases of unsuccessful opposition or administrative revocation, provided that the grounds for such procedures can be the subject of invalidation procedures.

PART V
DISPUTE PREVENTION AND SETTLEMENT

Article 63

Transparency

1. Laws and regulations, and final judicial decisions and administrative rulings of general application, made effective by a Member pertaining to the subject matter of this Agreement (the availability, scope, acquisition, enforcement and prevention of the abuse of intellectual property rights) shall be published, or where such publication is not practicable made publicly available, in a national language, in such a manner as to enable governments and right holders to become acquainted with them. Agreements concerning the subject matter of this Agreement which are in force between the government or a governmental agency of a Member and the government or a governmental agency of another Member shall also be published.

2. Members shall notify the laws and regulations referred to in paragraph 1 to the Council for TRIPS in order to assist that Council in its review of the operation of this Agreement. The Council shall attempt to minimize the burden on Members in carrying out this obligation and may decide to waive the obligation to notify such laws and regulations directly to the Council if consultations with WIPO on the establishment of a common register containing these laws and regulations are successful. The Council shall also consider in this connection any action required regarding notifications pursuant to the obligations under this Agreement stemming from the provisions of Article 6 *ter* of the Paris Convention (1967).

3. Each Member shall be prepared to supply, in response to a written request from another Member, information of the sort referred to in paragraph 1. A Member, having reason to believe that a specific judicial decision or administrative ruling or bilateral agreement in the area of intellectual property rights affects its rights under this Agreement, may also request in writing to be given access to or be informed in sufficient detail of such specific judicial decisions or administrative rulings or bilateral agreements.

4. Nothing in paragraphs 1, 2 and 3 shall require Members to disclose confidential information which would impede law enforcement or otherwise be contrary to the public interest or would prejudice the legitimate commercial interests of particular enterprises, public or private.

Article 64

Dispute Settlement

1. The provisions of Articles XXII and XXIII of GATT 1994 as elaborated and applied by the Dispute Settlement Understanding shall apply to consultations and the settlement of disputes under this Agreement except as otherwise specifically provided herein.

2. Subparagraphs 1(b) and 1(c) of Article XXIII of GATT 1994 shall not apply to the settlement of disputes under this Agreement for a period of five years from the date of entry into force of the WTO Agreement.

3. During the time period referred to in paragraph 2, the Council for TRIPS shall examine the scope and modalities for complaints of the type provided for under subparagraphs 1(b) and 1(c) of Article XXIII of GATT 1994 made pursuant to this Agreement, and submit its recommendations to the Ministerial Conference for approval. Any decision of the Ministerial Conference to approve such recommendations or to extend the period in paragraph 2 shall be made only by consensus, and approved recommendations shall be effective for all Members without further formal acceptance process.

PART VI

TRANSITIONAL ARRANGEMENTS

Article 65

Transitional Arrangements

1. Subject to the provisions of paragraphs 2, 3 and 4, no Member shall be obliged to apply the provisions of this Agreement before the expiry of a general period of one year following the date of entry into force of the WTO Agreement.

2. A developing country Member is entitled to delay for a further period of four years the date of application, as defined in paragraph 1, of the provisions of this Agreement other than Articles 3, 4 and 5.

3. Any other Member which is in the process of transformation from a centrally-planned into a market, free-enterprise economy and which is undertaking structural reform of its intellectual property system and facing

special problems in the preparation and implementation of intellectual property laws and regulations, may also benefit from a period of delay as foreseen in paragraph 2.

4. To the extent that a developing country Member is obliged by this Agreement to extend product patent protection to areas of technology not so protectable in its territory on the general date of application of this Agreement for that Member, as defined in paragraph 2, it may delay the application of the provisions on product patents of Section 5 of Part II to such areas of technology for an additional period of five years.

5. A Member availing itself of a transitional period under paragraphs 1, 2, 3 or 4 shall ensure that any changes in its laws, regulations and practice made during that period do not result in a lesser degree of consistency with the provisions of this Agreement.

Article 66

Least-Developed Country Members

1. In view of the special needs and requirements of least-developed country Members, their economic, financial and administrative constraints, and their need for flexibility to create a viable technological base, such Members shall not be required to apply the provisions of this Agreement, other than Articles 3, 4 and 5, for a period of 10 years from the date of application as defined under paragraph 1 of Article 65. The Council for TRIPS shall, upon duly motivated request by a least-developed country Member, accord extensions of this period.

2. Developed country Members shall provide incentives to enterprises and institutions in their territories for the purpose of promoting and encouraging technology transfer to least-developed country Members in order to enable them to create a sound and viable technological base.

Article 67

Technical Cooperation

In order to facilitate the implementation of this Agreement, developed country Members shall provide, on request and on mutually agreed terms and conditions, technical and financial cooperation in favour of developing and least-developed country Members. Such cooperation shall include assistance in the preparation of laws and regulations on the protection and enforcement of intellectual property rights as well as on the prevention of their abuse, and shall include support regarding the establishment or reinforcement of domestic offices and agencies relevant to these matters, including the training of personnel.

PART VII

INSTITUTIONAL ARRANGEMENTS; FINAL PROVISIONS
(omitted)

* * *

Table of Cases

Index

References are to Sections